STUDIES IN IMPERIALISM

general editor John M. MacKenzie

Established in the belief that imperialism as
phenomenon had as significant an effect on the ⟨
on the subordinate societies, Studies in Imperialis. ∪eeks to
develop the new socio-cultural approach which has emerged
through cross-disciplinary work on popular culture, media
studies, art history, the study of education and religion,
sports history and children's literature. The cultural
emphasis embraces studies of migration and race, while the
older political and constitutional, economic and military
concerns are never far away. It incorporates comparative
work on European and American empire-building, with the
chronological focus primarily, though not exclusively, on the
nineteenth and twentieth centuries, when these cultural
exchanges were most powerfully at work.

Imperialism and music

MANCHESTER
UNIVERSITY PRESS

AVAILABLE IN THE SERIES

Imperialism and music

BRITAIN 1876–1953

Jeffrey Richards

MANCHESTER
UNIVERSITY PRESS
Manchester and New York

distributed exclusively in the USA
by PALGRAVE

Published by **MANCHESTER UNIVERSITY PRESS**
OXFORD ROAD, MANCHESTER M13 9NR, UK
and ROOM 400, 175 FIFTH AVENUE, NEW YORK, NY 10010, USA
http://www.manchesteruniversitypress.co.uk

Distributed exclusively in the USA by
PALGRAVE
175 FIFTH AVENUE, NEW YORK, NY 10010, USA

Distributed exclusively in Canada by
UBC PRESS
UNIVERSITY OF BRITISH COLUMBIA,
2029 WEST MALL, VANCOUVER, BC, CANADA V6T 1Z2

British Library Cataloguing-in-Publication Data
A catalogue record for this book is available from the British Library

Library of Congress Cataloging-in-Publication Data applied for

ISBN 0 7190 4506 1 hardback
     0 7190 6143 1 paperback

First published 2001

10 09 08 07 06 05 04 03 02 01   10 9 8 7 6 5 4 3 2 1

Typeset in Trump Medieval
by Best-set Typesetter Ltd., Hong Kong
Printed in Great Britain
by Bookcraft (Bath) Ltd, Midsomer Norton

CONTENTS

For John Clegg

GENERAL EDITOR'S INTRODUCTION

Music is more than the food of love. It can also be the sustenance of patriotism and of ideology, the accompaniment of ceremony, conflict and acts of commitment. Throughout the world, those in authority and command have invariably revealed themselves to the sound of music. Political parties rouse their followers with musical invocations of the national sentiments and ideological nostrums to which they aspire. For music heightens the consciousness, often creating extremes of ecstasy or melancholy. It has the capacity to play upon the emotions and arouse its hearers to unaccustomed cheers or tears.

It is not surprising, therefore, that music should have played a major role in the life of a global ideological phenomenon like the British Empire. When the British were accused of being a people without music, the accusers invariably based their charge on the classical norms of continental Europe. As it happens, that accusation became more and more threadbare as the nineteenth century wore on, but in any case the British were exponents of many other forms of music that lay beyond those narrowly defined criteria. Jeffrey Richards explores these forms, and much else, in this refreshingly original book. It is full of material little known or understood hitherto.

It can truly be said that the sun never set on musical events in the Empire, in the characteristic contexts of the military, the Church, the theatre, the ceremony, the exhibition, the festival, and, as time wore on, the concert hall, the wireless and the cinema. Music and word settings carried complex layers of meaning, and these are thoroughly explored here. Music could convey the ideas and emotions that were supposed to bind the Empire together. Tours and other media carried such musical ideas to the further corners of the wider world. Imperialism disseminated western musical traditions as much as it did language, ideas, science, museums, sport and much more. But, as so often happened, it was modified in the process. Imperial sentiment was often counterpointed with developing national allegiances in the so-called white dominions, as the career of Peter Dawson neatly exemplifies. Sometimes it picked up the local colour of indigenous musical traditions, albeit converted for western ends. By the later nineteenth century, a world musicology (with some eighteenth-century antecedents) was beginning to develop which would be greatly extended in the course of the twentieth.

This is the first full-length study of the musical world of the British Empire. It stands for itself; but, as with so many pioneering works, it will also act as a remarkable quarry for future scholars. As it amply demonstrates, music has to be recognised as one of the central characteristics of the cultural imperialism of the late nineteenth and early twentieth centuries.

John M. MacKenzie

INTRODUCTION

When I set out on this project, longer ago than I now dare to remember, I did so with a grandiose, one might almost say imperial, plan. I would research and write about music of all kinds, from high culture to popular culture, which expressed ideas about and promoted the concept of the British Empire. I would write about other music in the Empire and its links with the motherland. I would write about anti-imperialism in music. As the work unfolded, this proved to be an impossibly massive undertaking. So I reluctantly abandoned the third aspect and much of the second aspect of my grand plan, to concentrate on the first – the expression in music of the ideology of the British Empire.

Although such eminent scholars as Linda Colley and Patrick Brantlinger have argued passionately for dating the beginnings of the cultural expression of the British imperial idea to the eighteenth and early nineteenth centuries rather than the second half of the nineteenth century, where much previous work had been concentrated, I have opted to cover a period roughly bounded by the dates 1876 and 1953: 1876 saw the passing of the Royal Titles Act which created Queen Victoria Empress of India – she was officially proclaimed Empress at a grand imperial assembly in 1877; 1953 was the date of the last imperial Coronation that we in Britain have witnessed or shall witness. It was not only that constitutionally Britain's monarch became an imperial ruler after 1876 but that the last decades of the nineteenth century saw the final flowering of an imperial ideology which was to find full expression in popular culture. This development coincided exactly with the emergence of the mass market and the English Musical Renaissance, two events which had a profound effect upon the creation, production and dissemination of British music. This congruence of events pointed me towards the time period I should study.

I approach the subject as a cultural historian rather than a musicologist. Therefore my primary focus is not analysis of the music but its cultural impact. I was particularly concerned to recover the contemporary responses to the music of imperialism. I therefore made extensive use of both *The Times* and *The Musical Times* as organs of record, their intoxicating pages recreating in vivid and immediate detail the feel of events and of music often long forgotten. I also drew extensively on the autobiographies and contemporary biographies of composers, conductors and singers for an insight into their attitudes and values, particularly with regard to the Empire.

The book begins with an account of the imperial music of Elgar and Sullivan and the establishing of an imperial musical idiom. It is followed by a sequence of chapters on the music composed for or utilized by official occasions: coronations, jubilees, exhibitions, tattoos, Armistice Day and Empire Day. Next, the book examines the imperial content of a range of musical forms: operetta and ballet, films, music hall songs, ballads, hymns and marches. The book concludes with a discussion of practitioners of imperial music: Sir Henry Coward and his Sheffield choir, the divas Emma Albani, Nellie Melba and Clara Butt, and the baritone Peter Dawson.

On the basis of cumulative empirical evidence, the book challenges a range of received views: the theory that neither Sullivan nor Elgar was inspired by the Empire; the assumption that the masses were uninterested in the Empire; the idea that Victorian hymns were not imperialistic; the belief that Britain after the First World War was anti-militarist and anti-imperial. The resulting volume will, I trust, help to open up to other researchers a hitherto neglected field of enquiry.

ACKNOWLEDGEMENTS

I have incurred many debts in the course of writing this book and have been substantially assisted by the librarians of the societies and institutions to which I have applied for information; I am grateful to them all. They include the British Library (Music Section); the Royal Commonwealth Society Library (Terry Barringer); the International Military Music Society (Philip Mather and Edward Bevan); the Vintage Light Music Society (Stuart Upton); the Theatre Museum, Covent Garden (Melanie Trifona Christoudia); the Sir Arthur Sullivan Society (David Eden, Stephen Turnbull); Sheffield City Library (Alison Derby); Cricklewood Library (Ian Johnston); the Peter Dawson Appreciation Society (Ron and Monica Hughes); the National Film Archive (Ali Strauss and Bryony Dixon); Aldershot Military Historical Trust (Mrs Sheila Noxon and staff); and Lancaster University Library (Thelma Goodman and staff). Professor Richard Taylor, Dr John Gardiner and Mr Philip Mather read individual chapters, and I am grateful for their constructive comments.

I am also indebted to the following individuals for advice and assistance of various kinds: Professor Harry Hanham, Dr Ruth Hanham, Professor Denis McCaldin, Dr Dave Russell, Professor Johanna Parry, Dr Andrew Spicer, Dr Mark Connelly, Dr James Chapman, Ms Dorothy Sheridan, Ms Pat Robinson, Dr John Wolffe, Dr Ian Bradley, Mr Bill Fuge and Mr Eric Norris. Professor John M. MacKenzie, my editor, has generously loaned me items from his own collection of books and imperial ephemera. I owe my greatest debt to my friend the pianist John Clegg, who gave up many hours of his time to play through for me imperial sheet music, recovered from second-hand book shops, which had lain unplayed and gathering dust for decades. The book is dedicated to him in gratitude. Bringing forgotten and neglected music back to life has been one of the pleasurable by-products of this investigation. All opinions, errors and omissions are of course my own.

Publication of this book has been made possible by a grant from the Scouloudi Foundation in association with the Institute of Historical Research.

I am grateful to Kim Latham for compiling the index.

CHAPTER ONE

Meanings:
Empire and music

Far-called our navies melt away;
On dune and headland sinks the fire
Lo, all our pomp of yesterday
Is one with Nineveh and Tyre

So wrote Rudyard Kipling in the poem *Recessional*, published in 1897 to mark the Diamond Jubilee of Queen Victoria, an occasion that retrospectively has been seen as the apogee of the British Empire. Kipling was concerned to warn his fellow countrymen against over-confidence and vainglory at this supreme moment of imperial celebration. Perhaps even he would have been surprised to learn that within a century all that imperial pomp would be 'one with Nineveh and Tyre' and that for the British population at large an Empire that was once ubiquitous in both popular and official culture has largely vanished from the public consciousness.

This was graphically confirmed in 1997 when the *Daily Telegraph*, to mark the centenary of the Diamond Jubilee, commissioned a Gallup Poll to discover the current extent of popular knowledge of British imperial history.[1] Asked in which countries General Wolfe and General Gordon died, 81 per cent and 80 per cent respectively either did not know or got it wrong. Asked who was on the British throne at the time of the American War of Independence and the Indian Mutiny, 79 per cent did not know or got it wrong. Asked who wrote the poem *Gunga Din*, 79 per cent did not know or got it wrong. When the answers were broken down by age group, it was discovered that among the minority getting the answers right, the highest proportion was in the 50-plus age group. For the young, the British Empire is now quite as remote as the Roman Empire – even more so, as Roman Britain is regularly taught in schools, the British Empire only rarely.

This present-day ignorance has been erroneously read back into the past by some historians who persist in reiterating the judgement made by Henry Pelling: 'there is no evidence of a direct continuous support for the cause of imperialism among any section of the working class'.[2] On the contrary, there is abundant evidence – the evidence of the marketplace. It is there in the record of how and on what people spent their money.

Every aspect of popular culture contrived to instil pride in the British imperial achievement: the regular exhibitions highlighting the produce and artefacts of the Empire; novels, stage melodramas and, later, feature films about gallant imperial heroes showing the flag and quelling the rebellious natives in far-off dominions; genre paintings like those of Lady Butler and the illustrations in a raft of magazines, postcards, cigarette cards and commercial packaging and advertizing; daily newspapers with an explicit commitment to Empire (*Daily Mail, Daily Express*); popular biographies of imperial heroes; juvenile literature in books and magazines promoting such a consistent imperial line that George Orwell in 1939 famously saw them enshrining, not to say embalming, a distinctively Edwardian mindset.[3] It was an image further inculcated at school via history textbooks and geographies of the Empire, by the uniformed youth movements and by a range of invented traditions and public rituals designed to promote Empire, in particular Empire Day with its religious services, processions, concerts and imperial displays. Many of the volumes in the 'Studies in Imperialism' series have recovered and explored in detail facets of this cultural expression of Empire.[4]

Under the circumstances, it is scarcely surprising that John Julius Norwich should recall of his 1930s' boyhood: 'Empire was all around us . . . part of the fabric of our lives. We were all imperialists then'; or that James Morris should conclude of the same period: 'Most Britons still considered [the Empire] all in all, as a force for good in the world and only a minority could conceive of it actually coming to an end.'[5] The novelist George MacDonald Fraser, who grew up in India and later served there with the British Army, set the subject in context:

> It is probably impossible for anyone born since 1950 to understand what it was like to be, and to think, British of the 1930s; equally impossible for anyone over sixty to conceive what it is like to be young today and have no imperial outlook . . . The child of 1939 had an imperial view, whatever his class (it is a massive error to suppose that imperialism was confined to the middle and upper classes; if anything it was stronger among the working class, and I speak from personal experience of the old Raj, where a colonel's imperialism was as nothing compared to the private soldier's). The British child of the 1930s thought that the Empire was terrific, giving him and his country a status beyond all other nations

[2]

– and he had the evidence to prove it on a world map that was one-fifth pink. The child of 1980 has no such evidence, but being a nationalist (and rationalist) of his own time, he takes his country's status as he finds it, without an Empire, so who needs it? It is a natural point of view, in which he may be encouraged by those revisionists who hold that imperialism was not quite respectable, and even positively evil.[6]

The fact that none of the major political parties seriously contemplated the Empire's dissolution until the 1940s suggests that such a policy would have commanded little electoral support, and even though the Labour Party gave India its independence in 1947, the Government expected to be ruling Africa for the foreseeable future.

Music

In view of the ubiquity of imperialism in fiction, painting, poetry and theatre, it would seem intrinsically likely that it has left its traces in music. Research indicates that there was a veritable ocean of imperial music from the classical to the popular during the nineteenth and twentieth centuries, most of it now forgotten. But music raises greater interpretative difficulties than the other arts.

There has long been a debate between the believers in pure or absolute music and those who believe that music is programmatic and referential. Stravinsky famously argued: 'Music is, by its very nature, powerless to *express* anything at all, whether a feeling, an attitude of mind, a psychological mood.'[7] Eduard Hanslick, the influential nineteenth-century Viennese musical critic, believed music was an end in itself and that listening to music involved the pure contemplation of beautiful sounds and not the representation, communication or stimulation of emotions. He wrote *The Beautiful in Music* to argue this case. This view has recently been revived by Peter Kivy, who argues that 'pure instrumental music, "music alone," as I have called it, is a quasi-syntactical structure of sound understandable solely in musical terms and having no semantic or representational content, no meaning, making reference to nothing beyond itself'.[8] Roger Scruton has taken a similar position. In his book *The Aesthetics of Music* he argues that music is 'not representational, since thoughts about a subject are never essential to the understanding of music . . . the meaning of music lies *within* it, it can be recovered only through an act of musical understanding, and not by an assignment of values'.[9] He understands music as a purely aesthetic experience, whose meaning lies in its structure and not in any outside associations.

The anti-representationalists thus comprise the formalists who believe that the internal structure of the music is what is important,

[3]

the aestheticians following Hanslick who believe in the pure beauty of sounds, and the purists who believe in the idea of 'absolute music' (a term coined by Wagner) and reject any extramusical associations. 'Absolute music' is seen as timeless, universal, transcendent, the product of individual genius.

But, as Lydia Goehr has shown, the whole idea of 'absolute music' is itself a historical construct, a product of the Romantic era.[10] Goehr argues that until the late eighteenth century

> theorists – philosophers, clerics, scientists – attributed to music specific 'extra-musical' meanings that rendered it a worthy contribution to a moral, rational, and religiously upright society. Music's meaning came from 'outside' itself. It derived either from music's cathartic ability to influence and sustain a person's religious, moral, and political convictions, or from its mimetic ability to imitate the nature of persons and the world.[11]

This continued to be an important strand in musical thinking throughout the nineteenth century. It is epitomised by the influential work of Rev. H.R. Haweis and is an explanation for the central role of music in the rational recreation movement, where concerts were promoted and choral singing encouraged in the belief that music was innately uplifting, improving and 'good for you'.[12] But in the late eighteenth and early nineteenth centuries, and as a direct result of the rise of Romanticism, theorists began to argue that music was a fine art, transcending its surroundings and reaching to the sublime. Musicians were heroically individualist artists; their music free of outside associations. This doctrine was the ultimate expression of 'Art for Art's Sake' and the celebration of the solitary genius, alone and complete unto himself. It has continued to hold powerful sway.

But there was an almost immediate reaction against this by artists who positively wanted to use music to express extra-musical ideas and who believed that the market required them to indicate to their public what they were about. If a composer gives his music a title – say The Imperial March – then he is evidently seeking to convey something specific to the audience. Liszt coined the terms 'programme music' and 'symphonic poem' to describe the kind of music to which names were given and which were *about* something. William Wallace, the notable Scottish composer of symphonic poems, defined it simply as 'music which attempts to excite a mental image by means of an auditory impression'.[13] Malcolm Budd describes this position as 'humanist' because it sees musical works as having

> a significance that can be explained only by their relation to what we are familiar with outside music. In these works there are embodied,

[4]

reflected, expressed, symbolised or in some other way presented phenomena that are integral to human life: we recognize moods, feelings,
emotions, attitudes and various other states and activities of our inner
life manifested in such a way that, if we are sensitive to their presence
and responsive to the manner in which music makes them present to
us, we value these musical works because of their essential human
reference.[14]

By this definition, music can be used to communicate individual but
universal feelings – love or loss of faith – or it can set out to capture
more generally the spirit of a place, a time or a nation. In the nineteenth century, some composers, such as Elgar, felt the need for both
types: absolute and programme music.

There are, however, those who believe that there really is no such
thing as 'absolute music' and that all music is about something.
Jacques Barzun wrote:

> Most Western Music has been composed 'about something' . . . the
> critical enthusiasm for the pure and absolute is the product of very
> recent estheticism. It belongs mainly to the second half of the nineteenth
> century . . . it appears as part of the hostile reaction to the modern world,
> as an expression of distaste for objective reality and common emotion.
> 'Pure form' in all the arts is meant to reinstate spirituality in the teeth
> of vulgar materialism and practical life.[15]

He compares music to literature. Both are necessarily programmatic,
both acting to express something deeper than the events they contain,
to express the essence of that experience.

Already in 1906 Professor Frederick Niecks had come to that conclusion. Having investigated the question at length in *Programme
Music in the Last Four Centuries*, he concluded 'all good music has
a programme . . . the artist whose forms are nothing but forms will
always leave his auditor or spectator cold'.[16] He argued that just as
vocal music necessarily has a programme in words, instrumental
music does too, even if the composer chose sometimes to conceal it.
He adduces the example of Weber's *Konzertstück* which the composer's correspondence revealed to have a specific and detailed programme of chivalric romance. Other examples might be cited, such as
Sir Hubert Parry's *Overture to an Unwritten Tragedy*, which was precisely the opposite, being inspired by *Othello*, and Vaughan Williams's
Ninth Symphony which was inspired by Hardy's *Tess of the
d'Urbervilles*, though that was never made public.

Equally, as Barzun points out, certain musical conventions have specific associations – slow pace and deep tone suggest sadness, seriousness, majesty; high notes in rapid time equal gaiety, joy, triumph,

celebration; certain keys and the minor scale show an affinity with darker and more pensive moods; other keys and the major scale, the opposite frame of mind.[17] Common sense suggests that both absolute and representational music exist. But this study is concerned exclusively with the representational.

A key question is how music affects listeners. Anthony Storr, in the authoritative survey *Music and the Mind*, expresses the convictions that music causes emotional arousal, 'a generally enhanced state of being', and that there seems to be a closer relation between hearing and emotional arousal than between seeing and emotional arousal.[18] Music, he says is a 'way of ordering the human experience', finding patterns of tone and melody to which audiences can relate: providing order and structure; stimulating feelings. In fact it has always been designed for that purpose. Music began by serving communal purposes, notably religious ritual and warfare, and has ever since been used as an adjunct of social ceremonies and public occasions. Both at coronations and cup finals, singing connotes belonging. Storr writes that the idea that 'music causes a general state of arousal rather than specific emotions partly explains why it has been used to accompany such a wide variety of human activities, including marching, serenading, worship, marriages, funerals, and manual work'.[19] He argues that music structures time and that, by imposing order, 'music ensures that the emotions aroused by a particular event peal at the same moment'.[20] He points out that music and speech are separately represented in the two hemispheres of the brain, with language processed by the left hemisphere and music by the right. 'The division of function', he concludes, 'is not so much between words and music as between logic and emotion'.[21] So the parts of the brain concerned with the emotional effects of music are distinct from those that have to do with an appreciation of its structure. The fact that people experience the effect of having tunes running through their minds is part of their imaginative inner lives. Individuals will react differently to music. It is reasonable to assume that each person in an audience will react differently according to personality, age, gender, experience, temperament. But music also functions within a shared culture, and until the gramophone and the wireless created the possibility of the solitary listener, music was designed to be experienced communally – and for the most part was so experienced, allowing for the emotion of a shared experience based on common denominators. Scientific research has recently suggested that many emotional identifications in music are shared. John Sloboda reports that in one classic series of experiments, people were played musical extracts that they had never heard before and were asked to choose, from a long list of emotional adjectives, the ones that best described the emotional character of the piece. It was found that there was broad general agreement between people of different backgrounds and age groups.[22] This is in part, he suggests, because music mimics certain aspects of life.

> For instance, when people or animals are dejected, they tend to move slowly, with drooping posture, and emitting low-pitched sounds. When they are exhilarated they move fast, with breathless high-pitched noises. And so on. If music displays some of these sound characteristics, we can't help but ascribe emotional characteristics to the music.[23]

Investigating whether or not listeners agree about the greatest points of emotional intensity within a work, Sloboda and his colleagues found that there was a common physiological response, a 'tingle' factor, at the same places in the music. They have identified ten musical features which have been found to recur again and again at moments of high emotion: harmony descending through the circle of fifths to the tonic, melodic appoggiaturas, melodic or harmonic sequences, enharmonic change, delay of the final cadence, new or unprepared harmony, sudden dynamic or textural change, repeated syncopation and a prominent event occurring earlier than the listener is prepared for. All this leads him to conclude that emotion is integral to our reception of music:

> It is rooted in our knowledge of the forms and structures within a musical culture, and the ways in which composers and performers manipulate these structures in order to fulfil or thwart expectations. Many of the processes we engage in when listening to music are semi-automatic responses which have built up in our brains by virtue of sheer immersion in the musical culture from birth.[24]

Nevertheless, music is not a universal language. The Western tonal system is only one of a number of different forms, and is very different from Indian and Japanese music. It is the product of specific cultural history.[25] Much more recently than in the other arts historians have begun to question the notion of art constituting 'an autonomous sphere, separate and insulated from the outside social world', the idea underlying much musical theory and musicology.[26] As Janet Wolff argues, 'culture . . . is a social product and the study of culture must accordingly be sociologically informed'. The history of art is the history of the circumstances which produced it.

In this context, what is the 'meaning of music'? Musicology can analyze the structure of a work but it cannot explain why it produced the effect it does. Music does not exist in a vacuum. The effect may change and the images the music produces may change as cultural circumstances change. For instance, Puccini's aria *Nessun Dorma* means for millions not the opera *Turandot* but the World Cup Final for which it was the theme tune, and as a result became a hit record. Composers go in and out of fashion, as cultural values and perceptions change: Elgar is a perfect example of this.

Interpretations of music in performance may vary – simply by playing the score faster or slower, louder or softer. Interpreters may follow exactly or depart radically from the intentions of the composer. There is a whole genre of performance interpretation books. But this book is concerned with a different kind of interpretation. Christopher John Ballantine argues for the organic inter-relationship of music and society: 'What actually happens is that social structures crystallize in musical structures; that in various ways and with varying degrees of critical awareness, the musical microcosm replicates the social macrocosm.'[27]

The meaning of music within the culture is defined by the understanding of the values of the culture by the composer, the performer and the audience. The composer cannot be immune to what is going on around him. For he – composers usually were men – is operating in a context determined by the role, aspirations, interests and views of the composer; the role and constraints of patronage; the role of the State (censorship, funding, control of institutions): the demands of the market; the nature of the consumer; the influence of class or national perceptions. 'Art', says Wolff, 'is a historically specific fact, produced in particular and contingent social circumstances. It can also be shown that the division between "high art" and . . . "popular art" . . . is based on social, rather than aesthetic, distinctions'.[28] There are many examples of this: the dominance of the oratorio as a form in nineteenth-century Britain was due to the social and cultural demands of that society; the different versions of Verdi's operas in Italy and France were responses to the different cultural demands of the two countries: the alteration of the setting of *Un Ballo in Maschera* from eighteenth-century Sweden to seventeenth-century New England and the transformation of *Stiffelio*, the story of a contemporary church minister, into *Aroldo*, the story of a mediaeval English crusader, were dictated by censorship.

The idea of the autonomy of music is contrary to the demands of the market, and the need of composers to earn a living by catering to the requirements of their patrons: to provide parlour ballads for home performance, special music for great public occasions, background music for theatres. There is evidence for the cultural interpretation of the meaning of works of music in the writings of composers and performers, in the reactions of audiences and in the views of critics –

important because they play a key role in interpreting and mediating the music for the audience. A cultural interpretation of music requires an examination of the entire range of music from 'serious' to 'popular'. This book is part of the movement to contextualize music and in particular to relate it to imperialism. To understand this relationship it is necessary first to outline the nature and structure of musical life in Britain.

Dave Russell, who has written the definitive work on popular music in Britain in the nineteenth century, sees three key processes in operation in the second half of that century: expansion, diversification and nationalization.[29] There was a dramatic expansion in all aspects of musical life. The number of professional musicians recorded by the Census rose from 19,000 in 1871 to 47,000 in 1911. In 1840 a piano was a luxury item; by 1910 there was an estimated one piano for every twenty members of the population. By 1900 there were more musical instruments, journals and societies available than at any time in the nation's history.

Music-making was everywhere: it was being performed in the home, in church, in school, at the seaside, in the parks, even in the streets. There were music festivals in many towns and cities; symphony orchestras in most big cities. There were travelling opera companies, choral societies, brass bands, musical comedies in the theatres, songs in the music halls, promenade concerts.

Despite regional variations, which remained strong, and the ever-present north–south divide, there was a process of musical nationalization underway. From the 1870s onwards, encouraged by the railways – which enabled music-hall artists, concert artists and orchestras to travel the nation with their repertoires and permitted the establishing of national contests for choirs and bands – there was an increasing unification of national musical tastes. The growth of the music publishing and instrument-making industries led to the promotion of national hit songs and hit music. Music was industrialized and commercialized as a genuinely national music culture emerged.

Musical life was organized on class lines and there was musical snobbery; but there were significant cross-class exchanges: music-hall songs sung in middle-class drawing rooms, operatic tunes sung in working-class music halls and concerts. There was a range of musical material which appealed to all classes: hymns, ballads, Gilbert and Sullivan operettas, marches, operatic arias.

Industrialization brought benefits for the working classes in terms of a reduction of the working week and an increase in wages, which gave them more time and money for leisure. The middle-class concern for 'rational recreation' led to the promotion of cross-class musical activities on a large scale.

The Great War proved to be a watershed in the musical life of Britain, for after it active music-making entered into a decline. The slaughter of the Great War reduced the available pool of male recruits for choirs and bands. The Depression cut the amount of money available for instruments, sheet music and the other necessities of musical life. The decline in religious observance and the growing secularization of society blunted the Protestant impetus towards religious music-making. Alternative leisure pursuits drew people away from the making of music to the consuming of entertainment: football, cinema and music hall.

There was still as much music around as before, though much of it was now generated mechanically by wireless, gramophone and cinema. There was a decline in concert-going, and the rise of modernism opened up a gulf between 'art music' and 'popular music' that has never been bridged. But there continued to be cross-class national music taste, fostered by the new mechanical media, and much of the standard Victorian and Edwardian musical fare – classical, popular and religious – could be heard on the BBC and on gramophone records. It continued to hold sway until the mid-1950s when the rock music revolution changed the world of popular music forever. As Simon Frith has suggested, popular music has social functions: it provides ways of managing the relationships between our public and private emotional lives; it shapes popular memory and organizes our sense of time; and it creates collective identity.[30] This could reasonably be broadened to include all music. For music plays a significant role in helping to define and foster a sense of national identity.

Musical identity

The nineteenth century was the century of musical nationalism, when countries like Russia, Hungary, Bohemia, Norway and Poland each developed a musical style that was seen to reflect the national identity. In Britain there began to be insistent calls for the promotion of English national music. But there was considerable prejudice against English music in Britain. Italian music dominated the opera, German music the orchestral field and French music the operetta stage.[31] However, more and more voices began to be raised in favour of English music.

Typically an editorial in *The Musical Times* (1 January 1887) set out the case for nationalism in music. 'This is an age of revived national feeling. On every hand we behold signs of a mighty movement of peoples towards a fuller appreciation of blood relationship, a common origin, and, as in fond hopes, a common destiny.' The writer pointed to the unification of Germany, the aspirations of the Slavs and Irish nationalism as evidence. He rejected the idea that music was universal. Racial, temperamental and climatic differences separated northern Europeans from southern Europeans, and these differences were reflected in their music.

> The roots of national music . . . lie deep down in the nature of the people to whom it belongs, and can only be eradicated by destroying the nationality. It is useless, therefore, to insist upon the claim of any 'classics' to be regarded as a universal standard . . . Each country, recognizing its own nature in its own music, should cultivate the art for itself, seize upon whatever is most distinctive and valuable in its own conception and expression, and endeavour to complete the edifice upon that best and surest foundation.

The writer admitted that we had no national music that was distinctive 'by peculiarities of structure' and which 'can instantly be recognized, like that of Scotland or Hungary'. The nearest thing we had was English folk-song.

> The tunes are simply constructed, of a manly and straightforward character, emphasized by definite, well-marked rhythm and regularity of phrase; and they combine strength and tenderness to a degree approached by no other national airs, save the kindred Germans, in which, however, sentiment predominates over strength . . . We have, therefore, a national style of melody, which has grown out of our temperament and circumstances, and is the natural musical expression of our feelings . . . But, as far as we are aware, no efforts are being made to infuse the English melodic spirit into works of higher culture.

Since the national music of the Slavic and Scandinavian countries was strongly based on folk music, and since the Welsh, Irish and Scots were recognized to have strong folk traditions, there was a natural and inevitable insistence on English folk music as the source of national music.

The Musical Times' editorial was echoed by Sir Hubert Parry's influential book *Style in Musical Art* (1911), in which he declared: 'the fact remains that when any people have strongly marked characteristics and any aptitude for musical expression, their music bespeaks them more truly than any other manifestation of the mind of man'.[32] He too turned to folk-song as most truly expressive of the English temperament, which he characterized as marked by 'simplicity, sincerity, tenderness, playfulness, innocent gaiety, healthy vigour'. To folk-song he added the music of Tudor and Jacobean England, which like folk-song was characterized by 'simplicity and unaffected tunefulness' and by the absence of 'passionate violence of intervals or rhythm or accents'.[33]

By the time Parry was writing, these ideas had become articles of faith, strongly upheld within the English Musical Renaissance, of which Parry was a leading member. It was the vision and energy of Sir George Grove and his campaign to promote English music and the notion of 'Englishness in music' which launched the English Musical Renaissance. Grove edited the monumental *Dictionary of Music and Musicians* (1879–89), which gave prominence to English music and became the bible of the English musical world. Repelled by the brutality and ruthlessness shown by the Germans in the Franco-Prussian War of 1870–71, he sought to break the stranglehold of German music on British cultural life. Grove's efforts, backed by the Prince of Wales and his musical brothers the Dukes of Edinburgh and Albany, led to the establishing in 1883 of the Royal College of Music, which became the powerhouse of the English Musical Renaissance. The Prince of Wales put this enterprise securely in an imperial context when, in a speech supporting the venture, he sought to involve in the enterprise leading figures in the colonies. He argued that the College could enhance 'colonial co-operation and sympathy' and promote imperial unity 'by inspiring among our fellow-subjects in every part of the Empire those emotions of patriotism which national music is calculated so powerfully to evoke . . .'. For he believed that music could provide 'an elevating source of enjoyment which is at the same time calculated to strengthen those emotions that have so much influence in perpetuating a common love of country'.[34] The Royal College of Music forged important links with the universities of Oxford and Cambridge, the Royal Academy of Music, the music publisher Novello, *The Musical Times*, the Carl Rosa Opera Company and the royal court. Grove became the first rector of the Royal College, but its leading musical influences were professors Sir Hubert Parry and Sir Charles Villiers Stanford. The Carl Rosa Opera Company was founded in 1875 to produce English opera and opera in English. Important concert series, like those of Sir August Manns at the Crystal Palace and Sir Henry Wood at the Queen's Hall, made a point of promoting new English music. Significant music critics and journalists campaigned for English music. The Purcell Society was founded in 1876 to resurrect the music and reputation of Henry Purcell as the last English composer of genius. In 1898 the English Folk Song Society was founded with Parry, Stanford, and Sir Alexander Mackenzie, principal of the Royal Academy of Music, as vice-presidents. It was to retrieve the folk-tunes which were to inform the music of a younger generation of composers like Gustav Holst and Vaughan Williams. But there were important figures outside the magic circle of South Kensington who also played their part in the assertion of English music, notably Sir Edward Elgar and Sir Arthur Sullivan.[35]

So if music represented the national identity, what was that identity? Prior to the English Musical Renaissance, the most successful and enduring English music was church music, in particular the oratorio, and this was the staple fare of the choral societies and provincial music festivals. Any composer who sought to earn his living from music was compelled to write oratorios. Their number was legion. The great master of the oratorio was Handel, and he, although German by birth, became a naturalized Englishman. His *Messiah* remained the most popular English oratorio of the nineteenth century and set the pattern for succeeding composers. But the whole structure of requiems, te deums and Anglican Church music, plus the host of hymns, Anglican and Nonconformist, established a definite and indisputable musical Protestantism as one key aspect of English identity.

The second element was the one created by the Musical Renaissance: 'Merrie England', an historical–pastoral tradition which drew its inspiration from folk music and folk dance and which looked to an idealized pre-urban England of the village but also to Elizabethan England, the first age of Empire, the age of Raleigh, Hawkins and Drake, the seadogs and the merchant venturers, of Shakespeare and Spenser, the masters of the English language, of the Protestant Reformation and the defeat of the Armada, and of a long-lived and revered queen, Gloriana, precursor of the Queen–Empress. It appealed across the political spectrum: to the Left with its celebration of the peasantry, the village community and the golden age before industrial capitalism; and to the Right with its glorification of the sea-borne Empire, the plucky little Protestant island under the presiding genius of the Virgin Queen standing alone against a tyrannical Catholic Empire. This historical–pastoral tradition was espoused by Vaughan Williams, Gustav Holst and George Butterworth, on the one hand, and by Edward German on the other.[36]

There was a third element – as popular in England as in Scotland, Wales, Ireland and Cornwall from where it drew inspiration – and that was the Celtic, the music of mists and mysticism, magic and mystery, gods and legends, fairies and giants, a kind of rejection of modern industrial society different from the construct of 'Merrie England'. This again appealed both to Left and to Right and inspired among others Sir Arnold Bax, Rutland Boughton, Sir Granville Bantock, Josef Holbrooke and George Lloyd.

But the great revival in English music, which some musical historians have dated to 1880 and the première of Parry's cantata

Prometheus Unbound and others to Parry's *Blest Pair of Sirens* in 1887, coincided exactly with the high point of the British Empire. One of the functions of music therefore was to express a British imperial identity. It presented a far more difficult task than that faced by the exponents of Protestantism, 'Merrie England' or Celtic mysticism, for it had to embrace England, Scotland, Wales and Ireland, as well as India, and the colonies, dominions and dependencies overseas. But what values were to be embodied in the music of imperialism?

Empire and imperialism

Belief and pride in Empire were steadily inculcated throughout the second half of the nineteenth century as a result of the development of the mass market and of well-developed and commercialized leisure industries, responding to the wishes of consumers as expressed through their purchases. The preconditions of the mass market were all in place by the second half of the century: rising real wages and greater leisure time for the mass of the people; concentrated urban markets; an efficient and integrated transport system in the railways; a breed of capitalist entrepreneurs willing to develop new leisure industries; and technological developments facilitating cheap mass production.[37]

The mass market sought to generate maximum profit by appealing to the lowest-common-denominator views of the majority. This development coincided with the growth of a specific doctrine of British imperialism. There can be little doubt that the primary motive in the growth of the British Empire was economic. The desire for profit can be seen to lie behind such diverse activities as the search for the North-West Passage, the foundation of the East India Company and the acquisition of Hong Kong. As the Empire grew, strategic imperialism developed, explaining the acquisition of the Cape of Good Hope and the expansion of British power in India, initially to protect the trading interest in Bengal. Altruistic imperialism played a very small part in the first phase of Empire, but with the need to develop a doctrine to justify the acquisition of Empire, it took on a major importance. The missionary impulse, the desire to bring the 'heathen' to the light of God, and the leadership principle, the idea that the British being the greatest race in the world had a duty to provide government and justice for 'inferior races', intertwined to create a continuing theme in imperial writing: the idea that the British ran their Empire not for their own benefit but for the benefit of those they ruled.[38]

The early Victorian attitude – consistent with the liberal philosophy of *laissez-faire* – was informal or free-trade imperialism. The

Manchester School of Cobden and Bright viewed territorial Empire as a liability and saw 'imperialism' (with its Napoleonic overtones) as the antithesis of the English democratic tradition and of free trade. But there was a seachange in the 1860s and 1870s. The Earl of Carnarvon drew a distinction between false imperialism – Caesarism, personal rule, militarism, vast standing armies, endless expense – and true imperialism – maintaining the peace, developing areas productively, educating the people towards self-government. This concept of duty and service merged with the evangelical desire to bring the 'heathen' to the light of God, with Dilke's popularisation of 'Greater Britain', the union of the Anglo-Saxon races in Britain and the white dominions, linked by common institutions, language, culture and traditions, and with a revived chivalry (service, duty, *noblesse oblige*). This was promoted by key figures of the age to produce a code for the ruling elite, who would be inspired by noble and selfless values, and to counteract the materialism of and the philistinism associated with the new industrial society. There was a rare convergence of belief between the intelligentsia and the masses as such leading figures as Ruskin, Froude, Seeley and Carlyle advocated the values and virtues of Empire.

A succession of great imperial events captured the public imagination: the suppression of the Indian Mutiny in 1857; the search for Livingstone; the purchase by Disraeli of the Suez Canal; the Abyssinian, Ashanti and Sudanese campaigns; and the proclamation of Queen Victoria as Empress of India in 1876. This was accompanied by a transformation in the standing of the army. Once regarded as 'brutal and licentious soldiery' and 'the scum of the earth', the army, like much of Victorian England, felt the impact of evangelicalism. The result was, as Olive Anderson has pointed out, that, by the mid-1860s, '[t]he British Army was ... more obtrusively Christian than it had been since the Restoration'.[39] Tommy Atkins the soldier came to rival Jack Tar the sailor as the popular icon of British masculinity. The arena for both to demonstrate their manliness and their Britishness was the Empire.

All of this reinforced and strengthened an idea of Britishness which had emerged in the eighteenth century, as Linda Colley has demonstrated.[40] She shows that a sense of specifically British identity was forged in the eighteenth century by a combination of historical forces. The United Kingdom of Great Britain was actually created in 1707 by the Act of Union which linked England, Wales and Scotland (Ireland was added in 1800). This unity was strongly reinforced and underpinned by a shared Protestantism. The succession of wars against France had the effect of emphasizing and consolidating British nationality and drawing a pointed contrast between Britain, defined as

[15]

Protestant, democratic, parliamentary, commercial and progressive, and France, defined as Catholic, aristocratic, absolutist, agrarian, backward and poor. The result of the wars was the acquisition of a vast overseas Empire – India, Canada, the West Indies – into which the Irish and the Scots enthusiastically opted as generals, rulers, traders and missionaries. Britain, as it emerged in the eighteenth century, was the product specifically of Protestantism, Empire, war and free trade.

It was not until the nineteenth century that intellectuals and ideologues caught up with popular instincts and ideas. When they did, they refined and articulated a doctrine of imperialism whose basic ideas, simplified and reiterated, percolated into popular consciousness: that the Empire was Britain writ large; that it was the embodiment and expression of a British character comprising of individuality, stoicism, a sense of duty, a sense of humour and a sense of superiority; that Britain was in the Empire for the good of its native peoples.

There were 'Little Englanders' on the Left and the Right. Little Englanders of the Left with their international perspective, idea of class war and detestation of jingoism saw Empire as a sham, a fraud and an exploitative despotism. Little Englanders of the Right, like Belloc and Chesterton, saw Empire as a plutocratic Jewish conspiracy that detached Britain from its true nature: Catholic, peasant and European. But both were minority views.

In his pioneering book *Propaganda and Empire*, J.M. MacKenzie identified 'an ideological cluster ... which came to influence and be propagated by every organ of British life in the period'. He identified this ideological cluster as militarism, monarchism, hero-worship, racialism and social Darwinism. 'Together these constituted a new type of patriotism which derived special significance from Britain's unique imperial mission.'[41]

This requires refinement in the light of subsequent historiography. We should certainly add Protestantism, with its doctrines of missionary impulse, the idea of the British as an elect and the sanctity of hard work, and perhaps substitute for militarism chivalry (which can be interpreted militaristically but also pacifically and defensively). Also Paul Crook recently has persuasively questioned the inclusion of social Darwinism, arguing that 'the myth of a Darwinized imperial discourse seems largely the creation of inventive new liberals ... who feared the authoritarian implications of an invasive social science based on biology'.[42] That cluster of monarchism, racialism, Protestantism, hero-worship and chivalry structures and informs the music of Empire just as much as it did other cultural forms.

The First World War marked a watershed in the depictions and promotion of the Empire. Before the war imperialism could be militaristic, expansionist and jingoistic, as represented in songs, stories and plays about scarlet-coated military heroes showing the flag. After the war, Empire was equated with stability, produce, peace and order, as epitomised by the BBC Empire Service, Imperial Airways, the Empire Exhibitions and the Empire Marketing Board. While juvenile literature continued to laud its military heroes in pre-war terms, films until 1939 more characteristically saw Empire's heroes maintaining the peace rather than pursuing aggressive expansion. But in either guise Empire remained resolutely a 'good thing', and integral to national identity. That was how the majority of the population understood it and such was the ideological context within which imperial music was to be produced.

Notes

1 The *Daily Telegraph*, 26 August, 1997.
2 Henry Pelling, 'British labour and imperialism', in H. Pelling, *Popular Politics and Society in Late Victorian Britain*, London: MacMillan, 1979, pp. 82–100. See also Richard Price, *An Imperial War and the British Working Class*, London: Routledge, 1972; John Belchem *Industrialization and the Working Class*, Aldershot: Scolar Press, 1990, p. 243; Bernard Porter, *The Lion's Share*, London: Longman, 1975, p. 200.
3 George Orwell, 'Boys' weeklies', *Complete Works*, London: Secker & Warburg, 1998, vol. 12, pp. 57–9.
4 John M. MacKenzie, *Propaganda and Empire*, Manchester: Manchester University Press, 1984; John M. MacKenzie (ed.), *Imperialism and Popular Culture*, Manchester: Manchester University Press, 1986; John M. MacKenzie (ed.), *Popular Imperialism and the Military*, Manchester: Manchester University Press, 1992; Jeffrey Richards (ed.), *Imperialism and Juvenile Literature*, Manchester: Manchester University Press, 1989; Paul Greenhalgh, *Ephemeral Vistas*, Manchester: Manchester University Press, 1988; J.S. Bratton, et al. (eds), *Acts of Supremacy*, Manchester: Manchester University Press, 1991; Robert H. MacDonald, *The Language of Empire*, Manchester: Manchester University Press, 1994; see also Paul Usherwood and Jenny Spencer-Smith, *Lady Butler, Battle Artist 1846–1933*, Gloucester: Alan Sutton, 1987; Martin Green, *Dreams of Adventure, Deeds of Empire*, London: Routledge, 1980; H. John Field, *Towards a Programme of Imperial Life: The British Empire at the Turn of the Century*, Oxford: Clio Press, 1982; Eric Hobsbawm and Terence Ranger (eds), *The Invention of Tradition*, Cambridge: Cambridge University Press, 1983; John Springhall, *Youth, Empire and Society: British Youth Movements, 1883–1940*, London: Croom Helm, 1977; Thomas Richards, *The Commodity Culture of Victorian England*, London: Verso, 1991.
5 MacKenzie, *Imperialism and Popular Culture*, p. 8; James Morris, *Farewell the Trumpets*, London and Boston, MA: Faber & Faber, 1978, pp. 315–16.
6 George MacDonald Fraser, *The Hollywood History of the World*, London: Michael Joseph, 1988, p. 137.
7 Igor Stravinsky, *An Autobiography*, New York: Norton, 1963, p. 53.
8 Peter Kivy, *Music Alone*, Ithaca, NY, and London: Cornell University Press, 1990, p. 202.
9 Roger Scruton, *The Aesthetics of Music*, Oxford: Clarendon Press, 1997, pp. 138, 211.
10 Lydia Goehr, *The Imaginary Museum of Musical Works*, Oxford: Clarendon Press, 1992; and 'Music has no meaning to speak of: on the politics of musical interpre-

tation', in Michael Krausz (ed.), *The Interpretation of Music*, Oxford: Clarendon Press, 1995, pp. 177–90.

11 Goehr, 'Music has no meaning', pp. 180–1.

12 Reverend H.R. Haweis, *Music and Morals*, London: W.H. Allen, 1888; and *My Musical Life*, London: W.H. Allen, 1886.

13 Frederick Niecks, *Programme Music in the Last Four Centuries*, London: Novello, 1906, p. 381.

14 Malcolm Budd, *Music and the Emotions*, London and New York: Routledge, 1992, p. 52.

15 Jacques Barzun, *Critical Questions*, Chicago: Chicago University Press, 1984, p. 81.

16 Niecks, *Programme Music*, p. 536

17 Barzun, *Critical Questions*, p. 82.

18 Anthony Storr, *Music and the Mind*, London: Harper Collins, 1992, pp. 24–5.

19 Storr, *Music and the Mind*, pp. 187, 182.

20 Storr, *Music and the Mind*, p. 30.

21 Storr, *Music and the Mind*, p. 35.

22 John Sloboda, 'Brain waves to the heart', *BBC Music Magazine* 7, 3 (November 1998), p. 32.

23 *Ibid.*

24 *Ibid.*, p. 33.

25 Richard Norton, *Tonality in Western Culture*, Philadelphia: Pennsylvania State University Press, 1984.

26 See for instance Richard Leppert and Susan McClary (eds), *Music and Society*, Cambridge: Cambridge University Press, 1989; Christopher Norris (ed.), *Music and the Politics of Culture*, London: Lawrence & Wishart, 1989; Alan Durant, *The Conditions of Music*, London and Basingstoke: MacMillan, 1984; Robert Stradling and Meirion Hughes, *The English Musical Renaissance: Construction and Deconstruction*, London and New York: Routledge, 1993; Dave Russell, *Popular Music in England, 1840–1914*, Manchester: Manchester University Press, 1997.

27 Christopher John Ballantine, *Music and its Social Meanings*, New York: Gordon & Breach, 1984, p. 6.

28 Janet Wolff, 'The ideology of autonomous art', in Leppert and McClary (eds), *Music and Society*, p. 5.

29 Russell, *Popular Music in England*.

30 Simon Frith, 'Towards an aesthetic of popular music', in Leppert and McClary (eds), *Music and Society*, pp. 140–3.

31 Nicholas Temperley, *The Lost Chord*, Bloomington: Indiana University Press, 1989, p. 6.

32 C. Hubert H. Parry, *Style in Musical Art*, London: Macmillan, 1911, p. 155.

33 *Ibid.*, pp. 156–7.

34 James Macaulay (ed.), *Speeches and Addresses of HRH the Prince of Wales*, London: John Murray, 1889, pp. 404–5.

35 Stradling and Hughes, *The English Musical Renaissance*.

36 Georgina Boyes, *The Imagined Village: Culture, Ideology and the English Folk Revival*, Manchester: Manchester University Press, 1993, pp. 63–93.

37 W. Hamish Fraser, *The Coming of the Mass Market, 1850–1914*, London and Basingstoke: Macmillan, 1981.

38 George Bennett (ed.), *The Concept of Empire*, London: A & C Black, 1967; Richard Faber, *The Vision and the Need*, London: Faber & Faber, 1966.

39 Olive Anderson, 'The growth of Christian militarism in mid-Victorian Britain', *English Historical Review* 86 (1971), p. 64.

40 Linda Colley, *Britons*, New Haven, CT, and London: Yale University Press, 1992.

41 MacKenzie, *Propaganda and Empire*, p. 2.

42 Paul Crook, 'Historical monkey business: the myth of a Darwinized British imperial discourse', *History* 84 (October 1999), pp. 633–57.

CHAPTER TWO

Sullivan's Empire

If there is one classical composer who has become identified with the Empire and the imperial idea, it is Sir Edward Elgar. But there was an imperial dimension also to the work of the man Elgar succeeded as the acknowledged leader of the British musical world – Sir Arthur Sullivan. Reporting his death on 22 November 1900, *The Times* declared:

> The death of Sir Arthur Sullivan, in his 59th year, may be said without hyperbole to have plunged the whole of the Empire in gloom; for many years he has ranked with the most distinguished personages, rather than with ordinary musicians. Never in the history of the art has a position such as his been held by a composer; and it was earned simply and solely by his own achievement, unaided by interest or side influence of any kind. For all the English-speaking races . . . Sullivan's name stood as a synonym for music in England.[1]

This being so, it is fascinating to find that Sullivan perfectly embodies the constellation of ideas that makes up the British imperial identity: patriotism, monarchism, chivalry, Protestantism, hero-worship and racial superiority. But he is also a clear example of the operation of multiple identity. Every person is a bundle of identities. Every individual describes himself or herself as being from a particular family or class, from a particular faith or political party, from a neighbourhood, town, county, country, nation, race, empire. Different aspects can be expressed at different times; but they can also fit together like a set of Chinese boxes.

Sir Arthur Sullivan was born in 1842 in Lambeth, his Christian name suggesting the influence of the revived cult of King Arthur and the memory of the great hero of the Napoleonic Wars, Arthur Wellesley, Duke of Wellington. Sullivan's grandfather was an Irish soldier from County Cork, who died a Chelsea Pensioner; his father, a military bandsman who later became chief Professor of Clarinet at the Royal Military School of Music at Kneller Hall. His mother, Mary Clementina Coghlan, was half-Irish and half-Italian. His biographers Herbert Sullivan and Sir Newman Flower claim that he inherited 'the tough Irish spirit of his grandfather', veteran Savoyard Henry Lytton calls him 'a warmhearted Irishman' and critic Hermann Klein talks of his 'Irish nature' and 'genuine Irish mother-wit'.[2] Sullivan was to acknowledge his Irish roots in his *Irish Symphony*, composed after a visit to Ireland though it is a work which owes as much to Mendelssohn and Schumann as to Irish folk-song. His final, uncompleted, operetta *The Emerald Isle* took him back again to the land of his forbears. Yet Sullivan thought of himself as English, and patriotically so. It can be seen in his fury at an episode which occurred when he was visiting Cairo in 1882. An English officer, challenged to a duel by an Austrian baron, bolted. Sullivan wrote to his mother: 'It has been a humiliation to all of us English here . . . Isn't it enough to make one's blood boil.'[3] His friend, Edward Dicey, the editor of *The Observer*, who was travelling with him, noted that the atmosphere in Cairo was extremely volatile and hostile to foreigners. There had been a revolt in the Egyptian army led by Arabi Pasha, and later in the year the Royal Navy bombarded Alexandria and General Wolseley crushed the rebels at Tel-el-Kebir. Dicey feared that Sullivan's 'staunch loyalty to England might get him into trouble'.[4]

This English patriotism extended to his devotion to and defence of English music. When the German Hans Richter was appointed in 1884 conductor of the Birmingham Festival, Sullivan wrote to Joseph Bennett, editor of the musical journal *The Lute*, calling the appointment 'a bitter humiliation for all us English' and suggesting that they should have appointed Cowen, Stanford, Barnby or even the Italian Alberto Randegger ('who is one of us, for all practical purposes') who 'would all have done the work well – a hundred times better than a German who cannot speak the language, who had never had any experience in dealing with English choruses and who knows none of the traditions of those choral works which form a large element in the Festival'.[5]

Signing himself 'A British Musician' he wrote to *The Times* during the Diamond Jubilee complaining bitterly about the lack of British music in the festivities' programme being played by the military bands. He was particularly incensed at the programme of the music for the review of colonial troops by the Prince of Wales at Buckingham Palace. It consisted exclusively of French, German and Austrian music: F. Wagner's march *Under the Double Eagle*, Herold's overture *Zampa*, two waltzes by Joseph Gung'l, *Weiner Reigen* and

Immortellen, and a selection from Offenbach's *Orpheus in the Under-world.* Sullivan wrote:

> The above might be an appropriate selection of music for a military review in Berlin or Paris, but it is not so apparent why such pieces should be chosen to welcome our colonial kinsmen to their Fatherland. I have examined several other similar programmes, and find to my astonishment that British music on these occasions (with two or three exceptions) has been totally ignored, the preference in all cases having been given to foreign productions. I have no idea of deprecating either German or French military music; some of the marches in particular are rich in melody and in accent . . . nor am I so exclusive as to wish that British music only should be performed at British musical entertainments; but on great national occasions it is not unreasonable to expect that the public should be reminded that British tunes do exist. I know of nothing more inspiring than *I'm Ninety-five, The Girl I Left Behind Me, Hearts of Oak, The British Grenadiers,* and our whole rich collection of Scotch, Irish, and Welsh national tunes; but most of these, at the recent Jubilee celebration, were conspicuous by their absence.[6]

Sullivan's most recent biographer Arthur Jacobs noted that his diary contained few references to public affairs or politics.[7] But Sullivan was conservative (with a small c), a monarchist and a patriot at a time when patriotism also embraced Empire. Having visited America, he expressed his distaste for that country, its system and values: 'ill-bred, rough and swaggering . . . no real lady or gentleman to be found . . . Republicanism is the curse of the country. Everyone is not only equal to but better than his neighbour and the consequence is insolence and churlishness in all the lower orders.'[8]

Sullivan had been an infant prodigy, already composing anthems and psalm settings while still one of the children of the Chapel Royal. He won the Mendelssohn Scholarship to the Royal Academy of Music and at Leipzig Conservatory earned his diploma with a highly praised suite of incidental music to Shakespeare's *The Tempest.* When it was performed in 1862 at the Crystal Palace, it caused a sensation and Sullivan was widely hailed as the great white hope of British music. His *Irish Symphony,* premièred in 1866 when he was still only 23, was proclaimed by *The Times* as 'the best musical work . . . for a long time produced by any English composer'.[9] There followed a cello concerto and the immensely popular *In Memoriam* overture. Then in 1871 he was teamed with W.S. Gilbert to produce the comic opera *Thespis,* initiating one of the most celebrated musical partnerships in theatrical history, Gilbert's brilliant wordplay and pungent satirical shafts being perfectly matched by Sullivan's gift for memorable melody and inspired musical parody. The Gilbert and Sullivan operas came to overshadow the rest of his work. Sullivan always maintained: 'My sacred music is that on which I base my reputation as a composer. These works are the offspring of my liveliest fancy, the children of my greatest strength, the products of my most earnest thought and most incessant toil.'[10] Seventy-six hymns were set to his tunes either original or arranged. They included alternative tunes to such standards as *Nearer, My God, to Thee* and *Rock of Ages*. But it is *St Gertrude*, his setting of *Onward Christian Soldiers*, which is best-remembered today. In his own lifetime, his oratorios *The Prodigal Son*, *The Martyr of Antioch* and *The Golden Legend* were much admired. But posterity has preferred the Savoy Operas. Both at the time and subsequently Sullivan was criticized for frittering away his talent on the operettas as well as on sentimental songs and ballads.[11] But he was a man without the inherited wealth of a Vaughan Williams or a Parry. He had to work for his living and to turn his hand to what the public wanted. However, he remained profoundly conscious of his position as the leader of English music, knighted by the Queen on the recommendation of Prime Minister Gladstone in 1883. So he continued to turn out his religious music, and he composed an English opera, *Ivanhoe*; he was planning another, *King Arthur*, at the time of his death.

Sullivan was devoted to the Queen ('Bless her, she is so kind and gracious'[12]) and took seriously his role as musical celebrant of crown and Empire. In this his career ran curiously parallel to that of the Poet Laureate Alfred, Lord Tennyson. Both men enjoyed the confidence and affection of the Queen. Both made their names and their fortunes by their artistic talents. Both appealed to the middle-class sensibilities of the age. Their work also overlaps at significant points. Sullivan set several Tennyson verses as songs: *St Agnes Eve, O, Swallow, Swallow, The Sisters, What Does Little Birdie Say?* and *Tears, Idle tears*. He provided incidental music for Tennyson's Robin Hood play *The Foresters* and set Tennyson's *Ode* for the opening of the Colonial and Indian Exhibition.

Both Sullivan and Tennyson produced work hymning monarchy and Empire. In Tennyson's case, this involved his celebrated poem *The Charge of the Light Brigade*, an epitaph for General Gordon, odes on the Golden Jubilee of Queen Victoria and the death of the Duke of Wellington, and the Arthurian epic *The Idylls of the King*, dedicated to Prince Albert and, according to Victor Kiernan, with 'an imperial dimension . . . visible throughout'[13]. Significantly, when Tennyson took his seat in the House of Lords, he sat on the cross-benches, explaining that he 'could not pledge himself to party thinking', wanting to be 'free to vote for that which to himself seemed better for the Empire'.[14] Monarchy and Empire cannot be seen as in any way separate. For, after 1876 and the proclamation of Victoria as Empress of India, Britain had an imperial monarchy, buttressed by ceremonial, which was the focus not just of national but of imperial sentiment.

Sullivan became a particularly close friend of the Queen's second son Prince Alfred, the Duke of Edinburgh, himself an amateur musician and strong supporter of English musical life. He dedicated his sacred cantata *The Martyr of Antioch* to Alfred and his oratorio *The Light of the World* to the Duchess of Edinburgh, Marie Alexandrovna. He dedicated his song *I Would I Were King* (1878) to Prince Leopold, Duke of Albany, Queen Victoria's youngest son.

His role of royal celebrant had begun as early as 1863 when, to mark the wedding of Albert Edward, Prince of Wales, to Princess Alexandra of Denmark, he composed *The Princess of Wales March* (dedicated to the Prince of Wales, and based on Danish airs), the song *Bride From the North* (to words by Henry Chorley) and the *Royal Wedding March*. But his role was confirmed spectacularly when in 1872 he composed his *Festival Te Deum* to celebrate the recovery of the Prince of Wales from his near fatal attack of typhoid. It was scored for soprano soloist, chorus, orchestra, organ and military band and divided into seven movements. It was dedicated to the Queen and performed at the Crystal Palace with 2,000 performers before an audience of 26,000. This genuinely joyous piece opens with Dr William Croft's solemn and sonorous *St Anne*, traditionally played to the Isaac Watts hymn *O God, Our Help in Ages Past* but here set to the new words of *God Have Mercy*. Sullivan, having provided confident and rousing choruses (*To Thee All Angels Cry Above* and *Glorious Company of the Apostles*), returns to *St Anne* for the climax and in a wonderfully bold and daring stroke counterpoints it with a jaunty military march, performed by military band. It somehow encapsulates the Victorian age musically: the devotion of the Protestant Church interwoven with the military swagger of imperial pomp, all in a work dedicated to the recovery of the Prince of Wales.

The Musical Times (1 June 1872) reviewed the *Festival Te Deum* with huge enthusiasm.

> With much of the breadth of Handel, some of the grace of Mozart, and an orchestral colouring almost unique in its masterly handling, this Te Deum ought to serve as a gratifying promise that English Music is blossoming into a Spring to be succeeded by a Summer, such as this land has not experienced since the death of Purcell.

It has rarely been heard since, which is a great pity as it is a bold, inventive, exuberant work.

But it was not just pieces directly related to royal events that encouraged Sullivan to display his monarchist sympathies. His opera *Haddon Hall*, set during the Civil War, displays Cavalier sympathies, satirizes the republican Roundheads and culminates in the restoration of King Charles II. His opera *Ivanhoe*, which was dedicated to Queen Victoria, culminates in the arrival of King Richard I, the raising of the royal banner and the hymning of monarchy. The Gilbert and Sullivan operetta *The Gondoliers* more directly satirizes republicanism and affirms the system of monarchy.

Both monarchy and Empire were deliberately promoted in the series of great exhibitions held in Britain in the second half of the nineteenth century and the first half of the twentieth century. The International Exhibition of 1871, marking the twentieth anniversary of the Great Exhibition, took place in the exhibition galleries of the Royal Horticultural Gardens, South Kensington. Thirty-two countries had been invited to display examples of their fine arts, manufactures, horticulture and scientific inventions. Among the examples were jewellery, mosaics, armour and carvings from India, but the principal emphasis was on Europe and the hope for peace.

The Exhibition was formally opened on 1 May by the Prince of Wales but was characterized by the confusion and disorganization that has been shown by Jeffrey Lant to characterize much of the public pageantry in the early and mid-Victorian periods.[15] A total lack of signposting resulted in many visitors failing to find the entrance; the unrehearsed performance of the 148th Psalm, sung to the tune of the Austrian national hymn, was disastrous, as the band and the choir performing it were so far apart that they were unable to coordinate their performance properly; the Lord Mayor of London tripped on his robes and fell down the steps of the platform; and the State Trumpeters drowned out the Prince's declaration of the opening. *The Graphic* pronounced the ceremonies 'flat and feeble'.[16]

There followed a concert, or 'Exhibition of Musical Art' as it was described by the official programme. The intention was to symbolize the friendship between Britain, France, Italy and Germany. The organizers had invited four leading national composers, Verdi, Auber, Wagner and Sterndale Bennett, to compose and conduct a work specially for the occasion. Verdi and Auber declined; Sterndale Bennett suggested that they get a younger composer, and Wagner did not reply. So, the works were commissioned from Ciro Pinsuti (Italy), Charles Gounod (France), Dr Ferdinand Hiller (Germany) and Arthur Sullivan (Britain). However, the whole thing took place in the shadow of the Franco-Prussian War, with new atrocities daily reported and France in turmoil.

The concert opened with Sir Michael Costa conducting the Overture to Weber's *Der Freischutz* ('a splendid performance', thought *The Times*[17]) and closed with him conducting the overture to Rossini's *Semiramide*. In between came the special pieces. First was Pinsuti's unaccompanied chorus to words specially written by Lord Houghton, a second-rate piece of versifying extolling the virtues of peace and hope. *The Graphic* thought the music 'ineffective and weak throughout'.[18] Gounod's *Gallia* was a setting for soprano, choir and orchestra of words from Psalm 130 – 'Out of the deep have I called thee, O Lord' – and the Lamentations of Jeremiah: 'How doth the city sit solitary, that was so full of people.' It was all too plainly a lament for the state of France. Gounod conducted it in tears and the piece received a standing ovation from the audience. He was followed by Dr Hiller, who conducted his *Triumphal March in D Major*. *The Times* thought it 'vigorous, rhythmical and to the purpose'.[19] But he was less warmly received than Gounod and left the building immediately after his performance.

Sullivan's contribution was the cantata *On Sea and Shore* to words by the playwright Tom Taylor. The theme was 'the sorrows and separations necessarily incidental to war', but to avoid contemporary resonances, the programme said, it had been deliberately set in the sixteenth century, against the background of the conflict between the Genoese and the Moors of North Africa. Opening with music that emulates the motion of the waves, like Mendelssohn's *Fingal's Cave* Overture, it has the Genoese sailors singing of their mission: 'Joys of the shore we must forego/ But ours are the joys of the sea/ To brave the storm and to sink the foe/ And the spoil of victory.' There is a yearning chorus of lament from the women at the departure of their men. The most striking part of the score, employing the instrument known as a Jingling Johnny, is the 'Moresque', Sullivan's exotic Moorish interlude which leads into a Moslem chorus of triumph and the call to prayer as the Moors vanquish the Genoese. The sailors, chained in the slave galleys, sing their defiance: 'Hold to Christian manhood, firm in Christian faith/ Faithful hearts make fearless hands, and faithful hearts have we/ The Christians 'gainst the infidel, chained though we be.' They break their bonds, seize the galley and sail home to joyous songs of reunion.

Although the theme, the wars of the cross and the crescent, is proto-imperial, the finale of the cantata is a paean to peace: 'Sink and scatter, clouds of war/ Sun of peace, shine full and far.' Selwyn Tillett sees it as Sullivan's *Land of Hope and Glory*.[20] It was certainly sung separately from the cantata as *The Song of Peace* in concert programmes. But unlike *Land of Hope and Glory*, it would never have been sung at football grounds, being far too elaborate and operatic in its trills, flourishes and repeats. There is no record of any performance of cantata or song between 1914 and 1984 when it was staged by Imperial Opera.

Far more full-bloodedly imperial were the events surrounding the Queen's opening, at the Royal Albert Hall, of the Colonial and Indian Exhibition on 4 May 1886. John MacKenzie has called it 'the first of the imperial "official" exhibitions, developed and funded with Government support, that culminated in Wembley and Glasgow'.[21] The proceedings at the 1924 and 1938 Empire Exhibitions at Wembley and Glasgow were to follow the pattern established at the Colonial and Indian, where music and pageantry were used to dramatize the idea of Empire. The Times (5 May 1886) observed that 'no public ceremonial honoured by the presence of Her Majesty has been surrounded by so much pomp or by such gorgeous accessories of State Pageantry as that witnessed yesterday in South Kensington'. It rhapsodized about the scene which presented itself in the entrance hall:

> Hardly a colour that could be mentioned was absent from it. The Yeomen of the Guard, in their picturesque costume, were drawn up to the right and left; the pursuivants and heralds, in their gorgeous silken tabards, stood near the vestibule; the State Trumpeters, in their tunic of ruby velvet, covered with heavy gold embroidery, and with their silver trumpets ready, were stationed behind the Prince of Wales's statue; a body of Lascar sailors, dressed in white and wearing red turbans, awaited the arrival of the Queen in the vestibule; and to and fro between these varied groups statesmen in Windsor uniforms, officers of high rank in scarlet tunics, and civilians in levée dress continually passed and repassed.

The Establishment was out in force, with the royal court, the aristocracy, politics, the Church and the colonies fully represented. Colonial flags flew at the entrance of the Exhibition. The Prince of Wales, President of the Commission which organized the Exhibition, welcomed the Queen by putting the Exhibition in context:

> In the Great Exhibition of 1851, your Majesty's colonial and Indian possessions were indeed represented, but their importance was then but little realized as their present greatness was at that time unforeseen. During the years that have elapsed since 1851 few greater changes have been wrought than the marvellous development of the outlying portions of your Majesty's Empire.

The Queen, in opening the Exhibition, expressed the hope that

> this undertaking may be the means of imparting a stimulus to the commercial interests and intercourse of all parts of my dominions, by

encouraging the arts of peace and industry, and by strengthening the bonds of union which now exists in every portion of my Empire.[22]

Music was to be used to consecrate the aims of the Exhibition, and so a concert was programmed as part of the opening ceremonies. It opened with the national anthem, the second verse being sung in Sanskrit. There followed an ode, specially written by the Poet Laureate Lord Tennyson, and set to music by Sullivan, who was conducting. With the hortatory refrain, 'Britons, hold your own', it celebrated the displays of colonial produce, reminded listeners of Britain's folly in fighting and losing the American colonies ('Unprophetic rulers they – / Drove from out ... the mother's nest/ That young eagle of the West') and made a rousing call for imperial unity ('Sons, be welded each and all/ Into one imperial whole/ One with Britain heart and soul!/ One life, one flag, one fleet, one Throne'). It was sung by the Canadian diva Madame Emma Albani and chorus. *The Times* reported that 'after each verse Her Majesty smiled her thanks to the singer and clapped her hands'. *The Musical Times* pronounced the music 'bright and spirited enough, but without much originality of idea'.[23] But with its stately main tune, rousing final verse and bold, repeated, recitative setting of the last line, it is a fitting *pièce d'occasion*. It was never to be performed again during the life of the Empire, but has now been recorded on CD.[24] The *Hallelujah Chorus* followed a prayer by the Archbishop of Canterbury for the continued unity of the Empire. Madame Albani then performed *Home, Sweet Home* which, said *the Musical Times*, 'was sung with such touching expression ... as almost to reconcile us to Bishop's sickly and commonplace ditty'.[25] *Rule, Britannia* was performed as the royal party left. The musical programme was in fact an appropriate blend of the royal, the imperial, the Protestant and the domestic sentiments that characterized Victorian public culture.

Sullivan was back on Empire duty in 1887 for the laying of the foundation-stone of the Imperial Institute. The Institute was built in South Kensington to provide a permanent exhibition, a library and information services of various kinds on the resources, social conditions and development of the Empire. Its purpose, as stated in its charter of incorporation, was 'to strengthen the bonds of union between all classes and races in Our Dominions and to promote a feeling of mutual goodwill, of a common citizenship'.[26] The Prince of Wales was an enthusiastic supporter of the project, seeing it as a chance to allow the Colonial and Indian Exhibition, which he had chaired, to continue on a permanent basis. Queen Victoria saw it as the completion of the work of the Prince Consort, the logical outcome of the 1851 Great Exhibition. Its funding by public subscription was one of the major projects of Golden Jubilee Year: £440,000 was raised, the money coming equally from Britain and the various territories of the Empire. A magnificent building in the Renaissance style was commissioned from T.E. Colcutt.

There was a glittering and prestigious foundation-stone laying ceremony on 4 July, 1887, attended by 10,000 people, including European monarchs, Indian princes and other great personages of the day. It was, declared *The Times*, 'a great event, an event in significance, in grandeur, and in the interest it excited', second only to the Golden Jubilee itself.[27] The Queen laid the foundation-stone with a silver trowel and the Archbishop of Canterbury gave thanks to God, 'for the abundance of dominion, loyal majesty and might of India and the colonies, wherewith even in this year of the jubilee, Thou hast multiplied the Empire of Our Queen and fortified it'. Sir Arthur Sullivan was once again conducting choir and orchestra. He conducted his own grand processional march from *Henry VIII* for the arrival of the royal party and *Rule, Britannia* for their departure. But the great set piece of the occasion was a new ode. The words were provided by Lewis Morris (1833–1907), a poet who is quite forgotten today but was sufficiently well-known to figure in eminent poetic company in Gilbert's lyrics for *Ruddigore*, when Robin Oakapple sings:

> As a poet, I'm tender and quaint –
> I've passion and fervour and grace –
> From Ovid and Horace
> To Swinburne and Morris
> They all of them take a back place.

He was a disciple of Tennyson and disappointed not to succeed him as Poet Laureate. But it was probably politics rather than poetry which kept him out. The job went to the Conservative Alfred Austin.[28] Morris was a radical Welsh lawyer, a Liberal who favoured Welsh home rule, disestablishment of the Church in Wales and social reform. He composed odes for the first Cooperative Festival in 1888 and the Trades Union Congress in Wales in 1901. He several times failed to get into Parliament but was knighted in 1895 at the nomination of Lord Rosebery. For all his political radicalism, he was a fervent imperialist; and, although not Poet Laureate, composed odes to mark royal and imperial occasions, *A Song of Empire* for the Golden Jubilee, odes on the marriage of the Duke of York, the death of the Duke of Clarence and the death of Canadian Premier Sir John Thompson, for instance.

His ode for the opening of the Imperial Institute was set to music by Sullivan and it was an even grander affair than the ode for the Colonial and Indian Exhibition. In consultation with Morris, Sullivan trimmed and paraphrased the ode here and there for ease of setting and he omitted an entire verse encouraging emigration ('Guide we their feet to where/ Is spread for those who dare/ A Happier Britain 'neath an ampler air'). Sullivan also interestingly substitutes 'England' on several occasions for Morris' 'Britain', but he retains 'Britain' for the final verse. This confirms the fact that for Sullivan, as for most nineteenth-century Englishmen, Britain and England were synonymous. Morris, as a patriotic Welshman, thought differently. But their collaboration is a celebration of the British imperial achievement, with the repeated chorus 'Worthy is she of praise', and beginning:

> With voice and solemn music sing,
> Loud let the pealing trumpets ring!
> Today our hands consolidate
> The Empire of a thousand years.

It acknowledges the role of war in the creation of the Empire:

> Soldier and sailor side by side,
> Her strong sons bravely dared and died.

Now it is not by war but by peace that 'we seek our realm's increase' and imperial unity, as embodied in the Institute. It ends with a paean of praise to the Queen ('First Lady of our English race'), her 'lost consort' and her son 'who has seen all thy Empire face to face', and asks God to 'Keep this Our Britain Great'. Herbert Sullivan and Sir Newman Flower in their biography of Sullivan, although claiming that Tennyson wrote the ode, presumably confusing it with the ode for the Colonial and Indian Exhibition, nonetheless note:

> Into the setting of the Ode Sullivan had woven the spirit of majesty and greatness of an Empire. Just as the mighty Handel before him had composed special music for coronations, royal weddings, for peace celebrations, so did Sullivan carry anew his mantle and reflect in his notes the dignity of a Queen.[29]

The music has an appropriate grandeur and soaring sense of triumph about it. The Prince of Wales wrote to Sullivan the day following the ceremony to thank him for composing the music: 'it met with universal approbation and the Queen was specially delighted with it'.[30] Once again, unheard for a century, it was given a concert performance in 1986 and has also been recorded on CD.[31]

The formal opening of the Institute by the Queen was on 10 May 1893. Twenty-five thousand people attended the event, and once again Lewis Morris composed an ode. It was printed in *The Times* and pub-

lished in the official programme but not set to music this time. Rhap-
sodizing on the building and its contents, it called for imperial
brotherhood and unity. Sullivan's contribution to the proceedings was
his new *Imperial March*. It opens with an arresting fanfare theme,
which is reworked with variations, but then goes distinctly off the boil
as the middle section lapses into Verdian operatic mode before returning to the heroic declamatory style of the opening. Sullivan's *Imperial March* failed to provide the imperial march idiom that was needed;
Elgar would do that with his *Imperial March*. Madame Emma Albani
sang the national anthem and the royal procession left to the popular
Coronation March from Meyerbeer's *The Prophet*, which had more of
a swing and snap about it than Sullivan's.

The Times declared:

> It has been often said that the English people have none of the dramatic
> and pictorial instincts which enable Continental nations to organise
> imposing pageants and to give a bright touch of colour to the dullness
> of everyday life. The stupendous popular demonstration on the occasion
> of the Queen's Jubilee was a sufficient refutation of this theory. But the
> brilliant success which attended the ceremony of yesterday ... afforded
> even more incontestable proof that Englishmen can, if they please,
> produce effects beyond the reach of communities in which pageantry is
> regulated by an omnipotent and omniscient government.[32]

The reception accorded the Queen and the royal family was 'an expression of a deep and durable sentiment that political theorists would be
unwise in discrediting or deprecating'. Equally, while the public may
not know too much about 'the nature, the advantages and the obligations of the British Empire', there was no doubt that 'the popular
feeling is entirely in favour of maintaining the Empire, and of drawing
closer the bonds of union between its component parts'.

The Imperial Institute was to suffer from underfunding throughout
its history, was taken over by the government in 1899 and shunted
from department to department, but did achieve some success in its
propaganda and educational activities, particularly through the use of
film during the 1930s, when it had its own cinema, opened in 1927,
and an extensive film library for use by borrowers. The magnificent
building housing the Institute was shamefully demolished in 1956,
apart from the campanile, and its activities transferred to the newly
established Commonwealth Institute.[33]

Sullivan made further contributions to the music of imperialism,
however. He composed the music for a Canadian national hymn,
God Bless Our Wide Dominion, to words by the Governor-General of
Canada, the Marquis of Lorne, who was the Queen's son-in-law.

[30]

God bless our wide Dominion,
Our fathers' chosen land;
And bind in lasting union
Each ocean's distant strand;
From where Atlantic terrors
Our hardy seamen train,
To where the salt sea mirrors
The vast Pacific chain:
O bless our wide Dominion.
True Freedom's fairest scene;
Defend our people's union;
God Save our Empire's Queen.

It was published in 1880, but was not adopted as the national hymn.

In 1897, for the Diamond Jubilee, he composed the official Jubilee Hymn, *O, King of Kings, Whose Reign of Old*. He rejected the verses offered by the Poet Laureate Alfred Austin, choosing to set instead the verses penned by William Walsham How, Bishop of Wakefield.

But his major contribution to the Jubilee celebrations was his ballet *Victoria and Merrie England*. It was commissioned by Alfred Moul, General Manager of the Alhambra Theatre, Leicester Square, who wanted him to provide something 'exceptionally splendid' for the Diamond Jubilee. The result was *Victoria and Merrie England*, 'a grand national ballet in eight tableaux', to a scenario created by Balletmaster Carlo Coppi. It opened on 25 May, conducted on the first night by the composer. It ran for six months, and Sullivan was paid £2,000 and a share of the nightly takings. Not only was it popular with the public but members of the royal family attended on nineteen occasions. From 8 July the entertainment also included a cinematograph film of the Jubilee procession.[34]

Two of Sullivan's most eloquent and well-informed advocates, David Eden and Selwyn Tillett, insist that he was a romantic nationalist rather than an imperialist.[35] There is no doubt that he was a romantic nationalist, something clearly reflected in his work. He composed incidental music to Shakespeare's *The Tempest, The Merchant of Venice, Macbeth, Henry VIII* and *The Merry Wives of Windsor*. He turned to the works of Walter Scott for his opera *Ivanhoe*, his cantata *Kenilworth* and the overture *Marmion*. He provided incidental music for Lord Tennyson's Robin Hood play *The Foresters* and for Sir Henry Irving's production of *King Arthur*. Tillett cites *Victoria and Merrie England* as being nationalistic rather than imperialistic. But this establishes a wholly false dichotomy between nation and Empire, whereas the two were closely intertwined. In fact, what *Victoria and Merrie England* makes clear is that the whole romantic history of Britain was leading up to its triumphant culmination in the Empire.

The early episodes are mythic and romantic. The ballet opens in ancient Britain with the processions and rituals of the Druids. The Genius of Britain enters and sees Britannia sleeping beneath an oak and predicts her future greatness, while the High Priest announces that Britannia is 'predestined to be the mother of a race which shall be mighty amongst the Nations of the world'. It is the same idea as that developed by Elgar in *Caractacus*. The sequence ends with Britannia awaking and embracing Britain's Genius.

The second sequence is a celebration of a May Day coming of age in Elizabethan England. The young heir is presented with a sword by his old uncle: 'With this I fought for Queen and Country.' There is a historical quadrille of Britons, Romans, Saxons and Normans, celebrating the racial mix of Britain. Robin Hood, Maid Marian and Friar Tuck, Morris dancers, hobby-horses, knights of the sword and rose maidens all dance and the sequence culminates in a dance around the Maypole.

A supernatural interlude has Herne the Hunter and his followers appearing during a storm in Windsor Forest. They set about a Yule Log Procession which is bringing home the symbol of Christmas. But Herne and his followers are routed by the Snow Fairy. 'Christmas in the Olden Time' has the Lord and Lady of the Manor entertaining guests during the reign of Charles II, with a procession of Boar's Head and Roast Beef, the peasants and retainers admitted to participate in the Christmas cheer and Father Christmas arriving to distribute gifts.

So far the scenes have stressed the inevitability of Britain's ultimate imperial glory, the joys of Merrie England (May Day and Christmas festivities), communality and aristocratic paternalism. The ballet evokes a mythic past (Druids, Robin Hood, Herne the Hunter) but links it to a heroic present. Sequence seven is a *tableau vivant* realization of the painting by E.T. Parris depicting the coronation of Queen Victoria in 1838. The final scene, 'Britain's Glory', has a military procession, headed by the Grenadier Guards, the Royal Irish Regiment and the Gordon Highlanders, followed by the Artists Volunteer Corps, 22nd Bombay Infantry, the Cape Mounted Infantry, Canadian Troopers and Australian Rifles. Then four groups, representing Europe, Asia, Africa and America and exactly reproduced from the sculptures at the base of the Albert Memorial, Hyde Park, enter. There is a procession of British sailors, Britannia enters, and finally the entire ensemble gather for the national anthem. The imperial intentions and dimensions of the climactic scene are inescapable. They represent the fulfilment of the destiny predicted in the first scene – an imperial destiny.

The delicacy, wit and inventiveness of Sullivan's score was widely praised, even though he had extensively re-used material from his 1864 ballet *L'Ile Enchantée. The Era* described it as

> one of the most splendid achievements which have ever been made at this popular place of amusement. It is not only a beautiful and gorgeous spectacle; it is a lesson in history and historical costume, accompanied by some of the best music ever written for ballet purposes . . . *Victoria and Merrie England* is a triumph, and is likely to be immensely popular during the forthcoming Jubilee.[36]

The Sun declared:

> Sir Arthur Sullivan's music is the music for the people . . . the melodies are all as fresh as last year's wine, and as exhilarating as sparkling champagne. There is not one tune which tires the hearing . . . All through we have orchestration of infinite delicacy, tunes of alarming simplicity, but never a tinge of vulgarity.[37]

Even *The Musical Times* called it 'a very pleasant example of his genius' and noted that 'there is an atmosphere of refinement and finished craftsmanship about . . . the ballet which can scarcely fail to exercise a salutary influence'.[38] The variety and joyousness of the score lies in the variety of dance forms that Sullivan introduces, his waltz, mazurka, galop, Morris dance, Maypole dance, quadrille and hornpipe, a mixture of the ballroom and the village green, all treated with inventive delicacy. *The Musical Times* singled out the storm music and the Yule Log Procession as the best music but observed that the Waltz of the Wood Nymphs was more popular with the audience. Familiar tunes were quoted in the music: *Rule, Britannia, The Roast Beef of Old England, A-Hunting We Will Go, A Fine Old English Gentleman* and *The Boar's Head* carol (*Caput Apri Defeo*).

For the Coronation tableau, Sullivan used his own *Imperial March* which received three curtain calls before the final sequence could unfold. This featured his *Union March*, in which Sullivan ingeniously combined *The British Grenadiers* (England), *St Patrick's Day* (Ireland) and *Scots Wha' Hae* (Scotland). Try as he might, he had been unable to fit in, as he had planned, *Men of Harlech*, so Wales remained unrepresented. *Home, Sweet Home* followed this march, then the delightful sailor's hornpipe from *Ruddigore, Rule, Britannia* for the entrance of Britannia and finally a rousing version of the national anthem.

But Sullivan's reputation rests still on the operettas he produced with W.S. Gilbert. They were toured regularly all over the United Kingdom, and they were popular all over the Empire and provided a potent musical link between the colonies and the motherland.

[33]

The D'Oyly Carte Company toured South Africa in 1896, 1902–3 and 1905–6. Australian impresario J.C. Williamson obtained a license to perform the Savoy Operas in Australia, where they were performed regularly from 1879. In 1927 the D'Oyly Carte Company made its first coast to coast tour of Canada playing to full houses and eulogistic reviews. There were further Canadian tours in 1928 and 1934. There were amateur performances of the operas all over the Empire.[39]

The Empire itself came in for the Gilbert and Sullivan treatment. One of the enduring points of appeal of Gilbert and Sullivan operas along with their memorable melodies and witty lyrics is that they are celebrations of England, Englishness and English institutions. There is satire, but it is largely affirmative and affectionate. Gilbert and Sullivan carefully cut out anything from their work which they thought might cause offence. Also, as J.B. Priestley has pointed out, it is a characteristic of the English to laugh at what they love most.[40] The application of self-deprecating humour allows the patriotic sentiment to be enjoyed and engaged in with gusto. A classic example of this is the rousing song *He Is An Englishman* from *HMS Pinafore*. It went round the Empire as a song of celebration so that when Sullivan accompanied the Duke of Edinburgh on his flagship *HMS Hercules* on a trip to Russia and sang *He Is An Englishman* in a ship's concert, Sullivan recorded that 'the whole crew to my astonishment sang the chorus'.[41] It is one of a series of resoundingly patriotic songs – *A British Tar Is a Soaring Soul* from *HMS Pinafore*, *When Britain Really Ruled the Waves* from *Iolanthe*, *The Darned Mounseer* from *Ruddigore* and the finale from *Utopia Limited*: *There Is a Little Group of Islands Beyond the Wave*. It is part of a tradition of apparently humorous patriotic songs which start out as satire and end up as celebrations. Noël Coward's *Mad Dogs and Englishmen* and Flanders and Swann's *Song of Patriotic Prejudice* ('The English, the English, the English are best') are other examples. As David Cannadine writes, the operas were 'a paean of praise to national pride and the established order'.[42] The opening nights of the Savoy Operas were great social events, and certainly received the stamp of approval of the Establishment. Queen Victoria had a command performance of *The Gondoliers* at Windsor. General Sir Garnet Wolseley, who inspired the song *I Am the Very Model of a Modern Major General*, used to perform the song as his party-piece. Two real-life Lord Chancellors, Lord Birkenhead and Lord Elwyn-Jones, were to perform the Lord Chancellor's song from *Iolanthe*. Admiral Lord Fisher, 'Jacky Fisher', went several times to *HMS Pinafore* and adored it. Even Oscar Wilde loved the send-up of himself in *Patience*.[43]

After the army, the navy, education, the law and politics, the Empire and the imperial mission came in for its dose of satire in *Utopia Limited* (1893), which was the penultimate collaboration and came after a period of estrangement. Sadly it was perhaps the weakest of the Savoy Operas. The music was pleasant enough but lacked any hit songs, although the depiction of the Utopian cabinet meeting as a Christy Minstrels' show was a lively interlude. It is hard to quarrel with the verdict of David Eden that the score 'in general terms fails to impress'.[44] This was due partly to the fact that Gilbert's libretto was lacking in drama or narrative drive and clearly failed to inspire Sullivan in the way that earlier works had done. Although many contemporary critics were so glad to see them reunited that they were indulgent – and Bernard Shaw with typical perversity pronounced *Utopia Limited* the best Savoy Opera yet – the *Pall Mall Gazette* was unsparing in its criticism.[45] It complained that Gilbert was merely imitating himself. 'It gave his book not merely a sense of cheapness, but a sense of fatigue, of weariness even to exhaustion. *Utopia Limited* is but the scrapings of the platter, the rinsings of the cup.' Others hinted that perhaps both Gilbert and Sullivan were beginning to repeat themselves. *The Musical Times* said of the opening night: 'the libretto of *Utopia Limited* seems a trifle dull, particularly in the first Act, and the music for the most part reminiscent rather than fresh'.[46] The critic thought the best of Sullivan's music came in Act 2, with its 'well built up *Finale*, a song caricaturing a tenor with a cold, an amazingly funny parody of a Christy Minstrel entertainment, and an unaccompanied concerted piece in which the composer is almost, if not quite, at his best'. This seems to have been the verdict of posterity, for after a first run in London of 245 performances it was to receive no professional production in the capital until 1975, a production which was recorded and which interestingly used Sullivan's *Imperial March* as overture, to create the right mood, given that the short existing prelude had been deemed 'meagre' by contemporary critics. It has been performed by amateur companies over the years and selections from the score have been available on records since as early as 1900.[47] As John Wolfson points out the imperial parallels would have been immediately apparent to contemporary audiences.[48] The South Seas were in the news as Britain had recently annexed Fiji and Tonga and the appearance of a Life Guard in full uniform in Utopia had a precedent in the presence of three Life Guards in a delegation to King Lobengula of Matabeleland several years earlier.

Utopia is a South Sea Island kingdom ruled by an absolute monarch, King Paramount I, whose inhabitants are languorous lotus-eaters whose every need is supplied by their monarch. But he has sent his daughter Princess Zara to Girton College, Cambridge, to gain mastery of 'all the elements that have tended to raise their glorious country to her present pre-eminent position among civilized nations'. Princess Zara returns to Utopia with representatives of those aspects of British society that have made the country great. They are the 'Flowers of Progress' who gave the opera its subtitle: 'Six representatives of the principal causes that have tended to make England the powerful, happy and blameless country which the consensus of European civilization has declared it to be'. They are Captain Fitzbattleaxe of the First Life Guards ('A British soldier gives up all. His home and island beauty/ When summoned by the trumpet call/ Of regimental duty'); Captain Sir Edward Corcoran KCB of the Royal Navy ('I'll teach you how we rule the sea/ And terrify the simple Gaul./ And how the Saxon and the Celt/ Their Europe-shaking blows have dealt/ With Maxim Gun and Nordenfelt'); Mr Blushington of the County Council ('All streets and squares he'll purify/ Within your city walls/ And keep meanwhile a modest eye/ On wicked music halls'); Sir Bailey Barre QC, MP, representing the legal system; Lord Dramaleigh, the Lord Chamberlain ('He'll cleanse our Court from moral stain/ And purify our stage'); and Mr Goldbury, company promoter. Their objective is to Anglicize the inhabitants of Utopia, who are 'when compared with Britain's glorious race/ But little better than half-clothed barbarians'.

The visitors are welcomed by the grateful natives:

> All hail, ye types of England's power –
> Ye heaven-enlightened band!
> We bless the day, and bless the hour
> That brought you to our land.
>
> Oh teach the natives of this land
> (Who are not quick to understand)
> How to work off their social and political arrears.

The country is now organized as a limited company (Utopia Limited), and completely Anglicized, the Army and Navy reorganized, the city beautified, social life purified. A law of libel is introduced which has the editors of scurrilous newspapers publicly flogged. But the reforms have left everyone too happy and healthy: the reform of the armed forces has ended war; the sanitary laws have been so successful that the doctors are out of work; the new legal system has abolished crime and litigation, so the lawyers starve. But Princess Zara remembers the missing element – government by party, 'at once the bulwark and foundation of England's greatness'. Once this is introduced, 'there will be sickness in plenty, endless lawsuits, crowded jails, interminable confusion in the Army and Navy, and, in short, general and unexampled prosperity.' So in future Utopia will no longer be a monarchy (Ltd) but a limited monarchy, which is much better. The would-be rousing finale begins with the opening bars of *Rule, Britannia*, which elsewhere in the score accompany any mention of Britain, and is a celebration of Britain and her world role:

> There's a little group of isles beyond the wave –
> So tiny, you might almost wonder where it is –
> That nation is the bravest of the brave,
> And cowards are the rarest of all rarities.
> The proudest nations kneel at her command;
> She terrifies all foreign-born rapscallions;
> And holds the peace of Europe in her hand
> With half a score invincible battalions.

It is, however, unmemorable – like much of the rest of the score.

Sullivan's final year was dominated by matters imperial. His most notable imperial contribution was a practical one, providing the rousing music for a setting of Kipling's poem *The Absent-Minded Beggar*, the proceeds of which went to Boer War charities. Kipling had given Sullivan the exclusive rights to set *Recessional* but Sullivan had found it too difficult. However, he provided a tune for *The Absent-Minded Beggar*. Sullivan and Flower record:

> The song took England by storm; it drove all other songs from the barrel-organs; tens of thousands of copies were rushed from the presses and sold for the benefit of soldiers' dependants, a fund the *Daily Mail* started and carried to a very successful conclusion. The Queen wrote to Sullivan for a copy; troops marched away to the troopships singing it.[49]

It received its first performance at the Alhambra Theatre on 13 November 1899. Sullivan recorded in his diary: 'conducted "Ab.M.Beg." at the Alhambra in the evening – packed house – wild enthusiasm. All sang chorus! I stood on the stage and conducted the *encore* – funny sight.'[50] In support of the fund, a patriotic brass band concert was held before an audience of 10,000 at the Albert Hall on 20 January 1900. It was organized by brass band impresario J.H. Iles, owner of *The British Bandman*, with ten brass bands and a cast of star singers; the proceeds to be devoted to the support of wives and children of soldiers recalled to the colours, and to relieve sick and wounded soldiers and sailors. The programme gives an insight into the kind of musical fare deemed appropriate for a patriotic concert at the height of an imperial war. It opened with musical selections played by the Band of the Royal Engineers, then moved on to *Onward, Christian Soldiers*, sung by Clara Butt, with massed bands, drums, grand organ and the audience joining in the second and third verses. Sullivan conducted. Later Clara Butt sang Sullivan's *The Lost Chord* with organ accompaniment and

Part One ended with Sullivan conducting the massed bands and drums in a vigorous march arrangement of *The Absent-Minded Beggar*.

Of the star singers, Edward Lloyd sang Thomas Moore's Irish ballad *The Minstrel Boy* and Braham's *Death of Nelson*, Andrew Black sang *Hearts of Oak* and Samuel Liddle's setting of *The Gay Gordons*. Emma Albani sang *The Blue Bells of Scotland* and Mozart's *Non mi dir* from *Don Giovanni*. Clara Butt sang Frances Allitsen's *There's a Land* ('There's a land, a dear land, where the rights of the free/ Though firm as the earth, are as wide as the sea') with an additional verse by Agnes M. Sibly:

> There's a Queen, a dear Queen, whom no Briton forgets,
> And upon whose dominion the sun never sets: –
> Who has governed by love, and has helped us to fight
> For conquest of evil and succour of right.
> Best reign! Blest reign! Longest! Strongest!
> This year of all years we'll sing and we'll pray!
> 'Glorious! Victorious! Thy Queen! My Queen!
> God bless her and keep her to-night and for aye.'

The individual brass bands played their usual repertoire: the overture to *William Tell*, selections from Weber's *Oberon*, Rossini's *Moses in Egypt* and Mendelssohn's *Elijah* plus a selection, *Wales*, arranged by J. Ord Hume. The London Kymric Ladies' Choir sang *The March of the Men of Harlech* and *Yr Haf* (*Summer*). Part Two of the concert opened with a specially composed fantasia on *God Save the Queen* and *Rule, Britannia*, arranged for bands by J. Ord Hume, and ended with *God Save the Queen*, Sir Michael Costa's version of the national anthem arranged for bands by J.M. Rogan of the Coldstream Guards, with Clara Butt and Emma Albani singing and the massed bands conducted by Sullivan, the audience joining in the last verse. It was a blockbusting patriotic extravaganza, and one which involved the whole spectrum of Victorian music, with brass bands, choirs, solo singers, and a programme which was careful to celebrate Britain and its component parts (Scotland, Wales, England and Ireland) individually, the monarchy, the army and navy and popular Protestantism, all in aid of a song and a fund to support the forces fighting an imperial war. It raised between £2,000 and £3,000 for the fund.

In February 1900 Sullivan conducted another massed military band concert at Her Majesty's Theatre in a 'patriotic picture' of Britain and her dependencies, again for charity. His last completed work was to be his *Boer War Te Deum*, commissioned in 1900 to celebrate the peace. Sullivan built it around his most popular hymn, *Onward, Christian Soldiers*, thus imbuing the Boer War with the idea of a Christian struggle against the infidel. It was eventually performed at St Paul's

Cathedral in the presence of the King and Queen at a Thanksgiving service for the end of the war on 8 June 1902.[51]

Incomplete at the time of his death was a final comic opera, *The Emerald Isle*, set to a book by Basil Hood, the best of the librettists he had tried since the split with Gilbert. Sullivan's sketches were orchestrated and the remainder of the opera set by Edward German to create a charming and tuneful work which opened at the Savoy Theatre on 27 April 1901 and ran for 205 performances.

It marked Sullivan's first and last operatic foray into the Ireland of his forbears and it took on a number of serious and highly contentious elements of British imperial rule in Ireland (the suppression of the Irish language, the expropriation of Irish landowners, the employment of informers, the sentencing of captured rebels to be shot) and gave them a comic and romantic treatment in a bid to neutralize their offensiveness.

The action takes place in 1800 against the background of the attempt by the Lord Lieutenant, the Earl of Newtown, to eliminate the Irish brogue and Irish customs. He has achieved a good deal of success by the offer of prizes for proper elocution: 'There is not a man nor a colleen here that could dance an Irish jig correctly, and say "Begorra" at the end of it with any conviction', complains the fiddler 'Blind' Murphy. The Lord Lieutenant's scheme is opposed by rebel leader Terence O'Brian. Unfortunately for him, his parents sold their estate to the Earl and had him educated in England at Eton and Oxford, so he too speaks with an English accent. So he hires elocutionist Professor Bunn to re-educate the locals in their Irish brogue. To complicate matters further, Terence is in love with the Lord Lieutentant's daughter Lady Rosie Pippin. She discovers that her father has been informed of a secret meeting of Terence and the rebels at the caves of Carrig-Cleena. He orders the 11th Regiment of Foot to arrest the rebels. But local colleen Molly O'Grady and Professor Bunn convince the soldiers, who are simple, superstitious, Devonshire peasants, that the caves are haunted by fairies, and they flee. Eventually, however, their courage returns and, rejecting Terence's claim that thay are 'playthings of unprincipled politicians', the soldiers arrest the rebels, who are sentenced to be shot. Lady Rosie reveals that she loves O'Brian, presenting her father with a dilemma. But this is actually resolved and reconciliation is achieved in the context of royalty and aristocracy. O'Brian reveals that he is descended from Brian Boru and the ancient Kings of Erin. The Lord Lieutenant reveals that Rosie is partially American, like much of the aristocracy – a reference to the trend of late nineteenth-century English aristocrats to marry wealthy American heiresses. Professor Bunn then resolves the dilemma by announc-

ing that since America is the friend of Ireland and the English aristocrats are partially American, there is no need for the Irish to rebel. It
would be absurd to shoot the rebels under the circumstances. The Lord
Lieutenant agrees, and all ends happily.

Sullivan furnished a score full of catchy Irish jig tunes ('Have you
heard the brave news that's goin' around?', 'If you want to appear as
an Irish type', 'Oh, have you met a man in debt and almost out at
elbows'?) and lilting romantic fairy music ('On the heights of Glan-
taun', 'Many years ago I strode/ Down the Carrig-Cleena road'). Edward
German contributed the *Song of the Devonshire Men* in his best
English pastoral vein, a Gilbertian patter song, '*Oh, the Age in Which
We Are Living*', and several charming romantic ballads. It never
achieved the success either of the classic Gilbert and Sullivan
operettas or of Edward German's subsequent collaboration with Basil
Hood, *Merrie England*.[52]

An important part of Sullivan's output, then, had been imperial; an
even larger part had been patriotic, and in the nineteenth century patriotism embraced not just Britain but the Empire. His patriotism may
even have cost him his life. His cousin B.W. Findon reported that,
already ill with bronchitis, 'he exposed himself to a piercing wind in
order to see the return of the City Imperial Volunteers' from South
Africa on 29 October 1900.[53] His bronchitis worsened, his heart failed
and on 22 November 1900, St Cecilia's Day, he died.

Despite being the leader of English music, the Queen–Empress's
favourite composer, and an undoubted monarchist and patriot, he had
failed to provide the musical idiom for the Empire. Neither his imperial Savoy Opera *Utopia Limited* nor his imperial ballet *Victoria and
Merrie England* found a lasting place in the repertoire. His imperial
odes were performed once, and then forgotten. His dominion hymn
for Canada was not adopted as the country's national anthem. His
Imperial March, while it did retain a place in the repertoire, was to
be eclipsed by the *Imperial March* of the man who definitively established the musical idiom of the Empire – his successor Sir Edward
Elgar. It may be that the musical world which produced Sullivan – his
initial inspiration being Schubert and Mendelssohn, and his later influences Gounod, Bizet, Massenet, Delibes and Offenbach – was simply
too light for the heavy business of Empire.[54] However, if he did not
provide an imperial idiom, it certainly is true to say, as did *The Times*
when he died, that his music was known and loved all around the
Empire and provided an important musical link. The sacred choral
works, the orchestral pieces, the songs, the hymns, the comic operas
were all part of the musical life of the Empire at all levels, and that in
itself is a major imperial contribution. Nothing is more symptomatic

of the centrality of Gilbert and Sullivan to imperial culture than the fact that their operettas were performed during the Siege of Mafeking to keep up the spirits of the defenders.

Many of the British composers of Sullivan's generation have been deeply unfashionable until quite recently, when new recordings of their music have been allowing for a positive reassessment of their achievements. Many of them contributed to the stock of imperial music. Sir Alexander Campbell Mackenzie (1847–1935) was born in Edinburgh and was a proudly patriotic Scot. His music celebrated his Scots' heritage, yet he drew on Dickens and Shakespeare for inspiration and also hymned the Empire in his 1887 *Jubilee Ode*, his 1902 *Coronation March*, his 1894 nautical overture *Britannia* and songs such as *The Empire Flag* (1887) and *An Empire Song* (1908). He toured Canada to enhance the musical links between Britain and the Empire and composed as a result a *Canadian Rhapsody* (1905) and four 'Canadian songs' (1907).

Sir Charles Villiers Stanford (1852–1924) was an equally passionate Irishman. He too composed a Jubilee ode (1887), *Carmen Saeculare*, and the ode *East to West* (1893). He made the magnificent settings of Henry Newbolt's *Songs of the Sea* and *Songs of the Fleet*, and he set to music imperial poems by the likes of W.E. Henley (*The Last Post*) and Conan Doyle (*The Frontier Line and A Ballad of the Ranks*).

Sir Frederic Cowen (1852–1935) was a true child of the Empire, born in Jamaica. He also spent six months as conductor of the Melbourne Centennial Exhibition in 1888–89 at which he conducted 260 concerts and performed his *Song of Thanksgiving*, specially written for the event. He composed the 1897 Jubilee ode *All Hail the Glorious Reign*, a *Coronation Ode* and a *Coronation March* (1902) and *Indian Rhapsody* (1903).

Sir Edward German (1862–1936), born in Shropshire of Welsh antecedents, completed Sullivan's opera *The Emerald Isle*, wrote his stirring fantasia on march tunes *In Commemoration* for the 1897 Jubilee, a 1911 *Coronation March* and several notable settings of Kipling poems (*Have You News of My Boy Jack?*; *Rolling Down to Rio*; *The Irish Guards*; *Big Steamers*), as well as the patriotic hymn *Canada* by Sir Harold Boulton. For none of these composers was the Empire central to their musical inspiration. It was, however, for Sir Edward Elgar.

Notes

1 *The Times*, 23 November, 1900.
2 Herbert Sullivan and Newman Flower, *Sir Arthur Sullivan: His Life, Letters and*

Diaries, London: Cassell, 1927 (1950 edition), pp. 6–7; Henry A. Lytton, *The Secrets of a Savoyard*, London: Jarrolds, 1922, p. 58; Hermann Klein, *Thirty Years of Musical Life in London*, New York: Century, 1903, pp. 192, 201.

3 Arthur Jacobs, *Arthur Sullivan: A Victorian Musician*, Aldershot: Scolar Press, 1992, p. 175.

4 Edward Dicey, 'Recollections of Arthur Sullivan', in Harold Orel (ed.), *Gilbert and Sullivan: Interviews and Recollections*, London: Macmillan, 1994, p. 83.

5 Jacobs, *Arthur Sullivan*, p. 199.

6 *The Times*, 20 July, 1897.

7 Jacobs, *Arthur Sullivan*, p. 58.

8 *Ibid.*, p. 135.

9 Quoted in Percy M. Young, *Sir Arthur Sullivan*, London: Dent, 1971, p. 41.

10 Jacobs, *Arthur Sullivan*, p. 223.

11 Ernest Walker, *A History of Music in England*, London: Oxford University Press, 1924, pp. 293, 295.

12 Jacobs, *Arthur Sullivan*, p. 383.

13 Victor Kiernan, 'Tennyson, King Arthur and imperialism', in Raphael Samuel and Gareth Stedman Jones (eds), *Culture, Ideology and Politics*, London: Routledge, 1982, p. 138.

14 Robert Bernard Martin, *Tennyson: The Unquiet Heart*, Oxford: Clarendon Press, 1983, p. 546.

15 Jeffrey Lant, *Insubstantial Pageant: Ceremony and Confusion at Queen Victoria's Court*, London: Hamish Hamilton, 1979.

16 *The Graphic*, 6 May, 1871.

17 *The Times*, 2 May, 1871.

18 *The Graphic*, 6 May, 1871.

19 *The Times*, 2 May, 1871.

20 Selwyn Tillett, 'On shore and sea', Sir Arthur Sullivan Society (nd), p. 13. This pamphlet gives a full account of the performance of the cantata.

21 John M. MacKenzie, *Propaganda and Empire*, Manchester: Manchester University Press, 1984, p. 102.

22 *The Times*, 5 May, 1886.

23 *The Musical Times*, 1 June, 1886.

24 Sir Arthur Sullivan, *The Masque at Kenilworth: Music for Royal and National Occasions*, Symposium, CD 1247.

25 *The Musical Times*, 1 June, 1886.

26 MacKenzie, *Propaganda and Empire*, p. 125.

27 *The Times*, 5 July, 1887.

28 Karl Beckson, *London in the 1890s: A Cultural History*, New York and London: W.W. Norton & Co., 1992, pp. 95–109.

29 Sullivan and Flower, *Sir Arthur Sullivan*, p. 171.

30 *Ibid.*, p. 172.

31 Sir Arthur Sullivan, *The Masque at Kenilworth*, Symposium, CD 1247.

32 *The Times*, 11 May, 1893.

33 MacKenzie, *Propaganda and Empire*, pp. 122–46.

34 For a full account of the ballet see Selwyn Tillett, *The Ballets of Sir Arthur Sullivan*, London: Sir Arthur Sullivan Society, 1998.

35 David Eden, *Gilbert and Sullivan: The Creative Conflict*, London: Associated University Presses, 1986, pp. 168–70; Tillett, *The Ballets*, pp. 22–3.

36 *The Era*, 28 May, 1897.

37 *Sun*, 26 May, 1897.

38 *The Musical Times*, 1 July, 1897.

39 Tony Joseph, *The D'Oyly Carte Opera Company 1875–1982*, Bristol: Bunthorne Books, 1994, p. 248; Martyn Green, *Here's a How-De-Do*, New York: Norton, 1952, pp. 57–65.

40 J.B. Priestley, *English Humour*, London: Longman, 1930, p. 16.

41 Jacobs, *Arthur Sullivan*, p. 164.

42 David Cannadine, 'Gilbert and Sullivan: the making and unmaking of a British "tradition"', in Roy Porter (ed.), *Myths of the English*, Cambridge: Polity Press, 1992, p. 19.

43 Ian Bradley (ed.), *The Annotated Gilbert and Sullivan*, Harmondsworth: Penguin, 1982, pp. 118, 192, 214.

44 Eden, *Gilbert and Sullivan*, p. 194.

45 Bernard Shaw, *Music in London 1890–94*, London: Constable, 1950, vol. 3, pp. 58–62; *The Pall Mall Gazette*, 9 October, 1893.

46 *The Musical Times*, 1 November, 1893.

47 Stephen Turnbull, 'Utopia Limited and the gramophone', in David Eden (ed.), *Utopia Limited*, London: Sir Arthur Sullivan Society, 1993, pp. 61–4.

48 John Wolfson, *Final Curtain: The Last Gilbert and Sullivan Operas*, London: Chappell & Company, 1976, p. 58. The 1975 production of *Utopia Limited* is on Decca London, CD 436 816–2.

49 Sullivan and Flower, *Sir Arthur Sullivan*, pp. 252–3.

50 Ibid., p. 252.

51 The *Boer War Te Deum* is available on *That Glorious Song of Old: Choral Music of Arthur Sullivan*, Cantoris, CRCD 2368.

52 There is a recording of this comic opera: *The Emerald Isle*, Sounds on CD, VGS 207.

53 B.W. Findon, 'Sir Arthur Sullivan: his life and music', in Orel (ed.), *Gilbert and Sullivan*, p. 314.

54 Eden, *Gilbert and Sullivan*, p. 168.

CHAPTER THREE

Elgar's Empire

Few composers have become so encrusted with myth and misrepresentation as Sir Edward Elgar. He burst on to the English musical scene in the 1890s, was hailed as the greatest English composer since Purcell and, by 1910, had established for himself an international reputation. That reputation dipped after his death in 1934. This was not unusual; it regularly happens to great composers. Sullivan, Parry, Vaughan Williams and Britten all suffered from it. But the process of reviving Elgar's musical fortunes has resulted in distortions of the man and his music that have taken on the status of orthodoxies.

First, there is the idea that Elgar was not really an imperialist or that he renounced imperialism or that his imperially inspired works are minor works. Michael Kennedy, who has taken the lead in seeking to downgrade Elgar's imperial inspiration, writes that for a long time Elgar the imperialist 'obscured the real Elgar, who was someone very different'.[1] Second, there is the assertion that Elgar's music – and by implication the Empire – was unpopular in the interwar period. Third, and linked, there is the theory that he dried up creatively after the death of his wife. Recent research has demonstrated all these orthodoxies to be untrue.[2]

The first thing to say is that Elgar was a patriot, a monarchist and a Conservative, and his imperialism was a logical extension of these values. After all, he signed a letter along with Milner, Roberts and Kipling protesting against Irish home rule and resigned from the Athenaeum Club when it elected Labour leader Ramsay MacDonald as a member. All this has been a profound embarrassment to his latter-day defenders. The revival of Elgar derived from two landmark events in the 1960s; Ken Russell's BBC television documentary *Elgar* (1962) and Michael Kennedy's book *Portrait of Elgar* (1968). The depth and sincerity of Russell's and Kennedy's love of Elgar are not in doubt; nor is the sensitivity of their interpretation. But in seeking to exculpate

Elgar from imperialism, they seriously distort the picture. If the idea that imperialism is something to be ashamed of or embarrassed about is abandoned and it is accepted as a cultural and ideological episode in British history, then it can be accepted as an element – and an important one – in the make-up of our greatest composer. Sir Arnold Bax, a later Master of the King's Musick and someone who knew Elgar ('he was kindness itself to a palpitating enthusiast of seventeen') recognized this complexity in his make-up. He wrote:

> Elgar was ingrainedly and invincibly English . . . and also, be it emphasized, an Englishman of his own particular generation. This is evident not alone in his love of nature (a trait, I think, inherent in almost every member of the island race,) and the somewhat melancholy mysticism . . . pervading *Gerontius* and *The Kingdom* . . . but also the precise opposite of these characteristics – the blare of jingoism and Kiplingesque and Rhodesian Imperialism so inalienably associated with the turn of the century and the period of Elgar's most fecund maturity. Difficult as it may be to reconcile these contradictions, the fact remains that the impulse to turn out such things as *Land of Hope and Glory*, the *Imperial March*, the *Coronation Ode* and the regrettable final chorus of *Caractacus* was an integral part of the make-up of this man, a representative, even an architypal [*sic*] Briton of the last years of Queen Victoria's reign.[3]

Ken Russell's documentary film *Elgar*, made in 1962 for the BBC art series 'Monitor', was one of the most popular television films ever made, and with its beautiful and imaginative visual imagery and creative use of Elgar's music it did much to revive that music in the culture of the day. But the Elgar it portrayed was an Elgar reconstructed for the 1960s. The unforgettable opening of the film, a small boy on a white pony galloping across the Malvern Hills to the exhilarating strains of the *Introduction and Allegro*, an image which was soon to appear on record sleeves, established a dominant theme in the film – Elgar was inspired by the countryside and in particular the countryside of Worcestershire. He starts out in Worcester and eventually returns there, and it always remains the source of his inspiration.

The film faithfully charts the struggle for recognition, the sudden burst of fame and his establishment in the Edwardian era as Britain's leading composer. But then come a succession of half-truths and distortions which recent research has seriously questioned. Elgar is appalled by the First World War, retires to Sussex to write string quartets and comes to hate *Land of Hope and Glory*, which had become a second national anthem during the war. Russell uses it as an ironic counterpoint to the scenes of slaughter in the trenches in one of the film's most powerful scenes. Jeremy Crump has shown that Elgar was active for much of the war period writing and conducting music for the war effort.[4] Michael Kennedy has pointed out that there is no evidence that he ever hated *Land of Hope and Glory*.[5]

The Russell film goes on to say that he came to regard official music as an 'abomination' and that after his *Cello Concerto* of 1919 he wrote almost nothing. It also alleges that the public was indifferent to his music in the interwar years. The researches of Jeremy Crump, John Gardiner and Ronald Taylor have demonstrated the opposite. And in fact after he became Master of the King's Musick in 1924 he turned out a succession of official pieces.

Kennedy's interpretation of Elgar is that the music is intensely personal and basically autobiographical, that later generations can see in it far more melancholy and greater complexity than contemporaries could. Kennedy picks up on Elgar's own description of the *Cello Concerto* as the key to interpreting his work:

> 'A man's attitude to life' was how he described the broken-hearted Cello Concerto. This directly personal appeal is the secret of his music. The technical expertise is but the means by which he speaks to the hearts of large numbers of his fellow-beings. What his message is will vary with each listener – perhaps he did not fully comprehend it himself. In *Gerontius*, the symphonies, *The Music Makers*, most of all in the Violin Concerto, are a human soul's hopes and regrets, disappointments and beliefs, universally shared experiences, strengths and weaknesses, faults and foibles.[6]

There is support for this in Elgar's own comments on these works. Of *Symphony No.1*, Elgar wrote to Walford Davies: 'There is no programme beyond a wide experience of human life with a great charity (love) and a *massive* hope in the future.'[7] Of *Symphony No.2*, he explained to the Chairman of Novello: 'The spirit of the whole work is intended to be high and pure joy: there are retrospective passages of sadness but the whole of the sorrow is smoothed out and ennobled in the last movement which ends in a calm, and *I hope and intend*, elevated mood.'[8] But Kennedy is not justified in moving from this evidence to argue: 'All the virtues and failings of Elgar's work are traceable to the man himself, not to the fact that he was an Englishman alive in the period of England's imperial noonday. He may or may not have accepted the age in which he lived . . . The issue is irrelevant.'[9] His music certainly transcended his age to live on by its own intrinsic merits. But the very fact that some of his most profound work is autobiographical means that he is constantly mingling the personal and the ideological, the public and the private. After all *Symphony No.2* was by Elgar's own admission intended as a tribute to Edward VII. Lady Elgar detected in the slow movement 'lament for King

Edward and dear Rodey'. Elgar had been profoundly moved by the death of Edward VII ('These times are too cruel and gloomy . . . that dear sweet-tempered King–Man was always so "pleasant" to me') and had been prostrated by the death of Alfred Rodewald ('I am heartbroken and cannot believe it . . . He was the dearest, kindest, *best* friend I ever had'[10]). Even when one examines the most personal works, the value systems are there in the music. *The Enigma Variations* contains a succession of delightful musical portraits of his wife and his friends. It culminates in his own self-portrait, EDU (Lady Elgar's nickname for him), a full-blooded, confident and triumphal image in the full imperial idiom. *The Music Makers*, Elgar's setting of Arthur O'Shaughnessy's *Ode*, celebrates the composer as lonely mystic and visionary. 'We are the music makers, and we are the dreamers of dreams' is the recurrent refrain, an idea that appealed to Elgar, but also 'we are the movers and shakers of the world for ever it seems'. (Elgar quotes from the *Enigma Variations*, *Gerontius*, the *Symphony No.1* and the *Violin Concerto* during the course of the score, indicating the nature of the piece as a personal statement.)

Quite clearly stated as one of the roles of the music-maker is that of bard of Empire:

> With wonderful deathless ditties
> We build up the world's great cities
> And out of a fabulous story
> We fashion an empire's glory.

On that last line, Elgar weaves in snatches of *Rule, Britannia* and *La Marseillaise*. The theme is elaborated in the fourth verse:

> A breath of our inspiration
> Is the life of each generation;
> A wondrous thing of our dreaming;
> Unearthly, impossible seeming –
> The soldier, the king, and the peasant
> Are working together in one,
> Till our dream shall become their present,
> And their work in the world is done.

This could easily be interpreted as the realization of the imperial vision enshrined in Elgar's music. Compare Kipling:

> We were dreamers dreaming greatly in the man-stifled town,
> We yearned beyond the sky-line where the strange roads go down,
> Came the Whisper, came the Vision, came the power with the Need,
> Till the soul that is not Man's soul was lent us to lead.

Here the mysticism and the imperial vision are directly linked.

[47]

The Russell–Kennedy view of Elgar has become inscribed into the popular consciousness because Elgar has become a dramatic figure in his own right, featuring in James Hamilton Paterson's novel *Gerontius* (1989) and David Pownall's play *Elgar's Rondo* (1993). Both fine works that movingly recreate the sensitive, depressive, highly strung composer, they also perpetuate the ideas that his pastoral inspiration was more significant that his imperial, that he gave up composing after his wife died, that he hated *Land of Hope and Glory*, and so on.

The 1960s, which saw the great Elgar revival, was pre-eminently a decade of social and cultural upheaval which rejected patriotism, militarism and imperialism and sought its inspiration in quite different directions. Essentially two strategies were adopted, therefore. The first was to separate the public from the private Elgar, to suggest almost a Jekyll and Hyde situation, with the public Elgar writing the patriotic ceremonial pieces, which are by definition inferior, and the private Elgar, inspired by the Malvern Hills and the Worcestershire countryside, writing humane, uplifting and inspiring autobiographical works about man's spiritual struggle – *The Dream of Gerontius*, the *Violin Concerto*, the *Introduction and Allegro*, etc. The latter are therefore the superior works and constitute the official canon. This operation also had the effect of helping to redefine 'Englishness', shifting the emphasis from imperial pomp to rural domesticity, from world-role to that of 'Little England'. This division into two Elgars had been suggested as early as 1935, by Frank Howes, and became something of an orthodoxy with those who wanted to acknowledge Elgar's greatness as a composer but were embarrassed by some of his music.[11]

The second strategy was to divide Elgar's career chronologically and see the young, brash, self-confident Elgar turning out patriotic music until the First World War; and, thereafter, a disillusioned Elgar, turning away from Empire, chivalry and war to melancholy, introspective retreat from the world and rejection by the music-loving public of the age. This period thus sees the composition of the *Cello Concerto* and the chamber music (which are acceptable by the standards of the 1960s). In this interpretation, Elgar's career is deemed to parallel the presumed climax of imperialism in the First World War and its subsequent rapid decline.

In both of these alternative readings, Elgar's career, personality and interests are being wilfully distorted to fit an *ex post facto* rewriting of history to minimize or eliminate elements in him or his work which a later age finds distasteful, but, which it finds distasteful, I would suggest, on a misunderstanding both of history and of imperialism. One of the classic cases of wilful misreading is that of Michael Kennedy, a man who evidently so detests imperialism that he is

[48]

willing to advance almost any argument in his endeavours to explain it away in Elgar's case.

Elgar's *Caractacus* (1898) was a deeply patriotic piece, a heroic cantata about the British race and its resistance to the Roman invader. It gives the lie at once to the distinction between the rural Elgar and the martial–patriotic Elgar. For this work celebrates the fighting spirit of the British, hymning swords and the clash of arms. It also celebrates the beauties of the English countryside, which is seen as the inspiration for the struggle. The cantata ends with a paean of praise to the future British Empire. It is clear then that the idea of two separate Elgars, one public and one private, one inferior and one superior, is essentially bogus. Elgar was equally inspired by the English countryside, by the idea of Empire, by martial glory and by patriotism. They cannot be separated out in any way that makes sense of Elgar's genius. The words of the finale, written by H.A. Acworth, are important:

> The clang of arms is over,
> Abide in peace and brood
> On glorious ages coming,
> And Kings of British blood.
> The light descends from heaven,
> The centuries roll away,
> The empire of the Roman
> Is crumbled into clay;
> The eagle's flight is ended,
> His weary wings are furled:
> The Oak has grown and shadow'd
> The shores of all the world.
> Britons, alert! and fear not.
> Tho' round your path of power,
> Opposing cohorts gather,
> And jealous tyrants lower;
> On – tho' the world desert you,
> On – so your cause be right;
> Britons, alert! and fear not,
> But gird your loins for fight.
> And ever your dominion
> From age to age shall grow
> O'er peoples undiscovered,
> In lands we cannot know;
> And where the flag of Britain
> Its triple crosses rears,
> No slave shall be for subject,
> No trophy wet with tears;
> But folk shall bless the banner,

And bless the crosses twin'd
That bear the gift of freedom
On every blowing wind;
Nor shall her might diminish
While firm she holds the faith
Of equal law to all men –
And hold it to the death;
For all the world shall learn it –
Though long the task shall be –
The text of Britain's teaching,
The message of the free;
And when at last they find it,
The nations all shall stand
And hymn the praise of Britain,
Like brothers, hand in hand.

When August Jaeger of Novello complained of the finale, Elgar declared that *he'd* suggested it, and added: 'I knew you would laugh at my librettist's patriotism (and mine) never mind. England for the English is all I say – hands off! There's nothing apologetic about me.'[12] Michael Kennedy writes on this:

> A stumbling block for the squeamish has been the final chorus 'The clang of arms is over' in which – somewhat incongruously, in view of the fact that the cantata is about a humbling British defeat – the end of the Roman empire is foreseen. Yet was it with ironical intent that Elgar based the music of this chorus on the theme of the Arch-Druid's deliberately false prophecy of Caractacus' victory?[13]

Of course it was not ironic, nor was the choice of theme in the least incongruous. Firstly, the final paean was a clear and unambiguous statement that the Druid's prophecy *would* be fulfilled in due course and that Britain *would* in the end triumph. The Roman triumphal march is in the Elgar imperial idiom confirming Britain's role as Rome's successor, which was in any case a commonplace of nineteenth-century political comment. Secondly, heroic defeats are part and parcel of Britain's self-image: the charge of the Light Brigade; the sinking of the *Birkenhead*; Gallipoli; Dunkirk; heroic defeats followed in the end by victory, and in the case of the murder of Gordon at Khartoum and the massacre of Sir Lewis Cavagnari's mission to Kabul, followed by the annexation respectively of the Sudan and Afghanistan. Kennedy's interpretation is absurd; but it is an absurdity typical of anti-imperial Elgarians. Kennedy has in fact even gone so far as to rewrite the words of the final paean, substituting an ode to the United Nations. Fortunately it is never used.

The problem is that people have misunderstood the meaning of imperialism, equating it with jingoism and exploitation. To apply the term 'jingoistic' to Elgar's work is to misunderstand his view entirely. His critics should have had more confidence in Sir Edward. Elgar's vision of Empire was clearly set out at the end of *Caractacus*: it is a vision of justice, peace, freedom and equality, of the *pax Britannica* and of the fulfilment by Britain of its trusteeship mission, to see the countries in its charge brought safely and in due course to independence – a far from ignoble dream.

Elgar's Empire was a fusion of three other elements in his world-view, his love of chivalry, his mystical Christianity and his patriotism. It is instructive to compare Elgar with Kipling. Indeed Elgar is on record as admiring Kipling's work, and many commentators, among them Sir Arnold Bax, Sir Charles Stanford, Sir Compton Mackenzie and Ernest Newman, have explicitly compared Elgar's music with Kipling's verse, though their work only overlapped directly when Elgar set *The Fringes of the Fleet*.[14] It is also significant that Elgar and Kipling were the last two artists of genius to have touched the hearts of the English people. The two men were very similar; both highly strung, intense and introspective; both prone to psychosomatic illnesses and depressions; both of a mystical and visionary nature. Both were self-made men and immensely hardworking. Both loved the English countryside, Kipling Sussex, Elgar Worcestershire. Both had a succession of fads and hobbies. Both adopted a self-conscious anti-intellectualism but both were widely read and deeply thoughtful. Both wrote letters in a slangy, hearty schoolboy fashion and had a fondness for nicknames and wordplay. Both married older women, mother figures who worshipped their genius and protected them against the outside world. But three things seem to me most important in explaining their nature and their imperialism.

First, they were outsiders. Kipling (although well-connected through his mother) was essentially a provincial (i.e. from British India), and had been educated at a public school designed specifically for the sons of hard-up officers; Elgar was the son of a Worcestershire tradesman, and furthermore was a Catholic. Neither of them had been to university. They felt their exclusion from the cultural establishment. Elgar took pleasure in cultivating hobbies that would cause Establishment eyebrows to rise (supporting Wolverhampton Wanderers FC; going to the races; flying kites.)

Second, as with many outsiders, both men identified with the dominant ideology and also were hungry for recognition. Kipling, who rejected almost all state honours, amassed honorary doctorates. Elgar

heaped up state honours and set his heart on becoming the first composer to earn a peerage. He managed only a knighthood, the Order of
Merit, KCVO and a baronetcy. (The dying Benjamin Britten received
the first composer peerage in 1976.)

Third, all their lives they remained essentially schoolboys. In 1921
Elgar confided to his friend Sir Sidney Colvin: 'I am still at heart the
dreamy child who used to be found in the reeds by Severn side with a
sheet of paper trying to fix the sounds and longing for something very
great.'[15] Similarly Frank Harris declared that Kipling 'had the prejudices and opinions of a fourth-form English schoolboy on almost every
subject coupled with an extraordinary verbal talent: the mind of a boy
of sixteen with a genius for expression', a view echoed by E.M. Forster
who wrote: 'There are at least two Kiplings. One of them is Kim, the
Little Friend of all the World, the other is also a boy but sneering and
cocky.'[16] It is clear that both Kipling and Elgar were brilliant examples
of that Victorian–Edwardian phenomenon, the *puer aeternus*, the
eternal boy whose literary embodiment was Peter Pan, which is why
they empathized so well with children (Elgar in his *Wand of Youth*
suites, his *Nursery Suite* and his *Starlight Express* music; Kipling in
Kim, the *Just So Stories*, the *Jungle Book* and *Puck of Pook's Hill*).
They were schooboyish in their love of jokes and japes, in their use of
slang and nicknames, in their pose of philistinism, and as boys they
responded instinctively to the grand heroic vision of the Empire. They
were also, like many boys, inveterate Conservatives, revering the
crown, the traditions and the history of their country, its glories and
its world-role. For all these reasons they revered the Empire. It is worth
noting that the same actor Alec McCowen has played the two men,
Kipling in the one-man play *Kipling* and Elgar in Pownall's *Elgar's
Rondo*.

It is a remarkable fact and one in many ways typical of Britain that
at the height of its global power and influence, when Britain was the
centre of the mightiest Empire the world had ever known, those key
cultural signifiers, the offices of Poet Laureate and Master of the
Queen's/King's Musick, were occupied by men who were, relatively
speaking, mediocrities. The Poet Laureate was Alfred Austin. When
he was appointed to succeed Alfred, Lord Tennyson, *Punch* summed
up the general opinion by announcing that Alfred the Great had been
succeeded by Alfred the Little. He was appointed essentially because
he was a good Tory. Kipling had been sounded out about the post, as
he was to be again when Austin died, but he declared himself incapable of writing official verse to order. It must have been a source of
continual frustration to Austin that Kipling became and remained all
his life the unofficial laureate, so that on Jubilee Day 1897 *The Times*

printed Austin's pedestrian and unmemorable effusion about the Queen and two days later Kipling's sonorous and unforgettable *Recessional* appeared and electrified the nation.

Similarly the office of Master of the Queen's/King's Musick was occupied by Sir Walter Parratt from 1893 to 1924. A much more considerable figure than Austin, Parratt was an organist and teacher, champion of the English Musical Renaissance but as a composer decidedly second-rate. To his credit, however, he was a keen champion of Elgar's music, and it was left to Elgar to provide the musical celebrations of Empire, just as Kipling unofficially provided the verse. Also, Elgar succeeded Parratt as Master of the King's Musick, in 1924.

Historically Empire may be many things: a vehicle for national ambition, for personal greed, for theories of racial supremacy; but the British Empire was also and at the same time for some people a vehicle for service, for the practice of a modern chivalry, for work, long, hard and thankless, in fulfilment of the Christian ethic on earth. Imperialism is never to be equated with mere jingoism, and it is absurd – and unhistorical – to do so. Jingoism is mindless chauvinism. It is the polar opposite of altruistic imperialism, which is effectively a religion. This had a strong appeal for Elgar, as his friend W.H. Reed recorded: 'Mysticism is a very strong trait in Elgar; it came out in all he did, and of course found its way into his music.'[17]

In the 1880s and 1890s a group of serious-minded young imperialists appeared who finally articulated the fully formed imperial religion. These were men like Curzon, Balfour and Milner, men who believed with Lord Rosebery that the British Empire was 'the greatest secular agency for good the world has ever seen'.[18] With them, imperialism transcends party lines and acquires the mystic appeal which is basic to true imperialism.

The nineteenth century, often seen as the age of faith, was in reality the age of crisis of faith, when Darwinism and Freudianism for instance undermined traditional beliefs. There were several reactions to this: atheism was one, a return to Roman Catholicism was another, and a third was the creation of a new religious faith, compounded of duty and Empire and incorporating the Protestant work ethic and a Calvinistic belief in the British as an 'elect'.

It was Lord Curzon, believing that in Empire we had found 'not merely the key to glory and wealth but the call to duty and the means of service to mankind', who defined the essentially religious nature of imperialism. He declared in 1907:

Empire can only be achieved with satisfaction or maintained with advantage, provided it has a moral basis. To the people of the mother state, it must be a discipline, an inspiration, a faith. To the people of the circumference, it must be more than a flag or a name, it must give them what they cannot otherwise or elsewhere enjoy: not merely justice or order or material prosperity, but the sense of partnership in a great idea, the consecrating influence of a lofty purpose.[19]

This sentiment is the inspiration behind the finale of *Caractacus*. The same fervent note sounds in the imperial writings of the twentieth century, with men like Leopold Amery declaring in 1924: 'Like the kingdom of heaven, the empire is within us. It means more than the practical advantages of a common citizenship and a common defence or than opportunities for advanced trade. It is a living faith, a faith that something can be done to raise the whole standard of man's life on this planet.'[20]

It was Kipling who in his stories and poems translated into dramatic form the concept of imperialism that had emerged in the writings of men like Curzon, Milner and Rosebery. Duty, discipline, obligation, self-sacrifice – these were the demanding ascetic concepts which informed the body of his work. He saw the duty of civilizing the world as a burden laid on the nation by God. He was under no illusion about it. It was a hard task, a thankless task, a burden shouldered by a small and dedicated band of men, whom he called 'the sons of Martha', and whose laureate he became, soldiers, engineers, administrators, policemen, 'a community of men of identical race and identical aims, united in comradeship, comprehension and sympathy'.[21] Their justification was their work and their work was performed in obedience to what Kipling called 'the Law':

> Keep ye the Law – be swift in all obedience,
> Clear the land of evil, drive the road and bridge the ford
> Make ye sure of each his own,
> That he reap where he hath sown,
> By the peace among our peoples let men know
> We serve the Lord.

This, too, is the essence of Elgar's Empire.

Perhaps a key to understanding his attitude to the Empire is his reaction to the Empire Exhibition at Wembley. He described to his friend Lady Stuart his attempts to conduct rehearsals as the Stadium was being prepared – '17,000 men, hammering, loudspeakers, amplifiers, four aeroplanes circling over etc. – all mechanical and horrible – no soul and no romance and no imagination'; and then his reaction at the sight of a group of real daisies on the Wembley turf: 'I was back in something sane, wholesome and *gentlemanly* but only for two minutes.'[22] It is clear that for him the Empire *was* a matter of soul, romance and imagination and something gentlemanly, and thus the antithesis of the huge artificial extravaganza that was Wembley.

Contemporaries correctly divined the appeal of the Empire for him. F.H. Shera wrote:

> In spirit Elgar is a romantic. The motto inscribed on the score of his early concert-overture *Froissart* 'When Chivalry lifted up her lance on high' labels him as such, but it does not give more than a superficial indication of the peculiar quality of his romanticism. It does, however, stamp him as an idealist, as does the characteristic *Nobilmente* . . . Where the romantic in general thinks of the past as an age of legend, Elgar thinks of it as an age of faith. Again, whereas the typical romantic turns instinctively away from his own age with its dark, satanic mills and hurrying city pavements, Elgar finds romanticism on the doorstep, in St. James's Park, amongst his friends. The British Empire, a battalion in full dress, a Cockney errand boy are for him fuller of romance than *La Belle Dame Sans Merci* or *Childe Harold* or *Deirdre*.[23]

Sir Compton Mackenzie, who was in no doubt of Elgar's genius ('by any standards that we know we must call Elgar a great artist'), wrote:

> It has always seemed to me that his music was an expression of the same state of mind as inspired Mr. Rudyard Kipling's poetry. I should describe both as romantics who had attempted to classicize their romance on the assumption that the British Empire, as revealed in all its outward glory in the Diamond Jubilee Procession of 1897, had at least as long a future before it as the Roman Empire in the reign of Augustus.[24]

Elgar and his Empire were steeped in chivalry. Interest in matters mediaeval and chivalric had revived as part of the whole Romantic reaction to the measured, passionless classicism of the eighteenth century. In the wake of the novels and poems of Sir Walter Scott, with their idealized and stylized picture of mediaeval chivalry, and of the massive revival of interest in the Arthurian legends, celebrated in poems, paintings and countless retellings of Malory, a living and meaningful code of life for the nineteenth-century gentleman had been fashioned. The image of the gentleman was reformulated as a latter-day version of the mediaeval knight, the embodiment of the virtues of bravery, loyalty and courtesy, modesty, purity and honour, and endowed with a sense of *noblesse oblige* towards women, children and social inferiors. This was to form the essence of the national ideology for over a century. By the middle of the nineteenth century the language and image of chivalry had been so far absorbed into the fabric of Victorian life and thought that it was automatic to see the gentleman exclusively in terms of the mediaeval paladin. The chivalric ideal was deliberately promoted by key figures of the age in order to produce for the nation and for the expanding Empire a ruling elite who would be inspired by noble and selfless values.[25] In practical terms, the march expressed his commitment to chivalric notions of warfare.

Although Elgar successfully mastered the oratorio, the symphony and the concert overture, there was one form which he made his own, which he chose, perfected and transformed into high art. It was the humble march, to which he gave a symphonic dimension. Robert Anderson concludes: 'Perhaps most characteristic of him are the great march tunes, mystic, ceremonial, solemn, patriotic, sprightly and vulgar, that are scattered throughout his work.'[26] Elgar told *The Strand Magazine* in 1904:

> I like to look on the composer's vocation as the old troubadours or bards did. In those days it was no disgrace to a man to be turned on to step in front of an army and inspire the people with a song. For my own part, I know that there are a lot of people who like to celebrate events with music. To these people I have given tunes. Is that wrong? Why should I write a fugue or something which won't appeal to anyone, when the people yearn for things which can stir them . . . We are a nation with great military proclivities, and I did not see why the ordinary quick march should not be treated on a large scale in the way that the waltz, the old-fashioned slow march, and even the polka have been treated by the great composers . . . I have some of the soldier instinct in me, and so I have written two marches of which, so far from being ashamed, I am proud.[27]

He also once declared that, were it not for his 'musical destiny', he would have become a soldier.[28] In old age, of course, he was famous for looking like a retired colonel. He planned, he said, a set of six marches, one of which was to be a soldier's funeral march. In the event he wrote five of the set, though he contributed a sombre and powerful funeral march to his incidental music to the play *Grania and Diarmid* by George Moore and W.B. Yeats.

Of the five *Pomp and Circumstance* marches, the first four were written in the Edwardian era (*No. 1 in D Major* and *No. 2 in A Minor* in 1901, *No. 3 in C Minor* in 1904, *No. 4 in G Major* in 1907). *No. 5 in C Major* followed twenty-three years later, but showed his inspiration in this vein undiminished.

The masterpieces of the set are *No. 1* and *No. 4*. *No. 1* with its unforgettable trio tune was a work which indelibly captured the spirit of the age. After he had composed it, Elgar declared: 'I have got a tune that will knock 'em – knock 'em flat.'[29] And knock 'em flat it did, when it was premièred at one of Sir Henry Wood's Promenade Concerts at the Queen's Hall. Wood recalled:

What *did* go down well was the first performance of Elgar's *Pomp and Circumstance* marches. I shall never forget the scene at the close of the first of them – the one in D major. The people simply rose and yelled. I had to play it again – with the same result; in fact, they refused to let me go on with the programme. After considerable delay, while the audience roared its applause, I went off and fetched Harry Dearth who was to sing *Hiawatha's Vision*; but they would not listen. Merely to restore order, I played the march a third time. And that, I may say, was the one and only time in the history of the Promenade concerts that an orchestral item was accorded a double encore. Little did I think then that the lovely, broad melody of the *trio* would one day develop into our second national anthem – *Land of Hope and Glory*.[30]

Sir Arnold Bax recalled in 1949 that as a young man he too was 'present on the very first occasion when the Empire's second National Anthem was heard at a promenade Concert':

That night Queen's Hall was invaded by one of London's most stupendous fogs, and Sir Henry Wood's back and the faces of the orchestral players were as figments in the baseless fabric of a dream ... At the end of *Land of Hope and Glory* there arose such a heartening din as could never before have startled the hall. The very fog was disturbed into dense and delicious whorls and eddies, and it seemed that the excitement would never abate.[31]

It has of course continued to feature down to the present day as an indispensable part of the Last Night of the Proms. *March No. 4* also has a noble and expansive trio that cried out for words to be set to it. They were in 1940, when A.P. Herbert composed *The Song of Liberty* around Elgar's tune as a rallying cry for the British at war. It was recorded by baritone Dennis Noble with chorus and the Band of the Coldstream Guards. Herbert's verse fitted awkwardly to the first section of the march, and although the chorus easily fitted the trio

> All men must be free,
> March for liberty with me,
> Brutes and braggarts may have their little day,
> We shall never bow the knee.

it never came close to matching the popularity of *Land of Hope* and was rapidly eclipsed by *There'll Always Be an England* as *the* popular march–anthem of the Second World War. As Michael Kennedy has written of the five marches:

The complete set, played one after the other, comprise [*sic*] a kind of suite, devoid of monotony except for the actual march form, consistently exciting rhythmically and scored with all Elgar's command of thrilling and poetic instrumental colour ... Nos 2, 3 and 5 ... are less fruity melodically than Nos 1 and 4 ... No. 2, for example, in A Minor is ... scored rather like a Schubertian *marche militaire* or a theatrical ent'racte. No. 3, like No. 2 also in the minor, is a subtle work, with a hint of mystery in its opening bars, and a trio section of lyrical and quite un-military charm. No. 5 ... is jovial.[32]

But he then characteristically seeks to undermine the genuineness of the inspiration of *No. 5* by suggesting that there is 'more than a touch of self-parodying, tongue-in-cheek humour in its final pages'. There is not. It is a totally convincing and confident endorsement of the style and values of the earlier works, and those were an affirmation of a cheerful militarism and imperial self-confidence. As Lady Elgar told August Jaeger of *No. 3*: 'The new march is *thrilling* – the most pacific friends were ready to fight.'[33] Elgar definitely set the style for marches on ceremonial occasions, so that William Walton's splendid marches *Crown Imperial* and *Orb and Sceptre*, written for the coronations of King George VI and Queen Elizabeth II, are decidedly Elgarian.

The series' title came from Shakespeare's *Othello*: 'the neighing steed, and the shrill trumpet, the spirit stirring drum, the ear-piercing fife, the royal banners, and all quality, pride, pomp and circumstance of glorious war'. The following lines by Lord de Tabley were taken as the motto for the marches as a whole:

> Like a proud music that draws men to die
> Madly upon the spears in martial ecstasy,
> A measure that sets heaven in all their veins
> And iron in their hands.
> I hear the Nation march
> Beneath her ensign as an eagle's wing;
> O'er shield and sheeted targe
> The banners of my faith most gaily swing
> Moving to victory with solemn noise,
> With worship and with conquest and the voice of myriads.

This is music inspired by that nineteenth-century phenomenon, the romance of war, war not as a matter of terror and mass destruction but as an arena for pageantry – scarlet coats, embroidered banners, fifes and drums – and as a vehicle for the noblest of instincts – courage, service, self-sacrifice, comradeship. Once again in this as in so many things, Elgar was a man of his time; for the nineteenth century was the era of Christian militarism, and although his greatest fame was in the Edwardian period, Elgar was essentially a Victorian, already middle-aged (44) by the time of the death of the Old Queen.

In the nineteenth century war was seen as a moral force and the profession of soldiering became a noble one. The evangelicals set out to demonstrate that it was possible to be both a professional soldier and a zealous Christian, and organizations and individuals set out to 'raise the tone of the troops', providing chaplains, chapels and bibles, creating role models of idealized Christian soldier heroes, notably Sir Henry Havelock and General Charles Gordon. The image of the Puritan soldiery of the English Civil War became a commonplace of military depictions. The result was, as Olive Anderson has pointed out, that by the mid-1860s, the 'British Army was . . . more obtrusively Christian than it had ever been since the Restoration'.[34] The Christianization of the army is paralleled by the militarization of Christianity. In the 1870s and 1880s, the Salvation Army, the Church Army and the Boy's Brigade were founded, complete with uniforms, titles and military ranks; at the same time there was a great vogue for military imagery in hymns. What was clear was that deep religious faith and patriotic militarism were felt to be wholly compatible, and they clearly co-existed in Elgar.

The nineteenth century's fascination with the Middle Ages and with chivalry gave us the glories of Gothic architecture, such as that magic citadel St Pancras Station, of Pre-Raphaelite painting, of poems like Tennyson's *Idylls of the King*, and novels like Conan Doyle's *The White Company* and *Sir Nigel*. Scott in particular was an inspiration. His novels were plundered by operatic composers, and he became a key figure of Romanticism. When Sir Arthur Sullivan came to write grand opera, he turned to Scott for his subject – *Ivanhoe*. Elgar also found inspiration in Scott. His first mature work, the overture *Froissart* (1890), was inspired by a passage in Scott's *Old Mortality* in which John Graham of Claverhouse speaks of his enthusiasm for Froissart's historical romances with their values of loyalty to the crown, pure faith in religion, hardihood towards the enemy and fidelity to lady-loves.[35] On the score, Elgar inscribed a line from Keats: 'when chivalry lifted up her lance on high'. *Froissart* glows with all the nobility, purity and splendour of the chivalric ideal. Elgar was to return again and again to the idea of chivalry, and elements of it can be found in *The Black Knight*, *Falstaff* and *The Severn Suite*. The *Worcester Herald* wrote of *The Black Knight*: 'Mr. Elgar has gone to the days of chivalry for his conception, and in his delightfully descriptive writing brings before us the imposing grandeur, the mysticism, and the romance of the period – a rare achievement in this prosaic age'.[36] Elgar's incidental music to Laurence Binyon's *Arthur* (1923) allowed the composer to explore that central chivalric myth, one which had inspired so many great Victorians from Tennyson, through Swinburne, Burne-Jones and William Morris, to Sir Henry Irving, greatest of Victorian actors, who commissioned a play on the subject towards the end of his career.

The idea of the Holy Grail in particular inspired the Victorians – the search for spiritual perfection. It was part of the 'call to seriousness' by which Ian Bradley characterizes the nineteenth century, the same idea that lies behind Longfellow's *Excelsior* (and Longfellow was a favourite poet of Elgar, the source of *King Olaf* and *The Black Knight*).[37] 'Excelsior' is what is embroidered on the banner with the strange device carried by the mysterious youth struggling through the Alps. What does 'excelsior' mean? It means the idea of life as a struggle, ever onwards and upwards, in search of perfection. Both the poem and the song based on it were drawing-room favourites in the nineteenth century. It crystallized the ideas of chivalry, mysticism and the heroic vision, which similarly lie at the heart of Elgar's Empire.

Dedicated imperialists invested their Empire with chivalry, and chivalric images were regularly associated with the Empire. Queen Victoria inaugurated orders of knighthood for her imperial servants: the Order of the Indian Empire, the Order of the Star of India, the Royal Victorian Order. In 1917 the Order of the British Empire was founded and just before the First World War a group of imperial enthusiasts set up the Round Table, in conscious imitation of the Arthurian knights. Baden-Powell originally planned to call his Boy Scouts 'The Young Knights of the Empire'.

Imperial heroes were regularly compared to knights. The greatest of them was Gordon of Khartoum, General Charles George 'Chinese' Gordon, who died on imperial service at the hands of the followers of the Mahdi in 1885. He became after his death effectively the patron saint of the imperial religion, a stream of biographies extolling his knightly virtues. One claimed that Gordon 'united all that is noble and chivalrous in man', another compared him to Sir Lancelot and Bayard, while a third claimed: 'Doubtful indeed it is if anywhere in the past we shall find figure of knight or soldier to equal him.'[38]

Gordon thus became the heroic ideal, a chivalric Christian martyr and mystic, who died in the service of others in a far-off land. It is significant, then, that in 1898 Elgar began sketching a Gordon symphony. So confident of his progress was August Jaeger that he put a notice in *The Musical Times* announcing it, in words which Percy Young says are Elgar's own and which give us some idea of Gordon's appeal for Elgar. The notice declares: 'The extraordinary career of General Gordon – his military achievements, his unbounded energy, his self-sacrifice, his resolution, his deep religious fervour – offers to a composer of Mr. Elgar's temperament a magnificent subject . . . moreover it is a subject that appeals to the sympathies of all true-hearted Englishmen.'[39] The use of the term 'temperament' is significant here. It suggests that Elgar very strongly identified with Gordon. In the event, Elgar did not complete the symphony, though most authorities agree that given Elgar's method of working it is likely that the sketches for this symphony eventually found their way into *Symphony No. 1* and *Symphony No. 2* and *The Dream of Gerontius*. After Gordon's death, his copy of Newman's poem *The Dream of Gerontius*, with certain special passages marked, circulated in the Midlands and many admirers transcribed the markings into their own copies of the poem. Elgar was presented with a copy, complete with the Gordon markings, at the time of his marriage in 1889. What appealed to Elgar about both the Gordon story and the *Gerontius* poem, I suggest, is the idea of Christian heroism, of the journey of a soul through danger and temptation, onwards and upwards, *excelsior*. Elgar poured all his intense feelings into *The Dream of Gerontius*, premièred in 1900. This may not be a directly imperial work, but it contains something of the spirit of Elgar's Empire, the idea of Empire as a vehicle for struggle and sacrifice. Certainly the Gordonian inspiration is undeniable.[40]

Undoubtedly *The Dream of Gerontius* was one of Elgar's major religious works, along with the oratorios *The Apostles*, *The Kingdom*, *The Light of Life* and the dramatic cantata *King Olaf*. What they all have in common is the notion of spiritual struggle, of the battle to fulfil the Christian ethic. As Abbess Astrid sings in *King Olaf*:

> Stronger than steel is the sword of the spirit,
> Swifter than arrows the light of the truth is,
> Greater than Anger is Love and subdueth.

Remembering the military imagery of nineteenth-century hymns (*Fight the Good Fight, Onward, Christian Soldiers, Stand Up, Stand Up for Jesus, Ye Soldiers of the Cross, The Son of God Goes Forth to War*, etc.), one cannot help but see this as a parallel struggle, the struggle of Christian heroes to impart the truth of their faith having many of the same features as the struggle of imperial servants to carry out 'the Law' and of chivalric heroes to find the Holy Grail. It is a battle against loneliness and isolation, hostility and despair, which can be applied equally to the Christian vocation, the imperial mission and the eternal predicament of the artist.

The third strand of the Elgarian worldview is *patriotism*. The symbol of the nation in this worldview was the monarchy. For the first three-quarters of the nineteenth century the monarchy had been deeply unpopular: monarchs had interfered in politics, and so became victims of scurrilous political cartoons; and the nation had witnessed in gruesome succession the madness of George III, the folly and extravagance of George IV, the unpopularity of Prince Albert and the increasingly excoriated withdrawal into seclusion of Queen Victoria.

Between 1871 and 1874 alone eighty-four republican clubs were founded.

Between the 1870s and 1914 all this changed. The monarchy returned centre-stage and moved above politics to become in reality the symbol of the nation, the focus of patriotic feeling, the embodiment of consensus and community, a position it has never lost since. It did so, for two principal reasons. Firstly, the monarchy, with its continuity, traditions and ancient trappings of power, came to seem a fixed point in a changing world, something to hold on to and look up to in an age of bewildering and rapid change, the age of the railways and the telegraph, electric lighting and the widening franchise. The mass media, the press and later the infant cinema, were mobilized to promote the cult of royalty, something else they have continued to do ever since.

But, secondly, the monarchy also became the lynchpin of the Empire at a time when imperialism was the dominant ideology. It was the only common feature in an extraordinary patchwork of colonies, protectorates, territories, dependencies, condominiums which never attained the formal precision and order of the Roman Empire, with which it was so often compared. As David Cannadine has written in a seminal article: 'From 1877, when Disraeli made Victoria Empress of India, and 1897 when Joseph Chamberlain brought the colonial premiers and troops to parade in the Diamond Jubilee procession, every great royal occasion was also an *imperial* occasion.'[41] The centre of London was rebuilt, with a range of grand new buildings, fit for an imperial capital, and an appropriate arena for the staging of spectacle and pageantry. The net result was adulation of Queen Victoria and King Edward VII, quite different from the low reputations of earlier monarchs.

From the 1870s onwards, there is a great development in ritual, pageantry and splendour, symbolizing the greatness of the nation and of the monarchy at its heart – the Diamond Jubilee of Queen Victoria and her funeral in 1901, the Coronation and funeral of King Edward VII, the Coronation and Durbar of King George V. In this whole movement, three individuals are singled out by Cannadine as playing vital roles. The first was Reginald Brett, Viscount Esher, the brilliant impresario who planned and organized every great royal event from the Diamond Jubilee to the Funeral of King Edward VII, single-handedly creating what has since come to be regarded as one of the continuing glories of Britain, something that the British can do really well: *official pageantry*. The second was King Edward VII, who loved dressing up, parading, ceremonial, medals and uniforms and who was directly responsible for the revival of the State Opening of Parliament as a regularly staged grand ceremonial occasion. The third was Sir Edward Elgar, who created the British ceremonial idiom in music, and did so successfully because it came from the heart. He loved the monarchy, ceremony, tradition. Processions, pageantry and pomp frequently figure in his music. This was one of the aspects of the appeal of chivalry, reinforced by his hobby interest in heraldry and mediaeval art.

Caractacus was dedicated to Queen Victoria and *Symphony No. 2* to the memory of King Edward VII. Elgar's *Imperial March* of 1897 was the smash hit of the Jubilee, catching the spirit of the age and the mood of the people so well that after its première at the Crystal Palace on 19 March 1897 it was played at the Jubilee State Concert and the State Garden Party at Buckingham Palace in 1897 and at the royal birthday celebrations in 1899.[42]

The *Coronation Ode* of 1902 is ceremonial music of the first rank, the lyricism and splendour animated by genuine emotion and belief. Michael Kennedy correctly calls it 'a masterpiece'.[43] Elgar was invited by Henry Higgins of Covent Garden to set A.C. Benson's *Coronation Ode* for the proposed Coronation Gala at the Opera House. Clara Butt had asked Elgar to set the trio theme of *Pomp and Circumstance March No. 1* as a song for her. Elgar now invited Benson to add a final verse to his *Ode* with words to fit the tune, intending it as a solo for Clara Butt at the gala. In the event the King's sudden illness caused the postponement of the coronation and the abandonment of the gala. But the *Ode* was eventually performed to great acclaim.

Elgar scored it for orchestra and soloists, organ and military band. But it would be a mistake to see it as jingoistic. It is a celebration of monarchy and a hymn of hope to all the virtues and qualities that were expected of the new reign – peace, prosperity, freedom. The work begins with a series of incantations, richly orchestrated, moving from grandeur to tenderness and back again, calling for the King to be crowned with life, might, peace, love and faith – 'Let the cries of hate/ Die in joy away; peace with kindly wealth/ Nurse of joy and health'. A second verse, simple and sincere, celebrates Queen Alexandra: 'Purest, stateliest, daughter of ancient kings'. When the *Ode* was revived for the 1911 Coronation, a new verse more appropriate to Queen Mary than to Queen Alexandra was substituted, a gentle paean to domesticity – 'True Queen of British homes and hearts'.

The third verse is brimming with martial vigour but it calls for preparedness rather than aggression: 'Britain, ask of thyself, and see thy sons be strong/ Strong to arm and go, if ever the war-trump peal', in order that Britain shall 'rest in peace, enthroned in thine island home'. Then follows an 'exquisite serenade', calling upon music, 'sweetest child of heaven', to bless the occasion. This leads directly to a moving and lyrical celebration of peace – a topical touch in the light of the end of the Boer War – 'give back the father to his children's arms'. The whole *Ode* culminates in the rousing *Land of Hope and Glory*. But it is not yet an imperial anthem. The introduction – 'Land of Hope and Glory, Mother of the Free/ How shall we extol thee, who are born of thee?' – is followed by an invocation of Britain's virtues ('Truth and Right and Freedom, each a holy gem/ Stars of solemn brightness, weave thy diadem') and a joyous affirmation of the ceremony of coronation ('Hearts in hope uplifted, loyal lips that sing/ Strong in faith and freedom, we have crowned our King').

Arthur Johnstone of the *Manchester Guardian* wrote after the *Ode*'s première at the Sheffield Festival:

> It is popular music of a kind that has not been made for a long time in this country – scarcely at all since Dibdin's time. At least one may say that of the best parts, such as the bass solo and chorus 'Britain, Ask of Thyself', and the contralto song and chorus 'Land of Hope and Glory'. The former is ringing martial music, the latter a sort of church parade song having the breadth of a national hymn. It is the melody which occurs as second principal theme of the longer Pomp and Circumstance march, which I beg to suggest is as broad as *God Save the King*, *Rule Britannia* and *See the Conquering Hero*, and is perhaps the broadest open-air tune since Beethoven's *Freude Schöner Götterfunken*. Moreover, it is distinctively British – at once breezy and beefy. It is astonishing to hear people finding fault with Elgar for using this tune in two different compositions, I find it most natural in a composer, to whom music is a language in which, desiring to say exactly the same thing again, one has no choice but to say it in the same notes. Besides, such tunes are composed less frequently than once in 50 years. How then can one blame Elgar for not composing two in six months? The chorus enjoyed themselves over it and so did the audience.[44]

Boosey, the publishers of the *Ode*, recognized the finale as a sure-fire hit, and at their request Elgar and Benson revived it for publication as a solo song, which was duly premièred by Clara Butt, becoming a regular part of her repertoire. It was in this guise that it became a truly imperial anthem. The verse, which is now rarely sung, ends with the lines:

> By freedom gained, by truth maintained,
> Thine empire shall be strong.

And the chorus, after the familiar introduction, celebrates the process of imperial expansion:

Wider still and wider
Shall thy bounds be set,
God who made thee mighty
Make thee mightier yet.

It was in this guise that it became the alternative national anthem.

Although the *Ode* was revived for the 1911 Coronation, Elgar also composed a new piece, the *Coronation March*. Far from the joyous spirit of the *Coronation Ode*, it is a dark, sombre and sonorous piece, somewhat in the spirit of Kipling's *Recessional*, a poem Elgar had seriously thought of setting to music in 1900. Despite being awarded the Order of Merit, Elgar, presumably in the grip of one of his periodical depressions, refused to attend the Coronation and forbade his wife to go.[45]

His next imperial commission, however, found him in somewhat better spirits. To celebrate that grand imperial occasion, the 1911 Delhi Durbar, impresario Oswald Stoll staged an 'imperial masque' at the Coliseum theatre. The *Crown of India* was written in blank verse by Henry Hamilton and Stoll persuaded Elgar to contribute the score. He also conducted the first fortnight of the run with an augmented orchestra. Elgar told the press: 'The subject of the masque is appropriate to this special period in English history, and I have endeavoured to make the music illustrate and illuminate the subject.'[46]

The subject was the glory and rightness of British rule in India. The book, which had received the approval of the King, consisted of two *tableaux*. In the first, *The Cities of India*, against a backdrop of the Taj Mahal, India is seen in state, surrounded by her daughter cities, Agra, Benares, Lucknow, Bombay, Madras, Hyderabad, Mysore, Gwalior and Allahabad. India was played by Nancy Price and the cities by other actresses. Delhi, attended by Tradition and Romance, and Calcutta, attended by Commerce and Statecraft, arrive late and dispute precedence. But St George announces the coming of the King–Emperor, and it is agreed to refer the matter to him. The second *tableau*, *Ave Imperator*, recreates the splendour of the Durbar. The King–Emperor and his consort enter; India does them homage. The native princes are presented and the King–Emperor listens to the rival claims of Delhi and Calcutta. Calcutta is supported by John Company, the personification of the old East India Company, and by the British heroes of Company days, Clive, Wellesley, Warren Hastings, Colin Campbell and the rest, and Delhi by the Moghul Emperors, Akhbar, Jehangir, Shah Jehan and Aurengzebe. The King–Emperor solves the dispute with Solomonic wisdom:

> Delhi to be his capital he names,
> And of his Empire, further makes decree
> Calcutta shall his premier city be.

A preliminary announcement in *The Times* declared that Elgar would be writing 'for the first time music to be (in the best sense) popular and for the secular stage'.[47] It was an announcement which *The Times*, heading its first night review 'Sir Edward Elgar's Masque', answered with a question:

> One naturally asks what Sir Edward Elgar has ever done which was not in fact popular in the best sense? . . . He is essentially a popular composer in his brilliant use of the orchestra, in his capacity for writing melodies which sound fresh . . . and most of all in the kind of literary ideas that appeal to him as suitable for music.[48]

The Times noted that all these qualities were present in the *Crown of India* music. The review singled out the *March of the Moghul Emperors* and the music by which the Princes of India assembled to receive the King–Emperor, seeing these pieces as having 'something of the energy and culminating power we have known in the *Pomp and Circumstance* marches, the Coronation Ode and the Imperial March of last year's Coronation'. This 1911 march was in fact the *Coronation March* but it is interesting and revealing that *The Times* should dub it the 'Imperial March'.

The Times pointed out that Elgar had failed to provide another *Land of Hope and Glory* in St George's song *Lift Aloft the Flag of England* ('well sung by Mr Harry Dearth'):

> Lift aloft the Flag of England!
> Hers it is to lead the fight,
> Ours to keep her still the Kingland,
> Keep her ancient Honour bright,
> Her manhood ever glorious,
> Her valour still victorious,
> Lift aloft the Flag of England,
> Break the wrong and make the right.

However, Agra's song to India, 'in which Miss Marion Beesley's voice was very effective', was 'one of the best numbers'. *The Times* concluded: 'The whole went well for a first performance . . . at the close the composer was called on to the stage and received hearty applause together with all who were concerned in the production'.

The score consisted of twelve different items, including songs, dances and marches, and Elgar selected five items for an orchestral suite, which received its first performance at the 1912 Hereford Festival with the composer conducting. Elgar's score included no authentic Indian music but represented Elgar's own created exoticism, evoked by the liberal use of tambourine, cymbals, drums and a gong specially devised by him for the occasion, and by the development of percussive rhythms. The suite begins with a meditative introduction and leads immediately into the whirling and captivating dance of the nautch girls. This is followed by and contrasted with the solemn and deliberate *Minuet in E Flat*, which accompanied the entrance of John Company. Then comes the *Warriors' Dance* with its cascading strings and 'barbaric' rhythms in G minor. The suite culminates with the splendid *March of the Moghul Emperors*, which combines stately majesty and exotic mystery in equal measure.

The Times's preference for the *Warriors' Dance* and the *March of the Moghul Emperors* was shared by Elgar himself, who specifically suggested them to the Gramophone Company in 1930 for recording.[49] In the event, the entire suite was recorded, with Elgar conducting. It became a popular item on the BBC in the 1920s and 1930s.

The *Crown of India March*, which accompanied the arrival of George V, was not included in the suite, though it was recorded in 1912, 1913 and 1928. With its opening fanfare and the incorporation of the song *Lift Aloft the Flag of England*, it is not one of the great marches, competent enough but repetitive and lacking the brilliance and inspiration of the *Pomp and Circumstance* marches.

All the pieces are in that style which Elgar so frequently adopted and for which he prescribed the direction *nobilmente*. Its greatest expression comes in the *Symphony No. 1*, so clearly an affirmation of the greatness of Britain that it would seem wilful perversity to disregard its inspiration. Whatever later critics may say of it, contemporary audiences recognized it as a musical expression of their age and its noblest aspirations. 'Never has a symphony become so instantly the "rage" with the ordinary British public as did this', recalled *The Times*. There were no fewer than eighty-two performances of it in 1908–9. Basil Maine, in his two-volume *Elgar, His Life and Works* (1933), writing against a background of highbrow disparagement of Elgar's work, dismissed because of its imperialist content and ineradicable Englishness, entered a robust defence:

> Neither the symphonies nor the concertos of Elgar are in any sense topical. But they cannot be completely appraised without a continual consciousness of the Edwardian Age which was their background. Indeed, no musician who has lived through that era . . . can be unaware of the close inter-relation of the music and the age . . . The national

ideals of the early years of the century could not but inform the music of a man of Elgar's cast of mind. They are implicit in many a phrase and episode. Implicit, but not blatant, self-conscious or obvious.[50]

In particular, Basil Maine acknowledged imperialism as a prime inspiration for Elgar:

> It is not easy for the present generation to realise how firmly Imperialism gripped the imaginations of those who were young men and women at the beginning of this century . . . A discussion of the pros and cons of Imperialism would be irrelevant . . . What is to the point is that, right or wrong, salvation or stumbling-block, Imperialism coloured the whole life of the nation during the early years of the century; and to say that Elgar's music during that period was coloured thereby is only another way of saying that it was a reflection of the nation's life. If this music appears to reflect the red and white and blue too vividly for present-day taste, it should not be forgotten that the colours accorded with the scheme and pattern of King Edward's reign.[51]

This even applied to his symphonies. Maine sees his *Symphony No. 1* as a *paean*, a celebration of the noble achievements of his nation; *No. 2* as an *epic*, a last exulting in the glories of an epoch that was closing, and the *Cello Concerto* as an *elegy* for the age that has passed.

> It can be freely admitted . . . that Elgar's symphonic works are the outcome and intense expression of emotional experience. The admission does not impair their status. Nor are they to be thought of any less account because the emotional experience underlying them can be related to a particular phase of national development.[52]

The idiom Sullivan had adopted for his imperial works was Italianate. The roots of the Elgarian imperial idiom lay in German Romantic music, in particular that of Brahms. But one of the most important influences on Elgar was the music of Sir Hubert Parry, of whom Elgar always spoke with the utmost admiration and regard. Because Parry's music fell dramatically out of favour after his death in 1918, the full extent of Elgar's debt to Parry has not been fully appreciated. When we listen now to Parry's *Blest Pair of Sirens*, his *English Symphony* and his splendid marches from *The Birds* and *Hypatia*, it is impossible to deny their seminal influence on Elgar's music. What Parry did, as Jeremy Dibble has shown, was to cross the Brahmsian symphonic influence with the diatonicism of the English church music of Samuel Sebastian Wesley and John Stainer to create a distinctively British style of grandeur and spaciousness which Elgar was to take up and develop further until it became so closely identified with him that the Parryan inspiration was forgotten.[53]

As Jeremy Crump has shown in his pioneering article on Elgar's reputation, the composer plunged himself wholeheartedly into the war effort. Crump says: 'the years from 1914 until the beginning of 1918 ... saw him as much involved in performance and composition as at any time and enjoying an unrivalled position in English musical life'. In 1916 the *Sheffield Daily Post* forecast: 'When the history of the Great War comes to be written the name of Edward Elgar will stand out as the one native composer whose music truly expressed the spirit of our people'.[54] Crump demonstrates just how true that was and how the devaluing of this phase of his career has been part of the creation of a reconstructed unhistorical Elgar.

Elgar composed pieces specifically for the war effort. There were tributes to our allies. Poland was celebrated in *Polonia*, a work dedicated to Paderewski, of which J.F. Porte, writing in 1921, said: '*Polonia* is one of the noblest and most brilliantly beautiful pieces that issued from Elgar's pen'.[55] Belgium was commemorated in the setting of three anti-German poems by the Belgian poet Emile Cammaerts: *Carillon*; *Une Voix dans le Desert*; and *Le Drapeau Belge*. Composer and Elgar biographer Thomas Dunhill recalled of *Carillon*:

> Nobody who heard that piece at that time can possibly forget the thrill which it produced. Recitations with music are seldom successful, but this one is triumphantly so. The music in itself is simple ... But it is charged with an emotional conviction which is not to be found in so intensified a form in any other of Elgar's compositions.[56]

Elgar provided stimuli to national patriotism. He set four Kipling poems, *The Fringes of the Fleet*, which successfully toured Oswald Stoll's music-hall circuit. He wrote the ballet *The Sanguine Fan* for a charity matinee. During the war, *Land of Hope and Glory* became an indispensable element of wartime patriotic concerts, so that the *Manchester Guardian* reported in 1917: 'Music hall audiences ... made one of Elgar's compositions their own long ago – the *Land of Hope and Glory* theme; and how fully it conforms to the requirements of permanent communal art may be gathered from the fact that few people are really aware that it is by Elgar'.[57] The symphonies also served to emphasize English identity. Crump reports that the Black Dyke Mills Band fulfilled over forty engagements with brass band arrangements of the Elgar symphonies.[58]

But Elgar also provided much-needed consolation. Clara Butt organized a remarkable Elgar Festival in 1916 in which *The Dream of Gerontius* was performed on six successive nights, to raise money for the Red Cross. At these concerts Elgar conducted his new work *For the Fallen* from his setting of poems by Laurence Binyon, a work which struck an extraordinary chord with the people.

Elgar set three of Binyon's poems, *The Fourth of August*, *To Women* and *For the Fallen* under the title *The Spirit of England*. They were set in reverse order; the second and third poems being premièred in 1916 and the whole set first performed in 1917. Elgar dedicated the work 'to the memory of our glorious men, with a special thought for the Worcesters'. Binyon had pressed Elgar to set them: 'think of the thousands who will be craving to have their grief glorified and lifted up and transformed by an art like yours'.[59] When Ernest Newman heard the result, he declared that Elgar's was the only music inspired by the war 'that expresses anything of what the nation feels in these dark days'.[60]

The prevailing mood of the music is at once one of pain and pride, of intrinsic nobility, suffering and sacrifice – but always for a just cause. The recurrent ideas in Binyon's text are 'splendour', 'grandeur' and 'glory'. The *Fourth of August* is characterized by a recurrent rising theme that signifies aspiration:

> Now in thy splendour go before us,
> Spirit of England, ardent-eyed.

The war has awakened something great:

> We step from days of sour division
> Into the grandeur of our fate.

Many have died but their cause was just:

> For us the glorious dead have striven
> They battled that we might be free.

The enemy is a clearly-identified Germany, ferociously denounced in the music and accompanied by the demons' chorus from *Gerontius*:

> The barren creed of blood and iron
> Vampire of Europe's wasted will.

It ends with a repeat of the opening verse in all its musical grandeur.

Then the women, their eternal lot to watch and wait, to hope and dread, to share the suffering and to accept with pride their menfolk's fate, are celebrated in music that achieves throughout a poignant tenderness.

> Your hearts are lifted up, your hearts
> That have foreknown the utter price.
> Your hearts turn upward like a flame
> Of splendour and of sacrifice.

To Women ends with a repeat of the *Spirit of England* motif, musically linking the women to the warrior heroes of *the Fourth of August*.

[70]

Finally, there is *For the Fallen*, which Basil Maine, writing in 1933, said was 'so loftily conceived that for many it has become a national memorial to which they instinctively turn every year on Remembrance Day'.[61] Taking his cue from the lines:

> There is music in the midst of desolation
> And a glory that shines upon our tears

Elgar sets much of the poem to the stately rhythms of a funeral march. It opens on a note of quiet dignity:

> With proud thanksgiving, a mother for her children,
> England mourns for her dead across the sea.
> Flesh of her flesh they were, spirit of her spirit,
> Fallen in the cause of the free.

When he comes to the verses which romanticize the fallen as youthful warriors, he moves into quick march rhythm, 'the sort of thing that ran in my mind when the dear lads went swinging past so many, many times', said Elgar:[62]

> They went with songs to the battle, they were young.
> Straight of limb, true of eye, steady and aglow,
> They were staunch to the end against odds uncounted,
> They fell with their faces to the foe.

The tempo slows down again for Binyon's most memorable lines: 'They shall grow not old, as we that are left grow old.' And a solo soprano voice repeats the haunting refrain: 'We will remember them.' The slow and solemn mood remains to the end, as the verses tell us the fallen are amongst the stars, 'moving in marches upon the heavenly plain' – 'To the end, to the end, they remain.' Their spirit has transcended death.

The young composer C.W. Orr wrote in 1931 of *For the Fallen*:

> Elgar summed up all that was worthiest in our pride and noblest in our grief in his setting of Binyon's *For the Fallen*; a work so poignant in expression that it seemed almost too painful to listen to during those times of agonised grief and suspense. Here was a masterpiece summing up the spirit of the time as greatly and memorably as did the orations of Pericles and the epigrams of Simonides. Elgar showed that he was the fittest Laureate of our 'proud thanksgiving' – the one musician who could best express patriotism without vainglory and sorrow without self-pity.[63]

But emphasizing that the First World War was an imperial war, Elgar conducted a peace pageant at the Coliseum Theatre in July 1919, in which *Land of Hope and Glory* and the *Imperial March* were played, and Britannia was seen acknowledging the colonies and dependencies.[64]

The idea that his music fell out of favour in the interwar period and that this somehow indicated a decline in popular imperial sentiment is mistaken on two fronts. First, his music did not fall out of favour; and, second, neither did the Empire. The nature of the imperial sentiment changed to meet changing times. After all Britain ended the First World War with a greatly increased Empire, and there was no demand domestically for its dissolution, as it was the source of Britain's global standing. Before the First World War, popular imperialism had had a confident, aggressive, militaristic tone as the scarlet-clad armies of Queen Victoria added more and more territories to her Empire. After the war and the slaughter of the trenches, imperialism was increasingly equated with peace, democracy and economic and commercial prosperity. Above all the Empire was seen as a prime force for world peace and order.

In appreciating the continuing popularity of Elgar's music, we have first to disregard the composer's own statements. Elgar was all his life chronically insecure and in need of reassurance. His wife had provided it in abundance, but after her death he continually lamented that no-one wanted his music. For example, when Basil Maine wanted to write his biography, Elgar wrote to him in 1931 saying: 'I fear that the interest in my music is too slight and evanescent to be worth such concentration as you propose to devote to it.'[65] Compton Mackenzie, founder of *The Gramophone* magazine, recorded his memory of Elgar saying to him at the Savile Club in 1923: 'I suppose you people in this magazine of yours have discovered that nothing I have written has the slightest value. However, you can say what you like about my music, for I am no longer interested in music.'[66] This was a regular refrain. But quite simply it was untrue.

Elgar had become unpopular with the 'Young Turks' of the musical intelligentsia and with the modernists who rejected wholesale the traditional approach to melody, harmony and structure. But these critics and composers were a distinct though vocal minority who were writing for each other and not for the general public which neither shared their views nor warmed to their music.

These critics were in no doubt about Elgar's genuine imperialism, and they hated his music because of it. But at the same time they both acknowledged his greatness and his appeal to the public. Cecil Gray, the Scottish music critic and failed composer, spoke for many in his generation in *A Survey of Contemporary Music* (1924). He began by establishing what was to become a regular trope in Elgar criticism: the distinction between 'the composer of the symphonies and the self-appointed Musician Laureate of the British Empire, always ready to hymn rapturously the glories of our blood and state on the slightest provocation. The one is a musician of merit; the other is only a barbarian, and not even an amusing one.'[67] He goes on to denounce the *Imperial March*, *The Banner of Saint George*, the *Coronation Ode*, the *Pomp and Circumstance* marches, the *Fringes of the Fleet* and *The Crown of India* ('undoubtedly the worst of the lot') as 'perfect specimens of that exotic growth called Jingoism which flourished with such tropical luxuriance in this country a quarter of a century ago, and is now, fortunately, almost extinct', adding that 'Elgar takes this aspect of his art as seriously as any other'. He went on to denounce imperialism as alien to Britain and as something which has infected Elgar's inspiration ('tainted by the phylloxera germ of Imperialism which has battened on the national vine'):

> This aspect of Elgar's art is not merely negligible . . . but has definitely exercised a pernicious and subtly contaminating influence over his whole work. For example, he concludes a work like *Caractacus* which . . . has much to commend it, with a chorus in which we are invited to brood on the glorious day which is coming when
>
> > The nations all shall stand
> > And hymn the praise of Britain
> > Like brothers, hand in hand:
>
> And many similar examples of the intrusion of this bombastic spirit, even into purely instrumental works, can easily be found. The final number of the *Enigma Variations*, for example, is undiluted jingoism . . . In the *Music-makers* . . . the whole intention of the work is obviously to give one clearly to understand, by means of elaborate quotations from his own work in the style of Strauss's *Heldenleben*, coupled with a reference to *Rule Britannia*, that he regards himself as one of those artists who, in the words of the poem on which the music is based, 'build up the world's great cities' by means of 'wonderful deathless ditties'. Now it is quite possible that the immortal *Land of Hope and Glory* tune may at some time or other have aroused such patriotic enthusiasm in the breast of a rubber planter in the tropics as to have led him to kick his negro servant slightly harder than he would have done if he had never heard it, and served to strengthen his already profound conviction of belonging to the chosen race; but however admirable and praiseworthy such a result may be from the point of view of empire building, it has no meaning whatever from the point of view of art, which . . . is eternally dedicated *ad majorem Dei gloriam*, and not to the greater glory of John Bull.[68]

As Gray admitted in his autobiography *Musical Chairs* (1948), both as a Scot and as an internationalist of Latin sympathies, he detested the

[73]

Englishness of English art.[69] So, even when Elgar was not being overtly imperial, his music did not find favour with Gray. He dismissed the oratorios ('the air is too heavy with the odour of clerical sanctity and the faint and sickly aroma of stale incense, and the little light there is filters dimly through stained glass windows . . . With all its spirituality and undoubted sincerity the atmosphere is sanctimonious rather than saintly, pious rather than fervid'); *Falstaff* ('He is not the Falstaff of Shakespeare but of his celebrated editor, Mr. Bowdler'); the overture *In the South* ('Italy seen through the eyes of a specially conducted Cook's tourist'). He finally does find some music to admire:

> Elgar's best achievements are the two Symphonies, the *Variations*, the string quartet, the *Introduction and Allegro* for strings. In them his consummate musicianship and amazing fertility of resource are given full play, unimpeded by literary and imaginative associations demanding a spiritual breadth and insight which . . . he conspicuously lacks.

He then goes on to compare Elgar to Delius, to Elgar's detriment: Delius is 'an artist before he is a musician'; Elgar is 'primarily a craftsman'; Delius

> appeals more to the cultured and imaginative section of an audience whose interest in art is not confined to . . . music alone . . . Elgar's personality and mentality are in many ways more readily accessible to the mind of the average audience than those of Delius.[70]

He finally returns to contextual interpretation and a dismissal of Elgar:

> The music of Elgar is essentially the musical counterpart of the literature and art of the Victorian era. This is probably the reason why it inspires such an extraordinarily violent antipathy and animosity in many of the present generation. Every age tends to react most violently against its immediate predecessor, and consequently the qualities which are most characteristic of the Victorian age are those which are most despised at the present time. On the other hand, while it is true that every artist must to some extent express his age, he is only a great artist in so far as he is able to rise above it; and it must be admitted that in the greater part of his output Elgar does not rise above it. He never gets entirely away from the atmosphere of pale, cultured idealism, and the unconsciously hypocritical, self-righteous, complacent Pharisaical gentlemanliness which is so characteristic of British art in the last century . . . Ruskin, Tennyson, Matthew Arnold, Walter Pater, Burne-Jones, Thackeray even . . . were all tainted with this spirit, and unfortunately Elgar has not escaped from it either. This it is which, more than anything else, just prevents Elgar from being a great artist. He might have been a great composer if he had not been such a perfect gentleman.[71]

I have lingered on Gray's criticism both because it was in many ways typical of the critical mindset of a particular circle and because it demonstrates how important is context in the evaluation of music. The rejection of Victorianism and imperialism by a generation of young critics conditioned the response. They saw the imperialism and hated it; but they also admired what they saw as non-imperial works. They recognized that Elgar's music spoke to the people.

F.H. Shera, Rossiter Hoyle Professor of Music at Sheffield University, in *Elgar: Instrumental Works* (1931), echoed Gray's prejudices and perceptions in somewhat less extreme form:

> No other composer . . . has more accurately voiced in music the thoughts of so large a number of his fellow-countrymen at different epochs. This may be a virtue or a vice, but it is a fact beyond dispute. Since 1897, indeed, Elgar has been the musical laureate of his country. The Diamond Jubilee produced the *Imperial March, The Banner of St. George* (1897) and *Caractacus* (1898). Imperialism gave us the *Pomp and Circumstance Marches* and the *Coronation Ode* (1901); and the epilogue of the Edwardian age is written in the *2nd Symphony*. The war brought *Carillon, The Spirit of England*, and *The Fringes of the Fleet*. Much of this music (not to mention *The Crown of India* (1912) and the Wembley music of 1924) has been allowed to fade into deserved oblivion, even though *Land of Hope and Glory* is still to be heard on Empire Day; but it had a value for its time far greater, surely, than such a work as Beethoven's *Battle of Vittoria* . . . And the older of us must acknowledge, in all humility, that to their own generation the imperialist sentiment of Kipling and Elgar alike made a genuine appeal. Which is of course the best possible reason for the present generation to scoff at it.[72]

Constant Lambert in the influential and widely read *Music Ho!* (1934) called Elgar 'the last serious composer to be in touch with the great public' and acknowledged Elgar's greatness but recognized a change of context.

> In Elgar, the first figure of importance since Boyce, we get an example of a composer, in touch both with his audience and his period, expressing himself nationally in an international language. It is more than probable that, but for the social and spiritual changes brought about by the war, Elgar would have been a more potent influence on English music than Vaughan Williams; but the aggressive Edwardian prosperity that lends so comfortable a backbone to Elgar's finales is now as strange to us as the England that produced *Greensleeves* and *The Woodes so Wilde*. Stranger, in fact, and less sympathetic. In consequence, much of Elgar's music, through no fault of its own, has for the present generation an almost intolerable air of smugness, self-assurance and autocratic benevolence.[73]

It is interesting to note the young Benjamin Britten dismissing Elgar's *Symphony No. 1* – 'I swear that only in Imperialistic England could such a work be tolerated' – after hearing it at the Proms in 1935; and in 1931 switching off a radio broadcast of *No. 2* – '1 min. of Elgar Symphony 2 but can stand no more'.[74] It is a practical expression of the lack of sympathy on the part of a section of the young intelligentsia. Nonetheless, as Jeremy Crump points out, there were no fewer than seven monographs on Elgar published during the 1930s, including Basil Maine's two-volume *Life and Works* – further evidence to refute the idea of neglect.[75]

But not all the young musical talents were so dismissive. In 1931 word reached England of an essay by Edward J. Dent, Professor of Music at Cambridge, in a German musical history in which the author, accusing Elgar of being a Catholic and 'having little of the musical culture of Parry and Stanford', dismissively declared: 'For English ears Elgar's music is too emotional and not quite free from vulgarity', and pronounced his orchestral works 'pompous in style and of a too deliberate nobility of expression'.[76] A letter of protest was organized by the critic Philip Heseltine (who composed music as Peter Warlock) declaring: 'At the present time the works of Elgar, far from being distasteful to English ears, are held in the highest honour by the majority of English musicians and the musical public in general.' It was signed by, among others, Hamilton Harty, John Ireland, E.J. Moeran, Landon Ronald, Albert Sammons, Beatrice Harrison, William Walton and Bernard Shaw, and was sent to all the leading newspapers in England and Germany.[77]

It has been widely reported, on the basis of comments from observers such as Bernard Shaw, that concerts of Elgar's music were poorly attended in the interwar period. Some may well have been, but this was not necessarily a reflection on Elgar's music. It may have reflected instead the general decline in concert-going which had followed the rise of the new mechanical media of music-making, the gramophone and the wireless. It also did not apparently affect the programming policies of concert organizers. Examining the period 1918–34, John Gardiner has ascertained that Elgar's music was programmed by the organizers of the Royal Philharmonic Society Concerts every year except for 1926, 1931 and 1932, and his music featured extensively every year in the Henry Wood Promenade Concerts. Indeed *Pomp and Circumstance March No. 1* was played every year between 1918 and 1934 except for 1932. Elgar's music was also played every year at the Three Choirs Festival between 1920 and 1934. *The Dream of Gerontius* in particular was done every year except 1922, 1925 and 1926.[78] This does not look much like neglect. Gardiner concludes on the basis of his research that Elgar was 'the *least* neglected British composer in London concert halls between 1918 and his death in 1934', performances of his works outstripping those of, for instance, Vaughan Williams, Walton and Bax.[79]

Elgar, despite his age, became a keen convert to the new media of wireless, gramophone and film. In 1931 he opened the new HMV Studios at Abbey Road, St John's Wood, with the first complete recording of *Falstaff*. But before he conducted that, he conducted *Land of Hope and Glory* for the Pathé Newsreel cameras, saying to the London Symphony Orchestra: 'Please play this as if you had never heard it before.' The same work inspired a full-length feature film *Land of Hope and Glory*, scripted by Adrian Brunel and directed by Harley Knoles. Featuring the distinguished stage stars Ellaline Terriss and Lyn Harding, it dealt with 'the effects of the war on a typical British family. It shows how its members, returned from the war, emigrate to the Dominions to seek a fresh life.'[80] The film premièred at the Plaza Cinema on Armistice Day 1927 and Elgar conducted his celebrated work as a prelude to the film at the cinema.

Elgar rapidly became an ever-present feature of BBC music broadcasting, a medium he applauded: 'To be able to hear, in your own home, all the important musical events of the day is the great advantage of wireless.'[81] Elgar himself was broadcast twenty-eight times conducting his own music, starting with his contribution to the opening of the Empire Exhibition at Wembley in 1924. Among his appearances were three Armistice Day concerts (1925, 1927 and 1932) at which he conducted his great wartime elegy *The Spirit of England*. This was accompanied in 1925 by the adagio from *Symphony No. 1*, the meditation from *The Light of Life* and *Pomp and Circumstance Marches Nos 1* and *2*, and in 1927 again by the meditation from *The Light of Life*. There was a special seventieth birthday concert of his music in 1927, and in 1932 an Elgar Festival to mark his seventy-fifth birthday. The concerts, broadcast from the Royal Albert Hall, took place on 10 November, 7 December and 14 December 1932. At the first, Elgar conducted his *Violin Concerto* and *Cockaigne* overture, and Sir Landon Ronald, the *Symphony No. 1*; at the second, Sir Adrian Boult conducted the *Enigma Variations* and the *Introduction and Allegro*, and Elgar conducted his own *Symphony No. 2*; and the third consisted of a performance of *The Kingdom*, conducted by Boult. In an article for *Radio Times* to launch the festival, Boult quoted with approval the *Grove* entry on Elgar:

Elgar's works hold the attention of his countrymen more decisively than do those of any other native composer. No English festival is complete

[77]

without him, every choral society and orchestra, from the smallest to the greatest, gives his music a large place in its repertory; and it will be no surprise if further works should come from his pen bearing the stamp of that personality which is so recognizable that from his name the adjective 'Elgarian' has been coined.[82]

On the night of the third concert, Sir Landon Ronald announced that the BBC had commissioned a third symphony from Elgar.[83]

Even more important for the popularity argument than Elgar's own performances are the live performances of his music on the BBC by others. Ronald Taylor has identified 5,110 performances of Elgar's music during the composer's lifetime, leaving aside *Salut d'Amour* and *Land of Hope and Glory* which were broadcast too often to be counted.[84] He has identified only ten items in Elgar's entire output that were not broadcast. Taylor concludes: 'On *most* days of the year, once the BBC Stations were all opened, it was inevitable that on at least one of the stations Elgar's music was being played.'[85]

It is significant that Elgar's imperial works were among his most regularly broadcast: the *Imperial March*, 65 times; the *Crown of India* suite, 102 times; *Pomp and Circumstance March No. 2*, 60 times; *Pomp and Circumstance March No. 4*, 92 times; and *Pomp and Circumstance March No. 1* too often to list. The *Pageant of Empire* songs were broadcast in whole or in part 25 times and the new *Empire March* 21 times. Elgar's music was regularly included in the Empire Day concerts, which almost invariably included the *Imperial March* and *Pomp and Circumstance March No. 1*.

Paralleling his wireless performances are his gramophone record performances. Elgar was signed by the Gramophone Company (which became EMI in 1931), and the recording manager, Fred Gaisberg, proudly recorded the importance to his company of their acquiring 'the prestige of England's greatest composer' and even more so the fact that he conducted his greatest works on record: 'Thus the greatest English composer has, for the first time in history, left to posterity his own interpretations of his works.'[86] The choice of repertoire for recording was dictated by commercial considerations. Bernard Wratten, who was in charge of repertoire, recalled:

> So far as Elgar's works were concerned we confined ourselves to a list of those most likely to be in demand on record. Obviously a list of best-selling works was self-limiting, by definition . . . It was essential . . . that we should be realistic; records were made in order to be sold and no useful purpose was served in recording works which would not sell.[87]

Both symphonies, the *Pomp and Circumstance* marches, the *Violin Concerto*, *Falstaff*, the *Crown of India* suite, *The Wand of Youth* suites, *In the South* and the *Nursery Suite* were among the works recorded. Again, not surprisingly, one of the best-selling Elgar records was that of *Pomp and Circumstance Marches 1* and *2*, which sold 11,731 copies between July 1926 and 1929.[88] Gardiner concludes that 'Elgar was . . . better represented on record than any other British composer between the wars'.[89]

The third myth that has been exploded is that he dried up creatively after Lady Elgar died in 1920 and did nothing worthwhile after that, part of the process of general disillusionment and disengagement from post-war British society. That myth has been spectacularly blown up by the success of Anthony Payne's realization of the *Symphony No. 3*. But there is more evidence even than this, though on its own this would be enough, and that evidence indicates that his old beliefs and values and inspirations were far from dried up.

Certainly for three years after Lady Elgar died he wrote nothing. But then, in 1923, he responded to an invitation from Laurence Binyon to provide incidental music for his play *Arthur*, just as Sullivan had done for Irving. The play was a retelling of the classic chivalric tale of knightly ideals and of the destruction of the Round Table. As Robert Anderson rightly remarks, it 'touched much of the essential Elgar'.[90] It had that nobility of theme that Elgar always found inspiring, and he responded with half-an-hour of beautiful music. He believed in it sufficiently to pay for the copying of the band parts and to supplement the small Old Vic orchestra with extra musicians at his own expense. He provided more music than was actually called for and he later proposed to rework some of the best themes in his *Symphony No. 3*. It was little heard after the play closed, but a recent recording of a suite made up from the music has confirmed it as a fine, rich and evocative score. He was asked to provide an overture and introductions for each of the nine scenes making up the play. He built the score around themes; heroic for chivalry; wistful for Elaine; sombre for Arthur; fearful for Guinevere; sturdy and inspiring for the fellowship of the Round Table. Among the high points of the score are the vivid and vigorous banqueting scene; the intricate battle music, complete with fanfares, charges and the interweaving of the chivalry, Elaine and Guinevere themes, and the final leave-taking of Arthur from Guinevere, his departure and death, represented by a solemn Gregorian chant theme, the slow and sonorous repetition of the chivalry theme and the tolling of the funeral bell.

Another threnody for a lost age of gentlemanliness was inspired by the commission in 1928 to provide incidental music for Bertram P. Matthews's play *Beau Brummel*, a vehicle for actor–manager Gerald Lawrence. The play, reported The *Birmingham Post*, 'idealized the character of Beau Brummel, and depicted him as a gentleman who is ready to sacrifice his life, his career, his friendship with the Prince Regent, to save a woman's honour'.[91] The music Elgar provided was 'elegant, courtly and "mainly sad"'.[92] But it remained unpublished apart from a delicate and melancholy minuet which was recorded the same year, with Elgar himself conducting. Some of the music was to be redeployed in his opera *The Spanish Lady*.

Having become Master of the King's Musick in 1924 he dutifully supplied 'official' music when it was required: the *Empire March* and eight songs for the *Pageant of Empire* at the 1924 British Empire Exhibition at Wembley, the carol *Good Morrow* to celebrate the recovery of King George V from his serious illness (1929); an ode on the unveiling of a memorial statue to Queen Alexandra, *So Many True Princesses Have Gone* (1932), with words by the Poet Laureate John Masefield and music of which Anderson says: 'His instinctive chivalry is here poignantly expressed in graceful melodic shapes as eloquent as they are apt.'[93]

Then, in 1930, came a last burst of creativity. He composed the charming *Nursery Suite* (dedicated to the Duchess of York and Princesses Elizabeth and Margaret Rose), a childhood piece worthy to stand alongside the *Wand of Youth* suites. The *Severn Suite* (1930) in four movements and a coda was composed for brass band and subsequently rescored for orchestra (1932), in which form it was recorded with Elgar conducting, his handling of the orchestra bringing out all the inventive richness of the musical texture. It was foursquare in his chivalric mode. It opens with an imposing introduction, *Worcester Castle*, which for Basil Maine evoked 'a procession in a pageant' and it moved directly to the vigorous toccata *Tournament*.[94] With fanfares proclaiming the initiation of the contest and drums marking the hoofbeats of the horses, it is a perfect evocation of a mediaeval tournament, the music building in pace and excitement as the iron-clad warriors charge each other, until the movement climaxes in a heroic flourish before the mood changes and it drops gently into the third movement, *Cathedral*, a fugal passage, spiritual, reflective and solemn. This in its turn modulates into a graceful minuet, *In the Commandery*, before returning for the coda to the grandeur of the opening, rounding off what has been a musical celebration of mediaeval Worcester, its pageantry, gallantry and spirituality. Also in 1930 there was a fifth and final *Pomp and Circumstance* march which had all the old fire and martial vigour.

Then, in 1932, he began work simultaneously on his *Symphony No. 3*, a piano concerto and the opera *The Spanish Lady*. The works had all taken shape in his head and Fred Gaisberg recalled in his autobiography that Elgar 'played for me excerpts from an unnamed opera he had underway, including a fine love duet set for soprano and tenor. During that same year he proudly played parts of a piano concerto and a beautiful slow movement and an intriguing scherzo of a Third Symphony.'[95] Elgar never lived to complete these works but left enough material behind for Dr Percy Young to prepare a performing version of *The Spanish Lady* and for Anthony Payne to complete the *Symphony No. 3*, revealing works of classic Elgarian quality.

Sir Barry Jackson had prepared the libretto for Elgar's opera and believed that, had he lived to complete it, it 'would have been among the half dozen of the world's greatest comedy operas'.[96] Elgar planned to 'out Meistersinger Meistersinger', and he had chosen as his subject Ben Jonson's play *The Devil Is an Ass*. A coruscating satire on the vulgarity, materialism, corruption and chicanery of Jacobean London, it evidently appealed to Elgar as a comment on the post-war world which he viewed with increasing distaste and which failed so signally to live up to his high romantic ideals. The story interwove the gulling of a vain dupe by crooked company promoters and the winning of the dupe's ward by her young admirer who disguises himself as a Spanish lady to gain access to her. The score has a youthful vigour and liveliness, tuneful and sprightly songs and some energetic and captivating dances: saraband, country dance, bolero and Spanish 'burlesca'. W.H. Reed recalled playing these with Elgar as the score was being composed.[97]

The unfinished *Symphony No. 3* had long been one of the most tantalizing of Elgar's legacies. Fred Gaisberg recorded in his diary that Elgar had played the whole symphony through to him on 27 August, 1933:

> The opening a great broad burst *animato* gradually resolving into a fine broad melody for strings. This is fine. 2nd movement is slow and tender in true Elgar form. The 3rd movement is an ingenious Scherzo, well designed: a delicate, feathery short section of 32nds contrasted with a moderate, sober section. 4th movement is a spirited tempo with full resources, developed at some length. The whole work strikes me as youthful and fresh – 100% Elgar without a trace of decay . . . The work is complete as far as structure and design and scoring is well advanced. In his own mind he is enthusiastically satisfied with it and says it is his best work.[98]

It is clear that the Symphony existed in his mind and he was able to play it through with assurance and enthusiasm. But when he died in 1934 what remained was a jumble of sketches, which he had earnestly requested on his deathbed should not be tinkered with. However, it was eventually to be completed by the composer Anthony Payne, with the blessing of the Elgar family. When it was premièred in 1998 it was rapturously received by the critics and the public alike. Geoffrey Norris of the *Daily Telegraph* summed up the general reaction when he wrote: 'It sounds like Elgar; it feels like Elgar. But the most important thing is that it has the powerful impact of *new* Elgar, living and breathing as his Third Symphony might have done if he had survived to complete it.'[99] The CD recording of the symphony became an instant hit.

Like Elgar's other symphonies, it is a work which reflects in music the complex nature of the man. It is autobiographical, but it is an autobiography which contains and expresses the values which had shaped his life and his music. Interestingly he drew for his main material on the sketches for his unfinished oratorio *The Last Judgement* and on the incidental music to *Arthur*, to which he was particularly attached. Payne talks of him being 'obsessed' with the banquet music from *Arthur*. The electrifying opening leads into a stunning first movement, which is marked *Allegro molto maestoso*, which Payne characterized as one of 'heroic vigour'[100] and which Geoffrey Norris memorably observed was 'starkly harmonized and with a raw, modal feel, conjuring up a sensation like the musical equivalent of some monolithic standing stone, windswept and awesome'.

The second movement was the *scherzo*, Elgar having reversed the original order of his second and third movements. Light-hearted and delicate with recurrent dance rhythms, this made great use of the *Arthur* banquet music and was conceived by Payne in Elgar's 'wistful light music vein'.[101]

The third movement, the *adagio*, drew its main theme from *The Last Judgement*, its effect described in a letter from Elgar to Ernest Newman as like 'opening some vast bronze doors into something strangely unfamiliar'. Payne deployed muted brass and muted strings to create 'an air of tragic stillness, occasionally threatened by ominous tensions', leading into Elgar's own 'well nigh unbearable' codetta with its solo viola finale.[102]

The fourth movement made extensive use of the *Arthur* music, in particular, as Robert Anderson noted, 'motifs associated with the idea of chivalry and more specifically with the King himself' who finally 'disappeared into the shadows en route for his final battle'.[103] After the celebration of the chivalric ideal and the burden of kingship it ends with a haunting diminution into silence.

Here distilled in this remarkable work we find the quasi-religious mysticism which remained even when his Catholic faith faltered, that nostalgia for the past which led him to produce in later life so much

music related to childhood and above all that never-failing commitment to chivalry by which he judged mankind and the world.

Kipling and Elgar were both geniuses. But like Wagner's their genius
came with ideological baggage that subsequent generations have found
unacceptable. One reaction to Kipling's unpopular imperialism has
been to write him out of the literary history of Britain. Another has
been to deny his imperialism and reclaim him as a modernist, revalu-
ing his later works for their psychological insight. The same thing has
happened to Elgar. As the greatest British composer since Purcell, he
could not be ignored; so he was reinvented.

There is undeniable melancholy and reflectiveness in Elgar's work,
which have led later commentators to see it as expressing dissatisfac-
tion with imperialism or the prediction of its end. Once again this is
anachronistic. Melancholy was an integral part of the imperial religion, the necessary melancholy that the mission calls for much sacrifice and so many casualties. Once again *Caractacus* gives us the clue,
for it contains both a thrilling call to arms, *The Song of the Sword*,
and an elegiac lament for the fallen, *Oh, My Warriors*.

It is of course true that, like all great artists, Elgar was often writing
about himself and his feelings. He called the *Cello Concerto* 'a man's
attitude to life'. *Falstaff* is deeply autobiographical; indeed Elgar told
Eric Fenby to inform Delius that 'I grow more like Falstaff every day'.
Falstaff, recalling as it does an idyllic youth in the west country, the
battles and the ceremonial of a public figure, the idealization of friendship (something so important to Elgar), and rejection and death, Elgar's
great fear, is a potent mingling of Elgar's memories, ideals, hopes and
fears. But significantly it includes both the public man and the private
man.[104]

The idea that the Great War represented a watershed leaving
him disillusioned with all his old ideas and that his music somehow
predicted the hollowness and eventual end of Empire is, historically
speaking, speculative nonsense. Kennedy asserts this idea while admit-
ting that neither Elgar nor his audiences were aware of it. Elgar's
ceasing to compose as much after the war as before is due far more to
old age, illness, and the profound blow of his wife's death, than it is
to the decline of his ideals.

What happened after the First World War was a dramatic split
between high culture, which became remorselessly hostile to Empire,
chivalry and honour, all the old pre-war values and verities, and
popular culture, which continued to endorse them. Elgar like Kipling
therefore ceased to be popular with the highbrows but remained
popular with the people, who continued to be steeped in
imperialism.[105]

The second false distinction is the one Kennedy describes as follows: 'The lonely composer walking on the heath, the poet who felt a companionship with swallows, the romantic artist who drew "inspiration" from the friendship of beautiful women; this is the true and secret Elgar and the best of his music reflects this side of the many-sided man.'[106] This is wholly misleading. The true and secret Elgar was also the man inspired by Gordon's sacrifice, by the noble vision at the heart of British imperialism, by the slaughter of the lost generation in the trenches, by the coronations and deaths of sovereigns, by the struggle for spiritual perfection. Elgar was one of a group of imperial mystics (Kipling, Buchan, Haggard, Newbolt were others) who responded equally to the beauties of their native countryside and the history, traditions and destiny of their nation. It is of course true that a piece of music can mean very different things to different audiences at different times. What people get out of Elgar now may be very different from what he intended. But to go from that to deny Elgar's inspiration, as Kennedy does, is unacceptable.

Far from being irrelevant as Kennedy argues, the fact that Elgar was an 'Englishman alive in the period of England's imperial noonday' is central to any understanding of him. Some artists may live cut off from the world, but Elgar was not one of them. He was inspired by the ideals and values of his age, pre-eminently chivalry, monarchy and the heroic vision of Empire. It is a vision that was grand, and one tinged with melancholy. It was also something which communicated itself meaningfully to a mass audience in a way no subsequent major English composer has done. Elgar himself called, in his inaugural lecture as Peyton Professor of Music at Birmingham University, for English composers to draw their inspiration 'from their own country, from their own literature . . . from their own climate', and he told his biographer Robert Buckley: 'my conception of a composer's duty includes his being a bard for the people'.[107] He practised what he preached.

Notes

1 Michael Kennedy, 'Elgar the Edwardian', in Raymond Monk (ed.), *Elgar Studies*, Aldershot, Scolar Press, 1990, p. 107.
2 See in particular John Gardiner, 'The reception of Sir Edward Elgar, 1918–1934: a reassessment', *Twentieth Century British History* 9 (1998), pp. 370–95; Ronald Taylor, 'music in the air: Elgar and the BBC', in Raymond Monk (ed.), *Edward Elgar: Music and Literature*, Aldershot: Scolar Press, 1993, pp. 327–55; and Jeremy Crump, 'The identity of English music: the reception of Elgar 1898–1935', in Robert Colls and Philip Dodd (eds), *Englishness: Politics and Culture, 1880–1920*, London and Sydney: Croom Helm, 1986, pp. 164–90.
3 Arnold Bax, *Farewell My Youth and Other Writings*, ed. Lewis Foreman, Aldershot: Scolar Press, 1992, p. 125.

4   Crump, 'Identity of English music', pp. 171–7.
5   Kennedy, 'Elgar the Edwardian', pp. 111–12.
6   Michael Kennedy, *Portrait of Elgar*, Oxford: Oxford University Press, 1982, p. 334.
7   Robert Anderson, *Elgar*, London: J.M. Dent, 1993, p. 330.
8   Kennedy, *Portrait of Elgar*, p. 237.
9   *Ibid.*, p. 183.
10 *Ibid.*, pp. 236, 159, 231.
11 Christopher Redwood (ed.), *An Elgar Companion*, Ashbourne and Sequoia: Moorland, 1982, pp. 258–62.
12 Percy M. Young (ed.), *Letters to Nimrod*, London: Dennis Dobson, 1965, p. 16.
13 Kennedy, *Portrait of Elgar*, p. 74.
14 Bax, *Farewell My Youth*, p. 125; Kennedy, *Portrait of Elgar*, p. 183 (for Stanford); Compton Mackenzie, *My Record of Music*, London: Hutchinson, 1955, p. 83; Ernest Newman, *Elgar*, London: John Lane, 1906, p. 47.
15 Kennedy, *Portrait of Elgar*, p. 15.
16 Andrew Lycett, *Rudyard Kipling*, London: Weidenfeld & Nicolson, 1999, p. 205; Harry Ricketts, *The Unforgiving Minute*, London: Chatto & Windus, 1999, p. 387.
17 W.H. Reed, *Elgar as I Knew Him*, Oxford: Oxford University Press, 1989 (1936), p. 138.
18 Jeffrey Richards, *Visions of Yesterday*, London: Routledge, 1973, p. 12.
19 *Ibid.*
20 *Ibid.*
21 Bonamy Dobree, *Rudyard Kipling: Realist and Fabulist*, London: Oxford University Press, 1967, p. 94.
22 Kennedy, *Portrait of Elgar*, pp. 300–1.
23 F.H. Shera, *Elgar: Instrumental Works*, London: Oxford University Press, 1931, pp. 6–7.
24 Compton Mackenzie, *My Record of Music*, p. 83.
25 Mark Girouard, *The Return to Camelot*, New Haven, CT, and London: Yale University Press, 1981.
26 Anderson, *Elgar*, p. 405.
27 Redwood, *Elgar Companion*, p. 123.
28 J.F. Porte, *Elgar and His Music*, London: Pitman, 1933, p. 5.
29 Anderson, *Elgar*, p. 49.
30 Sir Henry Wood, *My Life of Music*, London: Gollancz, 1946, p. 154.
31 Bax, *Farewell My Youth*, p. 126.
32 Kennedy, *Portrait of Elgar*, p. 187.
33 *Ibid.*, p. 219.
34 Olive Anderson, 'The growth of Christian militarism in mid-Victorian Britain', *English Historical Review* 86 (1971), p. 64.
35 Newman, *Elgar*, p. 128.
36 Anderson, *Elgar*, p. 177.
37 Ian Bradley, *The Call to Seriousness*, London: Jonathan Cape, 1976.
38 Girouard, *Return to Camelot*, p. 229.
39 Young (ed.), *Letters to Nimrod*, p. 25.
40 Jerrold Northrop Moore, *Spirit of England: Edward Elgar in His World*, London: Heinemann, 1984, p. 60.
41 David Cannadine, 'The context, performance and meaning of ritual: The British monarchy and the "invention of tradition", c.1820–1977', in Eric Hobsbawm and Terence Ranger (eds) *The Invention of Tradition*, Cambridge: Cambridge University Press, 1983, p. 124.
42 Young, *Letters to Nimrod*, p. 63.
43 Kennedy, *Portrait of Elgar*, p. 172.
44 *Ibid.*, p. 171.
45 Jerrold Northrop Moore, *Edward Elgar: A Creative Life*, Oxford: Oxford University Press, 1984, pp. 338–9.
46 *Ibid.*, p. 629.

47 *The Times*, 7 March, 1912.
48 *The Times*, 12 March, 1912.
49 Jerrold Northrop Moore, *Elgar on Record: The Composer and the Gramophone*, London: EMI, 1974, p. 113.
50 Basil Maine, *Elgar: His Life and Works*, London: Bell & Sons, 1933, vol. 2, p. 156.
51 *Ibid.*, 2, p. 300.
52 *Ibid.*, 2, p. 303.
53 On Parry's creation of a distinctive English style, see Jeremy Dibble, *C. Hubert H. Parry*, Oxford: Clarendon Press, 1992, pp. 253–8, 276–8.
54 Crump, 'Identity of English music', p. 171.
55 J.F. Porte, *Sir Edward Elgar*, London: Kegan Paul, Trench Trubner, 1921, p. 165.
56 Thomas F. Dunhill, *Sir Edward Elgar*, Glasgow and London: Blackie, 1938, p. 160.
57 Crump, 'Identity of English music', p. 173.
58 *Ibid.*, p. 175.
59 Moore, *Elgar*, p. 674.
60 *Ibid.*, p. 697.
61 Maine, *Elgar*, vol. 2, p. 240.
62 Anderson, *Elgar*, p. 204.
63 Redwood, *An Elgar Companion*, p. 272.
64 Anderson, *Elgar*, p. 140.
65 Monk (ed.), *Elgar Studies*, p. xvii.
66 Mackenzie, *My Record of Music*, p. 83.
67 Cecil Gray, *A Survey of Contemporary Music*, London: Oxford University Press, 1924, p. 78.
68 *Ibid.*, pp. 79–81.
69 Cecil Gray, *Musical Chairs*, London: Hogarth Press, 1985 (1948), pp. 18–19.
70 Gray, *Survey*, p. 91.
71 *Ibid.*, pp. 92–3.
72 Shera, *Elgar: Instrumental Works*, pp. 6, 10.
73 Constant Lambert, *Music Ho!*, London: Hogarth Press, 1985 (1934), pp. 233, 240.
74 Humphrey Carpenter, *Benjamin Britten*, London: Faber & Faber, 1992, pp. 69, 39.
75 Crump, 'Identity of English music', p. 180.
76 Quoted in Maine, *Elgar*, vol. 2, p. 278.
77 Moore, *Elgar*, pp. 289–90.
78 Gardiner, 'The reception of Elgar'. See also John Gardiner, 'Aspects of Elgar's reception in England, 1918–34, unpublished MA dissertation, University of Kent, 1996.
79 Gardiner, 'Reception of Elgar', p. 376.
80 *The Times*, 9 November, 1927.
81 Taylor, 'Music in the air', pp. 332–3.
82 *Radio Times*, 30 November, 1932.
83 Humphrey Burton, 'Elgar and the BBC', *Journal of the Royal Society of Arts* 127 (March 1979), pp. 224–36.
84 Taylor, 'Music in the air', p. 337.
85 *Ibid.*
86 Fred Gaisberg, *Music on Record*, London: Robert Hale, 1947, p. 233.
87 Moore, *Elgar on Record*, p. 96.
88 Gardiner, 'Aspects', p. 21.
89 Gardiner, 'Reception of Elgar', p. 380.
90 Anderson, *Elgar*, p. 271.
91 *Birmingham Post*, 6 November, 1928.
92 Anderson, *Elgar*, p. 272.
93 *Ibid.*, p. 206.
94 Maine, *Elgar*, vol. 2, p. 247.
95 Gaisberg, *Music on Record*, p. 233.
96 Sir Barry Jackson, 'The Spanish Lady', in Redwood (ed.), *An Elgar Companion*, p. 229.
97 Reed, *Elgar as I Knew Him*, pp. 91–2.

98   Moore, *Elgar*, p. 816.
99   *Daily Telegraph*, 16 February, 1998.
100 Anthony Payne, *Elgar's Third Symphony: The Story of the Reconstruction*, London: Faber & Faber, 1988, p. 66; *Daily Telegraph*, 16 February, 1998.
101 Payne, *Elgar's Third Symphony*, p. 66.
102 *Ibid.*, pp. 76–87.
103 Anderson, *Elgar*, p. 342.
104 Kennedy, *Portrait of Elgar*, pp. 334, 258.
105 John M. MacKenzie, *Propaganda and Empire*, Manchester: Manchester University Press, 1984.
106 Kennedy, *Portrait of Elgar*, p. 162.
107 Edward Elgar, *A Future for English Music*, ed. Percy M. Young, London: Dennis Dobson, 1968, p. 51; Robert Buckley, *Sir Edward Elgar*, London: John Lane, 1905, p. 48.

CHAPTER FOUR

Music for official occasions: coronations and jubilees

The national anthem and Rule, Britannia

Any consideration of official music must begin with the national anthem. It was an indispensable part of all official occasions for which music was specially provided: coronations, jubilees, royal weddings and funerals; the great exhibitions; the annual celebrations of Empire Day and Armistice Day. The national anthem has a particular significance. Where other countries' anthems celebrate the fatherland ('Deutschland, Deutschland, über alles' or 'Allons, enfants de la patrie') or the flag ('The star-spangled banner'), the British national anthem celebrates the monarch – 'God Save Our Gracious Queen'. This is of immense constitutional and emotional significance. It identifies the nation with the sovereign and vice versa, something reflected in the official name of the country – the United Kingdom of Great Britain and Northern Ireland (UK for short).

It is also no coincidence that the national anthem was the product of a threat to the established order. The national anthem was first sung in something like its present form at the Theatre Royal, Drury Lane, in 1745 at the height of the second Jacobite rebellion aimed at unseating the Protestant Hanoverian dynasty and restoring the Catholic Stewarts, ousted in 1688. The song was arranged by Dr Thomas Arne, musical director of the theatre and the composer of the other great national tune *Rule, Britannia*. It was performed on stage first after a production of Jonson's *The Alchemist*, and as the newspapers reported: 'The universal Applause it met with, being encored with repeated Huzzas, sufficiently denoted in how just an Abhorrence they hold the arbitrary Schemes of our invidious Enemies, and detest the despotick Attempts of Papal Power.'[1] The original version of Arne's song ran:

> God bless our noble King,
> God save great George our King,

> God save the King,
> Send him victorious, happy and glorious,
> Long to reign over us,
> God save the King.

He had discovered the words in the *Thesaurus Musicus*, published in 1744, where the original first verse ran:

> God Save our Lord the King,
> Long Live our noble King,
> God save the King.

and the second verse was the still existing:

> O Lord Our God arise,
> Scatter his Enemies
> And make them fall;
> Confound their Politicks,
> Frustrate their Knavish Tricks,
> On him our Hopes are fixed
> O save us all.

The success of the song led to the publisher of *Thesaurus Musicus* bringing out a new edition in 1745 with revised words and a third stanza. The first verse now begins:

> God Save Great George Our King,
> Long Live Our Noble King,
> God Save the King.

and the third verse:

> Thy choicest gifts in store
> On him be pleased to pour
> Long may he reign,
> May he defend our laws
> And ever give us cause,
> With Heart and Voice to sing,
> God save the King.

As it stood, it was a resounding plea to God to preserve the King against internal rebellion and foreign invasion and to identify the crown with the Constitution ('May he defend our laws') against the prospect of arbitrary and despotic government. Ironically, Dr Arne was a Catholic and many of his co-religionists were supporting the Young Pretender, Charles Edward Stewart.

The anthem was widely published in song collections and journals. It was extensively sold by street hawkers. It was regularly sung in theatres, called for by the people, and with a few minor changes ('O save us all' became 'God, save us all'; 'On him our hopes are fixed' became 'On thee our hopes are fixed') it formed the anthem as it stands today, though regrettably the second verse is now rarely sung. It became 'God save our gracious King' in 1830 on the accession of William IV: he was the first King not to be called George since 1745, thus invalidating the first line. King William was replaced by Queen Victoria in 1837 and the formulation was finally settled as 'God Save our Gracious Queen/ Long Live our Noble Queen' in the latter part of Victoria's reign.

A fourth verse was briefly in vogue at the time of the rebellion, but was rapidly abandoned thereafter:

> Lord grant that Marshal Wade
> May by Thy mighty aid
> Victory bring;
> May he sedition hush,
> And like a torrent rush,
> Rebellious Scots to crush,
> God Save the King.[2]

Its popularity with all classes survived its immediate matrix. It effectively became the national anthem in the 1780s and 1790s during the illnesses of King George III when the public sang it in sympathy with the King and also to demonstrate opposition to the Prince of Wales's campaign for the Regency.

Throughout the late eighteenth and the whole of the nineteenth century verses were regularly added to commemorate specific events, though they rapidly faded after those events: verses to celebrate George III's marriage to Queen Charlotte; to celebrate George III's recovery from illness; his Jubilee and his survival from assassination; to celebrate the Coronations of George IV and William IV and the marriages of Queen Victoria and the Princess Royal (verses by Tennyson), the Queen's widowhood, her survival of attempted assassination, the Golden and Diamond Jubilees and the Coronation of Edward VII. Many of the early nineteenth-century verses had markedly anti-French sentiments.

Almost from the first there was controversy about the origin of both words and tune, documented in an extensive literature.[3] But there seems little likelihood of firmly discovering the identities of the author of the poem and the tune's composer. The most likely solution is that Arne took over and adapted to Hanoverian use what was originally a Stewart anthem ('God Save Great James our King'), composed and performed at the time of William of Orange's invasion. It then became a Jacobite song, with words uniting a set of poetic themes involving the sovereign that date back to the sixteenth century. The musical theme is a galliard (a sixteenth-century dance tune), its composer unknown, though it resembles a keyboard piece by the Elizabethan composer John Bull. Both tune and words emerge from a common musical and poetical memory crystallized at the time of James II but taken over and definitively appropriated in 1745.[4]

The anthem as it stood was distinctively national. But towards the end of the nineteenth century there began to be expressed the desire for an imperial dimension. The 1887 Jubilee verse began to express it:

> Sorrow and joy her lot,
> Yet thee she ne'er forgot
> Wife, Mother, Queen,
> Purity, Love and Grace,
> Have met in sweet embrace,
> Blessing the human race,
> Our Empress Queen.[5]

Sydney G.R. Coles rewrote the whole anthem on imperial lines as *God Save Our Empress Queen* in 1892. So too did Canon F.K. Harford.[6]

> God save our gracious Queen,
> Long live our Empress Queen,
> God save the Queen.
> Send her victorious, happy and glorious,
> Long to reign over us:
> God save the Queen.
>
> O Lord our God arise.
> Scatter her enemies
> And make them fall.
> Bid strife and envy cease, brotherly love increase
> Filling our homes with peace,
> Blessing us all.
>
> Thy choicest gifts in store still on VICTORIA pour,
> Health, might, and fame.
> Long to her people dear, subjects her sway revere,
> Nations afar and near
> Honour her name.
>
> Through joy – through sorrow's hour,
> Thou, LORD, her guiding power
> Ever has been.
> Still bid Thine orb of day beam where her footsteps stray;
> Still let thy favouring ray
> Shine on our Queen.
>
> Guard her beneath Thy wings,
> Almighty KING OF KINGS,

SOV'REIGN UNSEEN.
Long may our prayer be blest, rising from East and West,
As from one loyal breast: –
GOD SAVE THE QUEEN.

Towards the end of the First World War, the Royal Colonial Institute ran a competition for an imperial verse for the national anthem. There were almost 400 entries. The prize was awarded to Captain Walter Inge for his entry:

> Wide o'er the linking seas,
> Polar and tropic breeze
> Our song shall bring,
> Brothers of each Domain,
> Bound but by Freedom's chain,
> Shout, as your Sires, again –
> 'God Save the King'.[7]

A 'Victory' version of the anthem with distinct imperial resonance was sung in 1919 at a Thanksgiving service held at St Paul's Cathedral, attended by the royal family, and was later included in the hymnbook *Songs of Praise* (1925):

> One realm of races four,
> Blest ever more and more,
> God save our land!
> Home of the brave and free,
> Set in the silver sea,
> True nurse of chivalry,
> God save our land.
> Kinsfolk in love and birth
> (variant version: Of many a race and birth,)
> From utmost ends of earth,
> God save us all!
> Bid strife and hatred cease,
> Bid hope and joy increase,
> Spread universal peace,
> God save us all!

None of them caught on. But evidence of the imperial significance of the anthem is provided by the facts that in 1882 H.H. Rajah Sir Sourindro Mohun Tagore translated the words of the national anthem into Sanskrit and Bengali and set them to twelve varieties of Indian melody; and in 1897, as an 'imperial souvenir' of the Diamond Jubilee, Habib Anthony Salmoné translated the third verse of the national anthem into 'fifty of the most important languages spoken in the Queen's Empire'.[8]

Periodically there have been sustained assaults on the national anthem. There was a fashion among literary luminaries of the Edwardian era for denouncing it. W.S. Gilbert thought it 'should be written entirely anew'; W.L. Courtney pronounced it 'wretched doggerel'; Sir Theodore Martin declared it 'wholly unworthy of the place it has so long occupied'; Theodore Watts-Dunton said 'the imbecility of the National Anthem has been a standing marvel for generations'; and J. Churton Collins proclaimed the national anthem 'a national disgrace'.[9] More recently, as part of the debate on the future of the monarchy, it has been again attacked and suggestions as disparate as commissioning Andrew Lloyd Webber to write a new one and adopting the signature tune of *Match of the Day* have been offered. Throughout the nineteenth century people had written alternative national anthems, among them Percy Shelley, Ebenezer Elliot, William Hudson and William Watson, almost all variations on *God Save the Land* and *God Save the People*. None caught on.

But no-one who has seen medal-winning Olympic athletes with tears coursing down their cheeks as the flag is raised and the anthem played, or seen the England football team and the massed fans lustily singing it at soccer internationals, can doubt its emotive power. It is its association with over 200 years of British history and its playing at all those official occasions which mark the ceremonial year, Remembrance Sunday, the Trooping of the Colour, the Last Night of the Proms, for example, that give it an emotional resonance which transcends any doubts about its musical or poetic excellence.

Critics might do well to heed the words which Beethoven wrote in his diary in 1813: 'I must show the English a little, what a blessing they have in their "God Save the King".'[10] To demonstrate this he composed a set of variations on the anthem for piano. Britain was the first country to have a national anthem; overseas visitors were struck by the fervour with which it was sung and soon continental countries emulated it. Twenty different European states adopted the tune and set their own words to it. *God Save the King* was also pressed into service as the first American national anthem, the tune set to the words *My Country, 'Tis of Thee* by Rev. Samuel Francis Smith (1831). It was replaced by *The Star Spangled Banner* in 1931.

The national anthem was incorporated into the introduction to Thomas Attwood's coronation anthem *I Was Glad*, sung at George IV's Coronation in 1821. It was played on the organ but not sung at Queen Victoria's Coronation. Thereafter, however, it accompanied her every appearance: sung by a choir of 1,000 voices at the opening of the Crystal Palace in 1851 and by 1,800 voices at the Palace's re-opening at Sydenham in 1854. A choir of 33,623 persons sang it at the Halifax

Sunday School Jubilee in 1856. By the end of the nineteenth century it was included in the hymn books of all the major denominations, and a number of other hymns were composed to its rhythmic structure.

But the national anthem could also provoke strong feelings. Patriotic artists were outraged when it was intimated to them that they should not perform it. This was particularly true in Ireland. But Dan Godfrey, Peter Dawson, John Mackenzie-Rogan and Emma Albani all at various times insisted on performing it. The anthem was hissed at the 1891 National Eisteddfod in Swansea. An Irish band attending the Irish Exhibition at Olympia in 1888 refused to play the anthem, its members claiming they would be unable to go back to Ireland if they were to do so. But it was enthusiastically sung on the visits of King Edward VII to Dublin in 1903, 1904 and 1907. In Canada, at a concert in Montreal in 1894, when the orchestra refused to play the anthem the Governor-General Lord Aberdeen stood up and began to sing it. The audience joined in and cheered.

At times of national crisis and national celebration the anthem would be sung with particular fervour. Lewis Winstock, having trawled through a host of diaries and memoirs, concluded: 'there is no doubt that in 1899–1902 *God Save the Queen* had an appeal that has never been equalled; even in World War Two it would be difficult to find anyone writing of a concert that "the event of the evening was *The Queen*"'.[11]

Writing in 1902, W.H. Cummings recounted the story of the massacre of Major Wilson and the Shangani River Patrol, in which the singing of the national anthem formed the tragic climax:

> During the Matabele war, in 1894, thirty-four Englishmen found themselves, after three hours' fighting, absolutely surrounded and hemmed in by the natives. The little band, commanded by Major Wilson, were all wounded and their ammunition was well-nigh expended; the Major, covered with blood from his many wounds, stood erect and continued to fire at the foe, assisted by a wounded comrade who stood by his side and loaded the rifles for him. The natives crawled along the ground and by degrees drew nearer the few surviving English, till at last the supreme and inevitable moment arrived when, in overwhelming numbers, they rushed in upon the devoted band who, of one accord, stood up, uncovered their heads, and joined in singing 'God save the Queen', and whilst so engaged were ruthlessly assegaied.

He concluded: 'it can, however be confidently asserted that its hallowed strains will continue to be fervently echoed and re-echoed by the many millions of peoples, throughout the world, who are proud of their allegiance to our beloved King and Emperor, Edward the Seventh'.[12]

No less a person than Sir Arthur Sullivan testified to the imperial significance of the national anthem. Speaking at the 1891 Royal Academy annual banquet, he declared to cheers from his distinguished audience that he wished to draw attention to an important attribute of music: 'its power and influence on popular sentiment':

> For that music is a power, and has influenced humanity with dynamic force in politics, religion, peace and war, no one can gainsay. Who can deny the effect in great crises of the world's history – of the Lutheran chorale, *Ein' feste Burg*, which roused the enthusiasm of whole towns and cities, and caused them to embrace the Reformed faith *en masse* – of the *ça ira* with ghastly association of tumbril and guillotine, and of the still more powerful *Marsellaise*? These three tunes alone have been largely instrumental in varying the course of history. Amongst our own people, no one who has visited the Greater Britain beyond the seas but must be alive to the depth of feeling stirred by the first bar of *God Save the Queen*. It is not too much to say that this air has done more than any other single agency to consolidate the national sentiment which forms the basis of our world-wide empire.[13]

Sullivan endorsed his judgement by including the national anthem as the climax of his Diamond Jubilee ballet *Victoria and Merrie England*.

There have been sets of piano variations on the tune of *God Save the King* almost from its first appearance: the earliest, apparently by Johann Christian Bach. Other sets are by Franz Hünten, Sigismond Thalberg, Johann Nicolaus Forkel, Dussek, Kalkbrenner, Czerny, Henri Herz, Brinley Richards: perhaps the most notable being by Beethoven, who also incorporated it into his *Wellington's Victory* battle symphony.

Weber used the anthem in his cantata *Battle and Victory* (1815) celebrating the Battle of Waterloo and in his *Jubilee Overture* (1818) composed for the fiftieth anniversary celebrations of Frederick Augustus III of Saxony, whose anthem it also was. There were sets of flute variations by Drouet, violin variations by Paganini, harp variations by Bochsa and Graille. A Clementi symphony (*Grand National Symphony*, c.1824) incorporated *God Save the King;* Thalberg composed a grand fantasia on *God Save the Queen* and *Rule, Britannia* (1837) and Liszt a *Grand Paraphrase* of the anthem in 1841. Brahms's *Triumphlied* (1870), celebrating Prussia's victory over France, used it in its guise as the Prussian anthem. Marschner used it in a concert overture in celebration of the baptism of the Prince of Wales in 1842. Gounod composed a wedding march for organ for the wedding of the

Duke of Albany and Princess Helena of Waldeck–Pyrmont using the anthem in 1882.

In Britain the version of the anthem orchestrated by Sir Michael Costa (1883) held sway throughout the latter part of Victoria's reign. It was superseded in the twentieth century by Elgar's arrangement. But there have also been arrangements by, among others, Sir George Elvey, Sir Henry Bishop, Sir Charles Stanford, Sir Joseph Barnby (for the Golden Jubilee), Sir Frederick Bridge (for the Diamond Jubilee), Sir Henry Wood and Sir Walford Davies (King George VI's Coronation), Gordon Jacob and Benjamin Britten (for Elizabeth II's Coronation).

It is a singular fact that both of Britain's premier national songs derived from the same composer – the leading English composer of the eighteenth century, Dr Thomas Augustine Arne. But whereas he merely arranged *God Save the King*, he actually composed what became almost the alternative anthem *Rule, Britannia*, of which the poet Southey wrote that it would be 'the political hymn of the country as long as she maintains her political power'.[14] It was the hit song of the masque *Alfred*, originally produced at Cliveden, the Thames-side mansion of Frederick, Prince of Wales in 1740, as part of the celebrations of the third birthday of his daughter Princess Augusta and of the commemoration of the accession of the Hanoverian dynasty to the throne. Originally only two acts and comparatively short, *Alfred* was continually reworked by Arne over the next fifteen years, added to and developed, as it was transformed from a heroic play with songs and musical interludes into a secular oratorio.[15]

The original plot has Alfred, fleeing from the Danes and taking refuge in Athelney in Somerset where he is eventually reunited with his wife Eltruda and confers with the Earl of Devon about a counter-attack against the Danes. He has a vision of the future greatness of Britain, with Edward III, Queen Elizabeth and William III appearing to him. Devon successfully defeats the Danes and Alfred takes command of the army to complete their rout. A bard sings *Rule, Britannia*.

In its original version, the masque was an allegory and a propaganda piece. Alfred symbolized Frederick, exiled from court because of his opposition to his father King George II and Prime Minister Walpole. He had become the focus of political and artistic opposition to the court, and among his artistic protégés were the poet James Thomson and David Mallet, who served at the Prince's under-secretary. Together they produced the text of the masque, though the words of *Rule, Britannia* were Thomson's alone. The text is informed by ideas in Bolingbroke's *The Patriot King*, the opposition's manifesto for a limited constitutional monarchy and a balanced constitution, in contradistinction to what was perceived as a Whig oligarchy and the factional monarchy of George II and Walpole. The spirits were hailed as representatives of the ideal of the *Patriot King*.

In the subsequent expansions and reworkings, much of this political propaganda was eliminated and it was transformed into a straightforward celebration of British heroism, as the English repel foreign invasion. In 1745 Arne expanded the piece for stage performance, turning it into three acts, adding a vigorous overture (with the familiar strains of the hit song interwoven). New characters were added, notably Edith, a Saxon maiden whose lover had fallen in battle with the Danes, and Prince Edward, the warrior son of Alfred, and the battle between Devon and the Danes was staged. By 1745 it had a more direct relevance to national political events, with Britain actually menaced by rebellion and invasion. Arne did further versions in 1753, 1759 and 1762. In the meantime, Thomson had died (1748) and Mallet, who falsely claimed to have reworked the whole text, made some further, if minor, textual emendations to fashion a stage play for David Garrick, who played Alfred, in 1751. The score was Arne's, though it was supplemented by Charles Burney. Garrick restaged it spectacularly in 1773, with the music prepared by Theodore Smith. Throughout all these changes and transformations, *Rule, Britannia* remained a constant feature, though removed from the bard and assigned to Alfred and Eltruda.

There is no doubt that *Rule, Britannia* is an imperial invocation. The original text is reproduced here, as is the speech following it in the masque:

When *Britain* first at heaven's command,
Arose from out the azure main;
This was the charter of the land,
And guardian Angels sung *this* strain:
'Rule, *Britannia*, rule the waves;
Britons never will be slaves.'

The nations, not so blest as thee,
Must in their turns, to tyrants fall:
While thou shalt flourish great and free,
The dread and envy of them all.
        'Rule,' etc.

Still more majestic shalt thou rise,
More dreadful, from each foreign stroke:
As the loud blast that tears the skies,
Serves but to root thy native oak.
        'Rule,' etc.

Thee haughty tyrants ne'er shall tame:
All their attempts to bend thee down,
Will but arouse thy generous flame;
But work their woe, and thy renown.
        'Rule,' etc.

To thee belongs the rural reign;
Thy cities shall with commerce shine;
All thine shall be the subject main,
And very shore it circles thine.
        'Rule,' etc.

The Muses, still with freedom found,
Shall to thy happy coast repair:
Blest isle! With matchless beauty crown'd,
And manly hearts to guard the fair.
'Rule, Britannia, rule the waves,
Britons never will be slaves.'

Alfred, go forth! Lead on the radiant years,
To thee revealed in vision.—Lo! they rise!
Lo! Patriots, heroes, sages, crowd to birth:
And bards to sing them in immortal verse!
I see thy commerce, *Britain*, grasp the world:
All nations serve thee; every foreign flood,
Subjected, pays its tribute to the *Thames*.
Thither the golden South obedient pours
His sunny treasures: thither the soft East
Her spices, delicacies, gentle gifts;
And thither his rough trade the stormy North.
See, where beyond the vast Atlantic surge,
By boldest keels untouch'd, a dreadful space!
Shores, yet unfound, arise! in youthful prime,
With towering forests, mighty rivers crown'd!
These stoop to *Britain's* thunder. This new world,
Shook to the centre, trembles at her name:
And there, her sons with aim exalted, sow
The seeds of rising empire, arts, and arms.

Britons proceed, the subject *Deep* command,
Awe with your navies every hostile land.
In vain their threats; their armies all in vain:
They rule the balanc'd world, who rule the main.

There were some minor textual emendations and three verses were dropped. But the principal change was one related to national developments. The original version contains the line 'Britannia, rule the waves', which is exhortatory. It was amended in the nineteenth century to 'Britannia rules the waves' which is affirmatory and reflected the new imperial reality. The song was an instant hit, published separately in 1742 as 'the celebrated Ode in Honour of Great Britain', ten years ahead of the rest of the score. Its success is evidenced by Handel's quoting from it in the *Occasional Oratorio* (1745–46), composed to celebrate the suppression of the Jacobite Rebellion.

Beethoven, self-proclaimed admirer of *God Save the King*, also wrote a set of piano variations on *Rule, Britannia* and incorporated it into his battle symphony *Wellington's Victory* as the 'theme tune' of the British Army. Wagner declared that the first eight notes of *Rule, Britannia* embodied the whole character of the British people and composed a *Rule, Britannia Overture*, which was completed and performed in 1837. He sent it to the Philharmonic Society of London but it was rejected and returned. It is arranged for a large orchestra and given the full Wagnerian treatment, characteristic of his later operatic overtures. There is, however, something rather ponderously Teutonic about it, and as a piece of music it is completely eclipsed by Sir Alexander Mackenzie's 'nautical overture' *Britannia*, which after a long period of neglect has recently been revived on CD and proves every bit as delightful as contemporary audiences had found it, true to the spirit of Arne's anthem, which Cummings calls 'strong, virile and characteristic'. It is composed of three original themes in the style of Dibdin's nautical songs, with a sailor's hornpipe interwoven, and out of the brilliantly orchestrated mix of these themes, the strains of Arne's anthem gradually emerge, as if coalescing and developing out of its musical context, the eighteenth-century songs and music of the sea. It is redolent of the sea and contrasts markedly with the heavy pomp of Wagner's which smacks more of court processional than of nautical celebration. Joyous and zestful throughout, its gradually increasing tempo culminates in a final grand, solemn, heroic conclusion. Sir Alexander Mackenzie recalled in his autobiography an episode that took place in the immediate aftermath of the Jameson Raid:

> The Overture also enjoyed the distinction of a political significance, quite unintentional, being attached to it. Immediately after Hallé's death (in 1895) I was invited to conduct some of the remaining concerts of his season in Manchester, Leeds and Liverpool. In the latter city the Overture met with so exceptionally warm an ovation that it had to be played a second time with the same result. In compliance with a third demand only the final pages were repeated. These boisterous encores were, however, not entirely due to an excessive appreciation of the music, because on that very day the German Kaiser's ill-judged telegram to President Kruger had become known, and *Britannia* had been made the vehicle of a patriotic demonstration rarely witnessed in a British concert room. The occurrence had an amusing sequel when the piece had been

selected, for a second time, to be played at Düsseldorf by the liberal-minded Buths, a few days later. A *Verbot* was issued and the offending work had the honour of being banned by the police.[16]

Rev. Rowland Hill used *Rule, Britannia* as the tune for a hymn in 1803 and Thomas Attwood appropriately included it in the opening and closing sections of the anthem *O Lord, Grant the King a Long Life*, composed for the Coronation of William IV, the 'Sailor King' in 1831. Thereafter, throughout the nineteenth century, often appearing together, *God Save the King/Queen* and *Rule, Britannia* were the twin anthems of nation and Empire. They were joined in the twentieth century by a third, *Land of Hope and Glory* by Elgar. It remains a remarkable fact that the three national anthems of the United Kingdom, whose identity was so strongly tied up with the Protestant succession, were composed by Catholics: Arne and Elgar.

Coronations

As Philip Ziegler wrote, 'The coronation of a British monarch is the event which brings him more dramatically than any other to the forefront of his people's consciousness.'[17] Since the monarch constitutionally and practically becomes ruler the moment his/her predecessor expires, a coronation fulfils some other function. It is the outward and visible sign of the compact between people and sovereign that is the essence of constitutional monarchy; the occasion at which the monarch, by swearing an oath, publicly affirms his/her commitment to uphold the laws and the Constitution, to maintain in the United Kingdom the Protestant faith and, in England specifically, the Anglican Settlement, and to ensure justice for the people. But co-existing with this process is the older sacred ritual in which the monarch is anointed as God's chosen instrument, obtains the symbols of kingship (sword, orb, sceptre, crown) and receives the homage of leading subjects. The widespread public participation of the people, especially since the introduction first of radio and then of television brought the ceremony directly into the homes of the monarch's subjects, makes it now more than ever an expression of the *community* of the realm, transcending differences of class, gender, ethnicity and religious belief.

The four Coronations that fall within the scope of this study, those of 1902, 1911, 1937 and 1953, also affirmed the unity and solidarity of the Empire. As the anthropologist Bronislaw Malinowski wrote of the 1937 Coronation:

The Coronation was, among other things, a large-scale ceremonial display of the greatness, power and wealth of Britain. It was also an occasion on which the unity of the Empire, the strength of its bonds, was publicly enacted . . . Even if the ceremony be taken at its lowest as a large piece of window-dressing, it might still have been well-invested expenditure. Psychologically, I think there was no doubt at all that the Coronation generated an increased feeling of security, of stability, and the permanence of the British Empire.[18]

The oath to defend Protestantism underlines the importance of that faith to the maintenance of Empire. It is an integral part of a hallowed religious service, which in the words of David Martin, is a form of 'sacred choreography, so carefully planned as to be invisible and seem inevitable', and which 'unites personal and universal, private and civic'.[19] Musically, the service combined the traditional with the new and provided an occasion for Britain's leading composers to signal their allegiance to the crown by contributing freshly composed works to the order of service. So the coronation became as much a celebration of British music as of British monarchy, each reinforcing and validating the other.

The Coronation of King Edward VII, 1902

The crowning of King Edward VII in 1902 was the first Coronation of a British monarch in the twentieth century and the first for over sixty years. There were few people then alive who had attended the previous Coronation, that of Queen Victoria in 1838. To mark the event, the historian J.E.C. Bodley was appointed to write an official account and to put Edward's Coronation in historical context. The resulting volume, *The Coronation of Edward the Seventh: A Chapter of European and Imperial History*, was published in 1903.

Bodley was in no doubt that this Coronation was a great imperial event. He proclaimed it 'the consecration of the imperial idea, conceived in the last generation of the nineteenth century', and declared that Edward VII was assuming a crown which 'had become an emblem of Empire wider than Darius or the early Caesars had ever dreamed of'.[20] London, he noted, was thronged with 'British subjects from the farthest corners of the earth . . . From Canada alone five thousand loyal visitors had come to London, while more distant Australia and New Zealand had sent many a shipload of colonists to salute the Imperial crown placed on the head of a new monarch as the emblem of the Empire of which they were proud to be citizens.'[21]

The capital was guarded by soldiers from Canada, Australia, New Zealand, the Cape and Natal, 'peacefully aided by dark warriors from our Indian Empire'. The New Zealand troops were accompanied by 'a body of loyal Maori warriors'. Bodley waxed eloquent on the subject of the native troops present in London for the Coronation:

The Maoris . . . were not the only soldiers of extra-European origin sent with the colonial forces to the Coronation. From North Borneo came a little band of Dyaks, sons of the head-hunters of the seas where the Pacific meets the Indian Ocean. The Sultan of Perak brought from the Straits, where it is always summer, his bodyguard of Malays. Ceylon sent its white-clad sinuous Singhalese; Fiji its bronze-tinted giants, clothed in crimson, white and blue. The black skins of many a branch of the great Bantu family were seen on the London pavement: Nigerians and Haussas from West Africa, Sudanese and Swahelis from the centre and east of the Dark Continent, wearing the uniform of the King's African Rifles. To them were added men of their race and colour who had never seen their native wilds, the descendants of West Indian slaves. The red tarbouch marked the Mohammedan guardians of Cyprus, and the yellow Mongol features of the Hong-Kong police told of England's post of observation in the farthest East. But the Orientals who attracted most attention wearing the King's uniform were . . . an imposing contingent of the native troops of the Indian army . . . To hail the Emperor of India it had sent to England representatives of a vast array of races and of castes. There were Tamils from Southern India, Telagus from the East Coast, Mahrattas from the Deccan, Brahmins, Jats and Rajputs from Oudh and Rajputana, Ghurkas from Nepal, Sikhs from the Punjab, Afridis and other Pathans from the wild borderland across the Indus, Hazaras from Afghanistan and Mussulmans of diverse origin and locality. The crowds admired the dark turbaned warriors in the brilliant attire of Lancers or Guides and felt a pride knowing that they formed part of the King's army.[22]

It was all a far cry from the Coronation on 28 June 1838 which, although Britain already possessed a substantial overseas Empire, was largely a domestic affair, with, says Bodley, 'not . . . much trace of imperial sentiment, as it was understood at the end of the Queen's reign'.[23] It was also chaotically staged, with the Queen being handed the orb at the wrong moment, the ring being put on the wrong finger, the service being prematurely halted and then re-started, and the elderly Lord Rolle falling down the steps of the throne while making his act of homage.

Edward's Coronation was carefully rehearsed but it encountered an entirely unexpected setback. Scheduled to take place on 26 June 1902, it had to be abruptly cancelled when the King fell ill and had to undergo an emergency appendectomy. It was re-arranged to take place on 9 August, by which time many of the foreign delagations sent specially to attend the Coronation had had to return home; their countries were represented by their London ambassadors. This had the effect of emphasizing the imperial nature of the event as the Coronation became, in Bodley's words, 'essentially a domestic celebration of the British race united by the influence of the Imperial Crown, which was for the first time assumed as a specific symbol of world-wide Empire'.[24] Among the 8,000 guests in Westminster Abbey were the Prime Ministers of Canada, Australia, New Zealand, Newfoundland and Natal; thirty-one Indian Princes and Princesses; eleven colonial bishops; the Paramount Chief of the Barotse; the Sultan of Perak; and representatives of all the colonies and dominions. Bodley reminds us that the Prince and Princess of Wales were attending the Coronation fresh from a tour of all the self-governing communities of the Empire, a journey of 50,000 miles from which had 'quickened the imperial sentiment of vigorous democracies, whose chief bond of union is their loyalty to the crown'; that the aged Archbishop of Canterbury, Frederick Temple, so feeble that he had to be assisted by two bishops, was the son of a governor of Sierra Leone and had been born in the Ionian Islands when they were a British protectorate; and that the key roles in the ceremony were taken by such notable imperial warriors as Lord Roberts of Kandahar, Lord Kitchener of Khartoum and Lord Wolseley of Tel-el-Kebir. He also reports that instead of being crowned, like his predecessors, with St Edward's Crown, Edward VII was crowned with the Imperial State Crown.

The Times shared Bodley's perception of the nature of the Coronation. Its reports of the events of Coronation Day returned again and again to its imperial nature.[25] It reported the rousing popular cheers that greeted the appearances of Lord Roberts, Lord Kitchener and the contingents of Indian and Colonial troops in the procession. The Band of the Royal Military School of Music, posted in Parliament Square, kept the crowd entertained with music, which included *Here's a Health Unto His Majesty*, Meyerbeer's *Grand March* from *The Prophet* and Sullivan's *Imperial March*. The triumphal editorial in *The Times* summed up its perception of the events:

Some of the most striking and conspicuous features of the Coronation of KING EDWARD are new in the history of the British monarchy and of the British race. KING EDWARD is the first of our Kings to be attended in his Coronation by an illustrious group of statesmen from our self-governing colonies, as he is the first to be accompanied by a number of the great feudatory Princes of India and to be escorted by splendid detachments of Colonial and Indian troops. The presence of our Colonial and Indian guests has been instinctively recognized by the people as a sign of the new place we have in the world. The rise of our great colonies, the creation of the Dominion of Canada and of the Commonwealth of Australia and the development of modern India under the direct government of the CROWN are the welcome fruit of our constitutional system as we have known how to apply it in the most diverse

[103]

conditions. Liberty and loyalty are to-day as deeply rooted and as strong of growth in the powerful communities which pay willing obedience to KING EDWARD across the Atlantic and in the Pacific, as they are at home; while in India hundreds of millions gratefully acknowledge the justice, the wisdom and the mildness of a sway incomparably better than Asia has ever witnessed in all the long course of her mutations. The late reign saw the beginning of a remarkable transition period, which promises to continue and perhaps to culminate in this generation or the next. In that period . . . mother country and colonies almost simultaneously awoke to a clear perception of their true interests and of the destiny marked out for them . . . They would know now as they have never known before that, whatever be the differences of race, or of history, or of creed between them, they are one people with a common inheritance, a common mission, and a common duty. They are bound to preserve the fabric of British polity and of British civilization.[26]

The order of service was based on that adopted for the Coronations of King William IV and Queen Victoria but it was shortened somewhat, even before the need to preserve the post-operative monarch from fatigue. The arrangements for the coronation music were in the hands of the organist of Westminster Abbey Sir Frederick Bridge. He decided to make the service a celebration of four centuries of English church music.[27] He utilized a choir of 430, an orchestra of 65, and 10 trumpeters for the fanfare.

The Times, reviewing the rehearsal of the music, observed tartly that the best pieces on offer were the oldest. Henry Purcell's 200-year old Let My Prayer Come Up, used for the offertory, was pronounced 'incomparably more beautiful than the church music of today'. There was praise, too, for Thomas Tallis's setting of the litany ('very beautiful'), the three-fold 'Amen' from Orlando Gibbons's anthem Great King of Gods, Handel's anthem Zadok the Priest, composed for the Coronation of King George II and used at every subsequent coronation, and the hymn Veni Creator Spiritus.

Of the works by modern composers included in the service, The Times pronounced the introit O Harken Thou, from Sullivan's The Light of the World, 'feeble', Samuel Sebastian Wesley's Credo, from his service in E, 'curious', Stanford's 1879 Te Deum 'familiar to all' and Stainer's Sanctus and Gloria, from his service in A, 'not inspired'. Three new settings had been commissioned. Sir Hubert Parry composed a magisterial new version of Psalm 122, I Was Glad When They Said Unto Me, We Will Go into the House of the Lord, which had been a part of every coronation ceremony since that of James I in 1603. He contrived to include the shouts Vivat Rex and Vivat Regina, and as Bridge recorded – rightly – it 'made a splendid effect'.[28] It has been used at every coronation since. *The Times* declared it 'the most beautiful of all the modern music used'. The newspaper's critic was less impressed by the other two pieces, a setting by Sir Walter Parratt of the *Confortare* 'Be strong and play the man: Keep the commandments of the Lord thy God and walk in his ways' ('a trifle . . . splendidly sung') and Bridge's own setting, as the homage anthem, of verses from Isaiah 49, 'Kings shall see and arise', which included the lines: 'Behold, these shall come from afar; and lo, these from the north and from the west; and these from the land in Sinim'.[29] *The Times* thought the setting uninspired but it is a clear biblical acknowledgement of the imperial nature of the coronation. Bodley thought that it 'seemed to foretell the glories of a world-wide Empire assembling its people from the ends of the earth'.[30]

Hymns were played and sung as various processions entered the Abbey. They included *Rejoice Today with One Accord* (sung to the famous Lutheran hymn *Ein' feste burg*) and *O, God Our Help in Ages Past*. During the many hours when the assembled guests in the Abbey had to wait for the arrival of the King and Queen they were entertained by a succession of marches: Wagner's *Kaisermarsch* (known in England as the *Imperial March*), Elgar's *Pomp and Circumstance March No.1*, and the coronation marches by Tchaikovsky, Gounod, Saint-Saëns, Mackenzie and Godfrey.

The Coronation inspired a good deal of occasional music. *The Times* observed sagely:

> 'Occasional' music, it is notorious, seldom reaches a very high level of importance; and the fact that the music chosen for the ceremonial itself has a rare degree of value should go far to compensate the poverty and inappropriateness of a good many of the works that have been published as supplementary to the selection actually made.[31]

The Times article does not mention the fact that the Master, the Wardens and Court of Assistants of the Worshipful Company of Musicians had offered a prize of fifty guineas for the composition of a suitable orchestral march for the coronation. There were 190 entries, and the judges (Sir Hubert Parry, Sir Frederick Bridge and Sir Walter Parratt) chose Percy Godfrey's *Coronation March*. Percy Scholes, who had to play it on the organ, thought it 'ineffective'.[32] Bridge later adapted the tune for the hymn *The King, O Lord, in Thee This Day Rejoices*, to words by Canon Armitage Robinson. Both hymn and march were performed in the preliminaries to the Coronation; it was advertized as available for the 1911 Coronation but thereafter it vanished from the repertoire.

There were other new coronation marches by Sir Alexander

Mackenzie, Frederic Cowen and Percy Pitt. Even the American John Philip Sousa, whose band had performed at Sandringham, made a contribution: his march was called appropriately *Imperial Edward*. A joyous free-wheeling piece, it included the opening bars of *God Save the King* played by the trombones in the trio section. *The Times* calling Pitt's march 'long and undeniably clever', declared severely that it 'hardly has the qualities that make for popularity, but its musical interest and the way the main theme is treated throughout must gratify people of musical taste'. *The Times* reserved its greatest praise for the *Coronation March* specially composed for the occasion by Camille Saint-Saëns, in recognition of King Edward's francophilia. It was scored for full orchestra, bells and, at the close, military band. Saint-Saëns came to England and rehearsed the orchestra, intending to conduct the piece at the coronation ceremony. But after the postponement he was unable to return for the rearranged date. It was nevertheless performed in the Abbey, conducted by Bridge. *The Times* thought the music 'thoroughly inspiriting, and a fine specimen of the composer's powers'.

> The principal theme, led up to by a short introduction of appropriately dignified style, is straightforward and jubilant, and a special interest attaches to the subject which serves as trio, for it is described as an English air of the 16th century; most students of English music will not find it very easy to identify the tune, but it is of fine, broad character, and is admirably treated. In accordance with an effective custom observed, if not originated, by Dr. Elgar in his two recent marches, the trio-subject, in the tonic key, forms the final section of the march.

The English air was the same one that Saint-Saëns had used in his opera *Henry VIII*. A *Coronation Song Book* for children's festivals was produced, with the usual entries to represent the four nations of the United Kingdom (*The Minstrel Boy*, *Bonnie Dundee*, etc.) but also Mackenzie's *The Empire Flag* ('a capital song set to words of higher literary pretension than most of the modern effusions in the volume'). Among the new works, *The Times* could find praise only for Dr Cuthbert Harris's *Heaven Bless Our Lord the King*, which had 'a tune that is easily learnt, though its resemblance at the close to "God Bless the Prince of Wales" is to be regretted'.[33]

There was a plethora of other coronation anthems, hymns and odes. But perhaps the most enduring work to be inspired by this Coronation was Elgar's *Coronation Ode*, planned for the special gala concert at Covent Garden Opera House that was cancelled when the Coronation was postponed. It was, however, successfully performed in Sheffield and Bristol and, reported *Hazell's Annual*, 'pronounced not only creditable to the composer's reputation, but in its breadth, fervour and patriotic ring, a worthy production for a great national event'.[34] It totally eclipsed the rival *Coronation Ode* composed by Frederic Cowen to lines by the Welsh imperialist poet Sir Lewis Morris and premièred at the Norwich Festival. Morris left his audience in no doubt about the coronation's imperial significance:

> No narrow realm it is to-day we own,
> Our little Isle, hearing the call of Fate,
> Thro' valour and wise statecraft mightier grown,
> Assumes a loftier state,
> Bearing o'er trackless land and unknown sea
> The war-worn ensign of the Free;
> And tho' with heavier weight the Imperial Crown,
> People and King bears down,
> From all the earth, by Love's enchantments bound,
> New ampler Britains kneel in homage round
> Twin hemispheres to-day from palm and pine,
> In loyal love combine:
> Their sons with ours have borne and fought and died,
> Their graves lie side by side;
> The vassal East to swell the pageant brings
> Her feudatory Kings;
> Ruler and peoples humbly kneel and pray
> A blessing from the gracious hand Divine,
> Their vows they take within this hallowed shrine;
> 'Tis a triumphant day!

The Times, reviewing the Norwich performance, was unimpressed, observing: 'The words, not in themselves very inspiring, have been put to music, which serves its purpose well enough for what is called an "occasional" piece, but they give little scope for the composer's special powers of fancy or dainty grace, and there is no very great cause to regret the improbability that this work will be often heard in the future'.[35]

The Coronation of Edward VII and its musical expression set a pattern that all three of the subsequent coronations of the twentieth century were to follow.

The Coronation of King George V, 1911

The Coronation of King George V on 22 June 1911, was, if anything, more imperial than that of Edward VII. The King's procession to Westminster Abbey was escorted by Colonial, Indian and British cavalry, commanded by Lord Kitchener of Khartoum. There were 60,000 troops lining the route between Buckingham Palace and the Abbey, including representatives of all the colonies: from the Bengal Lancers to the

Victoria Mounted Rifles, from the Gurkhas to the 7th Quebec Hussars, from the Transvaal Scottish Volunteers to the Malta Infantry and Royal Artillery. In the parade of standards, Norman Davies noted that 'for the first time the overseas dominions were being given the same prominence as the four home countries; and India was at the heart of things'.[36]

The Times, declaring that London offered 'a unique theatre for a display of the pageantry of Empire', again rhapsodized about 'the Imperial Idea':

> Once more we have to extend our horizon and to regard this ancient Monarchy as the mother of nations and the centre of a worldwide Empire, held together by no bonds of conquest and no assertive central authority, but by some force which none of us can properly name or define, impalpable and intangible as gravitation, yet, like that mysterious force, maintaining the system intact while allowing for all the perturbations due to the minor interactions of the several parts . . . it is no mean tribute to the informing genius of our institutions that through their ancient forms the great Dominions of the CROWN can join us not only in the symbolical pageant of the Coronation, but in the processional march of the ages. Gradually, but surely and naturally, they fall into step without compulsion and almost without conscious volition, because they are of the same blood and the same fibre, only superficially affected by external conditions, and the same old music to which we have been marching for eight hundred years thrills along their nerves and impels them to consentaneous motion. In that lie the greatness and permanence of the Imperial idea, and the secret of its hold among men living in the most various conditions and drifting further with each generation from close personal connexion with the Mother Country . . . We must . . . recognize that an Empire founded in a special and unique manner upon consent is an Empire founded upon character . . . it is the product of the inner character of millions upon millions of undistinguished people who, generation after generation, have been content to do inconspicuously the duty that lay nearest them. It can be maintained only by conserving the fundamental integrity and earnestness of purpose which went to its building.[37]

Sir Frederick Bridge was once again Director of Music and his aim, as in the 1902 Coronation, was to provide an all-British programme for the actual service.[38] He assembled a choir of 400 performers, selected from leading church choirs. The first ceremony of the day, the procession of the regalia, was undertaken to two well-loved and traditional hymns, *O, God, Our Help in Ages Past* (sung to Croft's *St Anne*) and *Rejoice Today with One Accord* (sung to the Lutheran hymn *Ein' feste burg*). Together they made, said *The Times*, 'dignified processional music'.[39]

Then a specially composed fanfare by J.E. Borland, with the old Scottish tune *Montrose*, cleverly woven in, introduced a sequence of orchestral pieces which were played while the arrival of the King and Queen was awaited. Walford Davies's *Solemn Melody*, 'sonorously scored for full orchestra', followed and later Frederic Cowen's *Prelude*. But the bill of fare was comprised principally of marches. Two new ones and a revised one were featured: the coronation marches by Frederick Cliffe, Edward German and Sir Edward Elgar. German's was reworked from his coronation march music for Shakespeare's play *Henry VIII* with a new trio added, and *The Times* observed that 'the whole thing has the directness of aim and certainty of effect which is essential to a good march. It suggests well-knit muscles and a straight back.' Cliffe's 'on the other hand rather halts between recollections of the style of Costa's once famous march in *Eli* and Tchaikovsky. It has little or no physical effect.' Elgar's *Coronation March* seemed to *The Times's* critic 'more a symphonic poem on the subject of Coronation than a concluding march' – a perceptive comment – but he praised 'the brilliant and sometimes glittering orchestration' and the symphonic sweep and intensity of the work. Also new was Sir Alexander Mackenzie's *An English Joypeal*, 'a sonorous work, built up to a dignified climax in the solid style', and including 'a good deal of finely-conceived orchestral colouring'. Also performed at this point were Meyerbeer's *Schiller fest-marsch*, Tchaikovsky's *March Solennelle* and Wagner's *Homage March*, with Elgar's *Imperial March* later accompanying the departure of the royal couple.[40] As on the occasion of the previous Coronation, the Musicians' Company offered a prize for the best coronation march. But none of the 200 entries was deemed worthy by the judges.

The actual service began with the arrival of the King and Queen to Parry's anthem *I Was Glad*, partially rewritten from its 1902 incarnation and now containing an orchestral introduction, 'more arresting and emphatic than was the original one'.[41] Then followed Tallis's *Litany*, a Purcell *Introit*, and Sir George Martin's adaptation of John Merbecke's setting of the Nicene Creed. The anointing took place to the singing of the hymn *Veni Creator Spiritus* and Handel's anthem *Zadok the Priest*. Immediately following the Coronation came Sir Walter Parratt's *Confortare*, "Be Strong and Play the Man" (previously performed in 1902) and, after the benediction and enthronement, the homage anthem, newly composed by Sir Frederick Bridge and making liberal use of *Ein' feste burg*. *The Musical Times* called it 'one of Sir Frederick Bridge's most notable contributions to processional marches'.[42] The service continued with Elgar's *Offertorium* ('O hearken Thou unto the voice of my calling, my King and my God'), 'beautifully set for this occasion . . . in a short but intensely expressive composition', the *Sanctus* by Dr Walter Alcock, Organist of the Chapel Royal, and the *Gloria in Excelsis* by Stanford, both also specially written for the occasion.[43] *The Times* thought the Alcock 'one of the most beautiful things' in the programme and the Stanford, with its bold, rhythmic qualities, 'a vigorous piece of manly writing'. The climax of the service was Parry's 'fine' new *Te Deum*, which worked in the melodies of *O, God, Our Help in Ages Past* and *All People that on Earth Do Dwell* and of which *The Times* declared 'the whole lofty design of the work makes it fit to mark the culmination of the greatest symbol we possess of our national faith, both religious and political'.[44]

Reporting on the event immediately afterwards, *The Musical Times* declared:

> The great State function was carried through with due dignity, splendour and solemnity in the presence of a vast concourse of notabilities representative of the whole vast British Empire and of practically every foreign nation on the globe. The imposing ceremony was one that kindled the imagination of all who were privileged to be present, and it was calculated to stir the pride of every patriotic Briton. To the musician there was an added gratification in the obvious indispensability of music, and it was a tribute to the genius of British composers that nearly all the service music was drawn from their works and that it proved to be so fit for its high purpose.[45]

The King pronounced himself 'very much pleased with the musical arrangements in the Abbey . . . he thought the music was beautiful and extremely well rendered'.[46]

The Novello publishing house used the occasion of the Coronation to promote the sales of the now-familiar patriotic part-songs, which included Cuthbert Harris's *Empire and Motherland*, Percy Fletcher's *For Empire and For King*, Dr Charles Harriss's *Chorus of Empire*, *Empire of the Sea* and *Sing, Britain's Sons*, Mackenzie's *The Empire Flag* and Elgar's *It Comes From the Misty Ages* and *Britons, Alert*. They also introduced the newly composed *Our Sailor King*, with words by Clifton Bingham and music by C.H. Lloyd:

> All hail to George, our Sailor King
> Long may he wear the crown,
> And to his mighty Empire bring,
> New glory, new renown.
> Throughout the world by land and sea,
> His loyal people sing,
> In homage to his majesty,
> 'God Bless our Sailor King'.

The Coronation of King George VI, 1937

The Coronation of King George VI, on 12 May 1937, was bound to be an event of momentous imperial significance. Both monarchy and Empire had been rocked by the abdication of King Edward VIII. The Coronation of George VI was an opportunity to affirm the strength and popularity of both and to banish doubts and anxieties.

The emphasis on Empire was to be found everywhere. The title page of the official coronation programme was headed by the coats of arms of South Africa, Canada, New Zealand, Australia and the Irish Free State, and contained the arms of forty other colonies and dependencies and the names of twenty-three further protectorates and mandated territories. The words of the coronation oath were changed.[47] In 1911 King George V had sworn to 'govern the peoples of this United Kingdom of Great Britain and Ireland, and the Dominions thereto belonging, according to the Statutes in Parliament agreed on, and the respective Laws and Customs of the same'. In 1937 King George VI swore to 'govern the peoples of Great Britain, Ireland, Canada, Australia, New Zealand and the Union of South Africa, of your Possessions and other Territories to any of them belonging or pertaining, and of your Empire of India, according to their respective laws and customs'. It was the recognition of the steady evolution of the Empire into the Commonwealth, something which was stressed by General Smuts, the acting Prime Minister of South Africa, in a widely reported speech:

> The King who is being crowned today is not the head of a central kingdom to which many other Dominions and possessions belong, but of a group of equal States, of whose free association together he is the common symbol. His kingdom has thus a meaning which no previous kingdom has ever had, and his crowning for the first time as sovereign of such a constellation of free states is a unique event in history. Here for the first time we have a King of Kingdoms spread over the globe.[48]

The King endorsed this view in his broadcast to the people of the Empire on the evening of Coronation Day:

> Never before has a newly-crowned King been able to talk to all his people in their own homes on the day of his Coronation. Never before has the ceremony itself had so wide a significance, for the Dominions are now free and equal partners with this ancient Kingdom, and I felt this morning that the whole Empire was in very truth gathered within the walls of Westminster Abbey ... To many millions the Crown is the symbol of unity. By the grace of God and by the will of the free peoples of the British Commonwealth, I have assumed that Crown. In me, as your King, is vested for a time the duty of maintaining its honour and integrity.[49]

But the free and equal association was essentially that of the *white* dominions: India and the wide range of colonies and dependencies remained resolutely imperial. And Empire was the predominant theme of the rhetoric, imagery and reporting. *The Times* had page after page of stories headed 'Empire Pageantry', 'An Empire's Devotion', 'The Empire's Homage', 'The King and the Empire', 'Day of Empire Rejoicing', and so forth. A specially commissioned sculpture *The Empire's Homage to the Throne* by Sir William Reid Dick was displayed at Selfridge's Store. One hundred thousand visitors from the Dominions were reported to be in London for the Coronation. A Rally of Empire Youth at the Royal Albert Hall, attended by 8,000 young people from all parts of the Empire and addressed by the Prime Minister, was organized for 18 May. The second half of the Rally was broadcast, as was a service attended by the same young people at Westminster Abbey the following day.

At 7.20 on Coronation night, the BBC broadcast 'The Empire's homage', an expression of 'homage and devotion to King George VI and Queen Elizabeth, from the assembled peoples of the Empire'. It was punctuated by fanfares specially composed by Arthur Bliss. It consisted of a series of messages of loyalty from dominion and colonial Prime Ministers and from the Viceroy of India. Lieutenant-General Sir Reginald Hildyard, Governor of Bermuda, expressed 'unswerving loyalty to . . . the Throne' on behalf of the colonial Empire. The Prime Minister of New Zealand, Mr. J.M. Savage, declared:

> The people of New Zealand, both Maori and Pakeha, join today with other British peoples in all parts of the world in proclaiming their allegiance to the King and Queen . . . The Crown is more than a symbol of Imperial unity. For us it is a cherished part of the common heritage we share with our kinfolk in other parts of the Empire.

Mr J.A. Lyons, Prime Minister of Australia, declared:

> Many of us, like children coming home to a great family reunion, journeyed from the far corners of the earth to this London, this centre of the Empire, this cradle of so many of the common ideals of our race. In this ceremony, of such deep significance to our Empire, it was my great privilege to represent the Australian people, and I speak, I know, for all of them, when I assure their Majesties that they have our undivided love, respect and loyalty.

Dr Ba Maw, Prime Minister of Burma, said:

> The Empire's joy this day is Burma's joy, and similarly the Empire's loyalty to the Throne is Burma's.[50]

The Coronation was attended by the Prime Ministers of Canada, New Zealand, Australia, South Africa and Southern Rhodesia, twenty-nine Indian princes, the Amir of Transjordan, the Chief Minister of Nepal, the Paramount Chief of Barotseland, and the Sultans of Zanzibar, Johore, Pahang, Trengganu and Negri Sembilan, and the procession included the usual array of Indian, dominion and colonial troops, who according to some observers elicited the loudest cheers from the crowds.[51]

As ever, the approach of the Coronation stimulated a flurry of music publishing, with the emphasis on royal and imperial themes. Elgar's *Coronation Ode* was re-issued in editions for female, boy and mixed voices, and with piano or orchestral accompaniment. Boosey & Hawkes issued a coronation music catalogue which advertized, among others, Mackenzie's *Britannia* overture, *Under the British Flag* – 'songs of the Empire, arranged by Kappey' – and Yvonne Adair's *Empire Suite* 'containing Assembly March, Here's a Health Unto His Majesty, Loudly Proclaim, Land of Hope and Glory, National and Patriotic Songs etc.'. Paxton & Co. advertized a new arrangement of *God Save the King*, by Herbert Pierce, *Zadok the Priest*, *Rule, Britannia* and the ceremonial march *With Pomp and Pride* by King Palmer. Arthur H. Stockwell Ltd. advertized Rubie Johnston's *Coronation Hymn*, R. Selby Cooke's song *O Noble King* and Bettie Lillie's march *Our Noble Monarch George VI*. Novello issued the *Coronation Song Book for Schools* and the official Coronation Order of Service.

The musical arrangements for the service were in the hands of Dr Ernest Bullock, organist of Westminster Abbey, in consultation with Sir Walford Davies, the Master of the King's Musick. It very much followed the pattern established by Sir Frederick Bridge for the two preceding Coronations. There was a choir drawn from the choirs of Westminster Abbey, the Chapel Royal, St Paul's Cathedral, St George's Chapel, Windsor, the Temple Church and other leading cathedrals and collegiate churches. The orchestra was made up of players from London's various orchestras.

The orchestra, conducted by Sir Adrian Boult, provided the music by which the congregation assembled. This part of the proceedings was not broadcast, unlike the service proper. Twenty-three items of music were performed during this part of the day's events. The music began with Handel's *Concerto in D*, arranged by Sir Hamilton Harty, and Gustav Holst's 'vigorous' *Marching Song* for orchestra, during which members of the royal family took their places in the Abbey. It had been decided that the arrival of foreign representatives should be accompanied by more cosmopolitan music and this included Saint-Saëns's

French Military March from his *Algerian Suite*, the prelude to *Khovanshschina* by Mussorgsky, the *Italiana*, a delicate sixteenth-century lute piece arranged by Respighi, Schubert's third *Rosamunde* entracte, the finale to Brahms's *Symphony No. 1* and the slow movement from *Symphony No. 3* by Sir Arnold Bax, who had been knighted in the Coronation Honours List.

Then the regalia was carried in, to the singing of the Lutheran hymn *Ein' feste burg*, the introit hymn *O Most Merciful* and the litany in Tallis's five-part setting, followed by the rendition by orchestra of Thomas Dunhill's 'dignified' *Canticum Fidei*, Herbert Howells's 'stirring' *The King's Herald* and the finale to Elgar's *Enigma Variations*.

The arrival of the royal Princes and Princesses was accompanied by Grieg's *Homage March* and Handel's minuet from *Saul*, the arrival of Queen Mary by Edward German's *Coronation March*, William Walton's new *Crown Imperial* march, the minuet from Handel's *Arminius*, the gavotte from Handel's *Otho* and the trumpet tune from Purcell's *Dioclesian*; and then, for the arrival of the new King and Queen, Elgar's *Imperial March*, a direct link back to the Diamond Jubilee.

The music critic H.C. Colles noted that what distinguished the Coronation of King George VI from those of George V and Edward VII was the prominence given to Tudor choral music, sung without orchestral accompaniment, a form which had undergone a major revival of interest following the English Musical Renaissance.[52] So the music for the service included William Byrd's *Creed* from his short service in English and the *Sanctus* from his Latin Mass, along with the traditional *Veni Creator Spiritus* and Handel's anthem *Zadok the Priest*. Stanford's *Gloria*, written for the Coronation of George V, was repeated, as was Parry's *I Was Glad*, in the form revised for that Coronation. For the act of homage four short pieces were selected, designed to span the centuries. They were: from the sixteenth century, Christopher Tye's 'stalwart' *O Come Ye Servants of the Lord*; from the seventeenth century, Purcell's 'intimate' *Hear My Prayer*; from the nineteenth century, Samuel Sebastian Wesley's 'melodious' *Thou Wilt Keep Him in Perfect Peace*; and, from the twentieth century, George Dyson's 'new and exceedingly effective' *O Praise God*.

The other new works along with Dyson's were Sir Edward Bairstow's introit *Let My Prayer Come Up into Thy Presence as the Incense*, Sir Walford Davies's *Confortare*, Dr W.H. Harris's 'reflective' *Offertorium* and the major new work, Vaughan Williams's *Te Deum*. Founded on traditional themes and embellished with trumpet flourishes, this highly characteristic work was approvingly described by *The Times* as a 'paean of rejoicing'.[53] The proceedings ended with the national anthem, and the royal procession left the Abbey to the strains of Elgar's *Pomp and Circumstance* marches. The fanfares throughout were the work of Dr Ernest Bullock, and were pronounced 'splendidly effective' by *The Musical Times*.[54]

But music was everywhere during Coronation Day, and we are able to get a flavour of the popular musical response to the event thanks to Mass-Observation, which was undertaking its first year's work as 'a nation-wide intelligence service', or rather an anthropological survey of the attitudes and behaviour of ordinary people. It mounted a full-scale operation to report on the preparations for 12 May, the events of the day, the activities up and down the country and individual reactions to the events. The results were published later in 1937.

The greatest innovation of the 1937 Coronation was the fact that it was broadcast by the BBC, which devoted the whole day to covering the processions to and from the Abbey as well as the service itself, with in the evening a forty-minute programme of messages of loyalty from the various countries of the Empire, the King's message to the peoples of the Empire, a coronation party featuring leading music-hall stars (Gert and Daisy, Mrs Feather, Clapham and Dwyer, The Two Leslies) and a performance of *Ye Tuneful Muses*, Purcell's 1686 'Welcome Song for His Majesty'.[55]

Mass-Observation reported that the broadcasting of the coronation has been 'the most potent means of unifying behaviour . . . It meant that a very high proportion of the population spent the day listening in and thus partaking of the central events.'[56] *The Musical Times* pronounced the broadcast day 'a triumph for the B.B.C.'.[57] As the broadcast went on, Mass-Observation reported that 'a certain number seem to have become bored and to have switched off, but others became increasingly moved, even to the point of tears (and this in the case of some of the more sceptical and hard-boiled). Music seems to have contributed a great deal to this access of interest.'[58] One of the Mass-Observers reported a female Lancashire factory-hand in her thirties saying of the Coronation's broadcast: 'This music is most stimulating. It upsets and stirs me but I like it.'[59]

It was reported that loudspeakers outside shops were pumping out songs: *Auld Lang Syne*, *It's a Long Way to Tipperary*, *Land of Hope and Glory*, *Yeomen of England* and *God Save the King*.[60] But there was also a good deal of spontaneous community singing, not least of the national anthem. It was reported that when film of the Coronation was shown in a Nottingham cinema, the audience stood 'spontaneously and naturally' during the singing of *God Save the King* in the Abbey. In a Birmingham bar, a man jumped up and began singing *God*

Save the King after the King's broadcast and everyone stood up and joined in. *God Save the King* was reported as being sung in a Swansea pub and by a torchlit procession in Prestwich.[61] *For He's a Jolly Good Fellow* was sung in Trafalgar Square and Regent Street and in a pub in Cricklewood.[62] In the streets of London and Birmingham *Land of Hope and Glory* was sung and on the day before the Coronation, in a Lancashire factory, the female machinists were 'singing (while machining) all the patriotic songs they could think of, *Land of Hope and Glory* and so on'. After work, six of them set off for London to see the Coronation. Interestingly First World War marching songs (*Tipperary, Pack Up Your Troubles*) figured strongly in the spontaneous renditions.[63] They had become a regular part of the repertoire of organized community singing events in the 1920s.

All was not sweetness and light in Coronation week. There was a bus strike in London, just as the 1911 Coronation had taken place amid a wave of strikes – docks, coalmines, railways – evidence that not the whole country had their minds on the inauguration of a new reign. But many, perhaps most, did. Philip Ziegler, analyzing the Mass-Observation evidence, concluded judiciously:

> People on the whole behaved as they might have been expected to do. Their participation in the Coronation was not as whole-hearted as the professional romantics would have had one believe, yet certainly far more enthusiastic than the cynic would find it easy to accept. Certain points seem irrefutable. Very nearly the entire adult population was aware of the Coronation and a vast majority was to some extent involved in its celebration. Of these some at least were initially hostile, but when it came to the point most of these were pleased to be participating. A genuine sense of common interest developed, transcending temporarily barriers of geography or social class. The Briton felt more conscious of being such and more proud of his nationality than had been the case for many years. He had been moved and excited by the Coronation, even though he may not have been very clear what excited him ... A deep, atavistic chord had been touched and the experience had been stimulating – even, for some, ennobling.[64]

This sense of pride extended beyond the boundaries of Britain to include the Empire. The *Birmingham Post* reflected a feeling that was experienced in many places on 12 May:

> The story of Birmingham's demonstration of loyalty to the King and Queen at their crowning is one that will be told and retold with pride in years to come. This was a day, it will be said, when England's second city showed, to the last man, woman and child, its devotion to the Throne and its pride in the Empire.[65]

The Coronation of Queen Elizabeth II, 1953

Princess Elizabeth was in Kenya, on the first stages of a dominions' tour, when she was recalled by news of the sudden death of her father King George VI on 6 February 1952. The Coronation of Queen Elizabeth II on 2 June 1953 marked not just the beginning of a new reign but of a new era, coming at the end of the period of post-war austerity. It was widely promoted as the 'New Elizabethan Age' and great hopes were expressed for an era of achievement and greatness, hopes which received a boost when Everest was conquered by a British-led expedition, news of which reached London on Coronation Day. The Queen shared this feeling, as she broadcast to Britain and the Commonwealth on the evening of Coronation Day, saying:

> I have behind me not only the splendid traditions and the annals of more than a thousand years but the living strength and majesty of the Commonwealth and Empire; of societies old and new; of lands and races different in history and origins but all, by God's will, united in spirit and in aim. Therefore I am sure that this, my Coronation, is not the symbol of power and a splendour that are gone but a declaration of our hopes for the future and for the years I may, by God's grace and mercy, be given to reign and serve you as your Queen.[66]

The day after the Coronation, *The Times* reflected on the event:

> The popular enthusiasm can never before have been so widespread and so intense. If the sense of Empire, which was so great at QUEEN VICTORIA'S golden jubilee . . . had vanished in a breathing space of time shorter than that of QUEEN VICTORIA'S own reign – a feeling of Commonwealth and community had taken its place. Yesterday's ceremonies and pageantry were both the inward and outward expression of the greatest coming together of free peoples freely associated that the world has ever seen.[67]

Constitutionally, it may have been the case that Commonwealth was replacing Empire. But despite the independence granted to India, this was still in many respects an *imperial* Coronation, and destined to be Britain's last. The souvenir programme for it, modelled directly on that for King George VI, had a title page headed by the coats of arms of the Union of South Africa, Australia, New Zealand, Canada, Pakistan, Ceylon and India (the latter out of the Empire but still in the Commonwealth), followed by the arms of forty other colonies, protectorates and dependencies and the names of ten more. Flowers from all round the Empire were gathered for the decorations. All of the countries of the Commonwealth issued special coronation stamps.

During the ceremony the Queen was arrayed in an 'Imperial Robe' and took an oath to govern the people of the United Kingdom, Canada, Australia, New Zealand, South Africa, Pakistan and Ceylon, and of her other possessions and territories. When she left the Abbey she had exchanged St Edward's Crown for the Imperial Crown. The procession back from the Abbey to Buckingham Palace included contingents from the armed forces of many colonies and Commonwealth countries. Besides the contingents from Canada, New Zealand, Australia, South Africa, Ceylon and Pakistan, there were detachments of the Royal West Africa Frontier Force, the Somaliland Scouts, the King's Own Malta Regiment, the Bermuda Rifles, the Sierre Leone Naval Volunteer Force, the Southern Rhodesia Armoured Car Regiment, the Hong Kong Auxiliary Air Force, the Falkland Islands Defence Force, the King's African Rifles, the Royal Malayan Navy, the Fiji Military Forces, the Royal Canadian Mounted Police and many more, marching to the strains of *Soldiers of the Queen*, *The British Grenadiers*, *Waltzing Matilda* and *Hearts of Oak*. There was a carriage procession of the Commonwealth Prime Ministers, which included those of Southern Rhodesia, India, South Africa, New Zealand, Australia, Canada and the United Kingdom; and a carriage procession of colonial rulers, including the Sultans of Selangor, Perak, Brunei, Johore, Zanzibar, Lahej and Kelantan, and Queen Salote of Tonga who, unlike the other rulers, insisted on driving in an open carriage, despite the rain, waving and beaming at the watching crowds. The *Daily Mirror* proclaimed her 'Next to our own Queen . . . the hit of the procession'.[68]

The Coronation provoked fervent protestations of loyalty from every part of the Empire and Commonwealth. The largest crowds ever seen in New Zealand thronged the streets of the principal cities to celebrate, and acting Prime Minister Mr Holyoake declared: 'We in the most distant of all her Majesty's dominions have always felt the deepest loyalty to the throne. It will always be so.' *The Times* reported 'the gay mood of Australians', 'Ceylon's fervour', Canada's pledge of 'fealty and service' made by Governor-General Vincent Massey and the 'warm felicitation' of the Governor-General of Pakistan: 'We all pray that your Majesty may be long spared to guide the destinies of your peoples along beneficent channcls.' Then there was a report that '[t]hroughout the British territories of south-east Asia the Coronation has been celebrated with enthusiasm and gaiety. In Government Houses and defended planters' bungalows, in Dyak long-houses and jungle camps, in clubs and humble streets, even in a detention camp for suspected Communists, people of many races and tongues joined together to show their loyalty to the Queen.'[69] There were military parades, processions, youth festivals, church services, civic

[118]

ceremonies; and, above all, millions all round the world gathered round their wireless sets to hear the coronation broadcasts.

As in the previous coronations, all of the music heard in the service in Westminster Abbey was British except for the hymn *Veni Creator Spiritus*. *The Musical Times* declared robustly:

> Let there be no quibbling about Handel's right to be called an Englishman, for he has no equal in voicing the corporate emotion of Britons on great national occasions. It was the same at the funeral of King George VI as at the Coronation of his daughter; Handel created the right atmosphere of dignity and confidence, of broad humanity and majesty, for participation in a ceremony charged with national community of feeling. And of course his anthem 'Zadok the Priest', took its inevitable place, for the seventh time at the coronation of British monarchs, at the anointing of the Queen.[70]

The composers represented stretched from Tallis to 1953, every century being represented in the music played before and after the actual service, with Sir Adrian Boult conducting the orchestra made up of the leading musicians of the day. There was *Greensleeves* from the sixteenth century; a trumpet tune by Purcell from the seventeenth; a minuet from Handel's *Fireworks Music* from the eighteenth; Elgar's *Nimrod* from the nineteenth; and Parry's *Jerusalem*, Holst's *Jupiter* and Butterworth's *Banks of Green Willow* from the twentieth century. As always there were marches: three of Elgar's *Pomp and Circumstance* marches, John Ireland's *Epic March*, Walton's *Crown Imperial* and two new ones – Walton's *Orb and Sceptre* and Sir Arnold Bax's *Coronation March*.

For the service itself, Parry's noble *I Was Glad*, composed for the Coronation of King Edward VII, and Stanford's sweeping and surging *Gloria*, composed for that of King George V, kept their places in the service, as did Tallis's *Litany* and Gibbons's *Three-Fold Amen*. Handel's *Zadok the Priest* accompanied the crowning itself. The *Credo* and *Sanctus* were by Vaughan Williams and taken from his 1923 *Communion Service in G Minor*. There were three homage anthems: the polyphonic *Rejoice in the Lord Alway* (attributed by some to Redford but by others to Anon.); Samuel Sebastian Wesley's serene *Thou Wilt Keep Him in Perfect Peace* and the Canadian Healey Willan's *O Lord Our Gouvenour*, specially composed for the occasion.

The new music included Herbert Howells's shimmering introit *Behold, O God Our Defender*, the gradual *Let My Prayer Come Up* by William H. Harris, the stirring confortare *Be Strong and of Good Courage* by George Dyson, the communion hymn *O Taste and See* by Vaughan Williams and the thrilling large-scale *Te Deum* by Sir William

Walton in his grandest manner. The national anthem was performed in Gordon Jacob's arrangement. The fanfares were all by Sir Ernest Bullock, who like J.E. Borland in 1911, contrived to include the Scottish tune *Montrose*.

There was one innovation in the musical arrangements, proposed by Vaughan Wiliams and endorsed by the Archbishop of Canterbury. This was for a congregational hymn to be sung during the offertorium. So Vaughan Williams made a new arrangement of *The Old Hundredth* with a trumpet descant. *The Musical Times* reported that 'the whole Abbey was flooded with the unison of the great hymn. The innovation was thus triumphantly justified.'[71] The music for the service itself, with its choir of 400, was under the direction of Dr William McKie, organist of Westminster Abbey, who was ultimately responsible for all the musical arrangements. *The Musical Times* reported that they went 'without a hitch. They might, like the choice of music, have been different; they could hardly have been bettered.'[72] If it was the last imperial coronation, it may *musically* have been the best, combining the finest compositions of previous coronations with some striking new music. The combination of Parry, Elgar, Handel, Vaughan Williams, Stanford and Walton ensured a musical texture for the pageantry, both secular and spiritual, that verged on the sublime.

The Archbishop of Canterbury, the Earl Marshal, the Prime Minister and the Cabinet had all agreed that there should be no cameras within the Abbey. But they were overruled by the Queen, who insisted that the ceremony be televised. It proved to be one of the great television events of the century. Every outside broadcast camera the BBC possessed was deployed and new transmitters were rushed into service. There was a surge in sales of television sets; tele-parties were staged and television owners invited in neighbours and relatives to watch the event. The service was relayed by loudspeaker to the crowds outside and was filmed for the newsreels and for the official Technicolor feature film of the event, *A Queen Is Crowned*, with its poetic narrative by Christopher Fry reverently intoned by Sir Laurence Olivier. Yet the majority of the population watched the event on television: 56 per cent of the adult population watched it on television, with a further 32 per cent listening to it on radio, a total of 88 per cent, making it the most widely seen and heard coronation in history.[73] Typically, opinion polls revealed that in February 1953 only 44 per cent of the population intended to watch the Coronation; by April this was up to 69 per cent and on the day was at least 88 per cent.

Popular music played its part in the celebrations. Dickie Valentine had a top-ten hit in June 1953 with the simple sentimental ballad *In a Golden Coach*:

> In a golden coach,
> There's a heart of gold,
> Driving through old London town,
> With the sweetest Queen
> The world's ever seen,
> Wearing her golden crown.
> As she drives in state,
> Through the palace gate
> Her beauty the whole world will see,
> In a golden coach
> There's a heart of gold
> That belongs to you and me.

Mass-Observation reported people singing the song in pubs and the *Daily Mirror* recorded that as the Queen and Duke of Edinburgh drove along Parnell Road, Poplar, on their first drive in public after the Coronation procession, they were serenaded by a choir of East End boys and girls, dressed in red, white and blue, and singing *In a Golden* Coach.[74]

The Coronation also inspired the composition and publication of *The Queen Elizabeth Waltz, A Waltz for the Queen, The Windsor Waltz, Coronation Rag* and *Queen of Everyone's Heart.*[75] *Crown Her Queen*, with words by Ernest Boyd Jones and music by Edward St Quentin, contained a verse with imperial overtones:

> O'er land and sea, from dawn to set of sun
> Borne on the breeze, her tale of 'Duty Done',
> Let nations bow, and sound from shore to shore
> Allegiance now as in the days of yore,
> So to the heavens glorious, send we a glad refrain
> 'Send her e'er victorious, The Queen! Long may she reign.'

Francis, Day and Hunter's *Coronation Album*, however, looked further back, including *Soldiers of the Queen, The British Grenadiers, Here's a Health Unto Her Majesty, Rule, Britannia, Land of My Fathers, Hearts of Oak, God Save the Queen* and *Auld Lang Syne.* The crowds in the streets spontaneously sang *Land of Hope and Glory*, and *There'll Always Be an England* was sung in pubs.[76] Thus in cathedral, pub and street, music sacred and secular, highbrow and lowbrow, was an integral part of the coronation celebrations, quickening the emotions, affirming allegiances, linking Empire, crown and people.

The jubilees

As David Cannadine has shown, by contrast with the sparse, irregular and badly managed spectacle of the earlier Victorian period, the grand tradition of British pageantry was invented in the last decades of the century, epitomized by the Diamond Jubilee of Queen Victoria and her funeral in 1901, the Coronation and Funeral of King Edward VII, the Coronation and Durbar of King George V.[77] In such events, says Cannadine, 'meticulous planning, popular enthusiasm, widespread reporting and unprecedented splendour were successfully allied'.[78] They underlined and affirmed the role of the monarchy as the symbol of nation and empire.

Queen Victoria's Golden Jubilee, 1887

The Golden Jubilee of 1887, eclipsed in the folk memory by the magnificence of the Diamond Jubilee ten years later, was nevertheless a turning-point in the history of the monarchy. The seclusion of the Queen following the death of Prince Albert had led to increasing discontent, but her proclamation as Empress of India in 1877 initiated a process of re-entry into public life that was completed by the Golden Jubilee. *The Times* declared:

> No constitutional monarch has shown a more consistent respect for popular liberties or a clearer conception of royal duties . . . Britons, in spite of a confirmed habit of grumbling, look upon their ancient institutions with steadfast affection and reverence, and their attachment to the monarchy has been blended with respect for the character of the QUEEN.[79]

A great throng of European royalty (the Kings of Belgium, Greece, Denmark and Saxony and the Crown Princes of Germany, Austria–Hungary and Portugal), plus a gaggle of Indian Rajahs and Maharajahs, descended on London. Newspapers noted the extension of the Empire since the Queen's accession in 1837. The year was marked by extensive charity fund-raising, in particular for funds for the Queen's Jubilee Nursing Institute and the Imperial Institute. The Queen backed the Imperial Institute. The Prince of Wales wrote to the Lord Mayor of London:

> I have ascertained that a public memorial which would illustrate the progress her Empire has made during her Reign would be more gratifying to Her Majesty than any personal or private tribute; and that the form which the Queen would most wish such a memorial should take would be an institution illustrative of the Arts, Manufactures and Commerce of Her Majesty's Colonial and Indian Empire.[80]

On 20 June the Queen arrived in London from Windsor and drove through cheering crowds to Buckingham Palace for a luncheon party for fifty royal persons. On 21 June she drove to Westminster Abbey for the official Thanksgiving service at which the choir sang the *Te Deum* composed by Prince Albert. There was a family lunch at the Palace with a march-past of naval bluejackets. In the evening there was a Jubilee banquet at the Palace, the Queen in a dress patterned with roses, thistles and shamrocks, and the next day, 22 June, there was the distribution of Jubilee Medals to the visiting monarchs, a delegation of ladies to present an address and 3 million signatures from those contributing to the women's Jubilee offering, and a visit to Hyde park for a jamboree of 26,000 school children, each of whom received a mug with the Queen's portrait on it. Six military bands provided light music, the children sang *God Save the Queen* and a large balloon inscribed with the name 'Victoria' floated upwards into the sky, leading one child to exclaim: 'Look! There's Queen Victoria going to heaven.'[81] Back at Windsor, amid crowds and bands, there was an unveiling by the Queen of a statue of herself, then dinner at the castle where she was serenaded by Eton boys. Over the next four weeks, there was a review of 28,000 Volunteers in Hyde Park, the laying of the foundation-stone of the Imperial Institute, a review of the army at Aldershot and the navy at Spithead, and a garden party given by the Prime Minister Lord Salisbury at his home, Hatfield. The Queen wrote in her diary at the end of 1887:

> Never can I forget this brilliant year, so full of marvellous kindness, loyalty and devotion of so many millions which really I could hardly have expected.[82]

The Queen had been extremely anxious about her Gorden Jubilee, but huge crowds gathered everywhere she went cheering enthusiastically. Society sculptor Lord Ronald Gower recorded his impressions of the day in his diary:

> *23rd June.*
> The great day – that of the Jubilee – has come and gone, and its triumphant success has been prodigious. Certainly the 21st of June 1887 must count as a red-letter day in English History, one to be gratefully remembered by all loyal Britons! . . . Piccadilly looked like a huge flower garden. London looked radiantly happy and the crowd most good-humoured and determined to enjoy itself thoroughly. When at length the Queen came, the enthusiasm was intense. I believe Her Majesty never looked more cheerful. The sight, the procession, all was worthy of the great occasion, and it was impossible for the most fault-finding to pick a hole in any of the arrangements of this great and superb show of Royalty and People.[83]

For the official Thanksgiving service, the procession of carriages containing Kings and Princes reached the Abbey to be greeted by peals of church bells, thunderous applause and the national anthem. Inside, there was a fanfare, the national anthem played by Dr Bridge on the abbey organ, a Handel overture as the Queen processed down the aisle, the singing of the Prince Consort's *Te Deum*; and, as she left, the march from Mendelssohn's incidental music to *Athalie*. There was a strong Germanic element here, admittedly; but Handel was a naturalized Briton, the Prince Consort was the Queen's revered husband and Mendelssohn her favourite composer. Nevertheless it was an indication that British music was not yet fully accepted for such occasions.

Biographies, poems and essays apotheosized Victoria as an ideal ruler, wife and mother. It marked the transformation in the fortunes of the monarchy from the nadir of the 1860s. A Jubilee song, *I Will Be Good*, was composed on the words allegedly uttered by the Queen upon receiving news of her accession, with the line:

> Let ev'ry English maiden make this her frequent prayer,
> that she the same high purpose may with her sovereign share.

Outside London, towns established funds for civic improvements in honour of the Jubilee; on Jubilee Day most towns had a service of Thanksgiving and a public event for the children or the poor, or both, and there were 350 Jubilee bonfires in the evening.

Music was a strong feature of the festivities, though *Hazell's Annual* (1887) thought that only two notable works emerged – Sir Alexander Mackenzie's *Jubilee Ode* and Dr Frederick Bridge's anthem written expressly for the Westminster Abbey service.[84]

The *Jubilee Ode* was the highlight of the Jubilee Music Festival at the Crystal Palace on 22 June. It had been composed by Mackenzie to words by Joseph Bennett at the request of the Crystal Palace Company. It was also intended for performance throughout the Empire on Jubilee Day, and the *Musical Times* declared it to be 'in some sort an imperial work'.[85] Mackenzie recalled that it was 'written, printed and despatched in time to be given simultaneously in Canada, Australia, Trinidad and Cape Colony'.[86] It was conducted at the Crystal Palace by August Manns and took forty-five minutes to perform. Mackenzie noted that although the performance was 'excellent . . . London offered greater attractions on the great day, and the concert was not largely attended'.[87]

The Musical Times thought the result 'splendid' and 'cleverly constructed', and noted that Bennett had achieved in his language 'tones of honest patriotism rather than courtier-like flattery' and that Mackenzie's music had a 'tone of manly vigour and honesty of purpose' which bore 'testimony to the sincerity with which the work had been undertaken and fulfilled'. It went on: 'The various sentiments expressed in the words are well represented in the music, loyalty to the sovereign, congratulations upon the prosperity of the vast Empire over which she rules, and a tender reference to the domestic virtues and affections of the sovereign as a wife, as a friend, as a mother, and as a Queen.' It thus reflects the three-part apotheosis that the jubilee represented.

The opening chorus proclaiming the news of the Jubilee and calling for its celebration throughout the Empire, *For Fifty Years Our Queen*, began with a passage in unison 'as if to show that there is but one accord in the offering of congratulations'. The 'joyous' phrase 'wild clanging bells and thunderous cannon' was expressed in jubilant strains which gave the chorus appropriate dramatic emphasis. The tenor solo, *O Queen, the People of Thine Home Lands Greet Thee*, which followed was designed to 'offer a placid contrast to the grandeur of the choral invocation which it follows'; but also, in conveying the affectionate greetings of the homelands, it declared an end to party strife for the duration of the Jubilee. As sung by Edward Lloyd, it had 'an exciting effect upon the audience'.

After this came the 'picturesque' chorus *Now Let the Long Procession Pass* in which the dominions, colonies, dependencies and, finally, India passed before the throne. Each of the colonies was represented by a characteristic musical phrase: sleigh bells accompanied the reference to 'sons of the Dominion' (Canada); 'semi-barbaric' melodies accompanied the reference to 'hill and plain 'neath Afric's burning sun'; and oriental tunes the reference to 'India's dusky sons'. In the section of the work which concentrated on the domestic life and personal virtues of the sovereign, *The Musical Times* declared that the composer had 'made his best endeavour to import beauty and life as an undercurrent of instrumental tone'. The result was 'some of the happiest and most inspired portions of his labour sung beautifully and expressively by Madame Emma Albani, who was very well received by the audience'. Finally 'A fine chorus, with a broad melodic theme', led up to the national anthem, 'newly and vigorously harmonised' and on this occasion accompanied by a discharge of cannon outside the building, 'booming in rhythmical cadence with fine effect'. *The Musical Times* thought it 'one of the most successful pieces of descriptive writing as yet produced by the composer'.[88] The *Daily Telegraph* thought the unaccompanied chorus prayer *Lord of Life and Light and Glory* 'solidly written and laden with rich yet not recondite harmonies', and the lead up to the national anthem to have been 'constructed with rare art . . . and [to work] on the feelings with immense power till "God save the Queen" comes in as an ultimate expression'. *The Standard* reported: 'The reception of the Jubilee Ode proved unmistakably that it had thoroughly taken hold of public favour and this is a fact agreeable to note seeing that the work is entirely of home growth.'[89] The *Ode*'s success at the Crystal Palace was followed by performances at the Norwich festival and at the Novello Oratorio Concert at St James's Hall. One of the hits of the Jubilee concert given by artists of the Royal Italian Opera at the Albert Hall on 2 July was Emma Albani singing her solo from the *Jubilee Ode*, conducted by the composer. It was 'enthusiastically received' and was the only English piece in the programme.

Mackenzie's *Ode* completely eclipsed all the others, notably *Carmen Saeculare*, written by the Poet Laureate Lord Tennyson and set to music, at Tennyson's request, by Charles V. Stanford. *The Musical Times* did not mince its words, declaring that 'nothing less musical or less adapted for music can be conceived. Poor in matter, awkward in structure, it might well be the despair of musicians.'[90] But it concluded that Stanford was to be congratulated 'upon the general manner in which he has discharged a task made irksome and well-nigh hopeless by circumstances beyond his control'.[91]

Tennyson's themes were similar to Bennett's and Mackenzie's. He praised the Queen's kindliness and womanliness, called upon 'the patient children of Albion, you, Canadian, Indian, Australasian, African', to raise their voices in praise of her Jubilee, hailed 'Fifty years of ever-broadening commerce! Fifty years of ever-brightening science! Fifty years of ever-widening Empire!' and called for the creation of an Imperial Institute, 'rich in symbol, in ornament, which may speak to . . . all the centuries after us, of this great ceremonial'. Interestingly Stanford reveals that it was at the Queen's request that Tennyson added the final lines – which Stanford deemed the 'finest in the poem'[92] –

> Are there thunders moaning in the distance?
> Are there spectres moving in the darkness?
> Trust the Hand of Light will lead her people.
> Till the thunders pass, the spectres vanish,
> And the Light is Victor, and the darkness
> Dawns into the Jubilee of the Ages.

So instead of ending on a triumphal note of celebration, it ends with the hope of God's aid during all the troubles of the world. It was performed at a State Concert at Buckingham Palace, where the orchestra and singers outnumbered the audience.

Stanford remained tactfully silent about the problems he faced setting Tennyson's lines, which *The Musical Times* pronounced 'very irregular, in some places quite fragmentary'. It was impressed by his attempt to give the piece unity by the use of a single melodic motif, set in the short orchestral opening, repeated with variations of form and pace during and worked up into a dramatic climax at the end of the piece. *The Musical Times* declared: 'Dr Stanford is seen at his best in these closing divisions. The words helped him but little, yet he appears at the full height of his great argument in music there, for his choral writing is of the loftiest.'[93]

The flood of jubilee odes stretched from Mackenzie's and Stanford's to less well-known but equally well-received efforts. The *Jubilee Ode* written for baritone solo and chorus by W. Bellyse Baildon, BA (Cantab.), and set to music by W. Harrison was presented to the Queen by the Pen and Pencil Club of Edinburgh. *The Musical Times* pronounced the words 'quaint, scholarly and original, qualities which are reflected and intensified in the music', and declared that it 'has all the effect of earnestness produced by music, which is the outcome of the labour of love'. The *Jubilee Ode*, published by Novello, with words by Juliette Heale and music by Helena Heale proved for *The Musical Times* that the composer 'possessed more than ordinary ability – far more, indeed, than the majority of lady musicians'. The text, 'an address of congratulation to Queen and people', was commended 'for its sound vigorous diction and freedom from all suggestion of fulsomeness'. Musically it consisted of one extended choral movement in 3/4 time, with a subsection which occurred twice in B flat: 'the principal theme, a broad Handelian figure, is eventually made the basis of a fugue which is developed at considerable length' and 'which . . . would do credit to any living composer'.[94]

But there was much other music, too. Sir Alexander Mackenzie composed a patriotic song for solo and chorus, *The Empire Flag*, to words by Stuart Reid and William Alexander Barrrett.

The Empire flag shall proudly brave the storms that fill the sky,
From war's rude shocks, from crested wave, from faction's party cry.
In peace or strife, for death or life, its folds remain unfurll'd;
Serene on high the flag shall fly, The mistress of the world.
An English tongue its praise shall sing, while loyal spirits call;
Nor Scot, Colonial, Kelt are we, But Britons one and all.

From far Australia's sunny land, the pulse beats warm and strong;
On Afric's shores, Canadian seas, is heard the patriot song:
In peace or strife, in death or life, we boast of English blood,
And England's Empire flag we'll bear thro' field and fire and flood,
An English tongue, its praise shall sing, while loyal spirits call,
Nor Scot, Colonial, Kelt are we, But Britons one and all.

From flowing Ganges' sacred founts, from islands of the main,
From rocky Zealand's misty mounts, is heard the fervent strain,

In peace or strife, for death or life, the banner proudly waves,
O'er worldwide Britain's happy soil, where free men live, not slaves.
An English tongue its praise shall sing, while loyal spirits call,
Nor Scot, Colonial, Kelt are we, But Britons one and all.
From North to South, from East to West, let hand to hand be given,
And from each loyal English breast, This song ascends to heaven,
In peace or strife, for death or life, while shines the radiant sun,
We'll guard each fold of the Empire flag, And stand or fall as one.
An English tongue its praise shall sing, While loyal spirits call;
Nor Scot, Colonial, Kelt are we, But Britons one and all.

The Musical Times (1 May 1887) declared:

ENGLAND possesses a large treasury of patriotic songs, most of which deal with the principle of loyalty in the abstract. These are known chiefly for their poetry, and rarely because of the music with which many are associated. It has been stated that two only live in the minds of the people – namely, 'Rule Britannia' and 'God Save the Queen' . . . all who know the literature of the country as exemplified in its songs can furnish proofs to the contrary in abundance if they are required. Additions are constantly made to the list of patriotic songs. The present year has seen many new ones inspired by the interesting occasion which is shortly to be celebrated. Dr MacKenzie's song, 'The Empire Flag', is a distinct and independent creation, for while the majority of the patriotic effusions recently produced have reference to that one event, they will be no longer available when it is past, and will enjoy no more than a local popularity, while his song is of a character which may secure a permanent acceptance for it. The words repudiate the notion that the various colonies are distinct nations owing allegiance to one power, but emphasise the unity of feeling which should belong to all under the protection of the Empire flag. The music is bold, spirited, and original, and enforces the manly, earnest expression of the words. Without suggesting any common form of sequence, the melody is impressive and easy to learn. Both words and music will be found available and appropriate for all gatherings of Englishmen throughout the world, especially of those who desire to see the Empire supported in its integrity, by the hands, in the hearts, and by the voices of the people.[95]

Novello published Dr Jacob Bradford's *The Song of the Jubilee*, a 'Thanksgiving cantata' for solo voices, chorus, orchestra and organ. *The Musical Times* commented that 'the multiplication of musical pieces composed to celebrate the fiftieth year of Her Majesty's reign may be accepted as a convincing proof of the acknowledged eloquence of the art to express the popular feeling'.[96] Bradford was a composer of an oratorio, numerous cantatas and anthems. The music of *The Song of the Jubilee* was said to be 'in every respect sympathetic with the subject it illustrates'. It opened with a soprano recitative, followed after a short instrumental introduction, by a *Te Deum* and chorale, to the tune *Gotha* composed by the Prince Consort. Then came a 'well-written and melodious solo' – *Grant the Queen a Long Life* – the stately movement of which was deemed to express the words with 'becoming dignity'. In the chorus which followed, the national anthem was 'effectively' deployed, the theme being treated as a fugue with some 'admirable' contrapuntal writing. A brief choral recitative for tenors and basses was followed by a duet, for soprano and tenor, with the quartet *The Queen Shall Rejoice* which was also commended 'for the easy flow of the vocal parts'; and the final chorus and fugue, *All Praise and Thanks to God*, formed a 'worthy' climax to a work which showed 'an intimate knowledge of the best school of sacred composers'.

Among other songs inspired by the Jubilee were *Who's For the Queen?* (words by F.E. Weatherly and music by Gabriel Davies); the grand choral march *God's Blessing on Our Sovereign Rest* by William J. Young with words by T.B. Leigh; William Hollingsworth's *Here's Life and Health to England's Queen*; Thomas Smith's anthem *He Set the Royal Crown Upon Her Head and Made her Queen*; and Dr J.C. Bridge's part-song *Great Britain's Sons and Daughters*, incorporating *Rule, Britannia* and the national anthem. *Victoria* was an ode for the Queen's Jubilee expressly composed for the leading singer of the day, Sims Reeves, by William Carter with words by Astley H. Baldwin, and sung by Reeves and Mary Davies with William Carter's choir at the Royal Albert Hall. It was truly imperial and was hailed by the *Standard* and the *Daily Chronicle*. The *Standard* (1 January 1887) wrote:

> As composition the Ode has considerable merit, the effect of the chorus in the repetition of Her Majesty's name at the end of each verse is good, and its performance during the coming year of celebration is likely to become general . . . Miss Mary Davies was rewarded by a storm of applause and a hearty encore.

The *Daily Chronicle* (1 January, 1887) reported:

> The Ode has bold and flowing tunefulness, together with a patriotic ring that must carry it into public favour during the next few months. Both words and music have indeed all the main striking claims to popularity, not the least important characteristics being the smoothness of the musical phrases and the adaptability of the work to small or large choral societies.

The ode ran as follows:

> All honour to thee, Empress Queen!
> So blest of heaven thy reign hath been,

That day by day, from shore to shore,
Thy subjects love thee more and more,
    Victoria!

For fifty years thine Empire Grand
Has gathered might from land to land:
Thy name is loved from sea to sea
And everywhere men honour thee,
    Victoria!

From Canada to India fair
We all for thee would do and dare:
Australia, Cape – all join to own
The glorious lustre of thy throne,
    Victoria!

O noble, tender, true and pure,
Thy fame for ages shall endure,
Thou truly great and wise and good,
Thou perfect type of womanhood,
    Victoria!

Thy people's love and faith are thine,
Far, far beyond all gems they shine:
Beloved Monarch – Mother – Wife,
God bless thee with eternal life,
    Victoria!

William Parker Robinson's part-song *O Noble Queen of England*, with music by T. Simpson, was pronounced 'very suitable for Sunday School marching or for brass bands'. Sir Herbert Oakeley set to music a jubilee lyric by the Earl of Rosslyn, *The Love that Lasts Forever*. Dr John Stainer composed both words and music for a madrigal for five voices, *The Triumph of Victoria*. *The Musical Times* (1 January 1887) thought the words 'thoroughly reflective of the feeling of the people' and that the music had 'all the bold simplicity which should characterize national compositions, combined with that true flavour of the madrigal which appeals to all music-loving Englishmen, and most appropriately recalls the day when, in these works, the virtues of a former Queen were glorified by the native composers of her reign'. It declared that:

The broad diatonic harmonies throughout the composition, the several interesting points of imitation, and the sympathetic colouring of the words will certainly make it a general favourite; and we conscientiously recommend it, not only as a worthy musical tribute to a Sovereign who for fifty years has reigned in the hearts of her subjects, but as a valuable contribution to the repertory of choral music.

The Musical Times celebrated the link between religion and patriotism when it declared: 'The Jubilee Services in Westminster Abbey, in St Paul's Cathedral, and in many places in Great Britain and the Colonies, demonstrated the value of music as a handmaid of religion, and as one of the most distinctive means of intensifying the expressions of loyalty.'[97] It had earlier declared the effect of the Jubilee on 'the usually calm and placid atmosphere of the organ loft' to be 'not a matter for surprise or regret' (1 May 1887) and proceeded to review the anthems inspired by the Jubilee.[98]

Hazell's Annual declared Dr Frederick Bridge's anthem *Blessed Be the Lord* to be one of only two pieces likely to survive from the Jubilee. 'Nothing could be less pretentious . . . and nothing more appropriate', thought *The Musical Times*. It opened quietly with a chorus 'in the orthodox church style', but then there was a dramatic transition from E to C as the organ launched into the first phrase of the national anthem. Later the Prince Consort's chorale *Gotha* was introduced as a *canto fermo* for bass solo with the chorus supplying the counterpoint. Bridge's anthem closed with a second rendition of the national anthem, this time in E. It was thus a musical encapsulation of monarchy, Protestantism and national identity. F.W. Hird's *Behold, O God, Our Defender*, consisting of several short movements with no solo voices, was 'spirited and melodious'. But A.M. Friedlander's *Hear, O God*, with its rondo form and recurring hymn-like theme, was pronounced 'decidedly commonplace'. Philip Armes's *Rejoice in the Lord*, written at the request of the Dean and Chapter of Durham, elicited from *The Musical Times* the comment that Dr Armes had 'risen to the occasion, and produced a piece worthy to take high rank among Jubilee music'. It began with a 'bold and vigorous chorus, developed at considerable length', and then a treble solo in 9/8 time, 'extremely refined and melodious', and finally an effective concluding chorus even more 'spirited and energetic' than the first. Dr John Stainer had two contributions. *Let Every Soul Be Subject Unto the Higher Powers* took its main text from Romans 13:1, which is a fundamental Biblical justification for the existing earthly hierarchy: 'Let every soul be subject unto the higher powers, for there is no power but of God; the powers that be are ordained of God.' *The Musical Times* thought the scoring 'full of picturesque colour' and the words 'powerfully and expressively set'.[99] It was constructed by Stainer as a series of interchanges with the solo voice or the choir answered by the full chorus.

It included a setting for solo and choir, with repeats for choir and congregation, of Godfrey Thring's hymn inspired by the Romans' text:

> O King of Kings, Thy blessing shed
> On our anointed Sovereign's head
> And looking from Thy holy heaven
> Protect the crown Thyself hast given.
> Her may we honour and obey,
> Uphold her right and lawful sway;
> Remembering that the powers that be
> Are ministers ordained of Thee.

It culminated in the national anthem, 'brought in so cleverly and with so much musicianly grace that no other Finale seems possible'.[100]

Let Every Soul Be Subject Unto the Higher Powers was one of the highlights of the Thanksgiving service held at St Paul's Cathedral on 23 June. It was attended by the Lord Mayor and city dignitaries. Stainer conducted the service, which included, along with his own anthem, Handel's *Dettingen Te Deum*, written in honour of the last victory in which a British monarch personally led his army into battle. The congregation was invited to join in *God Save the Queen*, which they did with 'a heartiness and fervour that it was impossible not to hear unmoved'. Stainer's second anthem, *Lord, Thou Art God*, was strictly speaking not for the Jubilee but for the Sons of the Clergy Festival. But Stainer included an optional coda utilizing the national anthem for the Jubilee. *The Musical Times* thought it 'emphatically one of the best efforts of the composer' with its 'fine and striking' opening chorus, 'beautiful' tenor solo and 'lengthy and splendidly worked out chorus'.

Also reviewed was Charles H. Lloyd's *Give the Lord the Honour Due*, intended for the Festival of Christ Church Diocesan Choral Association in New Zealand. With two lengthy choruses and an intervening trio, with a good deal of elaboration in both voice parts and accompaniment, *The Musical Times* implied that it might be beyond the capabilities of 'colonial church singers'. Sir George Elvey's *Behold, O God, Our Defender*, Handelian in style and 'distinctly of the old school', according to *The Musical Times*, was nevertheless spirited and well written, and 'shows a rare knowledge of the effects to be gained by comparatively simple and straightforward means'.

In addition to these great national pieces, local church composers were hard at work making their contributions. William Haynes composed his *Festal Te Deum and Jubilate* for the Jubilee service in Priory Church, Malvern; George Prior his *Thanksgiving Te Deum* for St George's Church, Ramsgate, and Dr William Spark his jubilee anthem

Behold, O God, Our Defender for the Great Stockport Sunday School Festival.

Many churches opted to repeat the music programme of the jubilee service in Westminster Abbey. But others made their own musical programmes for their Thanksgiving services. In London, for instance, St Agnes's Church, Kennington, opted on 26 June for Handel's *Zadok the Priest*, Stanford's *Te Deum* and Sullivan's *Processional March*. St John's Church, Fulham, chose Bridge's Jubilee anthem *Blessed Be the Lord Thy God*; Palmer's *Service in F*, Tallis's *Responses*, and concluded with Costa's version of the national anthem with an additional verse by Mr Baring-Gould to mark the special occasion. St John's, Waterloo Road, featured Handel's *The King Shall Rejoice*, Smart's *Te Deum* and Mendelssohn's march from *Athalie*.

Other churches put on special Jubilee festivals. St Columba's Choral Society gave a special recital at St Columba's (Church of Scotland), Pont Street on 1 July, performing Sullivan's *Festival Te Deum* and Handel's *The King Shall Rejoice* with Weber's *Jubilee Overture* performed on the organ. On 28 June, St Stephen's Choral Society gave a Jubilee Concert at St Stephen's Church, Walworth, performing the Jubilee Anthems by Bridge and Stainer, Weber's *Jubilee Cantata*, the *Hallelujah Chorus*, Jackson's *Te Deum*, and Costa's national anthem arrangement.

It was not just Britain that rejoiced, but the Empire as a whole. There were Jubilee services at the British churches in Paris and at the Embassy Church (21 June) where the service included Mr McMaster's specially composed *Jubilee March*. The Jubilee service held on 21 June at the Collegiate Church of St Paul, Malta, was notable for all the denominations of English Protestants on the island combining in common worship.

A national Jubilee concert at the Albert Palace on 20 June, consisting of several compositions by the Prince Consort, included a version of the national anthem sung in five Indian languages. A Hebrew version of *God Save the Queen* (*El Sh'mor Hamalko*) was prepared by D.M. Davis, Choirmaster of the West End and St John's Wood Synagogue, for use in synagogues throughout the Empire in Jubilee Year, and was accepted by the Queen.[101] Ernest Slater, Organist of St Paul's Cathedral, Calcutta, composed the Jubilee anthem *All the Kings of the Earth Shall Praise Thee* for the State Thanksgiving service in St Paul's Cathedral, Calcutta, on 16 February 1887.

A 'Grand Jubilee Concert' in the Town Hall, Grahamstown, South Africa (20 June) included Handel's *Zadok the Priest* and the oratorio *Judas Maccabaeus*. At Bandon, County Cork, two concerts were given by the Young Men's Association in honour of the Jubilee (28 and 29

June). A large orchestra and an eighty-voice choir performed *O Noble Queen* by T. Simpson, the *Royal Choral March* by William Young, *Great Britain's Sons and Daughters* by J.C. Bridge, *Advance, Britannia* by West, Mackenzie's *The Empire Flag* and the *Hallelujah Chorus*. The Band of the Royal Munster Fusiliers played selections including *War March of the Priests* from *Athalie*. The national anthem was sung at the beginning and the end, 'the whole audience rising and joining in heartily'. An address congratulating the Queen on fifty years of a reign marked by the 'wise fulfilment of her duties as Constitutional ruler' was adopted and would be presented to the Queen by the Earl of Bandon.

In Port of Spain, Trinidad, a Jubilee concert for the benefit of the poor was given on 25 June at the Prince's Building and included Handel's *Coronation Anthem*, Mackenzie's *Jubilee Ode*, the national anthem and Mendelssohn's *Hymn of Praise*. MacKenzie's *Ode* was also performed at the Exhibition Building, Melbourne, by the Philharmonic Society under George Peake. 'There was a very large attendance and the occasion had something of State dignity and importance', reported *The Musical Times*. It won general praise in the press, with the exception of the *Melbourne Age* whose regular music critic, Mr Plumpton, had produced his own *Jubilee Ode* which was done in the same programme.[102]

In Toronto, Canada, on 30 June a Jubilee service at the Metropolitan Church with Mr Torrington's amateur orchestra and the United City Choir included the national anthem, the chorus and three solos from the *Jubilee Ode* by Mackenzie, Dr Bridge's *Jubilee Anthem* and a jubilee song specially composed by Mr Torrington.[103]

In Wellington, New Zealand, on 17 June, the Harmonic Club's concert included Weber's *Jubilee Overture* and the official Jubilee service held at St Paul's Cathedral Church included Dr Stainer's *Jubilee Anthem*, *Zadok the Priest*, and *God Save the Queen* 'which the whole congregation sang with great fervour'.[104] The Demarara Musical Society on 19 September performed extracts from the *Jubilee Ode* of Mackenzie, borrowing the score from the Music Society in Port of Spain, Trinidad, which had performed the complete *Ode*, and on 16 September a Jubilee concert was held at the Philharmonic Hall in the presence of the Governor with a selection from the *Jubilee Ode* of Mackenzie, Mackenzie's *The Empire Flag*, Dr J.C. Bridge's new Jubilee chorus *Great Britain's Sons and Daughters*, Alfred J. Caldicott's new Jubilee song *The Queen, God Bless Her*, Purcell's *Come If You Dare*, and selections from Sullivan's operas, 'all showing a very laudable ambition to make the concert as thoroughly characteristic of the occasion as possible, and to give really national and truly patriotic music the prominence it deserves'.[105]

But the absence of appropriate British orchestral music was evidenced by the final concert of the Philharmonic Society's season (25 June) and by the Richter concert on 20 June. The Philharmonic concert, conducted by Sir Arthur Sullivan, comprised Mendelssohn's *Italian Symphony*; Sullivan's *Overture di Ballo*; and Beethoven's *Piano Concerto in C* played by 10-year old virtuoso Josef Hoffman. It included in reference to the Jubilee Weber's *Jubilee Overture* in which, noted *The Musical Times*, 'the English national anthem is introduced with fine effect'.[106] The year, 1887, was also the centenary of Weber's birth. In point of fact the *Jubilee Overture* was composed by Weber in 1818 to celebrate the fiftieth year of the reign of Frederick Augustus III, King of Saxony. The tune identified by *The Musical Times* as *God Save the Queen* was in fact the Saxon national anthem *Heil dir im Siegerkranz* which was set to the tune of the English anthem. The Richter concert also included it along with Mendelssohn's *Scottish Symphony*, Wagner's *Siegfried Idyll* and Beethoven's *Leonora Overture*.

The Ashford Orchestral Society gave their eleventh popular concert on 25 June and included *God Save the Queen, Rule, Britannia* and H. Smart's *Victoria*. A grand Jubilee Concert at Herne Bay Town Hall (9 June) included the national anthem, *Rule, Britannia*, MacKenzie's *The Empire Flag*, Stainer's madrigal *The Triumph of Victoria* and E.A. Cruttenden's *The Queen, God Bless Her* duet with harmonium obligato. The Salisbury Vocal Union (14 April) performed William Carter's *Jubilee Ode* and Stainer's *The Triumph of Victoria* and the fourth and last of Mr Stockley's concerts in Birmingham (21 April) included Weber's *Jubilee Overture*.

In Altrincham, Cheshire, a free concert was given in the Market Hall on Jubilee Day by a specially assembled orchestra of local musicians, who performed a programme of songs, glees, solos and orchestral selections. The highlight of the programme was a new march, *Victoria Regina*, composed by the orchestra's conductor Mr D. Colley. It combined the tune of the national anthem with musical phrases from the chorales *Coburg* and *Gotha*, composed by the Prince Consort and utilized by special permission of the Queen, the effect being 'very impressive'.[107]

Not all composers were willing to jump on the jubilee bandwagon. Hans Richter invited Hubert Parry to write a Jubilee overture for his concert series. Parry replied: 'If I had not the most invincible repugnance to it I should gladly do it . . . But what with Jubilee buttons and

Jubilee cards, and Jubilee Anthems and Jubilee hymn tunes, and Jubilee bunkum of all sorts, I cannot bring myself to join the company.'[108] Richter proposed instead a performance of his *Cambridge* symphony and Parry made extensive revisions for the performance which brought the symphony an ovation from the audience. But a new work was forthcoming. Charles Stanford wanted to perform Parry's *The Glories of Our Blood and State* as part of the Bach Choir's concert celebrating the Jubilee. But the committee thought that the line 'sceptre and crown must tumble down' inappropriate for such an occasion and so a new piece was commissioned. The result was *Blest Pair of Sirens* derived from Milton's *Ode at a Solemn Music*. 'Blest pair of sirens' became 'one of the most popular English vocal works of the age'.[109] Performed on 17 May 1887 at St James's Hall, it received a rapturous reception and many have dated the birth of the English Musical Renaissance to this occasion. Brahms, in particular the *German Requiem* and *Song of Destiny* was always an influence on Parry – and some critics claimed to find *Blest Pair* Brahmsian.[110] But Parry had moved beyond Brahms to create the distinctive new style that Elgar was to label *nobilmente* and which was to become the musical idiom of the heyday of the Empire. It is a situation replete with irony, as Parry was an anti-imperialist, hostile to jubilees and jingoism, and yet he directly inspired, in a work commissioned for the 1887 Golden Jubilee, what would become recognizably the Empire's musical style.

Queen Victoria's Diamond Jubilee, 1897

If there is one date and one event which can be taken as the apogee of the British Empire, it is Queen Victoria's Diamond Jubilee in 1897. 'Imperialism in the air – all classes drunk with sightseeing and hysterical loyalty', wrote Beatrice Webb in her diary, evoking the atmosphere all over Britain in the summer of 1897.[111] It was a moment at which the British collectively rejoiced not just in the longest reign in the history of the British monarchy but in the power and extent of the mightiest Empire since the fall of Rome. Odes poured from the pens of poets great and small. From Gibraltar to Rangoon, from Hudson's Bay to the Falkland Islands, people gathered to sing and dance, to feast and revel. In Britain itself, parades and processions, gala concerts and church services, public dinners and private parties, a review of the navy at Spithead and of the army at Aldershot, all taking place in glorious sunshine – 'Queen's weather' as it was dubbed – testify to the genuine cross-class nationwide consensus that Empire was Britain's destiny.

It was Joseph Chamberlain who had suggested that the occasion should be primarily an imperial celebration. The Queen was happy to agree, and the presence of foreign monarchs was vetoed, partly to exclude the Queen's grandson Kaiser Wilhelm II, who had expressed his support for the Boers. European royal families were represented by the sons and brothers of the reigning monarchs. Otherwise it was an occasion for a gathering of imperial troops from all parts of the Empire. Writing in 1903, J.E.C. Bodley said that it was at the Diamond Jubilee that 'the imperial idea, which had long been growing in the nation, first touched the imagination of the populace, as it cheered the citizen soldiery of young colonies guarding the venerable mother of all the Britains'.[112]

Music was central to all the celebrations. *The Musical Times* rhapsodized:

> The thoughts and feelings which have so recently thrilled the hearts of Britons all over the world have found their highest expression through the divine art of music. The celebration of Queen Victoria's sixty-years' reign – this unique event in our nation's history – has called forth an unprecedented outburst of jubilant strains, and millions of Her Majesty's loyal subjects, young and old, have raised their voices in notes of joy and gladness.[113]

The celebrations began on 19 June 1897 with a Grand Military Tattoo at Windsor Castle, where seven regimental bands performed, along with drum, pipe and fife music, the *Coronation March* from Meyerbeer's *The Prophet*, the medley *Reminiscences of All Nations* and the new patriotic overture *Loyal Hearts* specially composed by Cavaliere Ladislao Zaverthal, Bandmaster of the Royal Artilllery. On Accession Day, 20 June, the Queen attended a Thanksgiving service at St George's Chapel, Windsor, at which Sir Arthur Sullivan's new Jubilee hymn *O King of Kings*, the Prince Consort's *Te Deum* and the familiar hymn *Now Thank We All Our God* were performed. On 21 June, the Queen travelled up to London, and on 22 June she despatched a telegraph message to all parts of the Empire ('From my heart I thank my beloved people. May God bless them') and then left Buckingham Palace to drive to St Paul's. The procession was led by the great imperial warrior Field Marshal Lord Roberts and included Canadian Mounties, Jamaica Artillery, Royal Nigerian Constabulary, the Cape Mounted Rifles, the New South Wales Lancers, Trinidad Light Horse, and New Zealand Mounted Troops, along with a variety of Indian troops. The service took place on the steps of St Paul's, with the Queen remaining seated in her carriage. The choir contained many of the most famous musicians of the day joining in the singing: Sir Arthur Sullivan, Sir Walter Parratt, Dr Hubert Parry, Dr Frederick Bridge, Alberto Randegger, Dr A.H. Mann, Barton McGuckin, John E. West, and Joseph Bennett. Sir

George Martin conducted his *Jubilee Te Deum*, and this was followed by the intoning of the Lord's Prayer, the singing of *All People that On Earth Do Dwell* to the familiar tune *The Old Hundredth* and then the first verse of the national anthem. Then the Archbishop of Canterbury on an impulse called for three cheers for the Queen. They could be heard in Trafalgar Square. The service was accompanied throughout by the military bands of the Royal Artillery and the Royal School of Military Music, Kneller Hall.

After the service, the royal procession returned to Buckingham Palace. That evening the Queen hosted a dinner party at Buckingham Palace where the centrepiece at the table was a nine-foot high crown made up of 60,000 orchids from every part of the Empire. On 23 June the Queen received loyal addresses from both Houses of Parliament and in the afternoon travelled back to Windsor.

Music was everywhere during the Jubilee. Two major exhibitions opened: the Victorian Era Exhibition at Earl's Court, staged by Imre Kiralfy; and the Imperial Victorian Exhibition at the Crystal Palace. Both contained music sections. Kiralfy's was the more impressive, with a great display of letters, manuscripts, instruments and the portraits of 200 musicians; the Crystal Palace's section was more limited but its centrepiece was the musical collection of the late Sir Michael Costa. The Earl's Court Exhibition was opened on Queen Victoria's birthday, 24 May, by the Duke of Cambridge, and the ceremonies included a performance, by the exhibition choir accompanied by Dan Godfrey's military band, of Frederic Cowen's commemoration ode *All Hail the Glorious Reign*. George C. Martin, the Organist of St Paul's, and J. Frederick Bridge, the Organist of Westminster Abbey, were knighted in the Jubilee Honours List. All the cathedrals and churches put on Jubilee Thanksgiving services.[114] On 21 May the Queen visited Sheffield and a choir of 50,000 children, accompanied by 'half a dozen or so judiciously placed bands', performed a programme of patriotic songs and Jubilee hymns under the baton of Dr Henry Coward.

Just as for the Golden Jubilee, every level of music celebrated the Diamond Jubilee. There was a raft of music-hall songs: *Let's Be Jubilant* by T.W. Connor, sung by George Beauchamp; *The Great White Mother*, by Gordon Noble and G.D. Wheeler and sung by Leo Dryden; *There's Only One Queen Victoria* by T.F. Robson and Will Hyde, sung by T.F. Robson and Ernest Ball; *Victoria – the Mother of Our Nation* by Paul Pelham and George Le Brunn and sung by George Lashwood; *Commemoration Day* by A.R. Marshall and A. Seldon and sung by Herbert Campbell; and *Sixty Years* by Alma Curzon, G.F. Howley and C.E. Howells, sung by Alma Curzon. There was an ocean of light music: the waltz *Victoria Regina* by Ernest Allan; the quick march *Our Queen* by H.M. Higgs; the descriptive imperial fantasia *Our Empire* by Charles Godfrey, Bandmaster of the Royal Horse Guards; the valsette *For Crown and Throne* by M. Daniel and G. Miller; W.F. Martin's *National March*; William Haynes's *Victoria Jubilee March* (which introduced the national anthem); Percy Pitt's *Coronation March*; Edward C. Doughty's march *Our Empress Queen*; and many more.

There were part-songs and choruses: the patriotic chorus *Victoria – Our Queen* with words by A.C. Ainger and music by Joseph Barnby (which in its turn inspired an orchestral march based on its themes by J.E. West); *The Queen – God Bless Her, One Queen, One Flag, One Fleet – A Federal Greeting* and *One Glorious Aim – A Federal Song*, aimed at promoting the idea of imperial federation, all by Myles B. Foster; and Caleb Simpson's *God Bless Our Queen*.

There were cantatas: *The Banner of St. George* by Elgar, Frederick Bridge's *The Flag of England*, and G.F. Huntley's *Victoria*. *The Times* noted that Huntley's *Victoria* was set 'to a rather hysterical libretto by Rev. Charles Kent, in which the death of Boadicea and the commemoration of the present year of grace are set side by side with quaint effect'.[115] A novelty in this piece was that the leading theme of the final chorus was constructed so as to represent the year number 1897, 'the numerical value of the notes being taken according to their place in the octave'. The result was a tune rather like the opening of the national anthem, *The Times* commenting indulgently: 'No harm is done by this example of fanciful mysticism.' There were odes: Frederic Cowen's *All Hail the Glorious Reign* and Sir Herbert Oakeley's *A Golden Reign*, and recycled from the Golden Jubilee, Stanford's *Carmen Saeculare* and Mackenzie's *Jubilee Ode* (with 'fifty' changed to 'sixty' in the text).

Empire was unquestionably the theme of the music. Frederic Cowen's *Jubilee Ode*, with words by Clifton Bingham, proclaimed:

> Ring out from spire and steeple,
> Ye bells, o'er sea and land,
> To Africa's plain across the main,
> To India's distant strand!
> Ring out in acclamation,
> Proclaim it far and near,
> In tones that roll from pole to pole,
> For all the world to hear!
> Victoria! Victoria!
> All tongues up-raise the strain;

[139]

Let earth rejoice with heart and voice,
And hail thy glorious reign!
Victoria! Victoria!

True Queen from that first morning
That crowned thee yet a maid;
True to thy trust when in the dust
The hopes of life were laid.
In times of peace devoted,
In sorrow's hour serene,
And trusting still to Heav'n's high will,
True mother, wife and Queen.

Her Empire's heart her sceptre,
Her people's love her crown;
Let History's page, from age to age,
Her glorious name hand down!
No traitor foe shall harm us,
No storm the state o'erwhelm,
While day to day, her people pray,
'May God defend her realm!'
Victoria! Victoria!
All tongues up-raise the strain;
Let earth rejoice with heart and voice,
And hail thy glorious reign.

Eaton Faning's *The Queen's Song*, to words by Sir Edwin Arnold, ran:

For this great Reign, now rounded
To three-score golden years,
With pride and joy unbounded
We raise a Nation's cheers;
So well-beloved, so Noble
Ere now was no-where seen;
Hail'd let her be till Sky and Sea
Respond 'God Save the Queen'
So true a Sov'reign Lady
Ne'er ruled all hearts before!
Rise up and praise Victoria's days,
The glorious years three-score!

Heaven send Her peace and glory!
And when a Crown above –
Fulfilling earth's fair story –
Is granted by God's Love,
Be this His grace to England
That, for her deathless sake
Reign after Reign as royal remain
And thence example take.

Then, o'er Her subject Waters,
Her realm, Her wave-linked Lands,
On Britain's sons and daughters,
And labours of their hands,
Sweet surety, strength and justice
Shall dwell, as now hath been,
And God above, this Isle will love,
Who loved and saved our Queen.

The whole Jubilee can be seen as an apotheosis of Queen Victoria, who was the focus of an unparalleled outpouring of adulation. She had become, while still alive, the tutelary goddess of the British Empire.

Also among the hits of the Jubilee was Elgar's *Imperial March* which was played at the State Concert at Buckingham Palace on 15 June and at the Royal Jubilee Garden Party at Buckingham Palace on 28 June, somewhat mitigating the wrath of those who complained that at the review of colonial troops at Buckingham Palace the music played was exclusively French and German.[116] The *Imperial March* was rapidly arranged for piano, organ and military band. Similarly successful was Bridge's Kipling setting *The Flag of England* which, after its triumphant debut and generally ecstatic reviews, was immediately announced for performances in Rochester, Stratford, Southend, Sittingbourne, Leamington, Chester and Exeter.[117]

Novello published a collection of twelve hymns for use in jubilee services, some with new tunes expressly composed for the words. The hymns included *English Hearts and English Voices*; *From Every Clime, From Every Shore*; *From the Deep Heart of Our People*; *God of Nations, Lord Almighty*; *Long Loved, Long Honour'd Queen*; and *O King of Kings, who Gives Power to All*; and the composers included Sir Arthur Sullivan, Sir George Martin, Sir Joseph Barnby, Sir Alexander Mackenzie, Sir Walter Parratt and Dr Charles Harford Lloyd. Dr. Jacob Bradford was particularly busy, recycling from 1887 the cantata *Song of Jubilee*, making a special arrangement of *God Save the Queen*, composing the hymn *Sovereign of All, Whose Will Ordains* and the *Commemorative March*, but sadly he died during the festivities.

The Times noted that the Jubilee had called forth 'a large number of 'occasional' compositions of various degrees of merit'. It singled out Elgar's *The Banner of St George* and Bridge's *The Flag of England* as works likely to keep their popularity after the Jubilee celebrations had passed. It thought Cowen's music to *All Hail the Glorious Reign* a good deal better than the words but 'not a very remarkable composition'. But Eaton Faning's *The Queen's Song* had 'a good deal of spirit' and Myles B. Foster's *The Queen – God Bless Her* 'a stirring tune that well deserves to be popular'. *The Times* disapprovingly observed that 'the glorious national hymn is likely to undergo various tortures during the next few months, but few will be more trying to its constitution that the waltz *Victoria* by D. Cameron, the very ingenuity of which is its chief offence'.[118]

Among the many commemoration concerts, there was a Queen's Hall Jubilee concert on 20 June at which four leading musicians conducted their own Jubilee compositions: Sir Frederick Bridge his Jubilee anthem *Blessed Be the Lord Thy God*, Frederic Cowen his *Jubilee Ode*, Sir George Martin his *Jubilee Te Deum* and *Antiphon*, and Eaton Faning his *The Queen's Song*. In addition, a full band and chorus under Alberto Randegger sang the *Hymn of Praise* and Randegger's setting of the 150th psalm.

The Royal Choral Society held its commemoration concert at the Albert Hall on May 6. The programme opened with Dr Bridge's new arrangement of the national anthem with a new second verse by the Dean of Rochester, the Very Reverend S. Reynolds Hole:

> O Lord Our God arise,
> Scatter her enemies,
> Make wars to cease;
> Keep us from plague and dearth,
> Turn thou our woes to mirth;
> And over all the earth
> Let there be peace.

The Musical Times commented: 'There are some conservative minds who may regret the banishment of the "knavish tricks" and aggressive spirit of the discarded verse, but it must be admitted that Dean Hole's lines are more consonant with the sentiment of modern Christianity.'[119] It failed, however, to replace the existing verse permanently.

Eaton Faning's *The Queen's Song*, 'reflective of the spirit of today', proved 'highly effective'. Handel's anthems *Zadok the Priest* and *The King Shall Rejoice*, both part of the 1838 coronation service, were performed, and Mendelssohn's *Hymn of Praise*. But the hit of the evening was Bridge's *The Flag of England*. *The Musical Times* commented: 'This is no mere *pièce d'occasion*, the words being appropriate so long as Englishmen take pride in the prestige of their flag; and the music possesses a vigour and emotional life, combined with masterly craftsmanship, that will assuredly long appeal to all cultured musicians.' Of the performance, it noted:

> The solo portion was sung by Madame Albani with much fervour, and the choristers have never fulfilled their duties with greater intelligence and ardour. At the close the enthusiasm of the audience was immense,

and the applause only ceased after Professor Bridge had been recalled four times to the platform and expressed his regret that Mr. Kipling was not present.[120]

The Philharmonic Society's Commemoration Concert on 17 June, described by *The Musical Times* as 'absurdly long', included Tchaikovsky's *Variations on a Rococo Theme*, Schumann's *Piano Concerto*, Mendelssohn's *Scottish Symphony*, Weber's *Jubilee Overture* and Sir Alexander Mackenzie's 'delightfully spirited, tuneful and humorous *Britannia* overture, the orchestration of which is as sunshine and pure gold'. There were two English novelties, Frederic Cowen's scena *The Dream of Endymion* and Edward German's English fantasia *In Commemoration*, 'an attempt at a musical expression of the proud thoughts engendered by the glorious event celebrated during the last month, and consequently laid out on a grandiose scale'. *The Musical Times* thought it 'vigorously jubilant during the greater part of its course, while there are portions in *quasi* pastoral style, and yet others in which a prayerful or at any rate reflective mood seems suggested. The themes, without being striking, are well chosen, some of them being full of charm.' But it was critical of the orchestration, which allowed the percussion instruments to dominate 'till their din overpowers almost everything else'. It urged him to reorchestrate it, for future use. *The Standard* and *Morning Post* both thought it 'clever', the *Daily Chronicle* 'thoroughly national in chararacter and very effectively scored', *The Times* 'essentially English', and the *Morning Post* thought he was seeking 'a sort of British equivalent of Wagner's *Kaisermarsch*, "that gorgeous musical glorification of the German Empire"'.[121] German took the advice to rework it and it re-emerged in 1902 as *Rhapsody on March Themes* and, performed at the Norwich Festival, was hailed as 'finely invented, admirably scored and splendidly effective', a judgement which still holds true today.[122]

The Royal Academy of Music's concert on the 10 June included a performance of Mackenzie's *Jubilee Ode*, conducted by the composer. William Carter's Jubilee Festival at the Albert Hall on 19 June included Dr Jacob Bradford's *Song of the Jubilee*, Carter's own *Thanksgiving Anthem* and *Jubilee Ode* and Helen, Lady Forbes's *Celebration Ode* ('unpretentious but effective').

All round the country there were Jubilee concerts, which often included specially written Jubilee novelties by local composers. The Kendal Festival, for instance, included a concert, conducted by Mary Wakefield, which, in a nice combination of patriotism and Protestantism, included Arthur Somervell's setting of *The Charge of the Light Brigade* ('sung with great spirit and loudly encored'), Bach's cantata *A Stronghold Sure* and Miss Wakefield's own 'loyal chorus' *Queen of the Sixty Years*.

The Weston-Super-Mare Philharmonic Society's Diamond Jubilee Concert on 6 May featured Handel's *Zadok the Priest* and a part-song, *The Splendour of the Reign*, by E.A. Dicks. The High Wycombe Choral Association's Jubilee concert on 26 April included Sullivan's *On Shore and Sea*, Mackenzie's chorus *Lord of Life* and Myles Foster's part-song *The Queen – God Bless Her*. The Ryde Musical Society linked the Diamond Jubilee to the Schubert Centenary, performing on 29 April Schubert's cantata *The Song of Miriam*, *Zadok the Priest* and Faning's *The Queen's Song*. The Staines Choral Society gave the first performance of Dr G.S. Huntley's Jubilee cantata *Victoria* on 14 May ('the work was very warmly received'). The South Hampstead Orchestra, conducted by Mrs Julian Marshall, gave an ambitious concert at the St James's Hall on 26 May which included Weber's *Jubilee Overture*, 'which has been heard several times of late in the metropolis by reason of its containing the strain of "God save the Queen"'.[123] There was an open-air Jubilee Festival at Scarborough on 25 June when the Scarborough Choral Society performed Cowen's *All Hail the Glorious Reign*, Faning's *The Queen's Song* and Stainer's *The Triumph of Victoria*.

The Church Sunday School Choir Concert at the Crystal Palace on 19 June, which brought together representatives from about 100 schools in London and the suburbs, performed a 'pleasing selection of sacred and secular pieces . . . with much spirit and general efficiency', notably a Jubilee ode, *Victoria, We Hail Thee*, composed expressly for the occasion by Mr W.S. Desborough. 'Being sung with much animation', it was 'well received'.[124]

In Birmingham, the Festival Choral Society under Dr C. Swinnerton Heap gave two free concerts at the Town Hall, both of them 'crowded'. The programme included Faning's *The Queen's Song*, Cowen's *All Hail the Glorious Reign* and Hollingsworth's glee *Here's Life and Health to England's Queen*. The Chester Festival opened on 21 July with a Jubilee concert which included *Zadok the Priest* and Sullivan's *Festival Te Deum*. The Three Choirs' Festival opened at Hereford in 14 September 1897 with a Jubilee programme: *Zadok the Priest*, Mendelssohn's *Hymn of Praise*, Beethoven's *Symphony in C Minor*, Saint-Saëns's *The Heavens Declare* and Charles Harford Lloyd's specially composed *Hymn of Thanksgiving for the Queen's Long Reign*. *The Musical Times* noted that 'refusing the course taken by Mr. Elgar, Dr. Lloyd . . . kept closely to the orthodox Church style', with well-constructed fugal choruses whose themes derived from the hymn tune *Bedford*. It was pronounced 'a notable example of present-day

Church composition, and . . . a fitting memorial of a great event'. It was generally well reviewed.[125]

Services and concerts were also held all over the Empire. In New Zealand, there were special Jubilee church services, featuring *Zadok the Priest*, Handel's *Hallelujah Chorus* and the national anthem. Mr Maughan Barnett's Musical Society gave a 'most successful concert at Wellington Opera House', which included Cowen's *Song of Thanksgiving* and an original cantata *A Song of Empire* (words by Arthur H. Adams, music by Maughan Barnett). The cantata, 'which is a favourable example of colonial talent, was enthusiastically received'.[126] At the Christchurch Opera House, the Christchurch Musical Union performed Mendelssohn's *Hymn of Praise* and a short programme of patriotic music, 'in the presence of an immense audience. Ringing cheers for the Queen followed the singing of the National Anthem, *Rule Britannia* also evoking great enthusiasm.' Mendelssohn's *Hymn of Praise* was also performed at a Jubilee service in All Saints Church, Palmerston North.

In Jamaica, the Kingston Choral Union performed Dr Bradford's cantata *Song of Jubilee* in the Parish Church on 13 July 'with marked success'. In Sydney, New South Wales, at the York Street Centenary Hall, the Jubilee concert included J.E. West's march *Victoria – Our Queen*, Eaton Faning's *The Queen's Song* and a 'dignified Jubilee hymn', *Sixty Years of Service Splendid*, composed for the occasion by the conductor W.L.B. Mote, 'which was well received'. Master Arnold Mote's organ solo, an original *Queen's Commemoration March*, 'also won acceptance'.

Harold Stidolph of Cape Town composed the words and music of a national Thanksgiving hymn which was sung in the cathedrals and churches of South Africa on Jubilee Sunday. The Queen graciously accepted a copy of the hymn. At home and throughout the Empire, opera house, music hall, concert hall, church and school responded with musical affirmations of the greatness of Britain, her Queen and her far-flung dominions.

King George V's Silver Jubilee of 1935

By 1935 King George V was in poor health, but his ministers thought it both fitting and politically expedient to stimulate popular patriotism and support for the monarchy and the Empire, and so Silver Jubilee celebrations were organized. There was a service of Thanksgiving at St Paul's Cathedral on 6 May 1935, the twenty-fifth anniversary of his succession to the throne. The streets were packed with cheering crowds, causing the King to record 'the greatest number of people in the streets that I have ever seen in my life'. The King broadcast to the nation from Buckingham Palace: 'The Queen and I thank you from the depths of our hearts for the loyalty and – may I say so – the love with which this day and always you have surrounded us.' There was a reception for the dominion Premiers at St James's Palace, of which Ramsay MacDonald wrote: 'Here the Empire was a great family, the gathering a family reunion, the King a paternal head.' The two Houses of Parliament rendered their homage at Westminster Hall and the King reviewed the fleet at Spithead. Visiting the poorer districts of London, the King was astonished at the warmth of his reception. 'I didn't realize they felt like this', he declared.[127]

Music as before played its part. But there had been a dramatic change in the nature and structure of British musical life since the Diamond Jubilee. In particular there had been a decline in active music-making. The number of choirs and bands, music festivals and live concerts had declined, and much of the music that people heard was now produced by mechanical means in films, on the wireless and on gramophone records. Portions of both the Silver Jubilee Thanksgiving service and the Royal Command Variety Performance were recorded and issued on records, a clear indication of the way things were going.

Nevertheless the music publishers poured out appropriate scores for the celebration of the Jubilee, many of them having seen service at previous royal/imperial occasions. There were part-songs like J. Barnby's *God Prosper Him – Our King*, F.H. Cowen's *His Majesty the King*, Percy Fletcher's *For Empire and For King*, Charles Harriss's *Chorus of Empire*, C.H. Lloyd's *Our Sailor King* and A.H. Brewer's *The King*. For schools, there were songs by T. Facer (*God Bless Our King and Country, Sons of the Empire, Hail to Our King*), Percy Fletcher (*A Song of Britain, Children of England*), W. Hayes (*May the King and Queen Long Reign*), Gustav Holst (*In Loyal Bonds United*), E. Boyce (*A Rhyme of Overseas*) and J.H. Maunder (*Raise the Song, Ye Loyal Voices*). There were Jubilee song books of national airs from England, Scotland and Wales. There was a special Jubilee edition of Elgar's 1902 *Coronation Ode*. Weber's *Jubilee Overture* was trotted out again because of its utilization of the tune of *God Save the King*. There was a surge of appropriate marches – Elgar's *Imperial March* and the *Triumphal March* from *Caractacus*, Bantock's *Festival March*, Stainer's *Jubilant March* and Stanford's *Marcia Eroica*, Percy Fletcher's *Festal Offertorium*, R.G. Hailing's *March Royale* and J.E. West's *Commemoration March*. There was a flood of anthems, again many of them veterans of previous celebrations, such as Mackenzie's *Lord of Life* and Stainer's *Let Every Soul Be Subject* from the Golden Jubilee of Queen

Victoria, Bridge's *Blessed Be the Lord Thy God* from the Diamond Jubilee, Parry's *I Was Glad* and Bridge's *Kings Shall Arise* from the 1902 Coronation and Handel's hardy annual *Zadok the Priest*.

But, in many ways, more typical of the new popular culture was the contribution of the cinema. There were film compilations from the major newsreel companies. Gaumont British's *The King's Jubilee*, Paramount's *Long Live the King* and Pathé's *25 Years a King*. Associated British Pictures produced a dramatized documentary of the events of the King's reign, *Royal Cavalcade*, with an all-star cast and four directors. It ended with massed choirs singing *Land of Hope and Glory* and *God Save the King*. The critics lavished praise on it. Sydney Carroll in *The Sunday Times* wrote:

> *Royal Cavalcade* is a full panorama of royal experience, admirably conceived, magnificently executed. It merges the pageantry of kings with the human story of the people . . . It renders due homage to the lives of our King and Queen, and is a tribute also to the mighty Empire over which they reign.[128]

But the established music forms of celebration continued to be observed. On 6 May 1935 there was a Silver Jubilee Thanksgiving service at St Paul's. It included *God Save the King*, the hymns *All people that On Earth Do Dwell*, *I Vow to Thee My Country*, and *O God of Jacob, By Whose Hand Thy People Still Are Fed* and the rousing *Te Deum* specially composed for the occasion by Stanley Marchant, the Organist of St Paul's.

A very different occasion took place on 29 October 1935 at the London Palladium: a Royal Command Variety Performance at which Stanley Holloway introduced a parade of music-hall veterans who had been stars when the King was crowned. Arthur Reece sang that anthem of imperial seapower *Sons of the Sea*. But the bill of fare was mainly a cavalcade of Cockney warmth, sentiment and humour, with Alice Leamar singing *Her Golden Hair Was Hanging Down Her Back*; Florrie Forde *Pack Up Your Troubles* and *Down at the Old Bull and Bush*; Gus Elen *Down the Road*; Harry Champion *Boiled Beef and Carrots* and *Any Old Iron*; Kate Carney *Three Pots a Shilling* and *Are We To Part Like This, Bill?* At the end, the artists all gathered to sing *Here's a Health Unto His Majesty* and *God Save the King*. The recurrence of *Here's a Health Unto His Majesty* during these years is no coincidence. The King had caught a chill while attending the Armistice Day ceremonies in 1928, had developed pleurisy and septicaemia and had very nearly died. It was a year before he recovered, and thereafter his health remained frail.

Popular music contributed its tribute. Eric Coates composed *Song of Loyalty* to words by his wife Phyllis Black ('May peace and love enfold you is the prayer within our hearts'). A lilting and sentimental ballad lacking the profundity of a real anthem, it was rapidly forgotten. Haydn Wood composed and conducted on record the lively *Homage March* which concluded with the strains of *God Save the King*. Dance-band leaders Harry Roy (*Jubilation Rag*) and Carroll Gibbons (*Let's Have a Jubilee*) recorded their contributions. Betty Driver recorded *Jubilee Baby*, celebrating the birth of a child in 1935:

> What an age to be alive in,
> What a world to live and thrive in,
> Jubilee Year, the Jubilee's here.

Cicely Courtneidge, who made a speciality of dressing as a soldier and singing rousing military anthems, recorded a specially composed song, *Gentlemen, the King*. With its swinging chorus, 'We're marching along and we're singing this song – Gentlemen, the King', it evoked a tradition of 'warriors old, Saxons true and bold' and of 'ships sailing through the ages' whose exploits will live forever. It concluded triumphantly:

> Then through the years a mighty Empire dawned upon the world,
> And from the Mother Country got its name,
> It's called the British Empire; it commands the world's respect
> And now today the toast is still the same – Gentlemen, the King.

King George V barely made it through his jubilee year, dying on 20 January 1936. There would not be another jubilee until the Silver Jubilee of Queen Elizabeth II, in 1977, by which time the Empire would be little more than a memory.

Notes

1   Percy A. Scholes, *God Save the Queen!*, London: Oxford University Press, 1954, p. 7.
2   William H. Cummings, *God Save the King*, London: Novello, 1902, p. 48.
3   See in particular Scholes, *God Save the Queen!*, and Cummings, *God Save the King*.
4   Scholes, *God Save the Queen!*, p. 101.
5   *Ibid.*, p. 126.
6   S.J. Adair Fitzgerald, *Stories of Famous Songs*, London: John C. Nimmo, 1898, pp. 407–8.
7   Scholes, *God Save the Queen!*, p. 142.
8   *Ibid.*, pp. 176–8, 172.
9   *Ibid.*, pp. 130–4.
10 Cummings, *God Save the King*, p. 1.
11 Lewis Winstock, *Songs and Music of the Redcoats*, Harrisburg, PA: Stackpole Books, 1970, p. 255.
12 Cummings, *God Save the King*, p. v.
13 *The Times*, 4 May, 1891.

14 Fitzgerald, *Stories of Famous Songs*, p. 175.
15 For the history of the masque and the song, see Michael Burden, *Garrick, Arne and the Masque of Alfred*, Lampeter: Edwin Mellen Press, 1994, and W.H. Cummings, *Dr. Arne and Rule, Britannia*, London: Novello, 1912.
16 Sir Alexander Mackenzie, *A Musician's Narrative*, London: Cassell, 1927, p. 197. The *Britannia* overture is included on the CD *Victorian Concert Overtures*, Hyperion, CD A66515.
17 Philip Ziegler, *Crown and People*, London: Collins, 1978, p. 43.
18 Charles Madge and Tom Harrisson (eds), *Mass Observation: The First Year's Work 1937–38*, London: Lindsay Drummond, 1938, pp. 114–15.
19 Tony Walter (ed.), *The Mourning for Diana*, Oxford: Berg, 1999, p. 197.
20 J.E.C. Bodley, *The Coronation of Edward the Seventh: A Chapter of European and Imperial History*, London: Methuen, 1903, pp. 201, 204.
21 Bodley, *Coronation*, pp. 4, 222.
22 *Ibid.*, pp. 226–7.
23 *Ibid.*, p. 142.
24 *Ibid.*, p. 239.
25 *The Times*, 11 August, 1902.
26 *Ibid.*
27 Sir Frederick Bridge, *A Westminster Pilgrim*, London: Novello–Hutchinson, 1918, p. 182.
28 Bridge, *Westminster Pilgrim*, p. 193.
29 *The Times*, 24 June, 1902.
30 Bodley, *Coronation*, p. 302.
31 *The Times*, 23 June, 1902.
32 Percy A. Scholes (ed.), *The Mirror of Music 1844–1944*, London: Novello/Oxford University Press, 1947, vol. 2, p. 882.
33 *The Times*, 25 October, 1902.
34 Lewis Foreman (ed.), *Music in England 1885–1920*, London: Thames Publishing, 1994, p. 65.
35 *The Times*, 25 October, 1902.
36 Norman Davies, *The Isles*, London: Macmillan, 1999, pp. 878–9.
37 *The Times*, 23 June, 1911.
38 Bridge, *Westminster Pilgrim*, pp. 231–6.
39 *The Times*, 19 June, 1911.
40 *The Times*, 17 June, 1911.
41 *The Times*, 19 June, 1911.
42 *The Musical Times*, 1 July, 1911.
43 *The Times*, 19 June, 1911.
44 *The Times*, 17 June, 1911.
45 *The Musical Times*, 1 July, 1911.
46 Bridge, *Westminster Pilgrim*, p. 236.
47 *The Times*, 11 May, 1937.
48 *The Times*, 13 May, 1937.
49 *Ibid.*
50 *Ibid.*
51 Humphrey Jennings and Charles Madge (eds), *May 12, Mass Observation Day – Survey*, London: Faber & Faber, 1987 (1938), pp. 120, 130.
52 *The Times*, 13 May, 1937.
53 *Ibid.*
54 *The Musical Times*, 1 June, 1937.
55 *The Times*, 12 May, 1937.
56 Jennings and Madge, *May 12*, p. 270.
57 *The Musical Times*, 1 June, 1937.
58 Jennings and Madge, *May 12*, p. 270.
59 *Ibid.*, p. 278.
60 *Ibid.*, pp. 110, 111, 127.

61 *Ibid.*, pp. 284, 291, 207, 237.
62 *Ibid.*, pp. 153, 163, 293.
63 *Ibid.*, pp. 152, 159, 201.
64 Ziegler, *Crown and People*, p. 68.
65 *Birmingham Post*, 13 May, 1937.
66 *Daily Mail*, 3 June, 1953.
67 *The Times*, 3 June, 1953.
68 *Daily Mirror*, 4 June, 1953.
69 *The Times*, 3 June, 1953.
70 *The Musical Times*, 1 July, 1953.
71 *Ibid.*
72 *Ibid.*
73 Ziegler, *Crown and People*, p. 111.
74 Ziegler, *Crown and People*, p. 120; *Daily Mirror*, 4 June, 1953.
75 Ziegler, *Crown and People*, p. 104.
76 *Nobody Minded the Rain: Coronation Day 1953*, BBC2, 2 June, 1983; Ziegler, *Crown and People*, p. 120.
77 David Cannadine, 'The context, performance and meaning of ritual: the British monarchy and the "invention of tradition", c.1820–1977', in Eric Hobsbawm and Terence Ranger (eds), *The Invention of Tradition*, Cambridge: Cambridge University Press, 1987, p. 124.
78 *Ibid.*, p. 134.
79 *The Times*, 20 June, 1887.
80 Jeffrey Lant, *Insubstantial Pageant*, London: Hamish Hamilton, 1979, p. 127.
81 *Ibid.*, p. 12.
82 Caroline Chapman and Paul Raben (eds), *Debrett's Queen Victoria's Jubilees*, London: Debrett's Peerage, 1977, p. 13.
83 Lord Ronald Gower, *Old Diaries, 1881–1901*, London: John Murray, 1902, pp. 56–7.
84 Foreman, *Music in England*, p. 36.
85 *The Musical Times*, 1 May, 1887.
86 Alexander Mackenzie, *A Musician's Narrative*, London: Cassell, 1927, p. 155.
87 *Ibid.*
88 *The Musical Times*, 1 July, 1887.
89 *Ibid.*
90 *The Musical Times*, 1 September, 1887.
91 *Ibid.*
92 Charles V. Stanford, *Pages From an Unwritten Diary*, London: Edward Arnold, 1914, p. 233.
93 *The Musical Times*, 1 September, 1887.
94 *The Musical Times*, 1 July, 1887.
95 *The Musical Times*, 1 May, 1887.
96 *The Musical Times*, 1 June, 1887.
97 *The Musical Times*, 1 August, 1887.
98 *The Musical Times*, 1 May, 1887.
99 *The Musical Times*, 1 July, 1887.
100 *Ibid.*
101 *The Musical Times*, 1 May, 1887.
102 *The Musical Times*, 1 September, 1887.
103 *Ibid.*
104 *Ibid.*
105 *The Musical Times*, 1 November, 1887.
106 *The Musical Times*, 1 July, 1887.
107 *The Musical Times*, 1 August, 1887.
108 Jeremy Dibble, *C. Hubert H. Parry: His Life and Work*, Oxford: Clarendon Press, 1992, pp. 258–9.
109 *Ibid.*, p. 249.
110 Bernard Benoliel, *Parry Before Jerusalem*, Aldershot: Ashgate, 1997, p. 72.

111   James Morris, *Pax Britannica*, London: Faber, 1968, p. 26.
112   Bodley, *Coronation of Edward the Seventh*, p. 30.
113   *The Musical Times*, 1 July, 1897.
114   Details can be found in *Musical Times* 1 July and 1 August 1897.
115   *The Times*, 16 Apirl, 1897.
116   Percy Scholes, *The Mirror of Music*, vol. 2, p. 878.
117   *The Musical Times*, 1 July and 1 December, 1897.
118   *The Times*, 19 April, 1897.
119   *The Musical Times*, 1 June, 1897.
120   *Ibid.*
121   *The Musical Times*, 1 July, 1897.
122   *The Times*, 25 October, 1902.
123   *The Musical Times*, 1 July, 1897.
124   *Ibid.*
125   *The Musical Times*, 1 October, 1897.
126   *The Musical Times*, 1 September, 1897.
127   Kenneth Rose, *King George V*, London: Weidenfeld & Nicolson, 1983, pp. 395–7.
128   *Sunday Times*, 14 April, 1935.

CHAPTER FIVE

Imperial days:
Armistice Day and Empire Day

Armistice Day

The traumatic experience of the First World War required both formal commemoration and ritualized mourning to salve emotional and psychological wounds. There was a need to signal and demonstrate a sense of loss, together with a sense of pride and a sense of gratitude, not just on a national level but on an imperial level. For the First World War was an imperial war, with Indian troops serving on the Western Front, Australians and New Zealanders at Gallipoli and British troops in Mesopotamia and Palestine. Britain and the Empire collectively lost a million dead.

The need and the desire for public ceremonial called forth a range of events. *The Times* reported: 'The Two Minutes Silence and the wearing of the Flanders poppies have become the dominating feature of the anniversary.'[1] Both had imperial origins. The proposal of the two-minutes' silence came from Sir Percy Fitzpatrick, who had been the British High Commissioner in South Africa during the war, and whose son had been killed at Beaumetz. In 1919 he submitted a memorandum to the Cabinet suggesting that a practice observed every day of the war in South Africa – a three-minute pause for reflection – should be introduced on the anniversary of the first Armistice Day at 11 a.m. on 11 November 1918, with the aims of reminding people of their common bond and to inform posterity of 'the meaning, the nobility and the unselfishness of the great sacrifice by which their freedom was assured'. The King and the Cabinet agreed, and on 7 November 1919 all newspapers carried a request from the King for an Empire-wide observance of a two-minutes' silence at 11 a.m. on 11 November: 'I believe that my people in every part of the Empire fervently wish to perpetuate the memory of the Great Deliverance and of those who have laid down their lives to achieve it.' It was universally

observed and made a tremendous impact, for it was the perfect combination of a public and a private event: everyone joined in but each
had his or her own thoughts. At 11 a.m. on 11 November 1919, church
bells tolled, traffic stopped, stores ceased to trade, men removed their
hats, telegraphs and telephones were stilled, people knelt in the
streets. 'Everywhere there was mourning, sorrow and thanksgiving',
reported *The Times*.[2] Thereafter the two-minutes' silence became the
centrepiece of the ceremonies on Armistice Day and of its successor
after the Second World War, Remembrance Sunday.

The British Legion was formed in 1921 by the merger of various veterans' groups. Its leader and dominant figure was Field Marshal Earl
Haig. The sale of poppies became a central feature of revenue-raising
for the Earl Haig Fund for Ex-Servicemen. The poppy had been immortalized as a symbol of the sacrifice of the servicemen on the Western
Front by the poem *In Flanders Fields*. It was written by Canadian
medical officer John McRae and directly inspired by the death of his
close friend Lt Alexis Helmer. McRae had served in South Africa in
the Boer War and volunteered in 1914 to serve in the First World War.
He served throughout the conflict; but, exhausted by his efforts, he
died of pneumonia and meningitis in 1918. His poem, published in
Punch on 8 December 1915, provoked an enormous public response.
It became known as 'the most popular English poem of the Great War'
but was just as popular in the United States and the Empire as in
Britain. It combined the ideas of sacrifice and loss with that of dedication to a cause.

> In Flanders fields, the poppies blow
> Between the crosses, row on row,
> That mark our place; and in the sky
> The larks, still bravely singing, fly
> Scarce heard amid the guns below.
>
> We are the Dead. Short days ago
> We lived, felt dawn, saw sunset glow,
> Loved, and were loved, and now we lie
> In Flanders fields.
>
> Take up our quarrel with the foe:
> To you from failing hands we throw
> The torch; be yours to hold it high.
> If ye break faith with us who die
> We shall not sleep, though poppies grow
> In Flanders fields.

The poppy, blood-red but continually reborn, was taken up almost at
once as a symbol of remembrance, first by American ex-servicemen.

Artificial poppies were manufactured in Northern France, and a French woman, Madame Guerin, suggested to the British Legion that it should use the sale of poppies for fund-raising, and this began in 1921. It rapidly became universal. By 1922 everyone at the Cenotaph ceremony wore a poppy. Showers of poppies were incorporated into the annual British Legion Festival of Remembrance and the wreaths laid at memorials on Armistice Day soon came to be made of poppies. Participation in the two-minutes' silence and the wearing of the poppy was democratic, universal and open to all.[3]

All over Britain and the Empire, in towns and cities and villages, schools, churches, sports clubs, railway stations and banks, war memorials appeared to act as foci for homage and pilgrimage. The language of their inscriptions, says Adrian Gregory, drew heavily on the pre-war rhetoric of God, Empire, King and country. The national monuments certainly stressed the imperial dimension of the war. The Cavalry Memorial in Hyde Park, 'erected by the cavalry of the Empire in memory of comrades who gave their lives in war 1914–1919', took the classic chivalric form of St George with raised sword triumphing over the dragon. It included bronze plates listing the cavalry regiments of Britain, India, Australia, Canada, New Zealand and South Africa which served. A Camel Corps' memorial in Victoria Embankment Gardens was erected 'to the glorious and immortal memory of the officers, NCOs and men of the Imperial Camel Corps, British, Australian, New Zealand and Indian, who fell in action or died of wounds and disease in Egypt, Sinai and Palestine, 1916–17–18'. The Royal Air Force memorial on the Embankment was dedicated to 'those air forces from every part of the British Empire who have given their lives in winning victory for their King and Country'. The Royal Navy Memorial at Portsmouth pays tribute to 'the abiding memory of those ranks and ratings of this port who laid down their lives in defence of the Empire and have no known grave than the sea'. The Five Sisters Window in York Minster was restored as a national monument to the 1,400 women of the Empire who gave their lives. It was unveiled by the Duchess of York on Wednesday 24 June 1925, and on the same day in Canada, Australia, Tasmania, New Zealand and South Africa memorial services to the women casualties were held. The Prince of Wales unveiled a *chattri* (a memorial dome) at Patcham on the site of the funeral pyre where the bodies of Sikh and Hindu soldiers who died of their wounds had been burned. Unveiling ceremonies usually took the form of a religious service which almost invariably included the hymn *O God Our Help in Ages Past*, 'the tribal lay of the British' as Adey called it, and the national anthem, a reinforcement of the link of God, King and country as the inspiration of the sacrifice.

Perhaps the two most notable memorials were the Cenotaph in Whitehall and the Tomb of the Unknown Warrior in Westminster Abbey. It was the suggestion of wartime padre David Railton to bury an unidentified body in Westminster Abbey with full military honours as a symbol of all those who had fallen. The Prime Minister Lloyd George was enthusiastic and persuaded the King, who was reluctant, to agree. The body was brought back in state from France, the coffin carried by twelve generals and admirals. One hundred VCs lined the nave of the Abbey, and the King led the mourners. It captured the imagination of the public and up to a million people eventually paid homage at the tomb. *The Times* declared: 'The Unknown Warrior . . . may have been born to high position or to the low; he may have been a sailor, a soldier, an airman; an Englishman, a Scotsman, a Welshman, an Irishman; a man of the Dominions, a Sikh, a Gurkha. But he was one who gave his life for the people of the British Empire.'[4] The epitaph on the tomb recalled the many who had given their lives 'For God, For King and Country, For loved ones, home and Empire, For the sacred cause of justice and freedom in the world'.

The interment of the Unknown Warrior was the centrepiece of Armistice Day 1920. But on the same day the King unveiled the Cenotaph, and this rapidly became the focus of national mourning on Armistice Day. The ceremony, which is still enacted on Remembrance Sunday, was more or less finalized by 1921. Detachments of the armed forces and military bands were stationed around the Cenotaph. Just before 11 a.m., the King and members of the royal family emerged to lay wreaths. They would be followed by the Prime Minister, members of the Government and the High Commissioners of the dominions. The two-minutes' silence followed at 11 a.m., and after a short religious service, with the entire assembly singing *O God Our Help in Ages Past*, there was a march-past of organizations and members of the public laying their own wreaths, to the familiar strains of First World War marching songs. The order of events changed after the Second World War, with the two-minutes' silence coming first and the wreath-laying following it. To this day, the music of the march-past draws not only on the First and Second World War songs but on the songs of the late nineteenth-century imperial wars (*Sons of the Sea, Soldiers of the Queen, Boys of the Old Brigade*).

By 1930 a musical programme for the Cenotaph was established which has scarcely been varied down to the present. It carefully included traditional songs from the constituent parts of the United Kingdom, 'the national airs of Great Britain': *Hearts of Oak, The Minstrel Boy, Men of Harlech, Isle of Beauty, David of the White Rock, Oft in the Stilly Night, Skye Boat Song, Flowers of the Forest* plus

Walford Davies's *Solemn Melody*, Purcell's *When I Am Laid in Earth* and Elgar's *Nimrod*. In 1926 and 1930 the dominions' Prime Ministers were present in person and in 1930 thirteen ruling Indian Princes attended. But identical services were held all over the Empire, and the occasion was undoubtedly used to foster imperial sentiment. For example, in 1923 the Australian Prime Minister Mr S.M. Bruce issued an Armistice Day message:

> Our duty is to keep the Empire strong, politically and economically, in order to enable us to carry out our large share in the work of the world's spiritual and physical recovery. For the world still looks to us to show the way, as it has long done. The faith of Australia is that the British race will not, and cannot, decline the duty and the privilege which go with our Empire's place in the van of civilized progress.[5]

Yet another form of remembrance was the pilgrimage to the battle-fields and to the cemeteries, established by the Imperial War Graves Commission. The pilgrims came from Britain and the dominions. King George V made his pilgrimage in 1922, depositing a bunch of forget-me-nots on the grave of Sergeant Matthews at Etaples at the request of his mother. The object of the 1928 British Legion Battlefields Pilgrimage was stated as being 'to offer homage to the million dead of the British Empire'.[6] In 1936 King Edward VIII unveiled the Vimy memorial as the high point of the pilgrimage of 8,000 Canadian veterans to Vimy Ridge. David W. Lloyd calls this 'the most important and largest Dominion pilgrimage' and argues persuasively that it constituted both an assertion of Canadian identity and an affirmation of its role in and contribution to the Empire. King Edward VIII participated as King of Canada, was welcomed by a Canadian Cabinet Minister and inspected a Canadian guard of honour, and *O, Canada* was played immediately after *God Save the King*. But then, after this event, the pilgrims travelled to London, where they were addressed by Prime Minister Stanley Baldwin, marched to the Cenotaph to the strains of *Land of Hope and Glory* and were entertained at a garden party at Buckingham Palace where the King appeared to cheers and the impromptu rendition of *For He's a Jolly Good Fellow* and *God Save the King*, demonstrating that Canadian nationalism was perfectly compatible with Empire membership and royalist sentiment.[7]

Even in Ireland – from 1921 the Irish Free State – there were Armistice Day commemoration services in Phoenix Park, where 80,000 people regularly gathered, wearing poppies, carrying Union Jacks and singing *God Save the King*, to lay wreaths at a memorial cross. There were incidents reported of Republicans snatching poppies. In 1930 a dozen young men tried to seize the Union Jacks. 'They were severely handled by the ex-servicemen and five of them had to be treated in hospital', reported *The Times*.[8] The ceremony was regularly led by General Sir William Hickie (at this time an Irish Senator) who had commanded the 16th Irish Division in France.

Music played a vital role in the construction of remembrance, in the evocation of memory, in the provision of consolation. Hymns were of course integral to Remembrance services, a reassurance of eternal life for the fallen, an affirmation of the Christian aspect of war. One new hymn became an instant fixture in the proceedings. It was played and sung every year at the Westminster Abbey service of Remembrance and in many other services too. It was Sir John Arkwright's *O Valiant Hearts*, which had been published only in 1919 in a collection entitled *The Supreme Sacrifice*. It was set to music by Charles Harris. His tune, says Oliver Neighbour, 'late Victorian in flavour and undeniably memorable, appealed strongly to the taste of the congregations, who made the most of it with heavy vibrato and portamentos'.[9] When *Songs of Praise* was published in 1925, the editors rejected Harris's tune and introduced two new settings, a complicated and difficult one by Gustav Holst called *Valiant Hearts*, and a simple adapted traditional tune by Vaughan Williams called *Valor*. *Hymns Ancient and Modern* preferred Dr Martin Shaw's *Julius*. None of them supplanted Harris's tune, which was duly printed with the hymn in *The Baptist Hymnal* in 1933. Harris's tune has continued to command public affection, and still features in Remembrance Day services.

The hymn, which compares the fallen to Christ crucified, memorably evoked chivalric images of service and patriotism:

> O Valiant hearts, who to your glory came
> Through dust of conflict and through battle flame;
> Tranquil you lie, your knightly virtue proved,
> Your memory hallowed in the land you loved.
>
> Proudly you gathered, rank on rank, to war,
> As who had heard God's message from afar;
> All you had hoped for, all you had, you gave
> To save mankind – yourself you scorned to save.
>
> Splendid you passed, the great surrender made,
> Into the light that never more shall fade;
> Deep your contentment in that blest abode,
> Who wait the last clear trumpet-call of God.

The other regularly used hymns were familiar and well-loved yet evoked a passionate and moving response when sung. *Abide With Me* became so much a part of the ceremonies that the words and musical notes of the hymn were included in the wrought iron work around the war memorial at Marazion.

At the service in Westminster Abbey for the burial of the Unknown Warrior in 1920 the choir unaccompanied sang *O Valiant Hearts*. The organist played *O God Our Help in Ages Past* and everyone joined in singing what *The Times* called 'the most helpful and encouraging of our familiar hymns'.[10] The service itself included *Abide With Me*, *The Lord Is My Shepherd*, *Lead, Kindly Light* and Kipling's *Recessional*, 'and the great wave of feeling which that hymn always arouses could be felt surging through the whole congregation and seen in many a woman, and even some men, finding expression in tears'. The following year it was *O Valiant Hearts* ('the now familiar hymn', *The Times* called it), *The Lord Is My Shepherd*, *O God Our Help in Ages Past* and *God Save the King*.[11] The service at Westminster Abbey, focused on the tomb of the Unknown Warrior, became as much a part of Armistice Day as the wreath-laying at the Cenotaph in the 1920s and 1930s. 'The double pilgrimage to the Cenotaph and to the Unknown Warrior's Tomb in Westminster Abbey has now plainly all the strength of an accepted tradition', reported *The Times* in 1927.[12]

On Armistice Day 1919 one of the most striking events occurred at the Mansion House where, fifteen minutes before 11 a.m., the Salvation Army Headquarters Band appeared on the balcony in the presence of the Lord Mayor and city corporation, and the great crowds in the street took up the hymns they played. *The Times* reported of *Jesu, Lover of My Soul* that 'it appeared as if all London had given voice to this hymn of solace and refuge'. 'Still more impressive was the singing of *Nearer my God to Thee* to the Horbury setting immortalized by the tragedy of the *Titanic*'; and 'then like a great *Te Deum* that rose from the throats of thousands the great hymn *O God Our Help in Ages Past*'. After two-minutes' silence and *The Last Post*, *Praise God From Whom All Blessings Flow* and the national anthem were played. In 1920 the band again played *Lead, Kindly Light*, *Rock of Ages*, *O God Our Help in Ages Past*, *Nearer My God to Thee* and the national anthem. *The Times* reported: 'The great crowd, bareheaded . . . sang with a fervour seldom, if ever, heard before'.[13]

In a sense, the memorials, the Cenotaph and the Tomb of the Unknown Warrior were for the bereaved, for those left behind. What was there for the survivors? During the 1920s there were repeated rows about the holding of victory balls and celebrations of the end of the war. Rejoicing was deemed by many inappropriate and remembrance more in keeping with the national mood. A great victory ball planned for the Albert Hall on Armistice Day, 1925 was cancelled and replaced by a service of Remembrance.

For several years the musical centrepiece of the British Legion's Remembrance activities was a work directly inspired by the war and now largely forgotten. It was written by the left-wing composer John Foulds, who created a fine and now rarely heard body of music, notably a superb piano concerto, the *Dynamic Triptych*. He set out to write 'a tribute to the memory of the Dead – a message of consolation to the bereaved of all countries'. Working between 1919 and 1921, he produced a large-scale cantata, the *World Requiem*, which his biographer Malcolm Macdonald describes as 'grand, noble, idealistic . . . of elegaic and benedictory tone, implicitly Christian but supra-denominational in spiritual focus'. Foulds set texts from the Bible, *The Pilgrim's Progress* and the work of the sixteenth-century Hindu poet Kabir to 'express a desire for a new era of peace which will prepare for the coming of the Kingdom of God'. Macdonald argues that Foulds 'strove to achieve a radiant, shimmering sound-fabric of extraordinary incandescence' and achieved 'some dazzlingly beautiful music'.[14]

Foulds made over all royalties from the *Requiem* for the first five years to the British Legion. The work was first performed on 11 November 1923 at the Albert Hall in aid of the Legion. The Prince of Wales, Prince George, Princess Louise and 'many representatives of the Dominions and of the Diplomatic Corps' were present. Foulds himself conducted a choir and orchestra numbering 1,250. Macdonald recalls:

> It was a tremendous success – with the general public. The audience was ecstatic, many of them in tears; the ovation at the end for Foulds lasted ten minutes, and literally hundreds of congratulatory letters arrived in the following days.[15]

The Times recorded:

> The scope of the work is beyond what anyone has dared to attempt hitherto. It is no less than to find expression for the deepest and most widespread unhappiness that this generation has known. As such it was received by a very large number of listeners who evidently had felt that music alone could do this for them. They found perhaps in the communal note of that choir of 1,200 the sympathy of which they stood in need and in the words . . . the consolation they hoped for.[16]

For the critics, the work was, however, an almost total failure, being dismissed variously as pretentious, monotonous and simplistic.

Its popularity with audiences ensured that there were repeat performances on Armistice Day in 1924, 1925 and 1926, when it was received with continuing enthusiasm. But then it was dropped, and it has never been performed since. Like Macdonald, Stradling and Hughes[17] believe there was a conspiracy against Foulds and his music.

[159]

They may well be right. Macdonald records that the *Daily Express* was 'particularly abusive and was to remain an implacable foe' of the work, and that in 1927 the paper began sponsoring the annual British Legion Festival of Empire and Remembrance. The likelihood is that the *Express* found the *Requiem* insufficiently 'Christian' and patriotic and too universalist for its taste. One sympathetic critic observed that it was 'not exclusively a religious work' and 'not a distinctively national work'. Foulds had set his face against musical nationalism in general and folk-song-based English national music in particular. He was to write in his 1934 book *Music To-Day*:

> Following the war, a period of somewhat exaggerated musical patriotism ensued. All countries participated. The author had best say at once that it is an attitude with which he has little sympathy. There are a number of persons in the musical world who look for the salvation of a country's music to the intensification of its national characteristics, and would base a new national music upon its old folk-songs. Frankly, I am not one of these . . . For present-day composers . . . to concentrate upon such . . . narrow nationalistic phenomena goes clean against the main evolutionary trend of the art. Only out of a new realization of world-wide emotional-mental solidarity . . . can the real music of the future be born.[18]

Bitterly disappointed at the fate of the *Requiem*, Foulds went abroad for several years. Returning in 1930, he found it impossible to get his serious music performed. His light music was regularly played on the BBC but his serious music was just as regularly rejected, as he complained to Dr Adrian Boult in 1933.[19] In 1935 he and his wife, long-time supporters of Indian nationalist aspirations, left for India where Foulds became Director of Music for All-India Radio, only to die of cholera in 1939. He remains one of the lost talents of English music.

The first *Daily Express*-sponsored British Legion Festival of Empire and Remembrance took place at the Royal Albert Hall on 11 November 1927. It was an immediate success. It was broadcast by the BBC and was to become a fixture in the radio schedules thereafter. But, significantly, this was also the first important occasion to be broadcast to the whole Empire by the new high-power short-wave transmitter at Chelmsford. The motive of the *Daily Express* in sponsoring the Festival was 'the necessity for renewing that comradeship that existed during the war and to remind the British Empire of the unpaid debt to those men still unplaced in civil life who served their country'.[20] It was attended by the Prince of Wales, himself a veteran of the Western Front, who addressed the assembled veterans as 'Old comrades and friends' and was received with prolonged applause and a chorus of *For He's a Jolly Good Fellow*. The Prince spoke of the way in which rejoicing at the Armistice had been replaced by a mood of remembrance and that there were both private and shared memories. He said that they should remember not only the dead but the living, the need to prevent future wars and to strive for peace. He concluded: 'Lastly, we can remember this great Empire, for whose honour and existence we fought, that this great Empire is alive and that comradeship is its vital spot. Only in such remembrance can we redeem the sacrifices of all those who served the name and cause of Britain in that great day, that great time of trial.' The speech was greeted by cheers and followed by a singing of *Onward, Christian Soldiers*.

The Festival of Remembrance was followed by a torchlit procession to the Cenotaph in Whitehall with the Band of the Irish Guards playing *There's a Long, Long Trail A-winding*. Then, gathered around the Cenotaph, the veterans sang *Abide With Me* and *God Save the King*, before *The Last Post* was sounded. This encapsulates the mixture of shared sentiments that the annual Festival of Empire and Remembrance was to evoke – comradeship, Christian faith and patriotism.

The event was an extraordinary and potent blend of populism and patriotism, of sentiment and faith, of the formal and the informal, the official and the unofficial. The ethos was distinctly different from that informing Foulds's *World Requiem*. The first part of the Festival involved the communal singing of the popular songs of the War. They were 'sung with a zest which only those who had sung them in far different and less inspiring circumstances are capable', said *The Times*.[21] Many of them were deeply sentimental: *Keep the Home Fires Burning*; *There's a Long, Long Trail A-winding*; *If You Were the Only Girl in the World*; *It's a Long Way to Tipperary*; *Take Me Back to Dear Old Blighty*; *Pack Up Your Troubles in Your Old Kit Bag and Smile, Smile, Smile*. There were orchestral pieces (Sir Alexander Mackenzie's *Benedictus*; Sullivan's *In Memoriam*; Vaughan Williams's *Folk Song Suite*; Chopin's *Funeral March*; and, interestingly, Foulds's *Keltic Suite*) and patriotic songs (*Land of Hope and Glory*; *Soldiers of the King*; *Boy of the Old Brigade*; *Hearts of Oak*).

The second half included hymns (*Abide With Me*; *Nearer My God to Thee*; *Lead, Kindly Light*; *O Valiant Hearts*; *Now Thank We All Our God*; *Jerusalem*; and Kipling's *Recessional*), prayers, a shower of Flanders' poppies and the recitation of Laurence Binyon's lines from *For the Fallen* – 'They shall grow not old as we that are left grow old'. *The Last Post* and the national anthem concluded events. The musical items all blended in a seamless web of memory, affirmation, regret, pride and unity.

Along with the other shared memories were the memories of Empire. In 1928 the Prince of Wales did not attend the Festival because he was in Nairobi, Kenya, where after laying a wreath at the Armistice Day ceremony he said that 'the service of remembrance in which they had joined that day united the whole Empire in a common thought more than any other annual ceremony',[22] and he spoke about this event and the bond it constituted when he addressed the Festival of Empire and Remembrance in 1929. The 1929 Festival included a *tableau* of Britannia and her Empire. The 1930 Festival was attended by the Indian Princes, including the celebrated cricketer Ranjit Sinjhi, who were in London for the Round Table Conference. The 1931 Festival featured J.M. Rogan's *Festival of Empire* fantasia which was woven together out of tunes and themes representing many of the constituent countries of the Empire, climaxing with England: Africa, Australia (*There's a Land Where Summer Skies*), Burma (*Kaya than*), Scotland (*Annie Laurie*), Fiji Islands (*Autiko mai na*), New Zealand (*God Defend New Zealand*), India (popular theme), Wales (*Land of My Fathers*), Ireland (*Killarney*), Jamaica (*Kalinka*), Canada (*O, Canada*), Hong Kong (Chinese flower song *Moolee Wha*) and England (*Sailor's Hornpipe, Land of Hope and Glory* and *Rule, Britannia*). In 1932 the King and Queen attended, and *Here's a Health Unto His Majesty* was sung. There were always representatives of the royal family, often the Prince of Wales and the Duke of York, at the Festival. There were many musical festivals of Remembrance following the same format.

The BBC played an important part in bringing the nation and the Empire together on these memorial occasions. From the outset Sir John Reith, the BBC's Director-General, wanted to broadcast the Cenotaph service. From 1923 the BBC was permitted to broadcast the two-minutes' silence and *The Last Post* at 11 a.m. In 1927 it broadcast the Armistice Day service from Canterbury Cathedral. But from 1928 the BBC was permitted to broadcast the whole Cenotaph ceremony, and it has remained a fixture in the broadcasting year ever since. In 1929 the BBC relayed it to Canada and in 1931 to New Zealand. The BBC also broadcast every year from its inception in 1927 the annual British Legion Festival of Empire and Remembrance.

But there was more. On 11 November 1927 the BBC broadcast an Armistice Day national concert from the Queen's Hall, directed by Sir Edward Elgar and Sir Henry Wood. The sombre programme consisted of *God Save the King*, Elgar's *Lux Christi*, Parry's *Glories of Our Blood and State*, Chopin's *Funeral March*, Elgar's *The Spirit of England* and the finale of Beethoven's *Symphony No. 9*. There was an internal BBC debate about the composers to be represented. Gregory quotes an internal BBC memo saying that all composers were to be British, except Handel and Chopin – who were as good as British and French; but in the event Beethoven was played.[23] The concert also included Lord

Balfour reading Pericles's funeral oration and General Sir Ian Hamilton reading *Let Us Now Praise Famous Men.*

On 11 November 1928, the Armistice Day concert was repeated, with the BBC Wireless Symphony Orchestra and Chorus under Percy Pitt. This time there were no German composers in the programme, which consisted of Liszt's *A Dirge for Heroes,* Gounod's *Judex,* Elgar's *The Spirit of England* and *Immortal Legions,* and Sullivan's *In Memoriam* overture. In 1929 the BBC opted instead for a production of R.C. Sherriff's powerful war play *Journey's End,* but on Armistice Day in 1930, 1932, 1933, 1937 and 1938 there were programmes of mixed music and poetry. Elgar featured strongly in these programmes and, in addition to them, Elgar conducted his own setting of *For the Fallen* on the wireless on 11 November 1932. On 11 November 1934 the whole of Elgar's *The Spirit of England* was played.

Bob Bushaway has argued that the theme of remembrance so permeated interwar British society that it defused those popular expectations and aspirations which elsewhere had led to revolution and nationalism.

> Throughout the inter-war period British society witnessed an annual event in which social and political unity was reaffirmed. Other views and criticisms of the Great War were regarded as doing dishonour to the dead. The chronology of remembrance was a powerful thread of continuity which linked individual and collective memory . . . Armistice Day became a point of reference for British society. The festivities of victory gave way to the sombre mood in which the sacrifice of the dead was renewed and to which Church, state and Crown did reverence. Through the annual act of remembrance the demons of discontent and disorder were purged and the mass of British society was denied access to a political critique of the war by Kipling's universal motto 'lest we forget'.[24]

At one level, he is right. But it is worth pointing out that revolution and nationalism flourished most strongly in those countries which had lost the war. Britain had won the war and needed to make sense of victory rather than defeat. Alex King provides an explanation for these circumstances:

> The idea of community was the basis on which a sense of validity, of meaning, for death in the war was constructed. Death could be made meaningful if it was seen as service to the community, as protection of it, purification of it, warning to it, or restoration of it to an older and better identity. Loyalty to one's community provided an explanation of death in the war, a reason for seeing death as having intrinsic value, and a proposal for action on the part of the living which would keep that value alive.[25]

The rhetoric of commemoration involved a web of community inextricably interlinked: 'the community of the dead with the living, of the dead amongst themselves . . . of all mourners, or of those who now had the obligation to ensure the sacrifices of war were not in vain, of the nation . . . and most especially of the localities from which the dead had come – their homes'. This is not something which is imposed. It is something which is spontaneous and deeply felt across classes. If Bushaway is implying that it was deliberately created in order to defuse discontent, then he is mistaken. It may have had that effect. But it was fostered and given form by men who shared the widespread feeling of the need to revere the dead, to ensure that they had not died in vain and to commemorate their sacrifice.

Music played an important part in such remembrance, triggering memories and focusing emotions, and it is worthy of note that the music derived from all genres and idioms and that frequently, as for instance at the Festival of Empire and Remembrance, all the different idioms met and mingled, just as did the classes. There were the soldiers' own marching songs, the reminder of comradeship and shared hardship and danger. There were the hymns, also participatory and communal, but reflecting more on sacrifice and service, on life after death and Christian fortitude. There was classical music, often elegiac and transcendent, seeking to translate feelings of loss and memory into pure musical form. If one were to choose an example of each of the three forms, still recognizable today and popular then because they answered the needs of the people and expressed in words and music their mixed emotions and reactions to the Great War, they would be *It's a Long Way to Tipperary*, *O Valiant Hearts* and Elgar's *The Spirit of England*. It was once again the apostles of Empire who found themselves in tune with the heart of the nation, as Kipling, whose son had been killed in the war, devised the simple and moving epitaphs (*Lest We Forget*, *Their Name Liveth For Evermore*, *A Soldier of the Great War Known Unto God*) that were carved on the memorials, as it was Elgar who found the melodies to enhance the emotions provoked by Laurence Binyon's unforgettable lines which were recited annually and movingly at British Legion ceremonies.

Empire Day

The whole notion of Empire was brought home to everyone by the institution of Empire Day, on Queen Victoria's Birthday, 24 May. It was the brainchild of Reginald Brabazon, 12th Earl of Meath, who in 1896 began campaigning for a specific day to be instituted to focus the mind of the nation on the values and virtues of the Empire. Meath's aim, as he explained in a letter to the Colonial Secretary Joseph Chamberlain, was

> to hasten the time when the whole Empire shall be more closely bound together than at present, by drawing the attention of the next generation to imperial questions, by giving them the knowledge which shall enable them to perceive the advantages of a closer federation, by stimulating the feelings of loyalty towards their common Sovereign, and by filling their minds with an affectionate regard for their fellow-subjects in other portions of the Empire.[26]

In a speech to launch the Empire Day Movement, he stressed that it was the antithesis of jingoism and sought to emphasize the duties and responsibilities that citizenship of the Empire carried, to promote the Christian spirit of peace and goodwill towards men and to ensure harmony and mutual tolerance between classes, races and political parties.[27] In consequence, much of the activity of the Empire Day Movement was directed towards the young, and Meath was delighted when in 1906 Kipling offered him the use of the verses he had composed for *Puck of Pook's Hill*:

> Land of our birth, we pledge to thee
> Our love and toil in the years to be;
> When we are grown and take our place
> As men and women with our race.

Seeing this and the succeeding verses as a catechism for Empire Day, he even suggested it should be set to music and distributed in pamphlet form.[28] In due course it received fourteen different musical settings and was included in four hymn books to the tunes *Truro*, *Richmond*, *Jubilee* and *Llangollen*. The idea of Empire Day was enthusiastically taken up across the Empire, and 24 May was declared a public holiday in Canada (1901), Australia (1905), New Zealand and South Africa (1910) and India (1912). It was not formally adopted by the British Government until 1916, but from then until 1958, when it was rechristened Commonwealth Day, it was a major annual event.

There were Empire Day church services, concerts and displays. It was particularly important in schools, where Empire plays and pageants, parades and drills were staged, and exhibitions of Empire products. Liverpudlian Frank Unwin remembered:

> At school in the 20s and 30s we celebrated Empire Day in a big way. The Scouts, Girl Guides and Boys Brigade all wore their uniforms. The playground was decorated with flags and bunting . . . After morning assembly we all marched into the playground where there was a pageant of boys and girls dressed in the national costumes of various countries of

the Empire. We sang all the patriotic songs including *Land of Hope and Glory* and the National Anthem as the Union Jack was unfurled. A half-holiday followed. And it always seemed to be sunny and warm on Empire Day.[29]

This kind of spectacle brought alive in a vivid and emotional way the meaning of Empire. It supplemented for children what they learned in the classroom where both history and geography lessons were geared to familiarizing pupils with the countries, peoples and produce of the Empire and the British heroes who had created it.

From 1927 to 1932 the *Daily Express*, which strongly supported the Empire and imperial causes, sponsored an annual Empire Day Festival of Community Singing in Hyde Park. Community singing was a major phenomenon of the 1920s. It was different from the choral tradition which like the brass band movement was surviving in diminished form after 1918, undermined by rival leisure attractions and the terrible loss of young men, the potential next generation of performers, in the Great War. Community singing was mass participation, unrehearsed, on the part of the individuals there gathered.

Ronald Pearsall suggests that the phenomenon began at football grounds and gramophone companies began recording these performances.[30] One such had 14,000 voices at Fulham's Craven Cottage ground singing *Land of Hope and Glory*. Community singing became a recognized part of the proceedings at the Wembley Cup Final until the 1960s when the orderly organized singing conducted from a rostrum was drowned out by the raucous ritual chants proclaiming rival loyalties and signalling the decline of the idea of community.

It was the *Daily Express* in 1926 which took up the active promotion of community singing, declaring that 'for the last one hundred and fifty years the British people have had little or no opportunity of meeting in public to sing without restraint. The *Daily Express* will awaken the power of song once more in Great Britain.'[31] It cannot be mere coincidence that all this took place in 1926, the year of the General Strike, an event which was the culmination of several years of post-war industrial unrest and considerable anxiety in high places about the social cohesiveness and political stability of the country. The mass singing was a clear sign of social cohesion. The idea of 'everyone singing from the same hymn sheet' had a symbolic as well as an actual importance. The range of songs sung on these occasions included genuine folk-songs, sea shanties, hymns, music-hall songs, American minstrel songs, drinking songs, wartime marching songs, anything with a catchy tune and simple chorus.

Community singing became associated with the Empire, thanks to the *Daily Express*. The *Express* may well have noted the enthusiasm with which the spectators joined in singing at various events at the Wembley Empire Exhibition. In 1927 the *Express* began to sponsor both the Empire Day Community Singing in Hyde Park and the British Legion Festival of Empire and Remembrance at the Albert Hall. Community singing was also introduced at the Aldershot Military Tattoo in 1927, sponsored by the *Daily Express*. In 1928 the *Daily News* sponsored the community singing and from 1930 to 1939 its sponsor was the *News Chronicle*.

On 24 May, 1928, the Hyde Park Empire Day Festival took place in the presence of the Duke of Gloucester. Crowds, massed 300 feet deep around the bandstand, participated vigorously in the choruses of a programme of patriotic songs. Dame Clara Butt was the soloist with the Bands of the Coldstream Guards and the Welsh Guards. She sang *Rule, Britannia, Land of Hope and Glory, Jerusalem* and *Onward, Christian Soldiers*, among other items. An attempt to broadcast a telephone message from the Prime Minister of Canada Mr MacKenzie King failed due to atmospheric conditions, but the Canadian High Commissioner in London, Mr P.C. Larkin, read his message to the assembled crowds:

> For many years the seas have divided the young households of the British Empire from the Motherland. Today, with the progress of aviation and radio communication, their waters no longer divide us. On this Empire Day Canada is proud to be associated with the British Isles and other nations of the Empire in proclaiming a common allegiance to His Majesty the King.[32]

On 24 May, 1929, the Festival began with the Massed Bands of the Coldstream, Irish and Welsh Guards playing *Pack Up Your Troubles, John Brown's Body* and *Tipperary*, with the crowd singing along. Then there was a Procession of Empire, involving Boy Scouts, Girl Guides, Chelsea Pensioners, National Naval Cadet Corps and the Legion of Frontiersmen, carrying the flags of the dominions. A procession of church representatives and massed choirs, headed by the Bishop of Kensington, entered to the strains of *Onward, Christian Soldiers*. The Union Jack and the flags of the Empire were broken out and Dr Malcolm Sargent conducted the massed bands, choirs and audience in *Land of Hope and Glory*. The Bishop of Kensington offered a prayer for the recovery of the King from his illness. Everybody present said The Lord's Prayer and the choir sang the anthem *The Heavens Are Telling*.

The highlight was an address by the Prime Minister Stanley Baldwin, which was broadcast by the BBC. He stressed the fact that the Empire stood for service, peace and loyalty to the Crown: 'His

Majesty is everybody's King.' After the address, the hymns *O, God, Our Help in Ages Past* and *Abide With Me* were sung and the proceedings concluded with the national anthem. It seems likely that the strong religious element in the proceedings derived from the desire to give thanks for the recovery of the King–Emperor.[33]

A similar programme of community singing, Empire procession, church service and hymns took place in 1930. In 1931 the procession of Empire consisted of a group of young women in the costumes of Canada, Australia, New Zealand, Africa and India, borne on litters through the ranks of the audience by a contingent of the Legion of Frontiersmen. Sir Edward Elgar conducted the massed bands and choir in *Land of Hope and Glory* and a specially composed poem, *The Exiles*, by Alfred Noyes was declaimed from her motor car by the actress Dame Madge Kendal, who was unable to ascend the dais due to the heavy rain.

Disaster struck in 1932, when the featured pageant was to be *A Vision of Empire*, produced by historian Arthur Bryant. The Festival had to be abandoned when thousands of people broke into the Hyde Park arena shortly before proceedings were due to begin at 9.30 p.m. This was no anti-imperial protest; it was the hordes of people wanting to participate in the community singing. The police tried for an hour to hold back the over-enthusiastic mob. The Regimental Band of the Coldstram Guards entered and the singing began, but the constant surges in the crowd threatened a disaster. Several women fainted and had to be removed by ambulance men. *The Times* compared the scene to the first Wembley Cup Final when mounted police had to control excess numbers of spectators. Shortly after 10.20 p.m. it was decided that the Festival would have to be abandoned. The microphones were not working because the wires had been trampled by the crowds. The producer appealed to the crowd through a megaphone not to panic and to 'behave like an English crowd'. The band played the national anthem and everyone stood still, the men baring their heads. The lights were switched off and the crowd dispersed peacefully. Despite the chaotic ending to the events, *The Times* was able to report with evident satisfaction that 'the crowd remained good-humoured and accepted the situation philosophically'.[34] There were no further Hyde Park Festivals of Empire.

There was controversy in Empire Day celebrations elsewhere in the country. In 1930 the Mayor of Harrogate, father-in-law of the prominent Labour politician Philip Snowden, objected to the presence in the Empire Day programme in his town of *Rule, Britannia* and *Hearts of Oak*, calling them 'boastful war songs'. They were deleted from the Official Programme but the local branch of the British Legion had them printed in a separate programme and they were sung prior to the arrival of the Mayor.[35]

The BBC played an important part in the celebration of Empire Day. The broadcasting service had been set up in 1922 with a monopoly and finance from a licence fee, following negotiations between the Post Office, which controlled the air waves, and the radio industry, which manufactured the equipment. The Post Office was anxious to avoid what it saw as the chaos of unregulated broadcasting in the United States and was concerned with the function of broadcasting as a public utility. But it had no philosophy, no overall vision. That was provided by John Reith, Director-General of the BBC from 1923 to 1938. His book *Broadcast Over Britain* (1924) provided a manifesto for public service broadcasting based on a firm set of principles: the maintenance of high standards; a unified policy towards the whole service; the preservation of a high moral tone; the spreading of culture, knowledge and education, and not just of entertainment; the promotion of inter-class harmony and national cohesiveness; creating an informed and enlightened public as part of the political process in a mass democracy. Contrary to what those detractors who dubbed him 'the Czar of Savoy Hill' claimed, Reith believed in democracy, but his definition of it was freedom of *access* rather than freedom of *choice*. He saw what he called 'the brute force of monopoly' as the best means of implementing his programme. So Reith advocated, worked for and in 1927 achieved the transformation of the British Broadcasting Company into the British Broadcasting Corporation, with a charter, a board of governors and a commitment to public service. This was the instrument through which Reith sought to implement his ideals, providing access to all that was best in music, drama and literature, creating a sense of community through the broadcasting of the great public events in the national calendar – royal, imperial, religious, sporting, political – and promoting an active sense of participatory citizenship by instilling a wider understanding of public affairs.

Promoting pride in and understanding of the Empire was one of Reith's aims. Reith described the broadcasting of the opening of the 1924 Empire Exhibition as 'the biggest thing we have yet done'. Thereafter until well after the Second World War Empire was a major theme in broadcasting. Nothing symbolized the role of the BBC as national unifier so much as the King's Christmas Day broadcast, which began in 1932 and brought the voice of the sovereign into homes all over the Empire. The King regularly emphasized the idea of Empire and nation as family and this was entirely in tune with Reith's conception of the BBC audience. By 1939 three-quarters of British households had a wireless set, and the wireless was instrumental in the promotion of a national culture that transcended class and social boundaries without diminishing their importance, that was middle-brow rather than middle-class and whose role was the expression of shared values such as patriotism, religion, chivalry, domesticity and a belief in law and order.[36] Lord Meath wrote in the *Radio Times* of the value of broadcasting to Empire awareness:

> Broadcasting under its present wise and statesmanlike direction has proved a blessing to the British nation, spreading unconsciously a sane knowledge, and adding much innocent pleasure to millions of people. On Empire Day, through its instrumentality, the sovereign and the citizens of these islands will be brought into the happiest and closest relationship, and the latter will enjoy the privilege of listening to the voice of the Prime Minister of their choice.

He declared the watchwords of the Empire Day Movement to be *responsibility, duty, sympathy* and *self-sacrifice.*

> These four watchwords express the spirit which will ensure the defence, honour and well-being of the whole Empire . . . but still more do they express the living spirit which should preserve it from the fate which has befallen the Empires of the past.[37]

The Prime Minister broadcast an Empire Day message every year until 1933. The BBC broadcast the Empire Day service, and until its demise in 1932 the annual *Daily Express* Empire Day Festival from Hyde Park. There was an annual Empire Day message for schools. Then, in 1933, following the institution of the new BBC Empire Service there began a major series of documentaries, produced in turn by broadcasting organizations of the Empire. It began with 'News From Home', featuring the daily life and institutions of Britain. But thereafter the programmes came from Australia (1934), Canada (1935), South Africa (1936) and India (1937). On Empire Day 1936 there was the first ever broadcast of readings from Kipling's works, vetoed by the author during his lifetime.

Music was an integral part of the proceedings. On 24 May 1924, the BBC broadcast on all stations 'A Commonwealth of Nations', a three-hour feature in song, story and episode, featuring popular songs 'that have played their part in building and consolidating the Empire'. They ranged from *The Golden Vanity* and *Lilibulero* to *Pack Up Your Troubles* and *Tipperary.*

On 24 May 1925, the Empire Day Thanksgiving service was broadcast from Wembley Stadium, and in the evening the Prime Minister gave a fifteen-minute talk on the Empire. The talk was preceded by Charles Godfrey's musical potpourri *Our Empire* and followed by

Elgar's *Pomp and Circumstance March No. 1*. Later, the Empire Day concert given by Sir Dan Godfrey and his Bournemouth Municipal Symphony Orchestra was broadcast. The programme, carefully constructed to represent the constituent parts of the United Kingdom, consisted of Elgar's march *Land of Hope and Glory*, Sir Alexander Mackenzie's *Britannia* overture, Stanford's *Irish Rhapsody*, John Foulds's *Keltic Suite*, German's *Welsh Rhapsody*, Charles Godfrey's selection *Our Empire* and his *Reminiscences of England*, and J.H. Amers's Scotch patrol *The Wee McGregor* and Irish Patrol *The Bhoys of Tipperary*.

On 24 May 1928, the Empire Day feature 'Round the World on Your Bugles Blown', broadcast from 7.45 to 9.00 p.m., was a programme of poetry and song celebrating the Empire. The music included Percy Grainger's *Colonial Song* (Australia), Alexander Mackenzie's *Canadian Rhapsody* and the traditional *Canadian Boat Song* (Canada), Gerard Cobb's setting of Kipling's *Mandalay* (Burma), Maori songs (New Zealand), West African, Zulu and Afrikaans songs sung by the Yoruba Singers (Africa), Grainger's arrangement of the *Londonderry Air* (Ireland) and Elgar's *Pomp and Circumstance March No. 1* (Britain).

On 24 May 1935, the BBC broadcast the first-ever Empire Day Royal Command Concert. Sir Walford Davies, Master of the King's Musick, wrote in the *Radio Times*:

> His Majesty, having in mind the value of the pursuit of music throughout the country and Empire at all times, but especially now when the healthy use of increased and even enforced leisure is becoming a world problem, has desired that this Command Concert should be devised to bring together picked 'musical troops' from the whole of the British Isles, to typify and help to encourage national music-making in as comprehensive and representative a way as possible.[38]

Choirs drawn from all parts of the United Kingdom, a cast of all-star singers and players drawn from a variety of orchestras including of course the BBC Symphony Orchestra, performed. The conductors included Sir Adrian Boult, Sir Henry Wood, Sir Hugh Roberton, Sir Landon Ronald, Dr Malcolm Sargent and Ralph Vaughan Williams.

The idea of the concert was to trace the history of British music through from the Middle Ages to the present, and so it began with *Summer Is Icumen In* and *Agincourt Song*, and proceeded through songs by Purcell and Arne, taking care to feature specifically Scottish and Welsh items: the Hymn *The Old 124th*, the Gaelic air *The Isle of Mull* and the Hebridean melody *The Road to the Isles* (arranged by Marjorie Kennedy-Fraser) for Scotland; and hymn tune *Caerllungoed*, the harp tune *Rising of the Lark* and the traditional air *Nos Colan* for Wales; to some imitation period works, Sullivan's overture *The Yeomen of the Guard*, Edward German's song *Oh Peaceful England* from *Merrie England*, Vaughan Williams's *Hugh's Song* from *Hugh the Drover* and Roger Quilter's song *Non Nobis, Domine*; and, finally, as a celebration of 'the musical leaders of the King's reign', Elgar's *Nimrod* and *Busyness* and the Irish air *My Love's an Arbutus*, Holst's *Jupiter* from the *Planets* suite and Parry's festival song *England*. This last work was set to a paraphrase by Sir Esme Howard of John of Gaunt's deathbed speech from *Richard II*, which ended:

> Grant, Lord, that England and her sister nations,
> Together bound by the triumphant sea,
> May be renown'd through all recorded ages
> For Christian service and true Chivalry.

In 1938, with King George VI now on the throne, a second Empire Day Royal Command Concert in the presence of the King and Queen was arranged for 24 May, and once again was broadcast. Sir Walford Davies wrote in the *Radio Times* that the aim of the concert was to encourage British music and benefit musicians, and that the programme would be 'representative British music such as all Britishers can together enjoy', along the lines approved by King George V for the previous concert.[39] It was to be music that was both popular and good, performed by invited musicians and broadcast to Britain and the Empire. The music was chosen by 'the great and good' of the musical world, a committee including Vaughan Williams, Sir Hugh Allen, Sir Henry Wood and Sir Adrian Boult. The orchestra consisted of members drawn from four other orchestras, the chorus made up of singers representing the different parts of the United Kingdom and the dominions and the conductors included Sir Hugh Allen, Sir Henry Wood and Dr Malcolm Sargent. Many of the pieces from the previous concert were repeated as the programme ranged from the Middle Ages to the present. It opened with fanfares specially composed by Sir Granville Bantock, Dr Ernest Bullock and Major Adkins, and among its madrigals, glees, part-songs, hornpipes, Scottish, Welsh and English airs and folk-songs were included also Purcell's chorus from the *Ode on St. Cecilia's Day*, Elgar's *Imperial March*, Delius's *La Calinda*, Bax's *Paean*, the finale to Vaughan Williams's cantata *Dona Nobis Pacem* and Parry's *Jerusalem*.

John M. MacKenzie has traced the internal battles at the BBC about Empire Day broadcasting, where, despite the enthusiasm of Reith, many disliked both tone and content.[40] But the dissenters were regularly overruled. The Second World War gave a boost to the Empire, and

Empire Day documentaries and concerts had the added purpose of cementing the imperial war effort. On 24 May 1942, the BBC Home Service broadcast an Empire Day Concert performed by the BBC Symphony Orchestra, conducted by Sir Adrian Boult. It consciously sought to represent the dominions by composers or performers, with Douglas Gordon Lilburn's overture *Aotearoa* (New Zealand), John Gough's *The Wallaby Track* (Australia), the *Dorian Fugue* for strings by Graham George (Canada), Mozart's *Piano Concerto No. 23* (first movement), with Etienne Amyot as soloist (South Africa). Britain was represented by Elgar's *Imperial March*, Delius's *Song Before Sunrise* and Vaughan Williams's *Pavane for the Sons of the Morning* from *Job*. On 24 May 1943, there was an 'Empire Day tribute in music and song' with the BBC Theatre Orchestra and Chorus under Stanford Robinson, and Tom Burke and Margaret McArthur as soloists. In 1944, 1945 and 1946 the Empire Day Movement and the *Sunday Empire News* organized Festivals of Empire at the Royal Albert Hall, with the King and Queen and/or Princess Elizabeth in attendance, and all broadcast by the BBC.

The celebration of Empire Day in 1944 fell shortly after close of the Dominion Prime Ministers' Conference, and all the visiting Premiers recorded individual messages for inclusion in the BBC's Empire Day feature 'The Empire Speaks'. There was an Empire Thanksgiving and Dedication service at St Paul's Cathedral, with an address by the Archbishop of Canterbury. The Empire Day Movement made 'special efforts' to organize celebrations in schools and youth organizations throughout the Empire. *The Times* gave prominence in its news pages to a letter from Viscount Bledisloe, President of the Empire Day Movement, and Lt Colonel Sir William Wayland, MP, its Chairman:

> Never before in the long and honourable history of the British Commonwealth and Empire has there been more abundant justification for expressing our profound and humble thankfulness to God for the existence and the unshaken integrity of our great Empire family. Never have our fighting comrades from the overseas territories of the British Crown shown a grander record of heroism, skill and resourcefulness than during the present war. Many of them complain – and not without reason – of the ignorance of the inhabitants of this old motherland regarding their country's history. Its peoples, its economic products, its ideals, and its ambitions. Let us grasp the unparalleled opportunity which Empire Day affords of showing them that we are mindful of them and their outstanding loyalty and prowess, conscious of our obligations to them and anxious on this occasion to give vocal expression to our feelings of respect and affection for them.[41]

The Empire Day Concert at the Royal Albert Hall, with Sir Adrian Boult conducting the London Philharmonic orchestra and Dame Myra

[173]

Hess as pianist, struck an unusual note, prompting *The Times* to observe:

> A matter of curiosity for the future historian might well be the pro-gramme of an Empire Day Concert at the Albert Hall in the fifth year of a war. Last night, after the National Anthem to salute the arrival of the Queen and Princess Elizabeth, we heard Mozart at his most joyful and finished, the *Impressario* Overture [*sic*] and the A major Piano Con-certo, Elgar at his subtlest, the *Enigma Variations* and Schumann at his most popular which is to say his most romantically German, the Piano Concerto. Even the one piece which might wear a conventionally patri-otic air, the exquisite *Shropshire Lad* Rhapsody by Butterworth, who was killed in the last war, celebrates *rus* rather than *patria*. It was Empire Day honoured indirectly and wisely by some of music's universal mas-terpieces rather than directly, with bombast and fanfare.[42]

The situation was rather different in 1945 when the Festival of Empire arranged by the Empire Day Movement and the *Sunday Empire News* was designed as a tribute to all those who had served the Empire in the European War. It included contingents from the diverse Empire forces. Above the organ a large crown was suspended bedecked by intertwined ribbons of red, white and blue in the shape of a V for Victory sign. Union Jacks and flags of St George were draped around the boxes. The King, the Queen and the Princesses attended. *The Times* reported:

> In effect it was an unofficial indoor victory parade and it was treated as such by the great audience which filled the tiers of seats surrounding the arena from floor to roof. It was an occasion of restrained patriotic fervour as the various contingents marched down a red carpeted dais from an entrance beneath the royal box to their allotted seats behind the plat-form on either side of the great organ in front of which were the massed bands of the Bridge of Guards . . . the greatest enthusiasm was roused when the marching reached its climax and there came the men of the Empire's fighting forces.

Boys of the Old Brigade, Hearts of Oak, Heroes All and the *RAF March* were among the tunes played. *The Times* declared:

> It was a worthy climax to the first part of the evening's programme. The rest with its tableaux, anthems, and hymns was soothing though impres-sive ceremonial following the fervour of the earlier proceedings.[43]

The notable feature of the 1946 Festival of Empire was a message to the youth of the Empire by Princess Elizabeth, broadcast during the interval:

What we are we owe to God's guidance and to the work of our forefathers all over the world, and in proof of this we have those common ideals of freedom, justice and humanity, which are to be found in every corner of our Empire. We cannot think that such a noble brotherhood can have come into existence for no object, or that it is not our duty to do everything in our power to make it flourish. I want to ask you, therefore, to remember this heritage, and to maintain these high ideals, not passively by words but actively by your deeds. Neither must we forget that for a year in this last war we of the Empire stood together and alone, and by doing so saved civilization.[44]

A pageant of youth was a principal feature of the Festival, which involved the Massed Bands of the Brigade of Guards, the Goldsmiths Choral Union and Symphony Orchestra and the Sadlers Wells Opera–Ballet Company which performed dances from Smetana's *The Bartered Bride*. There was also, as in 1945, a march-down of contingents of Empire forces.

But the interest diminished after the war. There was a brief fillip with the Coronation of Queen Elizabeth II, the last great imperial coronation, and there was an Empire Day concert broadcast on the BBC Light Programme on 24 May 1952, with Sir Malcolm Sargent conducting and a thoroughly imperial bill of fare: Elgar's *Pomp and Circumstance Marches No. 1* and *No. 4*, Sullivan's overture *di Ballo*, Walton's march *Crown Imperial*, Edward German's three dances from *Henry VIII*, three Shakespeare songs by Roger Quilter, Vaughan Williams's *Fantasia on Greensleeves*, *Onaway, Awake Beloved* from *Hiawatha's Wedding Feast* by black British composer Samuel Coleridge-Taylor and Australian Percy Grainger's arrangement of an *Irish Tune From County Derry*. It looked back to the musical programmes of the interwar years. The future, though, was to be a story of decolonization, the emergence of the Commonwealth and a rapid waning of interest within Britain and on the part of the BBC in musical celebrations of Empire.

However, for at least half a century, the great ceremonial events in the life of the nation, the coronations and jubilees, the annual Armistice Day and Empire Day celebrations, had been steeped in the imagery, rhetoric and music of Empire. These events had been officially organized and approved, although there is abundant evidence that they were enthusiastically supported, participated in and enjoyed by a large proportion of the population at large.

Notes

1 *The Times*, 12 November, 1927.
2 *The Times*, 12 November, 1919.

3   On the rituals and institutions of Armistice Day, see in particular Adrian Gregory, *The Silence of Memory: Armistice Day 1919–1946*, Oxford: Berg, 1994; and Alex King, *Memorials of the Great War in Britain*, Oxford: Berg, 1998.

4   *The Times*, 12 November, 1920.

5   *The Times*, 12 November, 1923.

6   Bob Bushaway, 'Name upon name: the Great War and remembrance', in Roy Porter (ed.), *Myths of the English*, Cambridge: Polity Press, 1992, pp. 151–2.

7   David W. Lloyd, *Battlefield Tourism*, Oxford: Berg, 1998, pp. 198–207.

8   *The Times*, 12 November, 1930.

9   Alain Frogley (ed.), *Vaughan Williams Studies*, Cambridge: Cambridge University Press, 1996, p. 231.

10 *The Times*, 12 November, 1920.

11 *The Times*, 12 November, 1921.

12 *The Times*, 12 November, 1927.

13 *The Times*, 12 November, 1919.

14 Malcolm MacDonald, *John Foulds*, Rickmansworth: Triad Press, 1975, p. 28.

15 *Ibid.*, p. 29.

16 *The Times*, 12 November, 1923.

17 MacDonald, *John Foulds*, p. 31; Robert Stradling and Meirion Hughes, *The English Musical Renaissance 1860–1940*, London: Routledge, 1993, pp. 207–8.

18 John Foulds, *Music To-Day*, London: Nicholson & Watson, 1934, p. 147.

19 Lewis Foreman (ed.), *From Parry to Britten: British Music in Letters 1900–1945*, London: Batsford, 1987, pp. 166–7.

20 *Daily Express*, 1 November, 1927.

21 *The Times*, 12 November, 1932.

22 *The Times*, 12 November, 1928.

23 Gregory, *The Silence of Memory*, p. 138.

24 Bushaway, 'Name upon name', pp. 160–1.

25 King, *Memorials of the Great War*, pp. 236–7.

26 Reginald, Earl of Meath, *Memories of the Twentieth Century*, London: John Murray, 1924, pp. 43–4.

27 *Ibid.*, p. 78.

28 *Ibid.*, p. 102.

29 Frank Unwin, *Reflections on the Mersey*, Leighton Banastre: Gallery Press, 1984, pp. 50–1.

30 Ronald Pearsall, *Popular Music of the Twenties*, Totowa, NJ: Rowman & Littlefield, 1976, p. 140.

31 *Ibid.*, p. 141.

32 *The Times*, 25 May, 1928.

33 *The Times*, 25 May, 1929.

34 *The Times*, 25 May, 1932.

35 *The Times*, 26 May, 1930.

36 On the social and cultural role of the BBC, see Paddy Scannell and David Cardiff, *A Social History of British Broadcasting 1922–39*, Oxford: Blackwell, 1991; J.C.W. Reith, *Broadcast Over Britain*, London: Hodder & Stoughton, 1924; D.L. LeMahieu, *A Culture for Democracy*, Oxford: Clarendon Press, 1988; John M. MacKenzie, '"In touch with the infinite": the BBC and the Empire, 1923–53', in John M. MacKenzie (ed.), *Imperialism and Popular Culture*, Manchester: Manchester University Press, 1986, pp. 165–91.

37 *Radio Times*, 22 May, 1925.

38 *Radio Times*, 17 May, 1935.

39 *Radio Times*, 20 May, 1938.

40 MacKenzie, '"In touch with the infinite"'.

41 *The Times*, 24 May, 1944.

42 *The Times*, 25 May, 1944.

43 *The Times*, 25 May, 1945.

44 *The Times*, 25 May, 1946.

CHAPTER SIX

Teaching the lessons of Empire: exhibitions and festivals

One of the great cultural phenomena of the age of Empire was the exhibition. From the Great Exhibition in 1851 to the Festival of Britain in 1951, these extravaganzas were an integral part of the cultural life of the nation, attracting bigger and bigger audiences. The Great Exhibition of 1851 attracted over 6 million visitors; the Colonial and Indian Exhibition of 1886, 5.5 million; the 1924–25 Wembley Exhibition, 27 million.[1] They embraced almost every aspect of culture, from high to low. As John M. MacKenzie puts it:

> The secret of their success was that they combined entertainment, education and trade fair on a spectacular scale. By the end of the century, they were enormous funfairs, coupled with, in effect, museums of science, industry and natural history, anthropological and folk displays, emigration bureaux, musical festivals, and art galleries, together with examples of transport and media innovations, all on one large site. They were a wonder of their age, highlighted in the press and other contemporary literature.[2]

For all the elements of entertainment and exotic escapism, however, the organizers never lost sight of the need to educate and inform. Introducing the second session of the Wembley Exhibition to the public in 1925, Lord Stevenson, Chairman of the Exhibition Board, wrote in an article headed 'A University of Empire' that Wembley is 'accomplishing an educational work of great national and Imperial importance', that 'appeal is made to every class of the community' and that a visitor would leave 'with a quickened sense of Imperial achievement and a feeling of pride when he remembers his citizenship'.[3] This could probably have been written about all the previous exhibitions. For, as Paul Greenhalgh has written, 'from 1851 onwards Empire was proudly and exhaustively displayed'. But he detects a change in attitude in the 1880s as the organizers moved from 'complacent pride in Empire to a propagandistic defence of it', as imperial and industrial rivalries and in particular the rise of Germany and the United States began to pre-occupy the authorities.[4] There was a series of government-sponsored exhibitions aimed at awakening among the public pride in and support for the British Empire. The aim of the Colonial and Indian Exhibition of 1886 was stated to be 'to give to the inhabitants of the British Isles, to foreigners and to one another, practical demonstration of the wealth and industrial development of the outlying portions of the British Empire'.[5]

But what is remarkable evidence of the popular appeal of the Empire and all things imperial is the fact that, alongside the official exhibitions, there was a succession of purely commercial ones, staged for profit by the remarkable Hungarian Jewish impresario Imre Kiralfy (1845–1919). He had made his name staging theatrical spectacles such as *Nero or the Fall of Rome* (1889) and *Venice – Bride of the Sea* (1891–92). In 1895 he set up London Exhibitions Ltd, and this company staged an exhibition every year from 1895 to 1907 at Earl's Court. In 1908 Kiralfy created a new exhibition ground at Shepherd's Bush, known as the Great White City, where his exhibitions continued until the war when it was requisitioned by the Government for military use.

Many of the exhibitions at Earl's Court and at Shepherd's Bush had imperial themes. The first one, in 1895, was the Empire of India Exhibition. It was followed by the India, Burma and Ceylon Exhibition, in 1896, the Victorian Era Exhibition, in 1897, the Greater Britain Exhibition, in 1899, the Franco-British Exhibition, in 1908, the Coronation Exhibition, in 1911, and so on. Aside from exhibitions of goods, these displays featured tableaux recreating heroic episodes from imperial history and scenes of human beings in their houses and villages – Maoris, Burmans, Iroquois Indians, Sinhalese, Somalis and Tartars among them. Particularly popular were Dahomeyan and Senegalese villages, from the French Empire, which appeared regularly at both British and French exhibitions. They functioned both as ethnographic curiosities and as confirmation of the theory of racial superiority which buttressed the European Empires.[6] The royal family was strongly supportive of the imperial exhibitions, whether official or commercial, and members of the royal family regularly opened and regularly visited them. Throughout this period there were also imperial exhibitions in many of the cities of Britain and eventually also throughout the Empire itself, with, for example, grand exhibitions at Dunedin (1925–26) and Johannesburg (1936). After the Great War, the 1924–25 Empire Exhibition at Wembley and the 1938 Empire Exhibition in Glasgow were the two principal imperial expositions in Britain itself. The emphasis of the 1951 Festival of Britain was very largely domestic, and confirmed the decline of the imperial sentiment that had animated the exhibitions before the war.

Music was a significant element in the entertainment provided at these exhibitions. For some, special music was provided for the opening. It is a measure of the importance attached by the Government to the 1886 Colonial and Indian Exhibition that it prompted a special ode by Lord Tennyson and set to music by Sir Arthur Sullivan (see chapter two) and the presence of Canadian diva Madame Emma Albani to sing the national anthem.

At most exhibitions military bands were ubiquitous. The trend over the years was that they should play more and more British music. It is striking how little British music is in evidence, for instance, in the daily musical fare of the Colonial and Indian Exhibition in 1886.[7] There were afternoon and evening concerts by the Bands of the First West India Regiment, the Scots Guards, the Coldstream Guards and the Royal Artillery. Of the sixty-three different musical items played, only seven were British: Balfe's march *Riflemen Form*, a selection from and a fantasia on Sir Arthur Sullivan's *The Mikado*, the march from Sir Michael Costa's oratorio *Eli*, Crowe's waltz *Fairie Voices* and two selections of 'Scotch airs' arranged by F. Godfrey. The rest of the musical menu was an attractive and tuneful collection of works by Rossini, Strauss, Offenbach, Gounod, Smetana, Schubert, Mozart, Wagner and Waldteufel.

By 1908 and Kiralfy's Franco-British Exhibition, the amount of British music had increased somewhat. The Bands playing were those of the Grenadier Guards, the Royal Horse Guards, the Royal Marines (Chatham) and the 79th Cameron Highlanders. There were selections from Sullivan's *Mikado*, *The Gondoliers*, *The Yeomen of the Guard* and *HMS Pinafore*, his ballad *The Lost Chord* and his 'graceful dance' from *Henry VIII*, Edward German's three dances from *Henry VIII*, three dances from *Merrie England* and the *As You Like it* suite, Balfe's overture *The Bohemian Girl* and duet *Excelsior*, a selection from Sir Julius Benedict's *Lily of Killarney*, Cowen's song *The Better Land*, MacFarren's *Tarantella*, and selections from Paul Rubens's musical comedies *The Dairymaids* and *Miss Hook of Holland*, along with works by Mendelssohn, Liszt, Wagner, Suppé, Grieg, Lehar, Massenet, Rossini, Dvořák, Gounod, Offenbach and Leoncavallo.[8] However, the 1911 Festival of Empire and the 1924–25 Empire Exhibition at Wembley made a specific attempt to promote British and Empire music as part of their propaganda offensive.

The 1911 Festival of Empire

The 1911 Festival of Empire has been completely forgotten, eclipsed in the popular memory by the 1924 Wembley Exhibition. But it was described at the time by *The Times* as 'the most elaborate advertisement of the resources of the British Empire that has ever been devised', and it was in many ways a dry run for the Wembley Exhibition.[9] It had been planned for 1910 but was postponed because of the death of King Edward VII; it then became a major attraction in the coronation year of King George V, 1911. Lord Plymouth, Chairman of the Festival Committee, said: 'The main ideal was that it was to be a gathering of the Overseas Dominions, to help us in Great Britain to realize the extent and the resources of the distant lands and peoples owing allegiance to KING GEORGE V, how we could best help them, and how they could best help us.'[10]

The Festival ran at the Crystal Palace from 12 May to 28 October and utilized the whole 250-acre site at Sydenham. There was an All-British Exhibition of Arts and Industries, a Fair of Fashions organized by the *Daily Mail*, a Boy Scout rally, a military tattoo and a series of national and intra-Empire sporting competitions. But the principal features were the exhibition, the pageant and the imperial concerts.

The Exhibition recreated the entire British Empire in miniature. Among its most eye-catching and talked about features were the three-quarter-sized replicas of the parliament buildings of the dominions which housed displays of the produce and manufactures of those countries. The South African building contained uncut diamonds worth £2 million loaned by the De Beers Company. India was represented by a domed palace containing 'an interesting and valuable collection of Oriental works of art'.

A miniature railway, the 'All Red Route', 1.5 miles long, linked the imperial scenes, which included a Malay village, a Jamaican sugar plantation, Canadian wheatfields and orchard, an Australian sheep farm, an Indian jungle 'well stocked with wild beasts' and a tea plantation, a Maori village, a great waterfall in the Blue Mountains of Australia and the gold and diamond mines of South Africa. There was a model imperial smallholding with information bureaux to dispense farming information to interested parties.

A series of tableaux sought to convey the histories of the component parts of the Empire. South Africa, for instance, was represented by the Great Trek, the meeting of Stanley and Livingstone, Cecil Rhodes negotiating with the natives and the opening of the Union Parliament by the Duke of Connaught.

There was a display too of big game trophies, 'probably the most representative of its kind that has been held in this country'.[11] It was limited to 'sporting animals killed within the British Empire'. The King loaned from his own collection two 'fine specimens of New-foundland caribou', the head of a musk ox, an Indian markhor and a thar. The Duke of Connaught loaned a selection of the animals shot during his recent East African tour, including a lion, a buffalo, an eland and an impala. Other big-game hunters to lend trophies included the Duke of Westminster, Lord Kitchener, Lord Lansdowne, Lord Lonsdale and the Crown Prince of Bhopal.

The Festival was opened on 12 May by the King and Queen who were accompanied by so many members of the royal family that the royal box had to be specially enlarged. The main feature of the opening ceremony was a concert. *The Musical Times* declared 'the loyal greeting accorded to their Majesties . . . when they opened the Festival of Empire . . . was probably unexampled in choral magnificence'.[12] A choir of 4,000 together with the Queen's Hall and London Symphony Orchestras and the Festival of Empire Brass Band, with Walter Hedgcock on the organ, provided the music. The music was arranged and directed by Dr Charles Harriss, with Sir Henry Wood, Sir Hubert Parry and Sir Alexander Mackenzie on hand to conduct their own compositions.

The Musical Times paid tribute to Harriss, 'the leading spirit and chief controller of the Imperial Choir scheme', as

> pre-eminently the right man in the right position. He is the man not only to conceive but to carry out great plans, and his spark of enthusiasm is almost radio-active in its power of kindling enthusiasm for others. The cheers which accompanied his arrival at the conductor's desk and his departure were a tribute of real admiration for his personality and his far-reaching ideals.[13]

An 'effective' fanfare of trumpets devised and conducted by W.H. Bell announced the arrival of the royal party, which was greeted by the whole audience and chorus rising and singing Elgar's arrangement of the national anthem. But there was a hiccup at this point, reported by *The Times*: 'Many of the singers forgot the repetition of the first part of the melody, and went on to the second part.' But *The Times* reassured its readers: 'The mistake, however, was soon rectified, surprisingly soon considering how large a body of singers had to be pulled into line; and as the whole attention was concentrated upon the Royal box it is possible that it passed unnoticed by many of the audience.' *The Musical Times*'s critic noted it, however, commenting that the anthem was impressively sung, 'except for an unpremeditated contrapuntal experiment'. Colonel John Mackenzie-Rogan, who was conducting the Band of the Coldstream Guards, recalled that 'the situation was saved by the presence of mind of Mr. Walter Hedgcock, the organist. All stops out, he crashed in with all the thunderous power of his mighty instrument, swamping orchestra and voices alike, until he was satisfied that a breakdown had been averted.'[14]

Harriss then conducted his own *Empire of the Sea*, which was sung 'with wonderful energy', a 'remarkable' achievement given that the music was 'so light in character . . . built chiefly upon a waltz rhythm which suggests the theatre rather than the concert hall'.[15] *Empire of the Sea*, 'an Imperial greeting for chorus and orchestra' with words by Wilfred Campbell and music by Charles Harriss, was dedicated to Earl Grey, Governor-General of Canada. It dated from 1909 and was a 'hands across the sea' celebration of Anglo-Canadian unity.

> Hail! Sons of the race, from afar!
> Joyous kings of the wind and the star,
> We daughters of Britain's glad Isles,
> Warmly welcome you home with our smiles,
> Laurels now we bear,
> From the true and fair.
>
> Come, from your far fields of foam!
> Farewell to sadness,
> Waken to gladness,
> Welcome to Britain, your home,
> To Britain, your home.
>
> Come, then, come to your own, in the Empire of the sea
> Might and joy never ending await the brave and free.
> Gales of power and promise blending,
> Winds of fortune e'er attending,
> Ocean lapping shores of stone,
> Ever to your own, ever to your own!
> Ocean lapping shores of stone
> To your own, ever to your own.

Sir Henry Wood then conducted his orchestral suite based upon themes of Henry Purcell, 'far too delicate to make any impression in such surroundings, and the beautiful playing was drowned in the noise of the crowds who were parading about among the side shows of the Palace'. However, where an orchestra failed to subdue the crowds, the commanding figure of Clara Butt succeeded, as she performed J.L. Hatton's song *The Enchantress*. *The Times* observed with awe: 'she is so well able to command the masses that . . . she could be heard without effort'.[16]

The one new work on the programme was Percy Fletcher's 'patriotic chorus' *For Empire and For King*, which had been awarded the
£50 first prize in an Empire Chorus competition sponsored by Harriss.
The Times noted approvingly: 'it was clear that he had gauged the conditions of performance cleverly, for it is conceived upon broad melodic
lines, with strong contrasts between the male and female choruses.
Moreover, it has distinct musical value; it rings true, and is not a mere
piling on of effect as such works often are.'[17] *The Musical Times* said:

> Seldom has the decision of judges in music competitions of this type
> been so widely approved. The broad, patriotic style of Mr. Fletcher's most
> natural method of expression, and both his verses and his music are
> characterized by their fluency. The latter contains no injudicious
> modernities or executive problems, but achieves artistic aims and intel-
> ligibility by its melodic flow and rhythmic variety. Its climax is trying
> for the soprano voice but it is hugely effective.[18]

Percy E. Fletcher provided both words and music for *For Empire and
For King*, which successively outlined the imperial obligations of men,
women and children in the form of verses inspired by established
gender roles and a vision of Empire based on peace and strength. For
the men:

> A Song of Victory and Might! A Song of Justice and of Right!
> Sung with firm determination
> To the manhood of the Nation,
> Who on hearing it may cry –
> 'We will live, and do, and die,
> 'Neath the flag unfurl'd on high,
> For our Empire and our King!'

For the women:

> A song of Motherhood and Love,
> With gracious influence from above!
> Sung with simple supplication
> To the women of the Nation,
> Who on hearing it may say –
> 'We've a part, which we can play;
> We must love, and we must pray
> For our Empire and Our King!'

For the children:

> A song of Comfort and of Peace!
> That whispers 'strife shall cease!'
> Sung with quiet consolation

To the offspring of the Nation,
Who on hearing it may know,
If in Wisdom's path they go,
Peace her blessing will bestow
On their Empire and their King.

The shared anthem is:

O Song of Peace and Love and Might,
Swell forth in paeans ever bright!
Thy matchless melodies entwine
In blended harmonies divine;
Thy message send from Pole to Pole,
Enflame each patriot's heart and soul,
Till from our Empire's wide domain
Shall rise an answering refrain;
Devoted millions join and sing,
'God Save our Motherland! God Save our Motherland!
Our Motherland and our King!'

Thorpe Bates performed *Drake's Drum* and *The Old Superb* from Stanford's *Songs of the Sea*. After this, the whole audience, including the King and Queen, rose to sing Kipling's *Recessional* to a hymn tune by J.B. Dykes. *The Times* declared its wish

that some tune which fitted more closely the accentuation as well as the feeling of the verse had been used, but as the intention had been that the audience should sing with the choir the first consideration was necessarily that they should be supplied with a tune which they were likely to know and this was satisfied by the choice of one which is associated with the popular hymn *Eternal Father, strong to save*. By about the third verse a good many of the audience were actually singing, and if they could only have found the courage at the beginning, the effect would have been an imposing one.[19]

The Musical Times thought that 'the earnestness with which the multitude of onlookers lent their voices to the majestic strain revealed the deeper sentiment that underlay the holiday-making'. Mackenzie's popular *Britannia* overture followed and then Clara Butt was the soloist in the singing of Elgar's *Land of Hope and Glory*. *The Times* noted disapprovingly that to some in the audience this was the climax of the concert and that 'a good many left their seats', thus missing 'two good things', Parry's *Processional March of Orestes* from *Hypatia* and Elgar's epilogue to *The Banner of St George*, 'It comes from the misty ages': 'These two works gave a strong ending to the concert: both are broad and sonorous, both have a fine impulse which suggests a higher ideal of patriotism than that of mere clamorous assertion, and for both, we may well be grateful.' *The Times* noted that apart from the mix-up in the national anthem, the choir sang throughout 'with certainty and a fine body of tone'. *The Musical Times* recorded that 'the audience, which was one of the largest that has ever assembled at the Palace, showed an equal interest in music in front of them and Royalty behind'.

Following the concert, the King and Queen drove round the exhibition and inspected the pageant performers drawn up in their period costumes. They were so struck by the sight of thirty Maoris that the royal carriage made an impromptu stop and the Maoris, delighted by the gesture, 'went through a wild dance of welcome, accompanied with bursts of national song'. 'Welcome to our distinguished guests from far beyond the skies' was the burden of their refrain, and they acclaimed the King for coming to them in his 'canoe'.

Reviewing the concert, *The Times* observed:

> In criticizing such concerts as these complaint is sometimes made that the programme is not sufficiently representative; and if it is looked at from the point of view of the present activity among British musicians, fault might be found with yesterday's programme, both because of what it contained and what it omitted. But it is possible to insist too much upon the representative aspect. The concert had nothing to do with the musical representation of different parts of the Empire; that will come later when in the course of the Festival concerts of music from England, Scotland, Ireland and Wales as well as the Colonies will be given. The opening concert had nothing to do but to give as forcible a presentation as possible of the patriotic ideal.[20]

Noting with approval the presence of works by Parry, Stanford, Elgar, Mackenzie and Wood, it observed: 'These five musicians certainly represent the noteworthy events in the renaissance of British music which has been so marked a feature of the time, and no one of them could have been spared from the programme.'

In its first leader, *The Times* put the Festival of Empire into its context:

> Yesterday marked, in a manner at once impressive, popular, national and Imperial, the opening of the Coronation period, which will make this year memorable in the annals of our race and Empire. It opened, as was fitting, with a function in which the KING and QUEEN were associated with the people of their capital, and in sentiment and sympathy at least with the people of all their far-flung Dominions, in the inauguration of a great symbolic Festival of Empire . . . Beyond all question the dominant note of the whole Coronation period will be the Imperial note. It began yesterday with the Festival of Empire, it will end many months hence with the unprecedented Imperial Durbar in Delhi – unprecedented in

this sense, that the EMPEROR OF INDIA will for the first time be present among his Indian subjects to proclaim his sovereignty over them. Its central and most impressive moment will of course be the historic ceremony of the Coronation itself in Westminster Abbey . . . But the Coronation itself, albeit the most ancient and hallowed function of our race and State, is all too narrow in its associations, and too circumscribed by the inexorable conditions of time and space, to represent in all their manifold impressiveness the ever-growing complexity in unity, and the ever-quickening self-consciousness of an Empire on which the sun never sets. That is why the dominant note of the Coronation of KING GEORGE V is, and is being made by the spontaneous instinct of all his people, an Imperial note of unparalleled volume and significance . . . hence everyone will welcome the happy coincidence which has enabled the KING to make the inauguration of the Festival of Empire the first public function of the period of his Coronation, and will appreciate that unerring sympathy of his with the Imperial instincts of his people.[21]

Thereafter there were weekly Empire concerts, which according to *The Musical Times* 'continued to uphold the high musical standard that marked the opening of the Festival'.[22] On 30 May there was a Canadian concert which featured a revival of Alexander Mackenzie's *Canadian Rhapsody*, but there was no Canadian archetypal composition. Instead it showcased the talents of Canadian singers Madame Emma Albani and Miss Edith Miller.

The following Tuesday an English programme of familiar works was given by English artists. On 13 June, there was an Australian concert. The main item on the programme was the *Symphony in E Flat* by George Marshall-Hall. Marshall-Hall, born in London in 1861, had been appointed the founding Ormond Professor of Music at Melbourne University in 1891 and had thereafter become a leader of Australian musical life. His 1903 symphony, first heard in England at a Promenade Concert in 1907, was given 'a careful interpretation' by Sir Henry Wood and the Queen's Hall Orchestra, but *The Times* found the piece wanting:

> Taken as a whole . . . the work has not sufficient variety of expression. The third, which is also the last movement, fluctuates too indefinitely between major and minor, and should have been in a lighter vein to contrast properly with the *Largamente*. There is also too little development of the themes for the symphonic form.[23]

Nevertheless, it found 'the broad extended theme of the *Largamente* . . . a beautiful piece of writing' and praised 'the solemn entry of trombones and drums in the *Vivace* and the beautiful cantabile phrase for the trumpets leading up to the climax in the second movement'. Also on the programme were a number of Australian performers, including

Peter Dawson who sang *Arm, Arm, Ye Brave*, and Percy Grainger who played a Liszt *Hungarian Fantasia* 'with his customary brilliance'.

Sir Alexander Mackenzie conducted the Scottish concert on 20 June with an all-Scottish programme, including his own *Burns Rhapsody*, William Wallace's symphonic poem *Villon* and Hamish MacCunn's overture *The Land of the Mountain and the Flood*. Choral singing was by the Glasgow Select Choir.

The black British composer Samuel Coleridge-Taylor conducted the South African concert on 27 June, featuring his own *entr'acte* from the incidental music to *Nero* and an overture by Havergal Brian.

Irishman Hamilton Harty conducted the Irish concert on 4 July with music by Irish composers: Stanford's *Irish Rhapsody No. 1*, Harty's own *Comedy Overture* and Sullivan's *Overture di Ballo* and *Masquerade Suite* from the incidental music to *The Merchant of Venice*. There were arrangements of traditional Irish songs by Wood, Stanford and Somervell, and original songs from two of Stanford's song-cycles, sung by Harry Plunket Greene 'with conviction and genuine feeling, but with intonation which was often far from perfect'. Joseph O'Mara sang an air in Gaelic from the Irish opera *Eithne*, by Robert O'Dwyer, and *Ochone, When I Used to Be Young* from Stanford's *Shamus O'Brien*, 'which was beautifully phrased and given with just the right mixture of comedy and pathos'.[24]

The Welsh concert on 11 July featured the Rhymney United Choir who performed Ambrose Lloyd's *Teyrnasoedd y Ddaer* and John Prine's *Efe a Ddaw*. The orchestral part of the concert, conducted by Edward German, included his *Welsh Rhapsody* and Walford Davies's *Festal Overture*. The *Country Dance* from Harry Evans's cantata *Dafydd ap Gwilym* was conducted by the composer and 'was very successful'.

The final Empire concert, New Zealand, was conducted by Sir Frederic Cowen. The programme included his own *Butterfly's Ball* overture and the second suite of *English Dances*, but also the adagio (*A Maori Lament*) from the *Symphony in B Flat* by Alfred Hill, born in Australian, but prominent in New Zealand musical life, and two movements from the New Zealand composer Arnold Trowell's *Cello concerto* with Trowell himself as soloist. The singers included a Maori, Ranginia.

Earnest efforts were made to find representative artistes and musical compositions, but not always successfully. London-born and newly knighted Sir Henry Wood conducted the Australian and Canadian concerts, and Sir Frederic Cowen, who was born in Jamaica but had spent six months in Melbourne, Australia, as a conductor, was drafted in for the New Zealand concert.

[187]

One of the great successes of the Festival was the Great Pageant of London and Empire, which was staged in twenty-seven scenes and four separate parts. It was advertized as

> The most gorgeous and elaborate spectacle ever attempted – a living picture of our Empire – from the dawn of history to the present day . . . This is indeed the Pageant of the Past Glories and Future Aims of the British Empire. A dream of colour; a vision of history; a moving, stirring and inspiring spectacle, such as the world has never seen before.[25]

Masterminded by experienced pageant-master Frank Lascelles, it featured 15,000 performers. It had originally been planned to recall London's part in the history of Britain, with the performers in each scene drawn from the different London boroughs, but in view of the Coronation and the general emphasis on the Empire, it was decided to add a fourth part, performed entirely by men and women of colonial birth, 'with the exception of the characters representative of the dark-skinned races', and to give the whole thing 'a wider and more Imperial outlook'. So its inevitable dramatic thrust was to suggest that the whole of the previous 2,000 years of British history had been leading up inevitably to the glories and grandeur of the British Empire. This was very much in line with Lascelles's own vision of the function of pageants. He had already staged full-blooded imperial pageants in Quebec (1908) and Cape Town (1909), and was to stage them in Calcutta (1912) and at the Wembley Exhibition (1924). A 1932 tribute to Lascelles spoke of the devotion of his life to an ideal which had 'brought joy to hundreds of thousands throughout the British Empire, as well as a sense of beauty and poetry, an appreciation of civic and patriotic values, and a sense of history and continuity which uplift the race artistically, mentally and spiritually'.

There had been a major revival of the pageant form in Edwardian England. This was largely as a result of the work of Louis N. Parker. Parker, educated at the Royal Academy of Music and subsequently music-master at Sherborne School, had gone on to become a successful playwright. But he returned to Sherborne in 1905 to stage a spectacular pageant recounting the history of the town. It had been a notable success, and Parker was in demand to create civic pageants for other towns and cities: Warwick in 1906, Bury St Edmunds in 1907, Dover in 1908 and Colchester and York in 1909. The Parkerian pageant was different from the old mediaeval pageants, which had been largely processional. Parker crossed the processional pageant with the Elizabethan chronicle play, and drew on his musical and theatrical experience, to create a new form. He had very clear views on the nature and structure of the pageant.

A Pageant is the History of a Town from its remotest origins down to a date not too near the present; expressed in dramatic form; that is to say, in spoken dialogue; in action; in song and dance where dance and song are admissible . . . it is based on authentic history, but it welcomes folklore and picturesque traditions. It is divided into episodes corresponding with periods in the town's history. Each episode is complete in itself, and is performed by a separate and independent cast. No episode must . . . play more than a quarter of an hour. The performance is continuous: there is no interval.

He also had a definite philosophy of pageantry:

A Pageant is a Festival of Thanksgiving, in which a great city or a little hamlet celebrates its glorious past, its prosperous present, and its hopes and aspirations for the future. It is a Commemoration of Local Worthies. It is also a great Festival of Brotherhood; in which all distinctions of whatever kind are sunk in a common effort. It is, therefore, entirely undenominational and non-political. It calls together all the scattered kindred from all parts of the world. It reminds the old of the history of their home, and shows the young what treasures are in their keeping. It is the great incentive to the right kind of patriotism; love of hearth; love of town; love of county; love of England.[26]

It was very important that all the participants should be voluntary and unpaid, apart from the orchestra which was made up of paid professionals. It was thus communal and democratic, a shared experience, but it was also subject to strict discipline and organization by the pageant-master. Its aim was both entertainment and education and Parker laid stress on the need to obtain historical accuracy in costumes, weapons and vehicles used. But from today's perspective much of the content would be mythic and folkloric rather than strictly historical. Gilbert Hudson, pageant-master of various Yorkshire pageants, echoed Parker's sentiments when he outlined the social objects of the pageant as class harmony, rational recreation, a shared sense of history.[27] All these objectives fitted the agenda of imperial propagandists. So, too, did the effect the pageant could have. The historian of pageantry, Robert Withington, wrote:

In these pageants history is made alive for us . . . They have an emotional appeal which is rarely equalled in the theatre. It would be a great play which could hold an audience for four hours, and leave such an impression that members of that audience became enthusiastic at the mention of the play five years later. Yet more than one pageant has accomplished this feat.[28]

It was only a short step from the inculcation of love of town, county and England to the promotion of love of Empire. That became the objective of the Pageant at the 1911 Festival of Empire. With a narrative trajectory from the Druids to the British Empire, the Pageant recalled Sir Arthur Sullivan's Diamond Jubilee ballet *Victoria and Merrie England*. London was associated both with the iconic figures of romantic nationalism (Alfred, Edward I, Henry V, Elizabeth I, Charles II) and hero-worshipping imperialism (Drake, Wolfe, Cook). The unity of the United Kingdom and its realms beyond the seas was one of the shaping themes of the show.

The music played an important part, underlining, reinforcing and animating the processions, marches and staged tableaux, and each scene was assigned to a different composer, though existing music was also pressed into use. The music was directed by W.H. Bell, born in St Albans in 1873, and who in 1912 was to move to South Africa as Principal of the South African College of Music in Capetown. He became a leader of South African musical life, composing among other works *A South African Symphony* in 1927.

The Pageant began with an evocation of 'Pre-Historic London' with a pastorale composed by Bell and a Druid prayer and processional music by Frank Tapp. The sequence of the foundation of the city unfolded to music by Tapp, *A Prelude*, *Hymn to Diana*, *Soldiers' Chorus* and *Finale*. It centred on a celebration of the naval victories of the Romano-British Emperor Carausius: ancient Britain prefiguring imperial Britain as in Elgar's *Caractacus*.

Scene 3, the 'Restoration of London' by Alfred, had incidental music by Cecil Forsyth, which featured an 'ancient barbaric folk-song'. The 'Recapture of London' from the Danes featured the music of Gustav Holst, in particular the songs *Raven Song*, *Biarkmal* and *In Praise of Oluf*. Paul Corder provided the music for the 'Norman Conquest': a *Mournful March* for Harold's departure for Hastings and a *Joyous March* for William's victorious entry into London. 'The Commune of London' had some 'very bright music' by Haydn Wood, with four numbers, including a lively dance. Bell himself provided the music for scenes 7 and 8: 'The Dawn of British Unity', which featured the Investiture of Edward as Prince of Wales, bringing the Stone of Scone to Westminster and the translation of a fragment of the True Cross, had the Welsh air *Ar Hyd y Nos* provide the accompaniment to the 'Proclamation of Edward', a march movement with *Vexilla Regis* in choral counterpoint for the 'Procession of the True Cross' and another processional movement for the actual 'Investiture'. Part 1 of the Pageant ended with 'The Age of Chivalry' and a tournament at Smithfield, with Bell providing *The Entry of the Populace*, a dance in 6/8 time, a *Knight's Entry*, a stately dance in 7-bar rhythm and a choral finale.

Part 2 began with 'The Canterbury Pilgrims and Wat Tyler's Rebellion', with music by J.B. McEwen which included a 'jovial' *Processional March*, 'some wild music' for the riot and a song for Wat Tyler's men. This was followed by 'The Victories of Henry V' with a triumphal march, featuring the Agincourt song *Our King Went Forth to Normandy*. The episode in which fifteen virgins sang a *Noel* to the accompaniment of six trumpets was pronounced by *The Musical Times* 'very striking'. Scene 3 featured Richard III leaving London, to a solemn march by Frank Bridge, the Battle of Bosworth with battle music by W.H. Bell and Henry VII entering London to a 'brilliant march movement with an effect of pealing bells' by Frank Bridge. Bridge also provided a minuet to accompany 'The First Discoveries' which featured the return of John Cabot from his travels. A pavane and a galliard were also included in this scene.

The 'London of Merry England and the Mayday Festivities' featured folk-songs and Morris dances arranged by Vaughan Williams. 'The Field of Cloth of Gold' utilized the Entry of the Populace, a brilliant March and an Entry for the Queen by Charles MacPherson. Part 2 ended with Elizabeth I knighting Drake and reviewing her troops at Tilbury. The knighting had some specially composed music by Hubert Bath but the Tilbury scene perhaps inevitably utilized Edward German's march from *Henry VIII* and *God Save Elizabeth* from his opera *Merrie England*.

Part 3 opened with a scene representing the trade of the East India Company. *The Musical Times* noted that Mackenzie's 'delightful *Britannia* overture enlivens the otherwise not thrilling scene'. 'The Departure of the Pilgrim Fathers' was accompanied by nautical music by Bell based on *The Golden Vanity* and an *Entry of the Pilgrim Fathers* that incorporated Orlando Gibbons' *Angels' Song*. 'The Meeting of the Old World and the New', showing Pocohontas at the Court of James I, used contemporary works by Byrd, Gibbons, Pilkington and Rossiter. 'The Execution of Charles I' was accompanied by music by Dowland and Edward German's *Pastoral Dance*. For 'The Restoration of Charles II', *Old Sir Simon the King* was used, but Balfour Gardiner provided some powerful and striking music for the Plague, the Great Fire and the Lord Mayor's Show. The death of General Wolfe at Quebec was accompanied by the *Dettingen Te Deum* and the *Dead March* from *Saul*, St Bartholomew's Fair by 'gay' dances by Frederic Austin. Part 3 ended with Captain Cook sailing from the Thames for the Pacific, the funeral of Nelson and the meeting of the allied sovereigns in London during the Great War, with music arranged from contemporary sources.[29] *The Times* reported approvingly:

[191]

Considering that it was the first performance, the pageant last night worked with quite extraordinary smoothness. There was sometimes a certain amount of delay in getting the various bodies of actors onto the stage, and a good many of them were apparently reluctant to leave it when their turn came to go. But on the whole the continuity of the action, or rather of the spectacle was well-preserved. And as a spectacle the scenes were a really great success. No pageant has ever presented such crowds of characters, and the extra size of the stage had made it possible for Mr. Lascelles to group them and deploy them with great effect, so that the eye is constantly delighted not only by the harmony of the colouring, but by the lifelike animation of the various scenes. There is very little talk by any of the characters, and not much that is really exciting by way of incident. And yet as a pageant the series of pictures presented are in almost every way more satisfactory than any of their numerous predecessors in London and elsewhere.[30]

The complaint about not much happening was repeated when the fourth and final part of the Pageant was staged. The first scene was the landing of Sir Humphrey Gilbert in Newfoundland, which he claims on behalf of Queen Elizabeth I. The second scene had Captain Cook landing at Botany Bay and distributing mirrors and knives to the aboriginal children who remain when their elders flee at the sound of gunfire. The British flag is raised and *God Save the King* sung. South Africa was represented by the landing of Van Riebeck in 1652 and the arrival of British settlers in 1820. The presence of Highland pipers among the arrivals gave the opportunity for the performance of Highland dances. New Zealand was represented by the arrival of *HMS Herald* and the conclusion of the Treaty of Waitangi between the Maoris and the British. *The Times* complained:

> This made five landing scenes: rather too many despite the fact that they reminded one that the greatness of England had always had one foot on sea and one on land. It was rather a relief to come to the Canadian episodes – the departure of the United Empire Loyalists in a variety of vehicles (including a sedan-chair) and the driving of the last spike of the Canadian Pacific Railway.[31]

The only Indian scene was the embassy of Sir Thomas Roe to the Court of Emperor Jehangir at Ajmere in 1616. 'It was a blaze of vivid colours and more applauded than any preceding episode.'

The original plan had been to have colonial composers score these scenes but this had not proved practicable and only two were actually recruited, A. Allen, the Organist of St John's Cathedral, Newfoundland, who provided music for the opening scene, including the choral ode *Newfoundland*, and Arthur Alexander, a New Zealand student at the Royal Academy of Music, who provided a 'powerful' march and a 'quaint' Maori dance.[32]

The culmination of the entire Pageant was the *Masque Imperial* in which the Genius of the World summons Britannia, who is lectured on her duty to the world. Bands of weary people who had without reward given their lives for their country pass by her. But Britannia is declared to have proved her worth and is rewarded by the 'Pageant of the Gain of Empire' in which all the performers from the Pageant's four parts, representing Britain's unfolding history and imperial destiny, gather and process into the Temple. The *Masque* was scripted by Francis H. Markoe with a score by Frederick Corder. Corder's music aimed to realize the descriptions and instructions in Markoe's script. *The Musical Times* gave an appreciation of the score. It began with a 'fine' overture with 'a mysterious Introduction in which the musical subjects struggle towards clear expression, which they presently achieve in a curious pastoral movement. The second subject is a long melody of a strange, haunting character, oddly syncopated.' Britannia is ferried across the lake by her attendant spirits of Meadow and Forest, of Lake and Stream, of Sky and Mist, of Cliff and Mountain, and of Ocean. Each group had its 'special section in a chain of short choruses, the first of which, sung by boys' voices, has a tune which the audience will probably go home humming'. The 'Pageant of the Gain of Empire', which followed, was accompanied by a version of *Rule, Britannia* which began as a double fugue and merged into 'a stately and swinging March. This has two subjects which work together, a Trio suggesting barbaric music, and a Coda in which Arne's tune is found to form a bass to the second subject of the March.' Finally from the Temple come the sounds of an anthem and Tallis's *Responses*. *The Times*, which did not mention the music, observed: 'The Masque itself is fine in intention and has the sincerity as well as the phantasy of the mediaeval mystery. But the speeches should be cut.'[33]

The Great Pageant of London and Empire was so successful that the Festival Council extended the performances from July, when it was scheduled to end, to 2 September. *The Musical Times* observed that the Pageant had given 'an opportunity for seventeen of our many able musicians to distinguish themselves'.[34] Significantly, a good number of them were from the younger generation of British musicians (Vaughan Williams, Gustav Holst, J.B. McEwen, W.H. Bell, Frank Bridge, Haydn Wood). But the music critic of *The Times* sounded a cautionary note. In an article entitled 'Musical patriotism' he reflected on what had happened to British music in recent decades:

The British race, as a whole, is no doubt at the present time of national festivity experiencing more or less the same emotions as in 1887, 1897 and 1902; but their musical expression is in many respects different. In 1887 musical patriotism hardly existed, and only very gradually has it become conscious of itself and its aims. But now the Imperialist spirit has seized on the art; political ideals colour much musical criticism, and there is growing up a demand that our musical youth shall be fed much more than hitherto on pure British-grown food. Wealthy music-lovers transport large bodies of singers many thousands of miles in order to bind the whole of the subjects of King George with artistic bonds; and many concerts – notably the remarkable series being given at the Crystal Palace – are definitely designed to foster the local pride of the various sections of the world under the British flag. The native composer is taking courage to hold his head higher and higher and to speak with his enemies in the gate in a tone of manly, not to say defiant, self-confidence ... No doubt, political movements during the past decade have helped all this on ... ideas have been in the air which, consciously or not, have certainly influenced art ... Nevertheless, an occasional pause for sober reflection is not amiss, especially at a time when the world of music, like any other, seems full of shouts and waving flags.[35]

He went on to argue for 'the principle of the open door in art, the cosmopolitanism of the great spiritual things', warned against music becoming 'not merely narrowly national but parochial', and stressed that 'all great art ... speaks a world language'; and, while British composers and performers should get fair play, they should not get preferential treatment simply because of their nationality. The very fact that the critic felt it necessary to deliver the warning in these terms confirms the extent to which music had become saturated with imperialism in the decades since 1887.

The British Empire Exhibition at Wembley 1924–25

The Wembley Exhibition was in many ways the culminating exhibition of Empire. It had been originally proposed in 1913 but was deferred by the outbreak of war, and when it was staged it was as an affirmation of faith in the Empire's future. The war was seen retrospectively as having vindicated the Empire. For the Exhibition was described in the Official Guidebook as the

Family Party of the British Empire – its first ... since the Great War, when the whole world opened astonished eyes to see an Empire with a hundred languages and races had but one soul and mind, and could apparently, without any of the mechanism of organization, concentrate all its power for a common purpose.[36]

[194]

It was mounted by a company specially set up for the purpose and headed by Sir James Stevenson, managing director of a distillery company who was rewarded with a peerage. The Prince of Wales was the President of the Exhibition and Head of the Executive Committee. Its stated aim was 'to promote the unity and prosperity of the British Empire'.[37]

A 216-acre site was acquired at Wembley and covered with Palaces of Industry, Engineering and Art, pavilions for the dominions and colonies, four conference halls, five restaurants and twenty-eight cafés, churches and meeting-houses of all the religious denominations, a football stadium, monumental lakes and gardens, a children's day-nursery and playground, an amusement park, a full-sized colliery in operation, a dance-hall twice the size of the Albert Hall, a full-scale reproduction of the tomb of Tutankhamun, a miniature railway – 'The Never Stop Train' – and a life-size Prince of Wales and his horse sculpted in Canadian butter. There was to be a Wild West Rodeo, a Boy Scout Jamboree and a Searchlight Tattoo. There were fifteen miles of roads, which were named by Rudyard Kipling (Pacific Slope, Atlantic Slope, Princess Path, Drake's Way, etc.), and two new railway stations, opened by the Metropolitan and LNER companies, served the Exhibition.

The Exhibition was officially opened by King George V on St George's Day, 23 April 1924. The ceremony was held in front of 110,000 people in the Wembley Stadium. The Prince of Wales, inviting the King to open it, declared:

> You see before you a complete and vivid representation of all your Empire. The Dominions, India, the colonies, the Protectorates and Mandated territories under your care, have joined together in the great task of presenting this picture of our Commonwealth of Nations. The Exhibition is thus the work of the whole Empire, and it shows the crafts-manship, the agricultural skill, the trading and transport organizations of all our peoples and all our territories. It gives also a living picture of the history of the Empire and of its present structure. It will suggest to the world, I truly believe, that the most powerful agency of civilization has its heart set upon peaceful aims and the good of mankind. The lighter side of the organization of a great Exhibition has not been neglected. It is essential to the success of such as this that it should be attractive; that it should encourage the desire for amusement as well as for educa-tion. The sports, the entertainments, the music, the arrangements for the comfort of our visitors have been carefully planned:

His hope was that the Exhibition would

> impress vividly upon all the peoples of your Empire, the advice that you have given them on more than one occasion, that they should be fully

awake to their responsibilities as the heirs to so glorious a heritage; that they should be in no wise slothful stewards, but that they should work unitedly and energetically to develop the resources of the Empire for the benefit of the British race, for the benefit of those other races which have accepted our guardianship over their destinies and for the benefit of mankind generally.

The King replied that the Exhibition presented to the world, 'a graphic illustration of that spirit of free and tolerant cooperation which has inspired peoples of different races, creeds, institutions, and ways of thought, to unite in a single commonwealth and to contribute their varying natural gifts to one great end'. He expressed the belief 'that this Exhibition will bring the people of the Empire to a better knowledge of how to meet their reciprocal wants and aspirations; and that where brotherly feelings and the habit of united action already exist, the growth of inter-imperial trade will make the bonds of sympathy yet closer and stronger'. He ended with the hope that 'it may conduce to the unity and prosperity of all my peoples and to the peace and well-being of the world'.[38] The emphasis of both speeches was thus on peace, trade, co-operation and understanding. The speech was heard over loudspeakers in the stadium and was recorded by HMV for transmission by the BBC in the evening. The Exhibition was open from 23 April to 1 November. It re-opened on 9 May 1925, and ran until 31 October. In all, over 27 million people visited the Exhibition. It cost £4.5 million to stage, and ended up losing over £1 million.

The opening ceremony was an appropriate mixture of religious, martial and imperial music. It was provided by the Massed Bands of the Brigade of Guards and the massed choirs from London and from St George's Chapel, Windsor. Sir Edward Elgar conducted the choirs. There were fanfares of trumpets, pipers from the Scots and Irish Guards and a twenty-one gun salute. Before the arrival of the King and Queen, the massed bands played marches: Kenneth Alford's *Voice of the Guns*, Thomas Bidgood's *On to Victory*, Leo Stanley's *The Contemptibles*, and Egerton's *The Third Battalion, Hearts of Oak, The British Grenadiers, A Life on the Ocean Wave* and the *Royal Air Force March* with the choir singing *It Comes From the Misty Ages* from Elgar's *Banner of St George*.

After the arrival of the King and Queen and the official welcome, the Bishop of London recited a special prayer beseeching God that 'our Country and Empire . . . may be a blessing to all mankind'. Then, after The Lord's Prayer, *Jerusalem* was sung by the massed choirs. The King opened the Exhibition and the Union Jack, and the dominion and colonial flags were broken out. The choir sang Purcell's *Sound of the World*. Then after members of the board, officers and workmen were presented, the massed bands played Elgar's *Imperial March* and the massed choir sang *Land of Hope and Glory*. The royal party left to *Rule, Britannia* and Graham's march *The Champions*.

On Saturday 24 May, Empire Day, in the presence of the Duke of Connaught, the League of Empire staged a great parade of military and youth organizations at Wembley, a trooping of the colour and, to end, a selection of music played by military bands and songs sung by 1,000 Boy Scouts. On Sunday 25 May, the King and Queen attended a Thanksgiving service at the Stadium, with massed bands of 1,000 men, a choir of 3,000 conducted by Sir Walford Davies, and a congregation of 100,000. A record number of members of the royal family were present. There was a special prayer and a silence of 'thanksgiving for Empire builders of the past and for prayer that the Empire builders of the present and the future may work together to further God's peace on earth'. The Archbishop of Canterbury gave an address that was broadcast by loudspeaker. The massed choirs and the congregation sang *All People That on Earth Do Dwell* and *Praise, My Soul, the King of Heaven*; the choirs sang Psalms 46 and 67 and the anthems *Let Us Now Praise Famous Men* and *Jerusalem*. Following the service, the military bands conducted by Lt H.E. Adkins, Director of Music of the Royal Military College, played Sullivan's *In Memoriam*, Mackenzie's *Benedictus* and Coleridge-Taylor's *Petite Suite de Concert*, the works of an Anglo-Irishman, a Scot and a black Briton. The service was broadcast by the BBC.

The Times reflected on the significance of the weekend's events:

> Yesterday and Saturday were days of dedication – dedication to the service of the Empire and dedication of the Empire to justice and to righteousness under the shadow of the MOST HIGH. Both ceremonies were worthy of the great conception they symbolised and hallowed. Both appeal to some of the strongest of human sentiments, both raise us above the pettier aspects of the present, and remind us that its deep significance comes from its place as a link in that 'great mysterious incorporation of the human race' which binds together the past and the future through all time. The sacred function of yesterday, celebrated before the largest congregation ever gathered in this island for common worship, and in silent communion with the millions who keep this day throughout the globe, raises us outside of time to the sublimest heights of all ... it was an Imperial consecration of all good that the Empire has done, and of all good that it purposes to do and that it may do.[39]

The massed bands that participated in these ceremonies were one of the hits of the Exhibition. Colonel J.A.C. Somerville, Commandant of the Royal Military School of Music, reported on the arrangements. He claimed that the series of concerts beginning on Empire Day and continuing until the end of May would constitute 'an experiment unique in the history of the military band'. For never before had a band performed continuously for a week, two performances a day, with marching and counter-marching by the band itself, 'all in the splendour of their pre-war uniforms. This in itself is a brave and stirring sight, appealing to the primitive fighting instincts latent in most of us, and to all that is associated with "the pomp and panoply of glorious war"', claimed Somerville, sentiments rather at odds with the stress on peace of the opening evening. The majority of the concerts would be conducted by Lt H.E. Adkins, who would have a corps of 300 drums and fifes and 100 pipers. The programme would be 'the best and most popular music hitherto published for military bands'. They included a number of first performances of works written directly for military bands or arranged for bands from existing orchestral music.

This programme included the *Toccata Marziale* and *Folk Song Suite* by Vaughan Williams. The *Toccata*, written specially for the occasion, was a short piece, described by Somerville as 'very interesting and thoroughly characteristic' of Vaughan Williams's style. *The Suite*, written during the previous year but only just published, was 'compounded of delightful and hitherto unfamiliar old English airs, and is certain to achieve an immediate popularity'. Then there was the *Vanity Fair* overture by Percy Fletcher, 'a tuneful and charmingly arranged work, well worthy of his reputation'. The *Gaelic Fantasy* by Lt B. Walton O'Donnell of the Royal Marines, scheduled to be conducted by the composer, was judged 'his most important work hitherto for the military band. It exhibits all his notable gifts of originality and distinction of ideas, and of extraordinarily clever, appropriate instrumentation.' Ethel Smyth's overture *The Wreckers* had been re-arranged for military band by Sir Dan Godfrey, whose instrumentation did 'full justice to this splendid overture'. *Mars* and *Jupiter* from the *Planets* suite, arranged by students at Kneller Hall, were 'tremendously effective in their new medium'. Holst had been commissioned to write a new piece for Wembley, and had begun, but he had been forced by illness to abandon the work. Bach's *Brandenburg Concerto No. 1* arranged for military band by Adkins and the C major *Organ Toccata*, arranged by Bandmaster D. Plater, together with a suite based on William Byrd themes, arranged for band by Gordon Jacob, showed that pre-nineteenth-century music could be adapted for effective band performance. J.E. Adkins's orchestral overture *Hibernia*, rearranged for band by his brother Lt H.E. Adkins, proved to be 'highly effective . . . written in a vigorous 12/8 rhythm'.[40]

Extant works by British composers Stanford, Mackenzie, Elgar, Sullivan, German, Somervell, Coleridge-Taylor, MacCunn, Wood,

Quilter, Kappey and A. Williams were included, along with those by foreign composers: Mozart, Weber, Beethoven, Schubert, Tchaikovsky, Brahms, Rimsky-Korsakov and, in particular, Wagner, who had one programme entirely devoted to his work.

The Musical Times testified that Somerville's confidence in his programme was not misplaced. It was, however, not impressed by the initial music offerings, reporting:

> There has been a certain amount of music of one sort or another at the Wembley Exhibition, but our art cannot be said to have figured adequately as yet in that great show of proud imperial activities and achievements. In fact the poorness of its representation looks like acquiescence in the outworn theory that in whatever pursuits the British people shine, it is not music.

But it made an exception for the bands.

> The best music came from the massed military bands which on Empire Day began a week of first-rate concerts, the musical value of which was not adequately appreciated by the daily press . . . The standard of execution and the quality of the music . . . brought fresh recognition of the good work of Kneller Hall, which nowadays may fairly be said to rank with the leading civilian schools of music. It is sad that the gallant bandsmen had a week of unsettled weather, which meant smallish audiences, and for themselves much discomfort.

Walton O'Donnell's *Gaelic Fantasy* was encored and *The Musical Times* pronounced *Mars* by military band 'superb' and said 'the transcriptions of Bach and Wagner were also well worth going to Wembley to hear'.[41] The band concerts received further praise when *The Times* surveyed the musical output of the Exhibition:

> Pageantry is a poor thing without its incidental music. And Wembley had its due appeal to the ear as well as to the eye. From the sounding brasses of the massed bands in the Stadium to the mechanical syncopation of the Amusements Park, there was always a musical accompaniment to the story of the Exhibition . . . it was the massed bands . . . that . . . set the opening ceremony to music; it was the bands once again that translated the emotional appeal of the Torchlight Tattoo into something tangible. It was, however, in the week devoted exclusively to their concerts that the massed bands of the Army came into their own . . . The whole contributed to a display in which was combined a curious mixture of rigid discipline and the artistic temperament . . . One treasures the memory of the sweeping breadth of *The Ring* transcriptions, in which the general effect followed the original scoring to a remarkable degree, alike with that of selections from Holst, Vaughan Williams and Coleridge-Taylor, which demanded the utmost delicacy of touch, especially in the wood wind.[42]

There were also bands from Sydney, Edmonton and Georgetown, British Guiana.

No imperial exhibition would have been complete without Dr Charles Harriss and his 10,000-strong Imperial Choir, and they gave six choral concerts at the Stadium. They began on 31 May with an Empire Day musical programme. This opened with Elgar's arrangement of *God Save the King* and included the chorale *Lord of Life* from Mackenzie's *Jubilee Ode*, Percy Fletcher's patriotic chorus *For Empire and For King* and Harriss's own *Empire of the Sea* (both which had been heard at the 1911 Festival of Empire), the chorus *Forward Through the Glimmering Darkness* from Parry's *War and Peace*, Elgar's *Land of Hope and Glory*, Brinley Richards's *God Bless the Prince of Wales*, Henry Purcell's *Come If You Dare*, and *Achieved Is the Glorious Work* from Haydn's *The Creation*. There was a new song with words by Dudley Beresford, set by Harriss, *England! Land of the Free!* and marked 'allegro marziale'. It emphasized love of England, imperial solidarity and cross-class participation in the imperial adventure.

> Dear England, that I love so well,
> The Empire of the free!
> Though in remotest lands I dwell,
> My heart still yearns for thee;
> Capped are the hills with snow-white crowns,
> Across the surging foam,
> With sunbeams kissing em'rald downs,
> Dear England is my home.
>
> Dear England! Name of priceless worth!
> For thee, her sons of old,
> Of high estate, and lowly birth,
> Were brave, and true, and bold;
> Shall it be said that Nelson, Drake,
> Who ploughed the salt sea main,
> Live not in us, who now partake
> Of what they died to gain?
>
> *Chorus*:
> England! Homeland! Land of the free!
> England, dear land, ever to me;
> Where the hearts of her sons ring true,
> With the love that we bear for you,
> You who come from over the sea,
> Kinsmen always, ever will be;
> Bound in chains with our love are we,
> For our homeland, Land of the free
> For our homeland, Land of the free.

The Times commented severely:

> It is an outrage on economy, the first principle of art, to set so huge and so fine a machine to crack a dozen nuts, of which a few were good, a few were shrivelled, and the rest bad ... if Imperial ideals can inspire nothing better than self-conscious rectitude decking itself out in senti-mental part-songs, we should be shy of asking the world to come and contemplate the spectacle.

But the performance was praised:

> Of the choral singing in the Stadium it is possible to speak with enthu-siasm. Dr Charles Harriss ... secured a surprisingly good *ensemble*, the articulation was excellent, and the tone throughout had a firmness and a ringing quality that only comes from a large body of good singers.[43]

On 14 June there was a Handel concert, with extracts from *Solomon*, *Judas Maccabaeus*, *Samson* and *The Messiah*. The miscellaneous programme of 28 June opened with the march and chorus *Hail, Bright Abode* from *Tannhauser* and included short choral works by Coleridge-Taylor, Harriss, Gounod, Barnby, Mendelssohn, Rossini and Sullivan. Mendelssohn Day (12 July) featured extracts from *Elijah*, *The Hymn of Praise* and *Athalie*, while the concert on 19 July had selec-tions from Haydn, German, Elgar, Bishop, Handel and Sullivan; and the final concert (9 August) was devoted to British composers: Sulli-van, Elgar, Parry, Holst, Coleridge-Taylor and Geoffrey Shaw. The overall effect was to celebrate Protestantism, Empire and British musical achievements.

The Pageant was one of the principal attractions of the Exhibition and was intended to bring home in vivid visual form the heroic history of the Empire. The Treasury contributed £100,000 to the costs; Prince Arthur of Connaught assumed the Presidency of the Administrative and Finance Committee and J.H. Thomas, the Colonial Secretary, was President of the Empire Pageant Council. Frank Lascelles directed the Pageant – as he had that in 1911 – for which Royal Academician Frank Brangwyn designed the scenery. Fifteen thousand performers were involved. The whole enterprise was dogged by bad weather: the opening was delayed, and it eventually ran from 26 July to 30 August and was frequently watched in the rain. Since the aim was to bring home the lessons of the Empire to the public, free seats and standing places were provided for 19,000 people at each performance, though the first performance was watched by 50,000 and the last by 60,000.

The Pageant was divided into three sections, and took place over three successive evenings. Adventure and discovery, romance and exploration, heroism and service were the recurrent themes. The music was a vital ingredient. As *The Times* reported:

The music of the Pageant was not easily selected. Many considerations had to be borne in mind. One of them – a surpassing consideration – was the size of the Stadium. In that vast area, compositions might be charming if they would be heard, but lost in the air would be so much waste energy. There is a great deal of music in the Pageant and as little speech as possible . . . Music pervades the various scenes.[44]

A choir of 400 and an orchestra of 110, drawn from three London orchestras, provided the music.

The first day, 'Westward Ho', was devoted to Canada and Newfoundland. It began with Henry VII giving John Cabot permission to sail west and Cabot's subsequent discovery of Newfoundland, followed by the exploits of the pioneers Cartier and Champlain, the armies of Wolfe and Montcalm clashing on the Plains of Abraham, the arrival of the Loyalists who sacrifice their lands in America rather than desert the British Flag, Canada's successful resistance to American invasion in the War of 1812 and the foundation of the Hudson Bay Company. A direct descendant of General Wolfe enacted the role of his famous ancestor. To accompany these scenes and impart the appropriate atmosphere there was a rich and varied selection of music. The first piece to be heard – and it was to be repeated several times during the Pageant – was Elgar's new *Empire March*, written specially for the Exhibition. It was followed in the Cabot–Henry VII episode by Edward German's *Country Dance* from *Nell Gwynn*, Frederick Rosse's *Doge's March* from *The Merchant of Venice* and Edward German's *Coronation March*. The pioneers were accompanied by Byrd's *The Earl of Oxford's March*, Sir Landon Ronald's prelude to *The Garden of Allah* and Coleridge-Taylor's *Hiawatha's Wedding Feast*. Then, as Canada's history unfolded, the score comprised melodies from George Clutsam and Hubert Bath's score *Young England*, their 1916 operetta about the exploits of Sir Francis Drake, the gavotte from Montague Phillips' operetta *The Rebel Maid*, Percy Fletcher's *Empire Song*, George Elvey's *Festal March*, Nicholas Gatty's march from his opera *Prince Ferelon*, Edward German's pavane from *Romeo and Juliet* and Arthur Sullivan's *Graceful Dance* from *Henry VIII*. For the finale, the music was Walford Davies's *Solemn March*, Mackenzie's *Benedictus*, Elgar's *Sursum Corda* and a medley of songs, *The Maple Leaf Forever*, *O Canada* and Fletcher's *For Empire and For King*.

The second day of the Pageant, 'Eastward Ho', opened with Elizabeth I and her people celebrating the English victory over the Armada. 'There is a crowd of over 2,000 men and women, who dance and revel in such sights as quarterstaff and jousting. They make a spectacle full of colour.' It began, like day one, with Elgar's *Empire March*, followed by Eric Coates's prelude *In the Meadows* and *In a Country Lane*, the dances from Edward German's *Merrie England* and his song *Long Live Elizabeth*, Percy Fletcher's march *The Spirit of England*, Henry Smart's *Te Deum in F* and finally Elgar's *Imperial March*. The next sequence showed seventeenth-century naval hero Admiral Blake in the Mediterranean routing the Barbary pirates, to the strains of Coleridge-Taylor's march from *Nero*, the song *Mariners of England* by John Pointer, John Ansell's overture *Plymouth Hoe*, Montague Ring's *African Dances* and Mackenzie's *Britannia* overture. Then it was on to the pageant of South Africa, with glimpses of Pharaoh's sailors visiting the Cape, Vasco de Gama, Jan Van Riebeck, the Huguenot settlers in the seventeenth century and the English settlers in 1820. The Battle of Blood River recreated the defeat of Dingaan and 10,000 Zulus by Pretorius and his 460 Boers in 1838. Then, after the quieter incidents of Dr Livingstone's career, came the last stand of Major Allan Wilson and the Shangani River Patrol against the Matabele, and ended with Cecil Rhodes concluding a peace treaty with the Matabele. These scenes were accompanied by Old Hottentot melodies, a Dutch boat-song, a Portuguese melody, Old Huguenot dances, Momet's *Bourée*, E.D. Barcroft's *African Suite*, 'Kaffir melodies', and an episode from Hamish MacCunn's cantata *Livingstone the Pilgrim*, Coleridge-Taylor's *Bamboula*, an extract from Parry's *War and Peace* and finally Elgar's *Land of Hope and Glory*.

The second day ended with India and the Ambassador of James I, Sir Thomas Roe, visiting Emperor Jehangir. It recreated an Indian market, complete with musicians, snake-charmers, dancing girls, dervishes and story-tellers, and featured a procession of elephants, camels, ox-carts and soldiers with Indian bands. The music was drawn from Elgar's *Crown of India* suite, Amy Woodforde-Finden's *Indian Love Lyrics*, Liza Lehmann's *In a Persian Garden* and Shandar's *Old Indian Dances*.

The last day, 'Southward Ho', opened with King George III commissioning Captain Cook to explore the Southern Seas, with Elgar's *Empire March*, Percy Fletcher's *Sylvan Scenes*, Dr Philip Hayes's *Minuet*, and Herman Finck's *Pageant March* providing the score. Then a New Zealand section recreated the Maori Wars in New Zealand and their eventual resolution, with full justice being done 'to the bravery and chivalry of those who were then the Empire's foes'. This sequence began with the New Zealand anthem, *God Defend New Zealand*, then sea shanties arranged by Richard Terry, W.G. James's song *When the Yellow Kowbai Blooms*, Eric Coates's *Merrymakers* overture, Granville Bantock's *Benedictus*, Alfred Hill's songs *Waiata Poi* and *Tangi*, J.D. Davis's march *Pro Patria*, Edward German's *Harvest Dance* and, again, Elgar's *Empire March*. This was followed by the pageant of

Australia, its discovery and exploration, the crossing of the Blue Mountains and, finally, to symbolize its great natural riches, '[w]ater-seekers strike a well, and as the stream gushes forth the Stadium becomes a mingling of vineyards, orchards, fields of grain and sugar plantations, crowds of girls bearing the grapes, the corn and other riches of the Dominions'. This section was accompanied by Percy Grainger's *Colonial Song*, Herman Finck's *March Blanc*, the Australian anthem *Advance, Australia Fair*, W.G. James's *Stockrider's Song*, George Clutsam's *Plantation Songs*, Handel's *Hallelujah Chorus* and Sullivan's *Imperial March*. The final sequence, a pageant of heroes, brought on a succession of imperial worthies, from Richard Coeur de Lion to the Antarctic explorers Scott and Shackleton, to the strains of E.H. Lemare's *Solemn March* played on the organ. The state barge brought the body of Nelson across the lake to be received in the funeral coach and conveyed across the arena, to muffled bells and minute guns. Elgar's reworking of *For the Fallen, With Proud Thanksgiving*, was performed by choir and orchestra. After this bells pealed, trumpets were blown, the band played Elgar's *Empire March* and the choir sang the *Te Deum* as figures and groups representing Britannia, the dominions and the dependencies followed the symbolic figure of the Child of the Future. *God Save the King* was sung and, as the parade departed, Herbert Bunning's setting of Kipling's *Recessional* was played.

The whole Pageant was an extraordinary operation. Each dominion had formed a committee to select the historical episodes for dramatization and another body, under the historian Sir Charles Oman, had then collected these selections and formed them into a dramatic narrative. The poet Alfred Noyes had composed a set of verses to accompany the action and Henry Jaxon had selected and orchestrated the music, assisted by I.A. de Orellana. An analysis of the musical score reveals that it begins and ends with Elgar's new *Empire March*, which is regularly repeated throughout to provide imperial continuity. Much music is taken from suites of incidental music composed for theatrical productions, which is not inappropriate given that pageants are very largely theatre without words. But the two dominant forms employed are the march and the dance, conveying at the same time the idea of discipline and joyousness in the imperial adventure. Due respect was paid to old enemies like the Boers and the Maoris. The organizers were also keen to point out the presence of dominions' composers such as George Clutsam, Alfred Hill and W.G. James among the contributors.

Musically the highlight of the Pageant was new work by Elgar. He was well represented by existing work. But he had been commissioned to provide new work for the Pageant: 'What we want is a March of Empire which will be the Leit Motive [*sic*] going through the three days programme.'[45] Elgar provided it in his *Empire March*. Robert Anderson argues that 'the music is forthright and apparently brimming with self-confidence. There is a good trio tune, livened by nice touches of imitation as it proceeds. The percussive splendour of the end was a brave attempt to mend times that Elgar knew were thoroughly out of joint.'[46] It never achieved the popular success of the *Pomp and Circumstance* marches, however, and although it was recorded in 1924 on the Columbia label by Percy Pitt and the BBC Wireless Orchestra, and much later had several new recordings after the Elgar revival, it seems to lack the genuine inspiration of the *Pomp and Circumstance* marches. The confidence sounds forced, the tone bombastic. It is Elgar imitating himself.

There was, however, more genuine feeling in the songs he set to verses specially commissioned from Alfred Noyes. *A Song of Union* for the Canadian section, celebrating 'the love that linked our realms in one', is, according to Anderson, 'a march in Elgar's boldest manner, with swaggering melodic line above an imperiously descending bass'.[47] *The Heart of Canada*, a song with unison chorus, impressed Anderson less: 'competent and sturdy, but of no significance beyond its occasion'.

There were six solo songs. *Shakespeare's Kingdom*, which described the poet's arrival in London, utilized 'Elgar's favourite rhythm'. *The Islands* celebrated New Zealand 'with an all-purpose diatonic robustness', the same tune being used in *Sailing Westward*, which is hymnlike. *The Blue Mountains*, celebrating Australia, was 'quietly effective without having penetrated far into Elgar's imagination'. *Merchant Adventurers* was 'vigorous and redolent of seaspray'.[48] *The Immortal Legions*, which accompanied the pageant of heroes, is sombre and deeply felt, with the orchestra echoing the solemn tread of the dead and the living who serve the Empire, and the lament of the dead rising to a triumphant note of celebration of lives of service and sacrifice.

Entertainment there certainly was, but *The Times* was certain that there was also education:

> The Pageant of Empire was a great deal more than a splendid spectacle. It was such a lesson in Imperial history as could have been taught in no other way with an appeal to the eye, to the ear and to the emotions that could hardly fail to strike even the least complacent citizen with deep and moving pride of race ... something was needed to bring home to man and child the history and meaning of our Empire and there is no question that the need has been worthily met.[49]

The dominions had their full share of the glory in the Pageant. But they were musically less well served elsewhere. A series of dominion concerts was initiated in one of the halls of the Palace of Industry on 31 May. *The Musical Times* reported:

> South Africa took the field first, and Canada followed a few days later. Then the concerts somehow ceased. To be frank, they were not well conceived or interesting. We heard a large number of vocalists, several quite good, a few excellent. But the general effect was that anyone with the right birth certificate could come and sing anything. And performances of *Ombre leggiera* and *Somewhere a voice is calling* did nothing to help the musical prestige of the Empire. The creative musicians of the Dominions seem at present to be of a retiring nature, and the executants were content with threadbare or shoddy products of the Old World.[50]

A different kind of pageant, and equally successful, was the Torchlight and Searchlight Tattoo which opened with an audience of 50,000 on 1 September. It was due to run until 13 September, but was extended by popular demand until 20 September. The final performance was attended by an estimated 80,000 people and *The Times* reported that 'all the performances of the Tattoo have been received with the utmost enthusiasm'.[51]

The Tattoo began with massed buglers sounding the Retreat and after the Retreat, the Massed Bands of the Irish Guards, the Corps of Royal Marines and the Central Band of the Royal Air Force with the Massed Pipe Band. They played a programme of music that included *The Londonderry Air* for Ireland, German's *Welsh Rhapsody* for Wales and the dances from German's *Henry VIII* and the overture *Plymouth Hoe* by John Ansell for England, with the skirl of the pipes representing Scotland. There then followed a recreation of the Mounting of the Guard at St James's Palace in 1824 to the strains of *The British Grenadiers*, with the new guard being led in by the Scots Guards' Band and Drums.

Next followed the Tattoo itself, with the massed drums and fifes, a Scottish choir, massed pipers and torchbearers, and highland dancers, accompanied by Scottish songs. Marching and countermarching by the Massed Bands of the Royal Marines and the Royal Naval School of Music followed. There was a firefighting display and then a simulated air raid as Number 32 Squadron of the RAF launched an attack, its aircraft picked out by searchlights, and apparently bombed a Tower at the West End of the Stadium which burst into flames. The firefighters then rescued people from the Tower and put out the flames. 'Bombs, gunfire and fire-engine bells blended in a riot of noise', reported *The Times*. 'The whole thing was extraordinarily "realistic" from the moment when the first maroon was heard to that when a spurt of scarlet flame in the sky showed that one at least of the raiding aeroplanes had been hit.'[52] On Friday 1 September one of the planes taking part had to make a forced landing and burst into flames, but pilot and observer escaped unhurt.

The climax of the Tattoo was a recreation of Balaclava, described as a 'military fantasia'. It began with the Russian Army on the march, displays of Cossack trick-riding and Russian dancing; scenes in the British camp at night with the singing of soldiers' songs; then the advance of the British and French regiments; the sounds of battle; the slow return of the wounded with Florence Nightingale superintending their care; a victory march and the final scenes of the army at rest. The Tattoo ended, as was customary, with the evening hymn *Abide With Me*, the sounding of *The Last Post* and the national anthem.

As in the Aldershot Tattoos, the programme – of which *The Times* reported 'those who saw it must have felt that rarely had they lived through two consecutive hours so densely packed with thrills' – contrived to combine scenes of modern warfare with recreations of famous battles of the past, at once a celebration of tradition, modern efficiency and the romance of war. The music was an integral element, *The Times* noting: 'from the moment when the first notes fill the Stadium, the sound of music is almost continuously present, blending with, and forming part of the general plan of the performance, or providing a background for it'.

The fact that many of the Exhibition events took place in pouring rain – that summer was one of prevailing bad weather – allowed newspapers to praise the discipline and determination of the performers, underlining the imperial character of the British race that was a unifying theme of the proceedings.

The national, multi-party, cross-class significance of the Exhibition was summed up by the Colonial Secretary, J.H. Thomas:

> As a member of the Labour party and of the Labour Government, I am proud of the British Empire Exhibition and proud of the Empire it embodies and represents. Its success – and of that success I am certain – is as dear to the hearts of the Labour Government as it was to the Governments, composed of men of different shades of political opinion, who were holding office when the movement that has come to such a magnificent culmination at Wembley was initiated. Nothing is more mistaken than the idea, prevalent in some circles, that Labour is hostile to the Empire and to the Imperial idea . . . Labour realizes that it has good reason to be proud of the British Empire. It knows the part that working-men have played in the building of the Imperial edifice. It realizes that

[207]

the foundations were laid, not only by traders and explorers, in search of wealth and fame, but also by humble men and women of British stock, who left these islands for distant parts of the world, seeking only to secure a livelihood that was denied them at home. Labour knows how these men and women toiling in the far places of the world, brought prosperity to those new lands as well as to themselves and made them part, as it were, of the homeland they had left. It is, perhaps, partly true that the masses of the working classes of Great Britain have not always been alive to the scope and diversity, the resources and possibilities, of the British Empire. That, however, is no fault of theirs. Very few of them have had any opportunity to acquire much knowledge of the Empire beyond what is conveyed by looking at the parts coloured red on a map of the world. Nothing has been conceived, far less carried out, so calculated to correct that excusable ignorance as the British Empire Exhibition. Wembley is a living lesson in Empire and in what Empire means and comprises. To millions of humble Britons it gives the opportunity of which they would never otherwise get of visiting the Empire.[53]

After the Second World War, there were to be no more imperial exhibitions in Britain. But imperial echoes were still to be heard in the dark continent. In Coronation year, 1953, the Central African Exhibition was held at Bulawayo in Rhodesia. It aimed to showcase the products of all the African colonies and to commemorate the centenary of the birth of Cecil Rhodes, the country's founder. The Exhibition was opened by the Queen Mother, was visited by 1 million people and included an impressive programme of cultural events: a pageant of Rhodesia and performances by Sir John Barbirolli and the Hallé Orchestra; Sir John Gielgud and his acting company; Sadlers Wells Ballet and Covent Garden Opera performing, among other items, Benjamin Britten's opera *Gloriana*. A special exhibition march was commissioned from the leading British light-music composer Eric Coates. The result was the march *Rhodesia*. Coates had originally called it *The Green Land*, but the Colonial Office persuaded him to rename it *Rhodesia* on the grounds that *Green Land* suggested jungle and there was no jungle in Rhodesia. The march, rousing and lyrical by turns, is recognizably the work of the composer of *The Dambusters March*, the *Eighth Army* march and *The Seven Seas* march and reflects the confidence and optimism still displayed by the settler community in Rhodesia in the early 1950s. It was, however, rarely heard following the Exhibition, and Ian Smith's unilateral declaration of independence in 1965 and the eventual independence and renaming of the country as Zimbabwe has ensured it has remained one of Coates's least-known marches.[54]

Notes

1 John Allwood, *The Great Exhibitions*, London: Studio Vista, 1977, pp. 179–85.
2 John M. MacKenzie. *Propaganda and Empire*, Manchester: Manchester University Press, 1985, p. 97.
3 *The Times*, 23 May, 1925.
4 Paul Greenhalgh, *Ephemeral Vistas*, Manchester: Manchester University Press, 1988, p. 58.
5 MacKenzie, *Propaganda and Empire*, p. 101.
6 On these exhibitions, see Breandan Gregory's 'Staging British India', in J.S. Bratton *et al.* (eds), *Acts of Supremacy*, Manchester: Manchester University Press, 1991, pp. 150–78; Greenhalgh, *Ephemeral Vistas*, pp. 90–5; MacKenzie, *Propaganda and Empire*, pp. 96–120; Donald Knight, *The Exhibitions – Great White City*, New Barnet: Knight, 1978.
7 Colonial and Indian Exhibition Daily Programme, Saturday 31 July, 1886.
8 Franco-British Exhibition Programme, Thursday 27 October, 1908.
9 *The Times*, 5 May, 1911.
10 *The Times*, 13 May, 1911.
11 *The Times*, 8 June, 1911.
12 *The Musical Times*, 1 June, 1911.
13 *Ibid.*
14 *The Times*, 13 May, 1911; John Mackenzie-Rogan, *Fifty Years of Army Music*, London, Methuen, 1926, p. 174.
15 *The Times*, 13 May, 1911.
16 *Ibid.*
17 *Ibid.*
18 *The Musical Times*, 1 June, 1911.
19 *The Times*, 13 May, 1911.
20 *Ibid.*
21 *Ibid.*
22 *The Musical Times*, 1 July, 1911.
23 *The Times*, 14 July, 1911.
24 *The Times*, 5 July, 1911.
25 *The Times*, 19 June, 1911. On the 1911 Pageant, see Deborah S. Ryan, 'Staging the imperial city: the Pageant of London, 1911', in Felix Driver and David Gilbert (eds), *Imperial Cities*, Manchester: Manchester University Press, 1999, pp. 117–35; and Deborah S. Ryan 'The man who staged the Empire: remembering Frank Lascelles in Sibford Gower, 1875–2000', in Marius Kwint, Christopher Breward and Jeremy Aynsley (eds), *Material Memories*, Oxford: Berg, 1999, pp. 159–79.
26 Louis N. Parker, *Several of My Lives*, London: Chapman & Hall, 1928, p. 279.
27 Robert Withington, *English Pageantry*, Cambridge, MA: Harvard University Press, 1920, vol. 2, p. 23.
28 *Ibid.*, p. 220.
29 The music for the Pageant is reviewed at length in *The Musical Times*, 1 June, 1911.
30 *The Times*, 9 June, 1911.
31 *The Times*, 12 June, 1911.
32 *The Musical Times*, 1 June, 1911.
33 *The Times*, 12 June, 1911.
34 *The Musical Times*, 1 June, 1911.
35 *The Times*, 20 May, 1911.
36 Allwood, *The Great Exhibitions*, p. 126.
37 Donald R. Knight and Alan D. Sabey, *The Lion Roars at Wembley*, London: Knight, 1984, p. 4.
38 *Ibid.*, pp. 12–14.
39 *The Times*, 26 May, 1924.

40 *The Times*, 24 May, 1924.
41 *The Musical Times*, 1 July, 1924.
42 *The Times*, 30 September, 1924.
43 *The Times*, 2 June, 1924.
44 *The Times*, 19 July, 1924.
45 Robert Anderson, *Elgar*, London: J.M. Dent, 1993, p. 154.
46 *Ibid*., p. 301.
47 *Ibid*., p. 284.
48 *Ibid*., pp. 294–5.
49 *The Times*, 20 September, 1924.
50 *The Musical Times*, 1 July, 1924.
51 *The Times*, 22 September, 1924.
52 *The Times*, 2 September, 1924.
53 *The Times*, 24 May, 1924.
54 Ian Phimister, 'Commonwealth, colonialism and the Central African Exhibition of 1953', paper presented at the Commonwealth History Seminar, 'Representations of Empire', Oxford, 18–19 May 2000. The march was recorded and has been included on a CD of Eric Coates's music, *17 Orchestral Miniatures*, ASV, CD WHL 2107.

CHAPTER SEVEN

'All the King's horses and all the King's men': the Aldershot Tattoo

Anyone in doubt about the extent to which imperialism had saturated British popular culture needs only to look to the Aldershot Command Searchlight Tattoo, which has been called 'the greatest military social event of the inter-war period'.[1] The Tattoo (the word derives from the Dutch) originated in the tradition of beating drums to summon troops back to their billets at night. The drums were eventually replaced by bugle calls sounded at 10.00 p.m. and known as *The Last Post*. Half an hour earlier *The First Post* sounded, and the custom grew up of musicians with fifes and drums marching up and down the barrack square playing a selection of tunes in between *First* and *Last Post*. This ceremony later became elaborated into large-scale musical entertainments, which involved military drilling, military music and in due course full-scale military pageants, as the half-hour between First and Last Post was extended to two hours.

It was the logical outcome of the fascination with military spectacle that gripped the British public in the nineteenth century. As Scott Hughes Myerly observes in his study of British military spectacle from the Napoleonic to the Crimean Wars:

> The imagery and spectacle of the British army is a symbolic vision that has elicited a fascination from Britons and significantly influenced the values and attitudes of both soldiers and civilians in the nineteenth century. For the military, this influence was pervasive ... The martial management art combined drill and discipline with other factors, and was then embellished and enhanced by the style of the dress and equipment to make a colorful, visually arresting image. This art was a fundamental dimension of all military routines, and the display was designed to make the maximum impact upon viewers and participants.[2]

Public fascination with the vivid and colourful regimental uniforms, the regular reviews, parades and drills, the formal rituals such as the

Presentation of the Colours, Trooping the Colour and the Changing of the Guard, and military funerals was matched by the popularity of commercial entertainments such as the equestrian dramas popular in the first half of the nineteenth century when the Battle of Waterloo and the Battles of the Crimean War were regularly staged at venues like Astley's Amphitheatre, founded by retired Sergeant-Major Philip Astley. Eventually the army itself took over this idea.

The prototype of this kind of entertainment was the royal tournament which provided the activities that were combined with the musical elements of the tattoo. The tournament was first staged in 1880 (the prefix 'royal' was added in 1885) as the Grand Annual Military Tournament of riding and swordplay. The idea of formal drills and displays was inspired by the annual camps of the Volunteers, the forerunner of the modern Territorial Army. The Commander-in-Chief, the Duke of Cambridge, gave permission for troops to be used and granted the event his patronage in return for a donation to the Royal Cambridge Asylum for Soldiers' Widows. The first two tournaments, in 1880 and 1881, were financial flops, due to the lack of press coverage and the repetitive nature of the routines. But the third, in 1882, was a success, thanks to the introduction of the musical ride in which riding drills were performed to music and changed formation with the alternating tempo of the accompaniment, and of the competition of the gun teams of the Royal Horse Artillery. The 1882 event made a net profit of £3,000 and thereafter was established as an annual event.

In 1883, at the fourth tournament, the musical ride was performed by the 2nd Life Guards, with, according to its historian P.L. Binns, 'the glamour of the performance being heightened in the eyes of the audience by the knowledge that some of the horses had participated in the cavalry charge at Kassassin in the previous year' as part of the Second Egyptian War to suppress Arabi Pasha.[3]

From 1883 onwards, there was formal organization, with rules and regulations and a permanent secretary, and the whole thing was under the direct control of the General Officer Commanding, Home District. The combination of extensive press coverage, the continuing interest and support of the royal family and the popularity of the spectacle made it a success. It was valued as a recruiting agent and as a fundraiser for service charities. But, according to Binns, it also performed an important role in bringing together the army and the public.[4] In the popular mind, the image associated with the army had long been that of 'brutal and licentious soldiery'. But a change of attitude began to take place after the Crimea, with William Howard Russell's despatches and Miss Nightingale's heroism, and was furthered by the stories and poems of Kipling celebrating the ordinary soldier on duty in the

Empire. The tournament helped this process by stressing the discipline and skill of the troops.

The participation of the cavalry was stepped up to increase the spectacle and cavalrymen were shown delivering despatches, evacuating the wounded and exchanging fire with the enemy. In 1885 for the first time a mock battle was featured, and this became a regular set-piece, staged by Lt-Colonel G.M. Onslow of the 20th Hussars, Inspector of Gymnasia for Great Britain. Each year a variation was introduced: an attack on a fort, a *zareba*, a mountain pass; and eventually a river crossing. These displays invariably culminated to great applause in a British victory, and the raising of the Union Jack to the strains of *Rule, Britannia* and *See, the Conquering Hero Comes.*

New weapons and vehicles were introduced to the public: the Maxim gun, the Gatling gun, the Screw gun. An armoured train appeared on specially laid tracks in 1887, and new units such as the Camel Corps and the army cyclists put on displays. Physical drills and gymnastic displays were introduced in 1888, performed to music, usually *Faerie Voices* and *Two Lovely Black Eyes.*

The tournament also helped to introduce the excellent army bands and their music to the public. In the early days, there was a different band every day during the tournament, but once the musical ride was introduced there was a resident band. For many years this duty alternated between the Bands of the 1st and 2nd Life Guards and the Royal Horse Guards' Blue Band. When the cavalry were featured, they brought their own bands; and so sometimes four regimental bands participated. The music of the Gilbert and Sullivan operettas was a perennial favourite at the tournament, and one year selections from all the operettas were played.

By 1890, the Royal Tournament had become part of the London season alongside Ascot, Henley and Lords. Edward VII, as Prince of Wales and later as King, attended regularly. In 1887, 87,000 people attended at a shilling a head, and by 1893 the number had risen to 120,000. In 1896 a naval display was added to the events, initially cutlass and gun drill. In 1907 competition between naval gun teams entered the programme. In 1905 the title of the event was changed to the Royal Naval and Military Tournament, and in 1906 it moved from the Agricultural Hall, Islington, where it had been held annually since its inception, to Olympia.

Until 1891, the content had been entirely domestic; but the organizing committee became increasingly concerned to inject an imperial element, and this began with the introduction of colonial troops. In 1891, a detachment of the Victoria Mounted Rifles from Australia appeared and were much admired for their 'drab-coloured uniforms and wide felt hats'. In 1893, detachments of the New South Wales Lancers and the Victoria Horse Artillery, in England for the opening of the Imperial Institute, participated. There was also a detachment of cavalry of the Indian Army, but then no further Indian participation until 1902 when displays were given by the 10th, 11th, 15th and 18th Bengal Lancers. The presence of colonial troops in London for the Diamond Jubilee led to there being a very imperial flavour to the 1897 Tournament, with the New South Wales Mounted Rifles demonstrating their ability to deal with bushrangers in the Burragong Valley; the North Borneo Police staging a Dyak war dance and the Cyprus Police giving a display of spear-throwing.

In 1899 the New South Wales Lancers and the 6th Dragoon Guards gave a demonstration of how to handle the dervishes of the Sudan. In 1908 the West African Regiment performed a native dance and then defeated an ambush and captured a stockade, after transporting their Maxim guns through the bush.

The second element was the staged battles. Colonel Onslow gave up organizing them in 1896. His re-enactments had been stylized military episodes, attacks on anonymous frontier forts or jungle stockades. After he retired, although imaginary episodes continued (a South African War episode with the siege of a Boer blockhouse, in 1904, and an Indian frontier incident of pursuit of rifle thieves, in 1911), real incidents from real imperial campaigns were also re-enacted, often with their original participants recreating them; thus in 1898 the capture of Benin was staged and in 1899 the capture of Passer Sala on the 1875 Perak Expedition.

The third means of projecting the Empire was the pageant. This was introduced as a permanent feature in 1895 and usually consisted of detachments in uniform, each representing a different period or episode, and concluding with a *tableau*. It was colourful and 'with a background of stirring music, it invariably received its full measure of public approbation'. Many of the pageant subjects were historical and imperial. In 1899 'Warriors of Britain' ranged from the Wars of the Roses to the battle of Omdurman (1897); 'Our Army' ranged from Blenheim (1704) to Tel-el-Kebir (1882). In 1898 'Shoulder to Shoulder' featured the army and navy serving side by side at Cadiz, Gibraltar, Alexandria and El Teb. In 1900 the Royal Regiment of Artillery staged its own pageant featuring uniforms and guns from the medieval bombard to the mountain battery screw guns of the Indian frontier campaigns. The 1901 Tournament celebrated the inauguration of the Australian Commonwealth and in 1903 the Delhi Durbar. *The Times* reported:

Par excellence the feature of the Tournament is the Pageant represent-ing the Durbar, which is shown with a realism of the most attractive kind. Elephants there are, and camels, the former gorgeously caparisoned. There are true elephants and *bone fide* camels . . . But the Oriental soldiery who rode and marched before the spectators – Lancers from Bhopal, Haidarabad, Gwalior, Judhpur, Mysore, Patiala, mail-clad Rajputs, and Bikanir camel men, infantry of Alwar, Bharatpur, Jhind, Kapurthala, Kashmir, Nabba, and Patiala – were picked men from English regiments. Still, so cleverly had they been selected, and so well were they made up, that the illusion was complete, and it was not aston-ishing that some spectators should ask how many of the performers were genuine Orientals and how many were British. In the vast majority of cases nothing but the brawny hands of the Britons, hands such as no Oriental could boast, betrayed their race. Of the show it may be said that from the moment when the procession began, headed by the State trum-peters, to that at which 'God save the King' sounded, while soldiers saluted and presented arms and mock native princes saluted, it was brave, gallant and gorgeous in an extraordinary degree. It will certainly 'go' like wildfire.[5]

But perhaps the most magnificent was the 1910 pageant 'Britannia's Muster', with Britannia presiding and representatives of almost all the regiments of India, South Africa, New Zealand, Australia and Canada. In the 1910 Official Programme, Lt-Colonel N. Newnham-Davis rhapsodized:

Britannia's Muster at the Royal Naval and Military Tournament is no mere pageant. It is the militant spirit of our Empire translated into flesh and blood. It is the living story of the thousand battles by sea and land which have given Britannia her outposts North and South and East and West. Ready to assist the Mother Country if called upon, and to help each other in the day of trial, one great family united in peace and united in war. India, Canada, Australia and South Africa grouped around Bri-tannia with the Navy and Army of all our lands formed in square about them speak of the allegiance of the Commonwealths and Dominions and Empires of our race to the Mother Country, and their salute to the Royal Standard tells of the reverent loyalty to His Majesty the King–Emperor which binds together all the races of men who are under British rule and the protecting shadow of the British flag.[6]

It certainly had the effect its organisers intended, if *The Times's* special correspondent is to be believed:

The *pièce de résistance* is . . . Britannia's Muster. I have not the small-est hesitation in saying that of the many displays that I have seen in the arena of the Naval and Military Tournament this is the most dignified and suggestive. The official description of the 'Muster' conveys not the smallest idea of the wealth of colour and the great suggestion of potential strength that the realization of Colonel Nugent's scheme has produced.[7]

Britannia, 'in the person of a young and pretty woman', was conveyed to the centre of the arena, in a car, supported by a lion, and drawn by a team of horses whose postilions were costumed as John Bull. Her heralds then summoned by trumpet 'the various units that hold inviolate her Empire'. The first to appear were the representatives of the home military forces, including every unit from the Life Guards to the boys of Richmond's Eagle Scout Patrol. Then came South Africa, represented by 'a car with an ostrich and a Kaffir' heading columns of colonial troops and Volunteers with 'whose names the South African War made us familiar'. Australia had a car with a gold-miner and a kangaroo, followed by its contingent. New Zealand followed Australia behind its own flag. Canada was represented by a car in arctic dressing. Finally India was summoned, and was represented by a Maharajah 'reclining in State beneath a gorgeous canopy . . . followed by 18 detachments in the brilliant uniforms'. The imagery attached to the different areas of the Empire is instructive, the common factor being exoticism and romanticism, but with the specific emphasis on luxury in India, profit in Australia and wilderness in Canada.

> This great muster is then marshalled in the arena round these triumphal cars. Then it is that the great thought that underlies Colonel Nugent's conception breaks upon the spectator. This huge arena is packed full, so that there seems to be no inch of space left, with the troops of our great Empire. Yet there are only five men from each unit. The immensity of our resources flashes upon one. The 'fiery cross' has gone forth. And this is the result. No, it is not all. There is still something else. Again the trumpet calls and the doors open. To the swinging lilt of 'A Life on the Ocean Wave' a guard of honour of blue jackets march in amongst their crowded brothers-in-arms. Then the Royal Salute is given as the Royal Standard is broken above the Royal box. It is truly a moving moment . . . The Native troops of India march in to the airs of 'Lilli-pilli-punia' and 'Zakhami-dil' . . . 'Britannia's Muster' is a spectacle of wonderful dignity and it should bring its lesson to us all. Not a lesson of Chauvinism, but one of confidence in our great power if we are only wise enough to know how to direct it. It will certainly delight the hearts of the 2,500 Boy Scouts who attend the evening performance today at the invitation of the chairman and committee.[8]

As it happened, the 1910 Royal Tournament took place simultaneously with an Army Pageant, staged for a week in the grounds of Fulham Palace. Officially opened by Field Marshal Lord Roberts, it presented the history of the British Army in a series of episodes ranging from the sixth to the early nineteenth century, from the Battle of Mount Badon to Badajoz, all directed by the actor Frank Benson. Proceeds were to go to the Soldiers and Sailors' Help Society. But these spectacles were beginning to give rise to misgivings among the military experts reporting on them. The military correspondent of *The Times*, who thought the show 'charmingly staged and capitally performed', concluded his account of the Army Pageant with a sombre note of warning:

> The military defence of the greatest Empire that has existed within the memory of man demands from the race that controls and dominates it every effort of which it is capable. Let no one think who visits the Army Pageant that the day of stricken fields is past, Empires comparatively as puissant as ours have been swept away when the art of government has been forgotten by their citizens. Civilizations brighter and happier than ours have become submerged by overflowing tides of barbarism when idealists, dreamers, and talkers have preferred rhetoric to reason, and pageant to preparation ... There are, and there will always be, hard nations, aspiring rulers, ambitious people, who will seize the first favourable occasion to snatch from tired or unready rivals their champion belt. Modern democracies, with their materialistic appetites, their rage for rights, and their neglect of duties, have not yet displayed, under the test of fire, their aptitude for ruling, not only Empires but themselves ... It is because the spectacle at Fulham Palace, grievously though it does, and unavoidably must, fall short of the realities of things, recalls at least the continual struggles through which the Empire has fought its way to a place under the sun, and reminds each one who witnesses it of his duty to a country which has done everything for him, that we can forgive anything that offends taste and the sense of historical reality, and wish the Army Pageant all success.[9]

The correspondent covering the Royal Naval and Military Tournament shared these misgivings:

> There is a very marked feeling abroad that the public's appreciation of the sacred duties of national defence is in danger of being lessened by a light-hearted cheapening of the best of our military traditions for the purposes of charitable and other gate-moneys ... As the public are in danger of forgetting the real object of the great annual military display, I may perhaps be forgiven if I state it again. The main object of the Royal Naval and Military Tournament is not to acquire funds for the enrichment of naval and military charities. This very worthy result is only a secondary consideration. The real object of the Tournament is to encourage skill-at-arms in the Naval and Military services – that is, to preserve, in the only way that our modern conditions of life and armament will

permit, the great traditions in skill-at-arms that at one time made the people of this country formidable throughout the known world.[10]

Nevertheless the Tournament continued in the form that had become established by 1900, a two-and-a-half-hour programme of musical ride, cavalry display, pageant, combined display with, in the morning, inter-service competition, drill and displays of bayoneting, riding and jumping. In 1914 the Tournament closed down and remained so for the duration of the war. It was revived in 1919 with the addition of RAF displays and became known from 1920 as simply the Royal Tournament. The Pageant was re-instated in 1920 but was now usually a history of a particular regiment. The Pageant was discontinued in 1938 and the Tournament itself in 1939. Once again, in 1947, it was revived, and it continued until 1999 when, in a shameful act of cultural vandalism, the Labour Government, in thrall to the shallow and widely derided idea of 'Cool Britannia', arbitrarily abolished the Tournament. Audiences wept as the colourful rituals and routines were performed for the last time and an event that was as much a source of pride, tradition and cultural togetherness as the Last Night of the Proms or the British Legion Festival of Remembrance was consigned to history.

One of the most popular features of the Tournament was the Tattoo performed by the Bands, Drums and Pipers of the Brigade of Guards. This made its first appearance in 1903 and thereafter became an integral part of the programme. It was devised by Lt-Colonel John MacKenzie-Rogan, Bandmaster of the Coldstream Guards. The arena was darkened, then various bands would enter escorted by torchbearers. The massed bands would play a short programme of music followed by *Rule, Britannia* and *God Save the King*, then *The Last Post*.

In terms of spectacle, however, the Royal Tournament was eclipsed in the interwar years by the Aldershot Tattoo. The Aldershot Tattoo dated back to 1894, when the Duke of Connaught, third son of Queen Victoria and recently appointed General Officer Commanding (GOC), Aldershot, arranged a tattoo for the entertainment of the Queen. It took the form of drill displays in the afternoon and torch-lit band performances in the evening. This eventually became part of the annual Aldershot Military Fête held in the grounds of Government House, the official residence of the GOC. The Fête became more elaborate each year as the programme grew to include sports contests, balloon ascents and physical training displays, as well as military drills. After darkness fell, the military bands would perform in the light of torches held aloft by ranks of soldiers marching between the bandsmen.

By 1914 the Aldershot Tattoo had become a major event, repeated over four nights, involving 1,500 bandsmen, pipers and buglers and twenty-three musical items from *The First Post* to *God Save the King*. The Tattoo was suspended during the Great War. The Government House Fête was not revived after the war, but in 1920 the Aldershot Command Tattoo was revived as a self-contained event, and because of its popularity was moved to Cove Common where a ridge provided a natural viewing-point for spectators. Both before and immediately after the war the Tattoo was staged in Ascot Week and began at 10 p.m., allowing time for the fashionable elements of society to drive over to Aldershot and witness the entertainment. After the war, aeroplanes staged aerial combat in the searchlights and there were displays by tanks. But the most significant innovation was the historical pageant, which began properly in 1925 with the re-enactment of the Battle of Waterloo.[11]

The popularity of the event grew steadily and a new venue was demanded. In 1922–23 a great horseshoe-shaped arena was created at Rushmoor, with a grandstand and rows of benches. Forty-three thousand people attended the performance in 1923. The Rushmoor Arena helped to transform the Tattoo into a major national event, reported in newspapers all over the Empire. In 1922 at Cove Common there had been 22,000 spectators; in 1929 there were 300,000. By 1926 an estimated 50,000 motor vehicles and 200 special trains brought visitors to the Tattoo. In 1927 the official programme was describing the Tattoo as 'an accepted feature of English life'.[12] In 1925 the BBC broadcast the Tattoo for the first time and in 1926 HMV began to record and release the music.[13] Proceeds of the shows went to military charities.

Members of the royal family attended regularly. In 1930, for instance, Queen Mary attended the final performance. King George VI and Queen Elizabeth attended twice in 1936, first the daylight dress-rehearsal with the little Princesses and again the final performance after dining with the GOC at Government House. The popularity of the event led to the number of performances being increased to five in 1925, six in 1931 and nine in 1939. The logistics of staging the Tattoo were formidable. Planning for next year began immediately after each Tattoo. The preparation of each display and pageant was allotted to a division, brigade or unit, with a military historian as historical adviser. The Royal Engineers' Searchlight Battalion provided the searchlights. About 5,000 troops took part in the arena programme, with a further 1,600 in the administration; 450 Boy Scouts from the local association escorted visitors to their seats. In 1935 Lt-Colonel H.H. Douglas-Withers, MC, was appointed the full-time Producer, and he wrote, researched and directed the whole event for four years. Programmes, at sixpence each, were printed by Gale & Polden, the army's printers, who also produced, at two shillings each, handsome illustrated souvenir brochures with beautiful coloured plates of specially commissioned paintings, often chivalric in content and imagery, photographs taken at daylight rehearsals of the Tattoo and reproductions of famous paintings. They also produced sets of black-and-white postcards of the big scenes in the Tattoo.

The pattern of the Tattoo remained constant throughout: military drills, physical training, modern warfare displays, massed bands and large-scale historical pageants reconstructing military episodes. What is striking is that many of them celebrated the Empire and the prominence of war and empire at a time of widespread pacifist sentiment is significant.

The role of the music was highly important. In the 1938 Official Souvenir Brochure, Lt-Colonel F.E. Whitton wrote:

> Ceremonial is part, and by no means an unimportant part, in the life of any civilized nation, and in any ceremonial in which the head of state is concerned it is obvious that much of the ceremonial must be executed by the armed, trained and disciplined servants of the crown – soldiers in other words. The essence of any ceremonial is faultless rhythm and it can be secured, not indeed solely but to the best advantage, by the employment of music. 1000 highly trained military musicians on parade, massed bands of the Aldershot and Eastern Commands, drawn up under searchlights in a solid square of scarlet and gold, present one of the most dazzling sights of this year's Tattoo.[14]

The Tattoo drew on the whole range of musical forms and idioms for its programmes: classical (a potted version of *Tannhauser* in 1934), traditional, military, musical comedy. Music from the Gilbert and Sullivan operettas featured in 1924, 1925, 1927 and 1928. In 1926 the massed bands played *Oriental Scenes* in which the music was overlaid with the muezzin's cry from the minaret (helpfully translated into English), and, although they were hardly oriental, five West African drums, captured at the palace of King Prempeh after the fall of Kumasi during the Ashanti War in 1874. 'The largest of these drums was originally festooned with a ring of human ears', the Programme tells us, leaving us in little doubt as to the validity of the British expedition to end such barbarism.[15]

The military marches were a central element. They included the hardy perennials: Holzmann's *Blaze Away* (1901), R.B. Hall's *Officer of the Day* (1905), Javaloyes's *El Abanico* (1910), E.E. Bagley's *National Emblem* (1905) and Sousa's *The Stars and Stripes Forever* (1896). The fact that they were either American or Spanish in origin made no difference: they had become part of the international military repertoire and the upbeat, optimistic, military rhythm was understood as underlining the ideas of patriotism and service. The work of the British composer Kenneth Alford was also regularly featured with compositions such as *On the Quarterdeck, Colonel Bogey* and *The Standard of St George*. Such British military band standards as Thomas Bidgood's *Sons of the Brave* (1889) and W.H. Turpin's cheery and rhythmic *Flag and Empire* also made regular appearances in the musical programme.

In addition to the old favourites, there was also new and specially composed music, often with a royal or imperial theme. *The Aldershot Tattoo March*, with its distinctive fanfare theme, was specially written for the 1933 Tattoo by Alfred James, Bandmaster of the 2nd Battalion, Somerset Light Infantry. Sam Rhodes, Bandmaster of the Royal Artillery Mounted Band, composed the stately and memorably tuneful *Golden Spurs* for the 1937 Coronation Tattoo, the title being inspired by an item of the coronation regalia. Denis J. Plater, Bandmaster of the 1st Battalion, Oxfordshire and Buckinghamshire Light Infantry, wrote *The March of the King's Men*, also for 1937. Trayton Adams, who had been Bandmaster of the 2nd battalion, Northamptonshire Regiment, since 1916 and had served in India, Ireland and the Sudan, was Musical Adviser to the Tattoo until 1939, even though he left the army in 1936. He composed the cheerful if repetitive *Crown and Commonwealth* for the 1937 Tattoo. He also later composed *Drake's Drum* and *The Keepers of the King's Peace* march medley. In 1938 the programme featured Bassett Silver's jaunty but distinctly dance-band-ish *Royal Review* and Alfred Young's *Tournament* (better known as *Royal Birthday*) which cleverly combined elements from *Here's a Health Unto His Majesty, Happy Birthday* and *God Save the King* (the phrase 'send him victorious, happy and glorious').[16]

The Aldershot Searchlight Tattoo of 1924 ran from 18 to 21 June and commenced at 9.30 p.m. each evening. It began with the sounding of *First Post* and this was followed by the marches *Bombay* and *Somerset*, neatly representing the imperial and the domestic aspects of the army. The massed bands then played a selection of music for thirty minutes. There was a different programme for the first two and the last two days. On 18–19 June, the bands played Percy Fletcher's grand march *The Spirit of Pageantry*, Wagner's overture *Rienzi*, Jessel's *Parade of the Tin Soldiers* and Cyril Jenkins's tone poem *Life Divine*. On 20–1 June they played the triumphal march *Cleopatra* by Mancinelli, two excerpts from *Petite Suite de Concert* by the black British composer Samuel Coleridge-Taylor, the serenade *Sizilietta* by Blon and, again, Jenkins's *Life Divine*. Then, after a fan of searchlights, there was the entry of the massed drum and fife bands, playing on the first two days the marches *Flag and Empire* and *Bianca*. The pageant element was the staging of a forced river crossing, 'a typical incident in modern warfare', as the programme put it. It involved two companies of engineers, machine guns and tanks, and aeroplanes. Next there was an illuminated military drive by the eighteenth battery of the 3rd Brigade, Royal Field Artillery, with musical accompaniment by the Band of the Royal Artillery Mounted. They played the slow marches *Post Horn Gallop* and *Royal Artillery*, the trots *Keel Row* and *Over the Sticks*, Suppé's *Light Cavalry* overture and selections from Gilbert and Sullivan.

The Tattoo always took care to emphasize the army's identity as British rather than simply English. The contributions of the Scots and Welsh were highlighted by the appearance of massed pipe bands and three sets of foursome reels, using such traditional Scots' tunes as *The Deil in the Kitchen* and *The Reel O'Tulloch*, and items by the 1st Battalion, Welsh Guards' Choir including *Men of Harlech*, *Land of My Fathers* and *The Soldier's Farewell*. There was a musical ride by the 13th/18th Hussars in uniforms worn in 1742 and 1815, a firework display, and the entry of the massed bands and torchbearers to a trio of Kenneth Alford marches, *On the Quarterdeck*, *The Great Little Army* and *The Vanished Army*. The finale, played by the massed bands, and with the audience requested to join in, was the hymn *Abide With Me*. Then came the sounding of *The Last Post*, followed by *God Bless the Prince of Wales* and *God Save the King*.[17]

Taken together, the programme of events and the accompanying music can be seen as a celebration of the romance of war, the Empire, the monarchy, Protestantism, tradition and a Britishness which specifically encompasses Wales and Scotland as well as England.

The pattern established in 1924 was to be followed until the last Tattoo in 1939. The performance always opened with the sounding of *The First Post* and ended with the sounding of *The Last Post*, and in the intervening two hours there would be selections of music by the massed bands, an illuminated drive by the Royal Horse Artillery, drills and evolutions, and a firework display; and the highlight would always be a large-scale military re-enactment. The performance always ended with *God Save the King*. In 1928 a physical training display was introduced and in 1929 half-an-hour of community singing, sponsored by a succession of national newspapers, before the Tattoo proper began.

It is worth noting the inclusion of the hymn *Abide With Me* which also became the FA Cup Final hymn. It was sung every year except 1926, when *The Day Thou Gavest, Lord, Is Ended* was substituted. The audience was always invited to join in. In 1927 Kipling's *Recessional* was sung as well as *Abide With Me*. The Official Souvenir Programme explained why:

The most ardent and the fiercest of imperialists, Mr. Kipling, yet saw, with a poet's vision that, to pride, humility and thankfulness should be joined. In *Abide With Me*, the note is the same but not nationalist; it is purely individual . . . Sung after *Recessional* by them the personal share of each individual spectator as a member of the British race is stressed. It is 'Lest *we* forget', but 'Abide with *me*'.[18]

This leaves the audience in no doubt of the link, in the minds of the organizers, between British national identity and Protestant Christianity.

In 1924 a modern river crossing was staged. The historical pageant began in 1925 with a staging of the Battle of Waterloo, followed by a modern warfare display. In 1927 it was the Battle of Blenheim followed by an air display and a modern attack on enemy trench and village. But the 1926 Tattoo had a sequence called 'Visions and Realities' – 'visions of the glorious past of England, from which sprang the high morale that forms such a glorious basis for our national prestige'. As the Programme described it:

> The scene opens with the entry of a modern British military detachment which goes into camp on the outskirts of an Oriental village. While the camp sleeps, guarded by its sentries, cloud-wreathed visions appear in which are seen glimpses of battles that have gone to the making of the map of Europe as well as of England and the British Empire.[19]

They dream then and see recreations of the Battles of Hastings and Agincourt, and the Charge of the Light Brigade: 'There is no need to presume general ignorance of a cavalry charge which Tennyson immortalized and the memory of which has inspired millions of Britons – civilians as well as military.'[20] The visions were accompanied by Jean Nougues' *Quo Vadis*, Moore's *A Highland Scene*, Kling's *Shepherds Life in the Alps* and Kappey's *Episodes in a Soldier's Life*. At the end of the visions, the realities – the oriental inhabitants launch a treacherous attack on the British camp but tanks, guns and planes are deployed to defeat them. There is then a march-past of the ancient and modern soldiers to Javaloyes's *El Abanico* and the regimental march of the King's Regiment, *Here's to the Maiden*.

The 1928 Tattoo deliberately sought to integrate the disparate items and give them a coherent rationale. For the first time a theme was introduced – the value of sacrifice. That rationale was set out in the Programme's foreword, which explains that the Tattoo is divided into three phases. The first portrays the origins and history of the ceremony of tattoo. The second, 'A retrospect of war', includes England's participation in the Crusades, 'that first English Expeditionary Force which left England with the avowed object of releasing the birthplace of Christ from the grip of the Infidel', and the capture of Badajoz in 1812, 'one of the earlier victories in a series of overseas campaigns waged in the cause of liberty'. The third phase, 'Preparations for war', includes physical training and military evolutions. The finale, 'War and Victory', gave a glimpse of the First World War:

> A hint of Menin Gate and the troops which marched through it, of the Hell of the Salient and of Memories of the Sacrifice which must be held so long as our Empire endures. The promise that the Empire shall endure and the Memories remain is given in the living Union Flag that lies across the Arena and in the fervour with which actors and onlookers, acknowledging the Source of the courage which has sustained the Empire through sorrow and distress, sing in unison:

> 'I fear no foe, with Thee at hand to bless;
> Ills have no weight and tears no bitterness;
> Where is death's sting? where, Grave, thy victory?
> I triumph still, if Thou abide with me.'

The introduction continues to outline the binding theme of the *tableaux*:

> Visitors, before they have read so far, will have realised that the *motif* running through the entire Tattoo is sacrifice, the Cross of Sacrifice. History saves us from attributing that spirit to the leaders of the various Crusades as their sole motive, but the Cross and the Cross alone must have inspired the bulk of the crusaders ... it drew to the banner of the Cross the mass of England's manhood, which, forsaking families and friends, sacrificed comfort and security, in the hope to free the Cross from the domination of the Crescent, to release the Shrine of the Founder of Christianity from the grip of the Moslem. Not all England's expeditions have been justifiable, for our ancestors, in the main, were not better than their times; but something more than greed of gain and lust of adventure has animated British arms and has made us the world's most successful colonisers. Justice, mercy and brotherhood have travelled along the trail with British armies, and the call of Freedom has awakened the spirit of sacrifice ... It was seen ... in 1914, when Freedom's call again was sounded. The reports from Belgium fired the modern Briton as the reports from Palestine fired his Anglian ancestors. He flung himself into the New Crusade which should take him from all he held dear to unknown horrors overseas. He embraced the Cross of Sacrifice with the heroic chivalry which came with Christianity to the tribes of Britain and which remained and is symbolized to-day in the crosses on our Union Flag of Empire.[21]

The music to accompany all this is interesting. The community singing was conducted by Eric Godley of the *Daily News* with words

distributed free on a *Daily News* songsheet. The songs were traditional, *Hearts of Oak, Annie Laurie, John Peel, All Through the Night,
Drink to me Only*, a mixture of Scottish, English and Welsh with an
admixture of American (*John Brown's Body, My Old Kentucky Home*)
and First World War (*There's a Long, Long Trail a Winding* and *Pack
Up Your Troubles*) songs. The massed bands entered playing, on 19, 21
and 23 June, a selection from Sullivan's *The Mikado* and, on 20 and
22 June, a selection from *Yeomen of the Guard*. The bands marched
off each time playing J.M. Rogan's *Bond of Friendship* march. The historical staging of the Tattoo was done to traditional anonymous tunes
such as *Cupid's Retreating Sergeant, The Queen of Hearts* and *The
Irish Hautboy*. The Crusades' sequence began with the summoning of
Barons and Knights to the standard by King Richard the Lionheart for
the Third Crusade in 1189. They are blessed by the Bishop, attended
by clergy, choir and pilgrims, and addressed by the King. There is a
vision of Jerusalem the Golden, the object of the expedition, they
march away and the sequence ends with Crusaders and Saracens in
conflict and Jerusalem in flames. The music used here is Wagner's
Knights of the Grail music from *Parsifal*, the *Nunc Dimittis* sung to
Tonus Peregrinus and a chanted semi-chorus from Elgar's *Dream of
Gerontius*. This is followed by a scene of the Duke of Wellington and
his officers hunting to hounds for relaxation in 1812 during the Peninsular War and then the storming of Badajoz and the raising of the
British Colours, with 'The Iron Duke' bowing his head in grief as he
'counts the awful price of victory'. The massed drums and pipes
entered playing the march *King George V's Army*, followed by a variety
of traditional Scots' reels and marches. The Great War sequence began
with bands playing *Pack Up Your Troubles, Tipperary* and *Keep the
Home Fires Burning* and the troops marching through the ruins of the
Menin Gate followed by two old Mark IV Great War tanks. There is a
simulated battle, complete with a twin-engined bombing aeroplane
and then, as the noise of battle fades, a field of Flanders' poppies surrounding a cross over a soldier's grave. The words 'Lest We Forget'
become visible 'to remind us that, though the price of war is heavy,
its lessons of self-sacrifice should and do instil nobler ideals that lift
the standard of civilization to higher levels'.[22] After this the band plays
and the audience is requested to join in the first verse of the hymn *O
God, Our Help in Ages Past*. Finally the 2nd Battalion of the East Yorkshire Regiment perform torchlight evolutions, in the first part forming
up the names of 'some of the great nations with compose the British
Empire' and then creating 'a living Union Flag in which the Christian
crosses symbolise the loyalty, the brotherhood and the spirituality
which are the salient characteristics of the nations of the Empire'.[23]

After this came *Abide With Me, The Last Post* and *God Save the King*. There could be no more potent demonstration of the way in which the cultural images of monarchy, Empire, Protestant Christianity, chivalry, hero-worship and war were blended and overlaid with music to create a definite image of the values and nature and history of British imperialism, with the Third Crusade, the Peninsular War and the Great War seen as linked.

The same themes were taken up in the 1929 Tattoo whose focus was the value of chivalry. The organizers' didactic intent is made clear in the Programme.

> Primarily the Tattoo which is presented this evening is intended for the entertainment and enjoyment of our visitors; but, while it aims to inter-est, it also aims to instruct, to illustrate the growth of an altruism which began with the Christian religion, and which, in subsequent centuries, has assumed strange and sometimes, apparently irreconcilable aspects. The theme of a military Tattoo must of necessity concern war, and to attempt to reconcile altruism with war would seem to be absurd. Yet a little delving below the surface of the three main spectacles of this Tattoo – 'The Crusaders', 'Waterloo' and '1914' – will discover a spirit of chivalry common to all three, that spirit which Tennyson saw in the Prince Consort and which he defined in . . . his introduction to the *Idylls of the King*:
>
> > 'Who reverenced his conscience as his king;
> > whose glory was redressing human wrong;
> > Who spake no slander, no, nor listen'd to it.'

So the key to understanding war is chivalry, defined as: 'the protection of the distressed, the maintenance of right against might and the personal character of a champion of Christianity, *sans peur et sans réproche*'. Chivalry, once the preserve of knightly orders, spread even further during the Middle Ages to inspire peasant as much as it did prince. It inspired all the participants in the Crusades, the Battle of Waterloo and 'the Empire's sons in tens of thousands' who rallied to the Colours in 1914 when Belgium was invaded by Germany. Even though Britain is at peace, chivalry can be seen in action in the League of Nations, the public-school code, the Rotarian movement, the Playing Fields Campaign and the Boy Scout's vow: 'I promise to do my duty to God and the King and to help other people at all times.'

> Founded on the tilting ring and the field of battle, may it not be that old-time chivalry shall, at some future day, lead to world-wide peace and universal brotherhood? Viewed in that light, the spectacles seen in the arena tonight are not photographs of war; but, rather they are indications of the steps by which poor, half-blind humanity is struggling from the

darkness to the light. The Christian religion, which imposed its laws upon the belted knights of ancient chivalry, extorted from them vows of self-renunciation; but no vows were needed in 1914 from our Empire's chivalrous sons, whose spontaneous and joyous sacrifice in 'redressing human wrongs', is hymned in those glorious lines of Rupert Brooke:

'Blow out, you bugles, over the rich dead!
There's none of these so lonely and poor of old,
But, dying, has made us rarer gifts than gold,
These laid the world away; poured out the red
Sweet wine of youth; gave up the years to be
Of work and joy, and that unhoped serene,
That men call age; and those who would have been,
Their sons, they gave, their immortality.'[24]

The community singing, led by Eric Godley, contained much the same repertoire as the previous year's, with the conspicuous addition of *Here's a Health Unto His Majesty*, attesting to the general concern about the illness of George V. The Programme contained the message of thanks issued by the King on 22 April to 'those who, in every part of the Empire, were remembering me with prayers and good wishes. The realization of this has been among the most vivid experiences of my life.'[25]

The historical reconstructions, which blended music, sound, movement and stylization for their effect, began with 'The Return of the Crusaders', an imagined late twelfth-century scene of word arriving at an English castle of the approach of the victorious Crusaders. Bells are rung and the equipment set up for a celebratory tournament, all to the background of Edward German's zestful *The Merry-Makers*. The Queen and her train emerge to greet the King and his Crusaders, to the strains of Gounod's *Agnes Radieux*. The King and Queen take their places on the dais to watch the joust, to the music of Wood's *Three Dale Dances*. Then, in the joust, an 'unknown knight' defeats three warriors and receives the laurel wreath of victory from the Queen. An ecclesiastical procession emerges from the castle, chanting Barnby's *Te Deum*. King, Queen and subjects kneel to receive the Bishop's blessing and after it, the *Dresden Amen* is sung. The lights dim as the whole company processes back to the castle to the *Pilgrims' Chorus* from Wagner's *Tannhauser*.

Scotland's warrior history was recognized in a 'Highland Episode' of 1314 staged by massed pipe bands, which enter to the march *Blue Bonnets Over the Border*. During the march a beacon flares from the castle keep, and runners dash off to summon the clans, bearing torches to symbolize the Fiery Cross, the sign summoning clans to battle. Four clans, in costumes of 1314, enter and march and countermarch to the march *My Native Highland Home*. This symbolizes the Battle of Bannockburn – there is no display of English and Scots clashing directly. Then, as the band ceases playing, the wail of the pipes is heard and a body of clansmen marches in escorting the bier of a dead chieftain. The clansmen with the massed bands join the procession and accompany the bier at quick step to the castle, forming an avenue of flaming torches, and the massed pipe bands disappear into the trees to the strains of the slow march *My Lodging's on the Cold, Cold Ground*.

The 1815 sequence begins with 'The Duchess of Richmond's Ball', after which comes 'The Battle of Waterloo'. The next sequence, 1914, opens with the Cloth Hall at Ypres, representing Belgium at peace, as a distant bell rings the Angelus. The *William Tell* overture depicts the passing from peace to storm and the sound of distant gunfire heralds war. The German song *Die wacht am rhein* is heard and the Cloth Hall is seen flaming. The battle music from the *1812 Overture* by Tchaikovsky symbolizes the war and rising above it the *Marsellaise* and the French marching song *Quand Madelon* as French troops march in; then, to *Hearts of Oak*, British naval detachments and to the historic soldiers' songs of 1914 – *Tipperary, Pack Up Your Troubles* and *Keep the Home Fires Burning* – columns representing the imperial forces of India and the dominions. The clamour of battle increases, accompanied by the battle music from Royal Marines' Bandmaster Jacob Kappey's *Episodes in a Soldier's Life* (1885) and climaxes with the figure of the Virgin on the Albert Cathedral crashing to the ground, recalling the wartime legend that the fall of the Virgin would foretell the cessation of hostilities. The scene ends in darkness and silence, 'leaving imagination to play upon the bloody gulf separating 1914 from the ultimate realization of Victory and Peace'.[26] Immediately after this Big Ben is heard sounding the eleventh hour of the eleventh day of the eleventh month – Armistice.

The grand finale has torchbearers from the 1st Battalion, Royal Warwickshire Regiment, forming up the Star of the Order of the Garter (to the strains of Kenneth Alford's march *The Vanished Army*) and then Crusaders, English troops of 1815 and 1914, Highland clans and pipers, massed bands and drums form up to the strains of *British Grenadiers* and receive and salute French troops under Napoleon who advance to strains of the *Marsellaise*. *Abide With Me, The Last Post* and *God Save the King* follow. The troops exit to Bidgood's march *Sons of the Brave*.

The theme chosen for 1930 was 'valour'. The illustrations were Queen Elizabeth I reviewing her troops at Tilbury before the Armada in 1588; the Regiment of the Coldstream Guards under General Monck in 1660 transferring its allegiance from the Puritan republic to King Charles II at the Restoration, and George II personally leading his troops to victory at the Battle of Dettingen in 1743: the link between crown and armed forces could not have been clearer.

The object of the Tattoo, said the Programme, was, firstly 'to assist the Commands' Charitable Funds'. Secondly it was devised 'to instruct, amuse, interest, entertain and comfort its patrons'; comfort because Britain faces as many vexations as she did in 1588, 1660 and 1743. 'May we not find comfort in the thought that, as British courage in the past has refused to envisage defeat, so courage will again carry Britain through trial and stress to ultimate victory.'[27] It also stresses the importance, in 1588, 1660 and 1743, of team spirit: 'That spirit has remained with the British Army in war and in peace.'

The 1588 sequence had Drake and his game of bowls on Plymouth Hoe, a distant view of the English and Spanish fleets in action and the review at Tilbury. The first scene was performed to *Peaceful England* and *Yeomen of England* from Edward German's *Merrie England, Come If You Dare, For England, Home and Beauty* and *Episodes in a Soldier's Life* by Kappey. For the final scene the music was from German's *A Princess of Kensington*, Handel's *Rinaldo* and Humperdinck's *The Miracle*, and the people sang *Brave Lord Willoughby* as they dispersed. The finale had the 2nd Battalion, Grenadier Guards, carrying torches, enter to the strains of *The British Grenadiers* and form up into the shape of the Victoria Cross, what the Prince of Wales had called 'That most enviable order' at the VC Dinner the previous November. Those words and the Victoria Cross appeared in the background, sketched in fire. The hymn *O Valiant Hearts* was broadcast in the arena and troops from the different eras lined up with modern troops around the VC formation for *Abide With Me, The Last Post* and *God Save the King.*

The 1931 Programme pointed out that in its earlier forms the Aldershot Tattoo was 'military spectacle pure and simple' but more recently *themes* had been chosen: 'sacrifice', 'chivalry', 'valour'. The theme for 1931 was 'discipline':

> A quality that has long been identified with our race, and which has enabled us as a nation in times of stress and peril to endure when the limit of endurance has apparently long been reached, and to succeed when success has appeared impossible. This great quality of a voluntarily adopted national and individual discipline depends on something higher and nobler than fear for its maintenance. It is deeply ingrained in the very fibre of the people, and plays an important part in their daily lives. It was much in evidence during the Great War when the people carried on their daily avocations, facing with unflinching courage losses, dangers and difficulties, and enabled the nation to face the grave difficulties of the post-war years.[28]

[229]

The national sense of discipline, according to the programme, has its foundations 'in the splendid military discipline introduced into Britain by the Romans, which enabled their Legions to overcome the brave but undisciplined tribes and hold the country in captivity for three hundred years'. In illustrating how the British have emulated that discipline, the Programme carefully makes no distinction of class or gender. Discipline has been shown on sinking troopships like *Birkenhead* and *Warren Hastings* and liners like *Titanic*; in many mining and other industrial accidents; by Florence Nightingale and Grace Darling; and today among the police, firemen, ambulance men, nurses and doctors, housewives, merchants and armed services.[29]

To illustrate the chosen motif, the Tattoo re-enacted 'the unflagging discipline' of Crauford's rear guard during the retreat of British forces to Corunna in 1809, and then the burial on the ramparts of Corunna of the British commander Sir John Moore, killed in the battle with the pursuing French. By contrast 'Engines of War' paraded a succession of primitive military machines, but culminated in a sequence of modern mechanized warfare, including anti-aircraft guns, tanks and machine guns. The big set-piece was 'The Romans in Britain', emphasizing the value of discipline in the landing of the legions and the defeat of Boadicea's rebellion. It opens with a Druid human sacrifice and Druids leading British resistance to Roman invasion; then Boadicea's rebellion and the destruction of Camulodunum; and finally the defeat of rebellion by disciplined legions and the pardoning of captives by the Emperor 'as an act of grace to a brave enemy'. All this was staged to excerpts from Verdi's *Aida* and the *Doge's March* from Rosse's music for *The Merchant of Venice*. The finale began with a Scots Guardsman standing with a Union Jack at the centre of the arena and then around a triumphal arch all the various participants lining up to Rogan's march *Bond of Friendship* and cavalry to Gounod's *Soldiers' Chorus*. The massed bands played *Abide With Me* and the arena was darkened to show only an illuminated cross in the distance. Then after the Roman city was illuminated, came the sound of *Last Post* and as the arena was again flooded with light, the national anthem and a medley of war tunes, before dispersal. *The Times* reported of the first night:

> The Searchlight Tattoo, which had a successful opening tonight, must rank high among military representations in recent years. In the development of episodes that provide striking contrasts there is pageantry with movement and brilliant effects are produced by coloured lights that flood the vast arena and filter through the trees of adjoining woods. The finished character of the first public performance suggested that episodes with themes inspiring dramatic action made a strong appeal to the

soldiers engaged in their representation. The well-ordered movement of the Tattoo provides a fine example of the results of training and discipline, and shows the soldier as a man of many parts – enthusiastic as an actor in the character of an ancient Briton or a Roman warrior, and efficient as a member of the British army.[30]

The Times's correspondent found 'The Burial of Sir John Moore' 'impressive' and 'The Romans in Britain' sequence 'thrilling'.

The theme of the 1932 Tattoo was the 'The Flag and Empire'. The Official Programme opened with a quotation from Kipling's *The Flag of England* ('What is the flag of England? Winds of the World declare') and the introduction concluded with Merrivale's *Sceptre of the Sea*:

> Hold, Britain, hold thy creed of old,
> Brave foe and steadfast friend,
> And still unto thy motto true
> 'Defy not, but defend'.[31]

The emphasis is on the non-aggressive nature of British patriotism. There is no doubt, however, of the pride in and the commitment to Empire.

The Programme notes that as the Aldershot Tattoo, 'with its deeply stirring motif of "The Flag and Empire"', is being presented, preparations are being completed for the Ottawa Conference, 'one of the most momentous conferences in the history of the British Empire'. The Tattoo would depict the 'glorious episodes which have gone to build up our great Empire', and the conference would meet 'with the one great desire to bring into even closer unity the great British Empire, of which we are all so justly proud'. This was the conference which finally introduced imperial trade preference and tariffs, a long-discussed economic measure but only enacted under the pressure of the worldwide economic depression.

The Programme declares that there have been many empires (Egypt, Persia, Assyria, Rome, Turkey and Spain) and 'each in turn has decayed and died as the love of luxury and soft living sapped the fibre and weakened the will of the dominating race'. However, the British Empire has been built on surer foundations, 'freedom, truth and justice'.

> Upon the noble sacrifices of its innumerable pioneers, the steadfast loyalty and courage of His Majesty's Forces, enforcing law and order in the remotest parts of the world, and the wisdom and high sense of responsibility of its statesmen and ministers, this great commonwealth of nations rests united under the Union Flag. The British Empire has won a position and prestige attained by no other empire and works for the benefit of mankind in general.

[231]

The Programme stressed the *British* nature of the Empire. The symbol of all that is best in the Empire is to be seen in the British flag, which is composed of the banners of St George, St Andrew and St Patrick.

> Each of these nationalities has given something to the British character that has enabled the heroes of history to achieve when success seemed impossible, to endure when hope was gone, to fight for the right without hatred, and to prize honour above personal gain. These characteristics of the British race have been largely in evidence in the building of the Empire, and it is the glory of the Army that in the building it has played so large a part. The sense of self-discipline so marked in the British race is splendidly expressed in the Army, the efficiency of which is based on its high standard of discipline . . . That is the spirit that has built up the great British Empire and brought honour to the flag.[32]

The Tattoo opened with the ceremony of retreat featuring a detachment of the Toronto Regiment of the Canadian Military Forces, the first time any dominion troops had taken part in the Tattoo. They were accompanied by the Band of the 2nd Battalion, the King's Regiment, and the Programme reminded the audience that the two regiments, Canadian and British, had fought side by side in 1812 in the war against the United States, a pertinent reminder of the long-standing and special ties of Britain and her dominions. The massed drums and fifes beat the Tattoo, entering to *Land of My Fathers* and preceded by the pure-bred Welsh goat, the mascot of the 1st Battalion, Welsh Regiment, 'a gift to the Battalion by His Majesty the King'. This was to emphasize the Welsh dimension not represented in the flag. The 'Massed Physical Training Display' was performed to 'popular airs known throughout the Empire'. These included *Daisy, Daisy*; *Hallo, Hallo, Who's Your Lady Friend?*; *All the Nice Girls Love a Sailor*; *K–K–K–Katie*; *John Peel*; *Sky Boat Song*; *Eton Boating Song*; and *John Brown's Body* – an interesting combination of folk-song and music-hall song. The cavalry ride was performed by the 5th Enniskillen Dragoon Guards to emphasize the Irish dimension. Scotland was represented, as ever, by Massed Pipe Bands and eighty-one dancers from the Gordon Highlanders performing a ninesome reel. The music included the marches *St Andrew's Cross*; *Scotland the Brave*; *The Cock o' the North*; and *Athole and Breadalbane Gathering*.

The battle re-enactment was Inkerman in the Crimean War, staged to music drawn from Tchaikovsky's symphonies *No. 5 and No. 6* and the *1812 Overture*, culminating in a 'realization' of Lady Butler's famous painting *The Roll Call* with a sergeant calling from the actual roll of the 3rd Battalion, Grenadier Guards, at the time of the battle.

'The Flag and Empire' sequence opened with the three saints,

George, Andrew and Patrick, whose crosses make up the flag taking up position to greet the 'Heroes whose spirit of adventure and patriotism built the Empire'. The choice of imperial heroes carefully included both army and navy. It began with Drake, Raleigh and Hawkins, the Elizabethan seadogs who fought Spain, and then Prince Rupert, Oliver Cromwell, Admiral Blake and the Duke of Albemarle, consensually including both sides in the English Civil War and stressing their victories against the Dutch. They were followed by the Duke of Marlborough and Admiral Benbow; then Lord Clive and General Wolfe who added Canada and India to the Empire; Sir John Moore and Earl Howe, Wellington and Nelson, from the Napoleonic Wars; Lord Raglan from the Crimean War; General Havelock and Sir James Outram 'who led our troops to victory in the Indian Mutiny'; General Gordon and General Wolseley whose campaigns led to the acquisition of African colonies; Cecil Rhodes; and finally Captain Scott and his 'brave comrades who died carrying the flag to the South Pole'. Each group, apart from the last, was accompanied by soldiers and sailors of the period with appropriate contemporary flags. During the procession, four visions 'representative of the Empire' were seen in the distance: Drake's fleet under full sail; an Indian city; the desert, Sphinx and Pyramid; and an Arctic expedition, iceberg and full-rigged ship. The band played a selection from Engelbert Humperdinck's suite *The Miracle* during this prologue, to emphasize the wondrous nature of the achievement. Then three episodes of 'our Empire story, typical of discovery, enterprise and hardships endured by the early pioneers', were portrayed. First there was Captain Cook landing in Australia and raising the flag; then Red Indians attacking a group of Canadian settlers in a log cabin. They were rescued by a detachment of the Royal Canadian Mounted Police (RCMP). Finally there was a re-enactment of the last stand of Major Allan Wilson and the Shangani River Patrol, overwhelmed and wiped out by a Matabele *impi* which advanced to war drums and war chants. The Programme noted that Major Wilson's personal galloper, Mr George Bowen, who had survived by being despatched to bring help, had approved the faithfulness of the recreation.

In the grand finale, which brought together the key themes, the Union flag flew and the three saints appeared and St George of England summoned forth 'the present-day successors of those who have founded the Empire and upheld the Flag in the past'. A line of replicas of the historical Colours of the British Army was paraded, escorted by the 1st Battalion, Welsh Guards, and the 2nd Battalion, Gordon Highlanders. Representatives of the forces of the Empire then lined up, from all the dominions plus the Bechuanaland Police, the RCMP and the Territorials. The Toronto detachment had pride of place. While all this was going on, marches were played: Javaloyes's *El Abanico*; Bagley's *National Emblem* and *Marlborough*; and Carter's *Dover Castle*. Following this the massed bands played *Abide With Me* while a cross was illuminated in the distance. Henry Ainley recited two verses of Kipling's *Recessional* and, after *The Last Post, Reveille* and the national anthem, the troops dispersed to a medley of war tunes and Alford's *On the Quarterdeck*.

A record 60,500 people saw the opening performance in fine weather, and *The Times* (13 June, 1932) reported:

> The triumph of the Tattoo in its appeal to the imagination of the public was shown by the varying moods of the audience. The spirit of each scene was quickly caught by the vast assembly. During some episodes there was frequent and enthusiastic applause, as, for example, when the massed bands performed in a blaze of changing lights. There were others that inspired profound and impressive silence, but at the end there was always an outburst of cheers.[33]

The 1933 Tattoo, whose Programme opened with Alfred Noyes's lines 'There is a song of England that thrills the beating blood', recognized the ravages of the Depression but believed it would be overcome:

> For the national spirit, buoyed up by hope, gleams with an undimmed brightness, while the loyalty of the nation to these splendid ideals of a true brotherhood of Christian forbearance, of goodwill, justice and cheerfulness, combined with the will to help the weak and a tolerance for the other fellow's point of view, will go far towards solving the great difficulties yet to be overcome.

Britain had avoided the unrest of other countries because of 'the spirit of loyalty that is so deeply ingrained in the British character . . . loyalty to our national ideals, loyalty to our fellow men, loyalty to our King and Country, and loyalty to our inner selves'. The same spirit inspires all ranks of the British Army and 'all the native troops serving under the British Crown'. So the year's theme was to be 'loyalty'.[34]

The historical episode chosen to illustrate the loyalty theme was the death of Gordon at Khartoum, 'the desert story of General Gordon's loyalty to his great mission of peace to the Sudan, his noble death and the beneficent results that have accrued by his self-sacrifice to the enslaved tribes of the North African desert'.[35] It took the form of three scenes: the final Dervish attack on Khartoum, the death of Gordon on the steps of his palace and the raising of the Dervish flag in place of the Khedival flag; then the Battle of Omdurman, avenging the death of Gordon; and finally the reoccupation of Khartoum, the raising of the British and Egyptian flags over the ruined palace, three cheers for the Queen and the service of remembrance for Gordon. The principal music in scene 1 and scene 3 was the *Funeral March* from Coleridge-Taylor's *Othello* suite, with, in the third scene, snatches of the British and Khedival national anthems for the flag raising, the hymn *For Ever With the Lord* and the lament *Lochaber No More*.

The theme of loyalty also informed the sequence 'The Bowman and After', of which phase one was the training of the English archers in 1415, which opened with a passage quoted from Shakespeare's *Henry V*, an 'olde English' inn and smithy, the nobility returning from a day's falconry and stag-hunting, and Henry V arriving to sentence three aristocratic traitors, Richard, Earl of Cambridge, Lord Scroop of Masham and Sir Thomas Grey, all guilty of disloyalty. They are condemned to death, degraded from knighthood, and marched off to execution. The representatives of the Church then bless the expedition to France. 'So the pageant fades away, leaving only the memory of the glory and beauty of our ancient chivalry and the skill and courage of the old English archers which helped to make our armies so successful'.[36] The music was drawn from Grieg's *Sigurd Jorsalfar* suite and the scene and prayer from Mascagni's *Cavalleria Rusticana*. Phase two, showing modern warfare, had an attack on an enemy position mounted by all the latest weapons, guns and planes.

The grand finale, with the Union Jack at the centre, had all the participants line up to *Le Rêve Passé* by Krier and Helmer, R.B. Hall's march *Officer of the Day* and the march of the South Staffordshire Regiment *Come, Lassies and Lads*, followed by *Abide With Me*, an epilogue spoken by Henry Ainley and *God Save the King*.

Empire was again the central theme in the 1934 Tattoo. The Programme set out the meaning of Empire:

> The ideals which the builders of the British Empire have ever kept steadfastly in view have slowly but surely been realized, and although there yet remains a great work to be done, sufficient has been accomplished to render the Empire one of the great living factors, if not indeed the greatest factor, in leading the world from its present condition of anxiety, unrest and suspicion towards that state of international goodwill and peace which alone can give mankind happiness and prosperity. Throughout the past few centuries, while the Empire has been brought into being, its influence in international affairs has steadily grown, and has invariably been exercised on behalf of the oppressed and weak. With the passing of time the benign influence has grown more powerful, and Nations are coming to regard the British Empire as the most important factor in maintaining the peace of the world, in adjusting differences, removing causes of irritations, and in lifting backward races to higher planes of Christian civilization.[37]

The British Army has played a vital role in this great work: 'its mission has ever been to protect the defenceless, to give relief to the wronged, and to ensure freedom from tyranny'. So the army played a 'noble role' in founding, building up, protecting and defending the Empire, the strength of whose bonds was demonstrated by the colonies rallying to the mother country in 1914. The set-pieces were the siege of Namur in 1695 and a review of his troops on Hounslow Heath by King James II in 1686 – a somewhat unfortunate choice of monarch in view of the stress on freedom from tyranny. An innovation was a potted version of Wagner's opera *Tannhauser* with the massed bands playing the hunting fanfare *O Star of Eve*, the *Grand March* and the *Pilgrims' Chorus*. *The Times*'s reporter (18 June 1934) asked 'What has all this to do with the army?' and answered himself by saying that it demonstrated the army's technical mastery of the staging of such events, but in fact, the theme of the opera, the conflict of sensuality and spirituality, and the victory of good over evil, could be seen to underline the continuing Christian emphasis of the Tattoos. The finale was 'The Rally of Empire', beginning with a torchlit display as torchbearers formed up around Britannia seated at the centre of a cross of St George and the world at peace, as ships of Britain move to and fro on their lawful occupations. Noise of war is heard, Britannia waves her trident to north, south, east and west; trumpeters sound *The Rally* and the troopship *Empress of Britain* is seen in the distance. The troops of the Empire march in to surround Britannia, troops from Australia, New Zealand, Canada, and, from India, Sikhs, Gurkhas, Punjabis and Baluchis. The first scene was accompanied by *Rule Britannia*, *A Life on the Ocean Wave* and Winter's selection *Martial Moments*; and the finale by Williams's *Blue Devils* and Hudson's *Gullianan*. *The Last Post*, *Abide With Me* and *God Save the King* followed, with a spoken epilogue:

> So passes another Pageant of Our Empire History. In gratitude we remember those who have toiled for us, in small things as in great, and have made our birthright in the Four Corners of the Earth. We offer tonight our praises and thanks to God through whom they have brought Help to the Weak, Justice to the Oppressed, Light and Health to the darkest places of the World, and Freedom to Men. Let us be worthy of our Great Heritage.[38]

Queen Mary, the Duke and Duchess of York, the Princess Royal and Lord Harewood attended the final performance, but heavy thunderstorms caused many of the visitors to leave before the end. At 413,000, the total number of visitors to the Tattoo was 85,000 down on 1933; but the numbers were back up, to 483,000, for 1935.

The year 1935 was that of King George V's Silver Jubilee, and the Tattoo's theme of 'Crown and Empire' was chosen to reflect 'the deep sense of loyalty to the Crown and pride in the Empire' which marked the celebrations of the Jubilee. The Tattoo's Programme announced:

> The *motif* running like a gleaming thread through the programme of the 1935 Tattoo, 'The Crown and the Empire', has been happily chosen, for it weaves into an inspiring entertainment a combination of beautiful music, historical pageantry and stirring action presented by troops of the British Army... The past few weeks have witnessed scenes of unbounded gratitude and joy for the many blessings that have been vouchsafed to the British Empire during the past twenty-five years and in no section of the community is the sense of gratitude and joy deeper and more sincere than in the British Army... it is right and proper that the Army should regard the Crown, symbolized by His Majesty King George V, as the font and inspiration of all loyal endeavours. In him they visualize the central figure of the great British Empire, in the growth and development of which so many of the units serving in the Aldershot Command and Eastern Command have played an heroic part, and having played that part are content to return to their unobtrusive places in the Empire's organization for the peaceful progress of civilization and the brotherhood of mankind.[39]

Having said all this, the Programme then goes on to assert, paradoxically: 'The Tattoo has no militaristic aims or propaganda. That spirit has never found place in the British Army, any more than in the hearts of the nation.' It stresses that the aims of the Tattoo were to demonstrate army fitness and discipline, benefit service charities and provide a summer night's entertainment. If that is not propaganda, it is hard to see what could be, and the message of the spectacle was certainly appreciated by *The Times* which devoted a leading article to it, headed 'Drums of Jubilee'. Calling the Tattoo 'deeply civilized and truly art', *The Times* declared:

> Illuminated between the darkened grandstands and the darker woods, the performers in the Tattoo are suspended for a few hours in a world that seems compact of fantasy. Yet, steeped as they are in romance by the music and the searchlights, they do not fail to impress the spectator with the real spirit of the Army of today. These masses of men, marching and counter-marching in obedience to no visible signal or audible command, constitute a marvellously harmonious, infinitely flexible instrument, which no War Lord's hand could wield, but which is ready to the purposes of King of England and his people... There is nothing in the Tattoo to hint at lust of conquest or delight in war... These men are keepers of the King's peace, sharing that honourable duty with all the civilians who watch them. And differing only in the perfection of

discipline that adapts them to their function. It is a discipline of a high order that belongs to free men.[40]

The Tattoo included a musical tribute to the King by, allegedly, the largest assembly of massed bands ever seen, drawn from twenty-four different regiments. It involved the playing of the traditional song *Here's a Health Unto His Majesty* as a slow march, the quick march *Royal Standard* by J.H. Keith and the specially composed band, trumpet and bugle march *The King's Champion* by Arthur Graham. *The Times*'s special correspondent reported:

> To hear this band playing music which is all by English composers (with the exception of a beautiful rendering of Chopin's *Polonaise in A*) against a scenic background that blends the fifteenth-century Tower of London, with the distant turrets of Windsor, and to the expressive poetry of the changing lights, is not only to repeat on a larger scale an enjoyment of past tattoos, but to realize in its fullness the peculiar significance of this one.[41]

The set-piece 'Battles Old and New' staged a modern attack on an enemy-held village and a stylized period battle enacted after the bands played a special arrangement of Eckersberg's battle suite *Waterloo*. It involved English, Scottish, Welsh and Irish brigades assembling to the strains of *The British Grenadiers* and *Men of Harlech*, the skirl of the pipes and the beat of Irish drums. No enemy was specified. There was a Scottish set-piece, set in 1778 when Kenneth MacKenzie, Earl of Seaforth and head of the Clan MacKenzie, raised the 1st Battalion of the Seaforth Highlanders, which took over the MacKenzie motto 'Cuidich'n Righ' – Help the King. Pipers marched, beacons fired and the bearers of the Fiery Cross rode out to summon the clans who gathered and shouted 'Cuidich'n Righ' as the regiment was raised. The finale 'Long Live the King' had four parts: in part one the soldiers' toast to the King and Queen was delivered to the background of Horatio Nicholls's *Cavalcade of Martial Songs*. Then, the symbol of kingship, the imperial crown, appeared lit up, and beneath it St George summoned all the regiments of the Tattoo to pay tribute to the House of Windsor. The crown was said to stand for chivalry, loyalty, freedom, ordered government, brotherhood and sacrifice. The music for this sequence was Roger Barsotti's *The King's Company*. There was a cavalcade of those sovereigns who prior to George V and Queen Victoria (who by convention could not be impersonated) had enjoyed Silver Jubilees: Henry I, Henry II, Henry III, Edward I, Edward III, Henry VI, Henry VIII, Elizabeth I, George II, George III, each accompanied by their sons, their bodyguards and the leading generals of their time, latterly including 'Founders of the Empire' such as Wellington, Clive and Wolfe. The music was Elgar's *Pomp and Circumstance No.4* and Albert Ketélbey's *State Procession*. Part 4, sung by the Choir of the 1st Battalion, Welsh Regiment, was *The Soldier's Hymn to the King*, composed by Poet Laureate John Masefield, and set to music by the Master of the King's Musick Sir Walford Davies, laying great stress on peace and with the chorus: 'O, Power, hear us as we sing, And bless Our Country and her King.' After *Abide With Me* and before the national anthem, there was an epilogue culled from the Second Book of Kings and the First Book of Samuel: 'And the Guard stood – every man with his weapons in his hand, round about the King. And Samuel said to all the people, See ye him whom the Lord hath chosen, that there is none like him among all the people. And all the people shouted, and said, "God save the King"'. *The Times*'s correspondent rhapsodized: 'What splendour, what variety and subtlety of colour! Once again the Army gives lessons to the pageant master and the stage director.'

The theme of the 1936 Tattoo was 'youth'. The Official Programme noted: 'Every country is now realizing the potential value of its educational and moral qualities, mainly for national purposes, but within the British Empire the priceless asset of Youth is being developed on the broader lines of universal human happiness, progress and prosperity.'[42] So, along with 'Hail and Farewell', which depicted the cavalry in action in the Great War with memories of the cavalry regiments of the past (to the music of Alford's *Vanished Army*, Myddleton's *Phantom Brigade* and *Auld Lang Syne*), there was a staging of the duel between Sir Henry de Bohun and King Robert Bruce at the start of the Battle of Bannockburn in the presence of the English and Scottish armies, a sequence, says the Programme, 'designed to link up the Scottish soldier of those stirring times with those successors of his who have chosen to bear arms in the defence of the Empire which they now share with an erstwhile foe'.[43] The historical recreation featured the Rangoon River Expedition of 1824 during the First Burmese War, based on a series of prints of the expedition drawn by J. Moore and published in London in 1835. *The Times* described it:

> As if some fine old coloured print had been brought to life, we see the British ships floating on a river of shadow, the red-coated, white-trousered infantry disembarking, and advancing in long lines with their colours to the storming of the stockade, and the final burning of a native village. It is an admirable reconstruction of antiquated tactics.[44]

There was the usual pageant of massed army bands, this time playing a programme including Sullivan's song *The Lost Chord* and marches both traditional (*The Minstrel Boy, Lillibulero*) and modern (*Sons of the Brave* by Bidgood, *The Watch Tower* by Herzer, *Mechanised Infantry* by McBain). *The Times* reported:

> The familiar massed bands' number, in which this time both mounted and dismounted bands participate, seems more stupendous than ever, girdled, as it is, by shining torches bathed in enchanted purple lights, and fading away at last into a stream of fleeting sparks that may well bring a lump into the throats of the onlooker with their eloquent suggestion of mortal transitoriness.

The climax of the Tattoo came in the recreation of the episode in 1284 when King Edward I presented his newly born son, the future Edward II, to the Welsh at Caernarvon, as their Prince. The English entered to Albert Ketélbey's stately and stirring *With Honour Crowned* and the Welsh to the always rousing *Men of Harlech*. This had the effect of celebrating both youth and the incorporation of Wales into the United Kingdom. The final *tableau* of this scene remained in place for the grand finale in which all the performers entered to Tulip's march *The Prince* and a column of young soldiers appeared bearing torches to the march, by Robinson, *State Trumpeters*. The soldiers, the Programme tells us, symbolize youth, physical fitness and the 'spirit of adventure', a spirit 'which has made the Empire what it is to-day and in the symbol they carry the flame to light the path of unselfish national service, which youth must surely tread, if we are to hold fast that great heritage bequeathed to us by our fathers'. It ends with the singing of *Abide With Me* and Kipling's *Children's Song* ('Land of our Birth, we pledge to thee/ Our love and toil in the years to be') and then the national anthem. The Programme declared confidently: 'Youth succeeds to a great heritage, bequeathed to them by past generations who built up the British Empire at the cost of great sacrifices. There is no doubt that that heritage is in safe keeping with the Youth of today.'[45]

The Times's correspondent was in reflective mood at this Tattoo, observing:

> Not one of the Aldershot Tattoos has failed to stir both imagination and thought; but in days as momentous for the future as those we are now living through it is impossible not to wonder, as we sit and watch, through what vicissitudes of destiny ... we may 10 years hence look back and remember the glorious ghosts of Rushmoor.[46]

Even if the organizers of the Tattoo did not regard their show as propagandist, others did. The Labour-dominated London County Council Education Committee passed a resolution in 1935 forbidding the attendance of children at military displays. In 1936 the Tattoo invited London schoolchildren to attend a show. Committee member Miss C. Fulford (Municipal Reform Party) urged the LCCEC to rescind its ban, pointing out that the object of the Tattoo was to raise funds for military charities and not for poison gas or guns, that the theme of the Tattoo was youth and service, and that it was a 'magnificent piece of pageantry'. But the Labour members of the Committee insisted that the pageant gave no hint of the horrors of war, and Charles Robertson, the Vice-Chairman of the Committee, said that 'they were not going to prostitute the souls, minds and bodies of those children in the beastliness of war. They were not going to Hitlerize their schools.' The ban remained in force.[47]

The following year, 1937, was Coronation year and the theme was 'loyalty to the Crown'. The Programme announced that it was 'clearly revealed in the opening item that brings into the Arena representative banners of all the Overseas Dominions and Dependencies'; that it was 'embodied in the wonderful music that gives the Tattoo its unique interest'; that it was 'present in various forms in all the items'; and that it was 'the dominating idea of the Grand Finale'.[48] So the Tattoo opened with a procession of over 100 banners of every dominion, colony and state of the Empire. They assembled to the slow march *Golden Spurs* by Rhodes and the quick march *Crown and Commonwealth* by Adams, the march *Captain Norman Orr-Ewing* by Ross, the traditional march *Corn Riggs* and the traditional march-past *Pibroch o'Donal Dhu* played by massed cavalry (dismounted) and massed pipe bands. They marched past to *Rule, Britannia*.

The coronation theme was maintained in the pageant of army music performed by the Massed Bands of the Aldershot and Eastern Commands marching and countermarching. Preceded by a fanfare, they entered to the march *Royal Standard* by J.H. Keith, advanced in slow time to the *Coronation March* from Meyerbeer's *The Prophet* and broke into quick-time for Plater's *March of the King's Men*, which had been awarded the prize in the competition for a special Coronation Tattoo March open to bandmasters of the Aldershot and Eastern Commands. The massed bands then halted to play *The Hallelujah Chorus* from Handel's *Messiah*, as the Empire banners were paraded again, and the banner-bearers remained in position as bands resumed their marching and countermarching to McBain's march *Sergeants-at-Arms*. There was a modern battle sequence, a re-enactment of the crossing of the Douro by Wellington's army in 1809, the lodging of the Colours in the days of King Charles I and a repeat of the 'Cuidich'n Righ' sequence from the 1935 Tattoo, with pipe marches including *MacKenzie Highlanders* and 25th KOSB's *Farewell to Meerut* to stress Scottish loyalty to the crown. The grand finale was 'The Challenge'. With a massive Golden Lion of Empire as the centrepiece, guarding the crown, 'the symbol of kingship, the chief and strongest link that holds the Empire together', a pageant built up around it of Royal Archers, Yeomen of the Guard and Household Troops responsible for the safety of the King. The banners of Empire were paraded again and with them this time the banners of all the English Kings since William I. 'The poetry of martial movement', *The Times* called it.[49] The assembly terminated with the appearance of the King's Champion, in full armour, to challenge those arrayed against the King. The remainder of the participants assembled. The music for this pageant was Ketélbey's *Royal Cavalcade* for the entry of bodyguard and banners, Barsotti's quick march *Coronation Tattoo* for the grouping of the performers, and German's *Long Live Elizabeth* for the entry of the Champion, with Elgar's *Land of Hope and Glory* for the epilogue, written by Dermot Morrah and spoken by actor Robert Speaight:

> Here then our trumpets of defiance ring
> Menace to all arrayed against the King;
> And here in line of battle round the throne
> We stand to guard what God has made our own.
> While freeborn nations from earth's farthest bound
> Take post beside him at the trumpet's sound
> Embattled for the hope that wars may cease,
> Circling the King with swords – to keep the peace.

Then, after *Abide With Me* and the national anthem, which, according to the Programme, emphasizes loyalty 'to the great Christian traditions of our Country, which have bound us together under the Crown', the troops exited to a specially composed march medley of popular navy, army and air force tunes by Trayton Adams, entitled *The Keepers of the King's Peace*.

Although the first night of the Tattoo took place amid thunder and rain, the week as a whole was a triumph. It attracted a record 621,500 spectators, and the last night, 19 June, proved especially memorable. The event was attended by the King and Queen and every seat was sold. *The Times* reported that their car was cheered all the way from Windsor to Aldershot and that they were received by the crowd of 77,000 'with prolonged cheering' and the 'fervent' singing of the national anthem.[50] This time *The Times* devoted two leaders to the Tattoo. The first, headed 'King's Champions', confirmed the national significance of the Tattoo as an event:

> Even the triumphal march of monarchy through the rich-hued calendar
> of the Coronation year cannot make pale the splendours of the gracious,

stately romantic pageant of the Aldershot Tattoo. Year by year greater multitudes submit themselves to the enchantment of this annual marvel ... They will be rewarded for the journey to Aldershot by something more than a majestic spectacle, unfolded against a background of lovely rural scenery in the peace of an English summer night. For they will have been given a glimpse of the spirit of the modern army, a vision of the true meaning of that military faith which certain men devote their lives to maintaining in the years of peace, in order that it may be communicated to the whole nation if the need should be imposed by the emergency of war ... The ideal of the Army is not war, nor are wars made by soldiers – at any rate by British soldiers. War is now a universal affliction, as hateful to soldiers as to all humane-minded men; and the function of the Regular Army is to withstand it ... the military virtues that hold the ramparts of civilization against it are themselves lovely and of good report; and it is of these things, the ultimate nobilities of human valour defying the powers of darkness, that the Tattoo, in masque and symbol, makes the demonstration ... All the men of that Army are King's Champions now ... The march with which the massed bands play them from the arena bears the title 'Keepers of the King's Peace'.[51]

A second leader, 'End of the Tattoo', followed ten days later. It pointed out that the Tattoo imposed no drain on public funds and was not part of any official recruiting campaign, but it added: 'Nevertheless among the six hundred thousand spectators this year, there must have been very many young men for whom the thrill of martial music and the brave panoply of scarlet and gold, which all felt, may have had a personal significance'.[52]

This stress on peace continued in 1938, emphasized in the poetic extracts which topped and tailed the introduction to the Official Programme. McKay's *Tubalcain* ('And men, taught wisdom from the past/ In friendship joined their hands') and Longfellow ('Peace! And no longer from its brazen portals the blast of war's great organ shakes the skies').

> Amid this universal unrest the British Empire exerts a powerful influence for goodwill and understanding, and most of the nations are looking with hope to this country, as in the past, to act as peacemaker and mediator. That England's unselfish efforts to promote and maintain peace in the world will succeed is the fervent prayer of all.[53]

So, along with an air defence display, a re-enactment of the assault and capture of Fort Moro, Havannah, in 1762, by English forces under the Earl of Albemarle, and a lantern display forming a giant Rose of England, the great set-piece was a recreation of the Field of Cloth of Gold, cementing an alliance between England and France in 1520, a clear piece of historical parallelism. The message was continued in the epilogue, written by Dermot Morrah, celebrating peace and friendship, and spoken by Robert Speaight as massed bands softly played Ivor Novello's *Rose of England*. Trayton Adams composed special marches for Henry VIII and François I; arranged traditional drum marches, Lumley Holmes's *The Passing Pageant* and Ketèlbey's *A State Procession* were also played. As always, there was also *Abide With Me* and *God Save the King*. The King and Queen attended the final performance, and the total attendance was 531,800.

The last ever Tattoo was in 1939, and the mood had changed then to one of preparedness, 'steady and strong' being the motto. The Programme opened with a quotation of Sir Francis Doyle's *A Private of the Buffs*: 'Vain mightiest fleets of iron framed/ Vain those all shattering guns/ Unless this England keeps untamed/ The strong heart of her sons'; and it ended with lines from Sir Henry Newbolt's *Drake's Drum*.[54] The imagery was all now of Elizabethan England, threatened by the might of the Spanish Armada. It opened with a symbolic sequence, 'Changing the Guard', as an old red-coated army with its antique weapons hands the Union Jack over to new khaki-clad mechanized forces. As the flag was handed over, so *O God, Our Help in Ages Past* was played. Along with fanfares and regimental marches, the marches *Changing the Guard* by Flotsam and Jetsam, *Clarion Call* by Hughes, *The Beacon* by Young, *Soldiers' Chorus* by Gounod and *The Isle of Beauty* (arranged by Adams) were performed. The imperial dimension remained in a sequence aimed at showing the co-operation between land and air forces and emphasizing 'the more humane, rather than the destructive role that the Royal Air Force can play in modern warfare'.[55] It took place on an unnamed frontier of the Empire, and involved rebellious tribesmen attacking a British political agent and his small escort. After air reconnaissance, troop carriers were used to fly in men and equipment to disperse the tribesmen and relieve the British force. But the big set-piece was Queen Elizabeth I reviewing her troops at Tilbury, staged to extracts from Edward German's *Merrie England* and Frederick Curzon's stirring *March of the Bowmen*. This had been recreated only two years earlier in Alexander Korda's historical epic *Fire Over England*, which drew clear parallels between Philip II's Spain and Hitler's Germany. The finale retold the legend of Drake's drum, with BBC commentator John Snagge recounting the legend, and Drake presiding over the lighting of the beacons around the coast of Elizabethan England, and then, as all the performers gathered, the modern battleship *HMS Elizabeth* was seen steaming slowly up the river, 'representing the lion-hearted spirit and iron determination to defend her realm and her people that animated the great Queen after whom the ship was named'.[56] As she passed, the ship hoisted Nelson's famous signal 'England expects that every man will do his duty'. This was staged to background music of *The Deathless Army*, *Boys of the Old Brigade*, *The Death of Nelson* and finally *Rule, Britannia*.

The King and Queen being on a State Visit to the United States, the Duke and Duchess of Gloucester attended the final performance, and the Tattoo chalked up a total of 504,300 visitors. As *The Times*'s correspondent reported: 'This year it has a mood for the times . . . it pervades the year's production, which artistically is as successful as any of its forerunners'.[57]

Once again, too, it prompted a first leader from *The Times* (12 June 1939), headed 'Drake's Drum': 'The Army stands nearer to the heart and nearer to the life of the people today than ever before in time of peace . . . he must be dull of imagination who does not feel the presence of the spirit of the Army to which the Tattoo, with skilful mixture of realism and symbolism, gives such eloquent expression'.[58]

But there were to be no more Aldershot Tattoos. The war ended it and, after the war, a different world emerged, in which such great imperial jamborees had no place.

There is no doubt that the appeal of the Tattoos was at one level as spectacular theatre. But there was more to it than that. It was undoubtedly a celebration of the romance of war. As one contemporary journalist described it:

> The glamour of the Aldershot tattoo delights and entrances with the witchery of an enchanted dream . . . A magic bugle calls light from the darkness, the glorious past marches proudly out of the crimson woods, and the heroes of old ride forth in shining armour, 'trailing clouds of glory'. We who seem to be sleeping in the shadows see as in a vision the golden legend of war – war cleansed of its ugliness and horror, war transformed and ennobled with the spirit of chivalry and the glamour of romance. The lustre of the past is over it all. It is a grand illusion produced by the magic of light and the spell of melody. Silver guns and golden spurs, jewelled armour and flaming swords, painted chariots and purple robes. Flowers of flame glow in a garden of light. Swiftly the scenes change like the elusive visions of a dream; the past mingles with the present, the old embraces the new, and always it is the story of war without pain.[59]

But it was war in an imperial context, and the Empire was clearly seen as the culmination of Britain's long and colourful history, a history whose highlights, according to the Tattoo, were the Roman invasion, the Crusades, the Armada and the long roll call of Britain's eighteenth- and nineteenth-century wars. Despite the organizers' protestations to the contrary, it was propaganda at its most potent and beguiling. It was carefully linked to contemporary events, the Ottawa Conference, the

Silver Jubilee, the Coronation, the Anglo-French alliance, the threat of war with Germany, and it evoked historical parallels and precursors to remind its audience of the role of the army in the national life. It put the Empire at the centre of its ideological project, an Empire whose governing values were specifically stated to be sacrifice, chivalry, valour, discipline and loyalty. The recurrent themes were the participation of England, Scotland, Ireland and Wales in the Empire, the role of the Empire in the maintenance of peace, the Christian inspiration of the imperial mission and the centrality of the crown to the whole imperial edifice. Music was deployed throughout to reinforce, underline and emphasize this concept. Almost all musical forms were represented, from opera to dance-band music, from Tchaikovsky, Wagner and Elgar through Gilbert and Sullivan, Ivor Novello and Albert Ketélbey to Flotsam and Jetsam, Horatio Nicholls and *The Eton Boating Song*. Ever present above all were hymns and marches. What they all had in common was that they were tuneful, stirring and evocative, and that together they helped to make palpable a vision of Empire that was romantic, uplifting, sublime.

Notes

1   W.J. Reed, *Aldershot Command Searchlight Tattoo*, Aldershot: Aldershot Military Museum, 1991, p. 1.
2   Scott Hughes Myerly, *British Military Spectacle from the Napoleonic Wars through the Crimea*, Cambridge, MA: Harvard University Press, 1996, pp. 166–7.
3   P.L. Binns, *The Story of the Royal Tournament*, Aldershot: Gale & Polden, 1952, p. 15.
4   *Ibid.*, p. 19.
5   *The Times*, 21 June, 1910.
6   Binns, *Royal Tournament*, pp. 73–6.
7   *The Times*, 21 June, 1910.
8   *Ibid.*
9   *Ibid.*
10 *Ibid.*
11 On the origins of Aldershot Searchlight Tattoo, see Reed, *Aldershot Tattoo*, pp. 1–2.
12 Official Programme of Aldershot Tattoo, 1927, p. 3.
13 A selection of the original HMV 78rpm recordings of music from the Aldershot Tattoo, 1932–38, is available on *Tattoo*, Beulah CD IPD9.
14 Official Souvenir Programme of Aldershot Tattoo, 1938.
15 Official Programme of Aldershot Tattoo, 1926, p. 5.
16 Philip Mather, sleeve notes, *Tattoo*, Beulah CD.
17 Official Programme of Aldershot Tattoo, 1924.
18 Official Souvenir Programme of Aldershot Tattoo, 1927.
19 Official Programme of Aldershot Tattoo, 1926, p. 9.
20 *Ibid.*, 1926, p. 11.
21 Official Programme of Aldershot Tattoo, 1928, pp. 5–6.
22 *Ibid.*, p. 27.
23 *Ibid.*, p. 29.
24 Official Programme of Aldershot Tattoo, 1929, pp. 6–7.

25 *Ibid.*, p. 27.
26 *Ibid.*, p. 25.
27 Official Programme of Aldershot Tattoo, 1930, p. 3.
28 Official Programme of Aldershot Tattoo, 1931, p. 3.
29 *Ibid.*
30 *The Times*, 15 June, 1931.
31 Official Programme of Aldershot Tattoo, 1932, p. 2.
32 *Ibid.*
33 *The Times*, 13 June, 1932.
34 Official Programme of Aldershot Tattoo, 1933, p. 3.
35 *Ibid.*
36 *Ibid.*, p. 27.
37 Official Programme of Aldershot Tattoo, 1934, p. 2.
38 *Ibid.*
39 Official Programme of Aldershot Tattoo, 1935, p. 2.
40 *The Times*, 17 June, 1935.
41 *The Times*, 14 June, 1935.
42 Official Programme of Aldershot Tattoo, 1936, p. 2.
43 *Ibid.*, p. 21.
44 *The Times*, 6 June, 1936.
45 Official Programme of Aldershot Tattoo, 1936, p. 2.
46 *The Times*, 6 June, 1936.
47 *The Times*, 25 June, 1936.
48 Official Programme of Aldershot Tattoo, 1937, p. 2.
49 *The Times*, 15 June, 1937.
50 *The Times*, 21 June, 1937.
51 *The Times*, 11 June, 1937.
52 *The Times*, 21 June, 1937.
53 Official Programme of Aldershot Tattoo, 1938, p. 3.
54 Official Programme of Aldershot Tattoo, 1939, p. 3.
55 *Ibid.*, p. 19.
56 *Ibid.*, p. 30.
57 *The Times*, 7 June, 1939.
58 *The Times*, 12 June, 1939.
59 Unidentified 1931 press cutting, Aldershot Military Historical Trust Tattoo Collection.

CHAPTER EIGHT

'Bring on the girls':
opera, operetta and ballet

Opera

From the seventeenth century to the present there have been an estimated 3,000 English operas.[1] Among them, there appear to have been no imperial operas. Admittedly English opera has always had a problem. There is currently no regularly performed canon of English, as there is of French, German and Italian, opera. This was not always the case. The nineteenth century produced three operas at least which were regularly performed up until the Second World War – Michael Balfe's *The Bohemian Girl*, Sir Julius Benedict's *Lily of Killarney* and William Vincent Wallace's *Maritana*. Gladys Davidson included thirty-five English operas in her collection of 154 which formed the current operatic canon in her 1940 publication *Standard Stories from the Opera*.

The problem English opera has faced has been the snobbery, ignorance and conservatism of opera-goers. In the nineteenth century they resolutely preferred first Italian, then French and finally German opera to English. So strong has this prejudice in favour of foreign opera been that Drury Lane insisted that Balfe's *The Knight of the Leopard* be translated into Italian before it could be performed and premièred in 1874 as *Il Talismano*. But there have been periodic flurries of interest in English opera. In the late nineteenth and early twentieth centuries the Carl Rosa and Moody–Manners Opera Companies regularly commissioned and performed new English operas. Many leading British composers regarded it as a matter of honour to produce at least one English opera, hence Sir Arthur Sullivan's *Ivanhoe*, Sir Alexander Mackenzie's *Colomba*, Sir Charles Villiers Stanford's *The Canterbury Pilgrims*, Sir Frederic Cowen's *Nordisa* and so forth. But the themes they chose were generally the standard romantic ones: drawn from Celtic and Norse myth, mediaeval English history, Scott's novels and

Shakespeare's plays. There was no shortage of exotic subjects, and operas were set in Spain, Arabia, Russia, Bohemia but almost never in the Empire. Apart from one short-lived comic opera by Sir Henry Bishop, *English Men in India* (1827), there was nothing. Operatic composers in Italy, France and Austria were not shy of the subject and interestingly they always dealt with the impossibility of inter-racial marriage due to the clash of traditions and cultures. These clashes almost always ended in the death of the heroine. Thus in Puccini's *Madame Butterfly* (1904), the devoted Cho-Cho San commits *hara-kiri* when abandoned by the American Lieutenant Pinkerton; and in Delibes's *Lakmé* (1883), the Indian girl Lakmé poisons herself when the English officer Gerald, whom she loves, returns to his army duties. In Lehar's *Land of Smiles* (1928), the Chinese Prime Minister Prince Sou Chong is left brokenhearted when his Viennese wife Lisel finds the call of her homeland too strong, and Chinese life too alien, and flees from her marriage to him.

Composer and critic Cecil Forsyth recognized this imperial absence in his book *Music and Nationalism* (1911). Writing from the perspective of a nationalist and out of a belief in the role of music to express the national spirit, he argues that the most permanent characteristic of English opera was 'an inability to express either the strength or purpose of our race'. 'We may safely say', he avers, 'that no single English Opera exists in which the English people recognize any full expression of themselves, of their aspirations, or of their national genius.'[2] He rejects the idea, advanced by some, that the English are not musical. He believes that there have been great English composers, though only as isolated individuals, such as Purcell, rather than in schools of music.

He suggests instead that great music is the product of interiorization (the imaginative energy turned inward) but that exteriorization, the turning of energy and imagination outwards, is inimical to music, and England 'has been expending her energy . . . in one special form of national exteriorization which is fundamentally and psychologically opposed to the production of music', that is to say, empire-building. It is not the mere possession of Empire but the expending of emotional energy on it that is the problem. Unlike England, Germany, 'unaffected by the calls of Empire', has built up 'an immense and noble artistic structure'.[3] But this argument does not hold water. Germany was not a country but many countries and unification rather than imperial expansion a prime preoccupation. Also, other countries such as France were empire-builders and they were not short of great composers, operatic and otherwise.

But when it comes to the history of English opera, Forsyth's other arguments are more valid. Italian opera became all the rage in eighteenth-century England because it was supported by the aristocracy for reasons of fashion and cosmopolitanism, and the reaction to this was either for English composers to produce imitation Italian operas or to develop an alternative, the English ballad opera, which was topical, relevant, often comic, and which mingled speech and song. So, says Forsyth, and with some justice, the story of English opera has been 'the history of a continual struggle between a foreign culture imposed on us by our own upper classes and a national popular culture which was at once more elementary in its nature, less self-conscious and (artistically) almost completely undeveloped'.[4] English opera composers had always found difficulty in getting their works performed.

There had been a serious shortage of decent librettists. Pronouncing the history of English opera books to be 'dismal', Forsyth argued that 'for the most part English Opera Books have, until lately, been written by a set of literary mongrels more careless and incompetent than any that has ever disgraced the literary annals of a country'. In the first half of the nineteenth century the libretti were largely melodramatic: 'fierce crowds of Banditti (belted and bewigged), with Moslems, Crusaders, Robbers, and Villains, figures of paint and pasteboard, all clutching their daggers and pistols as they tip-toe on to the 1-2-3-4 of the music'. Even when librettists improved in the second half of the century, they still employed fake antique dialogue, Wardour Street language.[5]

Even if libretti improve, he argues, there will still be the same problems in the twentieth century as in the eighteenth: aristocratic patrons prefer foreign opera, English composers still seek success by imitating foreign models and the mass audience pursue the popular entertainment equivalents of the ballad opera. For English opera to flourish, what is needed is a receptive audience, composers in sympathy with the needs and aspirations of the people, better librettists and funding from state or local government or charitable concerns. Then it would be possible to produce opera which reflects the national spirit. The sources of inspiration to which the English composer should turn are outlined:

> the magic of his atmosphere, the infinite variety of his scenery, his woodland-ways and sweetly running waters, the noble silent cottages that hold his folk-lore, the little happinesses of his home, the drawn curtains and the blazing fire; the heavy magnificence that glows through his slowly moving dreams of Eastern Empire, the august procession of his saints and heroes passing through his imagination like an army of torchmen; even the sea itself that is at his feet winter and summer calling aloud for an expression which it has never yet known.[6]

So a true operatic expression of that national spirit would encompass the countryside, the Empire, heroes and the sea. They have not yet, Forsyth argues, been properly expressed. In the twentieth century British composers took up the challenges of the pastoral (Vaughan Williams's *Hugh the Drover*), the nautical (Dame Ethel Smyth's *The Wreckers*) and the heroic (Lennox Berkeley's *Nelson*), but the Empire remained firmly outside the operatic world.

Ballet

Classical ballet likewise eschewed the Empire. But there was one exception where ballet met Empire at the high noon of imperialism. Ballet was an integral part of nineteenth-century theatrical life and entertainment. It was a familiar element in opera productions in the first half of the nineteenth century but when the vogue for it passed, in the 1860s, the ballet found a home in the emerging music halls, and none more so than in the two flagship music halls in Leicester Square, the Alhambra, which opened in 1860 and boasted a capacity of 3,500, and the Empire, which opened in 1884. The emphasis of the ballets was topicality and spectacle. Their appeal, unlike opera, was to a mass audience. They were specifically English ballets and not French, like the opera ballets. They were unsubsidized and depended on audience patronage for success. They ran nightly, usually for six months,

Ivor Guest, who has made a detailed study of these ballets, observes: 'Many of them were carefully thought out productions of not inconsiderable merit, and artistic standards certainly rose as the audiences acquired a taste for ballet.'[7] The music-hall ballet was killed off by the impact of the Diaghilev Company, which set new artistic standards of excellence, the rise of revue to supplant the mixture of variety and ballet at the music halls and the impact of the First World War which changed so much in both life and art.

The Alhambra had opened in 1854 as the Royal Panopticon of Science and Art, a Moorish-style building housing lecture rooms, galleries and laboratories, a temple of rational recreation. But by 1856, with too few visitors, the venture had failed. It was purchased by E.T. Smith, lessee of Drury Lane, renamed the Alhambra Palace and was re-opened in 1860 as a music hall. Frederick Strange took it over in 1864 and adopted a policy of including ballet in his programmes. The ballets drew for their themes on familiar elements: the exotic (Spain, Russia, Scotland, the Orient); fairy tales and legends; love stories; with a fondness at the Alhambra for large-scale water-cascades, fountains and ice effects. The music was generally supplied by one or other of the successive music directors and was usually arranged from existing melodies. None of the musical scores has entered the permanent repertoire.

The Theatres Act of 1843 forbade the music halls to stage ballets with plots because that would make them stage plays; so they were *divertissements*. The attraction was the spectacle, settings, topical themes and skimpily clad females in full flight. Strange eventually secured a full theatrical license, remodelled the Alhambra as a theatre with stalls and re-opened the venue in 1871, enabled to stage fully plotted ballets. From 1872 to 1884 the Alhambra pursued a policy of staging comic opera, extravaganza and ballet. The prestige of the ballet rose due to the German-born Georges Jacobi, Musical Director from 1872 to 1898, apart from a brief intermission in 1883–84, under a succession of different managements. He composed the music for almost every ballet performed during that time – forty-five in all – scores that Guest pronounces 'competently written and eminently danceable'.[8]

There was one imperial ballet in the 1870s, *Nana Sahib* which debuted on 1 April 1872. It was a revival of a ballet created four years earlier in Vienna with musical score by Giovanni Panizza and Matthias Strebinger. It centred on the arch-villain of the Indian Mutiny, Nana Sahib, and his desire for an Englishwoman, Ophelia, a member of a hunting party led by the Governor-General. She is seized and carried off to Nana's harem. But the beautiful bayadere Zita, Nana's previous favourite, sacrifices her life to rescue the women, and the Goddess of Vengeance and Justice appears to chastise Nana Sahib for his sins. It included a hornpipe by English sailors (danced by a female chorus) in the streets of Cawnpore, a procession in the Governor-General's Palace and a finale in the temple of Brahma. The story is fiction but highlights the villainy of Nana Sahib and a horror of miscegenation. *The Times* noted that the plot was 'of the sketchiest character, and filled with violent but pleasing improbabilities'. However it omitted the massacre at the boats, one of the most notorious horrors of the Indian Mutiny. The reviewer praised the ballet's 'richness of setting, its continuous flow of incident and its brilliancy of costume. For something between an hour and an hour and a half processions of rich dresses flit on and off the stage, each more glittering and many coloured than its predecessor, yet with sufficient interval and accident between to prevent the display from sinking into a mere succession of transformation scenes.'[9] It constructs the Orient as rich, exotic and treacherous.

For the most part, modern themes were eschewed. The themes of the ballets were butterflies, birds and fish; Spain, Japan and Turkey; carnival; and fairies. In 1882 the theatre burned down; after it had reopened, it reverted in 1884 to a music hall. But ballet had been so successful that it was retained when comic opera was dropped. Expensively designed, staged and produced, the ballets became a highlight, and were particularly admired for processions and military routines. The ballets had now a detailed narrative line.

The ballet *Le Bivouac*, which opened on 22 December 1885 as a Christmas attraction, was a choreographed sequence of military drills. *The Times* reported:

> No barrack yard drill could be more accurate than the training which these stalwart female battalions have been put through under the direction of M. Hansen, with their brilliant evolutions and groupings. All branches of Her Majesty's services are represented, Irish jigs and Scottish reels alternating with English dances and hornpipes.

The newspaper noted, interestingly, 'the whole stirring up the house to a fever of patriotic enthusiasm'.[10]

These military drill type entertainments were both attractive and responsive to the public mood. The success of *Le Bivouac* led to an augmented version, *Our Army and Navy* (1 April 1889), in which choreographer Carlo Coppi rearranged the dances to what Guest called 'a panorama of high Victorian jingoism in the shapely form of superbly drilled Alhambra girls'.[11] The ballet ran for almost a year. *The Times* called it

> a great military and naval pageant . . . where the numerous *corps de ballet* represent all the various sections of the British forces from the Grenadiers to the Devil's Own. Many elaborate evolutions are gone through together with characteristic dances, to an accompaniment of popular airs, arranged by M. Jacobi. There is also revived in this connexion a grand representative gathering of the armies of the different countries of Europe which was produced some time ago under the title *Le Bivouac*. The whole spectacle is of the most picturesque and stirring description.[12]

In 1897 Sullivan's specially commissioned Diamond Jubilee ballet *Victoria and Merrie England* was staged. Ballet historian Mark E. Perugini recalled it as 'a huge success . . . one of the finest "patriotic" productions ever seen on the London stage'.[13] In 1898 Georges Jacobi retired as Musical Director and was succeeded by George W. Byng who provided the musical scores for the Alhambra ballets thereafter. Imperial politics began to feature increasingly. *A Day Off* (24 April 1899), which was chiefly about a day-trip to Boulogne, culminated with a 'Grand Valse Politique' in which the dancers impersonated the various countries in their international and imperial jostlings for power and advantage. The programme contained a precise analysis for the benefit of spectators:

[253]

France receives her foreign visitors. The first to arrive is Russia, who is most cordially welcomed. The Powers representing the Triple Alliance enter and are surprised to find Russia is the first and favoured guest. All interest is now centred on China, who in her endeavours to be most pleasing to all nations, accidentally pushes against Germany. That power immediately demands reparation for the insult, and tears off a sleeve from her rich mantle. Her appeals to Russia for sympathy only cause that nation to take the other sleeve so that matters will be equalised. At this moment England enters and protests strongly against the outrage, telling them that China is not for one nor the other, but is for the benefit of the world (The Open Door). To show them fully her meaning she takes off the greater portion of China's garment, the other nations dividing the rest of her once gorgeous apparel, leaving China almost bare. To con- ciliate poor China, England offers her a railway. China is delighted with the toy until Russia presents her with one of greater value. A most important visitor is announced – India. While France coquets with England, Russia seizes the opportunity of taking to himself such a rich and influential partner. England's attention is called to these designs, and taking India upon her arm, Russia is warned that India is for England alone, and interference in that quarter will not be tolerated. Turkey enters bringing Egypt and Greece, whom he holds in bondage, Italy strongly protests against the indignities shown to Greece. Russia and France take advantage to pay their attentions to Egypt, but again England bars the way saying that she still has another arm for the protection of that country. Spain enters, trying to keep two unruly children in order, viz. 'Cuba and the Philippines'. They break away from her jurisdiction, so Uncle Sam intervenes and finds they are more than he can manage. The other nations offer to assist him, but are kept at a distance by England.[14]

The ballet ended with what *The Era* called 'a dashing gallop, full of fiery vigour and "go"'.[15]

It was a cynical and accurate distillation of *realpolitik* of the late nineteenth century. But by the end of the year, with the Boer War in full flow, the Alhambra's manager A. Dundas Slater decided to replace the Christmas pantomime with a morale-boosting patriotic extrava- ganza. *Soldiers of the Queen*, which opened on 11 December 1899, was a military pageant devised by a pseudonymous army officer billed as A. Sol Dato. The programme called it 'a series of Military Snapshots'. It was set on the Queen's Parade, Aldershot, between sunrise and sunset, and the snapshots began with *Reveille* and the Changing of the Guard featuring the Gordon Highlanders. Then in the stables there was a Troopers' Dance. This was followed by a dance by Tommy and his Sweethearts, a dance of visitors and officers, a dance with Drums and Fifes, a Dance with Tutor and Pupils, Extension and Lance Drill per- formed by troopers of the 12th, 16th, 17th and 21st Lancers, a veteran's visit to his son, and Highland Dances by the Gordons. A comic song, *Murphy of the Irish Fusiliers*, specially written by Robert Martin and composed by George W. Byng, was performed by Clarence Hunt. Physical drill was performed by the Irish Fusiliers, the King's Royal Rifles and the Buffs. The First Aid Dance 'The Girls They Left Behind' was performed by soldiers and their girls. Then there was a parade of troops as Ian Colquhoun sang *Soldiers of the Queen*. Finally there was an entrance by the General Staff, an Inspection and a Grand March by the combined Bands of Infantry, Drums and Fifes, the corps de ballet, chorus and auxiliaries. This involved over over 250 performers representing twenty-eight regiments, including such fashionable outfits as the Life Guards and the Dragoon Guards, but carefully also including Irish units (Royal Irish Fusiliers, Royal Dublin Fusiliers, Royal Irish Lancers), Scottish units (Royal Scots Greys, the Gordons, Scots Guards), the colonies (New South Wales Lancers) as well as the Militia and the Army Medical Corps. *The Sketch* declared it 'excellent but it is not ballet'. But, whatever it was, the critic was won over by it completely:

> By reason of its clever arrangement, sparkling music, bright colouring and the keen, untiring interest that everybody takes in the work, a sketch that could hardly be more ephemeral holds the spectator from start to finish. It suits the hour, and will give everybody who is excited an excuse for enthusiasm. . . . Though the proceedings are no more than a playful copy of everyday military life at home, they are sufficiently realistic to bring a thrill to the least enthusiastic spectator, and I am sure that the precision, the almost military efficiency, of the *corps de ballet* will earn the praise of those most competent to award it – the officers of the services, who know all the varying possibilities of drill.[16]

He also noted that George Byng had welded old and new popular airs and original music into 'one harmonious whole', proving himself 'a refined and scholarly musician'. Another critic, observing that the Alhambra management had 'a finger on the public pulse', remarked that 'the lady lancers with their trim smart steps, their shapely headdresses, and the fearless handling of their redoubtable stage lances, were held to bear the palm'. He also recorded that Ian Colquhoun's performance of *Soldiers of the Queen* 'rendered the house hoarse with applause' and that Kipling and Sullivan's *The Absent-Minded Beggar*, 'which has become as much a part of London life as the hum of traffic', had been added to the proceedings and sung 'well, though rather nervously' by Harrison Brockbank.[17] The show ran for forty-seven weeks and was revived on 16 December 1901, as *Soldiers of the King*. It was quite evidently in tune with the mood of music-hall patrons.

[255]

For Coronation Year, the Alhambra produced the ballet *Britannia's Realm* in a prologue and four scenes. It was devised and produced by Charles Wilson, and choreographed by Carlo Coppi to a score specially commissioned from Landon Ronald, then a young composer and later a leading conductor and Principal of Guildhall School of Music. Mark Perugini recalled it as 'one of the best planned and most extraordinarily sumptuous productions ever seen at the Alhambra, long famous for the splendour of its effects'.[18] It opened on 16 June 1902 and ran for forty-six weeks. The official synopsis in the Programme is a perfect illustration of imperial myth and rhetoric.[19]

The aim of the ballet was 'to illustrate within the necessary limits the history of the development and progress of the British Empire'. It opens in the Abode of Fame with Britannia contemplating her masterpiece 'Progress'. Envy and Malice arrive, seeking to destroy it. But Justice appears to order the forces of evil to bow to the mighty influence for good. Father Time then reminds Britannia that 'the fulfilment of her great destiny must be the work of the coming years'. Four scenes follow. The first is set in Africa which 'has not known the beneficent influence of progress and civilization', specifically the Sudan. An African mother and her children are seized by slave raiders but are released by Britannia. Then 'from out of the midst of savagery and ignorance rises in the glory of a new era England's monument to her dead hero – the Gordon College at Khartoum. This typifies the spread of enlightenment.'

The second scene is set in India, 'with her splendid palaces and minarets silhouetted against a glowing eastern sky, her brilliant flowers flaming in the radiant sunshine. Eloquent of her wealth are those who represent the rulers and people of her states and provinces.' Dancing girls and attendants are ordered to reveal the riches of the land and the Ballet of Jewels, with dancers representing sapphires, pearls, turquoises, rubies and diamonds, takes place.

The third scene is set in Australia, billed as 'true to the Motherland'. A colonial family gathers for a mid-day meal 'in the glare of high noon'. The soldier lover of the daughter of the family is leaving Australia 'to answer the call of the Motherland'. The son of the family obtains his mother's consent to go, too, and 'departs with his friend to fight the battles of the Mother Country'. 'This', says the synopsis, 'is Australia's splendid proof of affection for the Mother Country – it stands as evidence of Britannia's wisdom in the work of Colonization.'

The fourth and final scene is set in Canada, where an Ice Palace has been built and skaters whirl on a frozen lake. 'To the scene of revelry come types of the people of North America in their strange costumes.' The ballet ends with a Homage to Britannia as the dancers form up in the crosses of St Patrick, St Andrew and St George to form 'the Union Jack of Old England'.

Apart from the characteristic slip, at the end, of equating Britain and Old England, this is a superb distillation of the myths, images and rhetoric of England: the ideas of progress, destiny, enlightenment, the wealth of India, the savagery of Africa, the loyalty of Australia, and the careful stressing of the Union at the end. Perugini noted:

> Probably nothing finer had ever been produced on the Alhambra stage for sheer magnificence than the Indian jewel scene, and the grand finale representing 'Homage to Britannia' and the formation of the Union Jack amid a display of electric light. It was an astonishing and impressive production and well deserved the enthusiasm with which, night after night, for some months, the ballet was received.[20]

Ronald's music was well-received, particularly 'the haunting music' he provided for the Canadian skating scene.

There was one more balletic celebration of Empire, *Our Flag*, which opened on 20 December 1909 and ran for twenty-three weeks, with music by George W. Byng. *The Times* noted that 'A *Rule Britannia* motif, plenty of pretty faces and dresses, and Mlle Britta's graceful and rhythmical dancing are the chief features of the new patriotic ballet *Our Flag*.' There was not much story but the reviewer liked 'the bright and tuneful music' of Byng.

The opening scene, 'with a background of the waves that guard our native shores, is an elementary lesson in the composition of the Union Jack, and shows how, after England has been presented with St George's Banner, the flags of St Andrew and St Patrick are respectively "offered" and "tendered" ["Hardly the words that one would choose to express the actual historical reality", *The Times* tartly commented] by Scotland and Ireland to complete the national "Jack."' The second scene, entitled 'Hands Across the Sea', has dancers representing colonial possessions (India, South Africa, Canada, Australia, West Indies, New Zealand and Hong Kong) combine in a series of kaleidoscopic dances. 'It is all very pretty and patriotic and the appearance of the various colonies and the presentation of a miniature Dreadnought in front of a well-painted scene representing Windsor Castle stirred the audience to quite a little display of enthusiasm.' The entire ballet was 'well received.'[21] The ballets ceased in 1912; the Alhambra went over to revue, and when it later reverted to variety it dropped the ballet. It became a theatre in 1931 and was demolished in 1936 to make way for the Odeon cinema.

On the other side of Leicester Square was the Alhambra's rival music hall, prophetically named the Empire. It was opened in 1884 and after a checkered start was taken over by leading impresarios George Edwardes and Augustus Harris, as a music hall. Its artistic triumvirate were Katti Lanner, Ballet Mistress from 1887 until 1905, Art Director and Production Designer C. Wilhelm, and, initially, French composer Hervé as Music Director. Hervé had in 1874 composed a dramatic symphony, *The Ashantee War*, which was performed at a Promenade concert. He was succeeded in 1889 by Leopold Wenzel as Director–Composer for the ballets. Lanner, Wilhelm and Wenzel had a fondness for 'topicals', often with an imperial dimension.

Round the Town, which opened on 26 September 1892 and ran for eight months, was typical. It was 'a representation of the more familiar sights of London streets', depictions of which were linked by Dr Birch, the schoolmaster, taking his pupils on a tour of London, including Covent Garden market, the Royal Exchange and Thames Embankment (complete with a Salvation Army band), and ending up outside the Empire theatre where 'somewhat incongruously', *The Times* thought, there was a ballet celebrating the Empire, with which the show itself ends. The ballet was *Daughters of the Empire*, and featured dancers representing England, Scotland, Ireland, Wales, India, Australia, Canada, Cape Colony, British Columbia, West Indies, Malta, Gibraltar, Hong Kong, New Zealand, Burma, a variety of British cities, plus Oxford, Cambridge, Windsor and Eton, four mercuries representing Commerce and finally Britannia herself, complete with trident. Despite the reservations of *The Times*, the ballet stressed the link between the everyday life of London and of the wider Empire, with a score by Wenzel incorporating 'familiar and illustrative airs'.[22]

The Girl I Left Behind Me (27 September 1893) was an example of cultural cross-fertilization. It was a balletic version of the typical Drury Lane melodrama for which Augustus Harris's regime was celebrated. It was billed as 'an up-to-date ballet' devised by George Edwardes and had a classic Drury Lane plot. A young gentleman, ruined by gambling on the horses, enlists in a Highland regiment and sails for Burma. There he distinguishes himself in the fighting and wins the Victoria Cross. The girl who loves him, and remained true despite her father's disapproval and the rejected advances of the villain, is united with him in a wedding finale. *The Times* thought that

> Epsom Downs on Derby Day, where the hero is 'cleaned out', and the embarcation of the regiment at the docks . . . are represented with entire success. The scenes in Burma, where the fighting is heard in the wings, are of a more conventional order; and so also is the grand wedding *fête* given at the close. But the ballet, as a whole, is exceedingly beautiful and interesting, the military evolutions of the mimic Highlanders being

conducted with marvellous precision, and the applause of the public is unstinted.[23]

There was a dream sequence in which the Spirit of Gambling contended with the Genius of Honour and Courage for the soul of the hero, plus sailors' dance, gypsies' dance, and a grand march, evolution and inspection of troops. It ran for fifty-four weeks.

The next imperial ballet was the Empire theatre's jubilee offering *Under One Flag* (21 June 1897), which ran for thirty-two weeks. Devised and produced by Katti Lanner, it consisted of two *tableaux*. The first, set outside Windsor Castle, represented a fête taking place at the outset of the reign with the *corps de ballet* in early Victorian costume, and specialized dances for dancers representing the Rose of England, the Thistle of Scotland and the Shamrock of Ireland. Wales was represented but not, apparently, by a flower. Then sailors and Highlanders arrived allowing for a hornpipe and Scottish dances. The second *tableau*, presided over by a statue of Victoria, was devoted to a homage to the Queen–Empress of 1897. Dancers representing the colonies paid homage to the statue: India, Canada, Australia, Cape Colony, West Indies, Malta, Gibraltar, New Zealand, plus Art, Science, Commerce, Industry and Britannia. It ended with the entire company joining in a grand cantata, performing a patriotic ode specially composed by the poet and critic Clement Scott. *The Sketch* praised the genius of Wilhelm, 'who for producing novel and charming colour-effects by costume renders every ballet entrusted to him delightful', and the music of Wenzel, who drew extensively on 'the splendid store of national melodies to be found in these islands, and has succeeded in blending and using strong measures with rich effect', and commented that the 'ladies of the *corps de ballet* do their work admirably'.[24] The two *tableaux* promote twin ideas of the unity of the nations of the United Kingdom in 1837 and the unity of the Empire in 1897, both focused on the person of the Queen.

A sequel to *Round the Town*, called *Round the Town Again* (8 May 1899), ran for seventy weeks. This time it reproduced scenes from Bond Street and Hyde Park, and a masked ball at Covent Garden, but opened at Charing Cross station with the return of victorious troops from the Sudan. Wenzel arranged a score from selections of musical comedies by popular composers such as Sidney Jones, Ivan Caryll, Lionel Monckton and Gustave Kerker. To add to the realism, Guardsmen from Wellington barracks were imported to supplement the dancers.

The Empire theatre's final imperial ballet, staged for the Coronation, was *Our Crown* (28 May 1902). It ran for thirty-three weeks, and Mark Perugini pronounced it 'a most brilliant production' and 'a conspicuous triumph'.[25] It consisted of two scenes and twelve *tableaux*. The first scene, set in the Caves of Memory, features the Muse of English History recalling the 'chief incidents' in the reigns of previous royal Edwards. These are symbolic events carefully chosen. In *tableau* 1 (1248), at Carnarvon Castle, Edward I presents his infant son, later Edward II, to the Welsh chieftains as Prince of Wales. In *tableau* 2 (1347), Edward III, at the intercession of Queen Philippa, spares the lives of the citizens of Calais. In *tableau* 3 (1471), set in Westminster, Edward IV visits Caxton's first printing press. In *tableau* 4 (1483), Edward V and his brother the Duke of York are held prisoners in the Tower. In *tableau* 5 (1552), Edward VI founds the Bluecoat School. Here the *tableaux* stress the role of the monarchy in the integration of Wales into the United Kingdom; in backing progress (the printing press) and education (Bluecoats School), and in showing clemency (Calais burghers). Legitimacy is stressed in the tragic fate of Edward V, murdered by Richard III. The narrative leaves out such contentious episodes as the Wars of the Roses, the conquest of Scotland and the Reformation, settling instead for reassuring folklore. Apart from his babyhood appearance, the gay King Edward II, who lost the Battle of Bannockburn, was murdered by his wife and her lover, and provoked civil war by promoting his male favourites is conspicuously omitted: that was not the kind of thing with which to greet a new reign.

In *tableau* 6, announced by the clarions of Fame, a messenger of peace now appears to summon the various colonies to contribute their resources to fashion a new imperial crown for King Edward VII. The Spirits of Commerce attend the revolution of the Globe, revealing in turn the gold of Australia, the rubies of Burma, the sapphires of India, the pearls of Ceylon, the diamonds of Cape Colony and the ermine of Canada. Each of the items is danced and the dancers finally combine in a grand ensemble to construct the crown.

The finale, London (1902), is set in the 'Royal Pavilion of the British Empire' where economic exploitation is legitimized by ritual. There is a procession of choirboys and heralds, Beefeaters and court functionaries, and a coronation to a stirring trumpet march, a dance of the Roses of England (red, pink and white), and the grand finale with *God Save the King*. The overture to the entire night's programme was the Coronation Prize March by Percy Godfrey, copies of which were on sale with proceeds to benefit King Edward's Hospital Fund.

The *Illustrated London News* considered that 'the ballet's success is assisted to a very large degree by M. Leopold Wenzel's striking score'.[26] The Programme reveals that Wenzel had selected the music for the historical *tableaux* from period scores in the British Museum, and the *Illustrated London News* noted his use of a chant from the year 1250, a song of victory from 1415 and a Christmas carol of 1460. Authentic Australian, South African and Canadian music was also deployed in the jewel scene. *The Times* proclaimed the ballet 'well worth seeing', admired the historical *tableaux* and the dance of the Roses of England, 'a really beautiful stage picture'. *The Times*, also noting the British Museum provenance of the historical music, thought Wenzel's score 'appropriate and bright', though adding 'the march at the climax owes rather too much to Dr Elgar's pomp and circumstance', confirmation that the Elgarian idiom was an instant success.[27]

The ballets continued until 1915, when the theatre went over to variety. It became a cinema in 1927, and remains so to this day. It is evident, if one takes the Alhambra and Empire ballets side by side, that Empire was a legitimate subject for popular culture and dance and that it was in the forefront of the popular mind at the time of great royal events, both theatres staging ballets to coincide with the Diamond Jubilee of Queen Victoria and the Coronation of King Edward VII. There are also recurrent themes: the association of Empire with progress; Empire as the logical culmination of British history; the unity of the Empire and within it the unity of the United Kingdom; the role of the army and the navy in the imperial context; but also the wealth and exoticism represented by the Empire.

Operetta/musicals

The modern musical grew out of the *opéra bouffe* of mid-nineteenth-century France, particularly the works of Jacques Offenbach. The dominance of the Paris of Offenbach was superceded by that of the Vienna of Johann Strauss and Franz Lehar, and Vienna in turn by the London of Gilbert and Sullivan and George Edwardes's Gaiety musicals. After the First World War, New York assumed the leading role, with both the Jazz-Age musicals of Gershwin, Kern and Cole Porter and the romantic operettas of Sigmund Romberg and Rudolf Friml sweeping the world.[28]

Although the traditional recipe for a hit musical has always been a good laugh, a good cry and a good tune, there was a difference of emphasis between the musicals of France and Britain's musicals: in France the accent was on sex, and in Britain it was on class. In British musicals and operettas, too, the Empire appeared where it was conspicuously absent from opera. The great age of operetta coincided with the high noon of Empire.

Although much of the Empire's depiction in musicals and musical comedies was comic, this should not be taken to denote disapproval.

Apart from the arguably healthy puncturing of pomposity, the comedy was rarely savagely satirical and was usually undertaken in a spirit of what J.B. Priestley called 'tender mockery', noting the specific tendency of the English to laugh at the things they love.[29]

This was on the whole the spirit also of Gilbert and Sullivan, who specifically aimed to avoid offence and whose satires on the army, the navy, the law and the aesthetic movement were happily attended by the victims of their mockery. Gilbert and Sullivan got round to the Empire in 1893 with *Utopia Limited*, which opened on 7 October and ran for 245 performances but never gained the permanent place in audience affections that earlier works had done; it has rarely been revived since. Rutland Barrington, who played the King of Utopia, thought the second act 'tedious' and 'not as full of fun as usual'.[30] (*Utopia Limited* is discussed in chapter two).

The musical comedy, which replaced the Savoy operetta, was associated with George Edwardes, 'Gaiety George', who perfected the new form at the Gaiety Theatre and at Daly's Theatre where his regime held sway for twenty years from 1894. His death in 1915 and the First World War put an end to the tradition. The ingredients were pretty girls, lavish costumes and sets, a formulaic romantic plot, music-hall comedy routines, hummable tunes and scripts with topical allusions, but also a regular injection of patriotism. He assembled a regular team of composers (Lionel Monckton, Sidney Jones, Ivan Caryll) and lyricists (Adrian Ross, Harry and Percy Greenbank), a scriptwriter (James Turner), and beloved performers who tended to repeat their characterizations in play after play. Rutland Barrington played a succession of comically pompous Oriental potentates, all variations on the Pooh-Bah character he had created in *The Mikado*, and Huntley Wright played a succession of comic malaprop Chinese, speaking and singing in pidgin English. The blend began with *The Shopgirl*, which opened on 24 November 1894 and ran for 546 performances. In a distinct spirit of 'dumbing down', out went the subtle and elaborate wordplay, the gentle satire of Gilbert and the richly allusive and inventively textured music of Sullivan. Musical comedy, with its straightforward tunes, music-hall jokes and broadly comedic routines, was rightly seen by purists as a fall from grace. But the shows were performed both in London and on tour in the provinces with equal success and can be said to constitute a theatrical taste for twenty years.

There was a particular vogue for things Japanese, a craze which gripped Britain from the 1860s to the 1920s.[31] *The Mikado* had first heralded it musically and *The Geisha* was widely seen as a sequel. Although the music of both is largely Western, Arthur Diosy of the Japan Society is credited with supplying a genuine Japanese march to

Sullivan (*Miya Sama*) for *The Mikado* and another to Sidney Jones (*Koi-wa-se-ni-sumu*) for *The Geisha*, and he trained the *Geisha* cast in correct Japanese deportment.[32]

The origins and meaning of the Japanese craze are complex. Japanese art and design had a powerful effect on Western artists. It received maximum exposure in a succession of international exhibitions: London (1862); Paris (1867, 1878, 1889); Philadelphia (1876); and Chicago (1893). Western designers were, according to John M. MacKenzie, captivated by 'the combination of refinement, elegance and simplicity' characterizing Japanese art, features that greatly influenced impressionism, the aesthetic movement and art nouveau.[33] Hundreds of travel books on Japan and a flood of photographs were published. Collectors began to amass Japanese prints, textiles and artefacts, and these were widely imitated and distributed commercially, Liberty's, the famous London store, being particularly known for its popularizing of Orientalist goods. In the Japanese musicals great pains were taken to establish authenticity of costume, setting, dance and movement. But the content could hardly be said to achieve the same authenticity. *The Mikado* was not about Japan at all: it was about Britain, satirized in Japanese settings. Japanese characters were invariably stereotypes: the comic Oriental or 'Jolly Jap' as Earl Miner calls him; the refined and delicate Japanese doll; the gallant *samurai*. Earl Miner argues that the ambiguous image of Japan appealed to the exotic needs of the Victorians who viewed it as 'an eastern country which was curiously civilized but hardly European, a nation of beautiful and refined but also enticing and "improper" women, a land which needed the benefits of civilization through trade and yet one which had a splendid culture to confer upon the West'.[34]

Once Commodore Perry had opened up Japan, in 1857, and the process of Westernization began under Emperor Mitsuhito (1852–1912), the Japanese adopted wholesale Western political structures, social and legal rules, and dress and manners. Japan became a model of modernization and was constantly held up to admiration by comparison with China and Russia, regarded as backward, feudal and repressive. The Japanese Empire had much in common with the British; indeed newspaper articles in the early twentieth century called Japan 'the Britain of Asia': both countries were islands; both had hereditary monarchies and aristocracies; both had parliamentary and cabinet government; and the Japanese had a code of chivalry (*bushido*) admired and recommended by Baden-Powell. Yoshisaburo Okakura's book *The Japanese Spirit* (1905), on the spiritual basis of Japanese military conduct, was widely read in Britain. In the Russo-Japanese war, British sympathies were with Japan. This was reflected in boys' fiction where the gallant, chivalric Japanese were the heroes and the benighted, cruel Russians the villains. History books favourably compared Japan to China.[35]

In fiction, Pierre Loti's 1887 book *Madame Chrysanthème* set a pattern: a French naval officer marries a Japanese woman and deserts her when he returns to his own land. This was the inspiration behind David Belasco's melodrama *Madame Butterfly* – and of Puccini's opera based on it – where the naval officer is American and the deserted wife commits suicide. It was also the inspiration behind *The Geisha*, which has a happier ending.

For not all liaisons ended tragically. Clive Holland's book *My Japanese Wife* (1895) recounted a successful and happy interracial marriage, ending with him bringing his wife back to England. Lafcadio Hearn argued that the most wonderful aesthetic product of Japan was not her ivories, bronzes or porcelains but her women, 'prepared and perfected by the old-time education for that strange society in which the charm of her moral being – her delicacy, her supreme unselfishness, her child-like piety and trust, her exquisite tactful perception of all ways and means to make happiness about her, – can be comprehended and valued'.[36] This is the image of Japanese and indeed of all Oriental women that appears in musical comedy, and it can be seen as an oblique comment on the rise of the New Woman. This exquisite doll-like creature, anxious to please her man, will have appealed mightily to all alarmed by feminism and the Suffragette Movement. So sometimes the hero dallied with her, but settled for his own race; and sometimes he married her, as the Hon. Harry Vereker happily sings at the end of *The Cingalee*: 'Cingalee, Cingalee, my wife for life is my Cingalee.'

There is a difference of form here: grand opera might end tragically; musical comedy must end happily. But there were two cultures, and musical comedy felt free to criticize Oriental customs (*suttee*, for example, and child-marriage), and its Oriental men were caricatures where its women were submissive china dolls. But often the Japanese and Chinese were used as vehicles to comment wonderingly on current London fashions and mores after the manner of *The Mikado*.

The Geisha, with music by Sidney Jones, lyrics by Harry Greenbank, and book by Owen Hall, staged to cash in on that fascination with all things Japanese which had also inspired *The Mikado*, had a phenomenal success. It opened on 25 April 1896, ran for 760 performances, and later toured Britain and the Empire. Although it remains popular on the Continent, *The Geisha* has not been revived on the stage in Britain since 1934. But its phenomenal success tells us something about theatrical taste. It had of course a tuneful score, attractive stars in Hayden Coffin and Marie Tempest, and impressive staging by George Edwardes at Daly's Theatre. It combines in classic proportions a laugh, a song and a tear. It celebrates the ritualized flirtations of Western sailors and Japanese geishas, as the geishas sing of 'Great big English sailor men' who 'Fight with any man they please/ Marry little English Miss/ Flirt with pretty Japanese'. The simple romantic plot has geisha girl O Mimosa San pursued by Lt Reggie Fairfax of the Royal Navy, pompous Provincial Governor Marquis Imari and dashing Captain Katana of the Imperial Japanese Army, a chivalric figure, 'truest of knights to trusty maid'. It ends with Reggie reunited with his English fiancée Molly Seamore who disguises herself as the geisha Roli-Poli to win him back. Molly is also courted by Imari but she tells him firmly: 'You thought I'd marry a Japanese marquis when I can get an English sailor?' Imari settles for marriage with French girl Juliette and O Mimosa San is united with Katana. The serious point behind the action is a critique of the Japanese tradition of polygamy and the philosophy, articulated by Imari, that in Japan love and marriage are two different things. The laughter is provided by comic Chinese malaprop Wun Hi, a Chinaman running a Japanese tea garden. He was played by Huntley Wright and had a characteristic pidgin song, 'Chin-chin-Chinaman, muchee, muchee sad/ Me afraid allo trade wellee wellee bad', which performed with a 'contortion dance' became a great hit. It was rapturously received and encored on the opening night.

The Times, calling it 'a marked improvement musically and dramatically upon all its predecessors', pronounced *The Geisha* 'a distinct and emphatic success'. *The Times*'s critic applauded the sets ('too high praise can hardly be given'), the dialogue ('often smart') and above all the music: 'The scoring is generally very refined and skilful, and more than once it rises to a high level of excellence.' Singled out for particular commendation were 'the madrigalian movement in the first finale', the 'really pretty and musicianly quartet *Woman's Queen of Everything*,' the Japanese chorus in the second act and the 'clever *lamentation chorus*'. Altogether *The Times* saw *The Geisha* as a landmark in the progress of Edwardes's musicals, evolving from 'the glorified variety show' into 'a form of dramatic entertainment similar in most respects to the real light opera'.

The appearance of a sparkling new performance of the show on CD vindicates *The Times*'s judgement of the score. It has considerable and consistent delicacy and charm, particularly in such songs as *The Amorous Goldfish*, *A Geisha Life* and *The Kissing Duet*. Also worthy of note are *Star of my Soul*, in idiom and rhetoric a full-blooded mid-Victorian love song, and the lively interpolated Lionel Monckton naval ditty *Jack's the Boy*. But perhaps the most enduring of its songs is the comic *Chin-Chin-Chinaman*, deeply politically incorrect but with an irrestistibly catchy tune. My grandmother was still singing it in the 1950s, half-a-century after she had first heard it. However, it is a good bet that almost no one has sung it in the last half-century before the issue of the new CD.[37]

There are verbal echoes of the master, W.S. Gilbert: 'Here's a delight-ful how-de-do'; 'childish versery/ might be worsery/ sweetly/ cursory nursery days'. But *The Geisha* is a very different kettle of fish from *The Mikado*. Gilbert and Sullivan's opera is a satirical vision of late-Victorian England, full of witty and clever patter songs, pointed parody and ingenious pastiche. Jones's musical, eschewing satire and verbal ingenuity, concentrates much more straightforwardly on romance and the exotic, constantly stressing the difference between Occidentals and Orientals and the 'otherness' of the Japanese. *The Geisha* is very much of its time; *The Mikado* is timeless. The result is that many of *The Mikado*'s songs remain current and many a Gilbertian phrase is still in common use ('I've got a little list', 'a short sharp shock', 'life is a joke that's just begun', 'to let the punishment fit the crime', 'the flowers that bloom in the spring, tra-la, have nothing to do with the case'.). While *The Mikado* can safely be regarded as a musical comedy masterpiece, *The Geisha* remains a lightweight if charming period trifle, with neither words nor music leaving any trace on the modern musical consciousness.

Even more decidedly downmarket among imperial musicals was *Morocco Bound* (music by F. Osmond Carr and lyrics by Adrian Ross) which opened on 13 April 1893 and ran for 293 performances, there-after touring the provinces. It was a parody of imperial expansionism. It centred on an Irish adventurer, known as Spoofah Bey, seeking to gain the music-hall concession in Morocco and fooling the Grand Vizier into thinking his guests are all music-hall stars; forcing them to do turns, impersonating the current stars of the halls. The star of the show was George Grossmith Jr as Lord Percy Pimpleton of the British Embassy, a classic silly-ass whose catchphrase, 'I think you're beastly rude, don't cher know', caught on.

Its success meant a follow-up, and Carr and Ross obliged with *Go-Bang* (10 March 1894), which centred on the search for the heir to the throne of the eastern country of Go-Bang. The ruler is known as the Boojam. British diplomat Sir Reddan Tapeleigh, KCSI, who had a song in praise of red tape, seeks to install Dam Row's secretary Narain, who duly turns out to be the rightful Boojam. Grossmith reappeared as another silly-ass, Lt Hon. Augustus Fitzpoop, whose song satirizing English double standards, *I Can't Make it Out a Bit*, was one of the hits of the show. It ran for 159 performances.

The same management put on *King Kodak*, with a score cobbled together by three different composers. Opening on 30 April 1894, it ran for only sixty-three performances. It concerned a British explorer, James South, who has discovered gold and set up his own country, Kodakoria, which he rules as the Kodak, a clear take-off of Cecil Rhodes. It involves his schemes to marry his daughter to a British Admiral's son and satirizes a number of contemporary phenomena. But it includes a Lord Deadbroke, stolen as a child by apes and now being raised as an English Lord. It predates by twenty years Edgar Rice Burroughs's creation of the story of a child who had been stolen by apes but later returned to become Lord Greystoke, *Tarzan of the Apes* (1914). Among all the farcical carryings-on and the satire of current happenings, it should be noted that the score included a straight patriotic number, *We've Faith in the Old Flag Yet*, by Lionel Monckton. The insertion of such patriotic songs became a feature of musicals.

Hayden Coffin was the reigning matinee idol of the musical comedy stage, and just as Richard Tauber had his personal hit song (*der grosse tauberlied*) in every Lehar musical, so Coffin had his own specially tailored hit-song which often did not belong to the original score but was interpolated by Coffin, with Edwardes's consent, and is evidence of how he was perceived and of what audiences expected of him.

Even if the musical had nothing to do with the Empire, events in the Empire might inspire the insertion of a song. *An Artist's Model* was running at Daly's in 1895. It was another Jones, Greenbank and Hall musical, which notched up 392 performances. During its run, the Jameson Raid was launched on the Transvaal and was foiled by President Krüger, to whom the Kaiser sent a congratulatory telegram. British public opinion was outraged, and Edwardes demanded a song from Henry Hamilton, who had written the words to the popular patriotic song *Tommy Atkins*. It was duly written, called *Hands Off*, and set to music by Frederick Rosse.

The song ran as follows:

> England, to arms! The need is nigh,
> The danger at your gate;
> In long array your foes ally –
> A league of greed and hate.
> Not ours the crime of war accurst,
> But once let war begin,
> They'll have to kill the Lion first
> Who'd wear the Lion's skin!
>
> *Chorus*
> Hands off, Germany! Hands off, all!
> Kruger boasts and Kaiser brags; Britons, hear the call!

Back to back the world around, answers with a will –
'England for her own, my boys! It's Rule Britannia still.'

Let Pinchbeck Caesar strut and crow,
Let eagles scream of 'War'
No jot we bate, no right forgo,
We've stood alone before.
When all the world was just as great
And we were half our size,
We faced the world in grim debate,
And blacked the bully's eyes.

The men of great Elizabeth
Were cast in heroes' mould;
Shall we then speak with bated breath
Of Jameson e'en as bold?
Our Drakes and Raleighs made some noise
For fame to dare and do,
And if they 'filibustered', boys,
We'll 'filibuster' too!

Go, tell the world our watchword now,
Let deep proclaim to deep,
The crown that shines on England's brow
Her sons' right hands will keep.
The Empire that our fathers got
It is not ended yet,
And on it, as the sun sets not,
No sun shall *ever* set.

It was, however, only sung in its full version on the night of its
introduction. Thereafter the theatrical censor intervened to remove
a number of inflammatory references. The chorus was rewritten as:

Hands off, all of you! Hands off, all!
Deutscher boasts and bantam brags; Britons, hear the call!
Back to back the world around, answer with a will –
'England for her own, my boys! It's 'Rule Britannia' still!'

In the second verse, instead of 'Pinchbeck Caesar', the words 'jealous
rivals' were inserted, and in the third, instead of 'Jameson' the word
'heroes' was inserted.[38]

Fairfax's song *Jack's the Boy* in *The Geisha* was a characteristically
breezy celebration of the British naval hero, by Lionel Monckton:

Jack's the boy for work,
Jack's the boy for play,
Jack's the lad, when girls are sad,
To kiss the tears away!

Hard as nails afloat,
Best of friends ashore,
Jack ahoy! You're just the boy
That all our hearts adore.

The Geisha's success prompted an inevitable follow-up: set in China, *San Toy* had music by Sidney Jones, lyrics by Harry Greenbank and Adrian Ross, and book by Edward Morton. It again starred Marie Tempest and Hayden Coffin, and ran for 778 performances, exceeding even *The Geisha*'s run. Once again its main thrust was romance: San Toy, a mandarin's daughter, is wooed by Captain Bobbie Preston, RN, son of Sir Bingo Preston, the British Consul at Pynka Pong, and by Fo Hop; but she catches the eye also of the Emperor, causing a variety of complications before San Toy and Bobbie are united. There was romance; there was comedy from Huntley Wright, doing his comic Chinaman act again, as Li.

Hayden Coffin was cast once again as the dashing naval hero. Coffin recalls in his autobiography that the Boer War was raging and George Edwardes decided a patriotic song needed to be added and he thought of *Tommy Atkins. Private Tommy Atkins*, a song composed by S. Potter with words by Henry Hamilton, had been made popular on the music halls by Charles Arnold. Edwardes inserted it into his musical *A Gaiety Girl* in 1893 and as sung by Hayden Coffin as Captain Charles Goldfield of the cavalry it had become the hit of the show, stopping the production every night:

Tommy, Tommy Atkins you're a good 'un, heart and hand,
You're a credit to your calling and to all your native land.
May your luck be never failing, may your love be ever true,
God bless you, Tommy Atkins, here's your country's love to you.

So Tommy dear, we'll back you 'gainst the world
For fighting or for funning or for work,
Wherever Britain's banner is unfurled
To do your best and never, never shirk.
We keep the warmest corner in our hearts,
For you, my lad, wherever you may be,
By the Union Jack above you! But we're
proud of you and love you.
God keep you, Tommy, still by land and sea!

Coffin wrote in 1930:

The simple words fit the music, which has a catchy air, and there is still a considerable sale for the song. If when singing in public, I give sailor songs, such as 'The Dover Patrol' and 'Jack's the Boy', a voice almost invariably calls out, 'Where does the army come in? Give us "Tommy Atkins".'[39]

This indicates the rehabilitation of the soldier in the popular affection, which was due largely to the Empire, and to the long-lasting affection in which some songs are held.

In 1899 Edwardes revived *Tommy Atkins*, with the insertion of some topical verses about the war, and gave it to Coffin to sing in *San Toy*. Coffin recalled that it 'fired the imagination of British audiences and made a strong appeal. On Mafeking night there was a memorable performance at Daly's. When I came to the end of *Tommy Atkins* the enthusiasm knew no bounds, and they did the maddest things, even going as far as throwing money on the stage.'[40] One of the shillings hit Coffin on the head. He retrieved it and had it cut in half. One half he gave to Barter Johns, 'the musical director who had contributed greatly to the revived success of the song by his masterful re-orchestration for this production'. The other half he kept on his own watch chain.

The political content of *San Toy* was greater than *The Geisha's*. It highlighted the cultural differences between West and East, with San Toy's nurse fleeing from the *suttee* pyre after her husband's death, her father Yen How hymning the delights of Westernization ('So we'll imitate the styles of the blessed British Isles') and Li, in his pidgin song *Chinee Soje-Man* (lyrics by Ross, music by Lionel Monckton), disparagingly comparing other nations' soldiers with the British (who were 'always dlilling, gettee shilling/ Evely day with beef and blead'), whereas the French were 'welly small' and 'lovee ladies' nussy maidies', Boer soldiers 'ugly lot/ dirty shirtee, goodeeshot' and given to shooting from any bush, and the German 'big about/ Eatee sausage, gettee stout'.

A Country Girl, written by Tanner, Ross and Monckton, and produced by Edwardes at Daly's on 18 January 1902, ran for 729 performances. It involved the romantic complications surrounding the love of Marjorie Joy, the country girl, and impoverished lord of the manor, Commander Geoffrey Challoner, RN (Hayden Coffin), who gets to sing *The Sailor Man*, celebrating the British sailor as the equal of the soldier: 'Oh he's all right at a sing-song/ And he's all right at a rag/ You should see him smile/ On a South sea Isle/ When he runs up the good old flag.'

The patriotism of audiences in these years is confirmed by Rutland Barrington in his account of the opening night of *The Geisha* in March 1904. The first act lasted two hours, and there was a long wait before the second act. The audience filled in the time by good-naturedly singing the national anthem and cheering the Queen and Princess Victoria in the royal box.[41]

The Belle of Cairo, which opened on 10 October 1896, had a book by Cecil Raleigh and F. Kinsey Peile, and music and lyrics by Peile, who was a former Indian Army officer. It received a mixed critical reception and ran for only seventy-one performances. But it was topical, set in Egypt against background of the war with the dervishes. Nephthys, 'the belle of Cairo', follows her sweetheart Sir Gilbert Fane of the 21st Cavalry to the front disguised as a boy servant. Among the songs was *The Gordon Boys*, in praise of military training for orphans. Fane, the hero, had a grand patriotic number, *An Englishman's Duty*, which was well received:

> An Englishman must march to glory,
> An Englishman must thrash the foe,
> Each Englishman repeats the story,
> As Englishmen have done, you know,
> No Englishman knows when he's beaten,
> Each Englishman does all he can,
> From days of Rugby, Harrow and of Eton,
> An English boy's an Englishman![42]

George Edwardes's next Gaiety production, *The Messenger Boy* (3 February 1900), with music by Lionel Monckton and Ivan Caryll, book by James Tanner and Alfred Murray and lyrics by Adrian Ross and Percy Greenbank, centred on the schemes of Tudor Pyke to prevent the marriage of Clive Radnor and Lord Punchestown's daughter by sending a messenger boy to Egypt with compromising letters; the inevitable farcical complications follow. It acknowledged the end of the Boer War with the inclusion of the patriotic song *When the Boys Come Home Once More*, and during the run *How I Saw the CIV* was added, celebrating the return from South Africa of the City Imperial Volunteers. It ran for 429 performances.

The Orchid, a musical play by James Tanner, with music by Monckton and Caryll, lyrics by Ross and Greenbank, was produced by George Edwardes at the Gaiety on 28 October 1903 and ran for 559 performances. It concerned the rivalry between Aubrey Chesterton, British Minister of Commerce, and a French Count to obtain a rare orchid. But the most intriguing fact about it was that actor Harry Grattan, playing Chesterton, was made up to resemble Joseph Chamberlain, complete with monocle. Chamberlain, who was Colonial Secretary from 1895 to 1903, was famous for his orchid buttonhole and monocle, his imperialism and his nickname, 'Pushful Joe'. Chesterton had a song, *Pushful*, which included the lines 'I stand up

[271]

for the Empire, thick and thin' and 'If the foes of Britain make a sudden disappearance/ That is all the product of my pushful perseverance'.

At Daly's, George Edwardes next produced *The Cingalee*, with a Tanner book, Monckton's music, and Ross and Greenbank's lyrics. It opened on 5 March 1904 and ran for 365 performances. This one was set in Ceylon. Ceylonese tea-planter Hon. Harry Vereker (Hayden Coffin) seeks to marry his estate worker Nanoya but has to get round her childhood marriage to a local potentate Boobhamba Chettur Bhoy. It featured beautiful sets, genuine Sinhalese dances and a clash of cultures. Just as *suttee* had been denounced in *San Toy*, so was child-marriage in *The Cingalee*.

There were plentiful imitations of the Edwardes formula of beautiful girls, romantic stories, topical allusions and tuneful scores: two, with music by Howard Talbot, opened within days of each other. *The Blue Moon* (book by Harold Ellis, music by Howard Talbot and Paul Rubens, lyrics by Percy Greenbank and Paul Rubens), began on tour but opened in London on 28 August 1905, and ran for 182 performances. It was, says Kurt Gänzl, the 'familiar story of the oriental singing girl and her British Navy lover and the comic high jinks which surround their path to wedded bliss'.[43]

The White Chrysanthemum (music by Howard Talbot, lyrics by Arthur Anderson, book by Leedham Bantock and Arthur Anderson), which opened on 31 August 1905 and ran for 179 performances, was a direct imitation of *The Geisha*. The hero was Lt Reggie Armitage, RN who succeeds in marrying his sweetheart Sybil Cunningham, despite his father's attempt to marry him to an American heiress. The action involves Sybil disguising herself as a Japanese girl. The show gave Admiral Sir Horatio Armitage a song celebrating the Japanese victory over Russia in the Russo-Japanese War ('. . . the gallant Mikado has checked her bravado/ And crushed her on sea and on land').

The Empire was most prominent, then, in Edwardes's musicals and their imitations in the late-Victorian and the Edwardian period. There was a late entry in the imperial cycle, the now-forgotten *The Song of The Drum*, written by Fred Thompson and Guy Bolton, which opened at the Theatre Royal, Drury Lane, on 9 January 1931. It starred Derek Oldham as Captain Anthony Darrell, Bobby Howes as comic relief Chips Wilcox, Peter Haddon as silly-ass 'Goofy' Topham and Marie Burke as glamorous spy Countess Olga von Haultstein. It featured spectacular and exotic sets which sent the critics into raptures, dance routines choreographed by Ralph Reader, and drills and marches reminiscent of Alhambra and Empire ballets. Originally it was to have been set in India, but this was forbidden by the Censor because of the current troubles in that country. It was therefore set in fictional

Huzbaria, an Eastern country under British rule where Captain Anthony Darrell is disgraced and loses his sweetheart, the colonel's daughter, and so goes in disguise to neighbouring Kahlek where an anti-British revolt is being plotted, to foil the enemies of the Empire.

The Broadway musicals *The Desert Song* and *Rose Marie* had enjoyed long runs at the Theatre Royal, Drury Lane, and this was an attempt at a home-grown exotic. *The Song of the Drum* had a score by Vivian Ellis and Herman Finck, with lyrics by Desmond Carter. Ellis was a somewhat unlikely choice as his musicals tended to be domestic romantic comedies like *Mr Cinders* and *Jill Darling*, but he contributed the tuneful songs, and Finck, the long-serving Musical Director of the Theatre Royal, contributed the dance music and atmospheric pieces.

Finck's music included the bazaar music, a syncopated Oriental piece reminiscent of Ketélbey's *In a Persian Garden* in quadruple rhythm which partially implies a triplet formation and develops into a jingling ostinato with distinct echoes of the bagpipes. His *Grotesque Dance* was another quasi-Oriental piece, slow, harmonically intriguing and syncopated. His *Wooden Shoe Ballet* translated tap-dance rhythms into quasi-Oriental music. His *Fan Ballet* was written in waltz time with a trilling *pas de deux* in the middle.

Ellis contributed the stirring march-time *Song of the Hillmen* (sung by Raymond Newell) and the rousing march-style *Song of the Drum* (sung by Derek Oldham.) There was the lilting and charmingly poised romantic ballad *You Looked At Me*, a lively duet, *I Must Leave My House*, a stately Viennese waltz song, *When I'm Dancing With You*, a conventional big romantic number *The Sun in My Eyes*, a wistful song of separation *Within My Heart* (sung by Marie Burke) and the harmonically rich and inventive *Sheila*.

The Times rhapsodized about the musical's 'look':

> *The Song of the Drum* presents spectacle as splendidly lavish as the most voluptuous eye could hope to behold. Huzbaria . . . is profusely touched with local colour and we see a good deal of it. From the elegance of the gymkhana, with its pretty swirl of Western frocks, we pass to the courtyard of a native house, three storeys high and seething in each storey with picturesque life, with maidens whirling and twirling in the frenzy of native dance, and from the decorous parade of scarlet-jacketed men and richly apparelled women in the regimental ball-room to the din and glitter of a bazaar in the native quarter. Wandering mendicants, charmsellers, and haggling vendors, passing rickshaws, donkeys, and goats – all the sights and sounds of the East of conventional romance are here, and once a real live camel pads the dustless stage with velvet hoof. When we cross to the adjacent country of Kahlek . . . we arrive at an Oriental

paradise, with a pearl-grey palace, its walls set with rubies and agates, jasper and cornelian gleaming with mysterious grandeur against a sky of lapis lazuli. There is no questioning the magnificence of this piece . . . we get originality as well as magnificence in Professor Ernst Stern's representation of the bazaar . . . a study in blue and gold and phosphorescent purple.

The reviewer praised the acting and singing but found the narrative 'as shallow a romance as could well be imagined'. It closed after a run of 131 performances.[44]

Vivian Ellis called *The Song of the Drum* his 'biggest disappointment'. He was critical of the choice of Helen Gilliland to play the Captain's sweetheart: 'poor Helen Gilliland, beautiful, Savoyard, Helen Gilliland, who was neither strong enough nor warm enough for Drury Lane'. Big music, he argued, required a big voice, which Helen Gilliland did not possess. But in the end, he concluded: 'The failure of *the Song of the Drum* was no particular person's fault, and certainly not Ernst Stern's or Marie Burke's. The whole thing was not good enough anyway, despite a tolerant press. The public soon find out for themselves, whatever the press say.'[45]

On Broadway in the interwar years, alongside the zippy, up-to-date, Jazz-Age musicals, there was a rich vein of European-influenced operettas. Where the musicals usually boasted contemporary American urban settings, the operettas were often set in exotic locales (China, Louisiana, Norway, the South Seas). The leading exponents of this form were the Czech Rudolf Friml and the Hungarian Sigmund Romberg who brought to the Broadway stage of the 1920s the full-blooded romanticism of late-nineteenth-century Vienna, much as Erich Wolfgang Korngold and Max Steiner were to bring it to 1930s Hollywood. They bathed the exotic locales in a stream of memorable melodies – by turns lilting and stirring – and their quest for the exotic sometimes took them into imperial territory.

There were three imperial operettas, two of them as successful in London as on Broadway. All three were scripted by Otto Harbach and Oscar Hammerstein II. It was producer Arthur Hammerstein who, considering the exotic location had not yet been used for a musical, hit upon the Canadian Rockies. This suggested in addition the red-coated Canadian Mounties as characters. Harbach and Hammerstein concocted a plot and Rudolf Friml and Herbert Stothart provided the score, which contained several songs that were to become popular standards: *The Indian Love Call*, *Rose Marie*, *Door of my dreams* and *The Song of the Mounties*. The show, *Rose Marie*, opened on Broadway on 2 September, 1924 and ran for 557 performances. It was to chalk up 851 performances at the Theatre Royal, Drury Lane, and

1,250 performances in Paris. It became the favourite show of the King–Emperor George V, who saw it three times during its Drury Lane run, and doubtless enjoyed the heroic presentation of the Royal Canadian Mounted Police.

The musical's plot was the familiar one of romantic complications. French-Canadian singer Rose Marie La Flamme, who works in a Saskatchewan saloon, is loved by wealthy Ed Hawley but is in love with gold-miner Jim Kenyon. Wanda, a half-caste Indian girl, who loves Hawley, kills her Indian lover Blackeagle and frames Kenyon for the murder. Hawley goes along with the plot in order to win Rose Marie for himself. Believing Kenyon guilty, Rose Marie is prepared to marry Hawley, but the truth comes out and the lovers are united. The crime is investigated by Sergeant Malone of the Mounties, and the role of the Mounties as Keepers of the King's Peace is celebrated in the stirring *Song of the Mounties*, with its affirmation that the Mountie always gets his man, 'dead or alive'.

When Metro–Goldwyn–Mayer came to film the show, starring its popular singing duo Jeanette MacDonald and Nelson Eddy, they retained the score but completely reworked the plot, putting the romance between Rose Marie and the Mountie Sergeant (rechristened 'Sergeant Bruce') at the centre of the action. In MGM's *Rose Marie* (1936), Rose Marie was a glamorous and temperamental opera star who goes up-country to help her brother, an escaped convict, on the run from the police. She falls in love with Sergeant Bruce but unwittingly leads him to her brother, who Bruce, putting duty before his personal feelings, arrests. Rose Marie suffers a nervous breakdown and loses her voice but she is restored to health and happiness by Bruce singing *The Indian Love Call* to her. It became the definitive film version of the show, even though *The Song of the Mounties* was rather thrown away by being sung by Nelson Eddy before a wobbly back-projection of his troop of Mounties. The 1954 remake of *Rose Marie*, despite having Technicolor, spectacular location-shoots and a virile performance by Howard Keel as the Mountie, was a lacklustre and uninspiring affair. It returned to something approaching the original plot, though adding a romantic triangle between Rose Marie, her lover and the Mountie. But this time the Mountie did not get his woman.

Oscar Hammerstein II and Otto Harbach with Frank Mandel provided the book for *The Desert Song* and Sigmund Romberg composed a score which contained such hit songs as *The Desert Song, One Alone, Romance, The Riff Song* and *Eastern and Western Love*. It opened in New York on 30 November 1926 and ran for 471 performances. Produced at the Theatre Royal, Drury Lane, in 1927, it notched up 432 performances, with Harry Welchman and Edith Day giving fondly remembered performances in the leading roles. It was successfully revived in the West End in 1936, 1939, 1943 and 1967.

The plot drew on the then-topical Riff Uprising against French colonial rule in Morocco in 1925–26. But it dealt with the issue by crossing two staples of romantic fiction: *The Sheikh* (white woman carried off into the desert by native ruler who turns out to be white) and *The Scarlet Pimpernel* (gallant adventurer masquerades as fop to deceive enemies).

The hero of *The Desert Song* is the 'Red Shadow', mysterious leader of the rebel Riffs. He is in reality Pierre Birabeau, who joined the French Foreign Legion in Morocco to prove himself to Margot Bonvallet, whom he loves. But refusing to raid native villages on a punitive attack at the order to the Governor, General Fontaine, known as 'the Butcher', he was dismissed the service. He fled to the hills and became leader of the resistance to the French ('I dreamed of being the Robin Hood of Morocco'), though his men are unaware of his identity. When Pierre's father, General Birabeau, becomes Governor, Pierre poses as an effeminate wild-flower collector at the Governor's palace while gathering information of use to the Riffs. Margot arrives in Morocco and, repelled by Pierre's pose, she agrees to marry Captain Paul Fontaine, son of the General. But the 'Red Shadow' carries her off to a palace in the hills, and she falls in love with him. Half-caste dancer Azuri, who loves Fontaine, discovers the identity of the 'Red Shadow' and leads General Birabeau and his men to the Shadow's hideout. Birabeau challenges the Shadow to a duel, but the Shadow refuses to fight his own father, for which he is proclaimed a coward and banished to the desert by his men. Birabeau orders him hunted down. Azuri then reveals to the General that the Shadow is his son. However, Pierre turns up to announce that he has killed the Shadow. He is reunited with his father and Margot, both of whom now know the truth, and they agree to work together for peace and reconciliation with the Riffs ('There is no need now for a Riff Robin Hood'). So, far from endorsing rebellion, *Desert Song* supports enlightened colonial administration.

In 1929 Warner Brothers filmed *The Desert Song*, choosing to make a virtually photographed transcription of the stage show and thus invaluably preserving a record of what the original show must have looked like. John Boles was in splendid voice as the Red Shadow, and the film was a huge hit, grossing $3 million worldwide.[46] Warner Brothers twice remade it. The 1943 version gave it a topical makeover. The hero (Dennis Morgan) had become an American Spanish Civil War veteran who doubles as a café pianist and the leader of the Riffs to oppose their enslavement by the Nazis who are building a railway across North Africa. The 1953 version, with Gordon MacRae in the lead, returned to something like the original plot but renamed the hero El Khobar. Richard Barrios suggests that at the height of the McCarthy era, no hero could be called the 'Red' anything.[47]

But the most remarkable of the three imperial operettas was the short-lived *Golden Dawn*, with book by Harbach and Hammerstein and music by Hungarian Emmerich Kalman, Austrian Robert Stolz and American Herbert Stothart. It opened on 30 November 1928 and ran for six months, but it was not produced in Britain and has never been revived. This is understandable, for it is an unbelievable and racist farrago with hand-me-down plot elements that must have seemed antiquated even in 1928. It was filmed by Warner Brothers in 1930 and was a box-office disaster.

It is set in German East Africa during the Great War and has the novel twist that the white colonial powers, British and German, join forces as captors and captives to keep the blacks in subjection. German Captain Eric and British Colonel Judson denounce paganism, slavery and human sacrifice in similar terms. The natives are all classic stereotypes: the high priest is a demented fanatic, the black overseer Shep is lecherous and cowardly and Mooda, a vengeful half-caste, seeking retribution on all white men because she was betrayed by one of them.

The racism is explicit and underpins the action at every point, although the score is tuneful and memorable in its late-romantic lushness and extravagance. But what is interesting is that *Golden Dawn* shares its racial stereotypes with the two other and better-known musicals. All three musicals have as a leading character a jealous, vengeful and unstable half-caste woman, (Wanda, Azuri, Mooda). Two of them have a leading character who is supposed a native but is really white ('Red Shadow', Golden Dawn), thus avoiding the danger of miscegenation. All three endorse the machinery of imperial rule. So while the Empire was conspicuously absent from the operatic stage, the musical and operetta stages resoundingly celebrated the virtues and values of imperialism.

Notes

1 Eric Walter White, *A History of English Opera*, London: Faber, 1983.
2 Cecil Forsyth, *Music and Nationalism*, London: Macmillan, 1922, p. 2.
3 *Ibid.*, p. 41.
4 *Ibid.*, p. 124.
5 *Ibid.*, pp. 152, 164.
6 *Ibid.*, p. 301.
7 Ivor Guest, *Ballet in Leicester Square: The Alhambra and the Empire, 1860–1915*, London, Dance Books, 1992, p. 8.
8 *Ibid.*, p. 27.
9 *The Times*, 2 April, 1872.

10 *The Times*, 29 May, 1886.
11 Guest, *Ballet*, p. 42.
12 *The Times*, 2 April, 1889.
13 Mark E. Perugini, *A Pageant of the Dance and Ballet*, London: Jarrolds, 1935, p. 227.
14 *A Day Off*, Alhambra Theatre Programme, 24 April, 1899.
15 *The Era*, 29 April, 1899.
16 *The Sketch*, 20 December, 1899.
17 Unidentified newspaper clipping, Theatre Museum file, *Soldiers of the Queen*.
18 Perugini, *Pageant*, pp. 229–30.
19 *Britannia's Realm*, Alhambra Theatre Programme, 16 June, 1902.
20 Perugini, *Pageant*, pp. 229–30.
21 *The Times*, 21 December, 1909.
22 *The Times*, 27 September, 1892.
23 *The Times*, 28 September, 1893.
24 *The Sketch*, 4 August, 1897.
25 Perugini, *Pageant*, p. 246.
26 *Illustrated London News*, 7 June, 1902.
27 *The Times*, 30 May, 1902.
28 Kurt Gänzl, *Musicals*, London: Carlton, 1995.
29 J.B. Priestley, *English Humour*, London: Longman, 1930, p. 16.
30 Rutland Barrington, *Rutland Barrington by Himself*, London: Grant Richards, 1908, pp. 94–5.
31 John M. MacKenzie, *Orientalism: History, Theory and the Arts*, Manchester: Manchester University Press, 1995, pp. 124–8; T. Sato and T. Watanabe (eds), *Britain and Japan: An Aesthetic Dialogue*, London: Lund Humphries, 1991.
32 Richard Traubner, *Operetta*, New York: Oxford University Press, 1983, p. 201.
33 MacKenzie, *Orientalism*, p. 124.
34 Earl H. Miner. *The Japanese Tradition in British and American Literature*, Princeton, NJ: Princeton University Press, 1958, p. 66.
35 Kathryn Castle, *Britannia's Children: Reading Colonialism through Children's Books and Magazines*, Manchester: Manchester University Press, 1996, p. 129.
36 Margarita Winkel, *Souvenirs of Japan: Japanese Photography at the Turn of the Century*, London: Bamboo Publishing, 1991, p. 18.
37 *The Times*, 27 April, 1896; *The Geisha*, Hyperion, CD A67006.
38 Hayden Coffin, *Hayden Coffin's Book*, London: Alston Press, 1930, pp. 106–8.
39 *Ibid.*, p. 101.
40 *Ibid.*, p. 122.
41 Barrington, *Rutland Barrington by Himself*, p. 140.
42 Kurt Gänzl, *The British Musical Theatre*, vol. I: *1856–1914*, London: Macmillan, 1986, pp. 604–5. Further details of all the musical comedies in this chapter can be found in Gänzl.
43 *Ibid.*, p. 876.
44 *The Times*, 10 January, 1931.
45 Vivian Ellis, *I'm On a See-Saw*, London: Michael Joseph, 1953, pp. 120–2.
46 Richard Barrios, *A Song in the Dark: The Birth of the Musical Film*, New York: Oxford University Press, 1995, p. 92.
47 *Ibid.*

CHAPTER NINE

'The sun never sets':
music for imperial films

The imperial melodramas which were a staple of the Victorian and the Edwardian stage were transferred largely intact to the silent cinema. The stage melodrama had orchestral accompaniment, with music signalling the entrance of characters, providing interludes and emphasizing dramatic climaxes. In the absence of dialogue, silent films were provided with continuous musical accompaniment which helped to structure and channel audience reaction by underlining the mood, pace and location of the action on the screen. In many cases this was drawn from the existing stock of musical scores and a repertoire of classical and light music themes appropriate for dramatic, romantic, comic and action scenes developed for use during film screenings. But, increasingly, special scores were composed to accompany major film productions, notably Joseph Carl Breil's score for *The Birth of a Nation* (1915) and Edmund Meisel's for *The Battleship Potemkin* (1925).[1]

When talkies were introduced in the late 1920s, films initially dispensed with special scores, partly because the technology was not yet sophisticated enough to mix music, dialogue and sound effectively, and partly because it was felt that audiences would be asking where the music was coming from if it was not obviously deriving from an on-screen wireless, gramophone or orchestra. But by 1933 the technological problems had been overcome and the success of scores specially composed for such films as *King Kong* led to the musical score becoming an integral part of the structure and nature of the sound film. Music was seen as valuable because of its ability to express emotion, establish mood and create atmosphere. It also bound films together scene by scene and helped to cue audience response. For these reasons Claudia Gorbman, in her admirable analysis of narrative film music, rejects the notion of music paralleling or counterpointing the action and sees it instead acting 'synergically' or by 'mutual implication' because of the way it mediated between the various elements on the screen and between the film and its audience.[2]

Long-time British film music director Muir Mathieson explained how it works:

> Music is and must always be a vital part of film art . . . Music can help to humanise the subject and widen its appeal. Music can make a film less intellectual and more emotional. It can influence the reaction of the audience to any given sequence . . . It can develop rhythmic suggestions from words. It can carry ideas through dissolves and fade-outs. It can prepare the eye through the ear. It can merge unnoticeably from realistic sound into pure music. It can shock. It can startle. It can sympathise. It can sweeten.[3]

Claudia Gorbman identified the principles lying behind the composition of the classical film score. First, it should not be heard consciously but should subordinate itself to the visuals and the dialogue, which are the primary means of telling the story. Second, it should set the moods and emphasize the emotions integral to the story being told. Third, it should provide referential and narrative cues for the audience, indicating for instance the historical and the geographical setting of the story, identifying individual characters, establishing and shading atmosphere, integrating and illustrating what is going on with musical rhythm imitating such actions as running, riding and climbing. Fourth, the music should provide continuity between shots, scenes and sequences. Finally, it should unify the film by repetition and variation of the basic themes it has established.[4]

The cinema rapidly established a set of musical referential conventions to suggest place. Gorbman summarizes some of them:

> Strongly codified Hollywood harmonies, melodic patterns, rhythms and habits of orchestration are employed as a matter of course in classical cinema for establishing setting. A 4/4 allegretto drumbeat (or pizzicato in bass viols), the first beat emphatically accented, with a simple minor-modal tune played by high woodwinds or strings signifies 'Indian territory'. A rumba rhythm and major melody played by either trumpet or instruments in the marimba family signifies Latin America. Xylophones or woodblocks, playing simple minor melodies in 4/4, evoke Japan or China. If one hears Strauss-like waltzes in the strings, it must be turn-of-the-century Vienna. Accordions are associated with Rome and Paris.[5]

The cinema also adopted the Wagnerian *leit motif* method, associating distinctive tunes with particular characters or groups, which are often set out in the title music, recur with variation throughout the film and are recapitulated at the end to provide closure.

Above all the music must be in a recognizable idiom which the audience can absorb without effort. The idiom of classical Hollywood was late-nineteenth-century European romanticism, tonal, tuneful, emotional, uplifting, the idiom of Puccini and Richard Strauss. It was imported into Hollywood by two Viennese émigrés, Max Steiner and Erich Wolfgang Korngold. Steiner is the man credited with virtually inventing the Hollywood film score with his atmospheric and richly textured music for such films as *King Kong* (1933), and Korngold is the man who brought prestige to the job of film composer.[6] As a Viennese *wunderkind*, he had been hailed as the successor of Richard Strauss and was an acclaimed operatic composer in Europe until the rise of Nazism forced him into exile. Around Steiner and Korngold gathered a remarkable group of composers of European or European immigrant origin, Dimitri Tiomkin, Franz Waxman, Miklos Rozsa, Alfred Newman, Victor Young, who ensured that the final flowering of late-nineteenth-century European romanticism took place in twentieth-century America.

Because this music was provided for the main form of commercial entertainment in the twentieth century, because it subordinated itself to the action and – for some – because it was expressed in a nineteenth-century idiom, it was long looked down on by critics. Only a scattering of lone courageous voices canvassed its virtues. But during the 1970s there was a major revival of interest in the music of Korngold. His film scores were resurrected and newly recorded.[7] In their wake, the work of all the great Hollywood composers was rediscovered and much of it made available again in new recordings, thanks to the painstaking reconstruction work of dedicated musicologists. A rich musical harvest has resulted.

The method of composition which evolved in Hollywood was for the composer to run a rough-cut of the picture in its entirety, then reel by reel, and, in consultation with director, producer, film editor and musical director, agree a set of cues and timings for the score. The composer would then write the required music rapidly. Owing to the speed required, the music would often be orchestrated by someone else, while the composer continued the task of preparing the main themes. The music would then be recorded with the film being run on a screen behind the orchestra; timings were made and the recorded music was finally dubbed on to the soundtrack and mixed with dialogue and sound effects. It was therefore in its final state when wedded to images and dialogue the ultimate example of programme music.

Music played an important part in the cycle of imperial films that began in Hollywood in 1935 with the enormous box office success, both in America and Britain, of Paramount Pictures' *Lives of a Bengal Lancer*, directed by Henry Hathaway. It was a swashbuckling north-west frontier adventure which owed more to Kipling than to its ostensible source, Major Francis Yeats-Brown's book of reminiscences and reflections. It was a film of action (pig-sticking; tent-pegging; rebel-crushing), but also of ideology. For the entire action of the film was structured by a justification for British rule in India. The *Daily Mail* (1 February, 1935) suggested that 'the film paid a remarkable tribute to the wisdom and courage which have marked British rule in India. It is a powerful and popular argument for the continuance of that rule.'

The film was deliberately aimed at both American and British audiences. For it is a striking fact that the three leading characters are played by American actors: Gary Cooper plays Lt Alan McGregor, a self-styled 'Scotish Canadian' from Alberta who joins the 41st Bengal Lancers in search of adventure; Richard Cromwell plays Lt Donald Stone, the son of Colonel Stone, Commanding Officer of the Lancers, but raised in America by an American mother who hated the service; and Franchot Tone plays Lt John Forsythe, son of a General and from a fashionable regiment. These characters – and with them the audience, both in Britain and in America – learn the British imperial mission from the senior Lancer officers, played by eminent British actors Sir Guy Standing and Sir C. Aubrey Smith. The British role in India is clearly stated to be protective ('We have 300 million people to protect') and dictated by the desire to maintain the peace.

Bengal Lancers has almost no background music. But what exists is credited to Milan Roder. Behind the titles, fanfares of trumpets symbolizing the British are interwoven with a sinuous Oriental melody reminiscent of Rimsky-Korsakoff's *Chanson Hindoue*, symbolizing the East. The film is punctuated by bugle calls, underlining the martial theme, and another Rimsky-esque passage over scenes in the palace at Gopal suggests Oriental luxury. The film ends with *God Save the King* as the DSO is awarded to Forsythe and Stone and the VC posthumously to McGregor who has been killed defeating the rebel uprising. *Sweet Lass of Richmond Hill* in march-time is played over the final credits, another reminder both of England and of her martial mission.

The success of the film sparked a major cycle of imperial films, to which all the leading studios contributed. Noting this phenomenon, Margaret Farrand Thorp wrote in her 1939 study of the American film industry:

> The immediate explanation of this burst of British propaganda is a very simple one. As continental audiences dwindled, Britain, which had always stood high, became an even more important section of the American movies' foreign public. It was highly desirable to please Great Britain if possible, and it could be done without sacrifice, for the American

[282]

public, too, seemed to be stirred with admiration for British Empire ideals. Loyalty as the supreme virtue . . . courage, hard work, a creed in which *noblesse oblige* is the most intellectual conception; those ideas are easier to grasp and very much easier to dramatise on the screen than . . . the problems with which the intellectuals want the movies to deal.[8]

But there was more to it than a simple economic explanation. Richard Slotkin, who rightly points out that the imperial cycle of films in Hollywood coincided with the contemporary absence from the screen of major westerns, sees the imperial epics as filling that intellectual gap, addressing the foreign affairs' concerns of the American public and creating a genre which could, by drawing on mythic and generic paradigms, actually appeal equally to British *and* American audiences. Slotkin writes:

> Thematically, these movies deal with a crisis in which civilization – symbolized by the Victorian Empire or its equivalent – is faced by a threat from an alliance between the opposite extremes of savage license and totalitarian authority. The Victorian or civilized order is embodied in a regiment or a military outpost whose values are nominally those of a liberal and progressive imperium but whose heroes are warriors and whose politics are those of a justified and virile patriarchy happily exercised over consenting white women and childlike brown faces. A fanatical . . . chieftain . . . is uniting the hill tribes against our regimental utopia . . . There is often a foreign power, an evil empire (Russia, Germany, Imperial China), working behind the scenes. . . . The only one who can save us is the hero, a soldier who straddles the border between savagery and civilization, fanaticism and religion, brown and white, them and us. And we are saved – though typically at the cost of the hero's sacrificial death. There is a striking and not fortuitous resemblance between this formula and the classic Indian-war scenarios of the Myth of the Frontier. In a sense the movies merely flesh out in fiction the ideological implications of the racial energies that won the West into the basis of an Anglo-Saxon alliance for the conquest and control of the undeveloped world.[9]

The ideological and structural similarities between imperial epics and westerns are underlined by the fact that several of the imperial films were actually remade subsequently as westerns: for instance, *Lives of a Bengal Lancer* (1935) as *Geronimo* (1939); *Four Men and a Prayer* (1938) as *Fury at Furnace Creek* (1948); *The Lost Patrol (1939)* as *Badlands* (1939); and *Gunga Din* (1939) as *Sergeants Three* (1961).[10] There are also strong ideological and casting similarities between imperial epic *Charge of the Light Brigade* (1936) and cavalry western *They Died With Their Boots On* (1941). In both Errol Flynn plays the sacrificial hero. The entry of the United States into the war in 1941 signalled an end to the imperial cycle and a dramatic return to the epic western as the vehicle for expressing the essentials of Americanism.

But where Slotkin stresses the Americanization of the ingredients of the imperial epic, I would argue that the Hollywood imperial epics are more properly seen as expressions of a shared culture. Hollywood certainly sought to make British Empire epics accessible to American audiences both by including American characters (or their Canadian surrogates) or by casting American actors in British roles. But both Britain and America had colonies. Both British and American cultures were strongly rooted in the codes of chivalry.[11] These values could be played out equally in the imperial epic and in the western. Providing musical scores in the late-nineteenth-century romance idiom further ensured the accessibility of the stories to both British and American audiences.

It was Warner Brothers' answer to *Bengal Lancer*, Michael Curtiz's *Charge of the Light Brigade* (1936), that acquired a virtually symphonic score. It was provided by Max Steiner and was his first for Warner Brothers, with whom he was to remain until his retirement in 1965. It set the pattern for future imperial scores. Steiner structured it around a set of themes illustrating specific elements of the film, interwove them, and in particular drew on familiar tunes to trigger a specific audience response. The film emulated *Bengal Lancer* by including a leopard hunt, featuring a sinister native potentate allied to the Russians and by having its hero killed at the end. But where *Bengal Lancer* was set in the present, *Charge of the Light Brigade* was set in the middle of the nineteenth century and incorporated a romantic triangle (two brothers in love with the same girl), resolved by the climactic charge. Anxious to maintain an authentic British flavour, Warners assembled a largely British cast (Olivia de Havilland, Patric Knowles, David Niven, Henry Stephenson, Nigel Bruce), headed by an Australian with an impeccable British accent, Errol Flynn. The film centres squarely on the exploits of the Bengal Lancers and is set largely in India, reworking episodes from the Indian Mutiny such as the Cawnpore Massacre and transferring the regiment to the Crimea only for the climactic charge.

The film opens with a verse from Tennyson's celebrated poem over the credits and the music, which blends the tune from the verse of *Rule Britannia*, a sprightly march theme and a barbaric, sinister, semi-Oriental theme for the villain Surat Khan, all of which recur throughout the film. During the course of the film, there is a charming love theme, and period waltzes and quadrilles for the Governor-General's Ball. In the scene in which Errol Flynn evokes England for his fiancée Olivia de Havilland ('Ascot, cricket, punting on the Thames') we hear

The Roast Beef of Old England, while over a stiff upper lip farewell between comrades David Niven and Errol Flynn music from the verse of *Rule Britannia* plays. Drums and bugles punctuate the action throughout. The actual charge, one of the most excitingly shot and edited sequences in all cinema, is the equivalent of one of the musical battle fantasies of the nineteenth century. The music begins slowly, steadily increasing pace as the charge builds up. It counterpoints Steiner's march of the Lancers, *The British Grenadiers* and *Rule Britannia* for the British troops, with the Czarist national anthem for the Russians. Bugle calls and cannon fire are mixed in and Tennyson's lines are flashed onto the screen.[12]

It is likely that Warners engaged Steiner for *Charge* on the basis of his score for RKO's *The Lost Patrol* (1934), for which he provided what was in effect a miniature symphonic poem, complete with running themes and variations and musical motifs for each of the key characters. This is clearly demonstrated by the suite prepared from the film score by John Morgan and recorded in 1995.[13] *The Lost Patrol* was directed by John Ford, and is an archetypal Fordian tale of male bonding and of sympathy and respect for soldiers and their lives. It tells the classic story of a British Army patrol in Mesopotamia in 1917, lost in the desert, surrounded by unseen Arabs and picked off one by one until only the sergeant is left.

In many respects, the patrol is made up of a cross-section of the sorts of men who joined up: a gentleman ranker known as George Brown (Reginald Denny), nicknamed 'Topper', a man with a fondness for women, horses and drink, two old sweats who have served in India and been reduced from Sergeant Major to the ranks for brawling and boozing, the Irishman Quincannon (J.M. Kerrigan) and the Scotsman Mackay (Paul Hanson), the brokendown Jewish ex-boxer Abelson (Sammy Stein), a religious fanatic, Sanders (Boris Karloff), a cheerful cockney cuckold, Hale (Billy Bevan), a garrulous ex-music-hall performer, Morelli (Wallace Ford), and Pearson (Douglas Walton), a starry-eyed nineteen-year old mother's boy inspired to join up by dreams of glory. Gradually, as the tension mounts, each reveals his inner self and then one after another they die. The sergeant (Victor McLaglen), the tough professional, alone survives to kill the Arabs and greet the relief column.

John Ford wanted no score for his film, but RKO, worried about the bleakly depressing nature of the tale, insisted, and Steiner's score adds considerably to the dramatic effect.[14] There are recurring themes: a sinister Oriental melody for the Arabs, a march for the patrol. There is illustrative music, set to the rhythm of foot-slogging and galloping. For atmosphere, there is a wordless chorus that chants along with

[285]

the night wind at the oasis. But most of all there are the characters' individual motifs: for Sanders, a hymn-like tune; for Pearson, a richly romantic theme; for Brown, a jaunty man-about-town promenade; for Hale the First World War standard *Pack Up Your Troubles*. For Quin-cannon, there is a lilting Irish melody; for Mackay, a musical version of the skirl of the pipes; and for Morelli a music-hall-type tune. They are repeated with variations at appropriate points in the narrative. Finally, when all are dead, the diverse motifs are interwoven and a snatch of *God Save the King* is added as a reminder that they died in the service of their country. The relief column arrives to the music of the verse of *Rule Britannia*. Over the graves, each marked by a gleam-ing sabre, *The Last Post* sounds. Steiner had wanted to end his score with the wistful playing of *Auld Lang Syne* and a dying fall. The recorded suite, arranged by John Morgan, does so. But the film itself omits *Auld Lang Syne* and – no doubt at the studio's insistence – ends with the stirring and upbeat *British Grenadiers* as the relief column departs from the oasis.

The employment both of traditional tunes and, in *Charge of the Light Brigade*, of Tennyson's lines links the films to the wider culture. Traditional tunes and popular poetry were taught at school and remained an integral part of the popular cultural memory. The use of Tennyson in *Charge* is paralleled in *Lives of a Bengal Lancer*. Lt Forsythe recites W.E. Henley's *England, My England*, and Lt McGregor's dying utterance is 'Poetry'. He has given his life in affir-mation of the sentiments expressed in Henley's poem. The young trooper Pearson in *The Lost Patrol* admits that he is 'mad about Kipling'. The film *Gunga Din* ends with Kipling himself composing his poem and the Commanding Officer reciting it at the funeral of the regimental *bhisti*. There is a rich form of intertextuality at work here, with the images, music and dialogue on film reinforced by traditional patriotic verse and melodies with their own associations which can deepen and enrich the audience's engagement with the films.

Perhaps the most Anglophile studio in 1930s' Hollywood was 20th Century–Fox, which was created from the merger in 1935 of 20th Century Pictures and Fox Film Corporation. *Clive of India* (1935), produced by 20th Century Pictures before the merger, pointed the way. The film idealized Robert Clive (Ronald Colman) as a paladin of Empire, a heroic individualist who in pursuit of his destiny disobeys orders from over-cautious or corrupt superiors and commits forgery, but always acts in the interests of the higher good. He does battle against native tyrants who oppress their own people and against vested interests which offend against the basic imperial principles of just and disinterested administration. It is all done in a spirit of stoicism, duty, dedication and good humour.

Alfred Newman's score includes as original elements a jaunty march behind the credits and an Oriental motif for scenes of native rulers Suraj-ud-Doulah and Mir Jaffar and for the captured war elephants. But he also makes much use of the traditional English melody *Drink to Me Only With Thine Eyes* as the love theme for Clive and his wife Margaret (Loretta Young). He uses *God Save the King* and *The British Grenadiers* in quick-time for the relief march to Trichinopoly and in double quick-time for the victory parade after the Battle of Plassey. There are drums and trumpets throughout the film to reinforce the martial theme. The film culminates in a vote in Parliament condemning Clive's conduct and he retires broken and ill to his house. But the Prime Minister, the Earl of Chatham (C. Aubrey Smith), arrives with a message from the King, expressing his gratitude that Clive has added a great new dominion to the Empire, and the film ends on an upbeat note with *God Save the King.*

John Ford was a professional Irishman who made a trio of anti-British films about the imperial oppression of Ireland (*Hangman's House; The Informer; The Plough and the Stars*) and turned his South Seas' drama *The Hurricane* (1937) into a powerful allegorical indictment of imperialism. But also as a 20th Century–Fox contract director he made a trio of imperial films: *Black Watch* (1929); *Wee Willie Winkie* (1937); and *Four Men and a Prayer* (1938).

Black Watch was made before the return of musical scores to films, but it prefigures the musical scores for imperial films by its use of folk-songs and pipe music performed as part of the action. *Black Watch* is set during the First World War. On the outbreak of war, Captain Donald King (Victor McLaglen) of the Black Watch is ordered to India where a foreign power is stirring up a rebellion of the hillmen, who plan to invade British India through the Khyber Pass, led by a mysterious woman, Yasmani (Myrna Loy), whom the hillmen worship as a goddess. King, posing as a cashiered British officer, joins the rebels but falls in love with Yasmani. King ensures that the rebellion is crushed, but Yasmani is killed and dies in his arms. Ford responds characteristically to the ritual of military life and in particular to the Scottishness of the central regiment. The pipes figure strongly. *Annie Laurie* (three times), *Auld Lang Syne* (twice) and *Loch Lomond* are sung by the soldiers during the course of the film, rooting the action securely in a Scottish tradition of comradeship and communality.

Interestingly, the same songs figure on the musical soundtrack of *Wee Willie Winkie*, based on Kipling's short story. The film starred

[287]

Shirley Temple as Priscilla Williams, granddaughter of Colonel Williams (C. Aubrey Smith), who arrives with her American mother at his fort on the north-west frontier and is taught by him the meaning of Empire: 'The Empire wants to be friends with everybody, to keep the Pass open and to bring peace and prosperity to everybody.' On the basis of this philosophy of Empire, Shirley intervenes in a frontier war to reconcile rebel leader Khoda Khan (Cesar Romero) to the Empire. Once again Ford turned it into a congenial project by making it a celebration of a Scottish regiment and of regimental life and loyalty. Alfred Newman's score opens with pipes and drums over the credits, establishing the Scottish military ambience, and features orchestral versions of traditional Scottish marches over scenes of the Regiment drilling. During the Regimental Ball, an orchestra plays *Annie Laurie*, *Loch Lomond*, *My Hieland Laddie*, *Comin' through the Rye*, *I Have Heard the Mavis Singing* and *Charlie Is My Darling*.

One of the central relationships in the film is that between little Shirley and gruff Sergeant MacDuff (Victor McLaglen). When he is mortally injured in battle, Shirley sings *Auld Lang Syne* to him and Ford stages his funeral procession past a field of crosses to pipes and drums, with the score intercutting *Auld Lang Syne* and *God Save the Queen*. When the Colonel goes up alone to see Khoda Khan, *God Save the Queen* is interwoven with an Oriental melody for the Khan. Consensus at the end is celebrated by a regimental march-past with the Colonel, the Khan and Shirley taking the salute. The final credits unfold to the strains of *Auld Lang Syne*.

Four Men and a Prayer (1938) was a fast-moving imperial thriller. It has a munitions syndicate – classic 1930s' villains – supplying natives with guns and stirring up rebellion against the British. Colonel Loring Leigh (C. Aubrey Smith) is framed, cashiered and murdered, but eventually his reputation is cleared by his four sons, an epitome of the English ruling class (RAF flying officer, barrister, diplomat and Oxford undergraduate). The film has almost no music. No composer is credited and musical director Louis Silvers almost certainly provided what there is: a few dramatic chords over key moments, *The British Grenadiers* over the opening and closing credits and, during a brawl in an Indian bar involving Irish troops, a broken pianola pumping out an Irish jig.

Wee Willie Winkie was the first of a 20th Century–Fox trilogy of imperial films starring Shirley Temple, a significant fact in promoting imperial sentiment given that she was the top box office attraction in Britain from 1935 to 1938 (inclusive) and single-handedly saved the Fox Film Company from bankruptcy. *Susannah of the Mounties* (1939), directed by William Seiter, had more or less the same plot as *Wee Willie Winkie*, but set this time in Canada and containing many of the same elements. It is 1884 and the Blackfoot Indians are opposing the activities of the Canadian Pacific Railway. The Royal Canadian Mounted Police seek to maintain the peace. The film evokes life on a Canadian Mountie post; there is a romance between Commanding Officer's daughter Vicky Standing (Margaret Lockwood) and gallant Inspector 'Monty' Montague (Randolph Scott), the counterpart of the romance between Mrs Williams and Lt 'Coppy' Brandes at the Indian fort in *Wee Willie Winkie*. Shirley is initiated into Blackfoot ways by an Indian boy hostage (Indian dances; the pipe of peace; blood brotherhood ceremony). When the Indians go on the warpath, thanks to the activities of the wicked Indian Wolfpelt, attack the fort and capture Montague, Shirley goes to the Indian camp, exposes the villainy of Wolfpelt and assures Chief Big Eagle and the Blackfoot that the Mounties want to be their friends. The film ends with a ceremonial smoking of the pipe of peace at the Fort by the two sides.

It lacks the rich musical texture of *Winkie* and had no specific composer. Fox Musical Director Louis Silvers provides the lightly scored background. The Canadian tune *The Maple Leaf Forever* is played over credits and the final scene of reconciliation, emphasizing the unity of Canada. The film contains authentic Blackfoot war dances, war chants and medicine chants. There is the familiar Indian-style music, identified by Gorbman, over the Indian camp and the Indian attack. In the film bugles represent the Mounties, and the raising of the Union Jack, with everyone stopping and saluting, is a key ideological moment; the Indians are represented by drums. Where *Winkie* has a Scottish flavour, this film has an Irish one. The Scottish male nursemaid role of Sergeant MacDuff is taken by Corporal Pat Hannegan, an old Irish sweat, in *Susannah*. He plays an Irish folk-tune on the mouthorgan while Shirley teaches Monty to waltz, and the band play the tune at the fort dance.

The Little Princess (1939) featured Shirley as a spirited English girl, reduced to poverty when her adored father is believed killed in the Boer War. She is rescued from her plight by a kindly aristocrat and reunited with her father by the intervention of Queen Victoria herself. The film, opening with the departure of the troops for South Africa to the strains of *Rule Britannia* and *Soldiers of the Queen*, including the popular celebrations of the Relief of Mafeking and ending with the divine intervention of the Queen–Empress and the playing of the national anthem, is a wholehearted and quite entrancing Technicolor affirmation of aristocracy, monarchy and Empire.

Fox also mounted a handsome tribute to Stanley and Livingstone in their *Stanley and Livingstone* (1939). As with the Temple films, it involves an American leading character being converted to an imperial role. Unlike the two earlier British films *Livingstone* (1925) and *David Livingstone* (1936), where the Scottish missionary was the central figure, here it is Henry M. Stanley, the American reporter.

The film is constructed from an American viewpoint, but also acknowledges the need to promote Anglo-American friendship. Stanley (Spencer Tracy) is asked by his employer James Gordon Bennett of the *New York Herald* to find Livingstone. Bennett defines his appeal to the public: a Christian missionary converting the heathen, an anti-slavery campaigner and great adventurer/explorer in 'Darkest Africa'. All these aspects of his career are highlighted in the film.

Stanley, having survived fever, native attacks and wild animals on an expedition which is the centrepiece of the film, finds Livingstone (Sir Cedric Hardwicke). Stanley accompanies Livingstone on his work, medical, missionary and exploratory, and is inspired by him. Back in England, the Royal Geographical Society rejects Stanley's claims and maps as false, but news arrives that Livingstone's body has been brought to the coast with letters mentioning Stanley and asking him to carry on his work. The film ends with Stanley returning to Africa to continue exploring and mapping. Livingstone had said: 'White men have seen Africa only through eyes of ignorance, and that means fear.' He wants to remove fear through his maps, so that doctors, teachers and pioneers will come and slavery will be abolished; in other words, the white man will fulfil his humanitarian mission.

The film vindicates Britain's imperial mission by showing the initially sceptical Stanley converted to it. In an impassioned speech to the Society, he explains that, although now an American reporter, he had been born in England, had grown up in poverty, learned to hate England and emigrated. But his faith in England has been restored by Livingstone. Leaving aside the use of England for Britain, the film clearly indicates that Americans, too, should love the British imperial mission.

The film's score was prepared by Musical Director Louis Silvers, from material in the Fox music library, and incorporated and re-used themes composed by Robert R. Bennett, David Buttolph, R.H. Bassett, Cyril Mockridge, Rudy Schrager and Silvers himself. For instance, the weird South American melody Cyril Mockridge composed for *The Adventures of Sherlock Holmes* turns up as accompaniment to a scene of Stanley racked by fever. Silvers uses background music as motif and as atmosphere. A march is played behind the credits, establishing the film as heroic adventure, and is repeated with variations throughout the action of the film, particularly over the footage of the expedition, filmed by a second unit in East Africa. There is a lilting love theme behind the scenes of Stanley with Eve Kingsley (Nancy Kelly), the fictional daughter of the British Vice-Consul in Zanzibar, who inspires him to continue his search. The garrulous scout Jeff Slocum who accompanies Stanley (Walter Brennan) is represented by the 'western' song *Oh, Susanna*. For atmosphere, there is an Oriental theme over scenes of Zanzibar, a wordless chanted chorus over scenes of a slave caravan encountered on the expedition, and throughout African drums and war chants; while in Wyoming we get the typical Indian music described by Gorbman.

The British imperial mission is given a clear Christian dimension in musical terms by the use of *Onward, Christian Soldiers* which is played whenever Livingstone appears or is mentioned. In an inspiring scene Livingstone is shown animatedly conducting his African choir in a rendition of Sullivan's hymn. This is wholly anachronistic, because it was composed only in 1872 and Livingstone could not have known it. But it has an immediate cultural and connotative significance for the audience. It also serves to underline the link between Livingstone and Stanley. For when at the end Stanley is seen marching across the map of Africa, discovering rivers, waterfalls and lakes, all of which are named after himself, it is to the stirring accompaniment of *Onward, Christian Soldiers*, indicating musically that he has taken up Livingstone's mission.

Korngold made his imperial contribution in a relatively minor Warners' imperial vehicle, *Another Dawn* (1937). It has a starry cast (Errol Flynn, Kay Francis and Ian Hunter), and reuses the Chukoti fort set from *Charge of the Light Brigade*, with added palm trees. The preface sets the tone and stance: 'A remote outpost a long, long way from Tipperary – where a handful of the King's best preserve a precarious peace among the warring natives, at the cost of much British blood spilled in the desert sand.' It is set somewhere in the Middle East in a fictional British protectorate, Dikut, commanded by Colonel Wister (Ian Hunter), who outlines his mission: 'One day Dikut will be a great, independent country because England had faith in it.' Until then, the British maintain peace and security for the peace-loving natives whose cotton crop is threatened by marauding Arabs under the neighbouring independent ruler Achaben.

The maintenance of peace is a running theme. But two more are foregrounded. There is the classic romantic triangle played out according to the rules of honour and duty. On leave in England, Wister meets Julia Ashton (Kay Francis), an American still mourning a lost love, and falls for her, although he knows she does not love him. She accepts his marriage proposal and agrees to accompany him to Dikut to support him in his work. Once there she falls for Captain Denny Roark

(Errol Flynn), a dashing Anglo-Irish officer, beautifully spoken and ravishingly handsome. He reminds her of her lost love. During a number of discussions over tea and at cricket matches they explore the situation but cannot bring themselves to do anything which would hurt Wister. Eventually Achaben dams the river and the natives are threatened with drought and death. A suicide mission is called for. Wister flies out his plane, bombs the dam, and is shot down in flames. He has done it to give the lovers another dawn: 'He went out the right way', says Roark. It is the 'forbidden love in the desert' theme, played according to Anglo-American rules, a snatched kiss in a moonlit garden and everyone behaving honourably. Wister knows of the love between Julia and Denny, but he also knows they will 'play the game according to the rules. You can't discard honour any more than you can love.' Wister, who is devoted to his duty ('It's a job of work, it must be done'), sacrifices all to save the natives. In the subplot, Private Wilkins, who fled under fire two years before, and is sent white feathers by the other soldiers, redeems himself when a patrol is attacked by Arabs, sacrificing his life to get an ammunition box to the survivors. The film, dismissed by latterday critics as tedious and dated, is nothing less than a full-blooded celebration of an entire value system, based on concepts of duty, service and honour.

The film ran for only seventy-three minutes, making it much shorter than any other Flynn vehicle of the period. Director William Dieterle had not wanted to do it and Warners seem to have been unsure whether to market it as a desert love story or an imperial thriller.[15] Evidently scenes in which Roark went to negotiate with Achaben had been shot but were cut from the film before release, suggesting a decision to emphasize desert love rather than imperial politics. Other scenes, too, were cut or shortened. In addition, Warners shot two endings, one in which Flynn made the supreme sacrifice and that, which they eventually used, in which Hunter did the same.

Korngold provided one of his most notable scores, which, reconstructed and restored by John Morgan and newly recorded in 1995, shows him at the height of his powers.[16] There are three principal themes which recur with variations throughout. The title music over scenes of the troops riding into the fort and Denny Roark landing his plane is the duty and heroism theme, resolute and determined. There is a surging love theme behind all Julia's romantic scenes with both Wister and Roark. The violins carry the main tune. Korngold liked it enough to reuse it as the first movement of his *Violin Concerto*, premièred in 1947 by Jascha Heifetz. There is an exhilarating riding theme with urgent trumpet fanfares, set to a galloping rhythm, for troop movements and horse-rides.

There are other passages which underscore either the atmosphere or the emotion. For the golf course meeting of Julia and Wister, there is a jaunty, playful theme; for the township, an exotic Oriental theme with tambourines; for the party at which Julia and Denny kiss, there is a lilting Bedouin love song with a Westernized Oriental rhythm. There is heavily percussive desert battle music building steadily in pace and volume as the action escalates; the sandstorm which symbolizes the growing passion engulfing Julia and Denny is captured in a musical equivalent of whirling, piercing and pounding desert winds. Korngold had originally created an elaborate final musical sequence for the film, working to the version in which Flynn sacrificed himself. It interwove the duty theme and the love theme, and brought them to a triumphant climax underlining the victory of both love and duty. But when the studio substituted the other ending, he had to settle for a shorter recapitulation of the love theme. The suite reconstructed from the music restores Korngold's original ending.

RKO Radio Pictures' *Gunga Din* (1939) was one of the best and most popular of the Hollywood imperial cycle. It combined rip-roaring action scenes, knockabout comedy and a strong justification for the British presence in India. It showed war as, by turns, comic, exciting and heroic, and depicted the Empire as a vehicle for manly adventure. Hollywood acquired the rights to the Kipling poem in 1936 and scriptwriters Ben Hecht and Charles Macarthur, working with director Howard Hawks, put together a script that blended the story of the heroic self-sacrifice of the regimental water-carrier Gunga Din with Kipling's concept of the Soldiers Three, Mulvaney, Ortheris and Learoyd, the archetypal Indian army privates, and added for good measure from the hit Hecht–Macarthur newspaper play *The Front Page* the running theme of a man trying to prevent his best friend from getting married and deserting his profession.

The whole thing was strongly cast in the tight-knit male comradeship mould of so much of Howard Hawks's work. But Hawks left RKO and director George Stevens took over the project. He reworked the script with writers Fred Guiol and Joel Sayre, incorporating the theme of the British campaign to suppress the religious strangling cult, Thuggee. The mission of the British is thus seen as being to protect the Indians. As soon as the Colonel realizes there has been a revival of Thuggee, suppressed by Colonel Sleeman fifty years earlier, he declares firmly: 'We must stamp this out immediately.'

The film was shot on a fifteen-week schedule at a cost of $1.9 million at Lone Pine, California, Hollywood's perennial stand-in for the north-west frontier of India, and at RKO Studios. The three soldiers, rechristened Cutter, Ballantine and MacChesney, were played by

Cary Grant as an irrepressible Cockney joker, Douglas Fairbanks Jr as a quick-witted swashbuckler and Victor McLaglen as a hectoring old sweat, with Sam Jaffe as a faithful Gunga Din who sacrifices his life to warn the regiment of ambush, and Eduardo Ciannelli as a sinister shaven-headed villain, the Guru. Where villains in imperial epics were usually suave Moslem frontier khans, here uniquely the villain was a Hindu fanatic, shaven-headed, *dhoti*-clad, looking rather like a demented Gandhi.[17]

Alfred Newman's score made a major contribution to the success of the film. A suite has been constructed from the music by William Stromberg and was recorded in 1994.[18] The film opens with a statue of Victoria Regina Imperatrix, a parade of regimental flags and Montagu Love as the Commanding Officer of the Lancers reciting the last verse of Kipling's poem and then behind the credits, we see a diminutive figure beating a large gong.

The title music opens with the first bars of the national anthem and then the main themes of the score are rehearsed. There is the very striking theme for Gunga Din, set to the word rhythm of the line 'You're a better man than I am, Gunga Din'. It modulates into the rollicking high-spirited 'Soldiers Three' theme and after the crash of a gong into the menacingly dark-toned Kali theme, with its slithering glissando effect like a shiver running down the spine. These three themes, with variations, run through the film. The 'Soldiers Three' theme is heard first as a solemn march accompanying an army patrol, later as a waltz at the Stebbins's dance, and regularly as speeded-up accompaniment to the action.

In the fight sequence at Tantrapur between the British soldiers and the followers of Kali, the 'Soldiers Three' theme and the Kali music are played against each other. The Scottishness of the regiment is emphasized by scenes of the regiment parading with pipers playing *Bonnie Dundee* and marching out singing *Will Ye No Come Back Again?* There are pipes and bugles throughout, and it is Din's bugle call which saves the regiment from ambush at the end. But traditional tunes and poetry also figure, as in *Bengal Lancer* and *Charge of the Light Brigade*. Private Archie Cutter marches into a Hindu temple full of rebels defiantly singing *The Roast Beef of Old England*. The climactic charge has Highland themes, the *British Grenadiers*, the 'Soldiers Three' theme and the Kali music, interwoven. At the funeral of Gunga Din, there are pipes, *Auld Lang Syne* and the Colonel reciting the newly composed Gunga Din poem. The film ends with the upbeat 'Soldiers Three' march over the credits.

When the film was first shown in Britain, Mrs Caroline Kipling, the author's widow, objected to the fact that her husband was shown in the film (played by actor Reginald Sheffield) accompanying the British forces to the climactic battle and later composing the poem in honour of Gunga Din. RKO, in deference to her wishes, deleted the scenes involving Kipling. They have now been restored, and so once again the film can be seen complete on video.

Perhaps the most notable film to chart the effects of the Empire and imperial responsibilities on the families at home was *Cavalcade* (1933). During the London run of his comedy masterpiece *Private Lives*, Noël Coward had discussed with impresario C.B. Cochran 'the idea of doing a big spectacular production at the Coliseum'.[19] Casting around for a suitable subject, he came by chance upon some old bound volumes of *Black and White* and *The Illustrated London News* at Foyle's Bookshop in Charing Cross Road. He bought them, and the first volume he opened contained a full-page picture of a troopship leaving for the Boer War. He knew he had found his subject – the story of a family told against the background of the great events of the period between New Year's Eve 1899 and New Year's Eve 1930.

It was the tunes of the period that came into his head first: *Dolly Gray*, *The Absent-Minded Beggar*, *Soldiers of the Queen*, *Bluebell*. As he wrote later in his autobiography:

> The emotional basis of *Cavalcade* was undoubtedly music. The whole story was threaded on a string of popular melodies. This ultimately was a big contributory factor to its success. Popular tunes probe the memory more swiftly than anything else, and *Cavalcade*, whatever else it did, certainly awakened many echoes.[20]

Coward drew on the memories of his friend G.B. Stern for the turn of the century events – Mafeking Night, the Relief of Ladysmith, cockney newsboys 'shouting victories and defeats along London streets', the illness and death of Queen Victoria. 'She remembered vividly, graphically, and became as excited as I was. Later on I dedicated the published play to her in gratitude', said Coward.[21] He drew on his own memories of family holidays at Bognor, First World War hospital trains at Victoria station, army recruiting songs sung at the Palace Theatre and on Armistice Day. The resulting show, *Cavalcade*, which eventually opened at the Theatre Royal, Drury Lane on 13 October 1931, was an epic in three acts and twenty-two scenes, cost 'an almost unprecedented' £30,000, and employed a cast and crew of over 400 for more than a year.[22]

The play opened just after Britain had gone off the Gold Standard and two weeks before a General Election ousted the Labour Government and installed a coalition National Government, dedicated to national reconstruction. The finale of the play, after a scene showing

[295]

the 'chaos and confusion' of the modern world, had the entire cast gathering against the background of the Union Jack to sing *God Save the King*. Coward, responding to the evident feelings of his audience, said in his curtain speech: 'I hope this play has made you feel that, in spite of the troublous times we are living in, it is still a pretty exciting thing to be English.' The reaction of the audience was one of patriotic ecstasy. The play garnered an equally enthusiastic press. Typical was the review by Alan Parsons in the *Daily Mail*. Noting that the first night's ovation was 'such as I have not heard in many years playgoing', he called *Cavalcade* 'a magnificent play in which the note of national pride pervading every scene and every sentence must make each one of us face the future with courage and high hopes'.[23]

On 28 October 1931, the night of the General Election, the King and Queen and the entire royal family attended the play – 'a thrilling, emotional event', Coward recalled. At the end, the entire audience joined the cast in singing *God Save the King*, and the King in the royal box received his own personal ovation.[24] Cynics suggested that Coward, whose image was that of an irreverent and worldly playboy, had written the play tongue-in-cheek. It was a view Coward totally rejected: 'There was certainly love of England in it, a certain national pride in some of our very typical characteristics.'[25]

Coward received many letters from people who saw in the play echoes of their own experiences.[26] The story was serialized in the *Daily Mail*. Gramophone records were made of the songs in the show. The film rights were sold to Fox Film Corporation for $100,000.[27]

Fox went to extraordinary lengths to achieve authenticity in its film version. It had the entire play photographed by Movietone News and shipped to Hollywood for reference purposes. An entirely British cast was assembled, including three of the performers from the London production (Irene Browne, Una O'Connor, Merle Tottenham.) A British director (Frank Lloyd) and scriptwriter (Reginald Berkeley) were recruited. The resulting film is an absolutely faithful recreation of the stage show with a few discreet additions (A Zeppelin raid on London, Edward Marryot's proposal to Edith Harris) and deletions (Edward's twenty-first birthday party.) The result, as *The Observer* noted, was 'the best British film that has ever been made – and it was made in America'.[28] James Agate wrote in *The Tatler*:

> *Cavalcade* is a grand film in all its aspects. It is a completely faithful reproduction of the spirit and letter of Noël Coward's original work. It conveys to the spectator exactly the same quality and quantity of emotion that the stage play did . . . In the matter of its photography, settings, crowd marshalling it is flawless . . . As a message for the times it

repeats Mr Coward's message exactly. As a precipitant of tears this film will not be easily equalled. And last though of course not least, as entertainment it is superb . . . never has a film been produced with greater magnificence or better discretion. The picture is totally without any trace of Hollywood, and, though made in America, is bone-English throughout.[29]

Seventy years after its appearance both as a play and as a film, it is possible to judge *Cavalcade* dispassionately. It is animated by a deep and genuine love of country – a country referred to throughout as England – but it is far from being jingoistic. It unsparingly shows the horrors of war and the sense of grief and loss that war brings with it. Much of this is suffered by Jane Marryot, who is the dominant figure in the play. Coward wrote: 'She seemed real to me and still does, a bit of my own mother and millions of others, too; ordinary, kind and unobtrusively brave; capable of deep suffering and incapable of cheap complaint.'[30] It is Jane who waits and who suffers while her husband serves in South Africa in the Boer War and while her son serves in France in the Great War. Mary Clare on the stage and Diana Wynyard in the film dominate the proceedings in this role, rather overshadowing the quietly devoted and undemonstrative husband Robert (Edward Sinclair on stage, Clive Brook in the film.)

The narrative cleverly interweaves the stories of the upper-middle-class Marryot family and of their servants, the Bridges. *The Observer* commented that *Cavalcade* evaded any truly constructive issues but that it was 'so close to the emotional memories of every British man and woman that it must sweep British audiences off their feet wherever it is shown'.[31] The truth of his observation is confirmed by the inclusion of *Cavalcade* in a week of plays put on by the BBC in October 1940 and chosen from those most popular with the listening audience.[32] It was again in tune with the feelings of that audience in the first year of the Second World War.

Cavalcade opens with the Boer War. Robert Marryot and his servant Alfred Bridges join the City Imperial Volunteers (CIV) and sail for South Africa. They return safely. Queen Victoria dies and her funeral procession passes the Marryots' house. Robert, who has received the Victoria Cross and a knighthood, participates in the funeral procession. In 1912, the Marryots' eldest son, Edward, and his bride Edith drown while on their honeymoon voyage on the *Titanic*. The younger son, Joey, serves in the army in the Great War, has a romance with Fanny Bridges, the Bridges's daughter, now a dancer, and is killed just before the Armistice. A montage of scenes depicts the anxieties of the 1920s. But the film, like the play, ends with Jane delivering her New Year's Eve toast to the future.

The Boer War and the death of the Queen are seen as the end of an era of security and self-confidence, one in which master and servant both fight for their country in South Africa and in which the family and the servants equally mourn Queen Victoria's passing. But after the war, encapsulating the new social mobility, the Bridges leave service to run a pub, Alfred takes to drink and is knocked down and killed in the street, and Ellen becomes a vulgar, snobbish parvenu, scheming to secure the marriage of Joey and Fanny. The narrative implies that the Bridges were happier and better off in service.

The music, as Coward recalled, is integral to the whole project, triggering memories, emotional responses and involvement in the film–play. *Land of Hope and Glory* is played behind the opening titles and then, on the departure of the CIV and the troopship, *Soldiers of the Queen*, *When Johnny Comes Marching Home* and *Auld Lang Syne*. The playing of *Soldiers of the Queen* and *Dolly Gray* on barrel organs in the street becomes intolerable to Jane as she awaits news of Mafeking, where her brother is trapped with the defenders and to whose relief Robert is marching.

Jane is attending a performance of a typical turn of the century musical comedy when news of the Relief of Mafeking is announced. There is a brilliant and accurate recreation of a George Edwardes-type show, featuring Coward's own pastiche songs *The Girls of the CIV* and *Lover of My Dreams*. At the Edwardian seaside, where the Marryots encounter the Bridges, the pierrots perform *I Do Like to Be Beside the Seaside* and *Take Me Back to Yorkshire*. Edith and Edward on board the *Titanic* for their honeymoon are accompanied to the strains of *Nearer, My God, to Thee*, to the American setting by Lowell Mason. As war breaks out in 1914, we see music-hall recruiting songs performed: *On Sunday I Walk Out With a Soldier* and *We Don't Want to Lose You*.

The war itself was represented by a graphic and powerful montage sequence – an endless procession of soldiers marches through an increasingly ravaged landscape to familiar marching songs, *Tipperary*, *Pack Up Your Troubles*, *Keep the Home Fires Burning*. Ironically intercut are the recruiting songs, the face of the music-hall singer in close-up, as more and more of the soldiers fall dead or wounded. The marching songs are drowned out by a cacophonous battle symphony which interweaves *The British Grenadiers*, the *Marseillaise* and *Yankee Doodle Dandy*, as the years flash past: 1914, 1915, 1916, 1917, 1918. Coward noted sadly that the irony of the war scenes was lost on the critics in the patriotic atmosphere of 1931.[33] The war ends with an Armistice Day sequence where, amid the tumult of the cheering crowds and to the strains of *Land of Hope and Glory*, Jane wanders brokenly mourning her dead son.

The 1920s is represented by a montage of fruitless peace conferences, re-armament, labour agitation, the preaching of atheism, intercut with poignant shots of blinded ex-soldiers basket-weaving and row upon row of white crosses in a war graves' cemetery. Fanny sings *Twentieth Century Blues*. But this fades as New Year approaches, the crowds sing *Auld Lang Syne* and the national anthem, and Jane proposes her toast: 'Let's drink to the hope that one day this country of ours, which we love so much, will find dignity and greatness and peace again'.

HMV issued both orchestral and vocal selections of the songs from *Cavalcade*. Coward introduced the orchestral selection with the words: 'These tunes are so inextricably woven into the pattern of the nation's history that no Englishman can listen to them without a strange pride and tenderness.'

The last film in Hollywood's imperial cycle was the appropriately named *Sundown* (1941), a taut and fast-moving thriller directed by Henry Hathaway, who had made the first film in the cycle, *Lives of a Bengal Lancer*. As in that film, American identification figures have been provided for the American audience. The hero, Bill Crawford (Bruce Cabot), a District Commissioner near the Kenyan border, is a Canadian from Ottawa, and he is assisted by the veteran American white hunter Dewey (Harry Carey). The film centres on the uncovering of a Nazi plot to run guns to the Shenzi tribe and to stir up rebellion against the British. The plot is scotched by a band of allies, comprising of the Canadian Crawford, the American Dewey, the British Major Coombes (George Sanders), who is killed, and the mysterious Zia (Gene Tierney), believed to be Arab, but in fact a half-French, half-English undercover agent.

Although there is a rather perfunctory march to accompany the patrol of the King's African Rifles, and there are bugle calls for *Retreat* and *Last Post*, the score by Miklos Rosza is almost wholly non-European, reinforcing the innate exoticism of the story. Much of the score comprises native music, which Rosza carefully researched. Native drums and African chants provide much of the background. War drums are used to send a signal to the British forces to attack the gunrunners' lair. There is sinister barbaric music for the Shenzi and a sinuous Oriental theme for Zia, maintaining musically the narrative fiction that she is an Arab. But Rosza used a musical saw to create the eerie feeling necessary in a premonition of death sequence. The whole story is set, like *Stanley and Livingstone*, in a Christian context. Dying

Coombes tells Crawford: 'The church and the army, they're both the basis of civilization: the church holds it together, the army defends it and the Crawfords make it good.' The film ends in a bomb-damaged church in London where the choir sings *Oh God, Our Help in Ages Past* and Bishop Coombes, having married Crawford and Zia, reads a poem sent him by his dead son, urging the maintenance of the faith until England wins. Poetry again.

There was a post-war imperial cycle in Hollywood but the films were now consciously historical rather than contemporary adventures. MGM produced a trio of Indian Empire films. There had long been plans to film Kipling's *Kim*, the story of the orphan boy torn between the Buddhist life of contemplation and meditation, personified by the Lama, and 'The Great Game', the English life of a secret service agent defending India against tribal unrest and personified by Mahbub Ali, Afghan horsetrader and secret agent. It finally reached the screen in 1951 after Indian Independence when, as the narrator tells us, the British Raj was 'already part of a legendary past'. It was a serviceable but not outstanding production, shot partly in India (Jaipur and Bundi) and partly in Hollywood, directed by Victor Saville and starring Dean Stockwell as Kim, Errol Flynn as Mahbub Ali and Paul Lukas as the Lama. It was very lightly scored by André Previn, who later with some justice described his score as 'expendable'.[34] It is mainly ethnic Indian music over the travelling scenes and the scenes of Lurgan training Kim for espionage duties, a few dramatic chords over the death of the Lama and the traditional tune *D'Ye Ken John Peel* in march-time to accompany scenes of the British regiment on the march.

Producer Pandro S. Berman, who, when he was at RKO, had overseen production of *Gunga Din*, tried to repeat its success at MGM in *Soldiers Three*, directed by Tay Garnett in 1951, and failed miserably. Where *Gunga Din* kept the balance between comedy and action adventure, *Soldiers Three*, apart from a rousing finale when Indian rebels seize the fort and are themselves besieged by the regiment under Colonel Brunswick, settles for broad knockabout farce, which is overdone and heavy-handed. The soldiers, all privates and long-serving members of the Rutlands, are all inferior to their spirited predecessors in *Gunga Din*. As Cockney Private Archibald Ackroyd, Stewart Granger does a hamfisted impersonation of Cary Grant's Sergeant Archie Cutter; Robert Newton's Private Bill Sikes is a re-run of his west country Long John Silver without the crutch; and Cyril Cusack's Private Denis Malloy is the traditional stage Irishman, full of booze and blarney. While their regiment marches back and forth across India, they spend their time boozing, brawling and scrimshanking; until at the end they help put down the uprising by Indian rebels and save the career of Colonel Brunswick (Walter Pidgeon, doing an unconvincing impersonation of C. Aubrey Smith).

Adolph Deutsch's lively score begins with a title sequence which, mingling an Irish jig and a cheerful march, sets the tone for the film. In the opening scene, the soldiers three pick a fight with kilted Highlanders and demolish a bar to the mingled strains of *With a Hundred Pipers and All, and All*, *The Campbells are Coming* and *Come Landlord, Fill the Flowing Bowl*. The latter tune, a musical symbol of the habitual drunkenness of the three heroes, is a recurrent theme. As the regiment marches back and forth *One Hundred Pipers* and an original rousing march by Deutsch are played.

When Brunswick's adjutant Captain Pindenny (David Niven) leads the soldiers on a raid to recover guns stolen by the Indians, and they lose their clothes crossing a river and have to don women's dresses, there is the musical equivalent of laughter on the soundtrack. They return to camp in the dresses to *Come Landlord, Fill the Flowing Bowl* in march-time. There is ethnic Indian music over scenes of Indian town life and shops; menacing mood music over the fort at night; attack music for the assault on the fort and again *Come Landlord* over the finale.

Allan Davis's *Rogues March* (1952) utilized Geoffrey Barkas's spectacular battle footage shot on location at the Khyber Pass in the 1930s for an uncompleted Gaumont British Kipling epic *Soldiers Three*.[35] It reworks the plot of *The Four Feathers* with two officers the rivals for the Major's daughter (Janice Rule). She agrees to marry one of them, Dion Lenbridge (Peter Lawford), who is then disgraced and enlists in the army as a private. He saves the life of his rival (Richard Greene), brings the news of the siege of the British garrison to headquarters and distinguishes himself in the final battle. Consequently he is restored to his rank and reunited with his girl. Like *Kim*, it has the added dimension of Russian intrigue to stir up Afghans against the British, a direct reference to the Cold War, which probably explains Hollywood's revived interest in the Raj.

The *Rogues March*, a surprisingly cheerful tune for such a solemn occasion as the drumming out of a traitor, is played in the introductory scene and over the final credits by a military band, and by drums and fifes over the scene of Dion being drummed out of the regiment. No composer is credited, and aside from some original music over the battle scenes, probably taken from the MGM musical library, the music is mainly traditional and likely to have been the work of musical director Alberto Columbo. *The Vicar of Bray* is played over the scenes of the lovers meeting and Dion proposing; *The Girl I Left Behind Me* and *Auld Lang Syne* over scenes of the departure of the troopship for India; *D'Ye Ken John Peel* over the entraining of the troops; and *Rose of Tralee* and *Little Brown Jug* at Queen Victoria's Birthday Ball.

British cinema, too, produced its imperial epics and its imperial scores. All the great British producers contributed to the 1930s' cycle, Alexander Korda at London Films, Michael Balcon at Gaumont British and Herbert Wilcox at RKO Radio Pictures. Balcon's imperial trilogy, *Rhodes of Africa* (1936), *The Great Barrier* (1936) and *King Solomon's Mines* (1937), is interesting because it deals with the economic aspects of Empire. This is worth noting, because we sometimes get the impression, due to the overwhelming military emphasis of Hollywood's imperial epics, that Empire films were about India, the army and the scarlet and gold heroics of the north-west frontier.

Rhodes of Africa, directed by Berthold Viertel, is a whitewashing biographical film about Cecil Rhodes, stressing his imperialist vision and his paternalistic concern for the natives. *The Great Barrier* is the story of the building of the Canadian Pacific Railway with heroic feats of exploration and engineering and a personal story of the redemption of two wastrels by work and sacrifice. *King Solomon's Mines* retells the classic Rider Haggard tale of the search for the legendary diamond mines in Central Africa. All three look back to the pioneering days of exploration, construction and profit, construed and legitimized as adventure. They evoke the romance of engineering, the romance of exploration, the romance of profit, and take care, at least in the first two cases, to stress the imperial dimension – Rhodes acquires his diamond mines in pursuit of his dream of an Africa united under British rule and the Canadian Pacific Railway is built to ensure that British Columbia remains with Canada.

Writing in 1948, Louis Levy, musical director on *Rhodes* and *The Great Barrier*, declared: 'These were semi-documentaries in the truest sense, and they place a great responsibility on the musical creator . . . it was extremely difficult to capture the true spirit of the film and to create and record music of the necessary degree of authenticity'. But he professed himself delighted with the music provided.

> Walter Huston's great role as Rhodes himself was supported, I like to feel, by accurate period music entirely in the theme of this fine colonial film. I can only say that I have had many hundreds of letters from South Africans who were charmed not only with the recreation of the man whom they loved so much, but with the music which helped the emotional appeal.[36]

In fact, the music for *Rhodes* is unremarkable, certainly by comparison with the lush Hollywood scores. *Rhodes* is quite lightly scored by the uncredited Hubert Bath. There is chase music over the Diamond Rush, native drums and Matabele chants as an ox-wagon is surrounded. There is a war dance of the young Matabele and trumpets versus native chants over the confrontation of the Pioneers and the Matabele. The pioneer column sets out to an heroic, jaunty march, punctuated by fanfares. The early part of the march is re-run, speeded up, over the Jameson Raid. This piece enjoyed an independent existence later outside the film as *The Empire Builders March*. Also as Jameson's men wait to begin their raid, they sing the music-hall song *Comrades*, which will have been familiar to audiences, and which also acknowledges music-hall imperialism.

Of *The Great Barrier*, Levy proudly writes: 'In the sweep of its story, the brilliance of its music, and the magnificence of its settings, *The Great Barrier* is a picture worthy in every way of the subject it portrays.'[37] Once again Hubert Bath scored the film but neither film nor score live up to Levy's retrospective accolade. The film opens and closes with *The Maple Leaf Forever*, to establish its Canadian locale. There is the cheery workers' marching song *To Work Up in the Rockies on the CPR*; heroic music over an expedition to find a pass across the mountains; and a romantic theme over the love scenes of Hickey and Mary. But perhaps the most interesting feature of the Gaumont British approach is Levy's insistence that the films are semi-documentary and his desire for authenticity, which marks the British films out from their Hollywood counterparts with their nineteenth-century musical romanticism.

King Solomon's Mines, directed by Robert Stevenson, was primarily a vehicle for Paul Robeson, whose character Umbopa, unlike in the book and the later Hollywood film versions, becomes the leading figure in the story. He is not only the mentor, protector, guide and adviser of the English explorers but he uses them to further his own restoration to the throne of his people; and the film ends with the whites leaving and Umbopa remaining as King of an independent black country. The score consists largely of three songs for Robeson, composed by Mischa Spoliansky with lyrics by Eric Maschwitz. They are magnificently sung by Robeson and confirm his centrality to the story. *The Wagon Song* is sung on the trek to the mountains; the majestic *Climbing Up* during the ascent of the mountains; and the war song *Kukuana*, complete with chants and drums, is sung as he rallies his men for battle with the usurper King Twala.

Alexander Korda's trilogy, directed by his brother Zoltan, was squarely about the defence and administration of Empire, both civil and military. The plots of all three films were strikingly similar. In *Sanders of the River* (1935), District Commissioner Sanders (Leslie

Banks) puts down a native uprising in Nigeria and rescues his faithful ally Chief Bosambo (Paul Robeson) from the evil King Mofalaba, installing him in Mofalaba's place. In *The Drum* (1938), Captain Carruthers (Roger Livesey) joins forces with the Indian Prince Azim (Sabu) to put down an uprising led by his uncle, the wicked Ghul Khan. In *The Four Feathers* (1939), a disgraced British officer Harry Faversham (John Clements) redeems his honour, assisted at the end by pro-British Chieftain Karaga Pasha, by helping to put down the revolt of the Khalifa in the Sudan and avenge the murder of General Gordon.

The score of *Sanders of the River* by the Russian Mischa Spoliansky, consists largely of native chants, recorded on location during the shooting of documentary footage for the film. There were three songs in which native chants were Westernized by Spoliansky and provided with lyrics by Arthur Wimperis. The documentary sequences include the Nuptial Dance for the Ochori Wedding sequence and the Lion Dance when the old King's warriors prepare for battle. Robeson, who is top-billed, sings – over the credits and during the film – *The Canoe Song*, with its refrain 'Ayee-oko' which hymns the Empire-building hero Commissioner Sanders:

> Sandi the strong, Sandi the wise
> Righter of wrong, hater of lies
> Laughed as he fought, worked as he played
> As he taught let it be made.

Robeson also sings *The Killing Song* as he initiates his son into warrior manhood: 'And smash, smite, slash, fight and slay'. Nina Mae McKinney as Lilongo, Bosambo's wife, sings the gentle and lilting *Congo Lullaby*: 'My little black dove, curl up in your nest of love.' Although Robeson retrospectively disowned the film as imperialist propaganda, his virile, charismatic and engaging performance as Sanders's loyal ally, together with the superbly performed songs, is a powerful boost to that same British imperialism.

The Drum, shot partly on location in Chitral on the north-west frontier, and based on A.E.W. Mason's novella, was clearly influenced by *Lives of a Bengal Lancer*. They share a similar opening (army patrol ambushed by tribesmen); the theme of a confederacy of border tribes against the British; polo match; Russian intrigue; and British officers disguising as natives to get information. But it adds a distinctively British theme: just as the friendship of Sanders and Bosambo, men of two races, underpins British rule in Africa, so the friendship of Indian boy Prince Azim and Cockney drummer boy Bill Holder justifies British rule in India.

Music itself is integral to the story, as Bill Holder gives Azim a personal drum signal, and he plays it to alert the British to an impending attack. Behind the credits there are nineteenth-century battle paintings, and John Greenwood's score mingles an Oriental theme and an Elgarian march, and a globe of the world spins, highlighting the Empire in pink and to minor-key variations of *Rule, Britannia*. Thereafter the film itself features a variety of musical forms and idioms. Bugle calls punctuate the film and pipes are prominent. Pipers lead the British mission into Tokot with *Campbellton Loch*. Scots soldiers at the Residency sing *Loch Lomond*, conveying the exiles' feeling when abroad. Fifes and drums lead the expeditionary force of British and Indian troops. There is genuine Indian music in Peshawar Bazaar and Ghul Khan's Palace. There is modern dance music played at the Governor's Ball and Mrs Carruthers (Valerie Hobson) sings *A Penny for Your Thoughts* at the British Residency in Tokot, just before Zarrullah's severed head is thrown through the window.

All of this stresses the mingling and the clash of different cultures. The United Kingdom dimension to the Empire is clearly stressed by the presence of English Captain Carruthers, the Irish Doctor Murphy and the Scots regiment. In a superb scene, the scarlet-clad officers toast the King–Emperor, amid the skirl of the pipes, and with the Pipe Major proposing the toast in Gaelic.

Perhaps the finest score for a Korda imperialist film, however, was the one provided by Miklos Rosza for *The Four Feathers*. At that time Rosza came closer than any other film composer working in Britain to matching the full Hollywood romantic style, and he went on to enjoy a long and distinguished career in American cinema. Ironically, he almost did not get the job. London Films' Musical Director Muir Mathieson did not think him capable of providing the score for such a British subject but Zoltan Korda insisted on him. Rosza repaid him with a score rich in atmosphere and dramatic power that contributed to the success of a film which garnered critical praise on both sides of the Atlantic. The *New York Times*, calling the film 'an imperialist symphony', observed:

> Mr. Korda, the Kipling of the kinema, has retaken the already twice-filmed *Four Feathers* of novelist A.E.W. Mason – and a fine stirring, gorgeously Technicolored job he has made of it too. In a week rich in action epics, African locales and good remakes, Mr. Korda has managed to plant the British flag higher than all the rest.[38]

The classic A.E.W. Mason story concerns Lt Harry Faversham of the Royal North Surrey regiment who resigns his commission on the eve of Kitchener's expedition to retake the Sudan in 1898. He is given four white feathers of cowardice by three brother officers and the woman he loves, Ethne Burroughs. Determined to prove himself, he goes out to the Sudan disguised as a native, redeems his honour, rescues the three officers and is united with Ethne at the end.

Harry learns the meaning of imperial duty when, in the key ideological scene of the film, Ethne expresses her horror at his decision to resign his commission and explains that they are not free to act as they might wish. They were born into a tradition, a code which they must obey because the pride and happiness of everyone around them depends on it. But what makes the film more complex, profound and tragic than either *Sanders* or *The Drum* is the subplot, the story of Captain Durrance, who is in a sense the real hero of the film, and is superbly played by Ralph Richardson. For where Harry wins everything, Durrance loses everything (his sight, his army career and the woman he loves – Ethne). His stoical acceptance of his fate demonstrates even more effectively than Harry's desert adventures the nature and strength of the imperial character.

Rosza's score for the film was the first of what he was later to call his Oriental period and which saw him score in rapid succession *The Four Feathers* (1939), *The Thief of Bagdad* (1940), *Sundown* (1941), *The Jungle Book* (1942) and *Sahara* (1943). Rosza studied indigenous music in the British Museum before setting out to create his score, and this influenced the whole flavour and tonal colouring of *The Four Feathers*.[39] The title music includes the main themes: the barbaric might of the dervish army, the romantic theme for Ethne, and an Oriental tune on flute and strings for Egypt. These recur with variations in mood and tempo throughout. But the dervish army theme, with its galloping rhythm and the use of trumpets, flute and cymbals, is the most effective of these. The British Museum studies yielded a traditional Sudanese boatman's song which is chanted by two choruses as background to the memorable scene of boats being hauled up the Nile. Elsewhere in the film specific passages heighten the emotion and atmosphere of key scenes. When young Harry retires to bed through the gallery hung with portraits of his military ancestors, distant, almost ghostly, trumpets sound and an eerie insistent theme suggests the weight of the past upon his shoulders. Period waltzes and polkas provide the background for Ethne's Twenty-First Birthday Ball. Particularly impressive is the music for the sequence in which Durrance loses his helmet, gets sunstroke and goes blind. As he stumbles helplessly among the rocks, he is accompanied by a pounding, dark-toned, passage of music with a sudden crash on an anvil to indicate the moment of irretrievable sight-loss. Later there is a delicately impressionistic passage evoking the changing moods of desert and river as the blinded Durrance is led to safety by the disguised Harry.

The whole score helps to emphasize the exotic background and the emotions at play among the characters. The more traditional British atmosphere is carried within the film by music played on screen: *The Girl I Left Behind Me* and *The British Grenadiers* played by bands accompanying British troops to their embarkation; *Auld Lang Syne* sung as the troopship departs; and traditional military marches played as Kitchener reviews the troops.

Herbert Wilcox had long cherished the idea of a film on the life of Queen Victoria. But the censors forbade it until the death of King George V. King Edward VIII personally sanctioned the idea, probably because his father had opposed it. But Wilcox had serious problems. His partners in Herbert Wilcox Productions, C.M. Woolf and his brother Maurice, were flatly opposed to the idea and there was extensive criticism of Wilcox's determination to cast Anna Neagle, his protégée and later his wife, as Victoria. So Wilcox bought out his partners, raised £100, 000, did a distribution deal with RKO Radio Pictures and acquired studio space at Denham Studios on credit from Alexander Korda. No royal locations were made available and the film was shot in five weeks flat. Its imperial significance is emphasized by the fact that its world première was held in Ottawa. Anna and Herbert were guests at a banquet hosted by the Governor-General, Lord Tweedsmuir (John Buchan), and were escorted by the Royal Canadian Mounted Police from Government House to the cinema. The film won the Gold Cup of All Nations at the Venice Film festival, was hailed by the press and was a box office hit. Wilcox immediately made a sequel in Technicolor, *Sixty Glorious Years*. He invited Sir Robert Vansittart of the Foreign Office to collaborate on the script and Vansittart acted as an intermediary with the Palace, securing permission for Wilcox to shoot scenes at Buckingham Palace, Windsor Castle, Balmoral, St James's Palace and Osborne. Vansittart said to Wilcox, in the wake of Munich: 'Wilcox, you've made a film that is a warm tribute to the British Empire and at a time when the first step has been shamefully taken to bring about its disintegration.'[40]

Victoria the Great is largely concerned with the first half of the reign, its touching and amusing picture of royal domestic bliss undeniably inspired by Laurence Housman's play *Victoria Regina*. *Victoria the Great* covers her proclamation, Coronation, courtship and marriage and deals largely with her partnership with Prince Albert in the administration of affairs. Victoria and Albert back Sir Robert Peel in his bid to repeal the Corn Laws so that the people can have bread, even though powerful vested interests and large sections of Peel's own party oppose it. Victoria and Albert stand for peace and oppose Palmerston's warlike policy, preventing him from provoking war with the United

States. But Albert dies and Victoria goes into seclusion, emerging to become Empress of India in 1877. Accepting the title, surrounded by her Indian Princes, Governor-Generals and Cecil Rhodes, she makes a speech, saying that it is her greatest wish to see her new subjects on an equality with the other subjects of the crown. She greets the assembled representatives of the Empire and tells them that she feels neither a Queen nor an Empress, but rather the mother or grandmother of a great family, and that is the proudest title of all: 'For the British Empire is one of the greatest families of mankind, which if it remains true to the principles on which it was founded: democracy, tolerance, freedom, may well move the destinies of the whole world.' This of course assumes that the British Empire was founded on the principles stated, which is debatable as far as history is concerned, but is central to the myth. The speech scene is the film's climax. The next scene is the last. The Queen at the steps of St Paul's acknowledges the cheers of her subjects on the occasion of her Diamond Jubilee. 'May God bless all my people', she declares. From black and white, the film bursts into Technicolor for the proclamation of Victoria as Empress of India, symbolizing the way in which the monochrome of everyday life was imbued with vividness, splendour and colour by the acquisition of Empire.

The film is a classic exercise in intertextuality. The music was arranged by Anthony Collins and the film draws on music, painting and literature to create its portrait of Victoria's reign. For her accession the film 'realizes' H.T. Wells's *Victoria Regina*, the celebrated painting in which Victoria in white, hair streaming down her back, receives news of her accession from the Archbishop of Canterbury and the Lord Chamberlain. The Coronation scene, 'realizing' Sir George Hayter's painting, incorporates actual music from Victoria's Coronation, including Handel's *Gloria* and Attwood's *The Queen Shall Rejoice*. Behind the Wedding of Victoria and Albert and subsequent domestic scenes, we hear Mendelssohn's *On Wings of Song*, a favourite tune of theirs. *God Bless the Prince of Wales* accompanies the birth of the Prince of Wales in 1848. Their departure on honeymoon on one of the new steam trains is accompanied by *The Homage March* from Grieg's *Sigurd Jorsalfar* suite. The Queen reads *Oliver Twist* and learns about the living conditions of her subjects. At Balmoral, with pipes playing, she dances an eightsome reel. Elgar's *Coronation Ode* is anachronistically played over the 1877 proclamation of Victoria as Empress of India and *Land of Hope and Glory* is sung over the final credits, evidence of the fact that by 1937 Elgar was indelibly associated with Empire in the popular mind. *Soldiers of the Queen* and *God Save the Queen* are deployed for the Diamond Jubilee.

Sixty Glorious Years chronicled Victoria's marriage and family life, the opening of the Great Exhibition, the repeal of the Corn Laws, the purchase of the Suez Canal, the Crimean War, the death of the Prince Consort, the retirement at Windsor, the death of Gordon at Khartoum, the Diamond Jubilee and the death of the old Queen. But where *Victoria the Great* had tended to concentrate on the relationship of Victoria and Albert, *Sixty Glorious Years* broadened the picture to become more of a portrait of the age, or those aspects of the age that fitted the myth. Once again the music was arranged by Anthony Collins and utilized much contemporary music, and the film is another example of intertextuality. It is linked by extracts from the Queen's diary, and there are quotations from Victorian poetry flashed up as titles. The whole gives the effect of a lavish pageant.

Again Mendelssohn's *On Wings of Song* accompanies scenes of the domestic bliss of the royal couple. Collins cheekily sets *Deutschland, Deutschland über alles* in waltz-time – and wholly anachronistically – as Albert and Ernest leave Saxe-Coburg Gotha for England. Strauss waltzes are played at the reception for the weddings of Victoria and Albert, and of Victoria, the Princess Royal, and Frederick, Crown Prince of Prussia. A passage from Dickens's *Sketches by Boz* about poverty in the slums is put onto the screen. The scene of the Opening of the Great Exhibition is a recreation of the official painting of the event by H.C. Selous. A Scottish folk-song is sung over scenes of the Highland Games at Balmoral. The Charge of the Light Brigade is staged with lines from Tennyson's poem flashed up on the screen, as in the Warner Brothers' film, though the charge wholly lacks the dynamic cutting and angle change of the Michael Curtiz epic. Queen Victoria visits her soldiers in a realization of Jerry Barrett's painting *Queen Victoria's First Visit to Her Wounded Soldiers*, a picture much reproduced in engravings.[41] Browning's lines 'Grow old along with me, the best is yet to be' ironically presages the death of the Prince Consort. Princess Beatrice plays Bach's *Jesu, Joy of Man's Desiring* on the organ while Albert lies dying. There is a strong Scottish element to stress the UK dimension (Highland Games, General Gordon and the Queen's servants Maggie and John Brown speaking with Scottish accents). There is a 'realization' of G.W. Joy's painting of the death of General Gordon. In 1895 Kitchener enters Khartoum after Omdurman, with Lionel Monckton's *Soldiers in the Park* playing. The film realizes G. Amato's painting of the jubilee procession at St Paul's. When it comes to the Diamond Jubilee in 1897, the lines flashed up are the uncredited 'From pole to pole a mighty shout/ Echoed from sea to sea/ For sixty glorious years has she reigned.' In the streets, black-faced minstrels sing *It Is the Navy, the British Navy* as the Queen leaves for St Paul's; *Sol-*

diers of the Queen is played during the procession; *O God, Our Help in Ages Past* is sung at St Paul's and *Land of Hope and Glory* as she returns to the Palace, a perfect musical encapsulation of the serious and the popular, the military and the Protestant, in the imperial ethos.

In 1901, the nation waits as the Queen is dying. 'Won't it seem funny without the Queen', says a man in the street. Wilcox inserted this little piece of oral history from personal experience, recalling a costermonger saying it to him as he bought a newspaper from him in 1901.[42] Dying, the Queen has a vision of her Coronation to the strains of *God Save the Queen*. Sullivan's *In Memoriam* is played over the coffin with the lines from Kipling's *Recessional* – 'The Captains and the Kings depart . . .' – flashed up. Wilcox's film is a perfect distillation of the popular memory of the Victorian Age as seen from 1938, involving Sullivan, Mendelssohn and Elgar, Dickens, Kipling, Tennyson and Browning, music-hall songs, hymns and familiar representational paintings. It both plays to and reinforces the popular memory.

The Second World War ended the imperial film cycle in Britain and America. The war promoted a new dominant ethos, eclipsing imperialism and rendering imperial epics unfashionable. The war was promoted as a war for democracy, a crusade which preached racial equality, self-determination and freedom. Its enemies were the cruel and racist tyrannies of the Third Reich and the Italian and Japanese Empires. It would be wrong to equate in any way the British Empire with the Axis powers. But they did share a fundamental belief in a racial hierarchy, an idea at odds with the Allied principle of the brotherhood of man and democratic government. This became an embarrassment when expressed in Hollywood films at a time when, for instance, India's role as a bulwark against Japanese aggression in Asia was crucial. Consequently the American Office of War Information scotched MGM's plans for a film version of Kipling's *Kim* and banned re-issues of *Gunga Din* and *The Real Glory*, a celebration of American imperialism in the Philippines.

In Britain, at the outbreak of war, comparatively little had been done by way of social and economic development to prepare the African colonies for the eventual independence that was always the stated aim of British colonial policy. This was due partly to economic restraint imposed by the Treasury and partly to the entrenched idea that nothing should be done that would interfere with the structures and practices of native life. But once war broke out, it became necessary to counter German propaganda about Britain's 'cruel and exploitative Empire' by projecting the image of a beneficent and constructive imperialism. Since this needed to be based on concrete reality, a positive programme of colonial development and welfare was initiated by the 1940 Colonial Development Act.

Even more pressing was the need to satisfy the Americans about the progress of the colonies towards independence. The war aims of the Allies, as embodied in the Atlantic Charter, included self-determination for all nations, and that view produced the attitude outlined by the American Under-Secretary of State Sumner Welles in 1942: 'The age of Imperialism is dead. The right of people to their freedom must be recognized. The principles of the Atlantic Charter must be guaranteed.'[43]

The Colonial Office had come to terms with the new imperative and by mid-1942 had evolved the concept of 'partnership' to replace the old idea of 'trusteeship', equality rather than dependence, and this began to be used regularly in public pronouncements. In July 1945, the Colonial Secretary Oliver Stanley made a statement of colonial war aims in the Commons, containing a specific pledge 'to guide colonial peoples along the road to self-government within the framework of the British Empire'.[44] Thus economic and social progress for the colonies became a goal recognized by all major political parties. But as Lee and Petter remark: 'The partnership doctrine sought to make dependence more palatable by portraying the colonial Empire as a system of co-operation animated by a desire for social and economic reform rather than a system of rule animated by a desire for good government.'[45]

The Colonial Office was aware of the need for positive propaganda to promote its new policy and commitment both at home and abroad. Public Relations Officer Noel Sabine decided on a major commercial feature film as the best vehicle. The task was passed to the Ministry of Information which commissioned a screen story from journalist E. Arnot Robertson to illustrate the policy.[46] The Ministry secured the co-operation of Two Cities Films, providing them with the story, official help and facilities in return for the right to approve the finished product. The result was the film *Men of Two Worlds*, which was written by Thorold Dickinson, Herbert Victor and Joyce Cary based on Robertson's outline. It was directed by Dickinson. But a twelve-week location trip to Tanganyika to shoot scenes resulted in only ten minutes of usable footage, as the Technicolor filmstock they were using deteriorated before it could be processed. The rest of the film was shot at Denham Studios.

Peter Noble, in his history of blacks in film, published in 1947, hailed *Men of Two Worlds* as 'historic' and 'revolutionary', a landmark in the mature and unpatronizing depiction of blacks. Dickinson was reported as believing that the film would be 'a potent weapon against discrimination'.[47] But the film is not really a race relations tract. There is no sign of white prejudice against Kisenga throughout the film. Any discrimination he suffers comes from his own people. The film is much more obviously a potent vindication of British colonial policy, which is what is was designed to be.

The basic theme of the film is the age-old conflict between back-wardness reinforced by superstition and progress via education. The characters are simply types, representing the different black and white viewpoints. The action of the film centres on the Government's wish to move the Litu tribe from their tsetse-fly infested tribal homeland to a new settlement area, part of a major programme aimed at elimi-nating sleeping sickness. The task of persuading the Litu to move is given to Kisenga (Robert Adams), who after fifteen years in Europe as pianist and composer returns to East Africa as a teacher. He is opposed by the Witchdoctor Magole (Orlando Martins), who uses all his powers to block the move. The film details the battle of wills between them. Magole wills Kisenga's father to die when he falls ill, thus discredit-ing the English doctor, Catherine Munro (Phyllis Calvert), who has treated him. Kisenga is shunned by the villagers, denounced by his sister and his mother and ordered to leave by the Chief. But he chal-lenges Magole to kill him, and the resolution of the action comes when Kisenga survives the challenge. Magole's influence is destroyed and the tribe is moved.

But Kisenga only survives the conflict because of the intervention of District Commissioner Randall (Eric Portman). Ill and depressed, haunted by guilt for his father's death, succumbing to superstitious fatalism, Kisenga is on the point of giving up when Randall saves him. He wills Magole to live and enlists the help of the local children to sing his chorale. Randall, shrewd, wise, experienced, humane, is the white father figure, the classic embodiment of altruistic imperialism. He incarnates the sensible and forward-looking policy of the Colonial Office. The obvious moral is that the whites still have a vital role to play in Africa, the white man's burden lives on, and Randall is really a latter-day Sanders of the River.

Music is integral to the film. In the original draft of the story Kisenga was a student. It was Dickinson's idea to make him a pianist and composer. He took this decision partly to help make the propa-ganda more palatable. He may also have noted the current vogue for concerto themes in films (the *Warsaw Concerto* in *Dangerous Moon-light*, the *Cornish Rhapsody* in *Love Story*, *The Dream of Olwen* in *While I Live*). He was also himself deeply fond of classical music.

Dickinson had the good fortune to secure the services of Sir Arthur

Bliss. Bliss found Dickinson 'a man of imagination, sensitive to music, and serious in aim' and the project 'rewarding'.[48] Bliss was given a set of recordings of African dances and songs made in Tanganyika by Austrian Jewish musicologist Hans Cory and utilized them as the basis of what John Huntley was to call in his book on British film music 'one of the finest film music works ever written'.[49]

One of the most important elements of the score is *Baraza*, a concert piece for piano, orchestra and male chorus, the composition of Kisenga, which he is first heard playing in the National Gallery in London in 1944. The word *Baraza* is Swahili, and means a discussion at a tribal council meeting. It includes a dialogue between trumpets and piano, Swahili chants from the male chorus and a thrilling piano cadenza based on drum rhythms, the whole piece consistently blending African themes and rhythms with European techniques and musical elaborations. Musically it also encapsulates the nature of the *Baraza*, the interchange of arguments and ideas, developing from reasoned and thoughtful discussion to passionate disagreement.

The credits unfold to the sound of African drums and a simple African folk-song sung by a female voice. With a sudden crash a discordant *agitato* piece of orchestral music bursts in to symbolize conflict and contrast. After the National Gallery performance of *Baraza*, Kisenga flies to Tanganyika and over this coming home sequence, with its aerial views of Mount Kilimanjaro, Bliss provides music that is measured and reflective, lyrical and majestic, balancing the joy of homecoming with the awareness of the magnitude of the work to be undertaken.

When the two non-professional Africans playing Kisenga's parents proved unable to produce the necessary emotions for their reunion with Kisenga on his return, Dickinson suggested that Bliss convey the emotion in his music, and the composer provided a passage of positive, joyous, tuneful music for the scene. But it is banked down so much behind the dialogue that it can barely be heard.

The music becomes central to the on-screen action when Kisenga composes a chorale for the children to sing, based on the folk-song heard behind the credits. It is performed with flute and xylophone accompaniment. Later, Randall and Kisenga play the tune side by side at the piano, their alliance visibly and aurally cemented by the music. The main tune from the chorale recurs repeatedly, slowly and threateningly, as Kisenga's terror of Magole grows, and triumphantly at the end, when he overcomes it.

Magole's appearances and actions are accompanied by a menacing theme, strongly reminiscent of 'the wandering sickness' music in Bliss's *Things to Come* score. There is a reminder of Western influence when, at the opening of the new school, the native band plays *Daisy, Daisy, Give Me Your Answer Do* and *Men of Harlech*.

Not only does the music play a key part in the action of the film, it also dictated the look of the film. The *Baraza* piece was completed and recorded before the opening concert sequence was shot, and Dickinson tailored the rhythm of his shooting and editing to the structure of the music, establishing the organic relationship between the members of the orchestra, the orchestra and the audience and of both with the black pianist.

Towards the end, in an imaginative hallucination sequence, shot with a tilted camera and Vaselined lens, Dickinson visually demonstrates Kisenga's fears (Magole's magic) and guilt (responsibility for his father's death), setting up a powerful conflict, mirrored in the music in the clash between the primitive beat of the tribal drums, representing his African heritage, and the European training.

But finally, when Randall brings in the children's choir to sing Kisenga's chorale and after Magole orders them away, Kisenga's sister and other loyal friends take up the song, Kisenga revives and survives. The final message is that music can heal and unify. The tribe depart to their new land to a triumphant choral finale.

Sadly, when the film was released in 1946, it was greeted by the English critics as a well-meaning but tedious bore, and several countries refused to distribute it. There was, however, praise for Bliss's score and a recording of *Baraza*, with Eileen Joyce (who played it for the film soundtrack) as soloist, was well-received, when issued in 1946.

After the war, the retreat from Empire began. India was granted independence in 1947; Britain withdrew from Palestine; uprisings convulsed Kenya, Malaya and Cyprus; and the so-called wind of change swept away Britain's African colonies, beginning with the Gold Coast in 1957, followed rapidly by Nigeria, Somaliland, Sierre Leone, Tanganyika, Uganda, Kenya and the Gambia. The final major imperial withdrawal would come in 1997 when Hong Kong was handed back to China. By then, the population of what remained of the Empire, which in 1944 had approached 800 million, had shrunk to 168,075.

The end of the war and the austerity that followed witnessed an increase in emigration to the so-called 'White Dominions' (Australia, Canada, New Zealand and South Africa) and this was reflected in the late 1940s and early 1950s in a cycle of what were, in effect, 'dominion westerns' featuring the exploits of settlers, explorers and fortune-hunters in Australia, New Zealand and South Africa. They highlight the romance and adventure associated with white settlement.

The most notable of these dominion westerns was a trio of Australian docu-dramas, produced on location by Ealing Studios and starring Chips Rafferty, who was seen as the Australian Gary Cooper. The Musical Director at Ealing, Ernest Irving, believed in recruiting the best of contemporary composers to write for Ealing's films, and during the war he had drawn on the services of William Walton, Lord Berners, Alan Rawsthorne, Gordon Jacob and Frederic Austin. He wrote in 1943: 'There is no reason why a master should write more effective film music than a hack, for artistic merit and authenticity of style have no "film value" per se, but it is pleasing to record that in point of fact they do.'[50] For *The Overlanders* (1946), he succeeded in recruiting John Ireland to write the score. It became the composer's last important work. Ernest Irving did the orchestrations from Ireland's manuscript short score.

Ireland, with his eyesight deteriorating and his finances depleted, duly undertook his one and only film score after viewing the completed film, which he admired for its documentary flavour and the expansive vistas captured by cameraman Osmond Borrodaile. He had to complete the score in six weeks when he would ideally have liked six months. He wrote: 'I am nearly *crazy* with overwork . . . Tho' terribly hard, *cruel*, work, this film is very interesting and exciting . . . it needs a lot of heavy symphonic music and what I have done is extremely good and will make an excellent concert suite'.[51] Ireland was right on both counts. Although he had never been to Australia, his score was praised for capturing the *feel* of the outback, and although Ireland joked about producing a *Sinfonia Overlandia* to match the *Sinfonia Antarctica* which Vaughan Williams had constructed out of his score for the film *Scott of the Antarctic*, it was in fact the Australian conductor Sir Charles Mackerras who put together the five-movement suite *The Overlanders* from Ireland's score. It was published in 1971.

The film, directed by Harry Watt, recreated a cattle drive across Australia from the Northern Territory to Queensland in 1942, to remove the cattle from the threat of seizure by the Japanese. Chips Rafferty starred as the leader of the drive. The action of the film encompassed all the perils and pitfalls of the journey: dangerous river crossings, stampedes, dried-up waterholes, blocked mountain tracks and accidents to the drovers.

Ireland's score is appropriately epic and heroic. It opens with a confident expansive march behind the credits which expresses the grand scale of the undertaking. This is followed by the 'scorched earth' music, a minor-key variation on the march, which captures musically the sensation of flames growing and engulfing the farmhouse as it is burned by the family preparing to leave with the drovers. Then we hear what becomes a recurrent theme of the film, the jaunty jogging rhythm which accompanies the cattle on the move. Almost all of

Ireland's score accompanies and enhances action scenes. The one major exception is the delicate and wistful love theme that accompanies the scenes between 'Sinbad', the sailor who hates the sea, and Mary, the female drover, between whom a romance springs up on the trip.

The music for the round-up of wild horses, or 'brumbies', swirls and surges with excitement and is followed by a quieter passage with a clarinet solo as Dan breaks-in one of the captured horses. Irving added a *pizzicato* violin countermelody to the clarinet solo in this sequence to boost the tension when the director objected to the reflective chamber-music texture of the passage.

The first stampede is a thunderous reworking of the jogging theme, with distinct echoes of Shostakovich as the cattle run wild and 'Sinbad' is trampled. The second stampede is accompanied by music that exactly mirrors the action on the screen: a gentle breeze gets up, the cattle get the smell of water and stampede towards a water hole. As the cattle are faced down by the drovers, the music falls away gradually and dies, to burst into life again as the drovers force the cattle to retreat to their original pasture.

The other significant section of music accompanies the hazardous crossing of a mountain range on a narrow track. The music is solemn, grave and apprehensive; then brassy chords indicate the finding of a fallen tree blocking the path. The music builds in urgency and tension as the drovers struggle to shift the obstruction, and it culminates in a triumphant crash as the tree falls down the mountainside, to open up the way.

In his orchestral suite, Mackerras selected five passages from the score, the march 'Scorched Earth' which utilized the title music and the music for the burning of the farm; romance: 'Mary and the Sailor'; intermezzo: 'Open Country', the jogging theme; scherzo: 'The Brumbies'; and the finale: 'Night Stampede'. This left two major passages unused and these were arranged by Geoffrey Bush as *Two Symphonic Studies*, with the mountain crossing music described very appropriately as 'fugue' and the second stampede as 'toccata'. The two arrangements indicate clearly the classical forms that Ireland had in mind as he set the film and produced one of the great British film scores. Both arrangements have been splendidly recorded.[52]

Narrative and dialogue predominated over music in Harry Watt's second Australian venture, *Eureka Stockade* (1949). This was a historical drama charting the Australian struggle for citizen rights in the mid-nineteenth century. The gold-miners, oppressed by extortionate license fees and police brutality, rebel and set up the Eureka Stockade, led by Peter Lalor (Chips Rafferty). The rebels are smashed by the army but public indignation throughout the colony leads to the granting of their demands (votes, land rights, the abolition of licenses). The film is careful to stress that the rebels remain loyal to the crown and are protesting about *local* misgovernment, and the final shot is of the Australian flag which combined the rebel ensign containing the stars of the Southern Cross with the Union Jack. John Greenwood's musical score is minimal, just short dramatic passages to underline a chase sequence, a lynch mob advancing on a hotel, the building of the stockade and the attack by the army.

Ealing's third Australian production was *Bitter Springs* (1950), directed by Ralph Smart. This film recounted the story of a pioneer family in 1900. Australian Wally King (Chips Rafferty), his family and workers, who include an indigent English music-hall artiste and a Scots carpenter, trek 600 miles to settle on land purchased from the Government. It turns out to be Aboriginal tribal land, and this precipitates conflict with the Aborigines; but after the farmhouse is besieged, a reconciliation is effected between the settlers and the natives. Ernest Irving called on Vaughan Williams to work on the score. Vaughan Williams provided thematic material which was developed and orchestrated by Irving. The film's credits ran: 'Music – Vaughan Williams, music supplemented, arranged and directed by Ernest Irving.' The title music is Vaughan Williams's, an optimistic, bouncy, up-beat march, which the composer dubbed 'Irving's march' and of which he wrote to Irving: 'What marvels you have done with my silly little tune.'[53] The marvels consist in the fact that the march, with variations, recurs throughout the film, faster, slower, grimmer, lighter, as the circumstances demand. It accompanies the whole of the trek in the first part of the film and returns in martial form as the troopers relieve the besieged farm house. Irving artfully re-used Vaughan Williams's sheep music from an earlier Ealing score for the pastoral drama *The Loves of Joanna Godden* (1947), commenting in his autobiography: 'after all sheep are sheep, and a little change in orchestral colouring will soon flip them over to the Antipodes'.[54] The manuscript score of *Bitter Springs* reveals that other passages were by Irving alone. The music for the cutting down of trees, sawing of wood and building of the house, with the music emulating the sounds involved in these activities, is Irving's. So, too, is the music for the scene of a boy being taught by an Aborigine to throw a boomerang; the music captures the flight of the boomerang. Particularly effective is the balletic music, set to a rhythmic flute tune, which accompanies the chasing of a baby kangaroo. The scores for all three of Ealing's

Australian 'westerns' stressed the heroism, adventure and romance associated with imperial pioneering.

But Ealing's greatest imperial film score came with the film *Scott of the Antarctic* (1948). Director Charles Frend had been 'especially inspired by Scott's last written message: "Had we lived, I would have had a tale to tell of the hardihood, endurance and courage of my companions which would have stirred the heart of every Englishman."'[55] In the film Scott (John Mills) sets out to reach the South Pole partly for the purpose of scientific investigation, but principally for patriotic reasons ('I think an Englishman should get there first'). He raises an expedition of like-minded souls, mostly naval personnel, some with imperial connections. They pit themselves against the terrifying forces of nature. They soldier on even after learning that the Norwegian Amundsen has set out for the Pole. Amundsen beats them to the pole and Scott and his four companions perish on the way back. In the hallowed tradition of the Englishman as gallant loser, Scott and his team display throughout what were deemed to be characteristic British attitudes under adversity – quiet determination, understatement, restraint, self-deprecating humour, stoical acceptance of defeat and disappointment. At the time of his death, in 1912, Scott was seen as an imperial hero, and that view persisted even when the film was released. The *Sunday Graphic* said: 'it is always an inspiring and noble film, and one that every man, woman and child in the British Empire must go and see', while the *Sunday Dispatch* declared:

> Such a film as *Scott* is welcome at a time when other races speak disparagingly of our 'crumbling Empire' and our 'lack of spirit'. It should make those who have listened too closely to such talk believe afresh that ours is the finest breed of men on this earth. And so it is.[56]

Ernest Irving, Ealing's Musical Director, had a clear vision of what the score should do:

> For an epic film on the scale of *Scott of the Antarctic*, I conceive it to be the function of the music to bring to the screen the hidden and spiritual illustration into which the camera, however ably directed, is unable to peer. The essence of heroism in the struggle to reach the Pole, and the sterner, because disillusioned, effort to get back to the base lay in the unbending spirit which endured day after day, hour after hour, mile by mile, yard by yard, unceasing, uncomplaining, unflagging. The camera has a hundred minutes to show these weeks of cracking strain and silent endurance and must portray them in action and dialogue. This is where music can step in as a spiritual ancillary to the spoken word or pictured scene, and the musician should be a composer who works on a scale comparable with the grandeur of the main theme.[57]

Vaughan Williams was his first choice for composer. Director Charles Frend and producer Sidney Cole readily agreed, Vaughan Williams was approached by Irving. Ursula Vaughan Williams recalled:

> He was at first reluctant to commit so much time but Irving was persuasive, and the idea of the strange world of ice and storm began to fascinate him . . . Apart from this he was excited by the demands which the setting of the film made on his invention to find musical equivalents for the physical sensations of ice, of wind blowing over the great, uninhabited desolation, of stubborn and impassable ridges of black and ice-covered rock, and to suggest man's endeavour to overcome the rigours of this bleak land and to match mortal spirit against the elements. For light relief there were the penguins and whales. There was to be music not only for the polar journey but also for the two women, Kathleen Scott and Oriana Wilson, so he had scope for many different kinds of tune.[58]

Vaughan Williams composed the entire score in two weeks, working to a draft script and ahead of receiving the formal list of music cues and timings, which was sent to him after he had already posted his score. But the location shooting for the film was not yet completed and the script was being revised still. Irving recalled: 'Nearly all the music had to be reshaped [after the final print was assembled, but this] was not so insuperable from the artistic point of view as it might seem, for the music is essentially right in the first place, and all the structural alterations were carried out under the censorship of the original architect'.[59] It was evidently not just the landscape and the opportunity for musical experimentation that fascinated Vaughan Williams. For the film, as constructed, is almost a secular analogue of *Pilgrim's Progress*. Scott's journey becomes another version of the journey of the human soul, which had long provided Vaughan Williams with inspiration, through the long gestation of his *Pilgrim's Progress* project and dating back as far as his setting of Whitman's *Towards the Unknown Region* (1907), which might almost have been an alternative title for *Scott of the Antarctic*.

Within the film itself there is an obvious religious element, with Oates laying down his life for his friends, Dr Wilson playing *Abide With Me* on his gramophone and the final letters of Wilson and Bowers, read on the soundtrack and expressing their belief in an afterlife. The final inscription on the cross, 'To strive, to seek, to find and not to yield', could have been Christian's motto in *Pilgrim's Progress*. It is no coincidence that he was working on the opera at the same time as he was developing Scott and the emerging *Symphony No. 7*. But we cannot wholly divorce the story from the celebration of English character under stress which was one of the film's structuring themes. The score for *Scott of the Antarctic* unquestionably represents the peak of Vaughan Williams's cinematic achievement. The film's title music contains the main theme, recurrent throughout the film, and symbolizing human endeavour, struggle both physical and spiritual, the great quest ever onward and upward. It is followed by a prologue, marked by Vaughan Williams 'the terror and fascination of the Pole', over scenes of the Antarctic landscape, eerie, glittering, icy, what Vaughan Williams called his 'Antarctic shimmerings', achieved by the use of glockenspiel, xylophone, vibraphone, celesta, harp and bells, and chanting wordless female chorus symbolizing the siren call of the Antarctic, the loneliness and wildness of the place, with its ever-changing treacherous beauty in a kaleidoscopic pattern of wind, snow, storm and cloud formation. After a snatch, barely heard, of the music for Kathleen Scott, behind a shot of her sculpting her husband's bust, and jaunty music for the assembling of the team in London, we get the voyage out to New Zealand and the Antarctic, marked by descriptive musical passages of ice-floes, whales and seals, ships at sea ploughing through the pack-ice, and the immensity of the great ice barrier. The mood of the film is lightened by jolly comic penguin music as they slide and waddle on the ice; the jaunty folk-song-like trotting pony theme brings a whiff of the English countryside into the Antarctic waste; and there is a triumphal surge in the music at the appearance of the Aurora Borealis.

As the explorers set out, we get the grim blizzard theme with the keening women's voices and wind effects. The climbing of the glacier employs the slow march theme of the titles, to give a musical equivalent of climbing and plodding. But it is never monotonous, due to the atmospheric weather colouring added and the cumulative effect of the repetition. The main heroic theme follows as they reach the summit.

On the last haul, the regular rhythms of the unending march return with a meditative passage as Scott is heard to ruminate about who to take on the final push. An ominous trombone burst greets the sight of Amundsen's flag. Then there is the long haul back, the rhythms of the march, the howl of the blizzard, the growing sense of despair – all captured in the music. After the deaths of Evans and Oates, the music falls silent and there is only the wind and the wordless female chorus. When the remains of the expedition are found, there is a fanfare as the words on the commemorative cross are picked out and the heroic final credits' music swells, symbolizing the triumph of the human spirit over death and pitiless nature. The film when released received mixed reviews. The photography and the music were universally praised.[60]

The story so gripped Vaughan Williams that he reworked the film music into his *Symphony No. 7, Sinfonia Antarctica*, which significantly was dedicated to Ernest Irving. The *Sinfonia* was written in five movements and there can be little doubt that they correspond to the phases of the film. The epigraphs he placed at the head of each movement clearly demonstrate that. The first movement, prefaced by an extract from Shelley's *Prometheus*, which he has also inscribed on the film score, universalizes the theme of the film and the symphony, the struggle of man against nature:

> To suffer woes which hope thinks infinite,
> To forgive wrongs darker than death or night,
> To defy power which seems omnipotent,
> Neither to change, nor falter, nor repent:
> This is to be
> Good, great, joyous, beautiful and free,
> This is alone life, joy, empire and history.

The movement opens with the film's main title theme which becomes the motto theme of the symphony, repeated throughout the first movement. Then comes the prologue from the film. The music for the scenes of the Antarctic is reworked, creating an extraordinary texture of sound, to evoke the heroism of human endeavour against the loneliness and icy desolation of the polar region. The movement ends with the triumphant finale tune from the film. The second movement, scherzo, with a quotation from Psalm 104 ('There go the ships and there is that leviathan whom thou has made to take his pastime therein'), represents the sea journey from England to the Antarctic, with ice-floes, ship music, whales and penguins music reworked from the film. The third movement, landscape, with a descriptive passage from Coleridge's *Hymn Before Sunrise in the Vale of Chamouni*, uses the iceberg, Ross Island and glacier-climbing music, climaxing in the conquest of the glacier with great peals of triumph on the organ, but drum and cymbal rolls, harp glissandi, wailing flutes, glockenspiel, celesta and piano to stress the nature of the landscape and the weather that they are fighting.

The fourth movement is headed by the superscription from John Donne's *The Sun Rising*, celebrating the strength of love. The movement represents first the recollections of the explorers. It develops Kathleen Scott's theme and the Oriana Wilson theme omitted from the film. The film includes a sequence on the trek back where Scott and Wilson recall their wives in flashback. The movement ends with the music for the death of Oates, whose sacrifice represents a different kind of love – the love of comrades.

The final movement, epilogue, with its quotation of words from Scott's journal, 'I do not regret this journey; we took risks; we knew we took them, things have come out against us, therefore we have no cause for complaint', represents the fatal last leg of Scott's journey. It opens with a fanfare of human defiance, then moves into blizzard music and the slow heroic march theme, as the wind and the female chorus assert themselves, until they are all that is left. The explorers have lost their battle but their spirit has conquered, as the first movement indicated. While he was working on *Sinfonia Antarctica*, Vaughan Williams referred to it as his *Scott* symphony and, given the programme of the music, it could be seen as a tribute to the visionary aspect of imperialism. As such, the *Scott* symphony, coming as it did right at the end of the imperial experience, was the counterpart of the unwritten *Gordon Symphony* of Elgar, which would, in the heyday of Empire, have commemorated the destiny, journey and death of an earlier imperial pilgrim.

Notes

1 Martin Miller Marks, *Music and the Silent Screen*, New York and Oxford: Oxford University Press, 1997.
2 Claudia Gorbman, *Unheard Melodies: Narrative Film Music*, London and Bloomington: BFI/Indiana University Press, 1987, pp. 30, 15.
3 John Huntley, *British Film Music*, London: Skelton Robinson, 1947, p. 163.
4 Gorbman, *Unheard Melodies*, pp. 73–91.
5 *Ibid.*, p. 83.
6 Christopher Palmer, *The Composer in Hollywood*, London: Marion Boyars, 1993, pp. 19, 53.
7 Brendan G. Carroll, *The Last Prodigy*, Portland, OR: Amadeus Press, 1997, pp. 367–70.
8 Margaret Farrand Thorp, *America at the Movies*, New Haven, CT: Yale University Press, 1939, pp. 294–5.
9 Richard Slotkin, *Gunfighter Nation*, New York: Harper Perennial, 1993, pp. 266–7.
10 Nicholas J. Cull, 'America's Raj: Kipling, masculinity and Empire', in C.E. Gittings (ed.), *Imperialism and Gender*, New Lambton, New South Wales: Dangaroo Press, 1996, pp. 85–97 elaborates on *Gunga Din*'s American appeal.
11 John Fraser, *America and the Patterns of Chivalry*, Cambridge: Cambridge University Press, 1982.
12 A suite from Steiner's *Charge of the Light Brigade* score prepared by John Morgan and recorded in 1994 is on Marco Polo 8.223608.
13 Marco Polo 8.223870.
14 Tony Thomas, *Music for the Movies*, South Brunswick and New York: A.S. Barnes & Co., 1973, p. 115.
15 Rudy Behlmer (ed.), *Inside Warner Brothers*, London: Weidenfeld & Nicolson, 1987, p. 72.
16 Marco Polo 8.223871.
17 Rudy Behlmer, *Behind the Scenes*, London: Samuel French, 1990, pp. 87–103.
18 Marco Polo 8.223608.
19 Noël Coward, *Present Indicative*, New York: Doubleday Doran & Co., 1937, p. 339.
20 *Ibid.*, p. 341.
21 *Ibid.*
22 Sheridan Morley, *A Talent to Amuse*, Harmondsworth: Penguin, 1974, p. 186.
23 *Daily Mail*, 1 November, 1931.

24 Coward, *Present Indicative*, p. 352.
25 *Ibid.*, p. 352.
26 Cole Lesley, *The Life of Noël Coward*, London: Jonathan Cape, 1976, pp. 144–5.
27 Morley, *A Talent to Amuse*, p. 196.
28 *The Observer*, 10 February, 1933.
29 James Agate, *Around Cinemas* (2nd series), London: Home & Van Thal, 1948, pp. 78–9.
30 Coward, *Present Indicative*, p. 343.
31 *The Observer*, 19 February, 1933.
32 Nick Hayes and Jeff Hill (eds), *Millions Like Us? British Culture in the Second World War*, Liverpool: Liverpool University Press, 1999, p. 79.
33 Coward, *Present Indicative*, p. 352.
34 André Previn, *No Minor Chords*, New York: Doubleday, 1991, p. 24.
35 Jeffrey Richards, 'Soldiers Three: the "lost" Gaumont British imperial epic', *Historical Journal of Film, Radio and Television* 15, 1(1995), pp. 137–41.
36 Louis Levy, *Music for the Movies*, London: Sampson Low, Marston & Co., 1948, pp. 131, 142–3.
37 Levy, *Music for the Movies*, p. 135.
38 *New York Times*, 4 August, 1939.
39 Miklos Rosza, *Double Life*, Tunbridge Wells: Baton Press, 1982, p. 72.
40 Herbert Wilcox, *Twenty-Five Thousand Sunsets*, London: Bodley Head, 1967, pp. 111–21.
41 Hilary Guise, *Great Victorian Engravings*, London: Astragal Books, 1980, p. 146.
42 Herbert Wilcox, *Twenty-Five Thousand Sunsets*, p. 9.
43 J.M. Lee and Martin Petter, *The Colonial Office, War and Development Policy*, London: Institute of Commonwealth Studies, 1982, p. 122.
44 *Ibid.*, p. 244.
45 *Ibid.*, p. 150.
46 For an account of the making of *Men of Two Worlds*, see Jeffrey Richards, *Thorold Dickinson and the British Cinema*, Lanham, MD: Scarecrow Press 1997 pp. 97–118.
47 Peter Noble, *The Negro in Films*, London: Skelton Robinson, 1947, pp. 128–36.
48 Arthur Bliss, *As I Remember*, London: Faber & Faber, 1989, p. 168.
49 John Huntley, *British Film Music*, p. 87.
50 Alain Frogley (ed.), *Vaughan Williams Studies*, Cambridge: Cambridge University Press, 1996, p. 143.
51 Muriel V. Searle, *John Ireland: The Man and His Music*, Tunbridge Wells: Midas Books, 1979, pp. 120–1.
52 John Ireland, *The Overlanders Suite*, Chandos, CD CHAN 8994; *Two Symphonic Studies*, Chandos, CD CHAN9376; sleeve notes by Lewis Foreman.
53 Michael Kennedy, *Works of Ralph Vaughan Williams*, Oxford: Oxford University Press, 1964, p. 590.
54 Ernest Irving, *Cue For Music*, London: Dennis Dobson, 1959, p. 175.
55 Michael Balcon, *A Lifetime of Films*, London: Hutchinson, 1969, p. 171.
56 *Sunday Graphic*, 5 December 1948; *Sunday Dispatch*, 5 December 1948.
57 David James, *Scott of the Antarctic: The Film and the Production*, London, 1948, pp. 144–5.
58 Ursula Vaughan Williams, *R.V.W.*, Oxford: Oxford University Press, 1992, pp. 279–80.
59 James, *Scott of the Antarctic*, p. 145.
60 Jeffrey Richards, *Films and British National Identity*, Manchester: Manchester University Press, 1997, pp. 318–19.

CHAPTER TEN

Sing a song of Empire

It was song that brought the Empire into the home. There were two staples of song in the second half of the nineteenth century: the drawing-room ballad and the music-hall song. It is sometimes said that the former was middle class and the latter working class, but this is an oversimplification. The drawing-room ballad was written for and aimed at the middle-class drawing-room but percolated down to the respectable working class. The music-hall song was written largely by middle-class writers to appeal to the shared sentiments of an audience that was largely working class but contained an increasing middle-class element for whose patronage the proprietors were making a distinct pitch, and music-hall songs percolated upwards to feature in middle-class musical evenings. Even if there were a class division between the consumers of ballads and the consumers of music-hall songs, the salient fact for this study is that both were steeped in Empire and there was a potent link between the two in Rudyard Kipling, who wrote poetry to the rhythms of popular songs and whose verses were set to music for performance both in the drawing-room and the music hall.

Music-hall songs

The music hall was the dominant popular cultural form of the second half of the nineteenth century. Music halls were not common before 1850 but were well-established by 1861 when the first purpose-built music hall was erected in London. Music hall grew out of pub entertainment. The 'free and easies', the informal sing-songs of eighteenth-century taverns, led to separate song and supper rooms being built on to pubs. From the 1860s onwards there were purpose-built music halls where food and drink were served and a chairman kept order. The music hall became the prototype of the modern entertainment industry, rapidly commercialized as capital was invested, advertising techniques were developed to promote stars, and a hierarchy of stars and supporting acts was evolved. By the 1870s many music halls were mounting shows twice nightly to maximise returns on investment. Initially music halls were independent operations, normally set up locally by enterprising publicans. But the railway system made touring possible and circuits developed with artistes touring regularly. By the 1880s and 1890s there were several nationwide circuits. There were also specific northern and southern chains, and many independent houses survived. Audiences included old and young, middle class and working class, male and female patrons; but the predominant element in the audience was the young, employed, unmarried adult.

The music-hall programme consisted mainly of songs, with occasional sketches which became more common in the twentieth century as music hall evolved into the aptly named 'variety'. Songs and choruses provided a shared experience, a chance for the audiences to express solidarity, to recognize and affirm their values, attitudes and aspirations. The writers of songs had to take into account the mixed nature of the audiences, the need for escapism, a catchy tune and sentiment, for it was the audience who 'made' songs and stars. So songwriters sought to dramatize general attitudes, and songs strongly reflected a set of regular themes: love (treated as romance), marriage (treated as a trap and a disaster), work (and how to avoid it), city life, food and drink, clothes and holidays. The values celebrated were comradeship, patriotism, luck and fatalism, a mild anti-authoritarianism, defined gender roles and the idea of an immutable social order.[1]

Dave Russell suggests that music hall's 'really close association with the flag' began in 1877 with the threat to Constantinople from the Russians during the Russo-Turkish War.[2] Gladstone's Liberals were anti-Turkish but Disraeli's Conservatives were pro-Turkish, viewing Turkey as a bulwark against Russian expansion and favouring war if necessary to protect Constantinople. This was the stance embodied in G.W. Hunt's celebrated *Jingo* song, performed by 'The Great MacDermott':

> We don't want to fight, but by jingo if we do,
> We've got the ships, we've got the men, we've got the money too,
> We've fought the bear before and while we're Britons true,
> The Russians shall not have Constantinople.

The song was an instant hit, 'phenomenally popular' according to journalist H. Chance Newton.[3] It was quoted in Parliament and in *The Times*. But it was not merely a London phenomenon: MacDermott sang it in provincial towns, too. G.W. Hunt was to be known as 'Jingo'

[325]

Hunt for the rest of his life. It is ironic that a song which actually stressed a reluctance to fight and a willingness to do so only in the last resort should have given birth to a word which came to mean belligerent ultra-nationalism.

The song also inspired the parody, sung by Herbert Campbell, *I Don't Want to Fight* (1879):

> I don't want to fight, I'll be slaughtered if I do,
> I'll change my togs and sell my kit and pop my rifle too.
> I don't like the war, I ain't no 'Briton true',
> And I'd let the Russians have Constantinople.

It is sometimes suggested that the popularity of this song is evidence of popular opposition to the war.[4] But this is to misunderstand the nature of parody in Victorian popular culture. Everything was parodied or burlesqued in the nineteenth century, especially things the Victorians loved. From Shakespeare and sentimental melodramas, which regularly had audiences in floods of tears, through to the latest popular song, everything was grist to the parodist's mill. It did not bespeak opposition but rather that typically English characteristic of humour which J.B. Priestley noted, the tendency to laugh at the things they love, in this case patriotism.[5] Also it should be noted that Henry Pettitt, who wrote the parody, was the author of some of the most gung-ho patriotic melodramas on the English stage, for instance *British Born* (1872), *Human Nature* (1885), and *A Life of Pleasure* (1893), and so was not in the business of undermining patriotic endeavour. There is no better example of the affirmative role of parody than Noël Coward's *Mad Dogs and Englishmen*. It was intended as an affectionate send-up (or, as Priestley would put it, "tender mockery") of the *pukka sahib* tradition but was rapidly transformed into and performed (by Coward, among others) as a celebration of the heroic English individualist.

The political mood of the halls was clear to contemporary commentators. Journalist J.B. Booth wrote:

> The music hall had a distinct function – it played the part of commentator on matters of public importance. The music-hall audience was an entity with very definite views. These views may have been crude, but they were simple, elemental, direct, as was the expression of them. So it came about that to a very large extent the songs of the halls represented popular criticism of the topics of the day, sometimes treated lightly, sometimes with portentous seriousness, but invariably from a purely national point of view. The patriotic muse was intensely pro-British; the nation had not yet arrived at the stage of apologizing for its existence, and there was still the comfortable belief that England was

the finest country in the world, and one Englishman was equal to half a dozen foreigners. The British soldier was the salt of the earth, and as for the British sailor – lions and bulldogs were tame by comparison when his country called him. Each foreign crisis inspired the music-hall bards anew; in the years between *We Don't Want to Fight, But By Jingo! If We Do!* and *Tipperary* lie chapters of history – not only of the music hall but of the nation.[6]

Another contemporary commentator, W. MacQueen Pope, calling the music hall 'the fount of patriotism', claimed:

> The patriotism which the Music Hall portrayed was not spurious, not cheap, flag-wagging, claptrap, done to get a round of applause. It was the true mirror of the ordinary man's state of mind, at a time when every English gentleman considered himself, not without reason, as good as at least three foreigners of any nationality whatever . . . He was on top of the world, although he knew little about the world, and to him the Union Jack was not something to be disregarded and guyed but to be saluted and revered.[7]

Booth and Pope evidently rather approved of the unapologetic nationalism of the halls. J.A. Hobson, who certainly did not, nevertheless agreed about the prevailing values being expressed when, at the height of the Boer War, he sought to analyse 'the psychology of jingoism':

> A gradual debasement of popular art attending the new industrial era of congested, ugly, manufacturing towns has raised up the music-hall to be the most powerful instrument of such musical and literary culture as the people are open to receive. Among large sections of the middle and labouring classes, the music-hall and the recreative public-house into which it shades off by imperceptible degrees, are a more potent educator than the church, the school, the political meeting, or even than the press. Into this 'lighter self' of the city populace the artiste conveys by song or recitation crude notions upon morals and politics, appealing by coarse humour or exaggerated pathos to the animal lusts of an audience stimulated by alcohol into appreciative hilarity. In ordinary times politics plays no important part in these feasts of sensationalism, but the glorification of brute force and an ignorant contempt for foreigners are ever-present factors which at great political crises make the music-hall a very serviceable engine for generating military passion. The art of the music-hall is the only 'popular' art of the present day; its words and melodies pass by quick magic from the Empire or the Alhambra over the length and breadth of the land, re-echoed in a thousand provincial halls, clubs and drinking saloons, until the remotest village is familiar with air and sentiment. By such process of artistic suggestion the fervour of Jingoism has been widely fed and it is worthy of note that the present

[327]

meaning of the word was fastened upon it by the popularity of a single verse.[8]

Hobson saw the imperialist message of the halls being reinforced by the press, the pulpit and the political platform, thus ensuring its dominance.

The question of whether music-hall songs reflected or constructed popular views is much debated. The most likely answer is that they did both. The music-hall proprietors were in the business of giving the public what they wanted and were not likely, whatever their own political opinions, to try to foist on the audience songs with sentiments which that audience rejected. It is also worthy of note that one of the most important music-hall chains, that of Edward Moss, christened all its music halls the Empire and eventually there was an Empire Music Hall in many of Britain's cities (thirty-five by 1914). Moss Empires became one of the leading players in the entertainment industry and no entrepreneur would risk putting off audiences by calling his theatres by a name with which the audiences could not identify.

Hunt's *Jingo* song was thus no isolated phenomenon. It was only the most famous of a clutch of songs inspired by the 1877 crisis, among them: *The Turkey and the Bear*; *We Mean to Keep our Empire in the East*; *True Blues, Stand By Your Guns*; *The Lion Wags His Tail*; *Hats Off to the Empire*; and *Here Stands a Post*. An older song, *The Union Jack of Old England*, first written and performed by Charles Williams in 1872, was revived 'with immense success' at the Standard Music Hall:

> The flag that lights the sailor on his way,
> The flag that fills all our foes with dismay,
> The flag that always has carried the day,
> The Union Jack of Old England.

For 'it had a swinging chorus, which was whistled and sung all over the town'.[9]

Evidently there was some mocking of music-hall jingoism in the press, for it prompted G.W. Hunt to pen a musical response, *Waiting For the Signal*, which referred to journalists who 'sneer about the "Jingoes" in hopes to raise a laugh'.

> If it's jingo to love honour, then jingoes sure are we,
> If it's jingo to love England, then jingoes sure are we,
> There are jingoes in our colonies who love the dear old land,
> Who are ready to when wanted by the brave old flag to stand,
> From her proud and right position England never will retreat,

[328]

And if cowards be amongst us, let them take a far back seat.
So we're waiting for the signal, directly up it runs,
Clear the decks for action, stand by the guns,
Our Army and our Navy, true British dogs of war,
Will make them cry peccavi the same as they did before.[10]

Thereafter imperial songs were an integral part of the music-hall pro-gramme. They were affirmative, positive, defiant and popular. There were recurrent themes. One was the solidarity of the Empire. The *Song of Greater Britain* stressed:

> Join hearts across the sea.
> In love and loyalty,
> For Englishmen are brothers, wherever they may be,
> No more 'tis little England,
> The island of the free,
> We fight for Greater Britain, our Empire o'er the sea![11]

G.W. Hunt contributed *If England to Herself Be True* (1879):

> The Afghan Wolf may friendship make
> With cunning Russian Bear,
> But the Indian Tiger's wide awake,
> And bids them both beware!
>
> The prowling foe on plunder bent
> By this should surely know
> The British Lion's not asleep
> As in the years ago.
>
> The dusky sons of Hindostan
> Will by our banner stand,
> Australia, aye, and Canada,
> Both love the dear old land!
>
> No foe we fear – we fight for right!
> No day we e'er shall rue,
> If England, dear old England,
> To herself be only true.[12]

Motherland or Australia Will Be There, which was in the regular reper-toire of both Tom Costello and George Lashwood, included the verse:

> Motherland! Motherland!
> Though your sons have crossed the sea,
> They have spread the Empire in your name –
> Great, glorious and free,
> Plant the flag, plant the flag,
> Let the world know 'tis our dream –

To never, never rest until
Our Empire is supreme.[13]

Similar sentiments were to be found in *We're Australians But Still Britannia's Sons*, *Sons of Our Empire*, *Sons of the Motherland* and *The British Bulldogs (Hail Our Empire's Unity)*.

Then, there were the regular celebrations of the flag, the British Lion, John Bull and Britannia: *Three Cheers for the Red, White and Blue*; *Under the British Flag*; *Why Rouse the British Lion?*; *The Lion Hearts of England*; *I Mean to Hold My Own While My Name's John Bull*; *John Bull's Letter Bag* with its lines 'Thank God we're Anglo-Saxons, and the Anglo-Saxon race shall rule the world'; *John Bull, Aren't We Loyal Now?* and *John Bull's Flags*. There were celebrations of Queen Victoria, particularly in her imperial incarnation: *Victoria – Empress Queen*; *Victoria, Empress of India*; *Victoria, England's Queen*; *Victoria, Our Queen*; *Victoria, the Mother of Our Nation*; *There's Only One Queen Victoria*, and *The Great White Mother*.

The Navy was a recurrent element in the imperial repertoire, its stance summed up by the perennially popular *Sons of the Sea*, written by Felix McGlennon and performed by Arthur Reece:

> Sons of the Sea, all British born,
> Sailing every ocean, laughing foes to scorn,
> They may build the ships, my lads,
> And think they know the game,
> But they can't build the boys of the bulldog breed,
> Who made old England's name.

Other popular songs eulogizing the navy included *The Lads in Navy Blue* ('It is the Navy, the British Navy, that keeps our foes at bay').

There was also a glut of songs about soldiers. In this, the music hall was merely echoing the cultural transformation of the image of the soldier that had occurred since the middle of the nineteenth century. The army, once much less popular than the navy, had been rehabilitated. It was as a result of a combination of powerful ideologies: the revival of the idea of chivalry; the implications of social Darwinism; and the impact of evangelicalism. War came to be seen as a moral force and the profession of soldiering as a noble one. The army was Christianized, and Christianity militarized. In the paintings of Lady Butler and her contemporaries, in the fiction of G.A. Henty and his imitators, in the poetry of Kipling, Henley, Sir Francis Doyle and Sir Arthur Conan Doyle, in the colourful despatches of the war correspondents, in the annual spectacular Drury Lane melodramas which often featured the latest imperial military campaign, the imperial soldiery came to be seen as the embodiment of manliness, patriotism, chivalry,

[330]

service, sacrifice, comradeship and courage. These ideas underlay such songs as: *Bravo Territorials; What Britishers Are Made Of; Boys in Khaki; Soldiers of the Queen;* and *The Boys of the Thin Red Line.* Dave Russell in a superb essay argues for 1880–1900 as the peak of soldier celebration and he discerns a variety of themes of approaches.[14] There are musical celebrations of real-life military heroes like Sir Garnet Wolseley (*Sir Garnet Will Show Them the Way; Success to Brave Sir Garnet Wolseley*), Colonel Fred Burnaby (*Burnaby the Brave; A Lion-hearted Soldier Was Colonel Burnaby; Homage to Colonel Burnaby*) and General Gordon, whose death as a Christian martyr was celebrated in G.H. MacDermott's *Too Late, Too Late,* a song whose lyrics stressed his commitment to service, duty and the protection of native races. There are songs about current campaigns but also many about previous campaigns viewed retrospectively from the positive revaluation of the soldiery: the Crimean War, especially the Charge of the Light Brigade, the Indian Mutiny, the Napoleonic Wars, particularly Waterloo.

By the 1890s the ordinary soldier was featuring regularly in music hall, a reflection in particular of Kipling's poetic rehabilitation of him. Then the 1890s' crop of 'Motherland' songs tended to stress the valour of the Indian troops (*India's Reply; How India Kept Her Word*), and the Fenian outrages of the 1880s prompted songs paying tribute to the loyalty of the Irish troops (*Why Do They Call Them Hooligans?; The Irish Are Always in Front; Bravo, Dublin Fusiliers; You Can't Call Them Traitors Now*). Certain regiments also came in for individual tributes: *The Gallant Twenty-Fourth* who had been slaughtered at Islandlwana in 1879; the Royal Artillery; the City Imperial Volunteers; and a variety of Highland regiments. Russell discerns three distinct images of the soldier in the music-hall songs: the soldier as Romeo (e.g. *There's Something About a soldier*); the soldier as warrior; the soldier as veteran. Analysing their content, he sees death being sanitized, language stylized, and the enemy rarely appearing in any detail. War is defined as 'gaining, defending and preserving honour both one's own and one's nation's', and manliness is celebrated, defined specifically as 'physical courage, fortitude, patriotism, stoicism, hardiness, endurance and selflessness'. It would be difficult to dissent from Russell's conclusion that the music hall presented a positive image of the soldier and his imperial achievement.[15]

One virtue in particular that was stressed was comradeship and this inspired the perennially popular *Comrades,* written by Felix McGlennon in 1890 and performed by Tom Costello. Costello was an Irishman born in Dublin but raised in Birmingham. Richard Morton in an 1897 biographical sketch described him as 'an out and out Irishman. He has all the wit, humour and pathos of his native country, and beyond all, is blessed with an Irish voice, soft, rich, persuasive and full of charm'. His songs, says Morton, are sung through the length and breadth of the United Kingdom 'and some of them have found their way to the uttermost ends of the globe'. This was particularly true of *Comrades*, which told of two boyhood friends raised together and joining the army together, one of whom saves the life of the other by taking a native spear thrust meant for his comrade and sacrificing his own life. The military campaign was necessary because 'England's flag had been insulted'. Morton recalled:

> He invested it with a wealth of feeling and pathos that went straight to the hearts of his hearers. It is a song of self-sacrifice . . . which . . . reaches the height of sublimity in the picture of the death of that comrade who died for his mate. Such an incident is common enough in the annals of British warfare, and will be repeated while the nation lasts and while men have hearts that can love.[16]

The song proved to be 'the keystone of his dramatic career', becoming 'almost . . . a national anthem'. Costello sang and acted it, and significantly broke with the stage tradition of the soldier always being in full uniform and armed by appearing as a soldier in barracks telling the story to his mates, wearing just a blue shirt and red trousers with his braces dangling. Morton says that the song was very popular with soldiers. Once, after it had been sung to a soldier audience at Chatham, two old military pensioners, who had been comrades for many years 'and had fought and bled together in England's battles', stood up in their places, 'grasped one another's honest hands and embraced and cried like a pair of lovers'. The rest of the audience cheered them. [17] Fascinatingly many of Costello's other popular songs were about the horrors of marriage (*At Trinity Church I Met My Doom*, for instance), a pointed contrast to the soldier's idealized love of his 'darling old comrade'.

Some performers became particularly associated with patriotic, imperial and military songs. One such was Charles Godfrey (1851–1900), a former melodrama actor who brought his dramatic skills to the music-hall stage and became, in H. Chance Newton's words, 'one of the most phenomenally successful artistes ever seen in the British music-halls'.[18] In a contemporary biographical sketch, Richard Morton attributed his success to 'an essential vitality in everything that he does, a naturalness and a big spark of human nature'.[19] His earliest success was a dramatic sketch, *On Guard* (1880). It had two scenes, divided by the playing of *Rule, Britannia* by the orchestra. In the first scene, Godfrey, in full uniform, sang a song about the

Battle of Balaclava, *Here Upon Guard Am I*, and, in the second, dressed as an elderly tramp, he delivered a monologue describing his attempts to get a night's sleep in the workhouse casual ward and being told 'You are not wanted here'. He replies: 'No, I am not wanted here – but at Balaclava, I was wanted there.' He later dies in a churchyard during a snowstorm. Chance Newton recalled:

> Godfrey's vigorous acting of the neglected old soldier in this sketch really raised vast audiences to an almost incredible pitch of enthusiasm. Alike in London and the Provinces I have seen him move the patrons of the 'halls' to volcanic excitement and to thunders of applause.[20]

The appeal of the sketch was the classic combination of melodrama, sentimentality and patriotism. It was performed throughout the 1880s and tapped into the same spirit as Kipling's poem *Tommy Atkins*, criticizing the neglect in time of peace of soldiers who have served their country in time of war. It celebrates the ordinary soldier as the real hero of Britain's overseas military campaigns.

Another of Godfrey's successes was *Fighting With the Seventh Royal Fusiliers* (1893), written for him by Wal Pink with music by George Le Brunn. Godfrey sings a story of the Battle of Inkerman and tells how the Russians dam a stream near the British camp, planning to force the British troops to surrender out of thirst. But, after three days, 'my dearest brother Fred' volunteered to breach the dam and he does so at the cost of his life, adding his name 'to the scroll of British glory'. The martial chorus ran:

> Oh! Fighting with the Seventh Royal Fusiliers.
> Famous Fusiliers. Gallant Fusiliers.
> Through deadly Russian shot and Cossack spears
> We carv'd our way to glory! Oh! Glory!

General Sir Ian Hamilton recalled in 1908 that the song 'produced such an overwhelming rush of recruits that the authorities could easily, had they so chosen to, have several additional battalions. As it was, recruiting for the regiment had to be closed for a year.'[21]

Godfrey's act also included carefully researched portraits of such British and imperial heroes as Drake, Nelson and Gordon. W. MacQueen Pope recalled that at one time Godfrey presented three different songs about three different heroes at three different music halls nightly, singing about Nelson at the Oxford, Wellington at the Canterbury and Major Allan Wilson of the Shangani River Patrol at the Tivoli. The Nelson song had Nelson asking if England was going to decline, warning that other nations were waiting to take her place and urging England to awake and prove that she is England still. All three were written by Charles H. Wilmott, 'one of the finest writers of lyrics the halls ever had', according to Pope, and set to music by George Le Brunn. All three were equally successful. 'Cheers filled all three halls for the songs and their splendid delivery by Godfrey' Pope recalled[22].

Britain's imperial destiny formed the inspiration for *It's the English-Speaking Race Against the World.*:

> We're brothers of the self-same race,
> Speakers of the self-same tongue,
> With the same brave hearts that feel no fears
> From fighting sires of a thousand years;
> Folks say, 'What will Britain do?
> Will she rest with banners furled?'
> No! No! No!
> When we go to meet the foe,
> It's the English-speaking race against the world.[23]

Even Godfrey's sentimental songs sometimes had a patriotic under-tow. In *The Golden Wedding* an old man looks back at fifty years with a devoted wife and mourns their only son who died a soldier for Britain, joining up because 'England requires soldiers to sustain her honour; you would not have me called a coward and a traitor'. Richard Morton was in no doubt about Godfrey's influence:

> In *On Guard*, in *England in Danger* and in *The Seventh Royal Fusiliers*, he successfully struck a keynote of British patriotism, and started a wave of national sentiment that it is no exaggeration to say has left its mark in the minds of the public. No other artist has aroused such enthusiasm, nor scored so heavily with the soldier and the sailor. Once, when Godfrey sang *Balaclava* in Portsmouth, the veteran pensioners presented him with a wreath of laurels in a hall that was full of our lads in red and blue. Sailors had even climbed the pillars supporting the galleries, in their anxiety for a better view of the proceedings. The National Anthem and *Rule Britannia* came again and again from loyal throats, and the cheers of Her Majesty's fighting men of both services, crowned a memorable scene unexampled in the history of the music hall.[24]

Godfrey, although generous and good-hearted, was like so many music-hall performers a heavy drinker and he died at the age of 49, his con-stitution undermined by alcohol, while trying to fulfil an engagement in Birmingham.

Leo Dryden (1863–1939), known as 'The Kipling of the Halls', both wrote (under his real name George Wheeler Dryden) and performed his own songs. His first hit-song, still being sung until at least the 1950s, was *The Miner's Dream of Home* (1891), an emigrant's lament for the people and places left behind. It was a sure-fire combination of a lilting melody and verses evoking aged parents, roaring fires, village bells and New Year's Eve. He went on to write *What Britishers Are Made Of*; *The Great White Mother*; *India's Reply*; *The Gallant Gordon Highlanders*; and *How India Kept Her Word*. One of his greatest hits, as popular with the troops as with the public, was the rousingly tuneful *Bravo, Dublin Fusiliers* (1899), which he wrote, composed and performed.[25] It was in the repertoire of three different music-hall singers.

The Boer War inspired a record number of songs of all kinds and represented perhaps the peak of imperial songwriting. Three of the most popular were not specifically written for the Boer War but struck chords that ensured their success. The classic 'soldier's farewell' song, *Goodbye, Dolly Gray*, with words by Will D. Cobb and music by Paul Barnes, was composed in 1898 for the Spanish–American War but achieved its major popularity with the Boer War, entering the repertoire of five different artistes. It celebrated the call to duty and the sacrifice demanded of the ordinary soldier. But its popularity was equalled by Leslie Stuart's *Soldiers of the Queen*. Originally written in 1881, it was included in the musical comedy *An Artist's Model* in 1895 and swept the country during the South African War. It was a supreme statement of imperial self-confidence, its chorus running:

> It's the soldiers of the Queen, my lads,
> Who've been, my lads, who've seen, my lads,
> In the fight for England's glory, lads,
> Of its world-wide glory, let us sing.
> And when we say we've always won,
> And when they ask us how it's done,
> We'll proudly point to every one
> Of England's soldiers of the Queen.

Charles K. Harris's *Break the News to Mother* (1897) tells a battlefield story. At the height of the battle, the regimental flag is lost, a youngster volunteers to retrieve it and does so at the cost of his life. The General arrives to see the dying hero and recognizes him as the son he thought safely at home, and the boy's words form the chorus:

> Just break the news to Mother
> She knows how dear I love her,
> And tell her not to wait for me,
> For I'm not coming home.

It was a potent combination of patriotism, sacrifice, duty and mother-love, and was in the repertoire of seven different singers.[26] The generals themselves were hymned in songs such as Harry Hunter and Edward Forrest's *Dear Old Bob*s (1900) (Lord Roberts) and *Cheer Up,*

Buller, My Lad (General Sir Redvers Buller). The latter, words and music by F.V. St Clair with an especially punchy chorus line, was published in 1901. It reflected the affection in which General Sir Redvers Buller, VC, was held, despite the fact that he presided over a succession of disasters and was replaced by Lord Roberts. Boer War veterans recalled the song being sung with feeling when Buller was removed:[27]

> Cheer Up, Buller, my lad,
> Don't say die.
> We'll know the reason why,
> To slight you some would try.
> You've done your best for England,
> And England won't forget.
> Cheer Up, Buller, my lad,
> You're not dead yet.

There was indeed a fashion among the working classes for naming their offspring after the generals and battles of the Boer War, a fashion which inspired the novelty song by C.W. Murphy and A.S. Hall, *The Baby's Name* (1900). Mrs Blobbs, considering a name for her new son, rejects the more obvious 'Jack' and 'Richard', and sings:

> The baby's name is . . .
> Kitchener, Carrington, Methuen,
> Kekewich, White;
> Cronje, Plumer, Powell, Majuba,
> Gatacre, Warren, Colenso, Kruger,
> Cape Town, Mafeking, French,
> Kimberley, Ladysmith, Bobs,
> The Union Jack and Fighting Mac,
> Lyddite, Pretoria-Blobbs.

J.B. Booth recalls that the chorus 'achieved enormous popularity'.[28] The songwriters were anxious to stress the full participation of the Irish in the conflict. So *Dear Old Bobs*, while stressing his democratic credentials ('He's pals with Tommy Atkins/ He's chums with all the nobs'), adds: 'He's Irish! He's British! And he's dear old Bobs.'[29] Similarly *He Was Only a Private Soldier* hymned: 'One of the rank and file, But he fought for the honour of England, like a son of Erin's Isle.'[30]

'Strange how potent cheap music is', wrote Noël Coward in *Private Lives*, and there is abundant evidence of the lasting potency of many of these songs. Coward himself employed *Soldiers of the Queen* for the Boer War scenes of his patriotic extravaganza *Cavalcade* in 1930 to capture the mood of the times. Writing his autobiography sixty-five years after he first heard the song, Herbert Wilcox was able to recall

[336]

from memory the words of the chorus of *The Baby's Name*, and Christopher Pulling could recall all the words of *Break the News to Mother* fifty years after a nursemaid taught them to him.[31] Most poignant of all, the last letter home of 16-year-old Jack Cornwell, who became a national hero when he died of his wounds after standing courageously by his gun during the Battle of Jutland in 1916 and was awarded a posthumous VC, contains a post-script which reads: 'Cheer Up, Buller, me lad, we're not dead yet' and 'Break the News to Mother', indicating the extent to which these music-hall songs had become an integral part of everyday family exchanges.[32]

The First World War saw the usual crop of recruiting songs (*Your King and Country Want You; We Don't Want to Lose You*) and imperial solidarity songs (*Australia Will Be There*), and pre-war songs such as *The Deathless Army* and *Boys of the Old Brigade* enjoyed a new lease of life; but the soldiers' own songs were lacking in the bombast of the nineteenth-century imperial war songs, and by the time the Great War ended the heyday of music hall and music-hall patriotism had passed and music hall was transmuting into variety. But imperialism simply migrated to the new media of cinema, wireless and gramophone.

Given the prominence of songs about soldiers in the music halls, it seems pertinent to ask what music the soldiers themselves sang. This was the question Lewis Winstock asked in his wide-ranging and exhaustively researched *Songs and Music of the Redcoats 1642–1902*. He concluded that the oldest surviving soldiers' songs were the product of Britain's eighteenth-century wars. Four of them are still recognizable today as popular signifiers of the army and army life. The earliest printed version of *The British Grenadiers* dates from 1745; but Winstock, who calls it 'the best known among British marches and war songs', believes that the tune is a late seventeenth-century march preserved orally.[33] The words would seem to date from the period after the 1707 Act of Union had created Great Britain, otherwise it would presumably be called *The English Grenadiers*. The rollicking tune is set to words proclaiming the British Grenadiers greater than all the world's great heroes, and lauding their courage.[34] From round about the same period comes *Over the Hills and Far Away* (traditional words and music). Believed to date specifically from Marlborough's campaigns ('Over the hills and o'er the main/ To Flanders, Portugal and Spain/ Queen Anne commands and we'll obey/ Over the hills and far away'), it celebrates army life as representing escape from scolding wives, noisy children and tyrannical masters.[35] It was still being sung during the Napoleonic Wars, and featured recently as the title music to the popular ITV drama series *Sharpe*, set in the Napoleonic Wars.

[337]

The Girl I Left Behind Me (words and music traditional), which Winstock dates to 1758, is the classic lament of a soldier for the sweetheart he has left behind. It has continued to be played regularly down to the present and has featured in films dealing with the British Army and the US cavalry. *Garryowen* (words and music traditional), 'written in praise of the moneyed young hooligans who ran riot in Limerick' and dating from 1770–80, is an unashamed celebration of boozing and fighting.[36] It was adopted as the regimental march of General George Armstrong Custer's Seventh Cavalry and has regularly been featured in films recounting their exploits and their tragic fate at the Battle of the Little Big Horn. Taken together, they represent a self-image of the soldier's life which combines a boastful assertion of superior courage and bravery, sentimental attachment to sweethearts, rejoicing in escape from responsibility and a defiant celebration of drunkenness and brawling.

When British forces left for the Crimean War in 1854, they were duly accompanied by the tunes *The British Grenadiers*, *Garryowen*, and *The Girl I Left Behind Me* plus *Rule, Britannia, God Save the Queen, Auld Lang Syne* and *Scots Wha' Hae Wi' Wallace Bled*. But the particular hit of the Crimean War, as much with the soldiers as with the public, was *Cheer, Boys, Cheer*. One eye-witness recalled that 'it was played by every naval and military band, sung in every ship and regiment, and whistled by every whistler', and Winstock says it 'enjoyed the same sort of popularity that *Tipperary* was to attain in World War One'.[37]

Cheer, Boys, Cheer (1852), with words by Dr Charles Mackay and music by Henry Russell, was a song of emigration. Rousing and eminently singable, it was the most famous of the 800 songs composed by Henry Russell, professional singer turned songwriter. He was to call his autobiography (published in 1895) *Cheer, Boys, Cheer* and he wrote there, confirming the contemporary evidence, that the song 'infused hope and courage in the breasts of our soldiers as they listened to its inspiring strains while embarking for the Crimean War'.[38] But it was only one of several songs he wrote to encourage emigration to the Americas.

The first verse, particularly applicable to departing soldiers, ran:

> Cheer, Boys, cheer! No more of idle sorrow.
> Courage, true hearts, shall bear us on our way.
> Hope points before us, and shows the bright tomorrow,
> Let us forget the darkness of today.

The song stressed patriotic love of England, the fortune to be made overseas and claims: 'The world shall follow in the track we're going/

The star of empire glitters in the west.' The British armies in 1854 were of course sailing eastwards, but that was a minor detail to set against the stirring tune and rousing chorus:

> Cheer, boys, cheer! For country, mother country.
> Cheer, boys, cheer! The willing strong right hand.
> Cheer! boys, cheer! There's wealth in honest labour.
> Cheer! boys, cheer! For the new and happy land.

Russell, who had sold the copyrights to all his most successful songs, recorded with gratitude that the publishers presented him with a silver plate, inscribed 'Cheer, Boys, Cheer' and a cheque for £10 in recognition of the enormous sales of the sheet music.[39]

Russell had a clear view of his object as composer; writing in his autobiography:

> It has ever been my object to make music the medium of common sense, by uniting it to good wholesome poetry; mine was a kind of recitative put to music, depicting everyday life in all its phases. I tried to carry audiences with me, heart and soul; to make them feel that I was not only singing to them, but I was telling them a story. A story that should rouse the noblest feelings that their hearts were capable of.[40]

Sincerity, accessibility, ennoblement and uplift were Russell's aims, and frequently enlightenment and education, as he wrote songs on anti-slavery themes as well as on emigration. With Mackay writing the lyrics, he composed *A Good Time Coming, Boys, To the West* and many others, even staging an entertainment, *The Far West*, in which a succession of songs against a succession of specially painted backdrops charted 'the emigrant's progress from the Old World to the New'. He claimed that the emigration songs 'had a beneficial effect on the public. They impressed on many a poor family the absurdity of clinging to a country, if that country refused them and their children bread. Hundreds, nay thousands, followed the good advice, and set out to seek their fortunes in the New World.'[41]

In 1891 impresario Sir Augustus Harris staged an eightieth birthday Henry Russell tribute at Covent Garden and the next day the *Daily Telegraph* published an article confirming Russell's own assessment of his career and significance. It described him as 'a melodist, who appealed to the heart of the people, more successfully, perhaps, than has any singer of his own songs during the present century' and the composer 'of a chain of ditties, which has long since encircled the civilised world, and the links in which are as strong as in the days of their first forging'. Despite modern musical developments in 'England, her colonies, and America', the love for 'the simple sentiment and straightforward melodies' of Russell had survived; Russell believed in 'songs that had a purpose' and their sentiment was 'always manly, never maudlin'. It recalled his campaign on behalf of emigration and recalled the memories of soldiers leaving for the Crimea and workers emigrating to the Americas, departing with his 'anthem of optimism' on their lips.[42]

Cheer, Boys, Cheer was also sung by British troops during the Indian Mutiny, which produced the extraordinary sight and sound of rebel sepoys playing British army tunes (*See, the Conquering Hero Comes*; *The Girl I Left Behind Me*; and even *God Save the Queen*), while besieging British garrisons. But there was no song on the British side as universally popular as *Cheer, Boys, Cheer* had been during the Crimean War. One of the more incongruous favourites was *Don't You Remember Sweet Alice, Ben Bolt?* (words and music by N. Kneass), a sentimental ballad evoking the memories of rural England, boyhood and the youthful sweetheart of an absent soldier. The British Army in India, while perpetuating the songs and ballads of the homeland, also took up some indigenous Indian themes. The most famous was the Pathan song *Zachmi Dil* (The Wounded Heart), which became the unofficial march of the Liverpool regiment. It turned out on closer investigation to be a lament of unrequited homosexual love:

> There's a boy across the river,
> With a bottom like a peach,
> But alas – I cannot swim.

The Empire's 'small wars' produced a crop of celebrations of the imperial soldiery and of imperial heroes which appealed equally to the general public and the soldiery. *The Noble 24th* (words by G.C. Anewick, music by V. Davies) commemorated the historic defeat of the British at Isandlwana by the Zulus ('Five hundred valiant English fought, and nobly fighting fell'). Its chorus was taken up and sung by the 24th regiment (the South Wales Borderers):

> All honour to the twenty-fourth
> Of glorious renown.
> England, avenge your countrymen
> And strike the foemen down.[43]

Kiss Me, Mother, Kiss Your Darling (words by L.C. Lord, music G.F. Root) is a deeply sentimental song sung by a dying soldier to his mother:

> Tell the loved ones not to murmur,
> Say I died our flag to save

And that I shall slumber sweetly
In the soldiers' honoured grave

This was actually being played by the band of the 94th Regiment, shortly before being wiped out by the Boers at Bronkhurstspruit in 1880.

During the Boer War, the soldiers' taste veered towards the sentimental. C. Rose-Innes reported: 'Mr. Atkins inclines towards mournful sentiment and such songs as *Break the News to Mother* were always favourites.'[44] The other favourites included *Comrades*, *Home, Sweet Home* and *Dolly Gray*. But the soldiers are also recorded cheerfully singing the self-confident *Soldiers of the Queen*.[45]

The First World War confirmed the soldiers' taste for the sentimental. For along with the parodies and satires, the soldiers' grumbling songs and the fatalism, there was a strong strain of sentiment tending to the wistful and the longing, with *Roses of Picardy*, *There's a Long, Long Trail A-winding*, *If You Were the Only Girl in the World*, *Let the Great Big World Keep Turning* and *Keep the Home Fires Burning*. Interestingly, the original version of Ivor Novello's hit had been titled, with overt patriotism, *Keep the Flag A-flying*, but this was abandoned in favour of the more domestic and intimate *Keep the Home Fires Burning*. But perhaps the two most popular songs were the cheerful marching songs *It's a Long Way to Tipperary* and *Pack Up Your Troubles in Your Old Kit Bag*.[46]

As in the First World War, so too in the Second, the popular hits were sentimental songs about parting, reunion and hopes for the future. Many of them were associated with the 'Forces' Sweetheart' Vera Lynn: *There'll Be Bluebirds Over the White Cliffs of Dover*; *Yours*; *We'll Meet Again*; *It's a Lovely Day Tomorrow*; and *When the Lights Come On Again All Over the World*. There were so many of these that an alarmed BBC, believing that such songs undermined the morale of servicemen, embarked on what the press dubbed 'the Anti-Slush War'. Songs and singers deemed too sentimental were dropped. To stiffen morale and fighting spirit, continuity announcers were ordered: 'when in doubt err on the side of marches.'[47]

The monarchy was celebrated in *The King Is Still in London* – 'The King is still in London, in London, in London/ Like Mr. Jones and Mr. Brown, the King is still in London town.' But the war added a new item to the stock of national songs, *There'll Always Be an England*, by Ross Parker and Hughie Charles. First heard in the summer of 1939, it became the first hit-song of the war and was played and sung for the war's duration and beyond.[48] It was an inclusive song, celebrating country, city and Empire.

[341]

There'll always be an England
While there's a country lane,
Wherever there's a cottage small
Beside a field of grain.

There'll always be an England
While there's a busy street,
Wherever there's a turning wheel,
A million marching feet.

Red, white and blue,
What does it mean to you,
Surely you're proud,
Shout it aloud, Britons awake.
The Empire too, we can depend on you,
Freedom remains, These are the chains, Nothing can break.

There'll always be an England,
And England shall be free,
If England means as much to you
As England means to me.

As so often, England is used here as a synonym for Britain. But its instant success indicates that it expressed a widely held national sentiment.

Popular ballads

Victorian and Edwardian popular ballads have been a subject of mockery and derision in the second half of the twentieth century, denounced as maudlin, stereotyped and sentimental.[49] But to take up such an attitude is both patronizing and ahistorical, to be guilty of what E.P. Thompson memorably called 'the enormous condescension of posterity'. The historian needs to judge them not by the anachronistic standards of the present but by their role, function and nature within Victorian and Edwardian society.

The drawing-room ballad was, as Derek Scott has demonstrated in his excellent book *The Singing Bourgeois*, a bourgeois construct, addressing the values, attitudes and opinions of the middle class, but one that percolated down to the working class to constitute a genuinely popular music.[50] The wide popularity of many of the drawing-room ballads should not be disparaged. The majority had strophic settings which repeated a simple melody for each verse, and had a catchy chorus or refrain which invited audience participation and was often the best-known part of the ballad. Their sentiments were in tune with those of their audience, and if we today no longer value the idealism, the purity, the nobility, the sacrifice and the sense of duty many of these ballads reflect, then so much the worse for us. As Nicholas Temperley writes: 'The emotion of the best Victorian ballads is genuine, and we need not be ashamed to respond to it.'[51]

Composing music for ballads was seen as an appropriate outlet for female composers, many of them denied other musical outlets. The themes they were expected to address, and did in large measure (love, children, marriage and jilting, religion), tell us something about the cultural construction of femininity. Scottish and Irish ballads, real and imitation, were popular because they hymned the beauties of nature, contentment with one's lot, rural bliss and a settled society. Sacred songs like *The Holy City* and *The Lost Chord* provided the spiritual uplift, and the exotic ballads (*The Arab's Farewell To His Steed*; *I'll Sing Thee Songs of Araby*) reflected the growing interest in travel, exploration and Empire and the construction of a fairy-tale realm known as 'The East', where romantic yearnings could achieve fantasy fulfilment.

With rising prosperity, the growth in the ownership of pianos and improvements in printing technology, the publisher Novello pioneered the production and sale of inexpensive music from the 1840s. Music publishing expanded in the later nineteenth century as publishers like Chappell, Boosey and Novello promoted concerts to showcase their latest ballads and paid royalties to leading singers to include them in their repertoire. Later, songwriters, who initially sold their songs outright, also received a royalty. So the price of sheet-music ballads fell from four shillings in the 1860s to three shillings in the 1870s to two shillings in the 1880s. Many of the leading composers of the day (Sullivan, Elgar, Parry, Stanford, Cowen) derived an important part of their income from ballads.

The heyday of the ballad was probably the period between the 1880s and 1920s. An examination of ballads from that period reveals the domination of themes of love, loss, dreams, parting, yearning, regret, separation and memory, with a combination of lilting melodies, an elevated sensibility and deeply felt emotion.[52] The repertoire of themes includes motherhood, childhood, romantic rather than sexual love, the countryside, family life. But along with these went the sea, the army and the Empire. The fact that it was possible to move from one subject to another without apparent incongruity, indicating how integral were patriotism and Empire to the popular mind, is demonstrated by the career of Fred E. Weatherly (1848–1929). Weatherly was one of the leading lyricists of the ballad, and 1,500 of his songs were set to music by leading song composers such as Eric Coates, W.H. Squire, Kennedy Russell, J.L. Molloy and Stephen Adams. He has left in his autobiography a record of the influences upon him and the sources of his inspiration.

He was born in 1848 in Portishead, Somerset, one of a family of thirteen, the son of a country doctor who found that 'from my earliest childhood, ships, books and music were my chief delight'. He had 'an exceptionally happy and fortunate childhood and boyhood' and he never lost his love of Somerset, which inspired his songs *The Green Hills of Somerset*, *Up From Somerset* and *Stonecracker John*. As a boy he played at highwaymen in the woods, listened to a school teacher reading aloud Scott's novels and dreamed of King Arthur and his knights, and John Cabot and his merchant adventurers. Such memories inspired his *Claude Duval* and *Highwayman Jack*. He loved the sea, and watched the ships sailing up and down the Bristol Channel, scenes which inspired *Nancy Lee* and *They All Loved Jack*. He remembered the gypsies camping in the countryside, hence *The Romany Lass* and *The Red Star of the Romany*. His mother told him stories of Inkerman, Alma and Balaclava, and 'of the little middy who took a boat crew ashore at Sebastopol and spiked the Russian guns'. This true story inspired the song *The Midshipmite*. He went to Hereford Cathedral School where he developed a love of cricket, theatre and church music, and discovered 'the wonderland of books'. He devoured the works of Marryat, Ainsworth, G.P.R. James, Dickens, Scott, Byron, Longfellow and Tennyson, as thorough a grounding in romantic literature as one could wish. His cathedral school background found expression in *The Holy City* and *Star of Bethlehem*. He went up to Oxford in 1867 where he rowed, was taught by Pater and discovered the poetry of William Morris, Swinburne and Rossetti ('What inspired me was the colour of it all'). He graduated in 1871, initially becoming a schoolmaster, but in 1887 he was called to the bar and embarked upon a long career as a barrister on the Western Circuit, combining his legal work with his prolific writing of verses and song lyrics. He recorded the sources of his inspiration:

> Something seen, something read of, something told; some tragedy, some comedy of life of which one has heard or in which one has taken part; knowledge of people's ways and peculiarities, love of beautiful things – the sea, the forest, the rolling hills, the working voices of the dawn, the solemn hush of the night – all these things and the power to appreciate them go to the making of songs.[53]

He testifies to the importance of his songs in binding together the Empire by their expression of a common sensibility.

> It is no idle boast when I say that my songs have been sung by millions all over the English-speaking world; it is not myself that I am praising

but my friends the musicians and the singers who have carried my words to the heart of the people. I do not claim to be a 'poet', I don't pretend that my songs are 'literary' but they are 'songs of the people' and that is enough for me.[54]

He was infuriated by the disparagement of popular ballads in favour of the new 'art song' or of the folk-songs being collected by Cecil Sharp and his followers. He passionately defended the ballad form:

Are such songs to be called 'inartistic', 'shop ballads' and so on, because they are popular? To call them so seems to me a form of intellectual pride. Such songs are popular because the people love them, the people sing them and buy them because they love them. The heart of the people is still simple and healthy and sound.[55]

He denounced the folk-song movement for collecting, expurgating and re-editing folk-songs and passing them off as genuinely popular songs, while ignoring 'the thousands of songs, simple, healthy, humorous, tender and sentimental, that have been sung during the last fifty years in concert rooms throughout Great Britain, her colonies and America'.[56]

So, along with the exotic (*Nirvana*), the love songs (*Thora*) and the rustic reveries (*Green Hills of Somerset*) went the imperial, the naval, the military and the patriotic. Many of his songs celebrated glorious death overseas in the service of king and country. *The Deathless Army* (1891), set by H. Troteré, is powerful and moving in its imagery of gallant troops in red and gold marching off to war amid drums and trumpets, followed by a phantom host of all those who had fought and died before them:

> Marching for the dear Old Country,
> Marching away to war,
> With the hearts they love behind them,
> And the flag they love, before.

Weatherly proudly recalled hearing it sung at the People's Palace, Bristol, at an Inkerman Anniversary:

The Bristol veterans, survivors of the Crimean expedition and of the Indian Mutiny, were standing to attention, bareheaded, their medals on their breasts. They were thinking, I am sure, of the dead comrades who lie in the Crimea and on the Indian hills, standing in the valley of the shadow waiting for the final Last Post to sound.[57]

Equally he recalled with pride the Bristol men marching off to the Great War in 1914 singing his lines:

[345]

> It's a rough, rough road we're going,
> It's a tough stiff job to do,
> But as sure as the tide is flowing,
> We mean to see it through.
> Who cares what the fight will cost us?
> Who recks of the shot and flame?
> We fight for the sake of England
> And the honour of Bristol's name.

Similarly *The Glory of the Sea*, set to music by Wilfred Sanderson, celebrated the sinking of a ship by the enemy with her tattered flag still flying, 'As she sank – for England's honour, and the glory of the sea' and hearing the news, a sailor's widow sings 'Thank God I gave my dearest to the glory of the sea'.

   Jack Briton (1910), set by W.H. Squire, celebrated the eternal British sailor:

> My name is Jack Briton and, as it appears,
> I've been at some fighting these three hundred years;
> For I does what I'm told, I'm a plain sort of chap,
> But it keeps a man busy when changing the map.

The equation of Empire with justice was highlighted in *Jack's Yarn*, set by Lewis Diehl. It was inspired by an Admiralty Order that runaway slaves seeking rescue on British ships be surrendered, an order defied by British seamen:

> "Every man is free" he cried
> "Where the British flag flies,
> And I'll never give him up" says he.

It was bought by an Irish singer with the Italianate stage name Foli, and when sung at the Crystal Palace caused a great demonstration in its favour. 'An immensely popular song of which millions of copies are said to have been sold', reported Harold Simpson.[58] These are just a few of Weatherly's patriotic ballads, and that they reflect his own genuine feelings is further underlined by his writing of the libretto for Joseph L. Roeckel's *The Victorian Age*, a cantata for the 1887 Golden Jubilee of Queen Victoria. It aimed to sketch in musical form the prominent features of the fifty years of 'Her Majesty's beneficent reign', which it took to be the spread of education, the extension of the franchise, the growth of trade, 'the useful lessons of war' and the development of the colonies.[59] The chorus *Ave Imperatrix* celebrated the solidarity of the Empire, with the colonists singing

The wide, wide sea may sever
Our homes from thine and thee,
But ever still for ever
Thy loyal sons are we.
Still brother calls to brother
Where'er our feet may roam
For thou are our great mother,
And Britain is our home!
Ave Imperatrix, Mother across the sea.
Ave Imperatrix, we send our hearts to thee!

But in addition to the original verses of the song lyricists, the works of many of the leading imperialist poets were set to music by composers and turned into parlour ballads.

Alongside the sung ballad, the spoken ballad also flourished in the nineteenth century. Ballads were declaimed as part of commercial entertainments but also recited at family gatherings, parish missionary and temperance meetings. The practice of public recitation was well established, sustained by anthologies of readings and books of instruction for would-be reciters. J.S. Bratton has sensitively and perceptively analyzed the whole phenomenon in her excellent pioneering work *The Victorian Popular Ballad*. She points out that heroic ballads were one of the staples of recitation and that there was an enormous appetite for them. They were infused with the same themes, sentiments and attitudes as the patriotic music-hall songs, and were devoured as eagerly. Sir Walter Scott (*The Lay of the Last Minstrel; The Lady of the Lake*) and Lord Macaulay (*Lays of Ancient Rome*) had revivified the old ballad form, setting the pattern for the genre with new ballads with a strong nationalist and patriotic flavour. As Bratton puts it:

> Most ballad writers derived from Scott and Macaulay the theory that all ballads past and present were written to immortalize the heroic deeds of the nation. Providing a standard of comparison for each individual to measure himself against, a source of pride for the passive members of society, a lesson for the young in the honour and traditions of the race, and when performed an active source of inspiration to further efforts.[60]

She identifies in the ballads a narrow range of story patterns embodying a common code of beliefs and behaviour. They focus on the ideal hero, whether famous (Lord Nelson, General Gordon) or unknown (the idealized common man of the armed forces, Jack Tar or Tommy Atkins). They stress his virtues of patriotism, bravery, stoicism, daring and honour. They frequently involve a tragic though noble end. They

[347]

seek to convey not a moral so much as a view of the world and a set of assumptions. As Bratton rightly points out, it is a distortion to regard these images as being imposed on the people in order to exploit them, 'for the emotions they expressed were those of the great majority of Englishmen of every rank, and the image of the heroic common man which they project was one which he himself aspired to and enjoyed'.[61] The popular ballads therefore played a vital role in sustaining the Englishman's self-image, in confirming the rightness of British rule over a quarter of the globe and in comforting 'the folks at home' when death was the outcome of foreign adventuring. The Empire was frequently the location for these heroic deeds, and they inspired a range of poems that were the staples of reciters throughout the nineteenth century. They include Tennyson's *The Revenge* and *Charge of the Light Brigade*, Newbolt's *Vitai Lampada* and *He Fell Among Thieves*, Sir Francis Doyle's *The Private of the Buffs* and *Saving of the Colours*, Gerald Massey's *The Relief of Lucknow* and Sir Henry Yule's *The Birkenhead*.

A number of famous ballads and poems were set to music and sung as well as being recited. W.E. Henley's *The Last Post* (1900) was impressively set by Sir Charles Stanford as a choral song, for mixed voices and orchestra. Celebrating those who died in the service of the Empire:

> Blow, you bugles of England, blow!
> That her Name as a sun among stars might glow,
> Till the dusk of Time, with honour and worth:
> The One Race ever might starkly spread,
> And the One Flag eagle it overhead!
> In a rapture of wrath and faith and pride,
> Thus they felt it and thus they died.

Henley's most famous poem, *Pro Rege Nostro*, better known by its first lines, 'What have I done for you England, my England', was set by Martin Shaw before the First World War, by Healey Willan in 1914 and by Vaughan Williams in 1941, the last two settings clearly prompted by the needs of war:

> Ever the faith endures,
> England, my England: –
> 'Take and break us: we are yours,
> England, my own!
> Life is good and joy runs high
> Between English earth and sky:
> Death is death; but we shall die
> To the song on your bugles blown, England.'

[348]

It is not now much remembered that Sir Arthur Conan Doyle was, in addition to being a novelist and short-story writer, also a poet and celebrant of Empire. His poems too were taken up by composers. They tell stories in a Kiplingesque idiom of heroic last stands and storming parties, of gallant public schoolboys who die for their country and administrators and officers who keep the Queen's peace in lonely outposts. In his *A Ballad of the Ranks* he paid his own tribute to 'Tommy Atkins'. It asked 'Who carries the gun?' and then ran through the variety of serving soldiers, Scots, Welsh, Lancashire, Yorkshire, Midland, Irish, west country, Londoner, united in comradeship, loyalty and service. It was set by Stanford in 1893 and Maud Valerie White in 1900. His *The Frontier Line* was also set by Stanford in 1893. *A Hymn of Empire* was composed for the Coronation of King George V in 1911 and set by Sir Frederic Cowen. It evoked in turn all the major components of the Empire, with the chorus:

> Set Thy guard over us,
> May Thy shield cover us,
> Enfold and uphold us
> On land and on sea!
> From the palm to the pine,
> From the snow to the line,
> Brothers together
> And Children of Thee.

The sea has always been a central element in popular song. The English love of the sea is linked to the sense of national identity. As Robert Louis Stevenson wrote: 'The sea is our approach and bulwark; it has been the scene of our greatest triumphs and dangers; and we are accustomed in lyrical strains to claim it as our own.'[62] Britain's naval history was an integral part of the Whig interpretation of history, the gradually evolving and improving story of the nation, as it proceeds from sixteenth to nineteenth centuries achieving democracy, commercial and maritime supremacy and an empire. In this version of history, rulers are extolled for their commitment to the navy, thus King Alfred who founded the English Navy and King Henry VIII who refounded it are given pride of place.

Naval heroes and naval heroism are celebrated in song and story from Drake, Hawkins and the Elizabethan seadogs defending the Protestant Reformation against attack by Catholic Spain through Cromwell's Admiral Blake, to the eighteenth-century admirals like Rodney, Benbow and Hawke and finally Nelson and his captains, victors of the epic struggle against Napoleon. Patriotic songs linked with the sea particularly take off in the eighteenth century. *Rule, Bri-*

tannia (1745) contains all the elements of the myth. The Seven Years War produces Garrick's naval anthem *Hearts of Oak* (1759).

Love of and mastery over the sea were seen by Victorian historians like Freeman and Froude as the key to Britain's racial superiority. Linked with the sea is Britain's position as an island, which leads to insularity and exclusivity, but also protects Britain from contamination by the outside world.

The English seaman becomes the epitome of British character and the Jack Tar, the symbol of robust and down-to-earth Englishness. T.P. Cooke, who as a sailor had seen service at the Battle of St Vincent, played William, the sailor hero of Douglas Jerrold's *Black-Eyed Susan* (1829), no fewer that 765 times and spent his twenty-five years' stage career incarnating similar maritime heroes; Jack Gallant, Jack Stedfast, Bill Bluff and Ben Billows among them. It was Tobias Smollett, himself a naval surgeon, who effectively invented the nautical novel and created the archetypal naval hero, Lt Tom Bowling, in *The Adventures of Roderick Random* (1748). Bowling was 'a man in whose speech is the salt savour of the sea, in whose personality is the breezy, open disposition of the seaman, all of the seaman's courage, all his simplicity, his generous prodigality, his spirit of comradeship, his simple philosophy, his practical sense'. He became the symbol of the nation. As Lord Palmerston said: 'When I want a man with a good head, a good heart, lots of pluck, and plenty of common sense, I always send for a captain of the navy.' Courage, discipline and character were the chief attributes bestowed by the naval career, according to the myth.

Both fictional and true-life stories of the navy cast their heroes in this mould. In the nineteenth century the maritime fiction of Captain Marryat, read by adults and children alike, the ballads of Charles Dibdin, whose most celebrated song was *Tom Bowling*, and the nautical melodramas all confirmed this myth. The pre-eminent naval hero was Nelson, who fulfilled the crucial quality: death at the moment of victory, to ensure immortality.[63] There was a particular surge of interest in Nelson in the last two decades of the nineteenth century as Britain's naval supremacy was challenged by rival powers. No fewer that ten biographies appeared and John Braham's *The Death of Nelson* (1811), with its famous refrain 'for England, Home and Beauty', remained a popular ballad. The centenary of Trafalgar, on 21 October 1905, was commemorated musically by the ballad cantatas *Trafalgar* by Hugh Blair and *A Song of Trafalgar* by Gerard Cobb, and by Sir Henry Wood's much-loved *Fantasia on British Sea Songs*. It was intended to provide a 'real popular climax' to a maritime Prom programme which included Mackenzie's *Britannia* and Wagner's *Flying*

Dutchman overtures, and songs such as *Hearts of Oak* and *Rocked in the Cradle of the Deep*. The *Fantasia* was so popular that it has been repeated in virtually every Prom season since, usually on the last night. On the two occasions when it was dropped, the outcry has been so great that it has promptly been reinstated.

The full version of the *Fantasia* – and sometimes an abbreviated version is played – begins with bugle calls: the admiral's salute, action, general assembly, landing party, prepare to ram and quick, double, extend and close. Then it moves through a succession of songs, each evoking a different mood: *The Anchor's Weighed* (with solo trumpet and trombone); *The Saucy Arethusa* (with solo euphonium); *Tom Bowling* (with solo cello); the hornpipe *Jack's the Lad* (with solo violin, flute and piccolo); *Farewell and Adieu, Ye Fair Spanish Ladies*; *Home, Sweet Home* (with solo oboe and harp); *See, the Conquering Hero Comes* (with solo horn); and *Rule, Britannia* (with organ and full orchestra).[64] Poets like Tennyson, Kipling and Swinburne continually extolled the sea, the fleet and the ordinary British sailor. But it was Newbolt who in his *Songs of the Sea* and *Songs of Fleet* achieved the greatest mythification, with his celebration of Nelson, Drake and the fleets of the past. They were set to music by Sir Charles Villiers Stanford.

Harry Plunket Greene, Stanford's son-in-law and biographer, notes the irony that 'Parry, English to the bone, sailor, swimmer, adventurer, never wrote a note in praise of salt water', but Stanford, who composed the ballad *The Revenge* as well as *The Songs of the Sea* and *Songs of the Fleet*, 'hated, or professed to hate, the sea'. It was not 'pleasure cruises in the Mediterranean or buffetings off the coast of Wicklow' that provided Stanford's inspiration. It was Newbolt's words and his own imagination. 'Irish though he was, with his romantic nationality showing through in every bar of absolute music, when he dealt with England on the sea he was as English as Tennyson or Henry Newbolt.'[65]

Plunket Greene himself gave the first performance of the *Songs of the Sea* in Leeds:

I shall never forget the enthusiasm of the chorus when we tried them through the first time, nor the cheers when he told the tenors that they could sing the F and top B flat (not in the original score) at the finish of *The Old Superb*. Everything went right on the night and *The Old Superb* taken at a break-neck pace whirled the audience off their feet. It was a joyous evening for all concerned and doubly joyous the next day when the *Yorkshire Post* said that '"the lame duck lagging all the way' had been more like the *Mauretania* on her trial trip"'. This is the only adverse criticism that I have ever received which delighted me.

[351]

Newbolt himself recorded his appreciation of the contributions of both Stanford and Greene to the musical version of his poems:

> (Stanford) was the most subtly appreciative critic and interpreter of poetry that I ever met with. Again and again he would receive my verses by the morning post, and set them before noon to irresistible music. I always felt that to hear those songs, given as Harry Greene could give them, was to be told secrets about myself, to see my own thought reflected with perfect accuracy but irradiated with the magic lights of a dream. He could set a ballad to a hornpipe so perfectly as to make my ears hear the wind in the rigging and my nerves dance, as it were, to my own tune. Better still, he could tell me in my own language what it means to some of us to sight the White Cliffs after a long voyage, and what it may mean to any of us to be Outward Bound at last.[66]

The settings are discussed in chapter fourteen.

The Newbolt poems proved a magnet for composers. *Drake's Drum* was set not only by Stanford but also by Sir Granville Bantock (1927), Samuel Coleridge-Taylor (1906), Walter Hedgcock (1891), Herbert Wrighton (1924), J.R. Wheeler (1939), George W. Chadwick (nd) and Arthur Farwell (nd). Bantock also set *Admiral Death* and *The Fighting Temeraire*. E. Markham Lee set *Admirals All* (nd) and Montague Phillips *The Death of Admiral Blake*. Of Newbolt's non-naval poems, *He Fell Among Thieves* was set by John Owen-Jones, *The King's Highway* by Stanford (1914), *Victoria Regina* by Charles H. Lloyd (1897) and *Vitai Lampada* by Florence Aylward (1900).

The most significant cross-over figure in the musical culture, sung in music halls, concert halls, drawing-rooms and pubs, was Rudyard Kipling. W.T. Stead's *Review of Reviews* had proclaimed him the 'Laureate of Empire' in 1896.[67] His position was succinctly summarized by Robert H. MacDonald:

> The importance of Kipling as the mythmaker of Empire cannot be over-stressed. He was the writer of the imperial hymns, he both spoke for and helped create the expansionist mood of the 1890s. Kipling beat the drum, but he also called his fellow-imperialists to a sense of responsibility and pride, reminding them of the mutability of all things, and the dangers of pride. He gave them a literature of the wider world, teaching them to appreciate 'The God of Things as They Are'; he gave dignity to the work of the engineer and the bridge-builder.[68]

J.S. Bratton – rightly in my view – sees Kipling as a popular poet whose work was 'the crown and epitome of the Victorian popular tradition, taking in all levels of the popular audience and uniting in his work all that is most expressive of the music-hall and drawing-room poetic conventions'. She believes he surpassed Scott and Macaulay 'by the force of his historical imagination and the skill of his handling of the rhetorical patterns they established'. She concludes:

> Most important of all, the roots of his gift lie beneath the superficial divisions of class and distinction of audience, so that the strength of his ballads is not confined to any section of the ballad varieties which he wrote, but is expressive of the unity which lay beneath them all and fed them from the same communal experiences and emotions.[69]

They were experiences and emotions which Kipling shared and sought to celebrate as the people's ballad-maker. It was the depth of feeling and the sense of complete identification with his subjects, coupled with his technical mastery and the grounding of his verse in popular rhythms, which secured his success.

Kipling drew for his mature poetry not on the models of Swinburne or Browning, who had inspired his juvenile efforts, but on popular rhythms and verse traditions. Charles Carrington identifies three sources of his poetic language. The first is the border ballad of Scott and Burns: 'The stylized imagery, the use of incantatory repetitions, the harmonics of a verse intended to be recited against a background of simple instrumental music, the turns of sentiment marked by a change of rhythm.'[70] The second source was the King James Bible and *Hymns Ancient and Modern*. Kipling, sent back to England from India by his parents, spent nearly six years in a Bible-reading and hymn-singing Calvinist household in Southsea. He called it 'The House of Desolation' and loathed it for its tyranny and lovelessness, but during the course of his stay he learned by heart 'a great deal of the Bible'.[71] Its stately sonorities became an integral part of his poetic imagination. Carrington calls *Hymns Ancient and Modern* 'by far the most popular volume of verse in nineteenth-century England' and noted that 'it was left to Kipling to adapt this genre of the popular hymn to the purpose of contemporary ballads'.[72] His third source was the songs the ordinary people were singing in the bar-rooms, barracks and music halls, and the tunes which imprinted themselves on his memory were American Civil War marching songs like *John Brown's Body*, *Marching Through Georgia* and *Tramp, Tramp, Tramp, the Boys Are Marching*, and music-hall standards such as *The Man Who Broke the Bank at Monte Carlo* and *Knocked 'Em in the Old Kent Road*.

When Kipling was writing one of his ballads, the ideas would form and a tune would be running through his head, and this rather than poetic metre would dictate its final form. Mrs Kipling would regularly confide to her diary: 'Ruddy was *singing* a new poem today'[73] (my italics). It has been possible to identify the musical inspiration for some of his verses. *Mandalay* was composed to the tune of a popular waltz; *Follow Me 'Ome* to the *Dead March* from *Saul*; *Birds of Prey*, to *Knocked 'Em in the Old Kent Road*; *'Shillin' a Day*, to *Villikins and his Dinah*; *Boots*, to *John Brown's Body*; *Ford at Kabul River* to *Tramp, Tramp, Tramp*; and *Danny Deever*, to the army song euphemistically known as *Barnacle Bill the Sailor*.[74] *The Widow's Party* can certainly be sung to *When Johnny Comes Marching Home*.

Their popularity with the public and their innate musicality made Kipling's ballads prime candidates for transformation into songs. Kipling's bibliographer James McG. Stewart traced some 273 different musical settings of Kipling, and there have been more since he compiled that listing and others he will have missed.[75] Perhaps the most famous collection of Kipling settings is the nineteen musical versions of the *Barrack Room Ballads*, published in three series in 1892, 1893 and 1897. Sixteen of the settings were by Gerard F. Cobb, a Cambridge don otherwise best known for writing church anthems. But he also established his imperialist bona fides with musical settings of Tennyson's *Charge of the Light Brigade* (1865), Newbolt's *The Gay Gordons* (1897) and E. Nesbit's *A Song of Trafalgar* (1900), as well as the march *The Charge at Dargai* (1898), celebrating the storming of the heights of Dargai by the Gordon Highlanders during a 'north-west frontier incident' in 1897.

Carrington sees the *Barrack Room Ballads* as the first adequate treatment of the English soldier since Shakespeare, and they did much to help transform the popular attitude to the army. Kipling dedicated them to Tommy Atkins, 'with my best respects', and faithfully chronicled the many aspects of the life of the soldier in the East, the loves and losses, the bravery and sacrifice, the drink and the boredom, the nerves and the sudden bursts of violence.

Cobb's three series were dedicated respectively to Lt General Sir Evelyn Wood, VC, described as 'former schoolfellow' of the composer, HRH The Duke of Cambridge, KG, and Field Marshal Lord Roberts of Kandahar, VC. They were an enormous success, earning encomia from the press and the nickname 'The Dibdin of the Army' for Cobb. The third series appeared in Diamond Jubilee year and *The Musical Times*, welcoming the sympathetic settings as simple, direct and effective, declared: 'The composer has again caught the wild, exuberant and reckless spirit which permeates the text ... and has acquired the power of increasing the dramatic significance of special points'.[76]

They are largely unknown today but would repay revival. Kipling had conceived *Mandalay* as a waltz and Cobb, recalling a lost romance in Burma and the sights and sounds and smells of the country, supplies for the soldier a delicate and evocative tune suggestive of the 'wind in the palm trees' and the tinkling temple bells. There is a rousing tribute to the gallant foe-man, *Fuzzy-Wuzzy*; the sombre, graphic advice of the old hand to the young soldier about the cholera, the heat, the fear, torture and death in *The Young British Soldier*; and the reflective *Screw Guns*. Australian baritone Peter Dawson recorded four of Cobb's settings. He also recorded Walter Hedgcock's 1899 setting of *Mandalay*, alternately sprightly and wistful; but both Cobb and Hedgcock were eclipsed by the 1907 setting by the American composer Oley Speaks, robustly set in march-time, which seems somehow more appropriate than waltz-time. This version can still be heard being sung today. Dawson himself, writing as J.P. McCall, made the definitive settings, vigorous and effective, of *Boots* (1928), *Route Marchin'* (1930) and *Cells* (1930).

Kipling ballads were also set by leading composers of the day. Sir Edward German set *The Irish Guards*, *The Just So Songs* and the rollicking *Rolling Down to Rio*. He also set in vividly melodramatic style in 1917 at the request of Clara Butt the poignant *My Boy Jack*, a series of urgent questions to the wind, 'Have you news of my boy Jack?', met by the mournful response 'Not this tide'. It builds to a triumphant finale and the vindication of sacrifice: 'He did not shame his kind/He was the son you bore.' Sir Frederick Bridge set *The Flag of England* in 1897. He had first heard it quoted in a sermon in the Abbey by Canon Farrar, who suggested he might set it to music. Kipling granted permission, and it became one of the hits of the Diamond Jubilee.[77] It was dedicated 'by gracious permission' to the Queen and received with enthusiasm by critics and public. Bridge had given each of the four winds a musical equivalent, the blustery north wind, the languorous south wind and so on. It was approvingly proclaimed by the *Daily Telegraph* 'tuneful, rhythmical and simple', and the *Daily Chronicle* said that it had 'thoroughly caught the spirit of the stirring and picturesque poem' and was confident it would 'speedily be in demand by choral societies . . . for it is marked by a freshness and energy not always apparent in compositions of this description'.[78] Walford Davies set *Our Lady of the Snows* and *Hymn Before Action*, earning the approval of *The Musical Times*: 'There is a healthy manliness in his music, which is at once inspiring and inspiriting.'[79]

The record for setting Kipling poems – some fifty in all – is surely held by the Australian composer–pianist Percy Grainger, who described himself as a composer 'whose musical output is based on patriotism and racial consciousness'.[80] He first encountered the poems in 1897 when he was studying in Germany and his father, feeling that 'the boy is getting too Teutonic', sent him several volumes of Kipling 'to tickle up the British lion in him'.[81] This initiated a life-long involvement with Kipling's works. Fellow-composer Cyril Scott believed 'no poet and composer have been so suitably "wedded" since Heine and Schumann than Kipling and Grainger', and one American critic, writing in 1916, dubbed Grainger 'The Kipling of Music'.[82] Many of the settings were first made in the 1890s but Grainger carried on revising, expanding and re-orchestrating them down to the 1950s. He also made several different settings of some faviourite texts.

There was a *Jungle Book* cycle, which included the heart-wrenching *Lukannon*, a white seal's lament for his fellows clubbed and shot to death by human hunters. But particularly striking and effective were his versions of Kipling's military and maritime ballads. *The Widow's Party* (1906), which he set for tenor, for male chorus and orchestra and as a piano piece, has a beguiling jauntiness which ironically counterpoints the gruesome catalogue of horrors endured by the soldiers involved in one of Queen Victoria's 'little wars':

> And some was sliced and some was halved,
> And some was crimped and some was carved,
> And some was gutted and some was starved.

Similarly, *The Young British Soldier* (1899), which unfolds the life awaiting the new recruit serving in the East (heat, violence, disease, drink and sudden death), does so with all the snap and jingle of a military march. Grainger made three different settings for *Soldier, Soldier*, in which a soldier's sweetheart enquires in vain for her dead lover.

The Anchor Song (1899) is an elaborate sea shanty, vigorous and virile, but underscored by the wistfulness of parting There is a heroic melancholy running through many of the sea songs, which tell of sacrifice and death in the service of nation and Empire: thus, for instance, *We Have Fed Our Seas for a Thousand Years* (1900), *The Men of the Sea* (1899), and the sombre and sonorous *The Sea Wife* (1905) which charts the lives and deaths of the numberless legion of seafarers sent across the world from their northern home.

Danny Deever (1924) is an ambitious setting of Kipling's grim account of the hanging in front of his comrades of a soldier found guilty of murder. It is percussive, dissonant and inventive, but fails to quite match Walter Damrosch's classic setting. Similarly Grainger's *Recessional* (1930) has an acceptably solemn hymn tune but fails to displace the memorable setting of Reginald de Koven. But Grainger is perhaps at his best in the visionary and elegiac poems, in the exquisitely wrought *Merciful Town*, in *We Were Dreamers Dreaming Greatly* (1899) and in *The First Chantey* (1899).

It was the Great War that brought about the only major collaboration of the two major laureates of Empire, Kipling and Elgar. Kipling wrote a small collection of poems, *The Fringes of the Fleet*, to boost morale, and Admiral Lord Charles Beresford asked Elgar to set it to music. Kipling, who was still mourning his son, killed at the age of 18 in 1915, reluctantly gave permission, and Elgar set four poems for four baritones and orchestra, dedicating them to Beresford. *Lowestoft Boat*, which looks to have been written by Kipling with 'A-Roving, A-Roving' in his mind, is an account of a fishing boat being fitted out with guns, and Elgar, who told Ernest Newman that he had aimed at a 'broad saltwater style', gives it all the swing and punch of a sea-shanty.[83] *Fate's Discourtesy*, with its broadly characteristic Elgarian melody, celebrates the ideas of comradeship, sacrifice and the subordination of the individual to the general good of the ship. *Submarines* is a slow, dark-toned, minor-key evocation of submarine warfare, with a pair of sandpaper blocks used to simulate the hiss of the water. *Sweepers* is a cheerful and jaunty celebration of fishing boats turned minesweepers accomplishing their task off the coast. The songs were performed, with Elgar conducting, as part of a variety bill at the London Coliseum, and were an enormous success. The delighted manager Arthur Croxton declared: 'In these songs you get the real right magic of British seafaring spirit, of the open air, of the sea.'[84] Elgar added as an encore a wistful setting of Sir Gilbert Parker's *Inside the Bar*, about a sailor yearning for his lass. He and his singers later toured the provincial music halls to equal acclaim, returning to the Coliseum in October 1917. The songs were recorded by the four singers with Elgar conducting. But then Kipling withdrew permission for the performances to continue, causing Elgar immense disgruntlement. But he later made a charming setting of *Big Steamers* (1918), at the request of the Ministry of Food. It was Kipling's account of the food supplies coming in from the Empire.

One of the most celebrated musical versions of Kipling was Sir Arthur Sullivan's setting of *The Absent-Minded Beggar*. This was Kipling's contribution to the well-being of the troops in the Boer War. He wrote a poem which stressed the cross-class nature of the army and the war:

> Cook's son – Duke's son – son of a belted Earl,
> Son of a Lambeth publican – it's all the same today!
> Each of 'em doing his country's work.

But he was particularly concerned with the plight of the working-class soldier and called upon the public in Britain to raise money to look after their families while they were away. It was published in the *Daily Mail* on 31 October, 1899, and they set up an 'Absent-Minded Beggar Fund'. Kipling recalled in his autobiography:

Sir Arthur Sullivan wedded the words to a tune guaranteed to pull teeth out of barrel organs. Anybody could do what they chose with the result, recite, sing, intone or reprint etc., on condition that they turned in all fees and profits to the main account – 'The Absent-Minded Beggar Fund' – which closed at about a quarter of a million.[85]

Sullivan's splendidly catchy tune, almost a descant on his *Onward Christian Soldiers*, was soon being sung and whistled all over the country.

Kipling settings were also popular in America and with American composers. Some of the settings became definitive. For it should not be forgotten that Kipling lived for a time in America and wrote his celebrated poem *The White Man's Burden* not, as many people believe, about the British in India but about the Americans in the Philippines. Britain and America shared a common cultural heritage and, in the late nineteenth century, a common imperial mission. Of the many settings of Kipling's *Recessional*, the best is undoubtedly that published in 1898 by the American operatic composer Reginald de Koven, inspiring, musically inventive and uplifting. Oley Speaks made the definitive setting of *Mandalay* and Walter Damrosch the definitive setting of *Danny Deever* (1897). Taking its cue from the *Dead March* from *Saul*, it is set as a dead march, rising to a splendid operatic finale. John Philip Sousa, the 'march king', made a setting of *Boots* in 1896.

Many of these settings were still current in the 1950s when American baritone Leonard Warren (1911–1960), acclaimed for his performances in Verdi – he died on stage during *La Forza del Destino* – recorded an LP of Kipling settings, magnificently performed, including *Danny Deever*, *Gunga Din*, *Rolling Down to Rio*, *Recessional* and *Mother O'Mine*, and preferring J.P. McCall's setting of *Boots* to the many others available.

Art song

Around the turn of the century there was a 'radical transformation in the aesthetic status of English song' and a conscious effort to develop a tradition of English art song marked by a refined sensibility.[86] Stephen Banfield, who has explored the phenomenon, sees a cluster of musical events around 1900 as symptomatic: the performance of Elgar's *Sea Pictures*, Somervell's *Maud* cycle and Roger Quilter's *Four Songs of the Sea*, and the foundation of *The Vocalist* magazine which between 1902 and 1905 sought to raise the level of English song. A group of influential composers began composing songs in this new idiom: Vaughan Williams, Holst, Bridge, Somervell, Parry, Elgar, Walford Davies, Ireland, Finzi, Charles Wood.

Art song, which tended to the spiritual, the introspective and the pastoral, generally did not feature the Empire. But in 1899, at the instigation of Master of the Queen's Music Sir Walter Parratt, a group of leading British composers, many of them distinguished exponents of the art song, contributed to a volume of choral songs, written and composed in honour of the eightieth birthday of Queen Victoria. The stated intention was to emulate the presentation of a collection of madrigals – *The Triumphs of Oriana* – to Queen Elizabeth I. 'The present collection is an attempt to express, in a more sedulous form, the same patriotic spirit which breathes so strongly through those ancient lays', says the Preface.[87] There is a strong imperial and monarchist tone to the collection.

Sir Alexander Mackenzie set *With Wisdom, Goodness, Grace*, a group of predictably prosaic verses by the Poet Laureate Alfred Austin to which Mackenzie does more than justice, with the rhythm of the music following the rhythm of the name 'Vic–tor–i–a!'. It begins solemnly and sonorously, stressing her qualities and commitment to democracy:

> With wisdom, goodness, grace, She filled
> For many years the Throne,
> And whatsoe'er Her people willed,
> That will She made Her own.

It modulates into a breezy sea-shanty tune, recalling Mackenzie's nautical overture, and appropriate to the maritime references. It concludes with a triumphal upbeat ending:

> Victoria! Victoria!
> Long may She live and reign!
> The Queen of our inviolate Isles,
> And the Empress of the main.

A.C. Benson provided much more florid words for *Out in the Windy West*, a song for six voices, set by Charles Villiers Stanford. It begins with a lively madrigal rhythm, with big choral writing throughout, dramatic pauses and the big dramatic finale 'Reign on, Victoria, reign'. The imagery is of an ancient pastoral land but with a maritime Empire ruled by the 'great Queen, whose name the Orient Oceans praise'.

Robert Bridges wrote *Hark! The World Is Full of Thy Praise* for Walford Davies. It begins solemnly, warms up to a jolly tune and goes faster and faster, speeding up on

> The world shall never tire to tell
> Praise, Praise, Praise of the Queen who reignéd well.

And it ends quietly on 'Regina cara'. It is full of counterpoint, a beautiful distribution of voices and a celebration:

> Honour, truth and growing Peace
> Follow Britannia's wide increase,
> And Nature yield her strength unknown
> To the wisdom born beneath thy Throne.

Sir Frederick Bridge set *For All the Wonders of Thy Regal Day*, words by Robert Offley Ashburton Crewe-Milnes, Marquis of Crewe, recently Lord Lieutenant of Ireland (1892–5) and later Secretary of State both for the colonies and for India, Lord Privy Seal and Lord President of the Council, and son of the poet Richard Monckton Milnes, Lord Houghton. It is a simple hymn-like tune which changes time half-way through and back again to fit the words

> We cling to this that thou has been
> In heart and home our Mother Queen.

John Davidson penned a veritable imperial ode in *The Seaboards Are Her Mantle's Helm*, inspired by a piece in the *New York Tribune* referring to 'The revered woman, who has for more than half a century been the unwavering friend of the republic and often its great benefactor, and who now, far more than any other living person, is the head and crown of the entire English-speaking world.' It is set by Sir George C. Martin, organist of St Paul's and composer of Anglican church music. His most important work was the Diamond Jubilee *Te Deum*, performed on the steps of St Paul's, scored for military band and 'Great Paul', the Cathedral bell. He provided a stirring Anglo-American anthem for the words:

> On the four corners of the world
> Her admirable throne is set,
> Established to endure.
>
> Most high, most dear, whom all degrees
> In all her workshops, all her marts,
> In all her courts revere, not these
> Alone are hers; but in all parts
> Where English speech and thought remain,
> Whatever flag floats on the breeze,
> Her tenderness and wisdom reign,
> Queen of the cities and the seas,
> Queen of all English hearts.

Who Can Dwell With Greatness! by Austin Dobson was set by Sir Hubert Parry in a nicely contrasted short piece, with music varying to meet the mood of the words. It opens sonorously with the line 'Who can dwell with greatness! Greatness is too high' and then into the jauntily pastoral 'Flowers are for the meadow, suns are for the sky'. The music is animated on the lines: 'Great in far dominion, great in pomp of years', and soft on 'Greater still as woman, greatest in thy years'.

The adulatory *Lady on the Silver Throne* by Edmund Gosse was set by A.M. Goodhart, a composer not to be found in the pages of Grove. It is a surging and yearningly romantic love song, Schumannesque in its intensity:

> Lady on the silver throne,
> Like the Moon, Thou art to me
> Something bright, august and lone.

A Century's Penultimate has words by Arthur C. James, developing the idea of an Empire on which the sun never sets and the unity of it to 'join hearts with hearts while threads that knit the seas/ Flash love and joy of brotherhood increased', all presided over by the Queen whose reign is 'of all our Reigns the longest and the best'. Charles Wood's music is fussy and busy with not much line or purpose. *With Still Increasing Blessings* has words by the Queen's son-in-law, the Marquis of Lorne, a playwright and poet and Governor-General of Canada. Arthur Somervell provided a hymn-like tune, excellent counterpoint and an arresting ending.

To Her Beneath Whose Steadfast Star has words by F.W.H. Myers, set by Edward Elgar, a simple, mystical piece, with distinctive and recognizable Elgarian cadences, nice variations in tone and mood, and an emphatic finale: 'Let the Queen live for ever.' It celebrates a reign which has seen an Empire, greater than Caesar's or Alexander's, created by the 'English' on their 'world-ingathering way' and fundamental changes which have dismayed some, but – perhaps tactlessly – it predicts an eventual reunion with her Prince in the great beyond.

A Thousand Years By Land and Sea by Sir Henry Newbolt, was set by Charles Harford Lloyd (1849–1919), precentor and music instructor at Eton. Rousing, coherent and nicely constructed, it is more Elgarian than the Elgar:

> A thousand years, by sea and land,
> Our race hath served the island Kings,
> But not by custom's dull command,
> Today with song Her empire rings.

Flora's Queen has music by Sir John Stainer to words by his eldest son, J.F.R. Stainer. It is not distinctive melodically, begins as a hymn, turns into a madrigal and ends on the emphatic paean 'Long Live Victoria!

Long may she reign!' It is full of floral imagery but ends with a stress on Empire:

> And hark, afar across the sea
> From clime to clime
> How kindred voices chime
> Joining the glad refrain
> In ever-swelling Harmony:
> 'Long Live Victoria! Long may she reign!'

The collection ends with *The Triumph of Victoria*, written in a self-consciously archaic 'Ye Olde Merrie England' idiom by T.H. Warren, though including a reference to 'Bright Sun, upon her empire setting never'. It was put to music by Sir Walter Parratt in humdrum rum-ti-tum fashion.

Of the thirteen composers ten were either already knights (Mackenzie, Parry, Martin, Bridge, Stainer and Parratt) or were to be knighted (Elgar, Stanford, Somervell, Walford Davies). It was a veritable musical establishment.

Fascinatingly, the exercise was repeated in 1953. A collection of madrigals and part-songs for unaccompanied mixed voices was commissioned by the Arts Council to celebrate the Coronation of Queen Elizabeth II and performed at the Royal Festival Hall at a special eve of Coronation Day concert in a programme which included madrigals from the original tribute to Elizabeth I, *The Triumphs of Oriana*. The composers contributing to this 'Garland For the Queen' were the leading composers of the day: Sir Arthur Bliss, Sir Arnold Bax, Michael Tippett, Ralph Vaughan Williams, Herbert Howells, John Ireland, Lennox Berkeley, Gerald Finzi, Alan Rawsthorne and Edmund Rubbra, setting texts by such poets as Christopher Fry, Louis MacNeice, Edmund Blunden and Walter de la Mare. The tone was celebratory in, for example, Bliss's *Aubade* ('Crown her with light'), Bax's *What Is it Like* ('Long may she reign') and Vaughan Williams's *Silence and Music* ('Rejoice'). But the imagery was overwhelmingly drawn from nature (dawn, the hills, the winds, spring, the birds, a summer night), and of imperial sentiment there was no sign at all. The musical world of this coronation tribute was as resolutely that of a pastoral Little England as the Queen Victoria collection's had been global and imperial. Music, like Britain itself, had moved on.

Conclusion

Some historians have insisted that the imperial element in music-hall songs is pure manipulation, right-wing propaganda foisted on the public (thus Senelick and Stedman-Jones).[88] Others have argued that the working classes were immune to imperial enthusiasms (Henry Pelling, Richard Price).[89] But this flies in the face of the evidence. After careful consideration, Dave Russell comes up with a judicious verdict from which it is difficult to dissent and which can with some confidence be applied to the whole broad field of popular song:

> The sheer weight of material must be stressed. There is *far* too much of it for it to be the result of music-hall writers creating, rather than, at least in part, capturing, a genuine sentiment. Similarly many of these songs were sung by top-flight performers and produced for them by leading writers. Such people were not prone to misread their audiences. Patriotism, broadly conceived, whether it be an interest in Empire, a hostility to Germany or a vague belief in British superiority, must have been a definite element in the consciousness of all classes between 1880 and 1914.[90]

Notes

1 On the history and nature of the music hall, see in particular Dagmar Kift, *The Victorian Music Hall: Culture, Class and Conflict*, Cambridge: Cambridge University Press, 1996; J.S. Bratton (ed.), *Music Hall: Performance and Style*, Milton Keynes: Open University Press, 1986; Peter Bailey (ed.), *Music Hall: The Business of Pleasure*, Milton Keynes: Open University Press, 1986. On music-hall songs, see Dave Russell, *Popular Music in England 1840–1914*, Manchester: Manchester University Press, 1997; Colin MacInnes, *Sweet Saturday Night*, London: MacGibbon & Key, 1967; Laurence Senelick, 'Politics as entertainment', *Victorian Studies* 19 (1975–76), pp. 149–80; Penny Summerfield, 'Patriotism and Empire: music-hall entertainment, 1870–1914', in J.M. MacKenzie (ed.), *Imperialism and Popular Culture*, Manchester: Manchester University Press, 1986, pp. 17–48; and Peter Davison, 'A Briton true?', in Peter Davison, Rolf Meyersohn and Edward Shils (eds), *Literary Taste, Culture and Mass Communications*, Cambridge: Chadwyck-Healy, 1983, vol. 8, pp. 165–79.
2 Russell, *Popular Music in England*, p. 146.
3 H. Chance Newton, *Idols of the 'Halls'*, reprint, Wakefield: EP Publishing, 1975 (1928), p. 81.
4 Kift, *The Victorian Music Hall*, p. 43; Bernard Waites, *Popular Culture: Historical Development*, Milton Keynes: Open University Press, pp. 71–2; Hugh Cunningham, 'The language of patriotism, 1750–1914', *History Workshop Journal* 12 (1981), pp. 25–6.
5 J.B. Priestley, *English Humour*, London: Longman, 1930, pp. 16–18.
6 J.B. Booth, *Life, Laughter and Brass Hats*, London: Werner Laurie, 1939, p. 34.
7 W. MacQueen Pope, *The Melodies Linger On*, London: W.H. Allen, 1951, p. 185.
8 J.A. Hobson, *The Psychology of Jingoism*, London: Grant Richards, 1901, pp. 2–4.
9 Booth, *Life, Laughter and Brass Hats*, p. 35.
10 Senelick, 'Politics as entertainment', p. 170.
11 Booth, *Life, Laughter and Brass Hats*, p. 36.
12 Summerfield, 'Patriotism and Empire', pp. 27–8.
13 Russell, *Popular Music in England*, p. 151.
14 Dave Russell, ' "We carved our way to glory": The British Soldier in Music Hall Song and Sketch, c. 1880–1914', in J.M. MacKenzie (ed.), *Popular Imperialism*

and the Military, 1850–1950, Manchester: Manchester University Press, 1992, pp. 50–79.

15   Russell, ' "We carved our way to glory" ', p. 68.
16   Richard Morton, Introduction, *Francis and Day's Album of Tom Costello's Popular Songs*, London: Francis, Day & Hunter, 1897, p. 2.
17   *Ibid.*, p. 18.
18   Chance Newton, *Idols of the 'Halls'*, p. 18.
19   Richard Morton, Introduction, *Francis and Day's Album of Charles Godfrey's Popular Songs*, London: Francis, Day & Hunter, nd, p. 3.
20   Chance Newton, *Idols of the 'Halls'*, p. 113.
21   C.R. Stone (ed.), *War Songs*, Oxford: Cliveden Press, 1908, p. xi.
22   MacQueen Pope, *The Melodies Linger On*, p. 391.
23   J.B. Booth, *The Days We Knew*, London: Werner Laurie, 1944, p. 39.
24   Morton, *Charles Godfrey*, p. 3.
25   Lewis Winstock, *Songs and Music of the Redcoats, 1642–1902*, Harrisburg, PA: Stackpole Books, 1970, pp. 255–6.
26   Michael Kilgarriff, *Sing Us One of the Old Songs*, Oxford: Oxford University Press, 1998, has singers' repertoires: *Bravo, Dublin Fusiliers*, p. 12; *Goodbye Dolly Gray*, p. 31; *Break the News to Mother*, p. 12.
27   Winstock, *Songs and Music*, p. 260.
28   J.B. Booth, *A Pink 'Un Remembers*, London: Werner Laurie, 1937, p. 119.
29   Russell, *Popular Music in England*, p. 159.
30   Winstock, *Songs and Music*, p. 251.
31   Herbert Wilcox, *25,000 Sunsets*, London: Bodley Head, 1967, p. 11; Christopher Pulling, *They Were Singing*, London: George Harrap, 1952, p. 129.
32   *This England* (autumn 1997), p. 63.
33   Winstock, *Songs and Music*, p. 29.
34   *Ibid.*, pp. 32–3.
35   *Ibid.*, pp. 36–9.
36   *Ibid.*, pp. 104–5.
37   *Ibid.*, pp. 168, 164.
38   Henry Russell, *Cheer, Boys, Cheer*, London: John MacQueen, 1895, pp. 13–15.
39   *Ibid.*, p. 199.
40   *Ibid.*, p. 194.
41   *Ibid.*, pp. 235–6.
42   *Daily Telegraph*, 13 October 1891.
43   Winstock, *Songs and Music*, p. 225.
44   Cosmo Rose-Innes, *With Paget's Horse to the Front*, London: John MacQueen, 1901, p. 97.
45   Winstock, *Songs and Music*, p. 252.
46   John Brophy and Eric Partridge, *The Long Trail*, London: André Deutsch, 1965.
47   Sian Nicholas, 'The BBC and its audience', in Nick Hayes and Jeff Hill (eds), *Millions Like Us? British Culture in the Second World War*, Liverpool: Liverpool University Press, 1999, p. 82.
48   S. Seidenberg, M. Sellar and I. Jones, *You Must Remember This: Songs at the Heart of the War*, London: Boxtree, 1995, pp. 28–9.
49   Ronald Pearsall, *Victorian Popular Music*, Newton Abbot: David & Charles, 1973, p. 91.
50   Derek Scott, *The Singing Bourgeois: Songs of the Victorian Drawing Room and Parlour*, Milton Keynes: Open University Press, 1989.
51   Nicholas Temperley (ed.), *Music in Britain: The Romantic Age, 1800–1914*, Oxford: Blackwell, 1988, p. 131.
52   Peter Cliffe, *Somewhere a Voice Is Calling: The Golden Age of Concert Ballads*, Cheltenham: Evergreen, 1997; Michael R. Turner and Antony Miall (eds), *The Parlour Song Book*, London: Michael Joseph, 1972; and Michael R. Turner and Antony Miall, *Just a Song at Twilight*, London: Michael Joseph, 1975.
53   Fred E. Weatherly, *Piano and Gown*, London: Putnam, 1926, pp. 138–9.

54 *Ibid.*, p. 138.
55 *Ibid.*, p. 142.
56 *Ibid.*, p. 146.
57 *Ibid.*, p. 226.
58 Harold Simpson, *A Century of Ballads*, London: Mills & Boon, 1910, p. 165.
59 Joseph L. Roeckel and F.E. Weatherly, *The Victorian Age*, London: Joseph Curwen, 1887.
60 J.S. Bratton, *The Victorian Popular Ballad*, London: Macmillan, 1975, p. 61.
61 *Ibid.*, p. 73.
62 Cynthia Fansler Behrman, *Victorian Myths of the Sea*, Athens: Ohio University Press, 1977, p. 26.
63 On the influence of the sea in British popular culture, see *ibid.*, and Charles N. Robinson, *The British Tar in Fact and Fiction*, London: Harrap, 1911.
64 David Cox, *The Henry Wood Proms*, London: BBC, 1980, pp. 51–2.
65 Harry Plunket Greene, *Charles Villiers Stanford*, London: Edward Arnold, 1935, p. 87.
66 *Ibid.*, pp. 134–5; Sir Henry Newbolt, *My World as in My Time*, London: Faber, 1932, p. 159.
67 Robert H. MacDonald, *The Language of Empire: Myths and Metaphors of Popular Imperialism, 1880–1918*, Manchester: Manchester University Press, 1994, p. 145.
68 *Ibid.*, p. 161.
69 Bratton, *Victorian Popular Ballad*, pp. 77, 87–8.
70 Charles Carrington, *Rudyard Kipling: His Life and Work*, Harmondsworth: Penguin, 1970, p. 413.
71 Rudyard Kipling, *Something of Myself*, Harmondsworth: Penguin, 1977, p. 14.
72 Carrington, *Rudyard Kipling*, p. 146.
73 *Ibid.*, p. 421.
74 *Ibid.*, pp. 418–21.
75 James McG. Stewart, *Rudyard Kipling: A Bibliographical Catalogue*, Toronto: Toronto University Press, 1959.
76 *The Musical Times*, 1 June, 1897.
77 Sir Frederick Bridge, *A Westminster Pilgrim*, London: Novello–Hutchinson, 1918, pp. 172–3.
78 *The Musical Times*, 1 June, 1897.
79 *The Musical Times*, 1 November, 1897.
80 John Bird, *Percy Grainger*, London: Faber, 1982, p. 57.
81 Malcolm Gillies and David Pear (eds), *The All-Round Man: Selected Letters of Percy Grainger 1914–1961*, Oxford: Clarendon Press, 1994, p. 275.
82 Lewis Foreman (ed.), *The Percy Grainger Companion*, London: Thames, 1981, pp. 52, 55.
83 Jerrold Northrop Moore, *Edward Elgar: A Creative Life*, Oxford: Oxford University Press, 1984, p. 706.
84 *Ibid.*, p. 710.
85 Kipling, *Something of Myself*, p. 113.
86 Stephen Banfield, *Sensibility and English Song*, Cambridge: Cambridge University Press, 1988, p. 2.
87 Various writers and composers, Preface to *Choral Songs in Honour of Her Majesty Queen Victoria*, London: Macmillan, 1899.
88 Senelick, 'Politics as entertainment', pp. 149–80; Gareth Stedman-Jones, 'Working-class culture and working-class politics in London, 1870–1900: notes on the re-making of a working class', in G. Stedman-Jones, *Languages of Class*, Cambridge: Cambridge University Press, 1983, pp. 179–283.
89 See Henry Pelling's 'British labour and imperialism', in his *Popular Politics and Society in Late Victorian Britain*, London: MacMillan, 1979, pp. 82–100. Richard Price, *An Imperial War and the British Working Class*, London: Routledge, 1972.
90 Russell, *Popular Music in England*, p. 160.

CHAPTER ELEVEN

'From Greenland's icy mountains, from India's coral strand': the imperial hymn

It became unfashionable in the 1960s and 1970s to talk about *national character* and *national identity* because of their perceived overtones not of race but of racial superiority, not of Empire but of imperialism, not of hierarchy but of a hierarchical status quo. But in the past decade, in the wake of the collapse of the Soviet Union and the rise of vocal and active nationalist movements all over the globe, there has been an upsurge of serious scholarly interest in questions of national identity and national character. This has resulted in scholars focusing attention on the role of religion in defining national identity, particularly British national identity. Three recent major works by leading scholars have highlighted this theme: Lionel Adey in *Class and Idol in the English Hymn* (1988); Linda Colley in *Britons* (1992); and John Wolffe in *God and Greater Britain* (1994). All of them have argued for convergence and consensus around a shared Protestantism which underpinned and pervaded the national ideology and the national identity, and which Adey calls 'a largely undeclared religion of nation, church, home and heart'.[1]

Linda Colley writes: 'Protestantism, broadly understood, provided the majority of Britons with a framework for their lives. It shaped their interpretation of the past and enabled them to make sense of the present. It helped them to identify and confront their enemies. It gave them confidence, even hope.'[2] Thus it was not the divisions within Protestantism but the division between Protestantism and Catholicism that was crucial in the eighteenth century, and much of the nineteenth. A popular Protestantism in the eighteenth century, rooted in the key texts of the Bible, Milton, Bunyan and Foxe, and reinforced by a succession of mythified victories against Catholicism (the Armada, the Glorious Revolution, the Jacobite rebellions), led the British to see themselves as a chosen people, equating the Israel of the Bible with the Britain of their day. It was expressed musically in the oratorios of Handel, a central component in the popular musical culture of eighteenth and nineteenth century Britain.[3]

The undoubted differences within Protestantism were subsumed in a popular anti-Catholicism and in the creation of the British Empire in which the home countries of England, Scotland and Wales, despite their different varieties of Protestant observance, all participated. The existence of the Empire reinforced the feeling, already deep-rooted, of the British as God's elect. 'When Britain first *at heaven's command* arose from out the azure main', said the alternative national anthem *Rule, Britannia*. 'God save our gracious Queen' said the actual national anthem, equating the nation and the monarchical system, a system which was by law Protestant and by dint of historical expansion imperial. Together monarchy, empire and Protestantism defined Britain and the British. Their world-role was the historical fulfilment of the mission imposed on them by God to bring Christianity, civilization and justice to the unenlightened areas of the globe. In the first half of the nineteenth century, evangelicalism was the shaping force of Britain's national ideology and national identity. In the second half of the nineteenth century, it was imperialism, but an imperialism that embraced evangelicalism and was seen as the working out of God's purpose.

What were the cultural expressions of this Protestantism? Hugh McLeod identifies three in particular which, 'to a considerable extent, crossed the boundaries of class, politics and denomination: knowledge of and reference to the Bible as a final authority; the love of hymns; and the observance of Sunday as a day set apart', and he goes on to say: 'In Victorian England hymns were the most universally popular art form and the nearest thing to a cultural inheritance common to women and men, working class and middle class, old and young, the sceptical and the devout.'[4]

The great hymnologist Erik Routley called the hymns 'the articulation of Christian worship ... the folk songs of the church militant ... the people's music'.[5] George Sampson argued that 'the hymn has been the poor man's poetry ... [t]he only poetry that has ever come home to his heart'.[6] An estimated 400,000 hymns were written between 1837 and 1901.[7] They became as much a part of the imaginative inner life of the people as any musical form. Their linguistic and musical rhythms were imprinted on the popular consciousness due to repeated hearings at Sunday school (attended by three-quarters of all British children), at school services, at church parades for the armed forces and the uniformed youth movements, and even in the home where hymns formed the largest single category of subject matter for pianola rolls. D.H. Lawrence confirmed this in an essay on hymns, recalling those he learned as a child and never forgot:

> They mean to me almost more than the finest poetry, and they have for me a permanent value, somehow or other. It is almost shameful to confess that the poems which have meant most to me, like Wordsworth's 'Ode to Immortality' and Keats' Odes . . . are still not . . . woven so deep in me as the rather banal Nonconformist hymns that penetrated through and through my childhood.

He saw the Nonconformist hymns as 'the clue to the ordinary Englishman'.[8]

Hymns were popular for the same reason as ballads and music-hall songs. They combined popular sentiments with melodies. They were particularly associated with childhood and recalled for many the security, the familiar routines, of home and family. It is no coincidence that *Home, Sweet Home*, which began life as an aria in Sir Henry Bishop's opera *Clari, the Maid of Milan*, had by the end of the nineteenth century achieved the status of hymn and was included as such in *The Fellowship Hymn Book* (1909). The words were as important as the tunes, which is why hymns are known usually by their first lines and not by the names of their tunes.

Hymns and hymn-singing were a distinctively nineteenth century experience.[9] The practice had only developed in the eighteenth century as part of the religious revival, with the Methodists particularly noted for hymn-writing and hymn-singing. But it was not until the middle of the nineteenth century that it became the norm in the Anglican Church. By the 1860s, the majority of churches of all denominations in England and Wales had abandoned the traditional gallery bands and the singing of metrical psalms for hymn-singing by the congregation, choirs in surplices and pipe-organs in what amounted to a musical revolution. Ian Bradley describes the introduction of hymns as a major feature in the services of all the main Christian denominations as 'a profoundly democratic and popular movement. The fact that the same verses were being sung to the same tunes in Eton College Chapel and Westminster Abbey as at the Rusholme Street Congregational Church brought a new egalitarian and ecumenical dimension to worship.'[10] Twelve hundred hymn books were published between 1837 and 1901. By the 1860s most denominations had their own authorized hymn book. The Anglicans never officially adopted a single book. But *Hymns Ancient and Modern* (1861) was to all intents and purposes such a book. It was being used by 70 per cent of Anglican churches by 1894 and was adopted for use in the army and the navy. *Hymns Ancient and Modern* established the principle that each hymn should have its own tune, overturning the old practice of having the same tune for many different hymns. There began to be a considerable cross-over between denominations. From the 1860s Free Church hymn books began accepting Anglican tunes and from 1889 *Hymns Ancient and Modern* included Methodist tunes. In some cases, however, different denominations preferred different tunes and it was possible to tell someone's denomination from their preferred tune to a particular hymn. Hymn book sales were enormous. *Hymns Ancient and Modern* sold 4.5 million copies in its first seven years, and W.T. Stead estimated in 1896 that 2 million hymn books were sold annually in Britain.[11]

Hymns became a leading form of popular verse, often taking inspiration from and reworking passages from the King James version of the Bible. But the language of the hymnal also influenced poetry, notably that of Kipling, several of whose poems were in their turn transformed into hymns and included in twentieth-century hymn books. When it came to the tunes, many were specially composed and the hymn tunes of J.B. Dykes, Arthur Sullivan, Joseph Barnby, Henry Smart, Henry Gauntlett, William Henry Monk and John Stainer became well-loved and long-enduring favourites. Most of these conformed to John Wilson's prescription for the successful hymn: the combination of 'singability' and 'memorability', a combination derived from the use of graceful melody, vital rhythm, interesting harmony and a structure that balances unity and variety.[12] But other tunes were shamelessly plundered from existing sources because of their memorable rhythms. The works of Handel were a favourite quarry, with, for instance, his triumphal *Hail the Conquering Hero* from his oratorio *Joshua* (later incorporated into his *Judas Maccabaens*) appropriated to fit the words of the hymn *Thine Be the Glory, Risen Conquering Son*, written by Swiss pastor Edmond Budry in 1884. Haydn's *Emperor Hymn*, more familiar as the German national anthem *Deutschland, deutchsland, über alles*, was fitted to John Newton's hymn *Glorious Things of Thee Are Spoken, Zion, City of Our God*, while Lvov's Russian national anthem *God Save the Czar*, was pressed into service for Henry Chorley's *God, the All-Terrible*. Rev. Rowland Hill even set the hymn *When Jesus First at Heaven's Command, Descended From His Azure Throne* to the tune of *Rule, Britannia*. The fact that these hymn tunes became deeply embedded in the popular consciousness is conclusively demonstrated by the First World War practice of fitting to hymn tunes words to express the discontents of the soldiery, J.B. Dykes's tune *Nicaea* for the hymn *Holy, Holy, Holy, Lord God Almighty* becoming

'Grousing, grousing, grousing, always bloody well grousing' and Charles Converse's tune for *What a Friend We Have in Jesus* being sung to the words 'When this lousy war is over'. Every unit had its version of Samuel Sebastian Wesley's majestic *Aurelia*, the tune for S.J. Stone's *The Church's One Foundation*. The most famous was 'We are Fred Karno's Army'.

The role of hymns in people's lives was eloquently expressed in the collection *Hymns that Have Helped*, edited and published in 1896 by the journalist W.T. Stead. He saw hymns as a major cultural link between Britain and her Empire, writing:

> The songs of the English-speaking people are for the most part hymns. For the immense majority of our people today the only minstrelsy is that of the Hymn-book. And this is as true of our race beyond the sea as it is of our race at home. . . . At this moment, on the slope of the Rockies, or in the sweltering jungles of India, in crowded Australian city, or secluded English hamlet, the sound of some simple hymn tune will, as if by mere magic spell, call from the silent grave the shadowy forms of the unforgotten dead, and transport the listener, involuntarily, over land and sea, to the scene of his childhood's years, to the village school, to the parish church.[13]

He claimed that his was the first hymnal to result from an investigation into what people actually sang and what hymns meant to them rather than to be compiled and prescribed by the authorities. The idea of a hymnal chosen by the people themselves was clearly greeted with some concern by the senior Anglican clergy contacted by Stead as part of an appeal to all classes of people for examples of hymns that had helped them. The Archbishop of Canterbury referred Stead to 'a hymnal which he himself had compiled many years ago'. The Dean of St Paul's declined to 'take part in compiling an unsectarian hymn-book'. The Bishop of Winchester thought any selection of hymns necessarily involved the explication of a personal spiritual autobiography which he himself was not willing to share with the public.[14]

From his enquiries, Stead came up with a list of 150 hymns based not on literary merit or doctrinal orthodoxy, but on popularity and effect on individuals. The single most popular hymn was *Rock of Ages*. It was the hymn asked for by the Prince Consort when he lay dying and which was translated into Latin, Greek and Italian by Mr Gladstone. It was sung by the passengers of the stricken vessel *London* as it went down in the Bay of Biscay on January 11 1866. When the magazine *Sunday at Home* did an opinion poll of 3,500 of its readers on the popularity of hymns, *Rock of Ages* came first. Interestingly the favourite hymns of many of the top people who replied to Stead also figure in the magazine's top 100. The Prince of Wales chose *Nearer, My God, to Thee* (seventh in the poll); the Duke of Cambridge, former Commander-in-Chief of the British Army, chose *Onward, Christian Soldiers* (forty-second in the poll); politicians John Bright and H.H. Asquith chose *O, God, Our Help in Ages Past* (nineteenth in the poll); Dean F.W. Farrar of Canterbury, *Forever With the Lord* (eleventh in the poll); novelist Mary Elizabeth Braddon, critic Richard Le Gallienne, General Sir Evelyn Wood and the Marquis of Ripon, the Viceroy of India, chose *Lead, Kindly Light* (fifteenth in the poll); and Dr J.E.C. Welldon, Headmaster of Harrow, *Hark, My Soul, It Is the Lord* (twenty-ninth in the poll). This confirms that hymns were a major means of producing a broadly diffused Christianity which was consensual and all-embracing. For as Henry Ward Beecher observed:

> There is almost no heresy in the hymn book. In psalms and hymns we have a universal ritual. It is the theology of the heart that unites men. Our very childhood is embalmed in sacred tunes and hymns. Our early lives and the lives of our parents hang in the atmosphere of sacred song. The art of singing together is one that is for ever winding invisible threads about persons.[15]

There is also clear evidence of MacKenzie's ideological cluster in Stead's collection, which includes the national anthem *God Save the Queen*, a collection of battle hymns (Luther's *Ein' feste burg*; Gustavus Adolphus's *Battle Hymn*; *The Battle Hymn of the Republic*; Cromwell's 'Battle Psalms'), hymns on the 'warfare of life' (*Onward, Christian Soldiers*; *Soldiers of Christ Arise*; *Forward! Be Our Watchword*) and missionary hymns (*From Greenland's Icy Mountains*; *Jesus Shall Reign Where'er the Sun*).

While hymns embodied Christian teaching on God the Father, God the Son and God the Holy Ghost, the four 'last things' (death, judgement, heaven and hell) and the basic elements of the faith, they also reflected the imagery, ideals and preoccupations of the eras which produced them. The eighteenth- and the early nineteenth-century hymns have a powerful strand of imagery centred on blood, wounds, bowels, agony and death, which the later Victorians found too graphic and gross for their taste and which Freudians have seen as evidence of repressed sexuality.[16] The Victorians preferred, on the one hand, the sentimentalized and idealized images of home, family, childhood and motherhood that reflected the cultural dominance of an ideology of bourgeois domesticity, and evocations of a rural golden age of sowing and reaping, shepherds, lambs and harvest which epitomized the powerful cultural reaction against the excesses of industrialization and urbanization; and, on the other hand, the military imagery of battles, banners, fighting, marching and missionary zeal to convert the heathen, which was a direct concomitant of British imperial expansion. The late twentieth century is often embarrassed by the military and imperial imagery that it finds deeply politically incorrect, and sedulous attempts have been made to eliminate it. There have been frantic rewritings to eliminate 'offensive' elements – the stirring 'Onward, Christian soldiers, marching as to war', for instance, being reborn as the banal 'Onward, Christian pilgrims, working hard for peace' – and some trendy vicars have banned well-loved hymns to the bewilderment of the older parishioners who grew up with them. The periodic storms which break out over the banning of O, Valiant Hearts or the dropping of Onward, Christian Soldiers from Remembrance Day services only serve to confirm the deep attachment people have to them.

Empire was at the centre of British national identity in the second half of the nineteenth century. The two dominant ideologies of the first half of the nineteenth century – evangelicalism and chivalry – cross-fertilized to provide a justification for an Empire which had been acquired initially for economic, strategic and political reasons. The evangelical missionary impulse, the desire to bring the heathen to the light of God, and the Calvinist idea of the elect, the British as the greatest nation in the world obliged to provide justice and good government for inferior races, intertwined with the chivalric vision of Empire as a vehicle for young Britons to demonstrate the virtues that made them gentlemen. The two ideals were linked by the idea that the British ran their Empire not for their own benefit but for that of those whom they ruled. Thus altruistic imperial evangelicalism and chivalry were linked by the concepts of service and duty. The embodiment of the new ethos was the monarchy, the focus of patriotic feeling and the lynch-pin of the Empire.

Although there were some hymns that were radical and concerned with oppression, poverty and the brotherhood of man (such as Ebenezer Elliott's When Will Thou Save Thy People and Edward Carpenter's England, Arise, the Long, Long Night is Over), they were in a distinct minority. Neither Elliott non Carpenter made it into Hymns Ancient and Modern. Ian Bradley has found that there was a dearth of hymns on the plight of the poor, on work and the working man, and on the communitarian values of mutual care and social responsibility; and he points out that the first hymnal to include a section on 'social service' was Songs of Praise, in 1931.[17] The majority of hymns, according to Susan Tamke, 'showed evidence of a profound inertia in social thinking', in other words support for the status quo.[18]

Monarchism

Stephen Wilson has argued that one of the functions of religion is the legitimization of the existing social order, and to this end has analysed the 1889 edition of *Hymns Ancient and Modern*.[19] He finds the deity *addressed* as 'God' in 305 hymns, 'Lord' in 350 and 'King' in 91. The word 'Lord' occurs 580 times and 'King' 123 times, and there are even a handful of imperial references – Hymn 306 declares 'for all the wreaths of empire/ Meet upon his brow' and Hymn 502 refers to God crushing Satan with 'His imperial strength'. Such hymns promote submissiveness to God's authority as a central Christian virtue, with paradise in the afterlife as the compensation for suffering in this world. One example will suffice to combine all these ideas: Caroline Noel's *At the Name of Jesus*, sung to William Henry Monk's *Evelyns*:

> At the name of Jesus
> Every knee shall bow
> Every tongue confess Him
> King of glory now;
> 'Tis the Father's pleasure
> We should call him Lord
> Who from the beginning
> Was the Mighty Word
>
> In your hearts enthrone Him;
> There let Him subdue
> All that is not holy
> All that is not true;
> Crown him as your Captain
> In temptation's hour;
> Let his Will enfold you
> In its light and power.
>
> Brothers, this Lord Jesus
> Shall return again,
> With His Father's glory,
> With His Angel train;
> For all the wreaths of empire
> Meet upon His Brow,
> And our hearts confess Him,
> King of glory now.

The widespread recognition of the principle of royalty cannot but have helped to entrench earthly monarchy, particularly one widely believed to be ordained and blessed by God as part of the Protestant settlement.

The link between the King of Heaven and the King of Britain, between the kingdom of heaven and the social hierarchy of earth, was explicitly made in two of the hymns included in Rev. Edward Bickersteth's widely utilized *Christian Psalmody*, published in 1833. The volume was enlarged in 1841 and revised and re-issued in 1858. Hymn 432 (anon., 1819) ran:

> O, King of Kings! Thy blessing shed
> On our anointed sov'reign's head:
> And looking from thy holy heaven,
> Protect the crown Thyself hast given.
>
> Him may we honour and obey,
> Uphold his right and lawful sway,
> Remem'bring that the powers that be
> Are ministers ordain'd of Thee.
>
> Him with thy choicest mercies bless;
> To all his counsels give success;
> In war, in peace, thy succour bring;
> Thy strength command – God save the King!
>
> And, Oh! When earthly thrones decay,
> And earthly kingdoms fade away,
> Grant him a throne in worlds on high,
> A crown of immortality.

Hymn 433 ran:

> Sov'reign of all, whose will ordains,
> The powers on earth that be,
> By whom our rightful monarch reigns,
> The minister to Thee.
>
> Guard him from all who dare oppose
> Thy delegate and Thee,
> From open and from secret foes,
> From force and perfidy.
>
> Let all for conscience sake revere
> Th'appointment of thy hand:
> Honour and love thine image here,
> And yield to his command.

It is worth noting that this hymn, included by the Anglican Bickersteth, without attribution, abbreviated and partly reworded, is by Charles Wesley and was still featured in its longer and fuller version in the *Wesleyan Methodist Hymn Book* (Hymn 465) in 1879, though it was not included in the 1933 edition.

Hymns Ancient and Modern was replete with royal hymns, many of them taken up by the Nonconformist hymnals. All were popular and well loved. Notable among them are *King of Glory, King of Peace, I Will Love Thee* (367), a George Herbert poem sung to *Salve Cordis Gaudium* by Bach, or to *Gwalchmai* by Joseph David Jones; *Praise to the Lord, the Almighty, the King of Creation* (382), translated by Catherine Winkworth from a German original and German tune of 1665; *O, Worship the King, All Glorious Above* (167), words by Sir Robert Grant, Governor of Bombay (1833), sung to *Hanover* by Dr William Croft (1708); *The King of Love My Shepherd Is* (197), words by Sir Henry Baker (1868) with tune *Dominus regit me* specially written for it by J.B. Dykes; *Let All the World in Every Corner Sing, My God and King* (375), another George Herbert poem, used with four tunes, by W.H. Monk, Basil Harwood, Martin Shaw and Erik Routley; *Teach Me, My God and King* (337), based on a poem by George Herbert, set to the traditional tune *Sandys*; *Praise, My Soul, the King of Heaven, to His Feet Thy Tribute Bring* (365), words by Henry Francis Lyte (1834), Sir John Goss's tune to it written in 1869. *All Glory, Laud and Honour, to Thee, Redeemer King* (98), translated by John Mason Neale from a poem by the ninth-century French Bishop Theodulph of Orleans, with the tune *St Theodulph* by Melchior Teschner (1615), stresses dynastic inheritance:

> Thou art the King of Israel,
> Thou David's Royal Son
> Who in the Lord's name comest,
> The King and Blessed One.

Hymn 254, written by L.B.C.L. Muirhead in 1899, and sung to the 1794 tune *University* (anon.), stresses 'The Church of God a kingdom is/ Where Christ in power doth reign' – a kingdom, you will note, and not a republic or a democratic syndicalist commune. Two well-loved hymns, *All Hail the Power of Jesus' Name* (217) and *Crown Him With Many Crowns* (224), both with rousing tunes, are extended celebrations of the idea of coronation. *All Hail* had words by Edward Perronet, and tune *Miles Lane* by William Shrubsole, published together in 1799. *Crown Him With Many Crowns* was written by Matthew Bridges in 1851, and memorably set to *Diademata* by Sir George Elvey for the 1868 appendix to *Hymns Ancient and Modern*; the tune was subsequently adopted by both *The Baptist Hymnal* and *The Methodist Hymnal*.

Militarism

While submissiveness to the King was one desirable Christian quality, another in the Victorian worldview was militancy in the propagation of the faith. This coincided with the prevalence of the idea, in the second half of the nineteenth century, that war was a moral force and the profession of soldiering a noble one. Professor J.A. Cramb declared: 'War is the supreme act in the life of the state.'[20] John Ruskin concluded that 'war is the foundation of all the arts, I mean that it is the foundation of all the high virtues and faculties of men', and he urged Britain's young soldiers to give to her 'a bright, stainless, perfect life – a knightly life'.[21] On the eve of the First World War, *The Nineteenth Century* published an article declaring that 'efficiency in war . . . is God's test of a nation's soul . . . Victory is the crown of moral quality, and therefore while nations wage war upon one another the survival of the fittest means the survival of the physically best.'[22]

The army, once regarded as 'brutal and licentious soldiery', came under the impact of evangelicalism, like so much of Victorian England. The evangelicals sought to demonstrate that it was possible to be both a professional soldier and a zealous Christian. Organizations and individuals set out 'to raise the tone of the troops', providing chaplains, chapels and Bibles, and creating role models of Christian soldier heroes. The pre-eminent example was Gordon of Khartoum, depicted in the celebrated painting by G.W. Joy going heroically to his death at the hands of the Mahdi's soldiers, a Christian martyr, a British warrior, the supreme exemplar of chivalry, courage and sacrifice.

The Puritan soldier of the Civil War became a commonplace of military imagery. Cromwell was rehabilitated and became a major English icon, celebrated among Carlyle's archetypal heroes. The result was, as Olive Anderson has pointed out, that by the mid-1860s 'The British Army was . . . more obtrusively Christian than it had ever been since the restoration'.[23] The Christianization of the army was paralleled by the militarization of Christianity. The 1870s and 1880s saw the foundation of the Salvation Army, the Church Army and the Boys' Brigade, complete with uniforms, titles and military ranks. The uniformed youth movements springing up in the wake of the Boys' Brigade invariably equated Christianity, chivalry and manliness.[24] It was not just Christianity but society as a whole that became permeated with the military ethos. Public schools had cadet corps; state schools, military-style drill as an integral part of the curriculum. In adult life, the Volunteers, the Militia and the Yeomanry all flourished. Post Office, Fire Brigade and Railway Company staff were put into uniform. Brass bands, in direct emulation of the military bands whose repertoire and style they shared, took up Ruritanian uniforms. All of this etched into the popular consciousness the dictum of Thomas Carlyle: 'Man is created to fight; he is perhaps best of all definable as a born soldier.'[25] The spirit in which war was to be waged was one of chivalry.

This is the context in which we need to examine the military imagery of hymns. The idea of a war against the Devil and the hosts of evil goes back to the New Testament. The equation of the Christian struggle against evil with real war against God's enemies by his new chosen people, the British, is explicitly made in the nineteenth century. Reverend Charles Kingsley, in his *Brave Words for Brave Soldiers and Sailors*, sent out to the troops before Sebastopol in the Crimea in the winter of 1855, argued that '[h]e who fights for Queen and Country in a just cause is fighting not only in the Queen's name but in Christ's army'; and that the

> Lord Jesus Christ is not only the *Prince of Peace*; he is the *Prince of War* too. He is the Lord of Hosts, the God of armies; and whoever fights in a just war, against tyrants and oppressors, he is fighting on Christ's side, and Christ is fighting on his side; Christ is his Captain and leader, and he can be in no better service.[26]

Adey's analysis of hymn imagery suggests that military imagery only appears regularly in hymns from the 1790s onward, making it largely a nineteenth-century phenomenon.[27] Susan Drain has argued that 'metaphors of warfare . . . were never so strongly taken up as in the latter part of the Nineteenth Century', and she notes a real increase in military imagery in the 1875 supplement to *Hymns Ancient and Modern*.[28]

Kingsley's sentiments became such a commonplace of religious pronouncements that J.A. Hobson devoted an entire chapter, 'Christianity in khaki', in his classic polemic *The Psychology of Jingoism* to tracing the involvement of Christianity with war and Empire. 'When has a Christian nation ever entered a war which has not been regarded by the official priesthood as a sacred war?' he asked. 'In England the State Church has never permitted the spirit of the Prince of Peace to interfere when statesmen and soldiers appealed to the passions of race – lust, conquest and revenge.' Instead of preaching peace and brotherhood, the Christian churches were preaching the ideas of 'the tribal God, the special race mission, the dominion of hate and forcible revenge'. Where the Nonconformist churches at least were divided about the Crimean War, he says, all the churches united in support of the Boer War, urging 'armed Britain to go forth in Jesus' name to slay their fellows and take their land'. He quotes from the sermons and speeches of leading clerics to justify his analysis. He points out that every soldier going to the front has been furnished with a copy of the New Testament decorated on the front with a Union Jack.[29]

Many of the militarist hymns were addressed directly to boys. Adey, analysing school hymn books of various kinds, concludes:

> The generation that fought the First World War had become conditioned to feeling for their country the reverence their forbears had felt for God, not denying Him but enlisting Him on its side. While this goes back to the 'God of battles' in the Old Testament, or the Puritan belief in Britain as the Second Israel, the drift of adults away from the churches converted it into a worship of two gods. They had come to view the Union Jack, a pattern of superimposed crosses, as equivalent to the Cross, a sign of ultimate value for which lives were well lost. Originally a feature of Dissenting, then of public school religion, this patriotic conditioning had by the accession of George V spread to all classes.[30]

The imagery of Christianity and of British imperialism are so intertwined as to keep slipping over from one to the other. The British flag was indeed composed of a mesh of crosses: those of St George, St Andrew and St Patrick. The celebration of banners was bound to suggest a double-image, as for instance in G.W. Doane's *Fling Out the Banner* (1848), set in *Ancient and Modern* to the eighteenth-century tune *Duke Street*, attributed to John Hatton:

> Fling out the banner! Let if float
> Skyward and seaward, high and wide;
> Our glory only in the cross,
> Our only hope the Crucified.
>
> Fling out the banner! Heathen lands
> Shall see from far the glorious sight,
> And nations, crowding to be born,
> Baptize their spirits in its light.
>
> Fling out the banner! Wide and high,
> Seaward and skyward let it shine;
> Nor skill nor might nor merit ours;
> We conquer only in that sign.

For all that the author was an American, the imagery could easily be interpreted as that of an expanding Christian Empire, and the last line recalls the story of the Emperor Constantine adopting the sign of the cross in his bid for Empire with the words: 'In this sign conquer.'

The Sunday School Hymnary, edited by Carey Bonner, published by the National Sunday School Union in 1905 and reaching its twenty-second edition by 1951, included a section for 'boys' meetings', replete with military and chivalric imagery. Hymn 384 was by Rev. F.A. Jackson, with music by Carey Bonner:

Fight for the right, boys, That's the thing to do;
Fight with your might boys, Plucky through and through;
Never mind your moods, boys, Never mind your skin,
Square your shoulders, set your jaw, And march right in.

You can all be gentlemen, courteous, kind and true;
You can have the strength of ten, if the right thing you'll do;
Never mind your feelings much, never mind the past,
Do the thing that's square today, First and last.

Hymn 385 had words by H.C. Beeching and music by A. Bryce:

God who created me, Nimble and light of limb,
In three elements free, To run, to ride, to swim;
Not when the sense is dim, But now from the heart of joy
I would remember Him: take the strength of a boy.

Jesu, King and Lord, Whose are my foes to fight,
Gird me with Thy sword, swift and sharp and bright,
Thee I would serve if I might – and conquer if I can
From day-dawn till night: take the strength of a man.

Hymn 386 had words by Walter J. Mathams and music by William Steffe:

From the heights where God is reigning rolls the ringing
    trumpet sound,
The men of Christ are waking and are leaping from the ground,
The mighty camp moves onward to the crowning battle bound.
For the Lord Christ leads us on.

The order of our marching is the Captain's 'Follow Me',
He advances on to conquest with His chosen chivalry,
With every man a hero we shall gain the victory,
For the Lord Christ leads us on.

Hymn 388 had words by Colin Sterne and music by H. Ernest Nichol:

Where the flag is flying, where the fight is keen,
Where the trumpet call is ringing,
There you find the soldiers, steady and serene,
There you hear the sound of singing.
Servants of the Master, scorning fear or flight,
Fighting for the Truth, the Life, the Light.
Soldiers of the Master, onward tread, yelling out the grand old
    story,
Ready day by day Jesus to obey, Soldiers of the King of Glory.

The enduring appeal of and to chivalry and the stress on chivalry's essentially religious nature lay behind Jan Struther's hymn *When a*

Knight Won His Spurs, set to a traditional English melody and first appearing in the 'children's section' of *Songs of Praise* (1931). It was reprinted in *The Life Boys' Hymnal*, published by the Boys' Brigade

> When a knight won his spurs, in the stories of old,
> He was gentle and brave, he was gallant and bold;
> With a shield on his arm and a lance in his hand
> For God and for valour he rode through the land.
>
> No charger have I, and no sword by my side,
> Yet still to adventure and battle I ride,
> Though back into storyland giants have fled,
> And the knights are no more and the dragons are dead.
> Let faith be my shield and let joy be my steed
> 'Gainst the dragons of anger, the ogres of greed;
> And let me set free, with the sword of my youth,
> From the castle of darkness the power of truth.

Perhaps the most celebrated of the military imagery hymns is the Anglican Rev. Sabine Baring-Gould's *Onward, Christian Soldiers*, written in 1864 for a children's Whit Monday procession and originally set to the tune from the slow movement of Haydn's *Symphony No. 15*. But it achieved its lasting popularity when set to the rousing tune *St Gertrude* by Sir Arthur Sullivan in 1871. Ian Bradley argues that 'despite its title *Onward, Christian Soldiers* is not a glorification of war; it is a stirring call to Christians to follow the Cross of Christ, and a powerful plea for Christian unity'.[31] It is all of that, but it is militaristic, too. Sullivan certainly thought so. After all he incorporated it into his Boer War *Te Deum*, written to celebrate the conclusion of that war. It is also used in the triumphant final scenes of two of the most notable films of the Second World War, *Mrs Miniver* and *A Canterbury Tale*, to urge the armies of Britain and her Allies on to victory against the Nazis. Whatever the words of the text itself, the popular perception of the hymn was as a call to arms. Its widespread popularity is attested by its inclusion in *Hymns Ancient and Modern* and in both *The Methodist Hymnal* and *The Baptist Hymnal*.

But *Onward, Christian Soldiers* is only one of the many hymns steeped in military imagery, some of them enduring and much loved. *Stand Up, Stand Up, For Jesus, Ye Soldiers of the Cross* was an American hymn. Written by Presbyterian Minister George Duffield in 1858 and inspired by the dying words of the evangelist Dudley Atkins Tyng, it was set to G.J. Webb's tune *Morning Light* (originally a parlour ballad) and became popular both in Britain and the United States. It was sung on both sides in the American Civil War and in Britain was included in *Hymns Ancient and Modern* and *The Methodist Hymnal* and *The Baptist Hymnal*.

Charles Wesley's *Soldiers of Christ, Arise and Put Your Armour On* appeared originally in 1749 at sixteen verses but was shortened to four by John Wesley in 1780 and thereafter appeared in that form in Methodist hymnals. But it was taken up by *Hymns Ancient and Modern* and *The Baptist Hymnal*.

Both ends of the religious spectrum embraced military imagery. At one end is *Hymns Ancient and Modern* where we find James Montgomery's *Lift Up Your Heads, Ye Gates of Brass* (1843), set to the tune *Crucis Victoria* by Myles B. Foster, with its 'holy war' in which 'the powers of heaven and hell engage', 'armies of the living God, sworn warriors of Christ's host' and a 'banner, brighter than the star that leads the train of night'; Bishop William Walsham How's *Soldiers of the Cross, Arise* (1863), set to Myles B. Foster's *Crucis Milites*, where the soldiers are urged to 'gird you with your armour bright', and warned 'Mighty are your enemies, hard the battle ye must fight'; Ada R. Greenaway's *Rise At the Cry of Battle* (1916), set to the tune *Battle Cry* by Alan Gray, urging 'Arm for the coming strife' and warning 'keen is the strife and long' and 'strive till the strife is over, Fight till the fight is won'; *See, the Conqueror Mounts in Triumph* (1862), by Bishop Christopher Wordsworth of Lincoln, nephew of the poet William Wordsworth, set to *Rex Gloriae* by Henry Smart, hails the risen Christ as 'Lord of battle, God of armies'. Even the carnage of the First World War did not blunt the chivalric imagery, and, later on, one of the best-loved hymns of Armistice Day services was Sir John Arkwright's *O Valiant Hearts* (1919), set in *Hymns Ancient and Modern* to the tune *Julius* by Dr Martin Shaw in memory of a brother lost in the war, but more popularly sung to the Nonconformists' *The Supreme Sacrifice* by Charles Harris. It proclaims of the fallen that their 'knightly virtue' is proved, that they had answered God's call to fight and had emulated the sacrifice of Christ, giving their lives for the good of mankind. There were many more military hymns. Adey argues that 'what conditioned the soldiers of Christ to become soldiers of the sovereign and ... to sacrifice themselves in war, was the activism and belief in progress evident in the swinging tunes and insistent themes of oneness and impending triumph common to *Onward, Christian Soldiers, Forward be our watchword* and many other hymns'.[32]

At the other end of the spectrum is the revivalist song book *Salvation Army Music*, edited by William Booth and published in 1880. There was little cross-over with Anglican hymnals. Recurrent themes in the *Salvation Army Song Book* are God's love; 'going home' to heaven, crossing the river to the 'bright and happy land'; Jesus as saviour, helper and refuge; man as sinner; the life of the pilgrim; eternal hope; the cross as the symbol of Christ's sacrifice; the 'crimson flood' of redeeming blood; the voyage of life on storm-tossed oceans; and, above all, warfare. Military imagery has been traced in 34 per cent of Salvation Army hymns: *I'm Glad I'm in This Army; Hold the Fort; Marching Along; Ye Soldiers of the Cross; A Soldier of the Cross; Sound the Battle Cry; Stand Like the Brave; The Trumpeters; Ye Valiant Soldiers* and so on.[33]

Hero-worship

Linked to militarism is hero-worship. The heroes of Protestant Christianity are the exemplars of Christian virtue and service, sacrifice and faith. One of the most notable hero-worship hymns is William Walsham How's *For All the Saints Who From Their Labours Rest* (1864), which blends militarism, evangelism and hero-worship. It was set to tunes by Sir Joseph Barnby (1869) and Sir Charles Stanford (1904), but both were superseded by Vaughan Williams's triumphant *Sine Nomine* (1906). In his *Hark the Sound of Holy Voices* (1862), Bishop Christopher Wordsworth specifies the heroes:

> Patriarch, and holy prophet,
> Who prepared the way for Christ,
> King, apostle, saint, confessor,
> Martyr, and evangelist.
> Saintly maiden, godly matron,
> Widows who have watched to prayer,
> Joined in holy concert, singing
> To the Lord of all, are there.

A very similar combination of the ideas of spiritual warfare, death and sacrifice is Reginald Heber's *The Son of God Goes Forth to War*, which celebrates their willingness to meet 'the tyrant's brandished steel, the lion's gory mane'.

There were sacrifice hymns for the saints on saints days – to St John the Evangelist, St Stephen the Protomartyr, St John the Baptist and St Paul. The most martial and nationalistic was in honour of St George. Written by Frederick William Newman, published in 1890 and set to Henry Smart's *Regent Square*, it was a chivalric call to arms:

> Jesus, Lord of our salvation,
> For thy warrior bold and true,
> Now accept our thankful praises,
> And our strength do thou renew,
> That, like George, with courage dauntless
> We may all our foes subdue.

Blazoned on our country's banner
England bears the knightly sign:
Lord, our fatherland empower,
That, endued with strength divine,
She may evermore with courage
Bear the standard that is thine.

Fill her youth with manly spirit,
Patient, self-restrained and pure,
Of thy cause the ready champions,
Never flinching to endure
Hardness for the name of Jesus:
So their triumph shall be sure.

Teach her manhood to confess thee
As the Master, Lord and King:
All their powers consecrated
To thy service may men bring,
And of loyal speech and action
Make to thee an offering.

Jesus, Lord, thou mighty Victor,
Thy all-glorious name we praise:
Thou art with us, God almighty:
'Midst our ranks thy shout we raise:
Where thy kingly war-cry soundeth,
Lead us on through all our days.

Missionary hymns

There is strong disagreement among scholars about the nature of missionary hymns. The standard view was established by Susan Tamke who acknowledges that there were 'some great missionary hymns written during the nineteenth century which asked simply and humbly for God's help in leading "the erring children" to God', and that, at the turn of the nineteenth century, 'a new type of missionary hymn, urging world peace and brotherhood and warning against arrogance' appeared, though 'it would be several decades before these hymns . . . became a noticeable quantity in the denominational hymnals'. Nevertheless 'a survey of nineteenth century hymns of foreign missions shows that the majority were not of this type. Most speak in terms of a condescending paternalism – "heathens", "rude barbarians" and "sin-darkened creatures" are phrases casually used to describe the subjects of foreign mission.'[34]

Lionel Adey fundamentally disagrees with this view:

The common impression that the Cross and the Flag went together is not borne out by the great missionary hymns . . . far more typical is a universalism that Watts and Montgomery caught from the Psalms . . . to judge from surviving hymn texts the chauvinism of missionaries has been much exaggerated . . . the keynote of the great hymns for overseas missions known to every Protestant churchgoer is not quasi-military conquest but universal love and liberation.[35]

But Adey is drawing a false antithesis between imperialism and Christian missions. Protestant Christianity was integral to British imperialism and British imperialism was a faith. Christianity was one of the bonds of Greater Britain and one of the justifications for Empire, as is clear from *God's Greater Britain* (1899), a collection of articles by leading Baptist Minister Dr John Clifford written during his world tour in Diamond Jubilee year, 1897. His reason for publishing them was to 'bind in closer union the far-sundered members of our vast Empire'. He celebrated 'the achievements of our British race', hymned the loyalty of the colonies to the mother country and to the crown, and preached the virtues of imperial federation, animated by a divine mission, for it was the duty of the British people to undertake 'the leadership of the moral and spiritual life of the world'. All the English-speaking peoples had a mission:

For we are called with a high calling . . . We must march in step. Ours is a single aim, a single task, the regeneration of Man. Our place is in the ranks of the great Anglo-Saxon missionary race, to whom is given the grace of preaching amongst all peoples the unsearchable riches of Christ. We are going to all men. They are coming to us. The world is becoming *one* . . . God chose us His colonizers and missionaries, for He had given us the stewardship of the five great principles on whose maintenance the progress of mankind depends.

These principles are liberty of conscience, reverence for truth, reverence for justice, compassion for the criminal and the ignorant, the poor and the lost and a sturdy independence. 'The people in possession of these principles and bent on incorporating them in the life of the world cannot be kept from empire by any forces whatever.'[36]

Anglicans took a similar view of the role of the Empire. The Anglican journal *The Churchman*, reflecting on the Queen's Golden Jubilee in 1887, pointed out that the growth of the Empire and of missionary endeavour had gone hand in hand:

We hold our empire as the gift of God . . . conferred on us, not through any merit of our own, but because it pleased Him to choose us as the instrument for spreading His glory among the nations. It was for this that, during the ages, His Providence moulded our composite race, and endowed it with the characteristics of enterprise, love of commerce, national persistency, capacity for rule and religious earnestness . . . he fitted these islands by situation and products to take the lead in universal, as distinguished from European politics: and for this too, when the time was come He gave us the priceless boon of 'the everlasting Gospel.'[37]

So the universalism was part and parcel of Empire and all part of God's plan. The Anglo-Saxon race had been chosen as the instrument of God's will. This became part of the popular consciousness, as evidenced by Thomas Jones Barker's 1861 painting entitled *Queen Victoria Presenting a Bible in the Audience Chamber at Windsor*. The grateful recipient of the Bible is a kneeling African chieftain, and Prince Albert, Lord John Russell and Lord Palmerston look on approvingly. This painting was turned into a popular print with the more suggestive title 'The Bible: That is the secret of England's greatness', and in this form it adorned many household walls, making clear the link of crown, Empire, race and faith.

Brian Stanley is therefore surely right when he argues that Christianity 'is inherently an imperial religion in the sense that it claims that the revealed truth of God was incarnated uniquely in the person of Jesus Christ, that all men and women are called to respond in repentance and faith to that revelation, and that the kingdom of God inaugurated in the coming of Christ makes absolute demands upon all people and all cultures'.[38]

Missionary activity was thus a key element of the faith. The modern missionary movement was born out of the evangelical upsurge of the 1790s when many important missionary organizations were created and launched a major offensive against heathendom and idolatry. The impulse faded after a generation, only to be revived with the rise of popular imperialism in the 1870s, the evangelical impact of the Moody and Sankey revivalist missions and the celebrity of Dr David Livingstone, who was effectively a Protestant saint and who mapped and explored Africa, seeking to combat slavery, promote legitimate commerce and convert the natives to Christianity. Concern on the part of the missionaries about the exploitation of the natives, the continuing menace of the slave trade, the effect of local native despotism and the threat from other nations' imperial ambitions led many, both Anglican and Nonconformist, to put their faith in and to press for formal British annexation of territory. This was a significant factor in the British acquisition of Uganda, Fiji, Bechuanaland and Nyasaland, for instance.

Missionary attitudes and values would change in the twentieth century with the rise of Communism and Islam, the effects of two world wars, the upsurge of pacifism and the decline of imperialism. But William Ellis of the London Missionary Society summed up the nineteenth-century consensus when he said: 'No man can become a Christian, in the true sense of the term, however savage he may have been before, without becoming a civilized man.'[39] Underpinning this dictum were, as Brian Stanley points out, four assumptions: faith in the idea of progress; confidence in the efficacy of civilization; the belief that the heathen realms were the domain of the devil; and that nineteenth-century Britain was the model of Christian society and culture which needed to be introduced to eliminate heathendom and all its attendant evils.[40]

It is in this intellectual and cultural context that we need to assess missionary hymns. The most famous of all missionary hymns, by common consent, was Bishop Reginald Heber's *From Greenland's Icy Mountains*, which contains all the assumptions underpinning the consensual view of missionary activity:

> From Greenland's icy mountains,
> From India's coral strand,
> Where Afric's sunny fountains
> Roll down their golden sand,
> From many an ancient river,
> From many a palmy plain,
> They call us to deliver
> Their land from error's chain.
>
> What though the spicy breezes
> Blow soft o'er Ceylon's isle,
> Though every prospect pleases
> And only man is vile,
> In vain with lavish kindness
> The gifts of God are strown,
> The heathen in his blindness
> Bows down to wood and stone.
>
> Can we whose souls are lighted
> With wisdom from on high,
> Can we to men benighted
> The lamp of life deny?
> Salvation! Oh, salvation!
> The joyful sound proclaim,
> Till each remotest nation
> Has learn'd Messiah's name.
>
> Waft, waft, ye winds, His story,
> And you, ye waters, roll,
> Till, like a sea of glory,

It spreads from pole to pole;
Till o'er our ransom'd nature
The Lamb for sinners slain,
Redeemer, King, Creator,
In bliss returns to reign.

It was famously written in twenty minutes in 1819, when Heber was Rector of Hodnet, for his father-in-law the Dean of St Asaph, who was preaching on Whitsunday in aid of the Society for the Propagation of the Gospel in Foreign Parts and wanted a new hymn for his morning service. Originally set to an Indian air, it later received specially composed tunes. But there was a denominational difference. Anglicans sang it either to Samuel Sebastian Wesley's sonorous and stately *Aurelia* or Thomas Clark's *Greenland* (1828), flowery, joyous, extrovert and uplifting. Methodists and Baptists sang it to Lowell Mason's plodding and prosaic *Missionary* (1824). In 1827, for reasons of metre, 'Ceylon's isle', was replaced by 'Java's isle', but the new reading failed to catch on and many hymnbooks retained the original: it perhaps had the advantage that Ceylon was part of the British Empire, whereas Java was not.

The original autograph text of the hymn was exhibited at the Great Exhibition in 1851. The 1870 illustrated edition of Heber's hymns describes it as 'universally admired' and W.T. Stead, in *Hymns That Have Helped*, in 1896 called it 'the favourite missionary hymn of the English speaking world'.[41] Ian Bradley observes that 'the imperialism and racial overtones implicit in the hymn came strangely from the pen of one so innocent and saintly as Reginald Heber'.[42] But this is to misunderstand the mindset of an age which believed that God had entrusted the British with a mission to Christianize and civilize the world, and that to do was a manifestation of love for the less fortunate peoples of the earth. Heber manifested just this commitment by becoming Bishop of Calcutta and dying there in 1826.

The twentieth century has become increasingly uncomfortable, however, with the imperial and racial overtones of the hymn, and has sought to banish it or at least cut it, removing the offending verse about the heathen. It appeared complete in *Hymns Ancient and Modern*, in *The Primitive Methodist Hymn Book* (1871), *The Presbyterian Hymnal* of 1882, *The Scottish Hymnal* of 1885, *The English Hymnal* of 1906 and *The Sunday School Hymnary* of 1905. It was still intact in the 1933 *Baptist Hymnal* but the 1933 *Methodist Hymnal* and the 1953 *Salvation Army Songbook* retained it only without the offending verse; while the progressive *Songs of Praise* (1931) dropped it altogether, a harbinger of things to come.

Some of the missionary hymns had a very long life. William

Williams's *O'er the Gloomy Hills of Darkness* of 1772 (sung variously to Thomas Clark's *Calcutta*, by Baptists; to Henry Gauntlett's *Triumph*, in *The Scottish Hymnal*; to Edwin Moss's *Ulpha*, in the 1882 Presbyterian *Church Praise*) did not make it into *Hymns Ancient and Modern*, but it was in Bickersteth's *Christian Psalmody* in 1833 and was still to be found complete in the 1933 *Baptist Hymnal*:

> O'er the gloomy hills of darkness
> Look, my soul; be still, and gaze;
> All the promises do travail
> With a glorious day of grace:
> Blessed jubilee! Let thy glorious morning dawn.
>
> Let the Indian, let the Negro,
> Let the rude barbarian see
> That divine and glorious conquest
> Once obtained on Calvary:
> Let the gospel
> Loud resound from pole to pole.
>
> Kingdoms wide, that sit in darkness,
> Grant them, Lord, Thy glorious light;
> And from eastern coast to western
> May the morning chase the night;
> And redemption,
> Freely purchased, win the day.
>
> May the glorious day approaching,
> On their grossest darkness dawn:
> And the everlasting gospel
> Spread abroad Thy Holy Name
> O'er the borders
> Of the great Immanuel's land.
>
> Fly abroad, thou mighty gospel,
> Win and conquer, never cease;
> May thy lasting, wide dominion
> Multiply and still increase:
> Sway thy sceptre,
> Saviour, all the world around.

This very much set the tone for the missionary hymns.

Charles Wesley targeted specific unbelievers with his hymns. The Methodist hymn (443) *Sun of Unclouded Righteousness*, directed at the 'Mahometans', says:

> The smoke of the infernal cave,
> Which half the Christian world overspread,
> Disperse, thou heavenly Light, and save

> The souls by that imposter led,
> That Arab-thief, as Satan bold,
> Who quite destroyed the Asian fold.

It was still in the 1879 edition of the *Methodist Hymnal*. Hymn 444, Wesley's hymn 'for the heathen', *Lord Over All*, contains the verse:

> The servile progeny of Ham
> Seize, as the purchase of thy blood;
> Let all the Heathens know thy name;
> From idols to the living God
> The dark Americans convert;
> And shine in every pagan heart.

There are three Methodist hymns directed to the Jews (450, 451, 452). *Almighty God of Love* (452) says:

> Send then thy servants forth,
> To call the Hebrews home;
> From East, and West, and South, and North,
> Let all the wanderers come
> Wher'er in lands unknown
> The fugitives remain,
> Bid every creature help them on,
> Thy holy Mount to gain.

Adey objects that it is wrong of Tamke and others to equate with Empire such hymns as Isaac Watts's *Jesus Shall Reign Where're the Sun Doth His Successive Journeys Run* (1719) or John Ellerton's *The Day Thou Gavest, Lord, Is Ended* (1870). But one of the best-known descriptions of the Empire was 'the Empire on which the sun never sets'. It does not take much imagination to see the kingdom of God on earth stretching from East to West, North to South, pole to pole, as the spiritual analogue of that physical Empire which was a manifestation of God's chosen race, the British, 'a nation God delights to bless' as Wesley called it (Hymn 466). Watts's hymn included the verse:

> Behold the islands with their kings,
> And Europe her best tribute brings,
> And crowds of Indian nations meet,
> To pay their homage at his feet.

Ellerton's hymn, set to the tune *St Clement* by Rev. Clement Scholefield (1874), appeared in *Hymns Ancient and Modern* and in the hymnals of the Presbyterians, Baptists and Methodists:

> As o'er each continent and island
> The dawn leads on another day,

The voice of prayer is never silent,
Nor dies the strain of praise away.

The sun that bids us rest is waking
Our brethren 'neath the western sky,
And hour by hour fresh lips are making
Thy wondrous doings heard on high.

When, on 30 June 1997, the Union Jack was lowered for the last time at the British Naval Base in Hong Kong at the 'Beating the Retreat' ceremony signalling the end of 150 years of British rule in the crown colony, and as the heavens wept uncontrollably, the band played *The Day Thou Gavest, Lord, Is Ended* – the day being the era of the British Empire.[43]

These hymns and others like them have to be seen in the context of divine favour and the imperial mission. While the Empire existed and flourished, it could properly be seen as working out God's divine purpose. Thus Bickersteth's *Christian Psalmody* (Hymn 434) could include the affirmation of divine favour:

While Britain, favour'd of the skies,
Recalls the wonders God has wrought;
Let grateful joy adoring rise
And warm to rapture ev'ry thought.

When wicked men combined their power,
And doom'd these isles their certain prey,
Thy hand forbade the fatal hour;
Their evil plot in ruins lay.

Again our restless cruel foes,
Resum'd, avow'd, a fresh design;
Again to save us God arose
And Britain owes the hand divine.

The undertaking of that mission by God's chosen people was cele-brated in J.H. Ellison's *O Living God, Whose Voice of Old* (written in 1901, included in *Ancient and Modern* in 1904, but out by 1922).

'Neath many a toil by land and sea
An English life is bending;
Lord, grant that they who onward press
To tasks of thy creation,
May onward bear through toil and stress
The faith that made their nation.

When the Empire declined and fell, the Church was forced to under-take a rethink. Different times confer different meanings. But to deny the imperial context would be both perverse and ahistorical.

Patriotism and nationalism

The identification of Britain with Israel and the favour of God's special protection, the importance of a Protestant monarchy and the established Protestant Churches meant that hymns inevitably played a part in celebrating the nation. The idea was encapsulated in Isaac Watts's *Shine, Mighty God, on Britain, Shine* which Bickersteth included in his 1833 *Christian Psalmody* but which fell out of favour later in the nineteenth century.

> Shine, Mighty God, on Britain, shine
> With beams of heavenly grace;
> Reveal thy power, through all our coasts,
> And show thy gracious face.
>
> Amid our isle, exalted high,
> Do thou in glory stand,
> And, like a wall of guardian fire,
> Surround our favoured land.
> May God our Saviour scatter round
> His choicest favours here,
> And let creation's utmost bound
> Behold, adore and fear.
>
> So let thy name, from shore to shore,
> Sound all the earth abroad,
> And distant nations know and love
> Their saviour and their God.

But it was another of Watts's hymns that became, in Adey's words, 'the tribal lay of the British', *O, God, Our Help in Ages Past*.[44] Written in 1714 at a time of grave anxiety about the future of the Protestant succession as *Our God, Our Help in Ages Past*, it was changed in 1738 by John Wesley to *O, God, Our Help* and set in 1861 in *Hymns Ancient and Modern* to Dr William Croft's majestic *St Anne*. Erik Routley observed that it is 'always to be heard on our great national occasions', and he cites as examples the funerals of Queen Victoria and King Edward VII, Mr Gladstone and Sir Henry Campbell-Bannerman and the Memorial service for King George V in 1936.[45]

It was at the end of the nineteenth century that hymnals began to include sections specifically chosen for national occasions. They appeared in *Hymns Ancient and Modern*, *The English Hymnal*, *The Methodist Hymnal* and *The Baptist Hymnal*. The national anthem *God Save the King/Queen* featured in all these sections, making its first appearance in *Hymns Ancient and Modern* in 1904.

Typical of such national hymns is Rev. John Ellerton's *Praise to Our*

God, Whose Bounteous Hand. He wrote it in 1870 and included it in the SPCK's *Church Hymns* (1871), of which he was co-editor. It entered *Hymns Ancient and Modern* in 1904 but was removed in 1950. In *Ancient and Modern* it was set to two existing tunes, Philip Hart's *Hilderstone* and the seventeenth-century German *Easter Song*. The *Baptist Hymnal* set it to the tune *Truro* from the 1789 *Psalmodia Evangelica*. In the Presbyterian hymnal *Church Praise* (1883) it was set to J.W. Elliott's *Church Triumphant*. It did not feature in *The Methodist Hymnal* or *The English Hymnal*.

Ellerton's text, with its distinctive Shakespearean overtones, celebrated the idea of God's protection for his favoured people and identified the nation with its ancient throne, its Christian faith and its burgeoning empire:

> Praise to our God, Whose bounteous hand
> Prepared of old our glorious land:
> A garden fenced with silver sea:
> A people prosp'rous, strong and free.

> Praise to our God: through all our past
> His mighty arm hath held us fast:
> Till wars and perils, toils and fears,
> Have brought the rich and peaceful years.

> Praise to our God: the vine He set
> Within our coasts is fruitful yet:
> On many a shore the offshoots grow:
> 'Neath many a sun her clusters glow.

> Praise to our God: His power alone
> Can keep unmoved our ancient throne,
> Sustain'd by counsels wise and just,
> And guarded by a people's trust.

> Praise to our God: though chastenings stern
> Our evil dross should throughly burn,
> His rod and staff, from age to age,
> Shall rule and guide His heritage.

There had long been national hymns. One of the most popular was J.R. Wreford's hymn, written to mark the accession of Queen Victoria in 1837. It was subsequently included in *The English Hymnal*, *Songs of Praise*, *The Baptist Hymnal* and *The Primitive Methodist Hymnal* but did not make it into *Ancient and Modern* until 1950. In *Ancient and Modern*, *Songs of Praise* and *The English Hymnal*, it was set to the anonymous eighteenth-century tune *Aberdeen*. The *Baptist Hymnal* set it to Joseph Barnby's *Holy Trinity*. The hymn invokes for Britain peace, prosperity and liberty under God's protection.

Lord, while for all mankind we pray
Of every clime and coast,
O hear us for our native land,
The land we love the most.

O guard our shores from every foe,
With peace our borders bless;
With prosperous times our citizens crown,
Our fields with plenteousness.

Unite us in the sacred love
Of knowledge, truth and thee:
And let our hills and valleys shout
The songs of liberty.

Lord of the nations, thus to thee
Our country we commend:
Be thou her refuge and her trust,
Her everlasting friend.

Rudyard Kipling added to the corpus of national hymns. His Diamond Jubilee poem *Recessional*, warning of complacency and vainglory at a moment of supreme triumphalism, was immediately transformed into a hymn, as was his poem of childhood dedication *Land of Our Birth* ('Land of our Birth we pledge to thee/ Our love and toil in the years to be'). *The English Hymnal* (1906) and *Songs of Praise* set *God of Our Fathers, Known of Old* to the early eighteenth-century tune *Folkingham*, slow and dignified. *The Baptist Hymnal* and *The Sunday School Hymnary* set it to Joseph Barnby's *St Chrysostom* with its distinctive harmonies. The Methodists set it to G.F. Blanchard's *Lest We Forget*, a very striking tune with unexpected cadential clases, to convey sombreness. One of the finest settings was by the American composer Reginald De Koven, who provided a memorable tune which was both solemn and uplifting. Its popularity in America emphasizes Kipling's transatlantic appeal. *Land of Our Birth* appeared in both *The Methodist Hymnal* and *The Baptist Hymnal* set to A.E. Floyd's tune *Land of Our Birth*; and in *Songs of Praise* to the rather uninteresting Welsh hymn tune *Llangollen*. Neither of the Kipling hymns made it into *Hymns Ancient and Modern*, despite *God of Our Fathers* being regularly sung at official occasions, such as the funerals of W.F. Massey, Prime Minister of New Zealand, Lord Milner and Kipling himself.

The revised *Ancient and Modern* (1950) did feature a new national hymn, *I Vow to Thee My Country*, composed in 1918 by Sir Cecil Spring-Rice, British Ambassador to Washington:

I vow to thee my country, all earthly things above,
Entire and whole and perfect, the service of my love:

[393]

The love that asks no question, the love that stands the test,
That lays upon the altar, the dearest and the best:
The love that never falters, the love that pays the price,
The love that makes undaunted the final sacrifice.

And there's another country, I've heard of long ago,
Most dear to them that love her, most great to them that know:
We may not count her armies, we may not see her King:
Her fortress is a faithful heart, her prize is suffering.
And soul by soul and silently her shining bounds increase,
And her ways are ways of gentleness and all her paths are peace.

Its subtle matching of selfless love of country and the devoted practice of Christianity struck an immediate chord in the aftermath of the
Great War and, set to Gustav Holst's stirring main theme from *Jupiter*
(renamed *Thaxted* for its hymnal incarnation), it became an immediate part of the public repertoire. It was, for instance, sung at the Silver
Jubilee service of King George V in 1935, at the funerals of Lord
Allenby, in 1932, and Lord Mountbatten, in 1979, and at the wedding
of Charles and Diana, Prince and Princess of Wales, in 1982, and at the
funeral of Diana, Princess of Wales, in 1997.

The role of the hymn in great national and imperial events has
entered the collective popular memory. Just as Kipling's *Recessional*
sounded that sombre note of warning to the Empire at the time of the
Diamond Jubilee, so two events in 1912 assumed a similar status of
warning against excess of pride in British achievement – the sinking
of the *Titanic*, and the disastrous failure of the Scott expedition to the
South Pole. Both were seen retrospectively as initial intimations of the
catastrophe that was to engulf the world in 1914, the reminders to a
settled, confident, ordered society of its impermanence and perisha-
bility. But at the same time both were seen as demonstrative of British
character and British stoicism, the keys to the creation and maintenance of the British Empire.

On the night of 14 April 1912, *RMS Titanic*, the biggest liner in the
world, hit an iceberg and sank with the loss of 1,500 lives, among them
W.T. Stead, author of *Hymns That Have Helped*. It was on its maiden
voyage and was believed to be unsinkable. 'God himself could not sink
this ship', one deckhand was reported as saying to a passenger. The
last instruction of the ship's master, Captain Smith, to his crew was
allegedly 'Be British'; in other words, behave calmly and dutifully. The
words were to be engraved on his memorial statue in Lichfield. The
passengers, the cream of Anglo-American high society, behaved
according to the chivalric code which they shared. American survivor
Colonel Archibald Gracie wrote: 'The coolness, courage and sense of
duty that I here witnessed made me thankful to God and proud of my

Anglo-Saxon race that gave this perfect and superb exhibition of self-control at this hour of severest trial.'[46]

Eight months later on 12 November 1912, the bodies of Captain Robert Falcon Scott and his companions were discovered. Scott's final message declared:

> I do not regret this journey, which has shown that Englishmen can endure hardships, help one another, and meet death with as great a fortitude as ever in the past ... we have been willing to give our lives to this enterprise, which is for the honour of our country ... Had we lived I should have had a tale to tell of the hardihood, endurance and courage of my companions which would have stirred the heart of every Englishman.[47]

The members of the expedition became national heroes because of their conduct. The action of Captain Oates in going out into the storm, to prevent his becoming a burden to his companions ('The act of a brave man and an English gentleman', recorded Scott), rapidly entered popular mythology.[48] The two tragedies became mythified as paradigms of good conduct, as exemplifications of that chivalry that was an integral part of the imperial spirit.

Both events also had a significant religious element. Scott held services on his expedition and recorded the 'lusty singing of hymns'; and there had been regular services aboard *RMS Titanic*.[49] Lt 'Birdy' Bowers's last letter to his mother expressed his faith that they would be reunited in heaven. Expedition survivors recalled Dr Wilson playing a gramophone record of Dame Clara Butt singing *Abide With Me* at the base camp. The film *Scott of the Antarctic* (1948) recreated this image, the words of the hymn making their icy fate all the more poignant.

Even more famous is the belief that the band of the *Titanic* played the hymn *Nearer, My God, to Thee* as the ship went down. This fact rapidly entered popular mythology. The British Musicians' Union sold copies of the hymn, bearing photographs of the members of the band, to raise money for the musicians' families. On 24 May 1912, Empire Day, the seven chief London orchestras put on a concert at the Royal Albert Hall in memory of the musicians who perished. Five hundred musicians performed, conducted in turn by Sir Edward Elgar, Sir Henry Wood, Landon Ronald, Thomas Beecham, Percy Pitt and Willem Mengelberg, who had travelled from Berlin to take part. Madame Ada Crossley sang *O, Rest in the Lord* from Mendelssohn's *Elijah*. The programme included Chopin's *Funeral March*, Elgar's *Enigma Variations*, Sullivan's overture *In Memoriam* and the third movement of Tchaikovsky's *Pathetique* symphony. But the *Daily Sketch* reported:

The supreme moment of the day came when Sir Henry Wood led the orchestra through the first eight bars of Dykes' version of 'Nearer, My God, to Thee' and then, turning to the audience, he conducted the singing to the end . . . Quite 10,000 people, intense with emotion, sang in unison what is now one of the world's most famous hymns, and the effect was such that women wept and men had difficulty in mastering their feelings . . . To two ladies sitting in a box near the Royal party the hymn made special appeal, and their emotion was evident. The last time they had heard it was from a small boat laden to the water's edge and the band was playing the hymn on the boat deck of the sinking Titanic.[50]

In recent years, however, there has been a sustained assault on the myth.[51] This has been based in part on the recollection of Wireless Officer Harold Bride that the band was playing *Autumn* and on the emphatic statement by survivor Colonel Archibald Gracie in his account, published in 1913, that *Nearer, My God, to Thee* was not played.[52]

But there is an explanation for this discrepancy of views. The proponents of the *Autumn* theory have always claimed that Bride referred to the band playing the Anglican hymn *Autumn*. In reality Bride never claimed this. He simply referred to the band playing *Autumn*. As a matter of fact people never refer to hymns by their tunes but always by their first lines or titles. It is also known that Archibald Joyce's popular waltz *Autumn* was part of the repertoire of the *Titanic*'s band, which had played light music up until the end to reassure the passengers.[53] So the playing of *Autumn* does not necessarily invalidate the playing of *Nearer, My God, to Thee* as the last musical gesture.

To set against Gracie's testimony, there is the statement of stewardess Violet Jessop, a survivor, who in a memoir written in 1934 recalled distinctly hearing the band play *Nearer, My God, to Thee*.[54] In addition there is the account of Herman Finck, Musical Director of the Theatre Royal, Drury Lane. His principal violinist was George Orrell, who had been Bandmaster on the *Carpathia*, the ship which raced to the help of the *Titanic* and picked up 700 survivors. Finck writes:

> From the survivors, he received the story of how the *Titanic*'s band, with wonderful courage, played 'Nearer, My God, to Thee' as the ship sank. 'The ship's band in any emergency,' he relates, 'is expected to play to calm the passengers. After the *Titanic* struck the iceberg the band began to play bright music, dance music, comic songs – anything that would prevent the passengers from becoming panic-stricken. The ship was so badly holed that it was soon obvious that disaster was ahead. Then various awe-stricken passengers began to think of the death that faced them and asked the bandmaster to play hymns. The one which appealed

to all was "Nearer, My God, to Thee". And soon the liner broke in two and sank, with fourteen hundred people on board; among them were the eight gallant musicians.'[55]

Mrs Sarah Flower Adams' hymn was published in 1841. Several tunes were fitted to it. But it became particularly associated with two tunes: *Horbury* (1861), by the British minister Rev. John Bacchus Dykes, and *Bethany* (1856), by the American Dr Lowell Mason. *Horbury* was most often used when the hymn was sung in Britain and *Bethany* when it was sung in America. This may explain the diametrically opposed memories of survivors. Colonel Gracie was American and Violet Jessop British, though raised in Argentina. Interestingly the three major film versions of the tragedy confirm this dichotomy over the tunes. The American film versions, both entitled *Titanic*, of 1953 and 1998 show the band playing *Bethany*, and the British version *A Night to Remember* (1958) uses *Horbury*. As the *Daily Sketch* reported, this was the version Sir Henry Wood conducted at the memorial concert. There is, however, a further complication. There was a third popular tune attached to the hymn, *Propior Deo* by Sir Arthur Sullivan, a tune favoured in particular by Nonconformists; unlike *Horbury*, which was the preferred Angican version, it never appeared in *Hymns Ancient and Modern*. *Titanic* Bandmaster Wallace Hartley was a devout Methodist, son of a long-serving Methodist choirmaster, and is known to have favoured this version of the hymn.[56] His relatives were so firmly convinced that this would have been the version chosen by him that they had the opening bars carved on the monument above his grave in Colne. Thirty thousand mourners attended Hartley's funeral in Colne and the Bethel Choir and Colne Orchestral Society sang *Nearer, My God, to Thee*. Sadly Sullivan's version is rather humdrum and undistinguished, and lacks the sense of uplift to be found in both the Dykes and Mason versions. However, when all the evidence is taken into account, it is much more likely that the band played a British version of the hymn (either Dykes's or Sullivan's) rather than an American version, and that would adequately explain discrepant memories without invalidating the legend.

The nation and its representatives came together to mourn these two tragedies. The *Titanic* memorial service was held on 19 April 1912 at St Paul's Cathedral, and in reporting it *The Times* recalled the words of Archbishop Tait: 'Always in their hours of strongest feeling men acknowledge that they need a church', and added that 'it is to the metropolitan Cathedral, the central church of the capital of England and of the Empire, that the thoughts of all are naturally turned at moments of national emotion'. *The Times* reported: 'Nothing could have been more timely, nothing more touching, nothing at once more solemn and consoling than yesterday's extremely beautiful and impressive service.'[57] The Lord Mayor and the City Corporation, government ministers and a strong array of Commonwealth high commissioners and foreign ambassadors attended, along with many ordinary people. The band of Kneller Hall played, and before the service began it performed Spohr's *Blest Are the Departed*, Mendelssohn's *O Rest in the Lord*, the andante from Schubert's *Unfinished Symphony*, *Power and Love* from Gounod's *Redemption* and *Judex* from Gounod's *Mors et Vita*. The service included the congregation singing *Rock of Ages* and *Eternal Father, Strong to Save*; the choir sang Psalm 5, 'Ponder my words, O Lord', Psalm 23, 'The Lord is my shepherd' and Psalm 90, 'Lord, thou has't been our refuge'. One of the most impressive moments came after the reading by the Dean:

> At its conclusion all rose and stood in solemn silence. There was a pause for a few moments, and then the almost painful stillness of the church was broken by the subdued sound of drums. Gradually, and almost imperceptibly at first, it grew louder, until the solemn rolling of the drums reached its climax, filling the church, and reverberating like thunder through the dome and lofty arches. Then it gradually diminished until it completely died away. Another pause for a moment or two and the trumpets sounded the first notes of the 'Dead March' from *Saul*. None of those who heard this stately dirge will ever forget the solemnity of the moment. The music was almost overpowering in its majestic grandeur, and it seemed to be the culmination of this service of sorrow and of hope.

The band played Beethoven's *Funeral March* as the mourners departed.[58]

The mood of grief was shared throughout the Empire. Although there were only ten Canadians aboard the *Titanic*, two of whom were saved, *The Times*'s Toronto correspondent reported that a public subscription had been opened and that there would be a memorial service in Toronto. 'There was a profound depression over the whole country as the full details of the disaster were published, but there was also something of a splendid pride in the conduct of the vessel's officers and passengers who "played the game" to the end.'[59]

The memorial service for the Scott Polar Expedition took place on 14 February 1913, attended by the King (in the uniform of Admiral of the Fleet), the Prime Minister, members of the Cabinet, high commissioners and ambassadors, as well as members of the public – 10,000 were unable to gain admittance and waited outside. 'In the reverence and sympathy exhibited by all classes of the people, it was a remarkable manifestation', thought *The Times*, commenting on the 'very real sense of personal loss' experienced by many members of the public.[60] The King had written to Scott's mother, expressing 'deep sympathy with you in the loss of your gallant son, who in the service of his country sacrificed his life'. The Band of the Coldstream Guards under Mackenzie-Rogan provided music, beginning with a British selection: Handel's *Largo*; Sir Alexander Mackenzie's *Benedictus*; and Sullivan's *In Memoriam* overture. *Rock of Ages* and *Jesu, Lover of My Soul* were sung by the congregation. The *Dead March* from *Saul*, its drum rolls so effective at the *Titanic* service, followed the reading and Beethoven's *Funeral March* was played as mourners left. A number of memorial services were held in Britain and throughout the Empire.

The British monarchy was directly hymned in compositions specifically prepared for royal occasions. None were more spectacular in their affirmations of Empire, monarchy and Protestant Christianity than the Golden Jubilee of Queen Victoria in 1887 and her Diamond Jubilee in 1897. The SPCK issued a special collection of jubilee hymns for 1887.[61] It began with the national anthem, *God Save the Queen*, with a newly composed verse by Rev. Francis Pott, celebrating the imperial dimension of monarchy:

> Through all these fifty years;
> Through all her joys and tears;
> Through peace and war;
> Thou hast upheld her throne,
> While round it love has grown,
> Binding vast realms in one,
> All the world o'er.

It included 'O, King of Kings, Thy blessing shed/ On our anointed sovereign's head' (1819), set to the tune *Winchester New*, and deriving from Bickersteth's 1833 *Psalmody*. Rev. John Ellerton added an extra verse to his *Praise to Our God, Whose Bounteous Hand*, to be sung to the tune *Helderstone*:

> Praise to our God, for Her whose sway
> Her isles commemorate today;
> On whose dear head and stainless crown
> Her millions call their blessings down.

Similarly Bishop William Walsham How added new verses to his *To Thee, Our God, We Fly*, which already called on God 'to guard and bless our fatherland', 'Give peace in our time' and bless with heavenly wisdom 'the powers ordained by thee'.

> Bless, Lord, our gracious Queen
> As in the long years past,

Her Guardian Thou hast been,
Protect her to the last.
O Lord, stretch forth Thy mighty hand,
And guard and keep our Fatherland.
The throne uphold with power
And wisdom from above;
And grant it for its dower
A Nation's loyal love.

It was to be sung to John Goss's tune *Bevan*.

Empire was clearly in the minds of those who wrote two new hymns for the occasion. I. Gregory Smith's offering ran:

Empress and Queen – whose rule extends
From those far climes, where breaks the day,
Beyond the western main, nor ends
Where dies the fire-tipped ray.
Through half a hundred changeful years
Her sceptre holds a sway serene,
Through storm and sunshine, hopes and fears –
God bless the Queen!

God bless the Queen! from shore to shore
Deep calls to deep and sea to sea,
To lift a loud, exultant roar,
A shout of Jubilee.
Their island Queen they will defend.
See! How they toss on high their spray –
And we with theirs our voices blend,
For her to pray.

God bless the Queen! most loved for this,
The holy brightness round her throne,
To those who mourn, the tenderness,
The stern, reproving tone
To vice, which unreproved might dare
To stalk abroad, with shameless mien.
O Father, hear a nation's prayer,
And bless our Queen!

Rev. John Ellerton contributed a children's hymn: among the nine verses, the following:

English children, lift your voices
To our Father's throne on high!
Many a land today rejoices
Many a coast prolongs the cry –
God save the Queen!

[400]

Dusky Indian, strong Australian,
Western forest, Southern sea,
None are wanting, none are alien,
All in one great prayer agree –
God save the Queen!

Dearly, Lord, her people love her,
Gladly hail her golden year;
Let thy shield be still above her,
Save from danger and from fear –
God save the Queen!

Spare her long through changing seasons
Still to rule her subject isles;
Guard her throne from wars and treasons,
Wild revolt, and secret wiles,
God save the Queen!

A volume of hymns for use during 1897, dedicated to the Queen and published by Skeffingtons of Piccadilly,[62] began with the national anthem, to which Martin Skeffington had added the extra verse:

Thou Who for threescore years
In sunshine, cloud and tears
Hast kept our Queen;
Still be her Guide and Stay,
Thro' life's uncertain way
Till dawns the perfect day;
God bless our Queen.

The volume consisted of hymns written and composed by Anglicans and included several originally written for the 1887 Jubilee and suitably amended.

God of Supreme Dominion, words by Rev. S.J. Stone and music specially composed by Sir John Stainer, was one of them: harmonically enterprising and with a stately, long-limbed melody.

God of supreme dominion,
From whom all power has birth,
Whose praise on eagle pinion
O'er sweeps Thine Heav'n and earth;
We lift one voice before Thee
From many a land and race,
And with one heart adore thee
For threescore years of grace.

Here, by the barriers olden
With front of silver sheen –

There, from the Islands golden –
From Orient lands between –
From isles of beauty sparkling
The Summer seas among –
From tracts with Winter darkling
Goes up the choral song.

These years, in tale excelling
All years of olden reign,
Their twofold story telling
Of blended joy and pain –
With equal grace upon her,
Like twain wings of Thy Dove –
Have crowned the Head we honour;
Have blessed the Heart we love.

Comes with prophetic morning,
With Peace afar and near,
With Hope our hills adorning,
This Diamond Marriage Year!
And hearts with praise o'erflowing
And souls that inly pray,
Great Queen and Nation going
Still on their stately way.

Praise for Thy long sustaining,
That held her firm in aim
Ever to keep unwaning
Our fair ancestral fame;
Praise for the sweet compassion
Which makes the wide world own
That love's divinest fashion
Is set on England's throne.

Lord, as her realm lies truly
'neath an unsetting sun,
As earthly meed all duly
Her stainless life hath won;
So when at last before Thee
She lays her kingdom down,
Christ's One Light be her glory
Christ's merit be her crown.

The Empire on which the sun never sets is clearly linked to the monarch chosen and blessed by God, people of many a land and race united in Christian faith, and a regime characterized by peace, hope, love and compassion. The Bishop of Ripon's *Lord of All Thrones* celebrated the Queen–Empress in eight verses, offering thanks to God, 'the Lord of all thrones', for imperial expansion, beneficent royal rule and unity.

> We thank Thee for the golden day
> Which crowns the sixty years
> Of lengthened sway and strengthened love,
> Of peace and vanquished fears.
>
> We thank Thee for the imperial soul
> True to the common weal,
> Wise, loyal, calm, and vigilant
> The growing breach to heal.
>
> We thank Thee for the subtle bonds
> In joy and sorrow wrought,
> Which knits the people and the throne
> As one in hope and thought.
>
> We thank Thee for the broadening rule
> O'er many lands and seas;
> For opened realms and added store
> Harboured with every breeze.

The music by Dr Frederick Bridge, Organist of Westminster Abbey, has a simple tune but an unusual and elaborate structure – a slow first and eighth verse and faster verses in-between, with first and last verses written in triple time and second through seventh in quadruple time, making it difficult to sing.

Canon H.D. Rawnsley contributed *Queen of Our Homes and Hearts*, celebrating the queenly virtues of Victoria, thanking God who gave her 'wisdom with the sword' and a policy of 'Peace with Honour'. This had two tunes but was difficult to set because the word-lines are of unequal weight. The better of the two is by Dr George Martin, Organist of St Paul's, a lively musical setting, varied and inventive, with a final triumphant declaratory two-line sequence: 'The people kneel to bless His hand/ Who made thee ruler of the land', leading in a different key back to the original tune. Sir Joseph Barnby's alternative tune is sonorous and harmonically interesting but with definite longeurs as he tries to match his musical line to the uneven words.

Rev. S.J. Stone's *One Wide Majestic Temple* celebrates the Empire as 'one wide majestic temple/ Our realm from sea to sea,/ Spreads 'neath the dome of heaven' and the monarch as 'the stateliest under sun', 'the guardian of our freedom', her 'duty grandly done'. It also boasts two alternative tunes. Sir George Elvey's is simple and traditional, almost commonplace, but Martin Skeffington's resembles a romantic song with lush chromaticism and untypical sophisticated changes.

[403]

Godfrey Thring's *From North to South* elaborates in detail on the imperial theme:

> From north to south, and east to west,
> Where'er thy children find a home,
> Raise, England, raise, a song of praise,
> And bid the gathering nations come,
> To celebrate, all seas between,
> The love we bear our Empress–Queen.
>
> For sixty years beneath her sway –
> God-guided as she e'er has been –
> Her sons afar, in peace and war,
> Have shared the glories of our Queen:
> Whose reign, O God, Thou'st deign'd to bless,
> And gird with truth and righteousness.
>
> The human griefs, and human tears,
> In which her widow'd years were school'd,
> Unlock'd the heart, and made it part
> Of that great Empire which she ruled:
> And, now, as decades onward move,
> Have crown'd her with an Empire's love.
>
> Then draw the cords yet closer still,
> And bid all lands and nations see
> That they are one, whose work's begun,
> Continued, ended, Lord, in Thee;
> And to Whose Wondrous Name we raise
> This thankful hymn of prayer and praise.

Myles B. Foster's tune is full of interesting, enterprising harmonic twists and cadences, and romantic modulation.

Shall Praise or Prayer? by Canon Henry Twells, set by the Master of the Queen's Musick Sir Walter Parratt, is a resounding failure, a simple, almost simple-minded, text, set to a clumsy and awkward tune, full of uneasy harmonic twists and odd modulations. Rev. S.J. Stone's hymn for children *O Lord of Lords*, with a simple jolly tune provided by William Henry Monk, offers up a 'festal Alleluia' for 'that Cross-Flag to every wind unfurled/ Beneath a sun that sets not in our world', for 'our Three-Realms-in-One, and Realms afar/ As deep responds to deep, and star to star', for 'Asian, Afric, Australasian shores/ Where Ocean, tuned to our great Anthem roars'.

W. Chatterton Dix's *To Thee, O God, Be Praise* elaborates on the support, guidance and blessing provided to the Queen by God, while bringing 'a people's heart-felt praise,/ For Queen Victoria's reign,/ Her heaven-sent length of days'. It was set to the German tune *Nun danket* ('Now thank we all, our God').

Jackson Mason's *Arise, O Church of England*, originally written for the 1887 Jubilee, was now revived, with its robustly romantic music by J.W. Elliott, with soaring melody and upbeat 'Amen', imperial in tone. It links the Anglican Church, God, Queen and Empire: 'Arise, O Church of England/ And sing from East to West/ His praise Who crowns our monarchs/ Who gives His people rest.' Verse three explicitly links crown and cross:

> Yes, peace in rich abundance
> Has flourished in her time,
> While with her flag, the Gospel
> Speeds on to every clime.
> Light from her sixty summers
> Dark Afric's shores have seen,
> And India's sons of freedom
> Give thanks for England's Queen.

W. Chatterton Dix's *O Blessed Trinity*, with tune by Martin Skeffington, difficult to sing because it has an irregular pattern of bars to fit an irregular pattern of words, calls on the blessed Trinity to 'bless and defend our Queen', 'Altar and throne protect, senate and rule direct'. Finally, S.J. Stone's *All the Mountain Heights*, also for children, traces Victoria's reign in verse from her 'maiden' accession through her 'loneliness and sorrow' to the triumph of her Jubilee:

> Ring it out from tower and steeple!
> Blazon it by flag unfurled!
> She is loved by all her people:
> She is honoured by the world –
> God Save the Queen.

The tune, by Sir John Stainer, ends strikingly with an interrupted cadence leading to the plagal cadence 'God save the Queen', sung on a rising rather than a falling note, like a triumphal Amen.

The volume is an extraordinary assemblage of the talents with its galaxy of knighted composers: Sir John Stainer, Sir Walter Parratt, Sir George Elvey, Sir Joseph Barnby; and both Frederick Bridge and George Martin, the two soon to be knighted in the Jubilee Honours. The hymn-writers were in the main stalwarts of *Ancient and Modern* and prolific writers of hymns, some of them classics: Rev. S.J. Stone (*The Church's One Foundation*), Canon Rawnsley (*Saviour, Who Did'st Healing Give*), Rev. Jackson Mason (*Fierce Raged the Tempest O'er the Deep*) and layman William Chatterton Dix (*As With Gladness, Men of Old*). Interestingly, an arrangement was made of six of the hymns for military band by Sir Dan Godfrey, ensuring a wider performance than simply in church.

The official Jubilee Hymn, appointed to be used in all churches and chapels on Sunday 20 June 1897, was specially commissioned from two leading practitioners, words by William Walsham How, Bishop of Wakefield, who was in fact dying, and was dead before Jubilee Day, and music by Sir Arthur Sullivan. Sullivan regarded it as 'a labour of love' and sought a tune to 'reach the hearts of the people'. The result was a splendid hymn, with ringing words and a simple, stately, memorable tune christened *Bishopgarth*. The Queen thought it 'pretty and appropriate'.[63]

> O King of Kings, Whose reign of old
> Hath been from everlasting.
> Before Whose throne their crowns of gold
> The white rob'd saints are casting;
> While all the shining courts on high
> With Angel songs are ringing,
> Oh let thy children venture nigh,
> Their lowly homage bringing.
>
> For every heart, made glad by Thee
> With thankful praise is swelling;
> And every tongue, with joy set free,
> Its happy theme is telling.
> Thou hast been mindful of Thine own,
> And lo' we come confessing –
> 'Tis Thou hast dower'd our queenly throne
> With sixty years of blessing.
>
> Oh Royal heart, with wide embrace
> For all her children yearning!
> Oh happy realm, with mother-grace
> With loyal love returning!
> Where England's flag flies wide unfurl'd,
> All tyrant wrongs repelling;
> God make the world a better world
> For man's brief earthly dwelling.

The tune was too good to lose and was later offered in *The Methodist Hymnal* as an alternative for the Harvest hymn by William Chatterton Dix *To Thee, O Lord, Our Hearts We Raise*.

These were *pièces d'occasion* but could be re-used. Rev. Henry Burton wrote a Jubilee ode for the Golden Jubilee of 1887, set to music by Sir John Stainer and sung at the Children's Home Festival in the Royal Albert Hall. Stainer wrote to Burton:

I was very much delighted with your words, and can only regret that they will cease to be 'current coin' in a few months' time. If you like the music I wrote, would it be possible to write a few verses of a patriotic hymn to the tune . . . I admire the bold rhythm of your verse, and venture to suggest that if that portion of the music were wedded to another set of words both might live a little longer than this year.[64]

Burton obliged with the hymn *O King of Kings*:

O King of Kings, O Lord of Hosts, Whose throne is lifted high,
Above the nations of the earth, the armies of the sky –
The spirits of the perfected may give their nobler songs:
And we, Thy children, worship Thee, to Whom all praise belongs.

Thou who didst lead Thy people forth, and make the captive free,
Hast drawn around our native land the curtain of the sea,
To make another holy place, where golden lamps should shine,
And human hearts keep loving watch around the ark divine.

Our bounds of empire Thou hast set in many a distant isle,
And in the shadow of our throne the desert places smile:
For in our laws and in our faith, 'tis Thine own light they see
The truth that brings to captive souls the wider liberty.

Thou who hast sown the sky with stars, setting Thy thoughts in gold,
Hast crowned our nation's life, and ours, with blessings manifold;
Thy mercies have been numberless; Thy love, Thy grace, Thy care
Were wider than our utmost need, and higher than our prayer.

It was sung to Stainer's *Rex Regum*, memorable, rich and harmonically interesting. It did not make *Ancient and Modern*, but it did appear in both Baptist and Methodist hymnals. It made clear that Britain and her Empire were chosen and blessed by God.

Perhaps the ethos of imperial Christianity is best summed up by Rev. F.A. Jackson's *Where the Flag of Britain Flies*, set to the tune *Syria* (anon., 1842). It was written for the *Sunday School Hymnary* in 1905 and was later incorporated into the 1933 *Baptist Hymnal*:

Where the flag of Britain flies,
In the lands across the seas,
Under dark or smiling skies,
In the warm or wintry breeze:
Lord of Hosts, Thy Sovereign Hand
Over all our comrades be,
Hear us from our Motherland
For our lands across the sea.

Far and wide Thy word be known,
On thy love, Lord, let us wait,
Let the Empire be Thine own,
By Thy gentleness made great;
By Thy will alone we stand,

[407]

We are strong alone in Thee,
Hear us from our Motherland
And the lands across the sea.

Through the Empire spread Thy Light,
Over all shed Thou Thy calm,
Arm us for our heavenly fight
By the oak, the pine, the palm:
One world-wide confederate band,
May we all be one in Thee,
Hear us from our Motherland
And the lands across the sea.

Notes

1 Lionel Adey, *Class and Idol in the English Hymn*, Vancouver: University of British Columbia Press, 1988, p. 10.
2 Linda Colley, *Britons*, New Haven, CT, and London: Yale University Press, 1992, p. 54.
3 On Handel, see Howard D. Weinbrot, *Britannia's Issue: The Rise of British Literature from Dryden to Ossian*, Cambridge: Cambridge University Press, 1993, pp. 408–45; Ruth Smith, *Handel's Oratorios and Eighteenth-Century Thought*, Cambridge: Cambridge University Press, 1995; Michael Musgrave, *The Musical Life of the Crystal Palace*, Cambridge: Cambridge University Press, 1995, pp. 27–57.
4 Hugh McLeod, *Religion and Society in England, 1850–1914*, London: Macmillan, 1996, pp. 100, 103–4.
5 Erik Routley, *Hymns and Human Life*, London: John Murray, 1952, pp. 3–4.
6 J.R. Watson, *The English Hymn: A Critical and Historical Study*, Oxford: Clarendon Press, 1997, p. 4.
7 Ian Bradley, *Abide With Me: The World of Victorian Hymns*, London: SCM Press, 1997, p. xii.
8 D.H. Lawrence, *Assorted Articles*, London: Martin Secker, 1930, pp. 155, 162.
9 On the subject of hymns and society, see Ian Bradley, *Abide With Me*; Lionel Adey, *Class and Idol*; Lionel Adey, *Hymns and the Christian Myth*, Vancouver: University of British Columbia Press, 1986; Susan Tamke, *Make a Joyful Noise Unto the Lord: Hymns as a Reflection of Victorian Social Attitudes*, Athens, OH: Ohio University Press, 1978; J.R. Watson, *The English Hymn*; Susan Drain, *The Anglican Church in Nineteenth Century Britain: Hymns Ancient and Modern, 1860–75*, Lampeter: Edwin Mellen Press, 1989.
10 Bradley, *Abide With Me*, pp. 45–6.
11 Tamke, *Make a Joyful Noise*, p. 2; W.T. Stead, *Hymns That Have Helped*, London: Masterpiece Library, 1896, p. 6.
12 John Wilson, 'Looking at hymn tunes: the objective factors', in Robin A. Leaver and James H. Litton (eds), *Duty and Delight: Routley Remembered*, Carol Stream, IL: Hope Publishing, 1985, pp. 123, 141.
13 Stead, *Hymns That Have Helped*, p. 2.
14 *Ibid.*, p. 3.
15 *Ibid.*, p. 7.
16 Donald Davies, *The Eighteenth Century Hymn in England*, Cambridge: Cambridge University Press, 1993, pp. 57–70; Gordon Rattray Taylor, *The Angel-Makers*, London: Heinemann, 1958, pp. 165–7.
17 Bradley, *Abide With Me*, pp. 124–8.
18 Tamke, *Make a Joyful Noise*, p. 9.

19 Stephen Wilson, 'Religion and social attitudes: *Hymns Ancient and Modern* (1889)', *Social Compass* 22 (1975), p. 215.
20 Quoted in Michael Howard, 'Empire, race and war in pre-1914 Britain', in Hugh Lloyd-Jones, Valerie Pearl and Blair Worden (eds), *History and Imagination*, London: Duckworth, 1981, p. 350.
21 John Ruskin, *Crown of Wild Olives*, London: George Allen, 1909, pp. 122–4, 164.
22 Quoted in H.W. Koch, *The Origins of the First World War*, Basingstoke: Macmillan, 1972, p. 344.
23 Olive Anderson, 'The growth of Christian militarism in mid-Victorian Britain', *English Historical Review* 86 (1971), p. 64.
24 John Springhall, *Youth, Empire and Society: British Youth Movements*, Beckenham: Croom Helm, 1977.
25 Thomas Carlyle, *Past and Present*, London: Chapman & Hall, 1905, pp. 163–4.
26 John Wolffe, *God and Greater Britain*, London: Routledge, 1994, pp. 227, 232.
27 Adey, *Class and Idol*, pp. 199–204.
28 Drain, *The Anglican Church*, p. 70.
29 J.A. Hobson, *The Psychology of Jingoism*, London: Grant Richards, 1901, pp. 41–62.
30 Adey, *Class and Idol*, pp. 193–4.
31 Ian Bradley, *The Penguin Book of Hymns*, London: Penguin, 1990, p. 332.
32 Adey, *Class and Idol*, p. 208.
33 *Ibid.*, p. 202.
34 Tamke, *Make a Joyful Noise*, pp. 135–8.
35 Adey, *Class and Idol*, pp. 197–202.
36 Dr John Clifford, *God's Greater Britain*, London: James Clarke & Son, 1899, pp. 167, 175.
37 John Wolffe, *God and Greater Britain*, p. 222.
38 Brian Stanley, *The Bible and the Flag: Protestant Missions and British Imperialism in the Nineteenth and Twentieth Centuries*, Leicester: Apollos, 1990, p. 184.
39 *Ibid.*, p. 160.
40 *Ibid.*, pp. 160–2.
41 Reginald Heber, *Heber's Hymns*, London: Sampson, Low & Marston, 1870, p. 80; Stead, *Hymns That Have Helped*, p. 72.
42 Bradley, *Abide With Me*, p. 128.
43 Tamke, *Make a Joyful Noise*, p. 131, claims that Queen Victoria personally chose *The Day Thou Gavest, Lord, Is Ended* for the Diamond Jubilee service in 1897. But I have found no evidence to support this.
44 Adey, *Class and Idol*, p. 208.
45 Routley, *Hymns and Human Life*, pp. 271, 278–82.
46 Walter Lord, *A Night to Remember*, London: Penguin, 1978, pp. 73, 117; Colonel Archibald Gracie, *The Truth About the Titanic* Stroud: Alan Sutton, 1994 (1913), p. 34.
47 Captain Robert F. Scott, *Scott's Last Expedition*, London: John Murray, 1936, p. 477.
48 *Ibid.*, p. 462.
49 *Ibid.*, p. 44.
50 *Daily Sketch*, 25 May 1912.
51 The most recent authority to question the authenticity of the *Nearer, My God, to Thee* story is Richard Howells (*The Myth of the Titanic*, London and Basingstoke: MacMillan, 1999, pp. 120–35). He suggests, among other things, that it developed out of the memory of the survivors of the wreck of the steamship *Valencia* singing that hymn in 1906. But that was only one of a number of reported hymn-singings on sinking ships, making the *Titanic* story more rather than less likely.
52 Bradley, *The Penguin Book of Hymns*, p. 283; Gracie, *The Truth About the Titanic*, p. 20.
53 Walter Lord, *The Night Lives On*, London: Penguin, 1986, pp. 119–27.
54 John Maxtone-Graham (ed.), *Titanic Survivor: The Memoirs of Violet Jessop*, Stroud: Alan Sutton, 1998, p. 132.

55 Herman Finck, *My Melodious Memories*, London: Hutchinson, 1937, pp. 109–10.
56 Lord, *The Night Lives On*, p. 123.
57 *The Times*, 20 April 1912.
58 *Ibid.*
59 *Ibid.*
60 *The Times*, 15 February 1913.
61 *Jubilee Hymns*, London: SPCK, 1887.
62 *Hymns for Use During 1897, Being the Sixtieth Year of the Reign of Queen Victoria*, London: Skeffington & Son, 1897.
63 George Earle Buckle (ed.), *The Letters of Queen Victoria*, vol. 3: *1896–1901*, London: John Murray, 1932, p. 147 (for Sullivan's comments) and p. 171 (for the Queen's).
64 James T. Lightwood, *Hymn-Tunes and Their Story*, London: Epworth Press, 1923, p. 203.

CHAPTER TWELVE

Imperial march

If there was one single musical form synonymous with the Empire it was the march. Most of the marches that form the basis of the repertoire of the military band derive from the period 1880–1914, the heyday of the Empire. As long as there have been armies, there have been musical rhythms (drumbeats, trumpet calls, fife tunes), to accompany them and to pace the tread of the marching troops, to inspire and to convey orders and commands. March music is defined by *The New Grove* as

> essentially an ornamentation of a fixed, regular and repeated drum rhythm. Stylistic traits of the march that seem to be present throughout its history include rhythmic patterns with regularly recurring accents built into phrases and periods, straightforward harmonies and textures, and unpretentious but often memorable melodies. The usually triadic melodic style and apparent preference for major keys of most march music may reflect to some extent the technical limitations of the wind instruments for which marches were written, many of which were limited to the notes of the harmonic series until well into the 19th century.[1]

The slow march was used for parades, exercises and reviews; the quick march, for manoeuvring; and the double quick march, for attacks.

The military band

The first full military band in England was formed in 1678, when Charles II decided to emulate the French bands he had encountered during his exile.[2] The military marches of the seventeenth and eighteenth centuries were generally ephemeral pieces knocked out by bandmasters as and when required, and in Britain were often adapted from the popular operas and oratorios of foreign composers.

There were two significant stimuli to military music at the end of the eighteenth century.[3] One was the influx of Turkish Janissary music, which was valued, says military music historian H.G. Farmer, 'for the better regulation of the march' and introduced the cymbal (1777), bass drum and tambourine (1781) and Jingling Johnny – or, more politely, *chapeau chinois* (1785) – a pole of small bells to enrich the sound palette of the band.[4] The second stimulus was the French Revolution and the Napoleonic Wars which led to the formation of new bands and the composition of marches for them by native British composers such as John Callcott, William Crotch, James Hook and John Mahon.[5] In the peace following the end of the wars, the crack regiments spent lavishly on their bands in inter-regimental rivalry. The full brass family was added to the line-up in the 1830s, previously dominated by the clarinet. Technical innovation in the construction and fingering of wind instruments extended the flexibility and range of timbre available for military bands. There is early evidence of an imperial dimension. According to Colonel J.A.C. Somerville, 'early in the nineteenth century the "chic" thing was to have a certain number of negro bandsmen, extravagantly dressed, who played the percussion instruments, but that disappeared at the time of the Crimean War'.[6]

Military band music was part of the explosion of popular music that took place in nineteenth-century Britain. The regimental bands moved from providing merely functional music for strictly military purposes to the performing of concerts for the public. As Lieutenant Albert Williams, Bandmaster of the Grenadier Guards, recalled in 1912:

> The advent of the annual exhibition, the popularity of the seaside holiday, Sunday concerts – winter and summer – playing in the public parks – all have contributed to render wind band music indispensable, while no gala, flower show, cricket match or even race meeting is considered quite complete without its bands.[7]

It was the flamboyant impresario–conductor Jullien who first brought military bands to public attention with his monster concerts. The first grand military concert was held at Chelsea in June 1851, with the Massed Bands of the Guards and Royal Artillery numbering 350 performers. *The Times* pronounced it 'admirable' but complained that, apart from the overture *Euryanthe* by Weber, the music was ephemeral – it included overtures and selections from Meyerbeer, Verdi, Bellini and Donizetti.[8] Military music was popular with the public because of spectacle, melody and patriotism, and in the nineteenth century this patriotism increasingly involved the Empire and imperialist sentiment. Farmer notes: 'In Britain the ceremonial of military music is closely linked with its glorious past.'[9] In Britain military music has been an integral part of the ritual events that structure the national year: the Trooping of the Colour (a ceremony invented largely in the nineteenth century); the Changing of the Guard at Buckingham Palace; the Ceremony of the Keys at the Tower of London; Remembrance Day services; Beating the Retreat; and military tattoos.[10]

There was a substantive improvement in the scope and quality of music from the middle of the nineteenth century. In the late eighteenth century bands were often maintained at the expense of the officers and were kept small. But many bandmasters were civilian, and frequently foreign. In 1854 the embarrassingly bad performance of British bands at a grand review of allied troops in the Crimea in 1854 led the Duke of Cambridge, the British Army's Commander-in-Chief, to bring all regimental bands under War Office control, to abolish civilian and foreign bandmasters and, after lobbying by British bandmasters, to establish a Military School of Music at Kneller Hall, Twickenham, to emulate the École Militaire Musicale in Paris and for the express purpose of training bandmasters and bandsmen for the British Army. It opened in 1857 and led to a general improvement in standards of professionalism. In 1845 the first military band journal was published, and others followed, which helped to standardize and disseminate military band scores. A further boost to military band music came from the wave of patriotism that swept over England at the time of the Crimean War and the establishment of the Volunteer Movement (1859), precursor of the Territorial Army. New staff bands such as the Band of the Royal Engineers (1856) were formed. Military band contests, particularly popular in Scotland, helped to sharpen standards of performance. From 1856 military bands were permitted to play in the London parks on Sundays and became a regular feature in the 1880s and 1890s. By the end of the nineteenth century, the average military band numbered 40–50 performers and had a huge repertoire of marches.

The role of Kneller Hall was significant. It was originally supported by regimental subscriptions but in 1876 the Government assumed total financial responsibility.[11] It became the Royal Military School of Music in 1887. After 1872 all British bandmasters had to obtain a Kneller Hall qualification. The Kneller Hall Band took part in all the great national and imperial occasions. Along with the Band of the Royal Artillery it accompanied the Choir singing the *Te Deum* at St Paul's in 1897 for the Diamond Jubilee of Queen Victoria. On the imperial front, it participated in 1900 in an Albert Hall concert to raise funds for widows and orphans of the Boer War; a Thanksgiving service at St Paul's for the return of the City Imperial Volunteers; the Nelson Centenary celebrations in 1905; and the *Titanic* memorial service at

St Paul's in 1912. It organized the massed military band display at the British Empire Exhibition at Wembley in 1924 and 1925. It performed at royal funerals (Queen Victoria, and King Edward VII), coronations (King Edward VII, King George V, King George VI and Queen Elizabeth II), and at the wedding of Princess Elizabeth and Prince Philip.

The royal family always took a particular interest in military music. In 1898 George Miller, Charles Godfrey and Ladislao Zaverthal, the three leading bandmasters, were given honorary commissions at the intervention of Queen Victoria herself. She thought that the rank, pay and pensions of the bandmasters were wholly inadequate. She believed that high demands were made on bandmasters in terms of their 'education, intellectual powers and culture', and that good bands were 'a necessary factor in the efficiency of the army'. The commissions were a recognition of all these factors.[12]

During the Second World War regimental bands were dissolved but were later reformed on the instructions of Churchill, who appreciated their morale-boosting value. The Royal Military School moved to Churchill House, Aldershot, and the Kneller Hall Band continued to be in demand for troop concerts and church parades. In 1946 it returned to Kneller Hall. Kneller Hall trained not only British bandsmen but bandsmen from all over the Empire and the Commonwealth, establishing a uniform standard of playing and a common repertoire.

The influence of military bands was enormous. Not only did they play in a variety of locations at home, so that the leading bandmasters became musical celebrities, but they accompanied regiments abroad and, in Farmer's words, 'made a solid contribution to maintaining the prestige of the British Empire'.[13] So integral to the musical life and taste of the nation were military bands that when the BBC was created and sought to cater for all musical tastes, it set up the BBC Wireless Military Band, which existed from 1927 to 1943, being conducted successively by Lieutenant B. Walton O'Donnell and Major Percy Sylvester George O'Donnell, two of the three celebrated O'Donnell brothers, all leading military bandmasters.

But the military band was also the inspiration for the brass band. In the wake of the Napoleonic Wars, bands sprang up all over the country. Towns, villages, manufacturing firms, collieries, police forces and fire brigades developed bands during the nineteenth century, all of them adopting military uniforms and sharing the repertoire. Rarely can a form of music have been subject to such contempt from musicologists, critics and aesthetes as was military music. Typical is the critic in the Blackwell History of British Music who indefensibly describes military band music as 'negligible'.[14] H.G. Farmer more accurately described it as 'the music of the people' and pointed out that military bands performed not only newly composed music but also transcriptions of art music, thus helping to acquaint working people with the classics.[15]

In *The Military Band*, George Miller, Bandmaster of the Portsmouth division of the Royal Marines, defined the kind of music military bands could play, linking it firmly to manliness, when he gave advice on composing for military bands:

> Subjects might be admirably suited to orchestral composition which would not suit the characteristic manliness of a military band. Softly, suggestive, half-veiled, indistinct and mysterious harmonic effects (too-early sunrises and too-late sunsets), possible on a highly sympathetic string orchestra, are not suited to the hard, matter-of-fact, plain speaking voices of the open-air band. Consideration must also be given to the people to whom the band usually plays, and subjects chosen that would interest them: the brain-workers, professional and business men who turn to music as a recreation, seeking a brief respite from the cussedness of things by a few hours in the park or a few days at the seaside; the hand-workers, soldiers, sailors, miners, factory-hands, potters, quarrymen, agriculturalists etc., whose music does not interfere with their occupation and is ever present, more or less. Those who do not know may think that this is not much of an audience to play to, or to compose for. It is certainly not acquainted with the latest 'idioms', but any composition in any style up to (say) the Wagner second period will be understood and receive the mead of appreciation it deserves. But the would-be composer is advised to avoid the 'greenery-yallery, Grosvenor Gallery, foot-in-the-grave' kind of music, and also the hypnotic, uncanny, exotic, Venusberg-y 'creations' of the New School. This is essentially chamber-music, and can be enjoyed only under the most luxurious conditions. The open-air band plays in equal temperament . . . therefore let the harmonic scheme be clear, intelligible and *modal*. Then in the working, do not be too minute in detail, remembering that the military band is frequently reduced to its 'foundation stops' . . . Assist the bandsman to a proper rendering and the audience to a proper appreciation of a composition, by its title and a 'programme' defining its poetic purport.[16]

Sir Vivian Dunn, a later doyen of military musicians, defined the essential qualities of the successful march in 1991:

1 The themes and subjects must inspire an impulse in all who hear them to want to march. To give uplift to tired feet, gladden the heart, and raise the human spirit and morale.
2 The very essence of the tunes must be cheerful, instantly recognisable and appealing, that can be sung or whistled easily.
3 The composer must have the gift of originality. To harmonise perfectly and add deft touches in counterpoint to his themes and sub-

jects bringing light and shade into a composition worthy of the art culminating in an example of the command of instrumental crafts-manship.[17]

Interestingly, while Dunn takes account of the developments of technique and technology which allow the creation of a greater range of effects, he like Miller stresses the importance of theme and subject.

Empire was explicitly one of the themes of military music. There were *Imperial Marches* by G.H. Dickens, Charles H. Ridee, S. Gatty Sellars and E.E. Bagley, and an *Imperial Britain March* by Thomas A. Chandler. Some of the composers were American, but their works tended to appear, like John Philip Sousa's *Imperial Edward* (1902), in the coronation year of either Edward VII or George V and thus explicitly to mark a great imperial occasion. There were *Empire Marches* by Charles LeRoy Abbott and R.W. Tulip and an *Empire Jubilee March* by Denis Wright.

Sir Edward Elgar's imperial works, *Imperial March, Empire March*, the five *Pomp and Circumstance* marches and the *Triumphal March* from *the Crown of India Suite* were rapidly arranged for military band and became band concert standards; as did arrangements of Sir Alexander Mackenzie's *Britannia Overture* and *Empire Flag March*.

One of the most enduring of imperial marches is *Imperial Echoes* (1913) by Arnold Safroni. Arnold Safroni was the pen-name of W.H. Myddleton, conductor, composer, novelist, dramatist and astronomer. As Myddleton, he composed the *Boys of the Old Brigade March*, the *HIM March* (1903) and *On Guard O'er the Empire March* (1904). As Safroni, he composed *Imperial March Chimes*, the *Sierra Leone March* (1907), *By Imperial Command* (1920) and *Call of the Empire* (1939). But his most famous composition was the rousing *Imperial Echoes*, once the signature tune of *Radio Newsreel* and the Empire Service of the BBC and still played as the regimental march of the Royal Army Pay Corps.

John Mackenzie-Rogan

The field of military music is so vast that it would need an entire book to cover the total imperial output. So I concentrate here on three doyens of the military bandsmen, whose successive careers and output resonate with imperial sentiment. If any bandmaster can be said to symbolize the musical expression of Empire it is Lieutenant-Colonel John Mackenzie-Rogan. His career coincided with the high-noon of Empire and his activities as conductor and composer, his organization of great public events and his imperial tours all underline the extent to which imperialism was an integral part of the popular mindset.

John Mackenzie-Rogan joined the 11th (North Devon) Regiment of Foot as a bandboy on 4 February 1867. He played the flute. He was a true Briton, son of an Irish father and a Scottish mother and himself born in the Isle of Wight. Like so many bandsmen, the Godfreys, the O'Donnells, the Millers, he was from a military background: his great-grandfather had fought under Marlborough; his father had joined the year before Waterloo ('it was the old man's tales of soldiery in foreign lands that fired the ardour of us boys to go soldiering too'); his step-brother had served in the Crimea and during the Indian Mutiny. His own younger son joined up in the second week of the Great War and was wounded at the Somme, and later served in the Indian Army. Rogan's own experience of the Empire began almost at once as his regiment was despatched to South Africa, and remained there until 1870. When Rogan joined, two-thirds of army bandmasters were foreign (mainly German) or civilian, and the repertoire of military bands was largely foreign. Looking back in 1926, he recalled:

> The programmes they played sound old-fashioned now. This would be the sort of thing: March, overture, mazurka, selection (operatic), quadrille, polka and galop. For the regimental officers' dances there would be, say: Lancers, valse, mazurka, quadrille, polka, galop – 24 items of that kind of thing. For the ordinary dances for N.C.O.'s and men: Quadrille, schottische, valse, varsoviana, lancers, mazurka, polka and galop. Our music was mostly written by foreigners; there was so little by British composers that was suitable. The only British music that the bands had were excerpts from Balfe, Vincent Wallace, Bishop, Macfarren, Calcott, Barnby, and a few others, including Hatton, whose part-songs were very popular. Operatic selections, overtures and so on, arranged for military bands, were chiefly by Offenbach, Mozart, Haydn, Beethoven, Gluck, Spohr, Meyerbeer, Donizetti, Mercandante, Rossini, Verdi, Gounod, Benedict, Weber, Kuhner, Nicolai, Auber, Flotow, Suppe, Adam, Boieldieu, Herold, Mendelssohn, Cherubini, Bellini and Strauss and Gung'l whose waltzes will run for ever in popularity . . . Taking the bands as a whole in those days, and for many years after, the standard of playing was as high as that of many of the military bands of to-day, and perhaps higher. Certainly individual playing was far better than it is now, though the quality and tone of some of the instruments was not so good. Modern instrumentation of course helped them.[18]

Operatic extracts and foreign marches and waltzes always remained part of the repertoire. But they were joined by British music: by Gilbert and Sullivan and the flourishing school of British operetta and musical comedy in the late Victorian and the Edwardian years, and compositions by British bandmasters, who began to flourish after the banning of foreign bandmasters and the opening of Kneller Hall to train British bandmasters. Rogan was one of them. Between 1877 and 1889 he was serving with his regiment in India; and when, in 1878 during the Eastern Crisis, 10,000 troops, including natives, were sent from India to Malta, Rogan wrote a march based on MacDermott's famous 'jingo song': *We Don't Want to Fight But By Jingo If We Do*. He gave a copy to the 26th Native Infantry Regiment, bound for Malta. When they returned to Poona, the Colonel told Rogan that the band had played the march on the deck of the ship on arrival in Malta and it had been loudly cheered by the troops on other ships nearby.[19] Between 1880 and 1882 Rogan studied at Kneller Hall, and when he left he joined the 2nd Battalion of the Royal West Surrey Regiment, the 'Queen's Regiment', in India. While in India, he wrote marches based on Indian native melodies. Visiting the Palace of Maharajah Sir Sourindro Mohun Tajore, CIE, an enthusiast for Indian music, he heard a number of beautiful Indian melodies sung and played. He wrote them down and when the Indian Princes came to England for the Coronation of King Edward VII twenty years later, a fantasia which Rogan based on these tunes and called *Melodies of Our Indian Empire* was played by the Band of the Coldstream Guards at a reception at Buckingham Palace.

Another by-product of Rogan's time in India was the march *The Bond of Friendship*, in memory of one of his bandsmen, Murray, who died of heat stroke en route from Calcutta to Burma on a troop transport in 1885.[20] It is the only Rogan piece to survive in the modern repertoire, its delicate and muted trio section hinting at loss and bereavement and contrasting with the rousing introduction, which emphasizes military service.

He was in Burma with his regiment from 1886 to 1888 and took down native tunes there, arranging the Burmese national anthem *Kaya Than* (*The Sound of the Trumpet*) for military band. He played his arrangements of Burmese airs with the regimental band, to the delight of the Burmese. But he remarked on the conservatism of the British soldier: 'The British soldier will sing what he knows and what he likes, but I do not think any power on earth will induce him to alter his tastes.'[21] When the troopship *Malabar* left for England with the regiment in 1894, at the end of their tour of duty, the band played *The Girl I Left Behind Me, Goodbye, Sweetheart, Goodbye, After Many Roving Years, Home, Sweet, Home, Auld Lang Syne, Rule, Britannia* and *God Save the Queen*, tunes which echoed round the Empire for successive generations as troopships ferried regiments back and forth to maintain the *Pax Britannica*.

In 1896 Rogan was appointed Bandmaster of the Coldstream Guards after scores submitted by forty candidates had been scrutinized by Sir

Arthur Sullivan, who was a great supporter of military band music, his father having been a professor at Kneller Hall. Rogan conducted the band at Hyde and Green Parks, state concerts at Buckingham Palace and levees at St James's Palace, and by request at regimental and brigade sports and cricket matches. Private engagements included flower shows, Earls Court exhibitions, agricultural shows and provincial concerts. The spectrum of events, and the class and geographical range which is typical of the military band across the board, show the unifying effect of the music on both the nation and popular musical taste. Rogan noted that some local audiences preferred 'popular music' and others the 'best music'.[22] Northern towns in particular preferred 'the best' to the 'popular' – this was almost certainly the effect of the brass bands and the choral singing traditions in the north. But the point is that the repertoire included both the 'popular' and the 'best'.

Rogan gives a fascinating first-hand account of the royal and imperial occasions to which he was party. The highlight was the Diamond Jubilee of 1897:

> There has been nothing quite like it since. Even the Great Peace after the Great War could not compare with it. Cities, towns, and villages began organizing their own separate festivities six months beforehand, that is to say, in the January of 1897 – Diamond Jubilee day was June 22. Not only were preparations made for the day, but so joyous was the spirit of the authorities and the citizens that dinners, dances, receptions and all kinds of entertainment were in swing months before the beloved Queen made her almost incredibly magnificent journey to St.Paul's for the Thanksgiving. It seemed as if the whole land had broken out into music and feasting. Naturally music was the art in which the delight and gratitude of the nation found its most common, indeed its unanimous expression.[23]

'We were high-pressure musicians for five whole months', recalled Rogan. There were drawing-room concerts at Buckingham Palace and levees at St James's Palace; on 26 May there was the Birthday Parade at Horse Guards; on 11 June the inspection of all the overseas troops by the Duke of Connaught; and on 25 June an Eton torchlit procession to Windsor Castle. By the Queen's instruction all the music to be played would be British, the choice to be left to Rogan: 'as there were no fewer than twenty songs and marches . . . [I] was kept very busy with arranging them all for my full band, with the drums, fifes and bugles of our 2nd Battalion added'. There was a Military Tattoo on 19 June with the Bands of the Household Brigade, the Royal Artillery and the Royal Engineers all taking part, an event 'spoilt by rain', he recalled. The same bands participated in the Military Review at Aldershot on 1 July. He described it as 'the busiest year of my life'. But the actual day of Thanksgiving – 22 June – was what stood out in his memory:

> Among all the magnificent sights the Thanksgiving on June 22 comes out clearly in my memory as incomparable. There was something bewildering, terrific about the whole thing . . . the scene outside St. Paul's – the serried mass of humanity, the blazing colours of the Church and military groups, the swelling mass of music, from the emotional roar of the crowd to the strains of the bands and the choirs – left an impression on me that at the time was almost stunning . . . Though it was the climax of months of thanksgiving, festivity and world-wide organization, the service itself was quite short, and all the more impressive for being short. A Te Deum, specially composed . . . was sung, also the 'Old Hundredth'. On the coming and leaving of the Queen the Coldstream Guards band played the National Anthem; the way in which it was taken up and sung by the vast crowd gathered around makes that particular rendering of 'God Save the Queen' the most majestic in my memory.[24]

In the evening the band played at the Crystal Palace:

> The crowd at the Crystal Palace was enormous – anything up to a hundred thousand – and all excited, happy and bent on enjoyment. They did not want any high-class music but something to which they could either sing or dance; they even danced to *Tannhäuser*. Hard worked as we had been . . . the good humour of that vast and joyous crowd reacted on us and we were as happy to play for them as they were to sing and dance to our music . . . That we felt the strain of this tumultuous culmination to months of fatiguing work I will not deny. At the same time, like good Britons, we were so very proud to have taken part in such a memorable event in the history of our glorious country that there was not a grumble amongst us.[25]

In 1900 Rogan became Senior Bandmaster of the Brigade of Guards, and was responsible over the next twenty years for the direction of all state music. During the Boer War the band were involved in a succession of entertainments to raise money for service charities, including Lady Lansdowne's at Covent Garden early in 1900 which raised £13,000. Another big performance on 18 February 1900 was at Her Majesty's Theatre when the Massed Bands of the Brigade of Guards assisted and Sir Arthur Sullivan was conductor-in-chief. The programme of music constituted a 'patriotic picture of Britain and her dependencies'. Each year there was a service for the fallen at St Paul's Cathedral. Rogan and his band played at every one. Then on Mafeking Day they were telegraphed for from the Crystal Palace where that evening there was to be a big gathering. There was no rehearsal and no programme, but

[F]or two or three hours we played nothing but patriotic and popular airs which many thousands joined in singing. A lot of these tunes had to be played from memory by the band and by Mr. Walter Hedgcock, the organist and musical director of the Crystal Palace. But whether it was *Rule, Britannia, The Men of Harlech, Come Back to Erin, Bravo, the Dublin Fusiliers, Annie Laurie* or *Soldiers of the Queen* mattered not to the vast crowd assembled, for they sang everything to the music of the band and the organ! That was a soul-stirring scene, an occasion when one felt proud to be a Briton. There was no roughness or horse-play; the people were gathered together purely and simply to give vent to their joy, and they did it in a sincere and whole-hearted way.[26]

It is significant that the tunes chosen reflected the constituent countries of the United Kingdom.

On 3 January 1901, Field Marshal Lord Roberts, idolized as 'Bobs' and victor of the Boer War, came home from South Africa and was met at Paddington by the Prince and Princess of Wales. As he stepped from the train, the Coldstream Band played *See, the Conquering Hero Comes*, and for the inspection of the guard of honour Rogan arranged a march which included the favourite Irish airs of Lord Roberts: *Oft in the Stilly Night, Let Erin Remember* and *Come Back to Erin*. Another noted bandmaster also marked the return of Lord Roberts. Cavaliere Ladislao Zaverthal, Bandmaster of the Royal Artillery Band, paid his own tribute. At the state banquet at Buckingham Palace that night where the Royal Artillery Band played, the programme included the triumphal march *Virtute et Valore*, named after Lord Roberts's family motto and composed by Zaverthal for the occasion. It contained a quotation from *See, the Conquering Hero Comes*. Also included were Zaverthal's setting of Kipling's poem *Bless You, Bobs* and another Irish selection, *Shamrock*.[27]

The band took part in the funeral procession of Queen Victoria on 2 February 1901, when Chopin's *Funeral March* and Beethoven's *Funeral March* were played alternately. For the Coronation of King Edward VII, Rogan had to arrange music for a state banquet, on 23 June, a coronation procession on 26 June and a gala performance at Covent Garden on 30 June. But the King's illness, which led to the postponement of the Coronation, resulted in the permanent cancellation of the gala at which the Sheffield Choir, the Band of the Coldstream Guards and a collection of star singers chosen to represent the dominions and the mother country were to have performed the national anthem arranged by Dr Edward Elgar and Elgar's *Coronation Ode*. The banquet went ahead without the King. There were also two inspections of the whole of the colonial and Indian troops who had come over for the Coronation, and Rogan wrote of having been instructed to prepare ... music suitable for each of the Dominions, for India, and for other Possessions. This, I may say, was a very heavy task, for it meant that I had to find appropriate music for thirty or forty different places in the Empire and fit it for the four bands of the Brigade of Guards, numbering some 250 performers. To accomplish this on time, I employed six music copyists and we all kept going night and day for forty-eight hours.[28]

For the Coronation on 9 August, bandmasters were given the choice of music and Rogan 'made a point of playing nothing but British music. My opinion is, and always has been, that on occasions of such a domestic patriotic kind, where you are appealing specifically to your own people, foreign music is out of harmony with the occasion and also quite unnecessary, seeing that we have a great national music treasure-field of our own.'[29] A flood of letters from the public endorsed his view.

In 1903, by invitation of the dominion's Government, the band visited Canada. It was the first time any military band from the British Isles had visited a dominion. The trip was approved by Colonial Secretary Joseph Chamberlain, the War Office and the King. 'It was in Canada that we first realized what "patriotic" music, so often spoken of with something like contempt by the high-brows in our own country, meant to those to whom this little island of ours is the greatest place on earth.'[30] They sailed on the liner *Parisian* from Liverpool and on deck the band played *Rule, Britannia, Auld Lang Syne* and *God Save the King*.

At the opening concert at the Massey Hall, Toronto, on 7 September, the band began with the national anthem and *The Maple Leaf Forever*, which they had to encore; and when, half way through the programme, the band played *Rule, Britannia*, it had to be encored twice. Rogan noted: 'That is how our national tunes go in the Dominions.'[31] The following day the band played at the National Exhibition to an audience of 40,000, and when performing a selection of patriotic music, '[the audience's] enthusiasm knew no bounds. The scene at the finish was indescribable.'[32] The band was mobbed, and Rogan himself only escaped with the aid of half-a-dozen policemen. Thereafter the band toured Ontario, Quebec and the Maritime Provinces, giving seventy concerts, during which it played the national anthem 150 times, *The Maple Leaf Forever* 120 and *Rule, Britannia* 126 times. 'It was quite a common thing for somebody to jump up in the middle of the programme and shout "Play 'The King'! and play 'Rule Britannia'" and we had to do it, the whole audience leaping to their feet and joining in.'[33] Band and bandmaster were invited to lunch by the Governor-General, the Earl of Minto, who declared that he had never witnessed such scenes of patriotic enthusiasm from all classes of the population. Rogan concluded:

> Throughout Canada there is an instinctive fondness for the best class of music. I have never known more attentive listeners, particularly during any melody of a patriotic character. At all our concerts we had very large audiences and when we played patriotic airs they nearly yelled themselves hoarse in the intensity of their feeling. Blood is thicker than water; to the people of the Dominion we represented, not the Coldstream Guards alone, but the British Army, with whom Canadians had been in proud comradeship throughout the long struggle in South Africa – and before. Since then that comradeship has been most nobly confirmed.[34]

In 1907 Rogan was awarded the honorary degree of Doctor of Music by the University of Toronto. He was described as

> the doyen of military music, one whose success as a composer and as an exploiter of British composers throughout the Empire is well known, one who has reached the highest possible position in the chosen branch of his profession, and who has done so much through the medium of his splendid musical organisation towards raising the standard of military music to a classical level.[35]

In 1911 after the Coronation of King George V, he and the band returned for two weeks to play at the National Exhibition at Toronto and in 1925 the Canadian National Exhibition invited Rogan to organize and conduct the massed bands in a military tattoo. The spectacle of which the tattoo was a part was called 'Ties that Bind' and the background was a giant set of St Paul's Cathedral. The opening day was for ex-servicemen, who attended in their thousands from all over the dominion. Having been addressed by Rogan, the ex-Servicemen spontaneously sang the national anthem and voted to send a telegram of loyalty to the King. Then on 'Young Canada's Day' 200,000 children assembled. 'They knew all the patriotic songs by heart, they were admirably behaved, and they bore the unmistakable stamp of a well-disciplined, self-respecting vigorous young nation.'[36] On the last night of the Exhibition he conducted the first performance of Dr Albert Ham's *Heroes of Canada March*, dedicated by special permission to Lady Patricia Ramsay, daughter of the Duke of Connaught, Governor-General of Canada between 1911 and 1916, and concluded with a strain from the national anthem. Warmly welcomed and well treated throughout, Rogan became a Vice-President of the Musicians' Association of Canada.

In 1907 an Irish International Exhibition was held in Dublin at which all the principal bands were engaged to play. The King and Queen visited the Exhibition and other parts of Ireland. The final piece on the last night of the Exhibition, at which the Coldstreams played, was a mixture of English and Irish airs, ending with *Soldiers of the King*, which was loudly cheered. Then the band of the 15th Canadian Light Cavalry marched up to the Coldstreams and played *Auld Lang Syne*. The Coldstreams replied with *Abide With Me* and then Rogan announced that the two bands would play *God Save the King*. 'It might have seemed a hazardous request to make in Dublin, but I believed in the power of music to awaken the better impulses of the human heart and therefore I was not amazed – as many frankly were – when the ten or fifteen thousand people around us sang the National Anthem so heartily that the two bands were almost drowned by the chorus of voices.'[37]

Rogan believed in utilizing the instruments of the band for maximum effect, particularly the drum:

There is music in the drum. It had always been part of my musical faith that the drum was an instrument of great potentialities when used not merely as a supplement to the rest of the orchestra, but as a separate and individual thing – an instrument that would, in its primitive and barbaric way, move the human heart even as the organ and the violin move it. My faith was confirmed by the approbation bestowed upon the drum effects which I introduced at the great memorial services at St. Paul's in 1902 for Cecil Rhodes the Empire-builder and the soldiers fallen in the Boer War. When I mentioned to Sir George Martin, the Cathedral organist, that I had the idea of writing special music for the drums, he gave me willing accord. As I heard it in my mind's eye, the music of the drums would open with a soft fluttering which would hardly be audible; gradually the whisper would rise to a tremendous thunder, then fade again to a delicate murmur and finally die away altogether, so that it might seem there had been a visitation in the echoing roof, as from another world. What I had in design was, in fact, music which would bring to memory that graphic saying of John Bright: 'The Angel of Death has been abroad throughout the land; you may almost hear the beating of his wings.' At those earlier services the solemn drum prelude did precisely what I had hoped. It was, however, at the funeral of King Edward that it had its highest emotional and, if I may say so, poetic effect. That was by far the most sorrowful State funeral which I have known. I wanted the drums to tell a story of their own, to reach the very deepest chords in the hearts of the mourning crowds.[38]

Rogan secured the services of all the side drummers in the Brigade of Guards (eighty in all). In addition he had 250 musicians from the four Bands of the Brigade of Guards and the Massed Pipers of the Scots Guards. He rewrote the prelude he had used for the Rhodes service. It was the first time anything like this had been done in the open, and it was an occasion 'we were anxious to mark in such a way that it would leave an impression on our countrymen which would never be forgotten'.

Rogan selected and King George V approved the use of Beethoven's *Funeral March*, Chopin's *Funeral March* and the *Dead March* from *Saul* by Handel, with the pipers playing *The Flowers of the Forest* and the music punctuated by the drum preludes. Rogan recalled:

> That the effect was what I had striven for I could see from the very first bars. The people had been talking quietly and reverently, but, as the soft waves of eerie sound fell upon their ears, and as the reverberations swelled and fell and rose again, I could see a great change come over them all. Whispers and movement ceased; men seemed turned to stone; tremulous women were in tears. The drums were carrying their awe-inspiring message into the hearts of us all, musicians as well as the rest. Each time the eighty drums played I observed the same effect; they did their work that day, almost terribly . . . in its magnificent solemnity that short march was the most profoundly moving in my experience.[39]

King George V concerned himself fully with the music of his army and personally approved the daily programme of music played at the King's guard-mounting. He even added his own suggestions. The band was engaged to play for the duration of the Festival of Empire at the Crystal Palace in May 1911.[40]

When the Queen Victoria Memorial was unveiled in May 1911, the choirs of St Paul's, Westminster Abbey, the Chapel Royal and St George's Chapel, Windsor, performed under the direction of Sir Walter Parratt, and the Massed Bands of the Brigade of Guards under Rogan accompanied the singing of *O God, Our Help in Ages Past*. The band played at the Investiture of the Prince of Wales with the Order of the Garter at St George's Chapel, Windsor. For the Coronation procession in June, arrangements for which were made by Lord Kitchener of Khartoum, the Coldstream Guards were stationed near Buckingham Palace and instructed to play before and after the procession passed. Around the Queen Victoria Memorial were assembled dismounted contingents of the Indian and colonial Guards of Honour. The programme of the band consisted of selections of the patriotic airs of England, Ireland, Scotland and Wales, the dominions, the colonies and India.

> When we came to the music that represented Canada, there was no holding the Canadian contingent of the King's Guard. Throwing military discipline to the winds, they swarmed round the band and joined in singing 'Maple Leaf' and 'O Canada', cheering so persistently that we had to repeat the numbers.[41]

A Thanksgiving service held at St Paul's a week after the Coronation included a special fanfare written at the request of Sir George Martin, the organist, and upon which Rogan was congratulated by Elgar, Parry, Mackenzie, Bridge and Martin. It was later much in demand. Throughout the events connected with the Coronation Rogan played only music by British composers.

On 4 August 1914, Rogan and his band were playing at the annual fête and flower show in Stourbridge. Informed that the declaration of war was due at 11 p.m., he appealed to the young men in his audience to join up and the whole audience sang *Rule, Britannia* and *God Save the King*.

He toured the country with his band. He estimates that their programme of patriotic music reached half-a-million people and each concert contained an appeal, sometimes by a local worthy and sometimes by Rogan, for young men to enlist.[42] The band also played at meetings to raise money for the War Loan scheme. The role of the bands in fortifying troop morale was appreciated and the Coldstream's Band did three tours of duty playing for the troops, in 1916, 1917 and 1918. They played to troops coming out of the line and at smoking concerts behind the lines, and to the wounded in hospitals. The Prince of Wales was a strong supporter of the venture and discussed in detail with Rogan the music to be played.

In 1917 Rogan celebrated fifty years in the army. He received congratulations from all over the Empire and a presentation at the Queen's Hall 'to mark the completion of fifty years' service in the Army and appreciation of his service to musical art during that period', a signed address and a cheque organized by a committee chaired by Sir Alexander Mackenzie and with a concert at which the Coldstream Guards' Band played and Sir Alexander Mackenzie, Sir Frederic Cowen, Sir Thomas Beecham, Edward German, Arthur Fagge and Rogan himself took turns in conducting.

Rogan stresses the role of music in recruiting and in war propaganda. 'It is no exaggeration to say that every note played by any and every military bandsman abroad helped in the great victory. Every note was a note of hope, confidence and friendship.'[43] He cited the visits of the Massed Bands of the Brigade of Guards to France and Italy which cemented Allied friendship.

Music was also deemed vital to troop morale, so the *Daily Telegraph* launched a fund for subscriptions for national bands for the New Army in 1915 and at one of the meetings in its support held at the Mansion House, presided over by the Lord Mayor of London, Rudyard Kipling spoke:

No one ... can say for certain where the soul of the battalion lives, but the expression of that soul is most often found in the Band. It stands to reason that twelve hundred men, whose lives are pledged to each other, must have some common means of expression, some common means of conveying their mood and thoughts to themselves and their world. The Band feels the mood and interprets the thoughts. A wise and sympathetic bandmaster . . . can lift a battalion out of depression, cheer it in sickness, and steady and recall it to itself in times of almost unendurable stress . . . Any man who has anything to do with the service will tell you that the battalion is better for music at every turn; happier, more easily handled, with greater zest in its daily routine, when that routine is sweetened with melody and rhythm . . . melody for the mind and rhythm for the body.[44]

Sir Frederick Bridge, who was present at the meeting addressed by Kipling, called for 'good rousing noisy marches and no classical stuff', giving as examples *Ninety-Five* and *Rory O'More*.[45]

A fourth function was to raise money for war charities. Rogan was responsible for the arrangements for all events involving the Bands of the Brigade of Guards. At a Red Cross concert at the Albert Hall in May 1915, organized by Clara Butt, 250 leading singers formed the choir, the Coldstream's Band accompanied, the King and Queen attended and £8,000 was raised. A grand concert in aid of the House-hold Brigade's Prisoners of War Fund was held at the Albert Hall in May 1916, and raised £5,000. The full Band of the Coldstream Guards, with Drums, Fifes and Pipers of the Brigade of Guards, took part in a Grand Patriotic Celebration at the Albert Hall in May 1918, when 8,000 sons and daughters of 'our fighting men' and 1,000 wounded officers and men were guests of the KK Empire Association. 'Very moving it was to a soldier's heart when boys, girls, wounded officers and men all joined in singing the refrains of the patriotic tunes we played.'[46]

He also organized and arranged a military tattoo with 350 performers for the *Daily Telegraph* and *Daily News'* matinée held at the London Opera House for the purpose of supplying the soldiers at the Front with plum puddings on Christmas Day. When Louis N. Parker produced his great spectacle *Follow the Drum* at the Coliseum in aid of the Lord Kitchener National Memorial Fund, Rogan arranged the music and the Coldstream's Band, with the Drums, Fifes and Pipers of the Brigade of Guards, played the tattoo. He made musical arrangements for the Victory Parade through London on 19 July. A Grand Concert was arranged to take place in Hyde Park in the evening featuring the Imperial Choir under Dr Charles Harriss, and to Rogan's disgust the band was ordered to put itself at the disposal of a 'civilian conductor' (unnamed, but clearly Dr Charles Harriss), which, over Rogan's protests, it did. The band performed, but Rogan recorded with some glee that it rained incessantly, 'which did not improve the quality of the music nor the public's enjoyment of it'.[47] In 1919 the band toured with Clara Butt and Kennerley Rumford, playing patriotic programmes. It played regularly at exhibitions in Scotland and England, and at Crystal Palace.

In 1920 Rogan retired. He had a personal audience of the King who promoted him to the rank of Commander of the Royal Victorian Order. Among the many tributes, Sir Alexander Mackenzie said he had raised the dignity and status of the bandmaster ('something like that which Irving did for his calling, you may be fairly said to have done for yours'). *The Times* called him 'the *doyen* of army bandmasters'. Sir Edward German, praising the military bandmasters 'who have done such splendid work in popularizing good British music all over the Kingdom and throughout the Empire', said that Rogan had done 'probably more than any other man, in raising the tone and status of military music in this country'.[48] He died in 1932.

Kenneth J. Alford

Mackenzie-Rogan was succeeded as the doyen of military music by Major Frederick Joseph Ricketts (1881–1945), known to his family as Joe but to the wider musical world by his pen name Kenneth J. Alford. Many regard him as the finest composer of British military marches, the British equivalent of the American 'March King' John Philip Sousa. All his marches are still part of the military band repertoire and they directly reflect his patriotic values and his experience as a career army musician.

Born in the East End of London, the son of a Shadwell coal merchant, he was orphaned in his early teens and falsified his age to join the army as a bandboy. His younger brother Randolph followed suit and earned himself a reputation as a composer of military music under the name of Leo Stanley. Leo's marches included *Alamein*, *The Contemptibles*, *Glory of Arnhem* and *Pageantry*. Young 'Joe' Ricketts joined the Royal Irish Regiment in 1895. He sailed with the regiment for India, where he served for seven years, surviving enteric fever and the ever-present threat from deadly cobras and witnessing the suppression of a Pathan revolt on the north-west frontier in 1897. In 1902 he participated in the durbar for the installation of Lord Curzon as Viceroy of India. Between 1904 and 1906 he studied for his bandmaster qualification at Kneller Hall, where surprisingly he was marked bottom of the class for his original march composition. In 1907 he married and in 1908 he took charge of his first band, that of the 2nd Battalion, Princess Louise's (Argyll and Sutherland Highlanders), which had been formed in 1881 by the merger of the 91st and 93rd

Highlanders. It was stationed near Bloemfontein in South Africa. In 1909 the regiment returned to Scotland but Ricketts and the band stayed on to participate in the ceremonies associated with the formation of the Union of South Africa on 1 January 1910.[49]

During the First World War, Ricketts's bandsmen were returned to service as stretcher bearers and medical orderlies. But with a band composed of overage musicians and bandboys, he spent the war giving concerts for service charities and other wartime causes, as a result of which he was mentioned in despatches. In 1920 the regiment, renamed the Argyll and Sutherland Highlanders, was sent to Ireland, where Ricketts survived two potentially lethal encounters with the IRA.

In 1927 Ricketts took over as Director of Music, Royal Marines' Depot, Deal, one of the finest military bands in the country. He succeeded Lt B. Walton O'Donnell, who was leaving to take up the job of Founder Conductor of the BBC Wireless Military Band. The band under O'Donnell had accompanied the Prince of Wales on his 1926 tour of the Empire.

In 1930, as part of the army economies, the Marines' Depot Band was disbanded and Ricketts was transferred to the Divisional Band at Plymouth with which he remained until he retired in 1944, turning it into a major musical outfit. During the Second World War, the band played at factories, service camps and defence establishments, and gave weekly concerts on Plymouth Hoe in the summers of 1941 and 1942. Ricketts was promoted to the rank of captain in 1935 and to that of major in 1942, but ill-health soon forced his retirement, and he died in 1945 after an operation for cancer.

His own experience was clearly shaped and formed by imperial service in India, South Africa and Ireland. The band and its music formed a link between the Empire and the mother country, in particular by its participation in imperial exhibitions. In 1911 the band performed during the Scottish Exhibition of History, Art and Industry in Glasgow, which was opened by HRH the Duke of Connaught. But in 1925–26 the Band of the 2nd Battalion, Argyll and Sutherland Highlanders went to New Zealand to act as house band for the New Zealand and South Seas Exhibition at Dunedin. The authorities had specifically requested a British Army band and presumably chose a Scottish regiment because of the strong links between Scotland and New Zealand.

The band performed twice a day for the duration of the Exhibition (17 November 1925 to 1 May 1926), entertaining some 3 million visitors. At a benefit concert for the band Ricketts and his band gave the first performance of his musical fantasia *Dunedin – New Zealand*, a picture of the Exhibition in music which was an instant hit. At the closing ceremony, the Exhibition Choir and the spectators joined in singing *Will Ye No Come Back Again?* and the band – at the demand of the audience – played the fantasia *Dunedin*, Alford's march *Colonel Bogey*, a selection from *Tales of Hoffman* and *God Save the King*.

With his Royal Marines' Band, Ricketts participated in the Canadian National Exhibition in Toronto in 1939, giving two concerts a day for three weeks and regularly performing *Colonel Bogey* at the request of the audience. At the conclusion of the Exhibition Ricketts directed a massed band of 400 at a Grand Tattoo, which included a spectacular musical ride by the Royal Canadian Mounted Police.

In Britain, the full military band repertoire, and Alford's marches in particular, became familiar as the band played in theatres and in parks, participated in great state and royal occasions, such as the Coronation of King George VI, and utilized the newest media to promote its music. In 1935 the band gained a contract with the BBC to play a fortnightly one-hour military music concert, which regularly featured Ricketts's own transcriptions of classical and operatic favourites. In 1939 the band produced a series of gramophone records of Alford marches.[50]

Alford's marches directly reflect his career and experiences. His biographer has identified 'an extensive but unpublished composition', *For Service Overseas*, which reflects those early years in the Empire.[51] His first march was *The Thin Red Line* (1908), which appeared when the Commanding Officer of the Argylls, Colonel A.E.J. Cavendish, asked him to compose a new regimental march, since the one used by the regiment, *Highland Laddie*, was used by several other Scottish regiments. Ricketts produced his excellent march, its title derived from the nickname bestowed on the 93rd Highlanders after the account by *The Times's* correspondent William Howard Russell of the regiment's heroic stand against the Russian Cavalry at Balaclava in 1854 during the Crimean War. It had been immortalized in Robert Gibb's painting, and was so now, again, in Alford's march, ingeniously based on the regimental bugle call. The march contained all those characteristics which Sir Vivian Dunn found typical of his work: 'quick repeated notes of the same letter name, a powerful subject in the brass in the minor key . . . a full-flowing, smooth and tuneful counter-melody in the tenor register'.[52]

The regiment did guard duty at Holyrood House during the Coronation visit to Scotland by King George V and Queen Mary. Ricketts's arrangement of the national anthem was played during the visit, and while in Edinburgh on royal duties he composed the march *Holyrood*, subsequently adopted by the Royal Air Force Regiment as its regimental march. It was the first of his royal occasion inspirations.

In 1912, he composed *The Vedette* march, an infectiously jaunty march complete with an engaging piccolo embellishment, which is a recollection perhaps of his service on the north-west frontier of India, where vedettes (mounted sentries in advance of outposts to observe the enemy) were in regular use. But it was while the regiment was stationed in Fort George near Inverness in 1914 that he composed what became his most famous march, *Colonel Bogey*, its name deriving from the fact that inspiration struck on the golf course. Its rhythmic structure was so appropriate for words that marching soldiers rapidly attached to it obscene lyrics, which were cheerfully sung by squaddies in both world wars. Cleaned-up lyrics were set to the music in 1939 ('Good luck and the same to you') but failed to eclipse the unofficial words. *Colonel Bogey* received a further boost when used as the march theme for David Lean's 1957 film *Bridge on the River Kwai* (in which two empires – the British and the Japanese – and their respective allies clash on the Burma railway).

By far the majority of Ricketts's marches were inspired by the First and Second World Wars and were seen by him as affirmations of his patriotism, as tributes to the fighting forces and as morale boosters. *The Great Little Army* (1916), dedicated to Field Marshal Sir John French, Commander of the British Expeditionary Force, was Alford's reply to the Kaiser's dismissal of the BEF as a 'contemptible little army'. It reflects in music a sense of pride and authority. The Battle of Jutland inspired both *On the Quarterdeck* (1917) and *The Middy* (1917), the latter's cheery echoes of an off-duty sailor's hornpipe mingling with the smart, swinging rhythm of official duties capturing the life of the middy perfectly. *The Voice of the Guns* (1917) was inspired by the Western Front. *The Vanished Army* (1919) was his personal tribute to the fallen of the Great War, a deeply felt piece with a lyrical and melancholy main subject which expresses both pride and loss and a nostalgic snatch of *Tipperary* in the minor key. In more light-hearted vein, two later marches looked back to the war: *The Mad Major* (1921), a celebration of the exploits of the eponymous army officer Major Graham Seton-Hutchinson, who won the MC and DSO for his exploits with the Machine Gun Corps, and *Cavalry of the Clouds* (1923), a tribute to the newly created Royal Air Force. The trip to New Zealand produced the exuberant march *Dunedin* (1928) and *Old Panama* (1929), inspired by the trip back from New Zealand through the Panama Canal and effectively incorporating Spanish rhythms.

His transfer to the Royal Marines inspired the richly textured *H.M. Jollies* (a service nickname for the Corps), which incorporated the bugle calls of the three divisions, Chatham, Portsmouth and Plymouth, and snatches of *Rule, Britannia*, *Hearts of Oak*, *A Life on the Ocean Wave* and a sailor's hornpipe. It was attending the Trooping of

[431]

the Colour in 1930 that inspired *The Standard of St George* (1930), which Dunn considers Alford's masterpiece, a stately and inspiring piece incorporating *Home, Sweet Home.*

In 1937 he composed a ceremonial march for the Marines, *By Land and Sea* (from the Marines' motto *Per Mare, Per Terram*), which includes the Royal Marines' bugle calls and their march *A Life on the Ocean Wave*. Then, during the war, he composed the majestic *The Army of the Nile* (1941), written as a tribute to General Wavell and his campaigns in the western desert, with its triumphant fanfares and snatches of *Rule, Britannia*. *Eagle Squadron* (1942) emphasized the Anglo-American alliance, paying tribute to the Americans serving with the RAF ahead of America's entry into the war. It has an appropriately breezy American flavour and adroitly combines elements of *The Star Spangled Banner, Rule, Britannia* and *The Royal Air Force Marchpast*. In 1944 he re-orchestrated and modernized the regimental march *A Life on the Ocean Wave*, originally arranged in 1881 by bandmaster J.A. Kappey. It is interesting to discover that Ricketts's first love was church music, and he wrote it throughout his career, including a *Te Deum*, a *Jubilate* and several hymn tunes. One of them, the *Vesper Hymn*, was recorded on the Golden Jubilee CD. The combination of Christianity, patriotism, militarism, hero-worship, monarchism and Empire makes him the perfect imperial composer.

Sir Vivian Dunn

The wheel comes full circle with Sir Vivian Dunn, the first military bandmaster to be knighted, and the last to emerge in the twilight of Empire. He was born Francis Vivian Dunn, in Jubbulpore, India, on Christmas Eve 1908, the son of Lieutenant William James Dunn, then Bandmaster of the 2nd Battalion, King's Royal Rifle Corps and later Director of Music of the Royal Horse Guards. W.J. Dunn was the only bandmaster to be awarded the Military Cross in the First World War. He wrote a number of marches, including *United Empire* and *Bravest of the Brave*. The Dunns were another military musical dynasty. William Dunn's father, Thomas Dunn, had been a band sergeant in the 1st Battalion, 33rd Regiment of Foot, had served in Abyssinia in the 1867–68 campaign and had married a Spanish girl while stationed in Gibraltar. William's brother, Augustus Joseph Dunn, became Bandmaster of the 2nd Battalion, Royal Irish Fusiliers and served in South Africa during the Boer War. His works include the march *For Country and Flag*. Vivian Dunn was trained at the Royal Academy of Music and served as a violinist in Sir Henry Wood's Queen's Hall Promenade Orchestra. In 1931 at the age of only 22 Dunn was commissioned as a lieutenant in the Royal Marines and appointed Director of Music of the Portsmouth Division of the Royal Marines' Band. The band played at the wedding of the Duke of Kent and Princess Marina of Greece in 1934, the funeral of King George VI in 1936 and the Coronation of King George VI in 1937. Throughout the Second World War, the band played at army camps, public concerts and on the wireless. After the war, Dunn and the band participated in two of the last great imperial tours: in 1947 the royal tour of South Africa by King George VI and Queen Elizabeth in *HMS Vanguard* and in 1953 the worldwide Commonwealth tour by Queen Elizabeth II and Prince Philip on *TSS Gothic*. In 1949, like Rogan before him, Dunn conducted his band at the Canadian National Exhibition in Toronto. In 1953, Dunn was appointed Principal Director of Music of the Royal Marines and head of the Royal Marines' School of Music at Deal. In 1961 he took a band to participate in the Independence celebrations in Sierra Leone, part of the progressive winding up of the Empire. He retired in December 1968 as a lieutenant-colonel, and in January 1969 he was knighted by the Queen. In 1976 he became the first President of the International Military Music Society. He died in 1995.[53]

Some of his sixty compositions reflect the imperial association of the last age of Empire. The *Cannatex* march (1949), cheerful and jaunty, recalls the band's visit to the Canadian National Exhibition. The royal visit to South Africa inspired the *Springbok March* (which incorporated Afrikaaner songs) (1947) and *Royal Vanguard* (1947). *Sarie Marais* (1953) was based on a song popular with the Boer Commandos and which a Royal Marines' general who had served in the Boer War introduced to Dunn. The spirited arrangement by Dunn became the official march of the Royal Marines' Commandos. The march *The Royal Regiment* (1978) was commissioned by the Canadians to celebrate the visit of the Prince of Wales to the Royal Regiment of Canada, of which he was Colonel-in-Chief.

Earl Mountbatten of Burma, the last Viceroy of India, had a long association with the Marines as Life Colonel Commandant of the Corps and was a great supporter of their music. Dunn was a great admirer of his and in his honour composed the splendid fanfare *Supreme Command* (1972), referring to his role as Supreme Allied Commander, South-East Asia, and the *Mountbatten March* (1972) which included snatches of *Rule, Britannia*, *A Life on the Ocean Wave* and the *Preobrajensky March*, once the march of a crack Czarist regiment commanded by Mountbatten's uncle and presented by him to the Marines in 1964 as their official slow march. After Lord Mountbatten's murder by the IRA in 1979, Dunn began work on the *Mountbatten Suite*, which was intended to comprise four movements

[433]

reflecting phases of its hero's life – prelude *Man of Destiny*, pastoral *Broadlands*, concert march *Man of Action* and epilogue *Classiebawn Castle*. It was never completed because the onset of arthritis in his hands made composing at the piano increasingly difficult. But two of the movements were to be performed separately, the pastoral *Broadlands* and in particular the noble concert march *Man of Action*, with its snatch of the music-hall song *Has Anybody Here Seen Kelly?*, as a reminder of the ship *HMS Kelly* commanded by Mountbatten and sunk off Crete during the war.

In addition to his compositions, Dunn made many arrangements for military band of existing works. These included Walton's orchestral marches *Orb and Sceptre* and *Crown Imperial*, Elgar's *Pomp and Circumstance March No. 4* and Leighton Lucas's *Amethyst March* (from the film *Yangtse Incident*, celebrating the escape of *HMS Amethyst* from Communist China in 1949). There were also arrangements of well-loved hymns: *Eternal Father*; *Fight the Good Fight*; *Onward, Christian Soldiers*; *O, Worship the King*; *Soldiers of Christ, Arise*; *A Safe Stronghold*; and *Love Divine, All Loves Excelling* – all expressions of that militant Protestantism which was an integral part of the imperial ethos.

Brass bands

The military band, whether regimental, militia or volunteers, was one of the inspirations for the civilian brass band. The brass band developed notably in the period 1830–70 due to a combination of circumstances: the invention of the piston-valve system which extended the range and subtlety of brass instruments; the promotion of music-playing by industrialists and others as an improving and civilizing activity; the popularization of brass by the flamboyant conductor–impresario Louis Jullien in his London concerts and provincial tours. But brass bands increased as music in general in Victorian Britain expanded, thanks to an increase in instrument manufacture, the reduction in price of sheet music, the development of musical education, the rise in the number of professional musicians, the popularity of tonic *sol-fa*, the entrenchment of the Victorian belief in the moral value of music and the deliberate promotion of bands and choirs as a way of bridging the gulf between classes.[54]

The development of brass band contests set the seal on the arrival of the new form. 'The contest is the thing that has brought the brass band into the greatest prominence and has been its greatest glory', recorded Russell and Elliot in 1936.[55] It was from the 1850s onwards that these contests developed and became great popular attractions.

Fifty excursion trains brought brass band enthusiasts to the Belle Vue contest in September 1888, and this was typical of the response such contests elicited. The bands played not just at contests but also at dances, concerts and public occasions, such as Sunday school walks, civic processions, the opening of public buildings and trades union galas.

The influence of the military bands upon the brass bands remained, not least in the colourful military-style uniforms that the bandsmen adopted. Russell and Elliot recalled:

> Uniforms – usually quasi-military in style, with peaked caps – are an indispensable part of the equipment of a modern brass band . . . During the seventies, bands commonly paid as much as sixty pounds for a set of uniforms – an immense sum to raise under the conditions then prevailing. By 1895, there were eleven prominent firms in different parts of the country devoting primary attention to brass band uniforms.[56]

Many military bandmasters were arrangers of music for brass bands and adjudicators at contests. Charles Godfrey, Bandmaster of the Royal Horse Guards, arranged the test pieces for the Belle Vue National Brass Band Contest for thirty years, from 1871 to 1900. The military bands, particularly after the establishment of Kneller Hall, set the standards of performance which the brass bands sought to emulate.

However, what is striking about the brass band repertoire is how little music referring to the Empire was played in the nineteenth century. The Cyfartha Band, whose repertoire details have survived, included nothing apart from the *Delhi Polka*. The test-pieces at the Belle Vue Contest from 1861 to 1900 contained nothing imperial. The programme for the Edinburgh International Exhibition (6 May–30 October 1886) at which a wide range of bands performed extensive programmes, yields only the *Indian Mail* galop, the *Camel Corps* polka and the march *The British Patrol*.[57]

The explanation for this lies in the nature of the brass band repertoire. The brass band played sacred music and hymns, popular dance tunes, overtures and marches, and above all operatic transcriptions. The works of Rossini, Bellini, Verdi, Donizetti, Meyerbeer and Gounod, joined latterly by Wagner, were staples of the brass band repertoire. Operatic selections provided the test-pieces at Belle Vue every year from 1861 to 1900. As has already been explained, the Empire was not among the subjects tackled by operatic composers.

'Serious' composers did not begin to compose systematically for brass bands until the twentieth century, and when they did, providing test-pieces for the Belle Vue and Crystal Palace Brass Band Contests, their choice of subjects reflected those of operatic composers – romantic nationalism (*Joan of Arc*, *Cromwell*, *Robin Hood*), Shakespeare (*Macbeth*, *Coriolanus*, *The Merry Wives of Windsor*, *A Midsummer Night's Dream*) and pastoralism (*Downside Suite*, *Severn Suite*, *Moorside Suite*). The only hint of Empire to be found is in Kenneth Wright's *Pride of Race* (1935), with its three movements, 'The Pioneers', 'Memory', and 'March: Pride of Race'.[58]

The bands, however, participated in the great celebrations of Empire, the Diamond Jubilee of Queen Victoria, the Coronation of Edward VII and the patriotic events associated with the Boer War. Perhaps their supreme imperial moment was the participation of eleven leading bands in the *Absent-Minded Beggar* concert at the Albert Hall on 20 January 1900[59] (see chapter two). It was not so much in the imperial content of their repertoire that the brass bands contributed to imperial solidarity; it was in their ubiquity throughout the Empire, performing a common repertoire. Trevor Herbert – rightly in my view – has argued:

> By the end of the nineteenth century, bands of one sort or another were found throughout the United States and the British colonies. Brass bands not only formed the basis for working-class culture in these countries, but also acted as a catalyst for all music culture as expatriate, garrisoned and protected communities strove to create oases of Britishness and 'civilization'.[60]

Brass-banding was an integral part of the imperial process, 'thunderous proof', say Trevor Herbert and Margaret Sarkissian, 'of western military and religious superiority'.[61] Every colony had its military bands. Police bands sprang up, too – in Canada (1876), Ceylon (1873), South Africa (1897), Barbados (1889) and Rhodesia (1897), for instance. Bands meant uniforms, order, discipline and regularity, and they acquired a shared Empire-wide repertoire of European romantic classics and British hymns, marches and popular music, such as Gilbert and Sullivan. As Herbert and Sarkissian argue, foreign bandmasters controlling native players was a paradigm of the colonial experience. But it was a complex process, with the natives taking what they wanted from the experience and not necessarily what their masters intended, and locally created bands composing their own pieces in their own idiom alongside the official repertoire. Nevertheless, the continuous life of military, police and missionary bands playing British hymns and marches throughout the Empire was a powerful enduring reminder of the imperial ideology.

Brass bands were even more potent as formers of musical bonds in the white dominions, direct links, along with choral societies, between Australia, Canada, South Africa, New Zealand and the mother country. Brass bands, for example, were established in Australia by the 1890s, modelled directly on Britain's, importing instruments and sheet music from the United Kingdom and participating in contests judged by British adjudicators.[62]

In 1926 Canadian Alfred Edward Zealley and Englishman James Ord Hume published an account of the leading military and brass bands in the Empire. James Ord Hume (1864–1932) was a Scot, born in Edinburgh, who had served as a military musician in the Royal Scots Greys, but left the army in 1890 to become a professional brass band conductor, composer and contest adjudicator. In that capacity he travelled all over the Empire. His nearly two hundred works included many with imperial connotations: *The Anglo-Oriental March*; the *Bab-el-Mandab March*; the *Diamond Jubilee March*; *For King and Empire*; the *General Buller March*; the *Grand Imperial March*; *Lads from Overseas*; *Laddie in Khaki*; *Our Glorious Empire*; *Rajputana*; *Soldiers of the Queen*; *Viva Victoria*; and *When the Boys Come Home*. Zealley and Hume declared the military band to have reached such a point of excellence that now it may be looked upon as 'the symphony orchestra of the open air'; that 'military music has now become a factor throughout the whole of the Empire' and 'our amateur bands (both Brass and Military) are now better recognized everywhere throughout our vast Empire'.[63] Among the celebrated bands of the Empire they listed the British Guiana Militia Band, founded in 1860; the West India Regiment Band, which wore a Zouave uniform designed by Queen Victoria in 1858; the Band of the Canadian Grenadier Guards (1906), uniformed exactly like their British counterparts; the Band of the Queen's Own Canadian Rifles (1862); from New Zealand, the Wellington Artillery Band and the Wanganui Garrison Band (1887); from Australia, the bands of the New South Wales Lancers (1888), the Malvern Tramways of Victoria (1911) and the Newcastle Steel Works of New South Wales (1914). There was reciprocation between these colonial bands and the mother country as well as the wider Empire. The British Guiana Militia Band and the West India Regiment Band performed at the British Empire Exhibition at Wembley in 1924. The West India Band also toured England in 1924 and performed at the Canadian National Exhibition in 1922. The Newcastle Steel Works Band also performed at Wembley in 1924, went on to win first prize at the Belle Vue Contest and third prize at the Crystal Palace Contest, touring South Africa and New Zealand on its way home. One of the most remarkable bands was the mixed brass and woodwind Kilties, a Scots-Canadian band, founded in 1900, which undertook a remarkable world tour in 1908–10, taking in Canada, Australia, New Zealand, India, Burma, Ceylon, Egypt, Fiji and Great Britain.

[437]

Both brass bands and military bands were called upon to tour. The Besses O'The Barn band toured the United States, Canada, New Zealand, Australia, South Africa, Hawaii and Fiji in 1906–7, the most extensive tour by any amateur British band to date. In 1912 the band toured Canada. The Black Dyke Mills Band toured Canada and the United States in 1906. The Band of the Royal Artillery of Woolwich performed for six months in New Zealand in 1913. The Band of the Grenadier Guards performed at the Canadian National Exposition in 1919. The Band of the Highland Light Infantry attended the inauguration of the Australian Commonwealth in 1900. The Band of the Scots Guards toured Canada in 1912 and 1922 and the Band of the Irish Guards in 1906 and 1913. The Band of the Royal Marines accompanied the Prince of Wales on his tour of India in 1875–76 and the Duke and Duchess of York on their grand colonial tour on *HMS Ophir* in 1901. The combination of touring and the British influence on style, performance and repertoire ensured that bands both military and brass helped to cement a sense of shared Britishness throughout the Empire.

Orchestral marches

The march entered the mainstream of art music through the opera and ballet of seventeenth-century France. Processional music had been part of Western drama since the inception of Greek theatre, and the theatrical march owes as much to that tradition as to the military one. Seventeenth-century theatrical march music allowed considerably more freedom in structure, phrasing and tempo than did the military march. Processions accompanied by march-like music were a feature of opera and oratorio. Handel's *Scipione*, *Judas Maccabaeus* and *Saul* all contain marches which acquired an independent existence. Indeed the march that opens *Scipione* was originally written as a parade slow march for the Grenadier Guards and is still used as such. Processional marches appear in the operas of Rameau, Gluck, Mozart, Bellini, Spontini, Meyerbeer, Verdi, Wagner, Prokofiev and Stravinsky. Mendelssohn's *War March of the Priests* from his incidental music to Racine's *Athalie* and the wedding march from *A Midsummer Night's Dream* became very popular. Beethoven's incidental music to *The Ruins of Athens* and *King Stephen* contain marches but he also wrote military marches specifically for the army.

There were wedding marches, Mendelssohn's and Wagner's being the most famous, and funeral marches: Handel's *Dead March* from *Saul*, Chopin's *Marche funèbre* from the *B Minor Sonata* and Beethoven's *Marche funèbre sulle morte d'un eroe* from the *Piano*

Sonata in A. These became familiar from their performance at great public events.

Towards the end of the century, the imperial march emerged as a distinctive orchestral genre. Sir Arthur Sullivan and Sir Edward Elgar both composed *Imperial Marches*. Such was the intoxication of the idea that youthful British composers Rutland Boughton, later a convinced Communist, and Josef Holbrooke both wrote *Imperial Marches* at the turn of the century. It remained a valid genre until after the Second World War, with Haydn Wood publishing his *Empire March* in 1942 and light-music maestro Eric Coates composing the march *Rhodesia*, for the Central African Exhibition in 1953.

Piano marches

Marches were a set feature of a largely forgotten musical genre – the battle fantasia. There was an established format for the battle fantasia, a programmatic piece of music recreating in musical form the events of a battle. The format was effectively established by the piano sonata *The Battle of Prague* by the Bohemian composer Franz Kotzwara. Published in Dublin in 1788, it was an enormous success in Britain, the USA and the Continent, and became a standard parlour piano piece throughout the nineteenth century. It established the form, beginning with the slow march for the arrival of the troops of the protagonists, here the troops of Prussia and the Holy Roman Empire, arriving to fight the Battle of Prague in 1757. This modulates into the word of command, then the shrill calls of the bugle and trumpet, the cannon's boom, and the fast and furious Prussian attack, with cannons, flying bullets and the rattle of musketry. Trumpets and kettledrums signal an attack with swords, and the thump of the sword blades over the galloping of the horses is rendered pianistically. The light dragoons advance, through heavy cannonade, running fire, the trumpet sounding the recall, the sombre sound of the cries of the wounded and then the victory trumpet. *God Save the King* (the Prussian national anthem) is heard, a Turkish quick-step for the leaving of the field and a speedy finale. All of this is indicated in the score. It is highly colourful and very pianistic, Mozartian in flavour.

There was an orchestral version of the form, perhaps the best-known example being Beethoven's *Wellington's Victory* (1813), also known as *The Battle of Vittoria*. It was composed as soon as news reached Vienna of Sir Arthur Wellesley's victory which expelled Napoleon's forces from Spain. It begins with drums and trumpets, followed by *Rule, Britannia* as the British advance, and then more drums and trumpets followed by the French marching song *Malbrouck s'en va-t-en guerre* (more familiar in England as *For He's a Jolly Good Fellow*). There is a French trumpet challenge and a British trumpet reply. The French advance. A battle is engaged, with a musical evocation of cannon and rifle fire and a cavalry charge. There is a storming march led by the British and then the battle sounds diminish, and *Malbrouck* returns, slow and solemn in the minor key, as the gunfire is silenced, to symbolize French defeat. There is a surge of triumph to celebrate the British victory and, as a climax, a set of variations on *God Save the King*, moving from quiet and slow to fast and loud. The combination of battle sounds and the use of key iconic melodies to symbolize the two sides and trigger the right patriotic response was standard. It was performed in the 1840s for Queen Victoria at Buckingham Palace with the Band of the Coldstream Guards, representing the British Army, and the Band of the Royal Horse Guards, the French. They moved through various rooms in the Palace to encounter the Queen's Band, whereupon the battle was musically enacted.[64]

The form inspired a whole genre of both orchestral and pianistic battle fantasies which eventually took on a decidedly imperial flavour. Thomas Thorley's *The Siege of Algiers* (1816) 'a characteristic divertimento for pianoforte . . . respectfully dedicated to the British Nation', commemorated Lord Exmouth's bombardment of the pirate city of Algiers in 1816. It comprises the introductory march, bugle calls, summoning the fleet commanders to consultation; then 'notice of bombardment', trumpets warning the natives to retire; 'cannons', general attack, 'flying rock', bombs, cries and groans, ships on fire, explosion, bugle horn to cease firing, trumpeters, cessation of arms, Britons triumphant, 'Huzza, Huzza, Huzza', *Rule, Britannia*, bells, and *God Save the King*.[65]

There was a *Battle of Waterloo* for military band, composed by A. Eckersberg, Bandmaster of the 4th (Royal Irish) Dragoon Guards at the time of the Crimean War. It became a favourite closing item of band concerts and was recorded in 1932 by the Kneller Hall Band under Captain H.E. Adkins. It opens with a blaze of fanfares, and then introduces the two armies with the *Marseillaise* and *The British Grenadiers*. Typically it celebrates the various elements of the United Kingdom with snatches of *St Patrick's Day*, *The Campbells Are Coming* and *Men of Harlech*. Then, after more fanfares, and drum rolls to signal a cannonade, there is furious battle music, cheers from the bandsmen, *See, the Conquering Hero Comes* and finally *Rule, Britannia*, with another rousing three cheers from the bandsmen to end.

One notable pianistic piece is Alexandre de Gabriele's highly impressionistic virtuoso and Chopinesque *Egyptian Patrol* – elaborate, bravura, full of Oriental echoes, key changes and inventive musical sounds. It begins with a soldierly Western march marked 'grandioso' but then intercuts this with distinctive Oriental tunes and themes, including in the middle a spare and undecorated passage clearly intended to evoke the immensity of the desert. Richly textured and with distinctive Oriental colouring, it covers the departure of an army patrol into the desert, where they discover the dead bodies of slaughtered comrades and then return. The march is constantly interrupted with incidental detail and changes of mood as the score signals 'murmurando', 'agitato', 'con dolore', 'strepitoso', 'con temerezza' as the patrol fulfils its mission.

The descriptive fantasia for piano of a battle or other military event became a stock item of the nineteenth-century musical repertoire. John Pridham's zestful piano fantasia *The Battle March of Delhi* (1857), a military divertimento 'descriptive of the triumphant entry into Delhi', boasted a sheet music cover picture of the victorious general entering the Indian capital with kilted Scots troops. Each separate element of the scene is signalled in the score. It opens with the clock of the Palace of the Great Mogul striking four, and then a gentle pastoral interlude to suggest the break of day. This is interrupted by the rumble of distant drums – a repeated low-toned trill – and then a return to the pastoral theme broken by the morning bugle call. The rumbling notes of the drums indicate the mutineers in possession of Delhi, and an Indian air which sounds more like an English country dance than an Oriental melody. Then a bass drum, and trumpet call, and 'the Mutineers are alarmed at the approach of the British cavalry' – jaunty, jogging, horse-riding music. The spirited cavalry march culminates in 'General Wilson's arrival at the Cashmere Gate': drums, gunfire from the mutineers, trumpet call for troops to form order of battle ('General Wilson orders an immediate attack') and there is a charge in musical form, the rumble of cannon and mortar, and the flight of the mutineers: musical notes indicate 'Hurrah, hurrah, hurrah, they fly', and then there are successive passages from *Smile On in Hope*, *Old England* and trumpets leading to *See, the Conquering Hero Comes* (marked 'majestic') and, after more trumpets, *The Campbells Are Coming*. Vividly, stirringly and economically, it told in musical form the story of the capture of Delhi. It was originally issued in 1857, re-issued in 1858, 1859, 1880, 1902 and 1904, and was still current in the 1940s as a veritable old war-horse of the parlour piano repertoire.

It is worth placing this in the context of Pridham's career. John Pridham was a prolific composer of piano music and his output ran the gamut of forms and subjects, a positive encapsulation of Victorian taste in the second half of the nineteenth century: the countryside (the fantasia *The Mill Wheel* and the mazurka *Queen of the May*); birds (the morceaux de salon *The Swallow's Farewell* and *The Skylark*, and the valse sentimentale *Le Papillon*); the sea (the sketch *A Seaside Sunset*, the rondo *The Moonlit Sea*); and flowers (quadrille *Alpine Blossoms* and valsette *The Rosebud*); the exotic (*Spanish Dance*, the fantasie *Cyprus* and *The Spanish Flower Girl* waltz); fairies (*The Fairy Lake*, *The Fairies' Flight* and *Danse des Fées*); and the ladies (the mazurka *Ada*, the waltz *Nellie* and the valsette *Ethel*).

He responded to topical events with *The Exhibition March* (1857) celebrating the Great Exhibition, *The Coronation of the Czar* (1883) evoking the Coronation of Czar Alexander III and *The Shah*, 'a grand divertimento descriptive of the Shah's visit to England' (1873). Partly topical but also, given the duration of their appeal, clearly ideological is a stream of pieces celebrating the monarchy, the military and the Empire. *The Battle March of Delhi* was only one of his descriptive fantasies. It was followed by *The Advance of Sir Colin Campbell* (1858), 'descriptive of the fall of Lucknow'; the 'military divertimento' *The Abyssian Expedition* (1868), 'descriptive of the battle and entry into Magdala'; and 'grand naval and military divertimento descriptive of the bombardment and occupation of Alexandria' (1882). On a smaller scale, but none the less celebratory, a succession of imperial heroes, imperial wars and royal and imperial occasions was commemmorated in *The Ashantee March* (1874), *General Havelock's Band March* (1858), *General Roberts' Indian March* (1879), *The Viceroy's Band March* (1869), the march *Khyber Pass* (1878), *Grand Review March* (1872), *The Royal Horse Guards March* (1878), *Attack March* (1872), *Imperial Cavalry March of the 9th Bengal Lancers* (1880), *The Empress of India's Grand Processional March* (1877), *Prince of Wales' Grand March* (1874), *Prince of Wales' Indian March* (1876), *Jubilee March* (1887), *Stanley's Grand March* (1876), *Duke of Edinburgh's Grand March* (1874), *The Days of Queen Victoria* (1856), a fantasia on *God Save the Queen* (1862) and the descriptive fantasia *Trooping the Colours* (1878). He was still hard at work at the end of the century, with the march *Our Soldiers* (1905), his last entry in the British Library Music catalogue. His piano composition *Lord Roberts' African March* (undated but clearly end of century), which opens with the piano equivalent of trumpet call and drums leading into the 'march pomposo', with distinct echoes of both Mozart and Bellini, and a final passage of trumpet calls shows him still mining the same vein he had been successfully exploiting since the Indian Mutiny. Anyone with a piano and the ability to buy sheet music could possess his work and participate vicariously in these great events, summoning them up musically in their own parlours.

But Pridham's piano music was only the tip of a musical iceberg which has been completely omitted from the musical map of the nineteenth century. Much of it is not even preserved in the British Library. Yet it represents an important strand in the popular music of the second half of the nineteenth century and one whose popularity tells us something of the mindset of those who purchased and played it. Even more prolific than Pridham was Ezra Read, whose output was dominated by the Empire and the monarchy, and by the march as their celebration. He flourished in the period 1895–1916, and he gave a precise musical definition of the Empire in his piano fantasia on popular melodies *The British Empire* (1900). It begins with the general salute of the British Army and then, in turn, runs through *The British Grenadiers, Hearts of Oak, Bonnie Dundee, Men of Harlech, Gary Owen, The Girl I Left Behind Me, Cock O' the North, The Sailor's Hornpipe* (the same one Sir Henry Wood used in his fantasia on British sea songs), *Rule, Britannia* and *God Save the Queen*. This evokes the army and the navy, carefully including Scotland, Wales and Ireland, and setting all in the context of Britain and the crown, a message underlined by the sheet music cover which sports the Union Jack and the Royal Standard. There were further descriptive fantasias: *War in Africa* (1900); *With the Colours* (1900); *With the Flag to Pretoria* (1900); *Return of the Troops* (1900); *Relief of Ladysmith* (1900); *On Active Service* (1900); *Sons of the Ocean* (1902); *The Victoria Cross* (1899); and *In Camp* (1902).

His marches were a prominent part of his output. He followed the standard march format, giving his marches a strong family resemblance. Usually in 6/8 time, with a rousing start, a gentle middle section and a triumphal finale, simple and uncomplicated in structure and in melodic line, and with the *oompah* element of the brass band that inspires them in the bass line.

Our Empire's Flag (not in the British Library) is rather repetitive, but the *Pekin Chinese War March* (1900), presumably inspired by the Boxer Rebellion, is more inventive and varied. The *Mafeking Heroes' March* is simple but not humdrum and with a whistleable central tune, and *The Relief of Mafeking* (1900) has a jaunty start, gentle middle section, repeat of the introduction and a big finish. In addition there are *The Ladysmith March* (1900), the *Transvaal Quick March* (1899), the *Khartoum War March* (1898), *The Pioneers' March* (1897), *Dr Jameson's Grand March* (1896), the quick march *Ashantee* (1895), the march *Baden-Powell* (1900), the march *Soldiers of the King* (1901), *The Victors Return* quick march (1902), plus the grand march *Australia* (1901), the quick march *New Zealand* (1906), the grand march *British Columbia* (1906), the *Commonwealth Federation* grand march (1901).

Australia, unlike much of his other work, is ceremonial, harmonically rich and grand and, unusually, it ends softly.

Royalty was celebrated in the *Coronation Day* grand march (1901), the *Diamond Jubilee* march (1897), *For Queen and Country* quick march (1900), *His Majesty* grand march (1901), *King Edward VII* grand march (1901), *King George V* grand march (1910), *Queen Alexandra* royal march (1901), *The Royal Marriage* grand march (1906). In addition there was the descriptive fantasia *The Coronation of King Edward VII* (1902), the cavatina *Victoria in Memoriam* (1900) and *Waiting for the King* (1902), 'a coronation cakewalk'.

The uniformed youth movement inspired a series of simple and jolly quick marches: *The Boy Scouts* (1909); the drill march *Boys' Brigade* (1908); *The British Boys* drill march (1911); *Cadets* quick march (1894); the *Church Lads' Brigade* drill march (1908); *The Gordon Boys* quick march (1894); and *The Church Parade* grand march (1907). His career climaxed with the First World War, during which he produced *The Belgian March* (1914), the song *Dear Old Bobs* (1916) in honour of Lord Roberts, the war march *Europe in Arms* (1914) and the descriptive fantasias *The Call to Arms* (1914), *The Fight for Freedom* (1914), *Fire! Fire!* (1915) and *War of the Nations* (1914).

Read was not the only 'March King' of the Empire. He had a rival in Fabian Scott, whose work was musically richer and more inventive. Fabian Scott was one of a raft of pseudonyms employed by Ernest Reeves, who published also under the names Allan R. Cameron (Scottish music), René Dubois, Frank Marsden, Paul Peronne, Leon Verré and Gladys A. Wood ('fairy music').

As Scott, he wrote *Bloemfontein March*, *Kimberley March*, *Ladysmith March*, *Mafeking March*, *Pretoria March*, *Imperial Volunteers March*, *March of Peace* (all in 1900), plus *The Night Attack* ('a military scene') and *Under the Union Jack* (1902), *Our Colonies* (1901), a descriptive fantasia based on the royal tour of 1901, *The Coronation March* (1902), *Our King*, a 'coronation barn dance for piano' (1902), and the naval fantasia *Departure of a Troopship* (1900). Under his own name, Ernest Reeves wrote *The British Empire* (1915), a 'patrol for piano' and '*Neath England's Flag* (1899), a 'march imperial for pianoforte'. His *Ladysmith March* (1900) in 4/4 time is harmonically exciting, with inventive triplet ornamentation and a central theme that is distinctly operatic and evokes memories of Bellini. *The Imperial Volunteers* has two different rhythms, a waltz tune in the middle, and is full of trills and triplets and very catchy. There is no doubt about the patriotic intent of these pieces. The *Ladysmith March* sheet music has a photograph of Sir George White on the front; just as Ezra Read's *Mafeking Heroes March* has a portrait of Baden-Powell and Theo

Bonheur's *March Transvaal* has Sir Redvers Buller on the cover. Max Werner's march *Our Heroes* (1900) was dedicated to Lord Robert and Lord Kitchener, and had portraits of the two, the Union Jack and the Royal Standard on the sheet music's cover.

It was widely believed, such was Britain's sense of musical inferiority, that foreign names carried more cachet, and many composers adopted foreign-sounding pseudonyms. Albert Ketélbey, born in Birmingham, accented his name, as did Henry Troteré, to acquire a foreign inflection. Theo Bonheur was the pseudonym of Charles Arthur Rawlings, who, like Fabian Scott and Ezra Read, was a turn of the century imperial celebrant. His songs include *Our King and Empire* (1902), *When the Boys Come Marching Home* (1900), *With the Colours* (1896), *The Bravest Boys of All* (1902), *The Boys Are Marching* (1899), *The Brave Patrol* (1899), *The King's Heroes* (1901), *Empress of the Sea* (1892), *The Battle Eve* (1898), *The Soldier Laddie* (1892) and *Sailors of the King* (1902). There were descriptive fantasias for piano – *The Dreadnought* (1906), *The Jellicoe Touch* (1914), *Our Army and Navy* (1903), *The Siege of Ladysmith* (1902), *The Prince of Wales* (1899); and there were many marches: *For the King* (1902), *The Grand Review* (1897), *Imperial Parade* (1898), *March to Pretoria* (1900), *March of the Troopers* (1895) and *Royal Naval Parade March* (1892). His *Transvaal March* (1900) in 6/8 time, is rather monotonous, run of the mill, rum-ti-tum stuff, though his *Queen's Review March* (1893) is vigorous and lively.

Leonard Gautier wrote descriptive pieces for piano: *The Battle of Omdurman* (1898); *Military Manoeuvres* (1897); *The Heroic Charge of the 21st Lancers at the Battle of Omdurman* (1898); *The Naval Review at Spithead* (1897); *The Queen's Guard* (1901); and *Battle of Atbara* (1898). In addition there were the popular marches *Our Heroes* (1901); *Star of Africa, The British Lion* (1901); *The Guards Are Coming Home* (1898); *Naval Exhibition* (1892); *On Guard* (1898); *To Khartoum* (1898); and *Victoria – Mother of the Nations* (1887). His grand march *King Edward's Coronation* (1901) is a set of variations of a four-bar tune that is jaunty enough but slightly monotonous. The grand march *Long Live Our King* (1901) included *Here's a Health Unto His Majesty*.

The imperial piano marches of the late-Victorian and Edwardian eras range in quality from the repetitive and the commonplace to the harmonically interesting, rich and inventive. At the undistinguished and unadventurous end of the spectrum is J. Warwick Moore's work, which includes *Colonial March* (1897), *Imperial March* (1901), *The Imperial Yeomanry March* (1901), *Royal Salute* (1892) and *Our Guards* (1890), and J.H. Lawrence's *The King's Colonials*, repetitive, unoriginal and commonplace. On the other hand, Mary Sloan's *Terrier Boys*

[445]

(1917), with its strong tune and incorporation of *Oh Where, Tell Me Where, Has My Hieland Laddie Gone*, is harmonically interesting and richly pianistic. Lionel Hume's *The British Outpost* march (1897) has a grand, romantic theme, well worked out and richly harmonic. Alphonse Latour's *General Wolseley's Grand March* is difficult to play but cohesive and with an interesting musical development. Edward C. Doughty's *Our Empress Queen* march, 'in celebration of the reign of Her Majesty Queen Victoria', in 4/4 time, is punctuated by pianistic fanfares and with an interesting melodic line, changing key in the middle section; it is operatic, full of trills and has distinct echoes of Meyerbeer.

J.H. Bridger's grand march *Isandula* (1898), dedicated to Major H. Pidcock-Henzell, was 'composed as a tribute to the conspicuous bravery displayed by the gallant regiment the 24th at the Battle of Isdandula, 1879'. Isandula is what the Victorians called the Battle of Isandlwana at which Lord Chelmsford's column was wiped out by the Zulus. Where almost all the other marches are triumphal, Bridger's march is a notable exception, full of sombre chords and a constant elegiac note. Much of it is in the minor key, giving it great poignancy. It is a lament with a nicely shaped melody and a Mozartian flavour.

George Jacobi, prolific composer of ballet scores, composed *The Queen's Jubilee Parade* (1897), a grand quick march 'in commemoration of the record reign of Her Most Gracious Majesty Queen Victoria (1837–97)'. It is rich and inventive, opening with a snatch of *God Save the Queen*, but then develops half-a-dozen different tunes – one wistful, one jaunty, one particularly good, and changes time at several points.

Stephen Glover was a prolific writer of romantic songs. But he also penned a long line of imperial and royal piano marches. Among them were *The Fall of Delhi March* (1857), *Hardwick's Indian March* (1857), *Napier's Abyssinian March* (1868), *The Oriental March of Victory* (1858), *Prince Arthur's March* (1850), *The Prince of Wales' March* (1859), *Princess Alexandra's Band March* (1862), *The Princess of Wales' March* (1872), *Queen Victoria's Band March* (1850), *Prince Albert's Band March* (1840), *The Sandringham March* (1863), *The British Cavalry March* (1894), *The British Grenadiers' March* (1894), *The Patrol March* (1894). Glover's marches, carefully characterized, were distinctively different from each other. His *Royal Camp March* (1854) is unusually almost entirely in the top half of the piano's register, full of trills and trimmings, apparently designed to indicate the feminine – the Queen reviewing her troops. *The Naval Reserve* (1861) is robust and rollicking with original rhythms. *The Coldstream Guards* (1859) is less original and more repetitive than the others. The

British Volunteers' March (1861) is lively, inventive and enthusiastic, conveying the twin ideas of service and hi-jinks which characterized the experience of the Volunteers.

Interestingly, the two different strains of military march can be heard inspiring the pianistic variety: the brass band (influencing Ezra Read particularly) and the operatic march (in particular the works of Bellini and Meyerbeer). But whatever the origin and whether good, bad or indifferent, what all these imperial marches invariably conveyed was the snap and jingle, the swing and the confidence of the imperial troops on the march.

These piano marches were for the home and the band marches were for the parade ground, the bandstand and the public concert. In the interwar years there were new outlets. In particular, there was the wireless. It was a measure of the popularity of military band music that the BBC in 1927 established the BBC Wireless Military Band, which remained a popular favourite until it was disbanded as an economy measure in 1943. It was formed by Lt Bertram Walton O'Donnell of the Royal Marines, who in 1937 was succeeded as Conductor by his brother Major Percy Sylvester George O'Donnell, also of the Royal Marines, who stayed with it until the end. Listener research in the 1930s indicated the high level of popularity enjoyed by brass and military band music, and King George V was a keen listener to band concerts.[66]

The BBC Wireless Military Band, like other leading bands (the Bands of the Coldstream Guards, Grenadier Guards, Royal Horse Guards, Welsh Guards, Royal Marines, Scots Guards), had recording contracts and recorded regularly for the gramophone. Many of their recordings remained available for years. To give just one example, Charles Payne's popular 1893 *Punjaub March*, with its Indian Empire associations, was recorded by the Band of the Coldstream Guards and remained available until 1950.

Notes

1 Stanley Sadie (ed.), *The New Grove Dictionary of Music and Musicians*, London: Macmillan, 1980, vol. 11, p. 650.
2 Nicholas Temperley (ed.), *The Blackwell History of Music in Britain*, vol. 5: *The Romantic Age, 1800–1914*, Oxford: Blackwell, 1988, p. 135.
3 H.G. Farmer, *Military Music*, London: Max Parrish, 1950, pp. 35–42.
4 H.G. Farmer, *The Rise and Deveopment of Military Music*, London: William Reeves, 1912, p. 74.
5 H.E. Adkins, *Treatise on the Military Band*, London: Boosey, 1958, p. 7.
6 Alfred Edward Zealley and James Ord Hume, *Famous Bands of the British Empire*, London: J.P. Hull, 1926, p. 12.
7 Farmer, *Rise and Development*, preface, pp. viii–ix.

8 *Ibid.*, p. 77.
9 Farmer, *Military Music*, p. 50.
10 Robert Giddings, 'Delusive seduction: pride, pomp, circumstance and military music', in John M. MacKenzie (ed.), *Popular Imperialism and the Military, 1850–1950*, Manchester: Manchester University Press, 1992, pp. 25–49.
11 For the history of Kneller Hall, see P.L. Binns, *A Hundred Years of Military Music*, Dorset: Blackmore Press, 1959.
12 *Ibid.*, p. 115.
13 Farmer, *Military Music*, p. 56.
14 Temperley (ed.), *Blackwell History*, vol. 5, p. 137.
15 Farmer, *Military Music*, pp. 65, 70.
16 George Miller, *The Military Band*, London: Novello, 1912, pp. 100–1.
17 John Trendell, *Colonel Bogey to the Fore*, Dover: Blue Band, 1991, pp. 90–1.
18 Lt Colonel John Mackenzie-Rogan, *Fifty Years of Army Music*, London: Methuen, 1926, pp. 7–8.
19 *Ibid.*, p. 72.
20 *Ibid.*, pp. 99–100.
21 *Ibid.*, p. 107.
22 *Ibid.*, p. 123.
23 *Ibid.*, p. 124.
24 *Ibid.*, p. 129.
25 *Ibid.*
26 *Ibid.*, p. 138.
27 H.G. Farmer, *Cavaliere Zaverthal and the Royal Artillery Band*, London: Hinrichsen, 1951, p. 135.
28 Mackenzie-Rogan, *Fifty Years*, p. 147.
29 *Ibid.*, p. 148.
30 *Ibid.*, p. 151.
31 *Ibid.*, p. 152.
32 *Ibid.*, p. 153.
33 *Ibid.*
34 *Ibid.*, p. 155.
35 *Ibid.*, pp. 155–6.
36 *Ibid.*, p. 158.
37 *Ibid.*, p. 165.
38. *Ibid.*, p. 167.
39 *Ibid.*, pp. 169–70.
40 *Ibid.*, p. 174.
41 *Ibid.*, p. 175.
42 *Ibid.*, p. 183.
43 *Ibid.*, p. 204.
44 *Ibid.*, pp. 184–5.
45 Sir Frederick Bridge, *A Westminster Pilgrim*, London: Novello–Hutchinson, 1918, p. 242.
46 Mackenzie-Rogan, *Fifty Years*, p. 227.
47 *Ibid.*, p. 233.
48 *Ibid.*, p. 248; Brian Rees, *A Musical Peacemaker: The Life and Work of Sir Edward German*, Bourne End: Kensal Press, 1986, p. 221.
49 Alford's biography is John Trendell, *Colonel Bogey to the Fore*, Dover: Blue Band, 1991.
50 Alford's *Complete Marches*, performed by the band of HM Royal Marine Commandos, is available on CD (Clovelly, CD102).
51 Trendell, *Colonel Bogey*, p. 13.
52 *Ibid.*, p. 95.
53 Dunn's biography is Derek Oakley, *Fiddler on the March*, London: Royal Marines' Historical Society, 2000; his most notable marches are on *The Martial Music of Sir*

Vivian Dunn, Clovelly CD 10394, performed by the Band of the Royal Marines, Plymouth.

54 On the history of brass bands, see Trevor Herbert (ed.), *Bands*, Buckingham: Open University Press, 1991; Roy Newsome, *Brass Roots*, Aldershot: Ashgate, 1998; John F. Russell and J.H. Elliot, *The Brass Band Movement*, London: Dent, 1936; Dave Russell, *Popular Music in England, 1840–1914*, Manchester: Manchester University Press, 1997, pp. 205–47.

55 Russell and Elliot, *The Brass Band Movement*, p. 77.

56 *Ibid.*, p. 165.

57 See Trevor Herbert, 'The repertory of a Victorian provincial brass band', *Popular Music 9* (1990), pp. 117–32; Robert A. Marr, *Music and Musicians at the Edinburgh International Exhibition, 1886*, Edinburgh: Constable, 1887; Russell and Elliot, *The Brass Band Movement*, pp. 169–70.

58 Newsome, *Brass Roots*, appendix 9, pp. 233–4.

59 Russell and Elliot, *The Brass Band Movement*, pp. 173–5.

60 Herbert, *Bands*, p. 5.

61 Trevor Herbert and Margaret Sarkissian, 'Victorian bands and their dissemination in the colonies', *Popular Music 16* (1997), pp. 167–81.

62 Duncan Bythell, 'The brass band in Australia: the transplantation of British popular culture, 1850–1950', in Herbert (ed.), *Bands*, pp. 145–64.

63 Zealley and Ord Hume, *Famous Bands of the British Empire*, p. 5.

64 Percy Scholes, *God Save the Queen!*, London: Oxford University Press, 1954, p. 242.

65 *Ibid.*, p. 245.

66 *BBC Wireless Military Band, Volume 3*, International Band series, sleevenotes by G.L. Frow and E.W.J. Bevan.

CHAPTER THIRTEEN

'Hearts across the sea':
the dominions' musical tour of 1911

Sir Henry Coward (1849–1944) was a classic Victorian, a self-made man from a humble background who rose to the top by his own efforts, a devout Christian (a Congregationalist), a non-smoker and life-long abstainer, profoundly patriotic and imperialistic. He was also Britain's leading chorus-master. Sir Dan Godfrey wrote in his autobiography that Coward's work was 'beyond praise':

> It is doubtful whether England has ever produced a better or more gifted choir trainer than Coward . . . Where choral technique is concerned, he is something of a superman. He has evolved, formulated, and put into practice a method of choral technique which has had the result of bring-ing about a revival of singing in chorus which has spread through the whole Empire. On all sides England is becoming vocal; choral societies are springing up on every hand, and the interest in choral music is growing with amazing rapidity. All this is due, primarily, to the example of Henry Coward.[1]

Coward's biographer J.A. Rodgers noted that he won through by 'sheer grit, fixity of purpose and a phenomenal application of systematic industry in overcoming difficulties' to which men of weaker fibre would have succumbed.[2] He had 'a purposeful and inflexible will', led 'a temperate life', had 'studied long and deeply' and 'endured hardships and material privations'.

> Dr Coward fulfils that attribute of greatness for he is emphatically origi-nal, in mind as well as in manner. A keen lover of nature, a follower of art, a staunch friend and tireless worker, Dr Coward has made a success of his life, first by the implicit belief in himself, and next by dogged, unswerving purpose backed by an infinite capacity for work.[3]

Coward was born in Liverpool, the only son of Henry Coward, a Sheffield-born cutler 'with a bent towards music' who became a banjoist and 'nigger minstrel', and his wife the singer Harriet Carr.

[450]

They toured for several years performing and then took over the Shake-speare Hotel, Williamson Square, Liverpool, where Henry was born. On his father's death when Henry was only 8, Harriet returned to Sheffield and Henry soon had to work to earn money. For twelve years he worked in the cutlery trade, developing 'that crowning asset of the self-made man, an implicit self-reliance. He made up his mind to "get on" and determined that no obstacle should daunt him.'[4] He had had little education and his spelling was deficient. So he taught himself spelling and shorthand and kept fit by early morning swims. 'To those early habits of clean living and solicitude for the welfare of his physique Dr Coward ascribes his present-day vigour . . . he boasts he has never had a headache in his life'.[5]

His musical career began when a lodger at his home taught him the flute. His Sunday-school teacher gave him violin lessons but he never learned the piano or the organ. He mastered tonic *sol–fa* and sang in the chapel choir; he attended performances by visiting opera compa-nies and taught himself the principles of harmony. He began teaching tonic *sol–fa*. By the age of 22, he was one of the best cutlers working in Sheffield. But he decided to become a teacher. He began as a pupil–teacher at Zion School, Attercliffe, Sheffield, at a salary of £20 a year. He took various teaching certificates to improve his educational standing, restricting himself to five hours' sleep a night. Within a year, he had become Headmaster of Tinsley National School, with an income of £80 a year, and there followed a succession of headmaster-ships until he reached the age of 40, in 1887. When the school he was heading closed, he made a major career shift into music.

He had founded the Sheffield Tonic Sol–Fa Association, later named the Sheffield Musical Union, and directed it for sixty years (1876–1933). He was a life-long advocate of tonic sol–fa and was President of the Tonic Sol–Fa College in London from 1929 to 1943. He taught tonic *sol–fa* classes five nights a week. He was appointed Conductor of the Sheffield Band of Hope Festivals, directing their annual demonstration by 3,000 children at the Botanical Gardens, and he conducted Whit Monday gatherings of 10,000–20,000 singers. In 1878 he became Con-ductor of the Sheffield Amateur Instrumental Society, the only per-manent orchestra in the city.

Having decided to gain musical qualifications, he went to Oxford and took B. Mus. (1889) and D. Mus. (1894) degrees, producing the cantata *Bethany* and the oratorio *The King's Error* as the exercises. The city of Sheffield subscribed in 1894 to pay for his D. Mus. robes as he was now a major figure in the musical life of the city. He was instru-mental in founding the Sheffield Festival in 1896, and when August Manns became its Conductor he became chorus-master, a position he

[451]

held from 1896 to 1908, achieving worldwide fame for the choir, as he sought to instil not just musical competence but 'expression, colour, interpretation, real musicianship'.[6] He had expected to become Conductor when Manns retired through ill-health but Henry J. Wood was appointed, keeping Coward on as chorus-master.

In 1897, on Queen Victoria's Diamond Jubilee visit to Sheffield, he conducted 60,000 scholars and teachers and nine bands in a programme of patriotic songs and jubilee hymns in Norfolk Park, Sheffield. *The Musical Times* reported that 'special mention should be made of the skill by which Dr Coward contrived with a huge baton to keep the mass together'.[7] In 1905 the Sheffield Festival Chorus under Coward performed before King Edward VII and Queen Alexandra at the opening of Sheffield University. They sang *God Save the King*, *Daughter of Ancient Kings* from Elgar's *Coronation Ode* and *O Gladsome Light* from Sullivan's *Golden Legend*.

In 1908 Coward gave up as chorus-master of the Festival because of the weight of other commitments, and these were prodigious. Not only did he lecture in music at Sheffield University and serve as musicmaster of Sheffield Training College but for fifteen years he was also music critic of the *Sheffield Independent*. He edited two hymnals for the Primitive Methodists, contributing many tunes. He was also appointed choral conductor of old-established musical societies: Huddersfield Festival Choral Society (1901), Leeds Choral Union (1905), Newcastle and Gateshead Choral Society (1906) and Glasgow Choral Union (1908). In addition to these permanent posts he was made chorus-master and co-conductor of the Newcastle Festival (1909) and the Southport Festival (1909). He directed the Aberdeen Festival in 1910 and conducted the Preston Choral Society for three seasons.

Coward's specific talent was for choral training. He took a Yorkshire chorus to Germany each year from 1906 to 1910. He published a definitive account of his techniques, *Choral Technique and Interpretation*, in 1914. He was unable successfully to conduct orchestras, and composition proved not to be his forté. Although he composed the cantatas *The Story of Bethany*, *Magna Carta*, *Victoria and Her Reign* and *Gareth and Linet*, Rodgers concluded:

> In a small form – a part song, a glee, an anthem . . . or a hymn tune (his setting of *Jesu, high and holy* in leaflet form reached a sale of over a million copies) his flow of ideas and his resources in handling them are equal to all requirements. But his fount of musical invention is soon exhausted: the trivial and the obvious are then drawn upon and the music speedily becomes mechanical and merely pedantic. *The King's Error* and *Gareth and Linet* fulfil all the obligations of the text-books. What they lack is true, innate musical qualities, imagination, and the

original thinking which can set aside a formula and utter an idea with freshness and point. The rough reception accorded by the critics to *Gareth and Linet* at the Sheffield Festival of 1902 must have persuaded Dr Coward that he was unwise in further pursuing the thorny path of a composer, for since then he has written nothing of any importance.[8]

He gave a practical demonstration of his patriotism by his participation in the cantata *Queen Victoria and Her Reign* (1885), which had a spoken narrative interspersed with songs. The text was by A.J. Foxwell and the music was composed and arranged by Coward, utilizing in some places melodies by Marschner and Zelter. It was wholly celebratory, declaring: 'There has probably never been a period in the history of the world when such vast and beneficent changes have taken place in all matters relating to the welfare of mankind, as in the reign of Victoria.' It goes on to hymn all the advances in the arts and manufacturing, the developments in science (steamboats, railways, the electric telegraph), the spread of education, religion and philanthropy, the rise in living standards and the passing of laws to protect workers and children. The spread of a divinely ordained Empire and its continuing links with the motherland figure too:

> We go to carry English thought
> And enterprise and skill
> To lands which heav'n has long reserved
> For English hands to till,
> To plant the flag of liberty
> On heights yet unattained;
> To consecrate by truth and right,
> Each peaceful conquest gained.
>
> Yet never will our hearts forget
> The soil from which we sprung
> Which feet of saint and sage have trod,
> And patriot-bards have sung!
>
> As leafy branches join to shield
> The stately parent stem,
> Old England's sons will still protect
> Her glorious diadem.

And at the centre of all this, inspiring it, encouraging it and blessing it, stands the revered figure of the Queen herself, the epitome of constitutional government and motherly compassion.

The Musical Times said of him that he was 'not a man of prepossessing appearance or address but was dark-visaged, stern of eye and always in a state of preoccupation'.[9] *The Dictionary of National Biography* recorded:

Coward's manner was brusque and his utterance awkward, for his mind moved too speedily for his power of self-expression. He was somewhat formidable at a first encounter, but those who came to know him learnt to admire his intense industry, his high sense of duty, whether religious, artistic, or civic, and to value his generous humanity.[10]

Rodgers says he was a blunt and forthright figure with 'an opinionative dogmatic manner, acquired through a triumvirate of despotic occupations – those of schoolmaster, musical critic, and conductor'. He was by nature autocratic. 'This was one of the secrets of his success.' He used sarcasm, rage and denunciation, but was underneath 'one of the kindliest and most warmhearted men in the world'.[11]

Despite the grim visage, he was three times married and had eight children, four boys and four girls. His obituary in *The Musical Times* noted that his 1911 world tour with his Sheffield choir was the high point of his career.[12] In 1933 Coward published an account of the tour, based on his own notebooks and the diaries of eight of the participants. 'The tour of the world' was, he believed, 'such a unique event, and its worldwide musical, ethical and political repercussions have been so marked', that it required a full account.[13]

The genesis of the tour was a deep concern about the unity of the Empire and the 'seeming neglect and indifference of the mother country to her expanding and sturdy children'. Coward noted:

> The British Governments in the past did not set very much store by the Colonies beyond a materialistic view. So long as they were a source of income there was no call for further thought. If they gave any passing trouble or expense they were regarded as a burden to the State. Neither was the British Empire visualized by the people at large.[14]

The wounds of the Boer War in South Africa, French-Canadian separatist feeling, and republican sentiment in Australia all required countering.

The hour produced the man – Dr Charles Harriss (1862–1929). Born in London and educated and trained in England, he migrated to Canada in 1880 to become a church organist in Ottawa. He later founded and directed the McGill Conservatorium in Montreal (1904–7). But in 1897 he married the wealthy widow of an iron magnate and, as *The Times* reported, 'her fortune enabled him to fulfil a long cherished dream of making music an effective link of Empire'.[15]

To this end he organized music festivals and tours, concerts and gala performances in Britain, Canada and other parts of the Empire. Harriss was, Coward noted, 'intensely British in sentiment and equally so for the propagation of the best type of British music' and wished 'to promote greater reciprocity of good feeling between the Motherland and her vigorous go-ahead stripling'.[16] In 1903 he invited Sir Alexander Mackenzie to tour Canada, playing only British music, because 'until then the Dominion had only seen German–American conductors and knew nothing of our music'.[17] It involved a massive amount of organization and financial outlay. Fourteen new choirs were raised and a number of existing music societies augmented. Associate conductors and executive committees in fifteen towns co-operated, and Mackenzie embarked on a fifteen-town tour, starting in Halifax, Nova Scotia and ending in Victoria, British Columbia. He successively conducted on the tour the Montreal Symphony Orchestra, the Chicago Symphony Orchestra, the Minneapolis Symphony Orchestra and a scratch orchestra in Vancouver recruited from Seattle and Portland, Oregon.

The Governor-General, the Earl of Minto, and his wife attended a public banquet at the State Opening of the music festival in Ontario. There were receptions by provincial lieutenant-governors all along the route and Mackenzie received an honorary doctorate from McGill University. At Moncton, where no choral work had ever been given, Mackenzie had the unique experience of having every item encored. At Winnipeg, the only work by a foreign composer admitted to the programme was Mendelssohn's *Elijah*, which was receiving its first-ever performance in the city. Among the most popular items on the tour were Elgar's *Banner of St George* and *Coronation Ode*, Parry's *Ode on St Cecilia's Day*, Coleridge-Taylor's *The Death of Minnehaha*, and Mackenzie's own *The Dream of Jubal*, *The Cottar's Saturday Night*, and *The Little Minister Suite*, the popularity of the latter two items a testament to Canada's large Scottish population. But Mackenzie noted that 'many important vocal and instrumental works by W.S. Bennett, J.G. Bennett, Cliffe, Coleridge-Taylor, Corder, Cowen, Elgar, German, Goring Thomas, Harriss, MacCunn, Parry, Sullivan, Stanford and William Wallace, had been introduced to an entire continent'.[18] The tour generated enormous enthusiasm, enhanced the musical life of Canada and inspired Mackenzie to write his *Canadian Rhapsody*, which was premièred at a Philharmonic concert in 1905.

In 1908, Sir Frederick Bridge, Organist of Westminster Abbey, was invited by Harriss ('a musician of ample means and high ideals') to tour Canada and give a series of lectures on English cathedral music, with the object of raising the standard of Canadian church music. Bridge wrote later: 'It was a delightful experience.' The tour included a meeting with the Prime Minister Sir Wilfrid Laurier, lunch with the Governor-General Earl Grey, the award of an honorary doctorate of music by Toronto University and a succession of invitations to luncheon clubs, which, he noted, 'invariably concluded with the National Anthem . . . a matter which always pleased and surprised me'.

There was a hiccup at the start of the tour when the Bishop of Montreal declined to allow him to lecture at the cathedral. But the Presbyterian Church of St Paul played host, and Bridge found he enjoyed his greatest success in the Presbyterian churches: 'I felt much at home in the Scotch atmosphere, meeting many Scotsmen who had friends and relatives in that part of Scotland where I spend my holidays.' He noted, however, that Canadian choirs tended to be all women, it being difficult to recruit boys. He felt that the Anglican Church was overshadowed by the Presbyterian and 'did not flourish here as by its great tradition it should have done'. Nevertheless, there were some 'excellent and enthusiastic musicians' among the organists of Canada, and he hoped to interest the Royal College of Organists in extending their activities to the dominion, but the report he made to the RCO on his return to London was ignored. Nevertheless, the selection of English cathedral music that he performed during his lectures, much of it unfamiliar, made an impact and helped to enrich the musical repertoire of Canadian churches.[19] In a different musical vein, Harriss also arranged for Lt Dan Godfrey and his military band to tour Canada.

In 1910 Harriss set up and became Director of the huge Imperial Choir, eventually 10,000 strong, which performed at the opening concert of the 1911 Festival of Empire, regularly gave Empire Day concerts and gave a series of concerts at the 1924 Wembley Exhibition. Harriss conducted his Imperial Choir in Hyde Park in the presence of the King and Queen on Empire Day, 1919, to celebrate victory and peace. The Choir was accompanied by the Massed Bands of the Brigade of Guards and admission was free. The result was 'by far the biggest gathering in recent years'. *The Musical Times* reported that the musical programme was appropriate to the occasion – 'music, simple, broad, with a good tune, and occasional unison passages'.[20] Its critic's view was that the most effective items were *Men of Harlech*, *Wi' a Hundred Pipers*, *Rule, Britannia* and the *Hallelujah Chorus*; the most popular were the *Soldiers' Chorus* from *Faust* and *Rule, Britannia*, 'the chorus of the latter being taken up and repeated many times'. The programme also included Sullivan's *Song of the Homeland*, *God Bless the Prince of Wales*, *The Minstrel Boy* and 'a couple of hymns'. The massed bands played Mackenzie's *Britannia* Overture and Elgar's *Pomp and Circumstance March No.1*, with the Choir singing *Land of Hope and Glory*. The programme thus represented all the different parts of the United Kingdom with a due acknowledgement of Protestantism, monarchy and Empire. The reactions of the crowd were reported:

> The good humour and orderliness were of the type we expect in an English crowd, but there were signs that much of the old stolidity had gone with other pre-war things. It was far more liberal with its expressions of approval than we should have expected. Thus each item was greeted by a tempest of hand-clapping, and the *Soldiers' Chorus* was re-demanded by a roar of 'encore' and cheers. The demonstration when the King and Queen mounted the rostrum was an amazing outburst – hats flew into the air, the National Anthem and *For he's a jolly good fellow* and the chorus of *Rule, Britannia* were being sung in a score of places at once; the man in the street, with no mind to sing, gruffly remarked in a general sort of way, 'Good old George! he's a real sport'; and the wife of the man in the street held up as many as possible of the younger and lighter offspring, who added a shrill quota to the hullaballoo. If any Hyde Park orators of the usual disgruntled type were in the neighbourhood they must have taken their tubs home – depressed.[21]

The concert was pronounced 'a triumph of organization', the crowds were delighted, and even if singing in the open air dissipated the sound somewhat, the occasion was more of a social one than a musical one, anyway.

Dr Harriss wanted a choir to follow up the Mackenzie visit and identified the Sheffield Musical Union's choir as the ideal candidate. He arranged for it to appear in London at a Queen's Hall concert, with the London Symphony Orchestra, conducted by Arthur Nikisch, Harriss himself and Coward, in the presence of the King and Queen and the Canadian Premier Sir Wilfrid Laurier. The success of the concert convinced Harriss that he had found the instrument he had been seeking 'to enable me to carry out an educational crusade in Canada, in order to set up an exalted standard of choral singing in the Dominion'.[22] So he arranged a tour of Canada by the choir in 1908, visiting Montreal, Ottawa, Toronto, Niagara Falls, Buffalo, St Catherine's, Hamilton, Brantford, London, Lindsey, Peterborough and Quebec. Coward recalled:

> This experimental venture was so successful musically . . . and the personal contact with two hundred singers from the Homeland created such feelings of cordiality towards the Old Country, that it precipitated the idea of fostering the development of 'Reciprocity' – Dr Harriss' favourite word – between the component parts of the British Empire – making brothers of all, and this, to be done on the 'plane of music'.[23]

Harriss now planned an Empire-wide tour for the choir, at the cost of £60,000, non-profitmaking since the choir were fee-less amateurs participating 'as a gesture of reciprocity and goodwill'. Harriss sought official backing for the project.

> With the enthusiastic support of Earl Grey, Sir Wilfrid Laurier, all the Canadian peers, the official representatives of each of the Dominions, and his own persuasive personality, he laid before the Colonial Office the political, racial and musical advantages which would accrue from the tour of two hundred choristers carrying the message of good will on 'wings of song' and reviving their dormant memories of the past in the old homeland.[24]

He needed government backing to secure the support of governors-general, governors, mayors and civic authorities, and he gained it. He spent twelve months visiting the dominions and setting up the tour, arranging dates, concerts and receptions. While Harriss was doing this, Coward was busy selecting the 200 singers 'who were to uphold the flag of England in all these places'. One hundred and thirty came from his Sheffield choir and the rest were drawn from the other northern choirs with which he was associated. They were all able to gain six months' leave of absence from their work. Many were teachers, granted leave by their education authorities for educational reasons. But there were also shopkeepers, businessmen and factory workers. Harriss ascertained from the committees of each city or town what they would like to hear, and eventually a list of eleven different programmes was drawn up, which eloquently confirm the common musical culture shared by the dominions. The programmes were:

1   Handel's *Messiah*
2   Mendelssohn's *Elijah*
3   Elgar's *The Dream of Gerontius*
4   *Gerontius* (finishing at 'Praise to the Holiest'); Epilogue to Sullivan's *The Golden Legend*; part-songs
5   Sullivan's *The Golden Legend*; Bach's 8-part unaccompanied motet *Sing Ye to the Lord*
6   Berlioz's *The Damnation of Faust*
7   Elgar's *The Kingdom*
8   Verdi's *Requiem*; Elgar's *Bavarian Highlands*
9   Harriss's cantata *Pan*; *Sing Ye To The Lord*; *The Bavarian Highlands*; Epilogue to *The Golden Legend*
10 Beethoven's *Choral Symphony*; Epilogue to *Golden Legend*; part-songs
11 Parry's *Blest Pair of Sirens*; Empire music and forty English part-songs; arrangements of English, Irish, Scottish and Welsh folk-songs, glees and madrigals for three or four miscellaneous programmes, among them such old favourites as Sullivan's *The Long Day Closes*, Parry's *There Rolls the Deep* and Bantock's *The Cruiskeen Lawn*.

The Empire songs consisted of Dr Charles Harriss's *Empire of the Sea*, Percy Fletcher's *For Empire and For King*, Elgar's *Banner of St George* and *Land of Hope and Glory*, Kipling's *Recessional* sung to a tune by J.B. Dykes, Purcell's *Come If You Dare* and Albert Ham's *Imperium et Unitas*.

Altogether the programmes contained 160 separate items, with an overwhelming sense of Protestantism dominant, along with that of the Empire, English art music (Elgar, Sullivan and Parry) and the folk music of the four home countries. There were 300 rehearsals. Coward recalled:

> The dominant idea of Dr Harriss was to establish in our Dominions and elsewhere the highest standard of British choralism. In this I heartily supported him, because I believe that choral singing is, and increasingly will be, one of the greatest forces in the social and moral uplift of the human race . . . there is in music a subtle, spiritual, psychological force, power or influence which will become more and more a vital factor in the progress of individual and national life.[25]

Writing from the perspective of 1933 and as a Victorian evidently at odds with the new age, Coward defended choral singing as the greatest form of music 'from a humanist point of view'. His reasons for this locate him precisely, culturally and politically. Choral singing, he thought, was possibly the most socialistic – 'using the term in its proper anti-Bolshevist sense' – of all the amenities of life, promoting as it does fellowship and friendship. It is the most *democratizing* force 'in [that word's] true political sense'. 'In all the choral societies I have had to control, the rich and poor, gentle and simple, the lady of high degree and the less exalted worker, mix together in happy companionship to the ousting of class distinctions.' The Great War had revealed that music, especially singing, was 'a wonderful promoter of morale and good health'. 'Membership of a choir provides a healthy, enjoyable "hobby" and prevents the degenerating tendency of becoming "inertiatics" through yielding to the passivity of merely listening or looking on, without any activity of body or mind.' Choralism is a 'strong bulwark against the baneful influence of atavistic jazz . . . However anyone can tolerate the sloppy, slithering, maudlin moans, supposed to be singing, astonishes me' and 'the debasing effect of the majority of American "Talkies"' with their 'low-down, decadent plots, lawless license, blighting revelry, debauchery, the defilement of the English language by the raucous "yah, yahing", the dethronement of high ethics for habitual unchastity, and the glorifying of "stars" who regard each successive divorce as an achievement'. He concludes: 'But the chief indictment of all this is the devastation it has wrought on the prestige of the White Races. It is horrible and humiliating to think about it.'[26]

The final public rehearsal of the Sheffield choir was held at the Albert Hall, Sheffield, on Saturday 11 March 1911, and this 'set the seal of preparedness on the choir for the responsible task of upholding the honour of the Homeland throughout "our far-flung Empire"'. After the final rehearsal, the choir and other invited guests were entertained at the Cutlers' Hall and the local MP, Stuart Wortley, delivered 'an eloquent address in which he dwelt on the imperial importance of the tour of the choir'. *The Musical Times* reported on the choir's musical qualities:

> The tone of the Choir is full and resonant. The sopranos are brilliant and the tenors also are conspicuously good. The contraltos have a peculiarly blendful quality, and the basses, although deficient in deep sonority, display many excellent qualities, not least of which are their full alertness and fluency. But it is not merely on fullness and beauty of tone that the Choir will rely in making its appeal to attention. The specialities of the Choir are its highly trained technique and interpretation.[27]

They sailed from Liverpool on 17 March aboard *RMS Victorian* and gathered on the quarterdeck to bid a tearful farewell to well-wishers, singing *God Save the King*, *O Gladsome Light* and *Auld Lang Syne*. On the voyage out they rehearsed solidly and gave two concerts for the Seamen's Orphanage, raising £25. The chorus travelled second-class but, 'with the consent of the Allan Company and by the courtesy of the first-class cabin passengers', they were granted free access to the first-class areas, and on the last night the Company put on a banquet for the choir.

The ship arrived too late for the scheduled afternoon concert in St John, but was in time for the choir to begin an evening concert at 9.45 p.m., singing non-stop until 11.45, after which there followed a reception at which 'thrilling speeches of loyalty to the King and Motherland and eulogies and thanks to Dr Harriss and the choir set our hearts aglow'. A special Canadian Pacific Railroad train was laid on to convey them from St John to Montreal, where there was an audience of 7,000 to hear *The Dream of Gerontius*, a performance which 'captured the public and the newspaper critics'. The two following concerts were equally successful, especially 'the Empire concert, at which national and patriotic music predominated'. The visit ended with a reception and supper at the United Yorkshire and St George's Club where speeches of welcome and congratulations and replies were given, some in Yorkshire dialect, and Yorkshire delicacies such as parkin were served; a perfect example of the theory of multiple identity in operation – Empire, Canada, Britain, Yorkshire, all operative as part of an easily accepted multiple identity.

The same sense of multiple identity can be seen in operation when the choir arrived in Ottawa and performed at the Parliament Building. They began by singing *O Canada*. Coward recalls:

> In parenthesis I may say that I had been requested officially to establish this piece as the National Song, and from what has followed, the singing of the Choir through the Dominion accomplished this ... The whole assembly, led by the Premier, Sir Wilfrid Laurier, clapped and clapped and shouted applause.[28]

They then sang Sullivan's *O Gladsome Light* and *God Save the King* (in Elgar's arrangement). 'This aroused further demonstrations. The tumult was glorious.' A Canadian MP was moved to publish a poem about the choir in the *Ottawa Free Press*. The last verse ran:

> O, Yorkshire lads and lassies from grimy Sheffield town,
> Where the smoke-stacks rise to heaven and the pallid factories frown,
> You have a nation's welcome beneath these northern skies,
> You silver-throated thrushes with the homeland melodies,
> The memory of your visit will linger with us long;
> You weavers of the Empire with golden threads of song.[29]

The Governor-General Earl Grey, and his party attended all the evening concerts. Sir Edward Elgar travelled out to Toronto to accompany the choir on the first leg of the tour. He hated the experience, writing to his friends: 'I loathe and detest every moment of my life here.' He was unwell and homesick, found the weather 'awful' and the people 'vulgar', and said he was only doing it for the money; but his presence added enormously to the imperial prestige and significance of the tour.[30]

In Toronto there were three concerts: *Gerontius*, conducted by Elgar ('a triumph'); *Pan*, conducted by Harriss; and an Empire concert, in which the Sheffield choir joined forces with two Canadian choirs – the Mendelssohn Choir and the National Choir – under six conductors:

> The Empire Concert, with its combined three choirs and six conductors, was a bumper in point of audience and enthusiasm which infected the singers with jubilation of spirit. The principals and orchestra had a good share in the praise awarded. The great number of military uniforms gave a spice of colour, variety and gaiety to the scene. The appeal of the Empire music to the patriotic feelings and the pronounced local pride in Dr Harriss, Dr Vogt, Dr Ham, Dr Broome and Mr Welsman – who conducted one piece each – kept up the excitement to fever heat and buoyed up the spirits of the performers to the last minute.[31]

[461]

The *Manchester Guardian*'s correspondent considered the choir to be superior in point of vocal tone to the choir that toured Canada in 1908, and singled out for praise Elgar's conducting of *Gerontius* ('remarkable for its devotional spirit and expressiveness').[32] Coward scrupulously printed both favourable and adverse press criticism in his book. There was much more of the former than the latter. But the billing of the choir as 'the finest choir in the world' sometimes led to adverse comment. St Catherine's was 'the one frosty setback of the Canadian tour. The hall was only half-filled by a dull, unresponsive audience, and the St Catherine's paper compared our singing with the local choir to our great disparagement.'[33] At Brantford, however, a *Welcome Ode* to the Sheffield choir was sung by the Schubert Society under its composer Mr Jordan and he was invited by Coward to conduct Elgar's *The Banner of St George*, the last item in the programme.

From Canada, the choir moved on to the United States. They performed in the Ohio State Legislature Building, Columbus, singing *O Gladsome Light, Moonlight, You Stole My Love* and *My Country, 'tis of Thee* ('which is sung to the tune of our National Anthem') with the result that 'the members of the House stood enraptured'.[34] Elgar conducted *Gerontius* in Cincinatti, received an ovation and was recalled again and again to the stage. The choir joined forces with the Cincinnati Symphony Orchestra and performed Verdi's *Requiem* under the baton of Leopold Stokowski 'The unmistakable success of the Festival musically and financially proved a tonic to the choir and a satisfaction to the responsible committee. It exalted the spirit of Dr Harriss, and cured myself of neuralgia, which had been troubling me for some time.'[35] In Indianapolis, all the main streets were decorated with British and American flags; Vice-President Fairbanks attended a reception for the choir and Elgar 'received and deserved the usual ovation' for his conducting of *Gerontius*. In Chicago the touring party was taken to the stockyards to see pigs being decapitated and turned into sausages ('Many of those present declined meat for a few days') and to a reception attended by the US Attorney-General Taft, brother of the President. At St Paul, Coward was taken by the Governor of Minnesota to a baseball match ('not to be compared with football or cricket'). Dr Harriss returned to London to conduct the opening concert of the 1911 Festival of Empire at the Crystal Palace, and planned to rejoin the tour in Australia. *The Musical Times* reported of the American leg of the tour: 'Our British singers were enabled to appreciate the warm and true-hearted fellowship meted out to them by their American cousins.'[36]

The choir now returned to Canada. At Regina, Saskatchewan, they visited the headquarters of the North West Mounted Police ('those splendid fellows to patrol the great North West and keep the King's Peace for over two thousand miles of territory') and at Saskatoon and Victoria, British Columbia, they were entertained by the 'Daughters of the Empire'. At Moosejaw, the speaker welcoming them declared: 'This visit would do more to cement the love of the Colonies for the Homeland than either Armies or Navies, and he longed to see Canadian stores filled with British goods and vice versa.'[37] At Calgary they visited an Indian encampment and sang to and danced with the Indians: 'It really was a unique experience, holding hands and dancing with real, live Red Indians.'[38] At Vancouver, the choir stayed aboard the *SS Zealandia* where they were officially greeted and sang on deck *O Canada*, *O Gladsome Light* and *God Save the King*, and the local military band responded with *The Maple Leaf*. They sailed in the steamer *Princess Adelaide* to Victoria, British Columbia: 'The most delightful and most English city in Canada – houses English, gardens English, sentiments English and English manners.' The scenery reminded them of the English Lake District and a cricket match between the male choral singers and the officers of the garrison was one of the highlights of the visit.

Finally on 19 May the choir sailed on *SS Zealandia* ('It seemed as if half of the inhabitants has come to wish us Godspeed'). The choir on deck sang *O Gladsome Light*, *Auld Lang Syne*, *O Canada* and *God Save the King*. 'Afterwards there was tremendous cheering from the quay and the steamer. Many were the affectionate farewells from the hosts of old and new friends, and not a few tears were shed on both sides by relatives who might never see each other again.'[39] Coward's verdict on the North American trip

Apart from the great public receptions, ceremonials and triumphs at concerts, etc., the thousand little acts of studied kindness, homely hospitality, gracious consideration, warm appreciation, and a strongly shown desire to be of service to us, touched our hearts and made us 'akin' to our cousins in America and brothers and sisters in Canada, in a much loftier sense than is expressed in the word 'kin'. In the heart-reaching actions mentioned above, we have been bound to them by the angel spirit aspect of kinship, based on the 'Sermon of Sermons', without any trace of the 'ape' and 'tiger' element of our primal nature. We cherish our memories of the *Stars and Stripes* and the *Maple Leaf* and can sing – and do sing – *My Country, 'tis of Thee* and *O Canada* with a fervour little short of that of Americans or Canadians.[40]

They were three weeks on shipboard 'although we were normally rated second class, we had most of the privileges of the first class in having the run of the ship and many of our berths being first class'.[41] They called at Honolulu where they gave an evening concert in the presence of Queen Lilioukalani and the choir sang the song of welcome she had composed. On Suva, the choir was given a Yorkshire dinner including Yorkshire pudding by exiled Yorkshire folk, and it gave a concert in the presence of the Governor of Fiji. It was 'crowded by well-dressed people, many of whom had come from other islands involving a week's journey, so keenly is the call of the Motherland felt by those who are exiled from "Home" '.[42] Passing the South Sea islands ruled by Britain, Coward recalled with pride the lines:

> Never was isle so little,
> Never was sea so lone,
> But over the sand and the palm trees,
> An English flag was flown.[43]

On 10 June, the choir arrived in Brisbane to be welcomed by the Premier of Queensland who assured them that the visit was a case not so much of 'hands across the sea' as 'hearts across the sea'. Coward replied: 'We are not coming to show how things should be sung, but as brothers giving of our best and wishing to cement the brotherhood of the British land overseas in the bonds of Reciprocity.'[44] In the evening concert at Exhibition Hall, the Brisbane Musical Union also performed. Then on to Sydney, where the choir was welcomed by bands playing *See, the Conquering Hero Comes* and *God Save the King*. Dr Charles Harriss rejoined them. The *Sydney Daily Telegraph* (13 June) devoted eight columns to the choir's arrival, declaring:

> People may say what they will about the relations existing between the colonies and the Mother-country . . . but while scenes like that which was enacted yesterday afternoon at the Orient Company's wharf are possible, whilst strong men can feel the chest tighten, the lip quiver . . . it is impossible for men to argue that sentiment is dead, and that the dream of a great united English-speaking race is gone . . . There was, below the veneer, something that showed Dr Harriss to have struck a right note when he said that he wanted to forge the bonds of Empire more tightly and more firmly than ever before.[45]

There was an audience of 5,000 at the Town Hall for the performance of the *Messiah*, including the Governor-General, the Earl of Dudley, and there were numerous encores, although this was not usual in oratorios. In co-operation with the Sydney Symphony Orchestra, the choir gave the first-ever performance in Sydney of Beethoven's *Choral Symphony*. The choir's last day in Sydney was the day before the Coronation of King George V, and the choir took part in the coronation festivities, performing on a platform in front of the General Post Office to an audience of 40,000 people:

It was a thrilling sight to see the upturned faces, every one expressing loyalty to the Crown in their very look. But this faded into insignificance when the huge crowd sang *God Save the King, Advance, Australia* and other patriotic songs. The silence which prevailed while the Choir sang some part-songs was a notable feature. But when, by request, we sang *Auld Lang Syne*, the crowd and the Choir made the welkin ring, and then cheers rent the heavens. It was a scene and demonstration of loyalty never to be forgotten.[46]

The choir left Australia for New Zealand on the *SS Wimmera* and encountered a violent storm during which the ship nearly sank and the passengers gathered in the saloon to pray and sing *Eternal Father, Strong to Save*. While at sea, on the night of Coronation Day, those singers 'who were physically able to do so' assembled in the saloon and sang *God Save the King*.[47] The long-term result of this storm was to deter Harriss from such gigantic enterprises in future.

The Australian pattern was repeated in New Zealand: warm welcomes, successful concerts, receptions from the Governor-General Lord Islington. The choir performed in Auckland, Wellington, Christchurch, Dunedin, Palmerston North and Invercargill, usually with local orchestras. There was a major row when, on the steamer *Mararoa*, travelling between the North and South Islands of New Zealand, half the party had to travel third class. The anger was assuaged by sovereigns handed out to the aggrieved travellers by Harriss.

Coward notes that:

In no country in which we had been did we hear the word 'England'. In the United States, and more especially in Canada, they always say 'The Old Country', while in Australia and New Zealand it is always 'Home' or the 'Homeland', spoken in touching accent. We then realized the force of Kipling's lines:

> We learn from our wistful mothers
> To call old England 'Home'.[48]

Then it was back to Australia, welcomed at Hobart by the Acting Premier of Tasmania; Melbourne where the choir's visit led to the formation of a Yorkshire Society in Ballarat where the Empire concert of national music 'attracted the largest audience of the week'; and Adelaide, where the Premier of South Australia welcomed them. Dr Harriss donated £100 to the building fund for a Melbourne Conservatory of Music. In Perth a row and a bad meal led to the choir threatening not to sing, but its members were mollified and all ended well, and 'thus we concluded our conquest of Australia in the Sacred Cause of Reciprocity' and won 'the affections of the sons and daughters of a vast continent by harmonious sounds and thus "strengthened" the bonds of harmonious feelings and sentiments between the Motherland and her sturdy, progressive offspring'.[49]

The choir set sail aboard the *SS Moravian* for South Africa, a fourteen-day voyage including a fearful storm. At Durban the choir received a magnificent reception from the Citizens Committee, giving four concerts and every one was successful both musically and financially. A special train took the choir to Pietermaritzburg, where the concert was 'a great success', and then to Pretoria, past reminders of the Boer and Zulu Wars. The party entered the city 'not in the panoply of hateful war, but holding the olive branch of peace, good will and reciprocity, by means of song', where it was met by Lord and Lady Gladstone, Lord and Lady Methuen, two musical societies and the President of the Yorkshire Society. The choir visited the graves of President Krüger and Prince Christian, but members were most moved by the row of iron crosses marking the graves of young British privates. Each cross was inscribed 'For the glory of His King and Empire'. In Johannesburg the choir was taken to the 'Kaffirs' Compound' to see a display of 'native war dances' and gave a children's matinée to 5,000 which culminated in 'Cheers for King George and South Africa'. In Bloemfontein choir members were again moved by the sight of the graves of 1,800 British soldiers, and the choir sang to the patients of Sydenham Leper Station. 'That an English choir should be received with such cordiality and enthusiasm in "the war area" after so short a time seemed to us to border on the marvellous. The more we think about it, the more wonderful it seems', wrote Coward.[50] In Kimberley the choir was joined by the Diamond Fields Musical and Orchestral Society for the Empire concert. Dr Harriss, who had established two singing scholarships for vocalists in Johannesburg, donated £100 towards the purchase of an organ for Kimberley Town Hall. In Capetown where the choir visited the colossal Rhodes Memorial and enjoyed a civic reception, a garden party, several trips and a dance given by the Festival Choral Associates, there were three choirs, three conductors and the Capetown Orchestra for 'Empire night', and the final performance of a tour in the course of which it was given 134 concerts. It was followed by a Thanksgiving service, conducted by the Archbishop of Capetown, held in the open and with the Sheffield choir singing so that the poor of Capetown might hear them. Immediately afterwards the choir boarded *SS Marathon* where, with a massive crowd to see them off, they sang *O Gladsome Light*, *Lead Kindly Light*, *For Those in Peril on the Sea* and *Auld Lang Syne*. The party sailed back to England and was rapturously received in Sheffield on its return. Harriss had budgeted for a loss of £25,000 but the tour broke even. A score of happy marriages resulted from the tour. Coward recalled:

> Dr Harriss was radiant with satisfaction. His two ideals – or obsessions – 1) the promotion of Reciprocity and 2) the propagation of the highest standards of choralism – had been achieved. The way in which Reciprocity had been received on all hands was proof of the potency of the principle throughout all the Dominions. The glowing tributes of the press in the USA, Canada, Australia, New Zealand and Africa testified to the influence of the singing throughout the Tour . . . The wide experiences gained by the unique privileges and special opportunities of the Tour have been of immense value to us all, and we have grasped more fully, both politically and imperially, the depth of the oft-quoted phrase of Kipling's [sic]: 'What do they know of England who only England know?' . . . And I rejoice that so much was done on the Tour by its means to cement the bonds of Brotherhood in the English Speaking World.[51]

There would have been further such ventures but war intervened. By the time it was over Coward was over seventy. But he carried on working in Yorkshire, giving up the Leeds choir only in 1929, Sheffield in 1931 and Huddersfield in 1932. He was knighted in 1926 and died in Sheffield at the age of 94 in 1944.

Notes

1 Sir Dan Godfrey, *Memories and Music*, London: Hutchinson, 1924, p. 128.
2 J.A. Rodgers, *Dr Henry Coward: The Pioneer Chorus-Master*, London: John Lane, 1911, p. 4.
3 *Ibid.*, p. 2.
4 *Ibid.*, p. 7.
5 *Ibid.*, p. 9.
6 *Ibid.*, p. 21.
7 *The Musical Times*, 1 June, 1897.
8 Rodgers, *Dr Henry Coward*, p. 48.
9 *The Musical Times*, 1 July, 1944.
10 *Dictionary of National Biography*, 'Sir Henry Coward', Compact Edition, Oxford: Oxford University Press, 1975, p. 2582.
11 Rodgers, *Dr Henry Coward*, p. 49.
12 *The Musical Times*, 1 July, 1944.
13 Foreword to Henry Coward, *Round the World on Wings of Song*, Sheffield: J.W. Northend, 1933.
14 *Ibid.*, p. 1.
15 *The Times*, 1 August, 1929.
16 Coward, *Round the World*, p. 4.
17 Sir Alexander Mackenzie, *A Musician's Narrative*, London: Cassell, 1927, p. 208.
18 *Ibid.*, p. 218.
19 Sir Frederick Bridge, *A Westminster Pilgrim*, London: Novello–Hutchinson, 1918, pp. 216–20, 296–303.
20 *The Musical Times*, 1 July, 1919.
21 *Ibid.*
22 Coward, *Round the World*, p. 5.

23   *Ibid.*
24   *Ibid.*, p. 6.
25   *Ibid.*, p. 11.
26   *Ibid.*, pp. 13–15.
27   *Ibid.*, p. 17; *The Musical Times*, 1 April, 1911.
28   Coward, *Round the World*, p. 30.
29   *Ibid.*, p. 31.
30   Jerrold Northrop Moore, *Edward Elgar: A Creative Life*, Oxford: Oxford University Press, 1984, pp. 612–14.
31   Coward, *Round the World*, p. 39.
32   *The Musical Times*, 1 May, 1911.
33   Coward, *Round the World*, pp. 48–9.
34   *Ibid.*, p. 57.
35   *Ibid.*, p. 62.
36   *The Musical Times*, 1 December, 1911.
37   Coward, *Round the World*, p. 82.
38   *Ibid.*, p. 95.
39   *Ibid.*, p. 105.
40   *Ibid.*, p. 103.
41   *Ibid.*, p. 106.
42   *Ibid.*, p. 117.
43   *Ibid.*, p. 118.
44   *Ibid.*, p. 119.
45   *The Musical Times*, 1 December, 1911.
46   Coward, *Round the World*, p. 127.
47   *The Musical Times*, 1 December, 1911.
48   Coward, *Round the World*, p. 141.
49   *Ibid.*, p. 158.
50   *Ibid.*, p. 177.
51   *Ibid.*, pp. 189, 198.

CHAPTER FOURTEEN

The Empire's queens of song:
Dame Emma Albani, Dame Nellie Melba,
Dame Clara Butt

Contemporaries never tired of stressing the extraordinary diversity of the Empire. Disraeli in 1878 said of the Empire:

> No Caesar or Charlemagne ever presided over a dominion so peculiar. Its flag floats on many waters; it has provinces in every zone, they are inhabited by persons of different races, different religions, different laws, manners and customs.[1]

There was not, in fact, one Empire but three: the 'Greater Britain' white dominions; the Indian sub-continent; and the African territories – each having its own special roles and problems. Within each of these divisions there was a patchwork of colonies, protectorates, territories, dependencies, condominiums. There was nothing approaching the formal precision and order of the Roman Empire, and Britain's Empire never remained static. New concepts constantly appeared: dominion status; trusteeship; mandates; dyarchy; and, finally, commonwealth. As latterday historian James Morris has observed:

> What was true of one colony was seldom true of another and there were in 1897 forty-three separate governments within the British Empire, displaying every degree of independence and subjugation and all manner of idiosyncrasy.[2]

As Britain sought to consolidate and centralize its control, there were, especially at the end of the nineteenth century, innumerable schemes for imperial federation, imperial defence systems, imperial customs' unions, imperial parliaments. But what statesmen and politicians overlooked was that there were stronger and more enduring links than any constitutional arrangements, certainly between the white dominions and even to an extent the non-white colonies – a shared culture. The Empire was linked by the use of the English language, by loyalty to the crown and by adherence to what we might loosely call Victorian culture, whose emblems were Dickens, Scott, Shakespeare and Tennyson, all of them revered wherever the English language was spoken. Literature linked the Empire. So too did drama. It was not just the acknowledged stars of Victorian theatre who toured the Empire (the leading dramatic actor of the age, Sir Henry Irving, toured Canada; the leading comic actor J.L. Toole toured Australia), travelling companies of English actors circled the globe, taking with them the Victorian repertoire of melodrama and Shakespeare. Music too linked the Empire, with a regular interchange of performers between the dominions and the mother country. It was not so much necessary that they performed an imperial repertoire, though some did; it was that they performed a repertoire that was shared and underpinned by common beliefs and values.

A number of key figures stand out in this process. Just as Queen Victoria was the female symbol of the mother country, the tutelary goddess of the Empire, a number of notable women singers also helped to bind the Empire together. They were invariably and conspicuously royalist, patriotic and imperial in their outlook.

Dame Emma Albani

The first was the Canadian soprano Emma Albani (1847–1930). Born Marie Louise Emma Cécile Lajeunesse, in Chambly, Quebec, of French-Canadian and Scottish ancestry, she was the daughter of a professor of harp, piano and organ. She studied in Paris and Milan, adopting Emma Albani as her stage name. She made her Covent Garden debut in 1872 and sang there nearly every season between 1872 and 1896, as well as singing all over the Continent. She played the leading soprano roles in the standard romantic repertoire: the Italian operas *La Sonnambula, Lucia di Lammermoor, Rigoletto, I Puritani*; the French operas *Hamlet, Mignon, Les Huguenots*; and such enduringly popular one-offs as Flotow's *Marta*, one of the few operas to have an English setting. She made a particular mark in the leading roles of the then new and controversial Wagner operas *Lohengrin, Tannhäuser, The Flying Dutchman, The Mastersingers* and *Tristan and Isolde*. But she was not only an operatic star; there were extensive provincial concert tours throughout the British Isles, and, deeply religious, she became a stalwart of the festival circuit, singing oratorios regularly for years at the Leeds, Birmingham, Norwich, Bristol and Three Choirs Festivals as well as the Handel Festival at the Crystal Palace. There she premièred many new English works by composers such as Sullivan, Elgar, Mackenzie and Cowen. In 1878 she married Ernest Gye, son of the operatic impresario Frederick Gye. She gave her farewell concert at the

Albert Hall in 1911 and retired to devote herself to teaching. So she had made her career in all the characteristic components of Victorian musical culture: Italian, French and German opera; English oratorio; and popular ballads.

Her autobiography *Forty Years of Song* (published in 1911), in which she gives her birthdate as 1852 rather than the actual 1847, is immensely revealing about her attitudes and her imperial role. Her publishers Mills & Boon stressed this in their catalogue: 'As Queen of Song she has reigned for forty years in the hearts of audiences in every quarter of the globe. Canada is the land that has the honour of having given her birth, so that the famous singer is a British subject and a true daughter of the Empire.'[3]

She is a fascinating example of multiple identity, something that was recognized by herself and others at the time, but identities that were mutually reinforcing. She quotes in her autobiography an article by Lady Hooper in *The New York World*:

> What an elastic nationality she possesses! In America she was American, and hailed from Albany. In England she was declared to be a Canadian and loyal subject of Her British Majesty. The French papers now state that she is a French woman.[4]

There was some truth in all of these attributions. She had spent four years (1864–68) in Albany, New York, during her late teens when her family moved there, and she was always greeted as a favoured daughter of the town when she returned. It made good commercial sense to emphasize whichever aspect of identity most appealed to her audiences. Later in the autobiography she recalls staying with the Canadian Prime Minister Sir John MacDonald in his beautiful house 'Earnscliffe' on the banks of the Ottawa, noting that 'it is now in the possession of Dr Charles Harriss, who is doing so much for music in Canada and the Empire generally'. She meets Sir Wilfrid Laurier, noting that he is loved equally by English and French Canadians, and praises him because 'he has done much to remove any little jealousies that may have existed between the two nationalities'. She goes on: 'I have married an Englishman and have made my home in England [elsewhere she refers to "our English festivals"] but I still remain at heart a French-Canadian.'[5] That may have been so, but she was a distinctly Anglophile and imperial one.

She is at great pains to acquit England of the old charge of being *unmusical*. Speaking of the triennial festivals, she declares: 'These festivals in England are a great institution, and go far, in my opinion, to contradict the assertion that the English, as a nation, are unmusical';[6] and of her concert tours she asserts:

it is wonderful to see how the publics of the provincial towns enjoy a good concert – how they flock to it, how silent they are during the performance of a piece, and how they show their pleasure when it is finished. I have always endeavoured to sing good music myself, and have always had as much good, even classical, music in my programmes as possible, but the public appreciate it all ... There is an enormous amount of money spent in England during the year on music, and this, combined with their great appreciation of it, is another refutation of the notion that the English are not musical.[7]

She is grateful for the continued affection of the British public, noting that the stars at Covent Garden 'became established in the affections of the British public. I use the word "affection" advisedly, for the English people take those who serve them well to their hearts, and never forget, even after long years, any who have won their admiration, and above all, their esteem ... the English public has been, and is, faithful and true to me'.[8] Next to her public Madame Albani loved a lord, claiming as personal friends a variety of aristocrats, including Lord Lathom, Lord Dudley, the Duke of Fife and the Duke of Westminster. Even more she loved a royal personage, and the autobiography is studded with admiring references to the various crowned heads before whom she sang.[9]

But pride of place was occupied by Queen Victoria, whose favourite singer she became. She gave her first command performance at Windsor in 1874, and afterwards the Queen sent her a pearl cross and necklace which she wore ever after as well as, later, a portrait of herself, in a silver and enamel case, accompanied by the words: 'I hear that you always carry my photograph with you in your travels. This one will be a more convenient one.'[10] She sang regularly at command performances at Windsor, Balmoral and Buckingham Palace. When, for several years, she holidayed in Scotland with her husband and son, the Queen would come to tea. She sang at the Silver Wedding party of the Prince and Princess of Wales in 1888 and at the festivities associated with the State Visit of the Emperor and Empress of Germany in 1891. Most movingly for her, as the Queen's favourite singer, she was asked to sing in the Memorial Chapel at Windsor over the coffin of the Queen as it lay for the weekend before its interment at Frogmore. She sang *Come Unto Him* and *I Know that My Redeemer Liveth*, accompanied by the Master of the Queen's Musick Sir Walter Parratt. The audience consisted solely of the new King and Queen and other members of the royal family. King Edward VII thanked her with tears in his eyes.[11] She recorded of Queen Victoria:

I need scarcely say that I deeply felt and as deeply reciprocated Her Majesty's generous attachment to me, of which I can never be sufficiently proud or sufficiently happy to have had the privilege of enjoying.[12]

She revealed that the Queen was particularly fond of Mendelssohn and Gounod and Scottish songs – *The Bluebells of Scotland* and *Annie Laurie* being special favourites.

Along with her attachment to the Queen went an attachment to the Queen's Empire. In 1886 she participated at the opening of the Colonial and Indian Exhibition by the Queen. It took place at the Royal Albert Hall, with the Queen and the royal family on the platform and behind them the orchestra and chorus, conducted by Sir Arthur Sullivan. Madame Albani recalled:

> The immense hall was full to overflowing, a great part of the audience consisting of representatives of the British colonies and colonials visiting or living in England, and it was a most striking thing and one never to be forgotten, to see our late Empress–Queen surrounded by nine thousand or ten thousand people belonging to every race and every religion on the face of the earth, and yet who were all her subjects. It brought home to one the extent and power of the British Empire.[13]

The music in which she participated symbolized the nature of the Empire. She sang with the chorus an ode specially written for the occasion by Lord Tennyson and set to music by Sir Arthur Sullivan, and in the *Hallelujah Chorus*. Near the end of the proceedings she sang *Home, Sweet Home*. This extraordinary mixture consists of a new piece of specially commissioned imperial music from two of the leading figures in Victorian culture; the most famous chorus from the talismanic score of Protestant England, *Messiah*, and that paean to domestic sentiment by Sir Henry Bishop which had become almost a second national anthem, a celebration of hearth and home and family, of the mother country recalled from abroad.

Home, Sweet Home runs through Albani's narrative like a binding thread and typifies the role of the hallowed and cherished sentimental ballad in linking together not only the different parts of the Empire but all classes within it. Her first encounter with the Empire after she began her singing career was in Malta, which she visited to perform in a programme of operas which included *L'Africaine, La Sonnambula, Lucia di Lammermoor, Robert the Devil* and *The Barber of Seville*; 'at that time local amusements were not too plentiful, so the opera was very popular'.[14] During the music lesson scene in *The Barber of Seville*, the English soldiers and sailors in the audience demanded she sing *Home, Sweet Home*. She did, and continued to do so on each night of the run, often having to encore it. She also added *The Last Rose of Summer* and *Robin Adair*. This demand for *Home, Sweet*

Home is an expression of the authentic voice of the Victorian imperial exile and it recurred with astonishing regularity. It figured in her first command performance for Queen Victoria in 1874 along with *Robin Adair*, *Caro Nome* and Gounod's *Ave Maria*. Lord Kitchener requested *Home, Sweet Home* at a dinner party given for her by the Governor-General of India at Barrackpore, and she sang it again at a reception given for her by a Parsee lady. In South Africa, she sang it to Zulu miners at Kimberley after they had performed one of their dances for her. In 1883, while on an operatic tour of the USA, she detoured to give concerts in Montreal, her first visit to her birthplace since she had left to start her career. She was rapturously received; and at her packed concerts, as well as French ballads and operatic extracts, she sang *Robin Adair* and *Home, Sweet Home*. She also sang the latter regularly at concerts in America, attributing this remarkable fact to the large number of English immigrants in America and the song's capacity for awakening memories of their past lives. It was also, she noted, the fact that the words were by an American, John Howard Payne, further evidence of a shared culture, transatlantic and Anglo-Saxon, which linked the United States with the Empire.[15]

Her links with the Empire continued. She sang the national anthem at the opening of the Imperial Institute in 1893, conducted by Sullivan, and in 1902 sang at a royal luncheon at Guildhall to celebrate the Coronation of Edward VII. But more than this, she toured. 'I can safely say that in the course of my long career I have sung in almost every corner of the British Empire.'[16] Wherever she went she was received and entertained by colonial governors and prime ministers, fêted and treated as visiting royalty, appropriate enough for the 'Queen of Song'. In 1889 on her first extended concert tour of Canada she was given lunch by the Premier of Quebec and stayed with the Prime Minister of Canada Sir John MacDonald. A second extended tour followed in 1896, taking in Winnipeg, Calgary, Vancouver and Brandon, and the programme included the garden and prison scenes from *Faust*, that favourite evangelical morality tale of the Victorian operatic repertoire. She had given *Faust* in its entirety at a command performance at Windsor before Queen Victoria. In 1898 and 1907 she toured Australia, and was received and entertained by governors all along the way. The second trip was extended to include New Zealand, Tasmania and India. She sang *God Save the King* at the King's birthday celebrations in Colombo and made a great success of her Indian concerts. She recalled:

Very few entertainments of any consequence take place in India and the audience consists entirely of English people. The natives do not understand our music, and only acrobats and jugglers appeal to them. I believe we had every English man and woman off duty at all our Indian concerts.[17]

But in the very next paragraph she declared proudly that half the stalls at her Bombay concert were occupied by Parsees. Her approach was resolutely patriotic. On her first tour of South Africa, she visited Johannesburg where she was told that President Krüger had forbidden the singing of *God Save the Queen*. At the end of her first concert, she defiantly sang it. It was taken up with enthusiasm by her audience. 'The police did not interfere, but I think that if they had, the Boer War would have begun prematurely', she wrote later.[18]

However not every concert ended so triumphantly. The bass Roland Foster recalled in his autobiography:

In later life she suffered serious financial reverses through the unsuccessful operatic enterprises of her husband, Ernest Gye, and was forced to emerge from retirement. Amongst other engagements she undertook a music-hall tour 'topping the bill' by virtue of her world-wide reputation. And thereby hangs a tale. With a voice impaired by the inexorable flight of time, her refined and cultured singing did not appeal to the plebeian audiences of some of the smaller towns that were visited . . . They would have preferred something more robust and roof-lifting . . . So their reception of the poor old lady was usually lukewarm and often decidedly cool. At one factory town she complained on the final night about the lack of enthusiasm throughout the week. 'I have never in all my life,' declared Albani, 'sung to such unappreciative audiences.' 'Eh, but you should hear "em when we've got somethin'" they really like,' replied the local manager. 'Why, last week I thought they'd bring the blessed roof down wi' their stampin' and whistlin' over Roscoe's performing pigs! They were champion, too! Best turn we've had this year.'[19]

That was in 1925 when she was 78.

Dame Nellie Melba, hearing of her plight, arranged a benefit concert for her in London. Sir Edward Elgar and Sir Henry Wood participated in it. In Canada, the Montreal French language daily *La Presse* organized a subscription and benefit concerts. All this enabled her to retire again. Also, in 1925 she was belatedly made a Dame of the British Empire. Her husband Ernest Gye was appointed CMG (Commander of St Michael and St George) but died within weeks. Dame Emma herself died in 1930.

Dame Nellie Melba

Albani's successor as reigning operatic diva was another colonial, Nellie Melba (1861–1931). Born Helen Porter Mitchell, the daughter of a Scots immigrant who made his fortune as a builder, she was trained in Melbourne, rapidly establishing herself as a successful singer. She went on to study in Paris and made her debut in Brussels as Gilda in *Rigoletto*. She subsequently became the reigning soprano at Covent Garden where she appeared every season but two between 1888 and 1914, her repertoire the popular French and Italian operas in which she took the roles that Albani had sung in *Lucia di Lammermoor*, *La Traviata*, *Faust*, *Rigoletto*, *Hamlet*, *Romeo et Juliette* and *Les Huguenots*. She made Mimi in *La Bohème* her particular role, ensuring its enduring popularity after an inauspicious start and singing it in her Covent Garden farewell in 1926. Two operas were written specifically for her: Herman Bemberg's *Elaine* and Saint-Saëns's *Hélène*, both dismissed by *The New Grove* as 'negligible'.[20] She never succeeded in Wagner. Her major attempt, singing Brünhilde at the Metropolitan Opera, New York, damaged her vocal chords, and she avoided Wagner thereafter.

Melba became the most famous living Australian, her career important evidence to Australians that they could hold their own with the products of the mother country. Oscar Wilde told her: 'I am the lord of language and you are the Queen of Song.'[21] Melba never let anyone forget that she was Australian. She declared proudly at the start of her autobiography: 'First and Foremost I am an Australian', and she called Australia 'the most beloved country in the world'.[22] The stage name 'Melba' was chosen to honour her home town of Melbourne, but characteristically she objected when other singers followed her lead by taking names to honour their native land, notably Florence Austral and Elsa Stralia. She was renowned for her use of 'the Australian epithet' (i.e. 'bloody') in her conversation.

Ivor Newton, who accompanied both Melba and Clara Butt, wrote that 'Clara Butt was the voice of the British Empire, but Nellie Melba was something more rare and dazzling, the idol and the ideal of audiences wherever European music was to be heard, from her native Australia across the globe.'[23] This is true, but also significant in the imperial context was her role as an advocate of monarchy and Empire.

Although she appeared in a number of royal command performances from 1890 onwards, Melba did not share Albani's reverence for Queen Victoria. 'I hated the bloody woman', she once said in private.[24] But even in her autobiography her dislike comes through, in a story of about how royal thoughtlessness once allowed a command performance at Windsor to overrun, delaying her return to Covent Garden so that she had to sing late and supperless.[25] But the dislike may also have been fuelled by the known fact that Emma Albani was Queen Victoria's favourite singer, and because it was Albani and not Melba who was invited to sing Marguerite in a royal command performance of *Faust*. There was also a distinctly royal chill when rumours began to circulate that she was having an affair with Louis Philippe, Duc d'Orléans, son of the pretender to the French throne. He was 20, had studied at Sandhurst and served in the British Army in India. But the affair threatened to become a public scandal. In 1882 in Australia Melba had married Charles Armstrong, youngest son of an Irish baronet and manager of a Queensland sugar plantation. Charles had accompanied her to England but they had become effectively separated by the time the Orléans affair began in 1890. However, he threatened a divorce action citing Orléans. Melba would have been ruined, and so the affair was terminated. Melba and Armstrong were eventually divorced in 1900.

She entertained much warmer feelings towards King Edward VII. Her biographer Agnes Murphy noted of her invitation to sing in the gala performance of Elgar's *Coronation Ode* that 'it was regarded as a felicitous circumstance that Melba, a daughter of the Empire, was available to shed the lustre of her art on an occasion of such great Imperial significance'.[26] But the King's illness necessitated the postponement of the Coronation and the cancelling of the gala. However on 11 June 1902, at a concert in aid of the King's Hospital Fund and in the presence of the Prince and Princess of Wales, Melba sang the first verse of the national anthem, Clara Butt the second and the entire audience the third, standing and waving Union Jacks. King George V and Queen Mary were at her farewell performance in 1926. Like Albani and Butt, she generally adored royalty and aristocracy.[27]

Like many Australians, she referred to England as 'home' and, despite proclaiming her pride in Australia, referred when talking about the English to 'us' and 'we'. She was proud when her brother Ernest volunteered to fight with the Australian forces in the Boer War and when her nephew Gerald Patterson, a captain in a British artillery regiment, won the Military Cross on the Western Front.[28]

Once she was established, she toured regularly around Britain, the United States, Canada and Australia. She did not like India, even though entertained there by the Viceroy, Lord Reading. She wrote: 'Frankly, the predominant emotion that comes to me when I recall India is a feeling akin to fear. I think of the teeming masses of natives dominated by so pathetically few of our own race, I think of the dark customs, the inscrutable eyes, the uncanny luxuriance of it all – and I shiver a little.'[29]

Her return to Australia in 1902 as a world celebrity was triumphant. She sang in the major cities of Australia, was entertained by Lord Tennyson, the Acting-Governor-General, state governors and mayors, and her reception everywhere she went was tumultuous. Agnes Murphy compared it to the celebrations attending the visits of the Prince and Princess of Wales for the inauguration of the Australian Commonwealth and 'those to celebrate the British successes at Lady-smith, Mafeking etc'.[30] Melba's biographer John Hetherington noted that throughout her visit she gave interviews to the press on 'the graciousness of the royal family and the everlasting durability of the British Empire'.[31]

In 1909 Melba made a sentimental tour of the 'back blocks' of Australia, 'perhaps the most remote outposts of the white race in any part of the world', a 10,000-mile trip through the small towns of New South Wales, Queensland, Tasmania and New Zealand. She recalled: 'I never had a more appreciative audience ... At every stopping place the village halls were packed, and at each place where I arrived they gave me a reception of which even royalty could not have complained.' She travelled around by train, receiving official welcomes from mayors and town councils, as choirs of schoolchildren would sing *God Save the King*, and local newspapers would be devoted to her visit ('The concert was such an event in their monotonous lives'[32]). In 1922 she staged concerts for the people in Melbourne and Sydney at cheap prices. In all, 35,000 people heard her sing at fifteen Melbourne concerts and more than 36,000 at fourteen concerts in Sydney.

Her imperial patriotism was given full vent during the First World War. She remained in Australia, working tirelessly for allied charities, particularly the Red Cross. Her concerts raised an estimated £100,000. She ventured out of Australia to tour Canada and the United States for similar purposes, and 'seized any chance that offered to impress the Americans with the sacred character of the British Empire's crusade against the Kaiser and German imperialism'. She was, says John Hetherington, 'an unsubtle patriot of the hang the Kaiser variety'.[33] In recognition of her war work she was made a Dame of the British Empire in 1918.

Melba sought to raise the level of serious music in Australia. In 1911, 1924 and 1928 she mounted in association with impresario J.C. Williamson full-scale operatic seasons in Sydney and Melbourne, telling the press: 'It has always been my ambition to present grand opera in Australia – grand opera such as is given in Covent Garden – and I trust the people here will all be pleased.'[34] In addition, she backed the Marshall Hall Symphony Orchestra, the leading Australian symphony orchestra between 1892 and 1912, and appealed to her fellow citizens to support it financially.[35] She gave singing classes at the Albert Street Conservatorium of Music in Melbourne and in her will left £8,000 for a Melba singing scholarship.

In addition to full-scale operatic performances she gave concerts, and these featured a judicious mix of operatic highlights and popular ballads. In 1909, her four concerts in Melbourne included the mad scenes from *Lucia* and *Hamlet*, *Ave Maria* and *The Willow Song* from *Otello*, *Sweet Bird* from Handel's *Il Pensiero*, extracts from *Idomeneo* and *The Marriage of Figaro*, Bishop's *Lo – Hear the Gentle Lark* and Landon Ronald's song-cycle *Summertime*. The 'back blocks' repertoire included the mad scene from *Lucia*, the aria *Ah! Fors e lui* from *La Traviata*, Arditi's *Se Saran Rose* and Tosti's *Goodbye*, *Comin' Through the Rye* and *Home, Sweet Home*. Wherever she toured, both in Britain and the Empire, her repertoire was a mix of operatic hits, modern French songs and old ballads.

Lindley Evans, her accompanist for several years after the First World War, recalled: 'She was happiest singing modern French songs, so you can imagine how she'd feel when some unsteady voice from the gallery would cry *"Home, Sweet Home*, Nellie". It happened all the time.'[36] In her autobiography, Melba complained about the conservatism of English audiences:

> Do you realise that the provinces are asking for exactly the same things as they demanded forty years ago? Do you realise that when I go to big towns which possess, according to popular tradition, such excellent taste, I am compelled time and again to sing the same old songs, and that whenever I endeavoured to put something new on the programme, I am regarded as positively eccentric? Do you realise that even now, in this year of 1925, wherever I go, I am being asked to sing Tosti's *Goodbye, Comin' through the Rye* and all the other old tunes that they have heard a thousand times? ... Why is it, of all countries in the world, we go on with the same old things in the same old way, distrusting anything that is fresh, unwilling ever to make any experiments? When I come to America, when I sing in Paris, or in Italy, I am overwhelmed with requests to sing works by hitherto unknown composers. None of these requests ever come to me in England. We are conservative to the point of madness.[37]

She seems not to have realized the value of popular song: the articulation of deeply held feelings, the reassurance of familiarity, the sense of shared experience and shared memory, the marriage of melody and sentiment, all of which made popular ballads so long-lasting in public taste.

Australia shared Britain's conservatism in the matter of songs. This led to a celebrated scandal involving Melba. In Clara Butt's authorized biography, published by Harrap in 1928, the author Winifred Ponder reported that when Clara was planning her first trip to Australia she discussed it with Melba, who said: 'What are you going to sing? All I say is – sing 'em muck! It's all they understand.' Melba in Australia was told about the inclusion of this remark, whereupon she contacted her lawyers and issued an indignant denial. Dame Clara was forced to announce that she has been misquoted and Harrap recalled the remaining 3,000 copies of the edition and deleted the offending passage. Ponder insisted that the remark was accurately quoted, and it certainly sounds like Melba.[38] Beverley Nichols, who ghosted Melba's autobiography, recalled: 'If only Australians could have heard how Melba used to rail against her own country! If only I had possessed a gramophone record of the mocking, bitter invective which she poured out upon Australia and everything Australian.'[39] But it was of course said in private and probably inspired by their lack of musical taste.

Home, Sweet Home was, according to Thérèse Radic, 'regarded by Australians as Melba's private property';[40] though in fact it had been a cherished part of the repertoire of both Adelina Patti and Emma Albani. It was one of those songs which transcended class differences and linked the colonies to the mother country. Melba recalled that when Lord Kitchener visited Australia in 1909 ('though he was the gentlest of men, with the voice of a poet rather than a soldier, he radiated strength'), he was fêted in Melbourne as an imperial hero ('the whole city went mad with excitement'). After a dinner at Government House he requested Melba to sing *Home, Sweet Home* because, he said, 'I've been an exile for eight years'. Melba said:

> I sang, the same song which I had sung many times before, to countless thousands in all parts of the world, but perhaps this time, the meaning was a little deeper, the sweetness of the melody more poignant, for I was singing for 'an exile' and I too had known what exile meant. When the song was finished, I looked across at Kitchener. He did not speak, but there were two big tears on his cheeks.[41]

In 1921 when she was on a visit to Norway and being entertained by the King and Queen, Prince George, the youngest son of King George V, arrived on a ship in which he was serving as a midshipman and sent a message asking for *Home, Sweet Home*.[42]

Melba inspired contradictory feelings in those who encountered her. Landon Ronald, who accompanied her regularly, found her 'simply splendid . . . full of fun, enjoying life, and being a very homely and very bohemian woman' with 'a rare gift of mimicry'.[43] Another accompanist, Gerald Moore, recalled that 'she enjoyed herself thoroughly by bullying the life out of me'.[44] Her fellow-Australian, the baritone Peter Dawson, who worked with her, disliked her and tells stories of her rudeness and egocentricity, concluding: 'From the nice Australian girl she became the spoilt snob of the musical world.'[45] Accompanist Ivor Newton recalled:

> Working with Melba was not easy: her strictness, perfectionism and technical mastery made demands on her colleagues and accompanist as exigent as those made on her own skill and temperament. But it was not necessary, when she was at work, to guard against difficult moods, tantrums and temperamental storms; she was too disciplined an artist to allow externals to interfere with work. What roused her anger was anything slovenly or inappropriate.[46]

She emerges as vain (she died of erisypelas, after a facelift that went wrong), capricious, inconsiderate and snobbish. 'Nobody in England or America had any idea of the intensity of the servant problem in the Southern Hemisphere', she announced in her autobiography.[47] But she was capable of great generosity. She sang like an angel and she sought continuously to raise musical standards in Australia. When she died in 1931, she was both a national and an imperial heroine. One newspaper reported: 'Never in the history of Melbourne – not even in the emotional stress of the war years – have the streets witnessed such scenes as marked Melba's funeral procession.'[48] A fife and drum band played Sullivan's *Onward, Christian Soldiers* and the Royal Victorian Liedertafel male voice choir sang Sullivan's *The Long Day Closes*. The Camberwell Boy Scouts, known as 'Melba's Own', lined the route. A trumpeter of the 8th Brigade, Australian Field Artillery, played *The last post*.

Dame Clara Butt

More notable in the imperial context even than Albani and Melba, however, was Dame Clara Butt (1873–1936). Where Albani was Canadian and Melba Australian, Clara Butt was English. Unlike the other two she was not a soprano or an operatic diva; she was a contralto and the leading female practitioner of the ballad concert. This gave her a more wide-ranging popularity than either of the other two. Sir Henry Wood described her as 'the idol of the concert public' and the *Dictionary of National Biography* calls hers 'a career of almost unexampled popularity'.[49] Roland Foster, who managed her 1913 world tour, said she 'occupied a unique place in the affections of the British concert-going public . . . She was, in fact, a great national figure, almost as well known to the people of the Empire as the Queen or the Prince of Wales.'[50] Peter Dawson, who worked with her, described her as 'a real singer of the people. Faultless diction, glorious quality – in fact she possessed a voice unequalled before or . . . since'.[51]

Her imperial significance was unquestionable. Ivor Newton, who accompanied her, called her 'the voice of the British Empire', and recalled: 'amongst my memories of her are those of the women in the artists' room of halls in lonely Canadian prairie towns, who dissolved into tears as they told her that they had heard her in Birmingham or Leicester many years before; she brought England back to them'.[52] Roland Foster concluded: 'It may truthfully be said that the Clara Butt–Rumford tours played no small part in cementing the bonds of fellowship and strengthening the ties which bind South Africa, Canada, Australia and New Zealand to the motherland.'[53]

Clara Butt was six foot two, statuesque, well-built and possessed a deep, resonant and majestic contralto voice. She was the daughter of a sea captain who later became a ship builder and ship broker in Bristol, where she was trained. She auditioned at the age of 16 for the Royal College of Music. Singing J.L. Hatton's *The Enchantress*, which ends with the lines 'Kings have trembled when I came/ Reading doom upon my face', she literally blasted the judges out of their seats and Sir Walter Parratt asked her to sing something quieter. Having been admitted to the Royal College, she performed in her last year in the College's production of Gluck's *Orpheus*. She was a sensation and *The Times* called her 'by far the best singer that has ever come from the Royal College of Music'.[54] The Prince of Wales called for a repeat performance, which was held at the Lyceum Theatre on 11 March 1893. Queen Victoria commanded her to sing at a State concert at Buckingham Palace, conducted by Sullivan. She sang Saint-Saëns's song *Mon coeur s'ouvre à ta voix* and received a letter of appreciation and a cheque for twenty-five guineas from the Queen. She subsequently sang at eight royal receptions and many aristocratic soirées. Like Albani and Melba, she adored royalty. She became a favourite of Queen Victoria and the Prince and Princess of Wales; a favourite too of the Empress Frederick, eldest daughter of Queen Victoria. Clara sang *Abide With Me* at the memorial service for Queen Victoria at Kensington Palace Chapel. Elgar's *Coronation Ode* was written with her in mind and she was to have sung it at the Coronation celebrations at Covent Garden. But when the Coronation was postponed, it was eventually given at the Albert Hall with King Edward VII and Queen Alexandra present. Clara not only sang in the *Ode* but, at the special request of the Queen, *The Lost Chord*. She was invited to sing the national anthem at the Coronation of King George V and Queen Mary in 1911 because 'the work of this great contralto has been so much bound up in representative English music that we have come to look upon her as the truly national singer'.[55] King George V stipulated that Clara should sing the national anthem at his Silver Jubilee, as she had at the Coronation. Ivor Newton said: 'When heard at a State occasion she was unforgettable.'[56] So regularly was she called upon to sing the national anthem at charitable events and special occasions (such as the opening of Tree's Her Majesty's Theatre in 1897 and the last night of *Chu Chin Chow*) that she jokingly told King George V that 'Died as a result of singing God Save the King' would be on her tombstone.[57] But it was Clara Butt who was responsible for the creation of the 'alternative' national anthem. She asked Elgar to turn *Pomp and Circumstance March No. 1* into a song for her. With words by A.C. Benson, *Land of Hope and Glory* became as closely associated with her as was *Abide With Me*.[58]

This association with the songs of nationhood was only too appropriate because, as her biographer Winifred Ponder recalls, within two years of her singing debut she had become

> a sort of institution for whom the English people had a proprietary, personal affection. And crowds would gather, not only to hear her, but to see her and watch her pass by. Very soon she was the biggest 'draw' on the concert platform; the name of Clara Butt was familiar throughout the world.[59]

Clara Butt became a symbol of something else of importance to the national image – domesticity. She married, on 26 June 1900, the popular baritone Robert Kennerley Rumford, who subsequently partnered her on her singing tours. A keen cricketer and golfer, Rumford was described by Sir Henry Wood as 'a typical English gentleman whose birthright shone through every bar he sang'.[60] Roland Foster said that they maintained the 'highest British traditions in their domestic and social relationships'.[61] She was offered St Paul's Cathedral for her wedding but preferred to be married, in her home town, at Bristol Cathedral, in the first marriage to be performed there for 100 years. It was a spectacular event – factories, offices and shops were given half-day holidays, special trains from London were laid on, church bells were rung and hundreds of presents received, including one from the Queen. Sir Arthur Sullivan was due to play the organ but was prevented by illness. However, his anthem *O God, Thou Art Worthy to Be Praised* was sung by Madame Emma Albani. Ivor Novello, whose mother Madame Clara Novello Davies was a guest, was a page boy. Nellie Melba was among the guests along with many notable singers of the day. Every newspaper covered the wedding. After it, Clara Butt became even more popular, embodying, says Winifred Ponder, 'the ideal of the simple domestic joys and virtues so near to the British heart'.[62] They had three children, Joy, Roy and Victor, but both sons ('splendid specimens of manhood', recalled Foster) were to predecease their parents.[63]

They remained a devoted couple, Rumford fiercely protective of his wife. When H.C. Colles, music critic of *The Times*, wrote something critical of Clara, he went to the newspaper's office and knocked Colles down.[64] They celebrated their silver wedding with a concert at the Colston Hall in Bristol, attended by the Lord Mayor and the council. Clara wore her wedding dress and Dr Malcolm Sargent conducted the orchestra.

Her popularity derived from her mastery of the popular ballad form. Ivor Newton wrote:

> Intellectuals always said that Clara Butt was no musician, and it is true that she was not a person of highly cultivated musical taste. But the music which suited her voice she sang very well; her diction was impeccable, and she had a remarkable power of projecting the words and emotion of a song, so that the audiences hung on her every word . . . In arias like Gluck's *Divinités du Styx* and Beethoven's *Creation's Hymn*, she was most impressive; she was always trying to improve her repertoire and was eager to learn new and contemporary songs which I found for her. But so long as her public loved her to sing ballads, she was never free to expand her interests in *Lieder*.[65]

Roland Foster defended her repertoire:

> Like other famous artists, Dame Clara had to endure her share of captious criticism and envious detraction. Her remarkable versatility was ignored, her magnificent renderings of classical arias overlooked by those 'superior' persons who blamed her for singing 'popular songs'. But why turn up one's nose at songs which express in an easily understood way the universal feelings of mankind – love, patriotism, religion, maternal tenderness, charity, hopefulness, joy in the beauty of Nature and in the manifold gifts of Providence? Clara Butt's singing of everyday songs brought happiness and delight to countless thousands, the grateful letters she constantly received during her last long illness being evidence of her substantial contribution to human happiness over a period of many years.[66]

Ivor Newton added a practical reason for her singing of ballads:

> She was at her best in the ballads which were then at the height of their popularity. Together with her extraordinary diction went a sincere love of religious songs or of songs with a moral. Her mastery of ballads was doubly profitable for her. Her audiences loved them as she did, and she contracted with their publishers to sing them, receiving a royalty on the sales of those she made popular; I believe that every copy of 'Abide With Me' brought her threepence. When I asked her why she had dropped one

highly popular song from her programme, she explained that she had made a contract with its publishers for a royalty on sales which continued for seven years; the contract had now expired, and she was not prepared to go on advertising the song. Generous as she was in her work for good causes, she was practical in all her business dealings.[67]

Clara Butt's greatest hit was Samuel Liddle's setting of *Abide With Me*. Winifred Ponder recorded in 1928 that:

> No song – with the single exception of *Home, Sweet Home* and Adelina Patti – has ever been quite so closely identified with a singer in the public mind as *Abide With Me* has been with the great English contralto. The percentage of concerts at which she has sung it is simply astounding, and even now, after more than thirty years, it is still first on the list of public favourites . . . the sound of the opening chords when the song was given unannounced, as an encore, was certain to call forth a spontaneous burst of applause from every audience.[68]

It became an integral part of the popular musical consciousness, evoking spiritual feelings, and summoning up memories of people and places. It was much played at the Western Front during the War and was a favourite in tuberculosis sanatoriums. All the Australian concerts demanded it. The composer Samuel Liddle was a fellow-student at the Royal College of Music and later Clara's accompanist. She asked him to write a religious song for her because 'of all created voices that of Clara Butt best expresses religious fervour'.[69] Liddle set Henry Francis Lyte's words, one of the best-loved of British hymns, *Abide With Me*. It is usually sung to William Henry Monk's tune *Eventide*. Liddle's setting converted it into a quasi-operatic aria.

She was also closely associated with Sullivan's *The Lost Chord*. When he heard Clara sing it, Sullivan told her: 'That is how I always meant it to be sung.' It was Queen Alexandra's favourite song and undyingly popular with the public.[70] Elgar's *Sea Pictures* was written for her, as were Frances Allitsen's *Song of Thanksgiving* and A.H. Needham's *Husheen*. Joan Trevalsa's *My Treasure*, a classic 'baby song', was not written for her but she found it and brought it out while her own children were still in the nursery. 'It caught on at once . . . Like *Abide With Me* it has had, and still has, an immense popularity among amateurs, and is a "best seller" in most English-speaking quarters of the globe.'[71] Her duet with her husband *The Keys of Heaven* was also very popular.

During the war, Clara wrote to Kipling saying that England lacked a stirring national song about the sea. She felt that he was the man to write it. Kipling replied that he was unable to oblige. But some months later he published the poem *Have You News of My Boy Jack?* in a newspaper. Clara sent a copy of the poem to Elgar, who declined to set it for 'personal reasons'. So she invited Edward German to her house, read him the poem and explained her idea about it. He set it, and she sang it throughout the war. It is a mother's appeal for news of a sailor son who has died in the war at sea but 'did not shame his kind'.[72] This was, like her rendering of *Abide With Me*, deeply moving. But there is something irresistibly comic in the account of the massive Clara singing Walter De La Mare's *A Little Bird* ('out from the ivy hopped a wee small bird, and that was me').

She became an enthusiast for records and, later, for broadcasting. Once the technique of recording had been perfected, she was able to endorse it: 'My records are in very truth the living voice of Clara Butt.' She recorded her great national songs (*God Save the King, Rule Britannia, Land of Hope and Glory, Home, Sweet Home*) and her popular religious songs (*Abide With Me, The Lost Chord, The Holy City*) and arias (*O Rest in the Lord* from *Elijah, O Divine Redeemer* by Gounod, *Softly and Gently* from *The Dream of Gerontius*) plus traditional folksongs (*Annie Laurie, Barbara Allen, The Minstrel Boy*) and the sentimental popular ballads hymning love, nature and parting (*Trees, Kashmiri Love Song, Love's Old Sweet Song, O Lovely Night, The Sweetest Flower, The Better Land, The Rosary*). This recorded repertoire of both Clara and Rumford went round the world. Winifred Ponder reported:

> They have . . . made a place for themselves in parts of the world where the singers' living voices have never been heard. In Java, where English singers are rare; in planters' bungalows in the Malay Peninsula; in Fiji and China and Borneo . . . in the Rhodesian highlands and the Australian bush – sooner or later, in the most unlikely places your host will produce with pride a 'Clara Butt' record.[73]

The recording of the national anthem which she sang at the Coronation of King George V and Queen Mary in 1911, accompanied by the Band of the Coldstream Guards, was at Clara's request issued at half the usual price, 'to bring it within the scope of a greater number of the King's loyal subjects'.[74]

She also saw wireless as a way of linking the world in peace and unity through song. She said:

> Some day one voice will do it. I want above all things that that voice shall be mine. I pray that when that day comes I may not be too old to sing a song that shall be heard in the back-blocks of Australia and New Zealand, on the Pacific slopes of America, in India, and the islands of the Southern Seas.[75]

Ponder records that part of her dream came true when, in a red, white and blue dress, she led the community singing and a choir of 10,000 in Hyde Park on Empire Day 1927. It was broadcast and though not all round the world, 'the spirit of the song, through the Empire's newspapers reached every corner of the earth where English is spoken, and our country is beloved'.[76]

Interestingly, despite her strictures about 'singing muck', Dame Nellie followed Dame Clara in committing some of her popular ballads to record. Like Clara, she recorded *God Save the King*, *Home, Sweet Home* and *O Lovely Night*, plus Tosti's *Goodbye*, *La Serenata* and *Mattinata*, Bemberg's *Nymphes et Sylvains*, Arditi's *Se saran rose*, *Auld Lang Syne* and *Comin' Through the Rye*.

Clara had some early success on the Continent but did not follow it up, unlike Melba and Albani. 'She preferred singing to British audiences', recalled Ivor Newton, 'and her success was equally great wherever the Union Jack flew – in Australia, Canada and Africa'.[77] Clara's awareness of her importance to the Empire and of the Empire's importance to Britain came on her first tour of the USA and Canada, in 1899. The Boer War was in progress and a Canadian contingent was serving with the British Army. 'Patriotic feeling in Canada . . . was running high', noted Ponder. Clara attended a meeting in Toronto addressed by Dr G.R. Parkin, Principal of Upper Canada College. A portrait of the Queen was projected on the screen and Parkin introduced Clara Butt from her box, declaring: 'It is pleasant to know that we have with us one whom the Queen dearly loves – Miss Clara Butt.' Clara stood and sang *God Save the Queen*, the audience of 4,500 people rose to sing it with her, 'and there was a scene of the greatest patriotic fervour, long remembered throughout the country'. Ponder recalls that Clara 'was deeply moved with her first realization of that greater love of country which is born from acquaintance with its empire – the knowledge that drew from Kipling the line, "And what should they know of England who only England know?" '.[78]

In 1907 she and her husband, their three children, nurses and concert party sailed for Australia. There was an enormous crowd to see them off. They were rapturously received in Australia:

> The sensational nature of her reception in warm-hearted Australia was a revelation. Wireless messages by the dozen, and letters by the score greeted her arrival. With her husband, she was elected to honorary membership of clubs and societies innumerable, and snowed under with invitations from Governors, Premiers, Lord Mayors, and public and private bodies of every description. They were besieged with requests to open bazaars and buildings, to present prizes to budding musicians, and to

make speeches upon every possible and impossible subject and occasion
... Not only were there crowds at the concerts and at the stations to
meet them, but people came for miles to railway-sidings to see their train
go through; mothers brought their babies and waited outside concert
halls so that Clara Butt might see and smile at them ... All sorts of
things were named after her, from roses and racehorses to soaps, per-
fumes and iced sundaes.[79]

It was in connection with this trip that Melba gave her celebrated
advice: 'sing 'em muck!'. But Ponder notes: 'Australian audiences, it
is interesting to note, proved as appreciative of the classical items ...
as of the more popular type of songs and ballads'.[80] The programme on
the 1907 tour of Australia included songs by Handel, Bach, Gluck,
Schumann, Schubert, Brahms, Grieg, Beethoven and Richard Strauss.
In 1911 the Rumfords visited South Africa and were fêted and at the
end of 1912 they started their first world tour – Canada, USA, New
Zealand, Australia and Tasmania. So great was their success in
America and Canada that they travelled back by the same route and
paid return visits.

Roland Foster, their tour manager, left a detailed record of his experience. He noted that they travelled like royalty in private saloon
carriages and that the wardrobe for the tour included seventy frocks
for afternoon and evening wear, each costing between sixty and one
hundred guineas.

> Their tour was attended by almost as much pomp and ceremony as a
> Royal progress. Vice-regal and civic functions in every capital; recep-
> tions, musicales and luncheons tendered by Royal Empire, Queen Vic-
> toria and other patriotic societies, women's clubs, musical organizations
> and theatrical performances in addition to formal dinner parties and mis-
> cellaneous invitations took up a large amount of time and seldom left
> the artists to their own devices, although – as is the custom with most
> great singers – Clara Butt made a point of having at least a couple of
> hours' rest during the afternoon on concert days.[81]

On the Australian tour there were seventy-eight concerts – in Melbourne, Sydney, Brisbane, Adelaide, Perth, Launceston and Hobart –
and a further nineteen in New Zealand. Total receipts from the
Australian tour exceeded £30,000.[82] The programmes of the tour were
carefully constructed: the best in vocal music in the first half, and
the latter part of the programme devoted to 'songs with a popular
appeal of which the public never seemed to get tired, judging by the
outburst of applause that inevitably heralded the opening bars of each
familiar favourite'.[83]

They returned in May, and in June 1914 made a re-appearance at a concert at the Albert Hall. Then came the war, and Clara threw herself into war work. Winifred Ponder recorded:

> No other woman could have done what she did, because the place she had made for herself in the hearts of the British public was unique, and gave her a power and an influence which she used up to the hilt on behalf of the war's victims. The visible result of her effort was a cash total running into hundreds of thousands of pounds, with the even more important factor that she had provided employment for hundreds who would otherwise have been penniless, and pleasure for thousands whose anxieties and worries the concerts she organized helped to alleviate.[84]

Kennerley Rumford offered himself 'and his new Wolseley car' for service with the Red Cross at the Front. Before leaving he and Clara gave a great concert at the Royal Albert Hall, all proceeds going to war charities. The entire proceeds of her autumn tour (£14,000) was devoted to the less fortunate. She organized a series of concerts throughout Britain, at hospitals, workhouses, asylums and homes for incurables, to give employment to musicians made workless by the war. She organized a series of concert parties touring small towns to raise funds for the Red Cross. She gave concerts for the Three Arts Women's Employment Fund, set up to provide assistance to women in the three arts adversely affected by the war.

A great spectacle, *The Pageant of Fair Women*, was staged at the Queen's Hall in 1915. Written by Louis N. Parker, it involved a mass of leading musical and dramatic artists and socialites portraying every part of the British Empire and its allies. Clara appeared as Britannia and her daughter Joy as the Sudan. It was a great financial success and was repeated a few days later. It was given again in Chiswick for two matinées in aid of Sir Oswald Stoll's War Seal Foundation – a scheme to provide flats for disabled soldiers and their families. One of the flats was named after Clara. She organized a week's run of *The Dream of Gerontius* in London, following two performances in Leeds for Red Cross funds. She wanted not only to raise money but to give people a spiritual experience. She declared:

> We are a nation in mourning, ... In this tremendous upheaval, when youth is dying for us, I want to give the people a week of beautiful thoughts, for I am convinced that no nation can be great that is not truly religious. I believe that the war has given us a new attitude towards death, that many who had no faith before are now hungering to believe that after death there is life.[85]

To achieve her end, she enlisted the aid of the Leeds Choral Union under Dr Henry Coward, the London Symphony Orchestra under Elgar, and leading singers. She sang the part of the Guardian Angel.

The King and Queen attended one performance, and Queen Alexandra and the King and Queen of Portugal another.

The Times reported that the occasion was 'unique among the many which have been held in London to aid the work of the Red Cross – unique in the fact that one could not for a moment lose sight of the serious intention of all concerned. The dominant idea was not the making of music for pleasure or profit. It was an act of commemoration for the dead with a message of comfort for "all tormented souls".'[86] The concert began with Elgar's arrangement of the national anthem, then his newly composed choral songs *To Women* and *For the Fallen*, setting poems by Laurence Binyon ('Both works made a finely serious impression and were finely sung', reported *The Times*). Then there came a performance of *The Dream of Gerontius*, which was 'generally admirable'. As *The Times* reported, these concerts raised £4,861.13s. 6d. but with the expenses of the undertaking 'necessarily heavy'[87] (£2,154.2s. 5d.), the sum handed over to the British Red Cross Society and the Order of St John of Jerusalem was £2,772.13s. 2d. Altogether, however, during the first five months of 1916, she handed over £5,365 to the charities.[88]

The most sensational of Clara's war efforts was the huge Red Cross concert at the Albert Hall in May 1916. She paid all the expenses and handed over £9,000 to the Red Cross. The Queen requested *Abide With Me*, and the King Sir Michael Costa's arrangement of the national anthem. Both were done, and Clara sang *The Lost Chord* and *Land of Hope and Glory*. There was a choir of 250 voices, the Massed Bands of the Brigade of Guards and almost every leading singer of the day. Madame Albani and Edward Lloyd came out of retirement to sing. Kennerley Rumford, on special leave of absence from the Front, appeared in khaki. Every member of the audience was provided with a small white satin flag. The flags were waved in unison to greet the King and Queen and also during the singing of *Rule, Britannia* by the whole audience. 'It was a spectacle which no one who was present will ever forget', said Ponder.[89]

In the same summer she mounted a concert at the Albert Hall for the benefit of wounded soldiers and sailors. Admission to the wounded was free. Members of the public were not admitted. Clara and Sir Frederick Bridge organized a concert at Westminster Abbey for blinded soldiers from St Dunstan's. Clara sang Sullivan's *And God Shall Wipe Away All Tears From Their Eyes*, from *The Light of the World*, and *Abide With Me*. In addition she toured Britain repeatedly, doing recitals and appealing for funds for the Red Cross. It was for this tireless work that Clara was made a Dame of the British Empire in 1920.

Rumford ended the war as a captain, having transferred from the Red Cross to headquarters' staff and, later, the Secret Service. He was twice mentioned in despatches. Roland Foster noted: 'It has always puzzled me why he did not receive a knighthood, because apart from his military service he was, like his wife, an Ambassador of Empire in the truest sense.'[90] Once the war was over, they resumed their imperial tours. In 1919, they toured Canada, the United States, New Zealand and Australia, to great enthusiasm. In Canada they found themselves booked to give a concert in Calgary on the same night as Dame Nellie Melba. Embarrassment was overcome by having a joint supper reception for them both after their concerts. Many patrons went to the first half of one and the second half of the other. The two Dames were conspicuously gracious to each other.[91] In 1923 there was another tour of Canada and the USA. Ivor Newton accompanied her:

> Wherever Clara Butt went, she was treated as the Queen of Song. In a hotel the manager himself would bring the register to her suite for signature. On trains she travelled in her own private compartment and top-hatted station-masters guided her to her place.[92]

In 1927 she was prominent in helping Commander Locker-Lamson to arrange his great anti-Communist rallies. At the end of 1927 on a private visit to India, she gave three big concerts. She visited Tagore, Annie Besant and Gandhi, singing *Abide With Me* at the latter's evening prayers. She was a guest of the viceroy, various provincial governors and of the great Ranjitsinhji, otherwise the Jam Sahib of Nawanagar, the first coloured cricketer to play for England. She sang the national anthem at a great banquet he held. According to Winifred Ponder, 'The effect Dame Clara Butt produced in India by understanding sympathy, as well as by her singing, cannot but have been of the highest values at the present difficult stage in Indian affairs. Press comment several times spoke of her "doing great national work" in this regard.'[93]

Dame Clara's final years were darkened by tragedy. She developed bone cancer and was often in great pain. Both her sons died. The elder son, then at Eton, died of meningitis in the summer of 1923 and the younger died while farming in Rhodesia in 1934. But Clara carried on, recording almost to the end and undertaking a final tour of Australia. She died on 23 January 1936 in the same week as Kipling and King George V, an extraordinary trio of imperial luminaries. As Roland Foster recorded:

> It is strange that three great figures who formed connecting links with the reigns of Queen Victoria and King Edward VII should have passed

away within a few days of one another – first Rudyard Kipling, the poet of Empire; then the King himself, ruler over that Empire; and finally Clara Butt, who did so much to kindle the fires of patriotism . . . wherever she went.[94]

In addition to her love of nation and Empire, she was deeply religious. She was a Christian Scientist and spoke frequently of the value and importance of religion. The power and beauty of her voice and her religious repertoire led one leading cleric to call her 'one of the greatest missionaries of our time'.[95]

In its obituary tribute *The Musical Times* said: 'The wonderful volume and steadiness of her voice, the ease and skill with which she directed it and her striking personality, all combined to make her the best known and most popular vocalist of the day', conceding that her strength lay 'in the breadth and simplicity of style rather than in range of interpretation . . . she was more in her element in the older oratorios and songs of the ballad type than in the more sophisticated side of her art'.[96] It was this combination of talent, personality, repertoire and belief in God, King and Empire that made her such a potent force for imperial unity.

Notes

1 Jeffrey Richards, *Visions of Yesterday*, London: Routledge, 1973, p. 10.
2 James Morris, *Pax Britannica*, London: Faber, 1968, p. 200.
3 Emma Albani, *Forty Years of Song*, London: Mills & Boon, 1911, catalogue p. 3.
4 *Ibid.*, p. 122.
5 *Ibid.*, pp. 212–13.
6 *Ibid.*, p. 71.
7 *Ibid.*, p. 200.
8 *Ibid.*, pp. 63, 68.
9 *Ibid.*, pp. 83, 109, 203, 107.
10 *Ibid.*, p. 94.
11 *Ibid.*, p. 205.
12 *Ibid.*, pp. 89–90.
13 *Ibid.*, p. 197.
14 *Ibid.*, p. 49.
15 *Ibid.*, pp. 269, 267, 270, 182, 216.
16 *Ibid.*, p. 263.
17 *Ibid.*, p. 267.
18 *Ibid.*, p. 270.
19 Roland Foster, *Come Listen to My Song*, London: Collins, 1949, p. 37.
20 Desmond Shawe-Taylor, 'Dame Nellie Melba', in Stanley Sadie (ed.), *The New Grove Dictionary of Music and Musicians*, London: Macmillan, 1995, vol.12, p. 100.
21 Nellie Melba, *Melodies and Memories*, London: Hamish Hamilton, 1980 (1925), p. 49.
22 *Ibid.*, pp. 1, 225.
23 Ivor Newton, *At the Piano*, London: Hamish Hamilton, 1966, p. 99.
24 John Hetherington, *Melba*, London: Faber, 1967, p. 22.

25 Melba, *Melodies and Memories*, pp. 52–4.
26 Agnes Murphy, *Melba: A Biography*, London: Chatto & Windus, 1919, p. 178.
27 Melba, *Melodies and Memories*, pp. 29, 80, 122, 217.
28 Hetherington, *Melba*, pp. 110, 201.
29 Melba, *Melodies and Memories*, p. 220.
30 Murphy, *Melba*, p. 190.
31 Hetherington, *Melba*, p. 115.
32 Melba, *Melodies and Memories*, pp. 178–9.
33 Hetherington, *Melba*, p. 179.
34 Thérèse Radic, *Melba: The Voice of Australia*, Basingstoke: Macmillan, 1986, p. 137.
35 *Ibid.*, p. 157.
36 Hetherington, *Melba*, p. 250.
37 Melba, *Melodies and Memories*, p. 232.
38 Radic, *Melba*, pp. 126–7.
39 Hetherington, *Melba*, p. 217.
40 Radic, *Melba*, p. 22.
41 Melba, *Melodies and Memories*, p. 185.
42 *Ibid.*, p. 219.
43 Sir Landon Ronald, *Myself and Others*, London: Sampson Low, Marston & Co., 1931, p. 168.
44 Gerald Moore, *Am I Too Loud?*, London: Hamish Hamilton, 1962, p. 62.
45 Peter Dawson, *Fifty Years of Song*, London: Hutchinson, 1951, p. 190.
46 Newton, *At the Piano*, pp. 100–1.
47 Melba, *Melodies and Memories*, p. 141.
48 Radic, *Melba*, p. 4.
49 Henry J. Wood, *My Life of Music*, London: Victor Gollancz, 1938, p. 41; *Dictionary of National Biography*, 'Dame Clara Butt', Compact Edition, Oxford: Oxford University Press, 1975, p. 2546.
50 Foster, *Come Listen*, p. 170.
51 Dawson, *Fifty Years*, p. 191.
52 Newton, *At the Piano*, pp. 99, 83–4.
53 Foster, *Come Listen*, p. 171.
54 Winifred Ponder, *Clara Butt: Her Life Story*, London: Harrap, 1928, p. 72.
55 *Ibid.*, p. 193.
56 Newton, *At the Piano*, p. 82.
57 Ponder, *Clara Butt*, p. 177.
58 *Ibid.*, p. 188.
59 *Ibid.*, p. 99.
60 Wood, *My Life of Music*, p. 41.
61 Foster, *Come Listen*, p. 171.
62 Ponder, *Clara Butt*, p. 134.
63 Foster, *Come Listen*, p. 171.
64 Newton, *At the Piano*, pp. 77–8.
65 *Ibid.*, p. 82.
66 Foster, *Come Listen*, p. 135.
67 Newton, *At the Piano*, p. 83.
68 Ponder, *Clara Butt*, p. 181.
69 *Ibid.*, p. 182.
70 *Ibid.*, p. 186.
71 *Ibid.*, p. 189.
72 *Ibid.*
73 *Ibid.*, p. 197.
74 *Ibid.*
75 *Ibid.*
76 *Ibid.*, p. 198.
77 Newton, *At the Piano*, p. 75.

78 Ponder, *Clara Butt*, pp. 125–6.
79 *Ibid.*, pp. 139–40.
80 *Ibid.*, p. 139.
81 Foster, *Come Listen*, p. 161.
82 *Ibid.*, p. 169.
83 *Ibid.*, p. 162.
84 Ponder, *Clara Butt*, p. 164.
85 *Ibid.*, pp. 167–8.
86 *The Times*, 9 May, 1916.
87 *The Times*, 19 July, 1916.
88 *The Times*, 3 July, 1916.
89 Ponder, *Clara Butt*, p. 169.
90 Foster, *Come Listen*, p. 171.
91 Ponder, *Clara Butt*, pp. 248–50; Newton, *At the Piano*, pp. 73–4.
92 Newton, *At the Piano*, pp. 75–6.
93 Ponder, *Clara Butt*, p. 254.
94 Foster, *Come Listen*, p. 170.
95 Ponder, *Clara Butt*, p. 17.
96 *The Musical Times*, March 1, 1936.

CHAPTER FIFTEEN

The troubadour of Empire:
Peter Dawson

It is often said that interest in the Empire waned after the First World War and that the general population was never much interested anyway. This is conclusively refuted by the career of bass-baritone Peter Dawson, who perfectly demonstrates the validity of the idea of each individual having multiple identity, outlined in chapter two. In the heyday of the Empire, it was possible to combine diverse identities without tension or incongruity. Peter Dawson was the great exemplar of this, being able to be simultaneously Australian, Scottish and British and to express these identities both separately and within the overall context of a truly imperial patriotism through the medium of song.

Peter Dawson was born on 31 January 1882 in Adelaide, South Australia, the eighth of the ten children of Thomas and Alison Dawson. Both his parents were Scottish and Thomas, originally from Kirkcaldy and later a seaman, had settled in Adelaide in 1863 and established a plumbing business. Alison Dawson ensured that all the children had musical training and Peter made his debut as a boy soprano at St Peter's Town Hall, Adelaide, at the age of 7. He joined the choir of St Andrew's Presbyterian Church, Wakefield Street, Adelaide, at 16 and studied singing with C.J. Stevens, founder and conductor of the Adelaide Choral Society. He began appearing in singing competitions and concerts, garnering appreciative notices. But when he left school, Peter joined the family firm as an apprentice plumber. Stevens, convinced that his pupil had a future as a singer, persuaded his reluctant father to send Peter to England to study. He sailed for England in 1902 and was taken on by the eminent British singer Sir Charles Santley with whom he studied for three years. Subsequently, the Russian singing specialist Professor Kantorez extended his range from one of E flat to D to one of E flat to A, converting him from a bass to a bass-baritone. Santley persuaded Madame Emma Albani to include Dawson in her touring concert party in 1904 and this launched him on his professional career. In 1909 he appeared in *The Mastersingers* at Covent Garden but he disliked singing in opera, considering it 'too much work for too little pay'.[1] On the other hand he enjoyed singing in oratorio, *Messiah* being a particular favourite, and in Gilbert and Sullivan he participated in the complete recordings of *Iolanthe*, *The Pirates of Penzance*, *The Yeomen of the Guard* and *Patience*. But he concentrated on his concert career, and by the 1920s had established himself as the leading ballad singer in Britain. Gerald Moore, who accompanied Dawson both on concert tours and on recordings for gramophone, recalled:

> Peter's sturdy frame and ruddy appearance belonged to an open air type of man: this was his nature and it came out in his singing . . . his *métier* was the ballad . . . I do not think anybody could sing such songs better than he, for he possessed a voice of such fine manly quality, had a good technique and . . . these straightforward songs came to him naturally.[2]

Dawson's singing was always characterized by a clarity of diction, a sincere and robust delivery and a consistently appropriate and never overstated emotional colouring.

While the majority of his appearances were in concert halls – and he appeared regularly in Sir Henry Wood's Promenade concerts, the Crystal Palace concerts and Chappell's ballad concerts – he also performed with success in the music halls and variety theatres, topping the bill at the London Palladium, playing thus to both middle- and working-class audiences. In addition, he toured extensively both in the British Isles and throughout the Empire. He never sang in the United States but undertook ten tours of Australia and six of New Zealand. He received a rapturous reception on his first return to Australia in 1909–10. He also toured South Africa, India, Burma and the Straits settlements.

Despite his touring, he admitted that he had become a household name as a result of his recording career. He wrote in 1951:

> My reputation as a gramophone artist was the dominating success of my career as a singer. Despite the many tours I made throughout the British Isles and the Empire, during the first twenty years of my career, there is no doubt that many more people know me through my gramophone records than my concerts.[3]

Latterly the wireless had joined the gramophone record as a means of reaching the widest possible public with songs. He was in no doubt of the value of these media:

Before the advent of the talking machine the musical knowledge of the masses was extremely limited . . . Today, thanks to the success of the gramophone and wireless, a vast public has become interested: good music and singing is heard regularly over the air. And make no mistake the operas and symphonies are really enjoyed by those people who we then referred to as 'the masses'.[4]

Dawson's view of his role and his material was clear and emphatic:

I regard myself as a singer of the people, and therefore understand what they need and expect. And let me say at once that their taste is not low. Sing good songs to them in the 'right' way and they will like and appreciate it. They are impatient of mannerisms and affectations. Above all they love words: a story in song.[5]

Clarity of diction, he believed, was one of 'the fundamental reasons for my success'.[6] He declared:

The greatest fault of modern singers is in their words – or lack of them . . . yet in my opinion the words of a song are quite as important as the music . . . a song is meant to tell a story – however simple it may be – and if the listeners cannot hear the words they will certainly not appreciate the song . . . It is only by experience that a singer learns to give to the story that he sings the same attention that he gives to the voice in which he is singing it. To make a success . . . a singer must get inside his song. His voice must be focused upon the story of the song.[7]

When choosing a new song, Dawson would recite the words aloud and if they appealed, he would sing them. He believed in singing in English even though he could sing, and had sung, in German, Italian, French, Russian and Spanish: 'Forty years' experience of British audiences has satisfied me that the vast majority of the British public like, or prefer, to understand the words of the song to which they are listening.'[8]

Dawson was in no doubt that the gramophone and the wireless had raised the standard of musical education:

What a revolution has taken place in the musical education of the peoples of the world! And that the public in Britain and the Empire are now sincere music lovers is proved by the immense increase in the sales of gramophone records of the better class music, such as piano concertos, orchestral symphonies, operatic *arias*, oratorios, art songs and the fine songs of some of the modern composers. Yes, we owe a great debt to the fine work of the B.B.C. in this direction, and for the magnificent recordings of the gramophone companies.[9]

He admired 'the wonderful progress made by the gramophone and the phenomenal advance made by wireless broadcasting', but admitted to

[497]

regret that the 'old fashioned homely function known as "the musical evening" when everybody must sing or play, has practically ceased to exist. I think it is a pity in some ways, for there are few pleasures like producing one's own music'.[10]

Dawson made his first recordings for the Edison Bell Company in 1904, his first record being a song called *Navajo* which was attributed to Leonard Dawson. It was the beginning of a continuous recording career stretching from 1904 to 1958. Initially he sang for a variety of record labels and under a variety of names. Most frequently he sang under his own name but he also recorded comic songs as Will Strong, light popular songs as Frank Danby and Scottish songs as Hector Grant. He signed for HMV in 1906 and sang exclusively for that label from 1912 to 1953, recording on the popular Plum Label rather than the more upmarket Red Label. By 1934 212 of his solo titles were in the HMV catalogue and his recording contract earned him £3,500 annually. In his autobiography he estimated that he had recorded 3,500 songs and sold some 13 million copies.[11] Subsequent estimates suggest sales of 25 million copies during his career.[12]

He made his wireless debut on the BBC on Australia Day, 26 January 1923, followed by a carol concert on 20 December 1924. He was to become a regular participant in the BBC's annual Australia Day concerts. Between 1930 and 1938 he broadcast thirty-two times and in 1938 and 1947 appeared on the fledgling BBC television service. In 1950 he made ten pre-recorded programmes for radio entitled *Fifty Years of Song* to be broadcast by the BBC's Light Programme in connection with the Festival of Britain. He also appeared in two films, *Chips* (1938), for which he also composed the music, and *Okay For Sound* (1938).

His recorded repertoire included popular classics. Among his personal favourites were *Largo al Factotum* from Rossini's *The Barber of Seville*, Mussorgsky's *Song of the Flea*, the prologue to *Pagliacci* and Mendelssohn's *I Am a Roamer*. But he also recorded Wagner's *O Star of Eve* from *Tannhauser*, *The Sword Song* and *Oh, My Warriors* from Elgar's *Caractacus*, *Iago's Creed* from Verdi's *Otello*, *Even Bravest Heart May Swell* from Gounod's *Faust*, Schubert's *The Erlking*, *Now Your Days of Philandering Are Over* from Mozart's *Marriage of Figaro* and a range of popular Handel arias such as *Honour and Arms*, *O Ruddier Than the Cherry* and *Why Do the Nations So Furiously Rage Together?*

Alongside these he recorded songs from current popular stage and film successes, shows such as *Maid of the Mountains*, *A Southern Maid*, *Sally*, *Our Miss Gibbs*, *Showboat* and *Chu Chin Chow*. Such showstoppers as *Stouthearted Men* from *New Moon* and *The*

Mounties' Song from *Rose Marie* were particularly suited to his style. When he recorded in the mid-1930s *Saddle Your Blues to an Old Mustang* and *We Saw the Sea*, he received, he recalled, hundreds of letters abusing him for wasting his talent – but the records sold well, he performed the songs with all the care and skill he put into the arias, and they stressed his range and his importance as what would now be called a cross-over artist who can move with ease between classical and popular music.[13]

He had a particular fondness for English *lieder*, writing that we had *lieder* 'every whit as good, as tuneful and musically profound as that of the German; and a dozen or more composers who have written and are writing songs of a standard which has probably not been reached in Britain since the Elizabethan era'.[14] He cited in particular John Ireland, C. Armstrong Gibbs, Thomas Dunhill and Roger Quilter, and he included in his permanent repertoire James Dear's *Sherwood*, Armstrong Gibbs's *Silver*, Vaughan Williams's *Orpheus With His Lute* and Somervell's *In Summertime on Bredon*. He recorded several of Vaughan Williams's *Songs of Travel*, and sang the role of the sergeant in the original recording of Vaughan Williams's folk-opera *Hugh the Drover*.

But his output showed the continuous imprint of the imperial cluster of values: patriotism, monarchism, militarism, racism, manliness, Protestantism and chivalry. His was a truly imperial patriotism. Throughout his life he remained a devoted and patriotic Australian. His Australian accompanist Will James described him as 'typically Australian in spirit, speech and attitude'.[15] But this in no way conflicted with his love of Britain, which he always referred to as 'the old country'.

He sang regularly and feelingly about Australia both in Australia and in Britain, and Australian songs were part and parcel of his repertoire both in Britain and throughout the Empire. He recorded, in England in 1938 and in New Zealand in 1942, Australia's unofficial national song *Waltzing Matilda*, an old army marching tune arranged by Marie Cowan and set to words by A.B. 'Banjo' Paterson and Cowan detailing the pursuit of a 'swagman' by a trooper. Dawson himself set several of Edward Harrington's Australian lyrics: the grim and powerful *Lasseter's Last Ride*; *The Bushrangers*, charting the dark deeds and eventual punishment of the Kelly Gang, and *Black Swan*; as well as Louis Esson's *Whalin' Up the Lachlan* and Mrs P. Carroll's *Grey Shades of Cobb and Co*. Mrs Carroll herself sent him *Grey Shades*, a celebration of the pioneer Australian stagecoach line, and he recalled: 'When I started to set the lines to music the words formed themselves into fantastic chordings and melody, underlying the soul of the country. I worked very hard to do justice to her fine lines.'[16] He also arranged for Australian poet Lindsay Gordon's six Australian *Bush Songs* to be adapted as song lyrics by the accomplished British lyricist Edward Lockton and set to music by his Australian accompanist Will James. He then recorded five of the six in London in 1927. Ironically, Lockton himself had never been to Australia. Instead he borrowed books on Australia from Australia House and immersed himself in the appropriate atmosphere to undertake the work.[17]

Dawson recorded and strongly advocated the virtues of *Song of Australia*, Carl Linger's 1859 composition, with words by Carol Carleton, as the Australian national anthem. He recorded it in London in 1932, and it sold widely in Australia:

> There is a land where, floating free,
> From mountain top to girdling sea,
> A proud flag waves exultingly – exultingly,
> And Freedom's sons the banner bear,
> No shackled slave can breathe the air,
> Fairest of Britain's daughters fair – Australia.

Dawson lamented that it was being contested by a rival, Peter Dodds McCormick's 1878 *Advance, Australia Fair*, which he claimed he had always declined to record.[18] In fact his memory failed him on this. He did record it, in London in 1931. *Advance, Australia Fair* also stressed the imperial link. The first verse recalled that 'gallant Cook from Albion sailed' to plant on Australian soil 'Old England's flag, the standard of the brave', affirming 'with all her faults, we love her still, Britannia rules the waves'. It goes on to celebrate the beauty and prosperity of the country, and promises that

> Beneath our radiant Southern Cross
> We'll toil with heart and hand
> To make our youthful commonwealth a prosperous happy land.

It was formally adopted as the Australian national anthem in 1974. Dawson himself also set to music Henry Baxter's *Australia – Home of the Brave and Free*.

His Australia is a land of cattlemen, pioneers, emigrants, gold prospectors, bush-rangers. But it is also a beautiful landscape, whose sights and sounds are regularly evoked: the bush, the rolling plains, the gum trees, the sprigs of wattle, the Southern Cross, the clear blue skies, kangaroos and koalas. It is a land of freedom, but of freedom within the Empire. All these aspects are memorably captured in the six Australian *Bush Songs*, five of which Dawson recorded. They constitute a superb series of sound pictures of Australia: the rousing call to action and the ride to *The Land of 'Who Knows Where'*; *Bush Silence*, the wistful and lilting evocation of the vast, wild, beautiful landscape; *Comrades of Mine*, a robust celebration of the joys of mateship and call for burial in that landscape where old memories can be lived after death; *Bush Night Song*, an evocative Australian nocturne, and *The Stockrider's Song*, an exuberant account of the ride home, the music evoking the galloping rhythm of the horses' hooves, after delivering the cattle to Queensland. After the heat, the dust storms and the long hard ride, they are 'riding, riding, riding home again' with a song on their lips and joy in their hearts.

The First World War saw Dawson stressing Australia's imperial connection. In 1917 he recorded in London Matson's solemn march *Australia*, hymning the soldiers coming from Australia and marching to glory, leaving friends, wives and sweethearts behind, for 'We must fight old England's foes'. He sang: 'In Belgium, France and the Dardanelles Australia has done her part and written her name in the scroll of fame that is dear old England's heart'; 'nothing can stop our daring boys when a stiff job lies ahead' and 'we will conquer or die with the men we have got from Australia'. As late as 1958 he was recording Ford's *Anzac Memorium*, singing in celebration of the glorious dead of Australia's participation in two world wars, the Southern Cross in the sky a reminder of the ultimate sacrifice of Christ and the need to maintain what they fought for. It is punctuated by a bugler blowing *The Last Post*.

The Second World War prompted an upsurge of patriotic songs, of which Dawson recorded and indeed wrote his fair share. Jackson's *Song of Australia* (recorded in 1940) celebrated the spirit of 'our valiant fathers' who came to settle 'in peaceful quest' and left 'this heritage of freedom to live for evermore' in Australia, 'mighty country of the free – thy heritage the noblest page of Empire's history', a call to faith and duty to defend the freedom bequeathed by the fathers, a wartime call to action in an imperial war. In the same year in Australia Dawson recorded Cohan's cheerful and catchy *Swinging Along the Road to Victory*, declaring: 'We mean to keep our Empire free' and 'we march beneath the Union Jack unfurled'. It mentions all the forces, army, navy, airforce and nurses, enlisted in the Empire's fight for freedom. Dawson himself composed and recorded in 1941 the equally jolly and upbeat *V for Victory*, based on the BBC radio signal utilizing the first notes of Beethoven's *Symphony No. 5*: 'Say it, sing it, play it, swing it, V for Victory.'

His deep love of Australia is attested in his solemn setting of Farrell's *This Land O'Mine* recorded in 1941: 'This land o'mine; this home of mine, this place on earth supremely blessed' and his lyrical setting of Lawson's *The Waratah and the Wattle* (recorded in 1958): 'Australia, Australia, most beautiful name, most kindly and bountiful land, I would die every death that might save her from shame.' In Dodd's *From the Outback to the Ocean* (recorded in 1951) he sang: 'From the outback to the ocean . . . it's the fairest land I know', 'a paradise on earth . . . Australia the most beautiful, the country of my birth'. The singing resounds with the same pride and sincerity with which he invested his musical settings.

Dawson's own conduct testifies to his imperial patriotism. By an extraordinary coincidence he was in Australia at the time of the outbreak of both the First and the Second World War. He was giving a concert at Goulburn, New South Wales, when the news of the declaration of war, on 4 August 1914, was received. Dawson announced the news to the audience from the stage. He recalled later:

> Their reaction was remarkable. Everyone started to cheer, and someone started to sing 'God Save the King', which the accompanist soon led with the piano. More cheering, and then 'Rule Britannia' was sung. More excitement and cheering, and again we all sang 'God Save the King'.[19]

The audience then dispersed. Dawson returned to England at once, anxious to help, and turned his talents to singing on behalf of war charities, fund-raising for War Comforts Funds and War Loan, and touring the hospitals to entertain wounded soldiers. But, anxious to do more, he returned to Australia, enlisted in the army as a private and, after training, was sent on a recruiting drive: 'I recounted many stories of how even the women of Britain were working, and how every man Jack in the old country was doing his best to pull off a victory.'[20] The Armistice was declared before he could see active service, and he returned to England to resume his career.

He was in Australia again when the Second World War broke out, and he remained there for the duration. At 57 he was too old to serve, and he resumed directorial duties at Thomas Dawson and Son, producing tins for military use, but he also toured the country in support of war funds and loan rallies, giving concerts for the American troops when they arrived. He welcomed their arrival: 'We know that the Old Country had her hands too full to be able to help us with troops.'[21] In 1942 he toured New Zealand. He wrote and recorded the war song *V for Victory* which he claimed to have been 'the biggest seller of any song in the history of Australia'; and he made a nationwide recruitment speech on ABC radio of which he was sufficiently proud to include it in his autobiography and which testified to his imperial patriotism.

In this war, which we are ultimately going to win, much depends on the young men of this great country, who are at present, for some reason or other, standing aloof and with deaf ears to the urgent call of King and Country.

The stoic heroism displayed by the British Expeditionary Force in its fight against overwhelming odds in Belgium and France is surely sufficient inspiration to every eligible person in the Commonwealth to rush headlong to the colours.

The response by the flower of the manhood of this country up to now has been magnificent, but not enough. This hanging back by the eligible men, this 'watching the other fellow do it' is a fatal mistake.

It has been said that Great Britain has always won the last battle. It has also been said that in the event of Nazi victory, America would protect Australia. *Don't you believe it.* Should such a calamity as a Nazi victory overtake us, it would be the end of us, and of everything worth living for.

Are you content to stand by complacently, and with the thought that everything will come right in the end? No I think not!

You are made of better stuff than that!

Nazi domination would be the end of the Christian era, and the cruel extermination of the British race. We are of the British race, and it is up to all of us to defend ourselves. The Nazis are out for world domination, just as Bismarck and Kaiser Bill were. Remember, there's only one good German, and he hasn't reached the ground from his burning bomber!

Unity is wanted here. Cut out party politics, and install a system of 'all for all'. How often have you joined together in singing:

> Rule, Britannia. Britannia rule the waves,
> Britons never, never never shall be slaves.

See to it, my countrymen. Would you care to see the Nazis come to our beautiful shores, to practise their well-known system of extermination by murder, and the rape of our womenfolk? Yes. Yes. It *is* as serious as that.

And it's now or never. It is up to you to join the mighty throng to liberate us all from the Nazi menace.

So, Johnny . . . get your gun . . . It's NOW OR NEVER!

He added: 'It served its purpose in rallying great numbers to the recruiting offices throughout the country.'[22] Of the war he wrote:

We were . . . sustained by the example of Britain. To say that we were proud of Britain would be an understatement. By this time we were overwhelmed with deep and sincere admiration and glad that we too were of the British race.[23]

This patriotism took artistic form in Dawson's determination always, or wherever possible, to sing in English and to promote British songs:

I have made a speciality of songs by British composers, and I find that audiences really enjoy them. They appeal irresistibly to the intelligence and although they demand a great deal of patience and practice I am sure that other artists would find it well worth their while to give good British songs a more prominent part of their repertoire.[24]

Although Australia was the major focus of his repertoire, he did not neglect the other dominions. He recorded the Maori song *Waiata Poi* ('Tiny Ball on End of String'), a setting by Alfred Hill of a traditional Maori song. He first sang it in 1914 but it became a hit in 1947 at about the same time as Gracie Fields made a hit of another Maori song adapted as *Now Is the Hour*, successes that may owe something to the post-war surge of interest in emigration to New Zealand. He adored New Zealand ('I found a remarkable spirit of *camaraderie* and its people exhibit a spontaneous friendliness that is lacking in so many other countries today') and the Maoris, singing to them in Maori *It's a Long Way to Tipperary* and *For He's a Jolly Good Fellow* as well as *Waiata Poi*.[25] He recorded in London in 1924 the New Zealand anthem *God Defend New Zealand*, ending it with *God Save the King*, again stressing the imperial connection. During the First World War, he recorded *Home, Canada, Home* and *Canada, March On* to celebrate the Canadian contribution to the Great War.

Monarchism

Dawson was a convinced monarchist, recalling with pride his meetings with members of the royal family and the fact that both King George VI and the Prince of Wales had collections of his records, as indeed did British Prime Ministers Churchill, Asquith, Bonar Law, Ramsay Macdonald and Stanley Baldwin, and the Australian Prime Minister John Curtin.[26] In his 1951 autobiography, he was at pains to stress that the new Australian Governor-General William McKell, although a 'rough diamond', firmly maintained 'loyalty to the throne'.[27]

Dawson recorded *God Save the King* in 1911 and in 1923 the newly composed *He's the Greatest Lad We've Ever Had* by O'Hara, a celebration of the Prince of Wales:

When you're looking for a man to lead the Empire to her goal,
When you're looking for a man to grip the Empire's very soul,
There is one renowned from sea to sea who nobly plays his part.
With the magic charm of youth, he holds the key to every heart
For the greatest lad we've ever had is the lad we're glad to know,
The greatest lad the Empire's had, that's why we love him so.

[504]

He is a true-born sportsman who plays the game
If winning or losing, his smile is the same.
So may he live – the greatest lad we've ever had –
God bless the Prince of Wales.

So we get the Empire, the monarchy and the 'gentlemanly code' fused in one person.

To celebrate the Coronation of King George VI, he recorded in 1936 a medley of patriotic songs, *Britain's Heritage*, which included *Hearts of Oak*, *Boys of the Old Brigade*, *Soldiers of the King*, *Private Tommy Atkins*, *The British Grenadiers*, *Red, White and Blue*, *The Lads in Navy Blue*, *Rule, Britannia* and *Here's a Health Unto His Majesty*. The provenance of the majority of these songs in the eighteenth and nineteenth centuries again stresses the continuity of the ideas of duty, service, patriotism and imperial commitment in the popular musical culture. Adams's *The Veteran's Song* (recorded in 1932) stresses loyalty to the crown. It opens with fanfare and drumbeat, and tells of an old veteran with a wooden leg and failing sight, who wants to stand to attention at his window as the King passes by: 'The King, the King is coming, Long Live the King, don't you hear the cheering, God bless the King is the nation's loving cry.' He declares: 'I fought for his dear old father – and I'd fight again for him', and bursts with pride when he hears the King say to his Marshal: 'Thank God when the young lads fall, sir/ We still have the brave old boys.'

Protestantism

The Protestantism underpinning the Empire found a full expression in Dawson's repertoire, as he recorded both hymns and sacred songs. He listed among his personal favourite songs *The Lost Chord*, *The Holy City*, *There Is a Green Hill Far Away*, *Christ Is Risen*, *Jerusalem*, *Nazareth*, *Bless This House*, *I Heard a Forest Praying*, *None But the Weary Heart* and *Little Prayer I Love*.[28] At the special request of Alba Rizzi, composer of *Little Prayer I Love*, he sang the song at her funeral. He recorded them all, along with Albert Ketélbey's *The Sanctuary of the Heart*, *The Sacred Hour* and *In a Monastery Garden*, and such well-loved hymns as J.B. Dykes's settings of *Nearer, My God, To Thee*, *Eternal Father, Strong to Save* and *Lead, Kindly Light*, Richard Redhead's setting of *Rock of Ages* and Bantock's setting of *The Lord Is My Shepherd*. He wrote and recorded his own hymn *The Lord Is King*. There was also an intriguing novelty, Lt Colonel J. MacKenzie-Rogan's *Church Parade*, which he conducted with the Band of the Coldstream Guards and Dawson and Ernest Pike singing. It consisted of some jaunty assemblage and dispersal music, church bells, an orchestral version of *I Know That My Redeemer Liveth* and Dawson and Pike singing in duet *Now Thank We All Our God* and *Christ Who Once For Sinners Bled*.

Gentlemanliness

Peter Dawson valued gentlemanliness, writing: 'There is no man quite like the cultured English gentleman. They are sincere, lacking in "side" and are wonderfully natural to all – whatever class – they meet.'[29] In India, where he found the Anglo-Indians intolerably snobbish, the social gulf between the army, the civil service and the businessmen likewise 'most distasteful' and declared that the segregation of clubs and dances 'just made me writhe',[30] he admired Lord Ronaldshay, the Governor-General, and Lord Lloyd, the Governor of Bombay, because they were gentlemen. Dawson described his teacher Sir Charles Santley as 'a grand English gentleman of the same culture as Sir Charles Villiers Stanford, Sir Walford Davies, Sir Edward Elgar and Sir Alexander Mackenzie'.[31] As a matter of fact, of these only Elgar was English: Stanford was Irish, Davies Welsh and Mackenzie Scottish. But, as so often in the heyday of Empire, *English* in this context meant *British*.

England

The England of which Dawson sang with such feeling and fondness was an idealized pre-industrial England, not the England of the industrial north nor that of the commercial metropolis but a rural and a seacoast England. It was an eighteenth-century England of dashing highwaymen (*Gentleman Jim*), daring smugglers (Kipling's *The Smugglers' Song* and *The Smugglers* by Popple) and scarlet-coated huntsmen riding to hounds (*Chorus, Gentlemen*), and a sixteenth-century England of Elizabethan seadogs, which he celebrated in his recordings of *Drake's Drum, Devon, O Devon, Drake Is Going West* and *Drake*, all hymning the Devon seadog who was in the vanguard of imperial pioneers.

Although there was a nod to Cumberland in *D'Ye Ken John Peel* (recorded in 1917), it was specifically a west-country England, celebrated most famously in *Glorious Devon, The Green Hills of Somerset, Devonshire Cream and Cider* and *The Cornish Floral Dance. The Cornish Floral Dance*, composed by Katie Moss after participating in the 'Furry Dance' at Helston, was the most popular of all Dawson's recordings. It sold more copies than any of his other recordings, was one of the most requested by audiences and was sung all round the Empire. Dawson himself thought that the *Floral Dance, Waiata Poi* and *Waltzing Matilda* were among his most successful songs because he put into them his love of Cornwall, New Zealand and the Maoris, and the Australian bush.[32] The song itself, aside from its insistent and captivating rhythm, is about the integration of an outsider into a celebration in a 'quaint old Cornish town'. The whole town is dancing, lovers are kissing, and 'I felt so lonely standing there' until a girl whirls him into the throng. The outsider is incorporated into the joyous, loving, communal celebration in a triumphant affirmation of tradition, rurality and communality.

Glorious Devon (words by Sir Harold Boulton and music by Edward German), while celebrating the joys of the countryside ('beetling cliffs by the surging main, rich red loam for the plough') and bygone heroes ('spirits of old world heroes wake, Grenville, Hawkins, Raleigh and Drake'), also stresses the manliness of the west-country man:

> Devon's the fount of the bravest blood
> That braces England's breed,
> Her maidens fair as the apple bud,
> And her men are men indeed.

It hymns the English racial diaspora and its imperial links:

> To ev'ry land the wide world o'er
> Some slips of the old stock roam,
> Real friends in peace, dread foes in war,
> With hearts still true to home.

There were two other songs particularly associated with Dawson, both of them hit songs from operettas that acquired an independent life of their own. Dawson recorded them both in 1929. *The Yeomen of England* came from the Edward German–Basil Hood operetta *Merrie England* (1902), a celebration of Elizabeth I and her England, and *The Fishermen of England* (1921) from the Montague Phillips–Gerald Dalton operetta *The Rebel Maid*, set in Devonshire amid the preparations of the local Protestants to welcome William of Orange and overthrow the tyranny of the Catholic King James II. The yeomen of England are the medieval bowmen who cherish English freedom – and where are they today? 'In homestead and the cottage they still dwell in England', an affirmation of the sturdy rural yeoman as the heart of England. In Phillips's rousing song, the fishermen of England similarly guard the liberties of the nation:

In tiny vessels they defy the perils of the deep
And scan the waters' dreary wastes with eyes that never sleep
[. . .]
And when the foes of England assail in fury blind
The children of the storm arise and leave their nets behind,
With merry oath and laughter and a smile upon their lips,
The fishermen of England go down to the sea in ships.

One significant sub-genre that Dawson also mastered and which was immensely popular in the interwar period was the song of the open road: songs celebrating freedom from restriction and responsibilities, lauding the fresh air and beauty of the countryside and highlighting the carefree life of the tramp, a key figure of interwar mythology who could be a figure of menace – deracinated, light-fingered, potentially violent – but could also be a romanticized free soul in touch with the true heart of England. It was a significant element of the rural myth which was part of the powerful cultural reaction to industrialization and urbanization.[33]

These songs, usually set to a tramping rhythm, were invariably tuneful, cheerful and evocative. Emblematic of them is Pat Thayer's *I Travel the Road* (recorded in 1931):

> My garden the gorse, my carpet the flowers,
> I travel the road, who cares.
> My candle the moon, my pillow the flowers,
> My slumber the night owl shares,
> A lark in the sky to call me at dawn,
> The scent of the breeze to wish me good morn,
> A gypsy am I, a wandering by, I travel the road, who cares.

In similar vein and equally tuneful were his recordings of Valerie May's *Song of the Highway*, Arale and Paul Andrew's *The Winding Road*, Samuel's *Jogging Along the Highway*, Lockton and Drummond's *The Gay Highway*, Gleeson's *The Tramp's Song* and Vaughan Williams's *The Vagabond*. Holloway's *Two Old Tramps* had the added poignancy of dealing with two Great War veterans, shabby and down-at-heel, but wearing their medals and 'tramping along as we did before, singing the songs that won the war'.

Scotland

Dawson's Scottish background remained important to him. He still had close relatives in Scotland. His uncle, Captain James Dawson, who lived in Glasgow, owned the Rock Shipping Line. Early in his career Dawson recorded under the pseudonym Hector Grant what would now be called cover versions of Harry Lauder's popular Scottish songs for Zonophone, a subsidiary label of HMV. In 1906, short of money, he toured the music halls as Hector Grant, complete with kilt and tam o'shanter, doing a Scottish comedy and singing act. He also composed his own ersatz Scottish songs such as *Lassie, Dinna Sigh For Me* and *Sandy, You're a Dandy* under the pen name of Hector Grant.

In his recording heyday, he recorded Josiah Booth's tribute to Scotland's national poet, *The Star O'Rabbie Burns, Auld Lang Syne,* Lady Nairne's *The Auld Hoose,* the traditional air *Turn Ye Tae Me* set to words by Christopher North and a medley of traditional songs, including *Loch Lomond* and *Annie Laurie* arranged by Henry Geehl. Dawson was in splendid form in Sir Frederic Cowen's robustly martial setting of Sir Walter Scott's 1820 ballad *March, March, Ettrick and Teviotdale.*

Ireland

The position of Ireland in the Empire was nothing if not ambiguous. The Irish provided many of Britain's greatest generals and a higher proportion of the enlisted men in the army than any other part of the United Kingdom. At the same time it had an active nationalist movement, campaigning both with and without violence for home rule or independence. But Irish songs, like Scottish songs, were popular throughout Britain during the nineteenth century. An article published in 1852 explained why. They were 'morally sound'. They were full of pictures of domestic peace and contentment. They celebrated the beauties of nature and the wild countryside that the Romantic movement had pronounced sublime. They were non-elitist, expressed honest sentiments and aimed at the widest audience.[34] There was a recognized formula for constructing an 'authentic' Scottish or Irish song, and throughout the nineteenth century and beyond genuine traditional ballads nestled side by side with newly manufactured songs which, by combining mentions of hills and lochs, shamrocks and heather with evocative place names, a few Gaelic words (macushla, mavourneen) and a poignant love story, homecoming, parting or memory of lost content, pressed all the right buttons and entered the repertoire.

Dawson had a big repertoire of Irish songs. They were, he thought, 'wholesome, stirring . . . and plaintive, reflecting the great character of the race'.[35] He prided himself on his mastery of the Irish dialect and always included an Irish song among his concert encores, invariably chosen from one of the following: *The Kerry Dance, Phil the Fluter's Ball, Molly Branagan, Lanagan's Log* and *The Pride of Tipperary.* He noted that he had sung them with equal success in England, Scotland,

Wales, Australia, New Zealand, South Africa, India and the Straits settlements, further evidence of a common Empire-wide musical culture.[36]

He always enjoyed singing in Ireland, but on one visit, when requested by the 'boys' of the IRA to sing *The West's Awake*, he cut the passage cursing England and had to be escorted back to his hotel for fear of reprisals. He commented on the Irish: 'I have always found them hospitable and friendly, but they are inflexible in their political and religious beliefs, and take these things far more seriously than we do in the old country, or in my own country of Australia.'[37]

His Irish recordings ran the full gamut from comic to tragic, from authentic ballad to manufactured song. They included Percy French's hardy perennials, *Phil the Fluter's Ball* and *The Mountains of Mourne*, the O'Brien–Wallace song *With My Shillelagh Under My Arm*, Thomas Dunhill's setting of Yeats' *The Fiddler of Dooney*, Lockhead's *The Pride of Tipperary*, Thomas Moore's *She Is Far From the Land*, Sir Charles Stanford's *Father O'Flynn*, Charles Wood's adaptation of the traditional air *The Jug O'Punch*, J.L. Molloy's *The Kerry Dance* and Hermann Lohr's *Away in Athlone*.

Dawson took particular pride in singing in dialect – cockney for Kipling, Irish for Irish ballads, Scots for the Scottish folk-songs and west country for his Devon and Cornwall songs. His advice to all singers, both amateur and professional: 'Master the dialect of a song before singing it in public.' It was part of the process of communicating to an audience his interpretation of the song's meaning. It also stressed the cultural diversity of the British Isles, a diversity that remained perfectly compatible with Empire, as his singing of these dialect songs all over the Empire demonstrated.

Orientalism

Dawson also performed his share of those highly perfumed and highly spiced Orientalist ballads that constructed the East as a world of romance and exoticism, of temple bells and fragrant blossoms, of dusky maidens sighing for lost or distant lovers, of teeming bazaars and singing birds, camel caravans and endless desert sand. He recorded such evocative items as *The Bedouin Love Song*, *The Lament of Shah Jehan*, *The Garden of Allah*, *Till the Sands of the Desert Grow Cold* and *In a Persian Market*. Perhaps the most famous of these compositions was the song-cycle *Indian Love Lyrics*, poems by Laurence Hope, set to music by Amy Woodforde-Finden. But Dawson's personal favourite was another Woodforde-Finden cycle, the less well-known but highly melodic *A Lover in Damascus*, with its hints of Eastern bells and flutes, and jingling camel harness.

The sea

Britain's was a maritime Empire, linked by, supplied by and defended by its fleet. The sea-song was an integral part of popular musical culture, and if he was known for anything in particular Peter Dawson was identified with the sea-song. Significantly in his only two feature film appearances he was cast as a seaman.

The pre-eminent imperial naval song-cycle was Sir Charles Villiers Stanford's setting of Sir Henry Newbolt's *Songs of the Sea* which was premièred in 1904 and sung by Stanford's son-in-law and biographer Harry Plunket Greene. Dawson recorded the cycle, one of his own admitted favourite repertoire items, in 1932–33. A perfect matching of words and music, the song-cycle captured the changing moods of the sea, the feelings and emotions of the sailors and a ringing pride in Britain's naval history. No one has ever bettered Dawson's recordings of these songs. *Drake's Drum* in vigorous march-time and with its refrain of beaten drums evokes the spirit of Drake, ever-ready to come to his country's aid in its hour of need. The wistful and reflective *Outward Bound* ('Earth-home, birth-home, with love remember yet/ The sons in exile on the eternal sea') is an anthem of aching longing for the country the singing sailor is quitting. The rumbustious *Devon, ODevon* pictures Drake battling through storms to victory ('Victory lit thy steel with lightning'). *Homeward Bound* is quietly meditative and suggests the peace and rest at the end of the long voyage home ('her storms forgot, her weary watches past'). Exhilarating and ever-popular is the foot-stamping, rip-snorting, spirit-lifting *The Old Superb*, charting the courage and determination of Nelson's oldest and slowest ship.

Stanford set a subsequent cycle of Newbolt's poems as *Songs of the Fleet* (1910). It has been less popular over the years than *Songs of the Sea* though the sequence is musically as rich, varied and sensitive as its predecessor. Dawson recorded several of them. *Sailing at Dawn*, mystical and shimmering, is an expression of absolute belief and confidence in the Royal Navy, its historic traditions and its timeless commitment to service and duty. *The Song of the Sou'Wester* is an exhilarating evocation of gale-force winds and driving spray. *The Middle Watch* is a haunting and haunted evocation of that desolate period between night and day when life – at sea as much as on land – is at its lowest ebb. *The Little Admiral* is a thunderous tribute to the inspiring spirit of Nelson as the patron saint of the Navy. The elegiac *Farewell* is a moving tribute to those who have died at sea to save their beloved homeland. Its sadness however is mitigated by the rising note of triumph at the end, which indicates that the sacrifice was justified:

> Far off they served, but now their deed is done,
> For evermore their life and thine are one.

The call of the sea is a recurrent theme in Dawson's repertoire. It is one of the motive forces of British naval expansion. Ramon's compelling *A Sea Call* ('Deep seas call me – I must go'), May's *Give Me the Rolling Sea* listing the attractions of the sailor's life – freedom, adventure, comradeship, distant lands and exotic locations – and Fraser-Simpson's rollicking *The Call of Sea* ('Give me the sound of the sea and the scent of the driving spray/ Give me the tide flowing free and the shores of a sunlit bay/ Give me wherever I be the sight of a sail unfurled') are typical. Dawson himself set Francis Barron's song *Fret-Foot* in which the sight of a ship moored at Stepney acts as a voice calling the singer back to the life he used to know on the sea and the exotic places he used to visit ('That's the road for me'). A truly imperial creation in this vein is the setting by the black British composer Samuel Coleridge-Taylor of verses by the Parsee poetess Sarojini Naidu, *Sons of the Sea*, which is about native boatmen and their love of the sea ('The sea is our mother, the cloud is our brother, the waves are our comrades all'), a richly coloured evocation of catamarans and nets, coconut glades and 'the scent of the mango groves'.

Naval history in its most heroic form figures strongly. Bevan's *The Admiral's Broom* celebrates seventeenth-century Admiral Blake's putting a whip on his mast as a symbol of his intention to whip the Dutch – 'that wherever we go, the world may know we ride and rule the sea' – after Dutch Admiral Van Tromp had placed a broom at his masthead. Wilfred Sanderson's *Drake Goes West* ('Drake is going West, lad') depicts a boy being urged to join Drake's expedition ('Whate'er be our fate, with Drake we'll win or die'). *Drake* ('A wonderful man was Francis Drake') celebrated his Devonshire origins, his treasure-gathering ('A pilin'up gold for England's Queen'), the game of bowls and the defeat of the Armada. Sir Granville Bantock's rollicking *Captain Harry Morgan* celebrated the exploits of the Welsh pirate, 'King of all the pirates that sail the Caribee', whose burning of Panama and capturing of wine, women and gold earned him 'immortal fame'. Morgan was of course eventually pardoned, knighted and ended his career as Lieutenant Governor of Jamaica, another case of pirate turned legitimate imperial functionary. Graves and Buck's stirring *Full Sail* (recorded by Dawson in 1937) sonorously celebrated the British naval tradition with 'memories of Raleigh and Drake, days when England was wide awake' (an oblique reference, presumably, to 1930s' appeasement) and the navy defending England, home and beauty, and displaying 'a love of the sea that never will die'.

The commercial basis of empires was charted in Martin Shaw's tuneful setting of John Masefield's *Cargoes*, with stately music for the quinquereme of Nineveh, with its cargo of ivory, apes and peacocks, sandalwood, cedarwood and sweet white wine, and the Spanish galleon coming from the Isthmus with diamonds, emeralds, amethysts, topazes, cinnamon and gold moidores, and the tune speeded up for the 'dirty British coaster with the salt-caked smoke-stack' and its cargo of Tyne coal, rails, iron ware and cheap tin trays.

Death at sea in the service of the nation remains a noble sacrifice, as classically expressed in Wilfred Sanderson's *The Glory of the Sea* (recorded by Dawson in 1933). It is a father's tribute to his son lost at sea. 'She sailed for England's honour and the glory of the sea', the ship 'that took my boy from me'. The ship was outnumbered but fought until sunk. 'Thank God, I gave my dearest to the glory of the sea.' He lies sleeping in the sea until the sound of the 'last trumpet shall give him back to me'.

Militarism

Dawson as composer always regarded *Boots* – rightly – as the one song he would be remembered for. But his other Kipling settings are, in fact, just as good. Kipling was the poet of the ordinary soldier, and Dawson, who had been a soldier himself, gave them a convincing martial flavour. It was his trip through India and Burma that directly inspired his settings. He travelled down the Grand Trunk Road, visited Rangoon, Simla and other Kipling locales.

> Everywhere I travelled in India I kept recalling Kipling. Every animal, scene, incident, cow, bird and elephant reminded me in some way of the great man's writings . . . I have always been a passionate admirer of Kipling's works but my visit to Burma and India inspired me to set more of his lines. To date I have set *Boots*, *Route Marchin'*, *Cells* and arranged a song scena of four songs on *Mandalay*. No man knew or saw more, in and about India and Burma, than Rudyard Kipling, and my advice to any visitors going to those places is to study Kipling. When you arrive you will find his pictures continually and forcibly recurring to your mind. A thousand times better, this poet, than all the guide books you might buy.[38]

He met Kipling once. Kipling expressed his appreciation of the setting of *Boots* and said: 'There is no-one I should like to hear sing one of my verses more than you, Mr. Dawson.' When Dawson replied that he hoped to do more, Kipling said: 'Well, Mr. Dawson, if they are as good as *Boots* we shall not quarrel.'[39] *Boots* was composed in the train on the way to a concert at Margate – the words, the necessity of a march-ing tune and the rhythm of the train wheels almost dictating the tune. It was launched at a Promenade concert, got an ovation and became an immediate standard. In 1937 Dawson sang Edward German's setting of Kipling's *The Irish Guards* at a dinner organized by the Kipling Memorial Fund, set up to provide scholarships at Kipling's old alma mater the Imperial Service College.

Dawson became the supreme interpreter of Kipling verse in song form. His settings and performances of *Boots*, *Cells* and *Route Marchin'* are masterly. He found the perfect musical equivalent of foot-slogging in *Boots*. It was recorded in America by Nelson Eddy in pref-erence to the other versions. *Route Marchin'*, set appropriately in march-time, is so good that you cannot imagine it in any other setting, and *Cells* is a rueful and fatalistic lament by an old sweat doing time for being 'drunk and resisting the guard'. Dawson recorded separate versions of the Oley Speaks, Gerard Cobb, Charles Willeby and Walter Hedgcock versions of *Mandalay* and compiled a song scena which incorporated them all. In all he recorded four of Cobb's *Barrack Room Ballads'* settings: *Fuzzy Wuzzy*, *Screw Guns* and *The Young British Soldier*, as well as *Mandalay*. His recording of Charles Mortimer's setting of *The Smuggler's Song* and Edward German's *Rolling Down to Rio* are definitive, gleeful and rhythmic. He recorded Walter Dam-rosch's grim and sombre setting of *Danny Deever* and, with extra-ordinary and moving tenderness, William Ward-Higgs's plaintive setting of *Follow Me 'Ome*, one soldier's poignant lament for a lost comrade: 'There was no-one like 'im, 'Orse or Foot . . . Take 'im away. 'E's gone where the best men go.'

One extraordinary recording venture Dawson was involved in was *The Wreck of a Troopship*, recorded in 1907. Although the ship is not named, the story is based clearly on the wreck of the *Birkenhead*, one of the great imperial tragedies turned into a moral lesson. In 1852 the troopship *Birkenhead* struck rocks off Simons Bay, South Africa. The lifeboats could only accommodate 138 and so were used to get the women and children to safety. The soldiers stood to attention as the ship went down; 454 men were lost. One of the regiments involved was the 74th Highland Regiment, and in the recording it is this regi-ment which is addressed by an officer as he calls on the men to meet death with faith and courage. The men sing *The Old Hundredth* and give three cheers for 'his gracious majesty the King' and *Rule, Britannia* is played as the ship goes down. The episode inspired two much-quoted nineteenth-century poems by Sir Francis Doyle and Sir Henry Yule and entered the imperial mythology as a tale of stoicism, service and sacrifice. It was clearly still current and recognizable as a subject for the fledgling recording industry. The recording was a favourite of King George V and was played regularly after dinner at Buckingham Palace, everyone present standing to attention at the end.[40]

But it was merely one of a now-forgotten genre. Recording pioneer Fred Gaisberg recalled in his autobiography:

> The star turn during the Boer War period was a descriptive record entitled *The Departure of the Troopship*, with crowds at the quayside, bands playing the troops up the gangplank, bugles sounding 'All ashore', farewell cries of 'Don't forget to write', troops singing *Home, Sweet Home*, which gradually receded in the distance, and the far-away mournful hoot of the steamer whistle. The record became enormously popular and eventually historic. It brought tears to the eyes of thousands, among them those of Melba, who declared in my presence that this record influenced her to make gramophone records more than anything else.[41]

In 1930 the Band of the Welsh Guards recorded *The Voyage of a Troopship*, a musical fantasia composed by its Bandmaster George Miller. It was performed complete with male chorus and sound effects. It opened with the sounds of the ships departing and snatches of *Auld Lang Syne* and *The Girl I Left Behind Me*. The progress of the ship through the Mediterranean was indicated by *Blow the Man Down*, *Santa Lucia, A Life on the Ocean Wave* and *We'll Rant and We'll Roar Like True British Sailors* (sung to the tune of *Farewell and Adieu to You, Fair Spanish Ladies*). Then after a musical version of a storm and a sailor's hornpipe, the ship arrives to the strains of *Rule, Britannia*. So both before and after the First World War these celebrations of British naval and military power were being produced by the record industry.

Dawson also joined an all-star cast of singers (John Turner, Webster Booth, George Baker, Walter Glynne, Edward Holland, Jackson Potter) who in 1932 recorded a series of songs newly written to famous old military marches, which, Dawson recalled, sold well – this in an inter-war period widely seen as anti-militarist.[42] All rousing, upbeat and tuneful, the songs evoke different aspects of army life. Alfredo Javaloyes's *El Abanico* (1911) is accompanied by a description of kit inspection and route marching in all weathers ('We'd be far better off in a home') and the perennial soldier's complaint: 'We work all day and we don't get much pay.' Charles Payne's 1893 *Punjaub March* is set to a verse which is an evocation of night in camp before a battle, the sentries on duty and the arrival of dawn before the departure for battle ('Comrades, we are marching to glory with a song on our lips, ever ready to follow the flag').

Hermann Starke's *With Sword and Lance* (1900) celebrates 'the soldiers of the King' returning in triumph, greeted by cheering crowds 'in splendid pageantry', 'with sword and lance on high, lifted to the sky', a riot of gold and scarlet, 'a famous sight to see, forward the Light Brigade, flower of chivalry'. The chorus runs:

> Honour and Arms on parade,
> In all our glory arrayed,
> Heroes of old seem to ride again,
> Names that resound like a grand refrain,
> Where gallant deeds are extolled,
> When silken banners unfold,
> Then still the story of war's romance
> With sword and lance be told.

Waterloo, Crimean War and African War victories and the names of the great regiments are all included in the song.

Sons of the Brave, set to Thomas Bidgood's 1889 march, celebrates the actual business of war:

> When the bugle sounds the clarion call
> From the countryside they are rallying all
> Ready, dare and serve whatever befall,
> Sons of the brave, the nation's pride,
> Marching with pride and cheerfulness,
> On the road that leads to victory
> Sons of the brave, and the nation's pride,
> They go to claim a hero's name
> In freedom's cause to conquer.

Side by side, the boys are 'swinging along with a cheery smile and a rollicking song into battle'. They march back without a song, thinking of the battlefield and the dead. But the cheerful marching tune connotes more of glory and heroism than of bereavement and loss.

Campbell's *The March of the Cameron Men* ('Whatever men dare, they can do'), adorned with fanfares and the skirl of the pipes, similarly celebrates the contribution of Scots soldiers to the Empire. Death in the service, noble and valorous, is a recurrent theme in the Dawson *oeuvre*. Thus he sings with great tenderness of *Trooper Johnny Ludlow*, telling of a handsome and gallant young trooper who ends up buried beneath a white cross in a foreign field.

The Last Patrol, recorded in 1936 but never issued, is a beautifully and evocatively sung story, recounting how Irishman Pat Clancy enlisted in the Army Corps in 1904, was shipped to Bombay and year after year served in India, a life of heat and marching, drill and sweat, growing old and grey in the service. But he loves the life and fears his imminent retirement ('Fighting, that's all I know'). A native shoots from ambush, Clancy rushes forward and is killed, fittingly for a soldier whose whole life has been soldiering, and who looks on retirement with dread.

Many of the best-loved and longest-lasting military songs confront the prospect of death directly but see it in Christian terms as leading to eternal life. What is interesting is that many of them long preceded the First World War and were sung and played throughout that war and recorded by Dawson after it. *The Trumpeter* (1901) celebrated the trumpeter calling *Reveille*, *Charge* and *Rally*. Those who do not survive the battle 'will hear it again in a grand refrain when Gabriel sounds the last rally'. Death in the service of your country will be rewarded by everlasting life – it is the message of 'the just war'.

The same idea lies behind *The Deathless Army* (1891), music by Henri Troteré, words by Fred Weatherly. The words conjure images of scarlet and gold uniforms, flags, drums and trumpets, patriotism, heroism, service and the promise of eternal life.

> Marching for the dear old country,
> Marching away to war,
> With the hearts they love behind them,
> And the flag they love before.

A phantom host accompanies the army, the men who had fought and died 'in the ranks of the brave old army'.

> Their souls will never die – they march in a deathless army
> [. . .]
> For the souls of heroes die not in the land that they adore.

This itself reworks the earlier *Boys of the Old Brigade* (1881), music by O. Barri and words by Fred Weatherly, a song recorded by Dawson in 1926.

> Where are the boys of the Old Brigade who fought with us side by
> side,
> Steadily shoulder to shoulder, steadily blade by blade,
> Ready and strong, marching along, like the Boys of the Old Brigade?

The answer to the question is 'over the sea, far away they lie, afar from the land of their love'. Nevertheless, 'they sleep in old England's heart'. They are soldiers who die on imperial service but who will never be forgotten. The song is still played annually today in the march past the Cenotaph on Remembrance Sunday.

[517]

Even a French song could be pressed into service when it tapped the same source of inspiration. Helmer and Krier's *The Soldier's Dream* (1906) was such a song, recalling the historic glories of the French Army, and was sung throughout the First World War. When Dawson recorded it in 1930, it was framed to serve as a tribute to our gallant allies. Dawson sings it as a cockney soldier on guard duty ('It's all in a day's work – mustn't grumble'), who encounters the spirit of France, spoken by Ralph Richardson, who tells him of the dead soldiers on the soil of France. 'The glorious dead are always at your side, fighting their battles anew' and Dawson sings of a vision of the dead – 'see them riding on to glory'. Not only did Dawson sing this anthem to the romance of war after the First World War, it was recorded anew by Josef Locke after the Second.

What is remarkable is that the same ideas of glorious death and eternal life were still being sung in new songs composed after World War One, something which runs directly contrary to the perception that interwar Britain was predominantly pacifistic and anti-war. *When the Guards Go Marching By* (recorded in 1931) tells of a sight 'you ought to see in London', the Guards marching by and stirring pride in the watchers:

> Fearless and bold, in their scarlet and gold
> With their colours waving high
> And you'll find the answer there
> To every maiden's prayer.

The upbeat march, including a snatch of *The British Grenadiers*, modulates into a sombre tribute to the phantom host who follow the Guards ('Those who fell in the war in Flanders fields'), still marching with them to the end of time.

The Menin Gate was completed in 1927. Surmounted by a British Lion, it is dedicated to 'the armies of the British Empire' who served from 1914 to 1918 in Belgium. It bears the names of 55,000 men 'who fell in war and have no known grave'. *The Last Post* is sounded for them every night at 8.00 p.m. It is a permanent reminder that it was an imperial war: 50,000 Irish soldiers, 30,000 from the south, 20,000 from the north, died in the war; as did 72,000 Indian soldiers, 68,300 Canadians and 60,000 Australians. They were all part of the 1.10 million British and Empire troops who died in the Great War.

The gate inspired the song *The Menin Gate* by Bowen, recorded by Dawson in 1930 and superbly sung with immense power and gravity to an organ accompaniment. The singer apostrophizes a sentry: 'What are you guarding, man at arms, why do you watch and wait?' The answer is that he is guarding the ghosts of the fallen who come to the

Menin Gate. 'They will march at midnight' singing 'the marching songs that let them laugh at fate'. 'Their souls will sing . . . the dead will wake at my call to arms and march through the Menin Gate'. Just as in the imperial nineteenth-century wars were evoked in Fred Weatherly's verses, so after the First World War the souls of the fallen, proud, united and singing, march on, yet another assurance of the eternal life for the fallen. Final confirmation of the justness of the First World War comes in Dawson's recording of *Christ in Flanders*, which evokes the appearance of Christ helping and comforting the soldiers in the Great War but still bearing 'the sword of God in his hand', showing which side he was on.

In a completely different vein was De Rance's remarkable and deeply moving account of survivors' guilt *The Journey's End*, recorded in 1929 and evidently inspired by R.C. Sherriff's play of the same name. It unsparingly evokes the grim images of the First World War to its haunting march-time rhythm:

> Shellfire – hellfire
> Creeping and weeping gas
> Trenches – stenches
> Broken and soaken mass
> Wipers – snipers
> Lit by a star-shell light
> Drowsy, lousy,
> Broken and soaken mass.

It embodies the lament of the sole survivor who had sworn to be with his friends:

> The journey's end with every friend
> We vowed we'd wend together
> The journey's end beyond the bend
> We'd all ascend as one—
> Now I wend without a friend
> The journey's end alone.

He longs above all to be back with them:

> Though they've passed on
> They'll never die,
> I can't forget,
> They're with me yet.
>
> Now they've passed on,
> Each man is gone,
> Their day is done,
> I linger on,

How I long to be back again
There amongst those men.

During the Second World War Dawson was once again singing of the need for heroic sacrifice, recording in Australia in 1942 Jack Lumsdaine's *England in the Morning*, about a bombing raid on Germany:

British bomber squadron, flying 'cross the Channel,
Nosing through the fog in the moonshine,
Heading for Dusseldorf, Bremen or Essen,
Then home again to England in the morning.

Altitude a thousand feet, bombs roll out behind—
Railway station, dockyard, are all a ruddy glow,
Just another stick or two, then it's time to go,
Back to England in the morning.

Listen to the BBC, then it is we learn
One British bomber failed to return,
Vale to the pilot, vale gallant crew
Your souls will be in England in the morning.

Dawson ends with a recitation:

England, our island home, land of the free,
England, unconquered yet, o'er land or sea,
Lord of the heavens above, answer our prayer
God keep Britannia's sons, Lords of the Air.

It was an emotional demonstration of solidarity of purpose between Britain and Australia but also one which drew on a long and well-established tradition of celebrating service, sacrifice, duty and eternal life.

Exile

Exile was a fact of imperial life, and 'homeland' songs, songs of yearning and exile, were a regular feature of Dawson's repertoire. Songs like *The Miner's Dream of Home*, *My Little Grey Home in the West* and *The Dear Homeland* were calculated to raise a tear whenever sung to an audience of exiles. *The Dear Homeland*, 'far across the sea/ I wonder if they miss me or they think of me', with its lilting melody and memories of far-off loved ones and long-cherished and much-missed scenes, is still deeply moving, evoking in words and music the ache of homesickness. *Calling Me Home Again* similarly encapsulates the emotions of a pioneer who has gone to Australia and there brands cattle and mines gold but in quieter moments finds: 'I often sigh for the days gone by, and the London fog and rain – and an English country lane' and a sweetheart left behind. At the end, he resolves to return home 'for my sweetheart's calling me, calling me home again'.

Jack O'Hagan's popular Australian song *The Road to Gundegai* (1921), which Dawson recorded in 1931, is a classic 'return home' song, with its infectious swinging melody and lyrics of memory and loss. There are memories of blue gums, sunny skies, an old bush house, old friends and 'my Daddy and Mother waiting for me'. A return there will put an end to roaming: 'When I get back there I'll be a kid again/ I'll have no thought of grief or pain.'

Dawson as composer

Dawson not only sang ballads; he wrote them. He composed an estimated fifty songs under a variety of pseudonyms, of which J.P. McCall was the most frequently used. The works cover precisely those areas which Dawson had made his own and they clearly reflect his own views and interests. There are the celebrations of Australia, her history and landscape (*Lasseter's Last Ride, The Bushrangers, Whalin' up the Lachlan, The Waratah and the Wattle, This Land O'Mine*). There are celebrations of the army (his settings of Kipling's *Boots, Cells* and *Route Marchin'* and of F. Barron's *Old Kettledrum* in which a retired veteran lovingly recalls the horse he left behind). There are celebrations of the sea (the rollicking pirate songs *Westward Ho!* and *The Jolly Roger*) and the countryside (*Tramping Through the Countryside*). There is his tribute to Scotland (a setting of Robert Burns's *McPherson's Farewell*). There are evocations of an idealized English past, in the pastiche eighteenth-century drinking-song *Festal Song*; in *Song of the Drum*, a pastiche eighteenth-century celebration of the martial music of the drum; and in *Prentice Lads O'Cheap*, which commemorates the drinking and wenching of the London apprentices in Tudor England. There is the sonorous hymn *The Lord Is King*, which imagines the trees, the streams and the winds singing the praises of God.

There are two songs of particular imperial significance. In 1934 he set and recorded in England A. Barker's lyrics *The Glory of the Motherland*, a rousing anthem for the Depression in march-time, which exhorts the people to remember the example of the past and work hard to get out of recession for the good of King and Empire.

> Gentlemen, gentlemen, how goes the world with you?
> Is your trade so slack, do the skies look black?
> Are the bills so overdue?
> What of the years of long ago?
> What of the times our fathers knew?
> Gentlemen, gentlemen, there lies the world for you

[521]

Singing the songs our fathers sang
With a rousing, rollicking swing,
Let us march along, with a courage strong,
And cheer for His Majesty the King.
We shall all win out, without the slightest doubt
If united we stand,
For the future of the Empire story
And the glory of the motherland.
Gentlemen, gentlemen, how does the world with you?
Let us work today, in a stirring way,
To a vision born anew,
List to the voice of the mighty plains
Where lies the Empire grand and true,
Gentlemen, gentlemen, there gleams the world for you.

Then in 1942 in New Zealand he performed his own composition *The Spirit of England*, dedicated to the 'land we love'. The song evoked the spirit of Drake, Nelson and Shakespeare, in affirming the belief that 'the spirit of England none can slay'.

Here's a toast to the spirit of England,
Let us boast of the spirit of England,
Lift your voices on high,
Raise your voice to the sky,
Give three cheers, give three cheers, for the spirit of England
Let us pray for the spirit of England
Till the day when the spirit of England
Shall shine through the night,
Like a beacon so bright,
Let us drink to the King and the spirit of England.

Dawson returned to England in 1947 and gave fifty-seven concerts, declaring that he was broke because of tax demands from Britain and Australia and the poor management of his finances. In 1951 he published his autobiography *Fifty Years of Song*. In 1954 he made a final tour of England and in 1955 his final English recordings. In 1955 he settled in Australia for good, making his final public appearances and his last recordings in 1958. He died of heart failure in Sydney on 27 September 1961 and was buried at Rookwood Cemetery, Sydney. Dr Cunningham Thom, Rector of St David's Presbyterian Church, Haberfield, said in his funeral address: 'He belonged to the generation of Kipling and Henley, and of those strong robust British poets and writers who were the voices of the then invincible British Empire and the then invincible British Army.'[43]

For fifty years Peter Dawson was a veritable troubadour of Empire. His popularity both in Britain and throughout the Empire demonstrates the persistence in the British public until after the Second World War of an essentially Victorian musical sensibility, a sensibility which was sentimental, nostalgic, patriotic, imperial, romantic and religiose. It was extended, strengthened and underpinned rather than eclipsed by the new mechanical media of gramophone and wireless; it was a culture, middle-brow rather than middle class, that communicated to a wide public a shared sense of values through song. There was no one to equal Dawson in singing *Glorious Devon, Old Father Thames, The Fishermen of England, The Cornish Floral Dance,* Stanford's setting of Newbolt's *Songs of the Sea* and the various settings, including his own, of Kipling's *Barrack Room Ballads.* They remained perennial features of his concert and recorded repertoire. He recorded many of his hits several times over the years to take advantage of developments in recording technique. The culture that Dawson represented survived until the rise of rock music transformed the musical scene. Beginning it in 1904, Dawson concluded his British recording career in 1955, the year Elvis Presley began recording – and the year before the Suez crisis demonstrated that the British Empire was no longer able to enforce its writ. Dawson's final recordings – imperial to the end – were the Australian ballad *Clancy of the Overflow* and his own song scena which incorporated all four settings of *The Road to Mandalay.*

Notes

1   Peter Dawson, *Fifty Years of Song*, London: Hutchinson, 1951, p. 22.
2   Gerald Moore, *Am I Too Loud?*, London: Hamish Hamilton, 1962, p. 38.
3   Dawson, *Fifty Years*, p. 30.
4   *Ibid.*, pp. 143, 23.
5   *Ibid.*, pp. 156–7.
6   *Ibid.*, p. 35.
7   *Ibid.*, pp. 183–5.
8   *Ibid.*, p. 186.
9   *Ibid.*, p. 146.
10 *Ibid.*, p. 147.
11 *Ibid.*, pp. 134–5.
12 Peter Burgis, *Peter Dawson – Ambassador of Song*, booklet with set of 10 LP records, EMI, Australia, 1982.
13 Dawson, *Fifty Years*, p. 133.
14 *Ibid.*, p. 187.
15 John D. Vose, *Once a Jolly Swagman*, Blackpool: Vose, 1987, p. 105.
16 Dawson, *Fifty Years*, p. 162.
17 *Ibid.*, p. 198.
18 *Ibid.*, p. 166.
19 *Ibid.*, p. 82.
20 *Ibid.*, p. 89.
21 *Ibid.*, p. 218.
22 *Ibid.*, p. 214.

23 *Ibid.*, p. 218.
24 *Ibid.*, pp. 187–8.
25 *Ibid.*, p. 80.
26 *Ibid.*, pp. 189–90.
27 *Ibid.*, p. 217.
28 *Ibid.*, p. 135.
29 *Ibid.*, p. 101.
30 *Ibid.*, p. 102.
31 *Ibid.*, p. 19.
32 *Ibid.*, p. 160.
33 See M.A. Crowther, 'The Tramp', in Roy Porter (ed.), *Myths of the English*, Cambridge: Polity Press, 1992, pp. 91–113.
34 Derek Scott, *The Singing Bourgeois*, Milton Keynes: Open University Press, 1989, p. 94.
35 Dawson, *Fifty Years*, p. 121.
36 *Ibid.*
37 *Ibid.*, p. 119.
38 *Ibid.*, pp. 105–6.
39 *Ibid.*, p. 106.
40 Kenneth Rose, *King George V*, London: Weidenfeld & Nicolson, 1983, p. 319.
41 F.W. Gaisberg, *Music on Record*, London: Robert Hale, 1947, p. 45.
42 Dawson, *Fifty Years*, p. 133.
43 Vose, *Once a Jolly Swagman*, p. 103.

CONCLUSION

During the period covered by this study, 1876–1953, the music of Empire was everywhere in Britain. It could be heard in music halls, concert halls, churches and cinemas; at coronations, jubilees, pageants, exhibitions and tattoos; in the park, at the seaside, on the wireless and the gramophone. With its unique capacity to stimulate the emotions and to create mental images, music was used to dramatize, illustrate and reinforce the components of the ideological cluster that constituted British imperialism in its heyday: patriotism, monarchism, hero-worship, Protestantism, racialism and chivalry. It was also used to emphasize the inclusiveness of Britain by stressing the contributions of England, Scotland, Wales and Ireland to the imperial project.

Music was written specifically to promote the idea of Empire, and music from other sources was used, for instance in pageants and tattoos, to bolster and underpin imperial ideology. At the same time, a common musical culture was disseminated within the Empire, partly by emulation of the home country but also partly by the activities of touring British bands, choirs, conductors and singers. This culture, based on the standard classical repertoire and the great oratorios, also included the sentimental ballads, popular hymns and stirring marches which reinforced in emigrants and exiles the feeling of being British.

What is particularly striking about the music of imperialism is that there were no operas and few symphonies hymning the Empire. The Empire inspired high culture far less than it inspired popular culture. Popular culture, with an eye to the market, gave people what they wanted, and the fact that popular music of all kinds was steeped in Empire indicates a widespread imperial sensibility among the consumers of that music. It is noticeable how often the staples of popular music – the ballad, the hymn, the music-hall song, the march – were referred to as 'the people's music'. By the same definition, the Empire was above all *the people's* Empire, a major element in their sense of identity and national pride.

INDEX